NUMBER THREE IN THE
*Amerind Foundation
New World Studies Series*
Anne I. Woosley
Series Editor

Great Towns and Regional Polities

Great Towns and Regional Polities

*in the Prehistoric
American Southwest and Southeast*

EDITED BY
Jill E. Neitzel

An Amerind Foundation Publication, DRAGOON, ARIZONA
University of New Mexico Press, ALBUQUERQUE

Library of Congress Cataloging-in-Publication Data

Great towns and regional polities in the prehistoric American Southwest and Southeast / edited by Jill E. Neitzel.
    p.   cm. — (Amerind Foundation New World studies series ; no. 3)
    "An Amerind Foundation publication."
    Includes bibliographical references (p.   ) and index.
    ISBN 0-8263-2001-5
1. Indians of North America—Southwest, New—History. 2. Indians of North America—Southern States—History. 3. Indians of North America—Southwest, New—Politics and government. 4. Indians of North America—Southern States—Politics and government. 5. Indians of North America—Land tenure—Southwest, New. 6. Indians of North America—Land tenure—Southern States. 7. Chiefdoms—Southwest, New—History. 8. Chiefdoms—Southern States—History. 9. Land settlement patterns—Southwest, New—History. 10. Land settlement patterns—Southern States—History. 11. Southwest, New—Antiquities. 12. Southern States—Antiquities. I. Neitzel, Jill E. II. Series: Amerind Foundation New World studies series ; 3.
E78.S7G74 1999
979′.01—dc21   98-40959
                                                                                                              CIP

Contents

Figures

Tables

Acknowledgments

Anumber of individuals and institutions helped to make the idea for this book a reality. Financial support was provided by a conference grant from the Wenner-Gren Foundation for Anthropological Research and a publication grant from the Amerind Foundation New World Studies Series. The Amerind Foundation provided generous institutional support throughout the various stages of grant writing, symposium organizing and management, and manuscript editing.

This project could not have been completed without the positive encouragement and thoughtful advice of Anne Woosley, Director of the Amerind Foundation, Inc. She enthusiastically welcomed the idea of holding a multi day seminar at the Amerind, helped to secure funding to support the seminar, and arranged for the resulting papers to be published. Anne's generosity cannot be understated. Her friendship has been one of the most personally rewarding aspects of this whole endeavor.

Two other Amerind Foundation members also made key contributions to the project. Maureen O'Neill handled with unwavering patience and thoroughness the innumerable logistical details involved in organizing the seminar and much of the computer work relating to the manuscript. Throughout the various incarnations of this project, Allan McIntyre, in his usual good humor, kept the editorial and production process moving forward and proved invaluable during the various phases of manuscript preparation and production. Julie Barnes Smith is owed a debt of gratitude for her illustrations and counsel on map production. During the final production process Linda Smalling of the Amerind provided proofreading assistance.

Many others helped along the way. Bruce Smith suggested the names of Southeastern archaeologists who became part of the project. Randy McGuire made the initial suggestion of reconvening the original Society for American Archaeology symposium for a week-long seminar at the Amerind Foundation. Useful advice was also provided at several critical junctures by George Gumerman.

A special thanks is owed to my original doctoral committee, Sylvia Gaines, the late Fred Plog, Geoffrey Clark, Gary Feinman, and Barbara Stark. Their questions prompted this whole endeavor.

In many ways this volume represents a synthesis of lessons learned from Fred Plog about how to study culture change and Gary Feinman about the importance of considering scale.

As always, my deepest gratitude is owed to my family. My mother, Jane Neitzel, and my husband, Willett Kempton, assumed my household and childcare responsibilities so that I could chair the Amerind seminar, and my children, Reuben, Judson, Hannah, and Isaac, provided me with a healthy dose of reality throughout this project.

Finally, I would like to dedicate this volume to the memory of Fred Plog, an innovative scholar and inspiring teacher of Southwest archaeology.

JILL NEITZEL

Preface

GREAT TOWNS AND REGIONAL POLITIES IS THE THIRD in the Amerind Foundation New World Studies Series. From its inception, the guiding philosophy of the Series has emphasized the synthetic perspective on the one hand and the atypical approach on the other. Researchers who have been actively working on key themes and problems in New World Archaeology are provided an opportunity to meet and deliberate such issues. Of equal import, however, is the prospect of exploring less commonly traveled avenues of investigation. Great Towns falls into the second category as it brings together two groups of scholars, Southwesterners and Southeasterners, seldom found occupying the same space but often discussing similar problems.

When Jill Neitzel initially broached the possibility of a seminar to expand the subjects introduced in a Society for American Archaeology symposium, it sparked an immediate positive chord with the original aims of the New World Series. How interesting it would be to explore prehistoric sociopolitical trajectories in two regions of the United States in which two communities of researchers have long argued for complexity among themselves, but scarcely ever from one group to the other. Archaeologists would be grappling with how prehistoric societies organize themselves politically and what were their symbols of leadership and power, some firmly entrenched in the great plaza at Pueblo Bonito or from a platform mound at Mesa Grande, while others have the familiarity of a view from Monks Mound at Cahokia, from Moundville, Etowah, or Kincaid. Discussions between Southwestern and Southeastern archaeologists were expected to focus on the building blocks of data including, for example, architecture, mobile material culture, mortuary patterns, or road systems and how such lines of evidence could be brought to bear especially on questions related to scale and organizational structure.

From the first day of formal sessions, conversations over meals, and informal gatherings it became clear, and this point was made by several participants, that the vocabulary used might be the same, but the meanings were not. What to some individuals defined the terms of town, polity, community, chiefdom, village, hamlet, and so forth was not consistent between Southwestern and Southeastern groups and, sometimes, was not even the same within a group. Of particular interest were the varying attitudes toward the validity of applying ethnohistoric records and ethnographies of indigenous peoples to prehistoric situations. Among the Southwestern archaeologists, there appeared an almost unanimous reticence (bordering on the suspicious) that ethnographic information concerning historic Southwestern peoples could be safely employed to make inferences about prehistoric situations. Curiously in seminar discussions, certain Southwesterners had no problem in drawing ethnographic comparisons between African or Asian settings and prehistoric Southwest contexts. In contrast, Southeastern archaeologists seemed to be less troubled in bringing data from the historical accounts of European explorers to bear on prehistoric reconstructions.

Alternatively, the Southeasterners at least in this group of archaeologists, were loathe to make Mississippian and Mesoamerican connections of any sort. If there were southern linkages, they cautiously posited the Caribbean or Central and possibly South America. Southwesterners were not at all shy about looking southward to Mesoamerica for any number of inspirations ranging from the domestic plant complex, to material culture, and certain expressions of religious form and symbol. Most intriguing, however, was the growing realization expressed by both groups of archaeologists that contact between Southwest and Southeast regions probably existed, particularly during the Late Prehistoric period. Moreover, this theme will prove to be an important subject of future research.

Another theme often remarked on related to the degree of chronological precision extant in many Southwest contexts and the lack of it throughout the Mississippian Southeast. The presence of dendrochronological sequences enables Southwestern archaeologists to address extremely specific issues of short term change in organizational structures, settlement distributions, and demographic patterns to name but three areas of study. The archaeological data generally do not lend themselves to such concomitant problem solving given the lack of chronological exactness that generally characterizes much of the Southeast.

The Great Towns and Regional Polities volume investigates these sociopolitical and many related topics through the work of its contributors. For the first time, a sustained effort is made to investigate and compare two regions—from specific small data sets to the macroregional—during the same time interval. This volume will provoke commentary and discussion, and these two factors among all others, will be the measure of its success.

ACKNOWLEDGMENTS

This volume profited by the excellent input of the staff of the University of New Mexico Press, especially the Director of the Press, Beth Hadas and Liz Varnedoe, Manuscripts Editor. At the Amerind Foundation our appreciation, as always, is extended to the Members of the Board: Wm. Duncan Fulton, Peter L. Formo, Michael W. Hard, Elizabeth F. Husband, Marilyn Fulton, George J. Gumerman, Peter Johnson, Sharline Reedy, and Lawrence Schiever. We also wish to acknowledge the generous support of the late R. Preston Nash.

ANNE I. WOOSLEY
THE AMERIND FOUNDATION INC.

Introduction

Jill E. Neitzel

Comparison is the lifeblood of archaeology. Any archaeologist who attempts more than simple description must make comparisons. This is true whether the goal is a straightforward chronology or an ambitious attempt to explain culture change. However, while comparison has been fundamental to archaeology since its inception, the kinds of comparisons employed have changed.

The New Archaeology of the 1960s brought two significant additions to the traditional use of comparison as a tool for doing culture history. One was the processual perspective, requiring the monitoring and comparing of different variables through time (e.g., Plog 1974, 1979). The other was an interest in how prehistoric groups were organized (e.g., Hill 1970a; Longacre 1970b). Models of regional analysis subsequently brought a key conceptual refinement to this interest in prehistoric organization with a recognition of the need to consider any social unit within its broader context (e.g., Flannery 1976; Johnson 1977). This volume combines the perspectives of processualists and regional analysts to compare sociopolitical developments in the prehistoric American Southwest and Southeast. The comparisons are systematic and comprehensive and they are done through time and at multiple scales.

For archaeologists working in the Southwest and Southeast, the value of comparative analyses has become increasingly clear (for the Southwest see Cordell and Gumerman 1989b; Crown and Judge 1991; Gumerman 1994; Upham et al. 1989; for the Southeast see Anderson 1996a; Barker and Pauketat 1992; Nassaney and Cobb 1991; Pauketat 1991; B. Smith 1978b, 1990). For the most part, comparisons have been intraregional, contrasting developments in different parts of the Southwest with each other and likewise for the Southeast. The chapters in this volume do present areal comparisons but from a different perspective and with a different goal.

The perspective expressed in the following chapters is multiscalar. The comparisons within and between the Southwest and Southeast pertain to successively larger spatial scales. This approach imposes systematization on the areal comparisons and facilitates considering the effects of developments at one scale with developments at other scales. However, this volume attempts more than simply presenting comparisons of areas within the Southwest and the Southeast. This volume's primary purpose is to compare systematically the Southwest with the Southeast.

For archaeologists working in the Southwest and Southeast, sociopolitical development has been a dominant theme throughout the past decade. Yet despite this common interest, there has been little formal interaction. As a result, the systematic comparisons of interregional developments have been virtually nonexistent. The chapters in this book are the product of an intensive effort to perform such comparisons.

By comparing sociopolitical developments in the prehistoric Southwest and Southeast, this volume contributes to the growing body of anthropological literature on chiefdoms (see Earle 1987a for a brief review). It documents both the tremendous diversity that characterizes societies with an intermediate level of complexity and searches for underlying commonalities. It also illustrates an important methodological improvement to the long tradition of comparative research in the chiefdom literature (e.g., Drennan and Uribe 1987; Earle 1989, 1991a,b; Goldman 1970; Kirch 1984; Sahlins 1958; Taylor 1974; Upham 1990a,b). The chapters demonstrate how the comparative approach can benefit from a perspective that is multivariate, diachronic, and multiscalar—comparing the trajectories of change in multiple variables at different scales and in different areas.

While the primary contributions of this volume are substantive and methodological, an underlying theoretical issue is raised but never resolved. The problem of how to explain the commonalities and variation of sociopolitical developments in the prehistoric Southwest and Southeast, is awaiting additional discussion. That task is beyond the scope of this project. However, this volume should aid efforts to achieve that goal by providing the comparative data necessary for evaluating existing cultural evolutionary models and perhaps for proposing new ones.

HISTORY OF THE PROJECT

The idea for this volume began with an inadequately answered question on my comprehensive exams. The question asked me to consider how archaeologists should study culture change. My answer described the need to focus on the diachronic relationships between different variables, such as between demographic, productive, and organizational changes. I supported my points using examples from the area I know best, the late prehistoric Southwest.

Although my committee passed me on my answer, I was not satisfied. The search for a better response must have continued in my unconscious, because months later I experienced a moment of insight: what had been missing in my answer was a consideration of the issue of scale. To explain changes in any prehistoric social unit, comparisons should be made not only between variables and areas, but also between scales.

This realization led me to appropriate broader scale comparisons that could apply to the Southwest. The Southwest should obviously be considered within the broader context of North America (Figure 1). Given that my graduate work had, in part, focused on the development of chiefdom-level societies, the obvious comparison would have been between cultural developments in the Southwest and those in the Southeast, the North American area most frequently cited in the chiefdom literature.

This idea of Southwest-Southeast comparisons lay dormant for nearly a decade. In 1991, I began to organize a symposium, entitled "Great Towns, Regional Polities: Cultural Evolution in the U.S. Southwest and Southeast" for the 1992 Annual Meeting of the Society for American Archaeology to be held in Pittsburgh. The topic for the symposium would be Southwest-Southeast comparisons. The focus would be on sociopolitical organization, and the format would be multiscalar.

The series of scales of to be discussed would be; the big site, the polity, the macroregion, and the world system. For each area of interest, a Southwestern archaeologist and a Southeastern archaeologist were invited to prepare a paper dealing with organizational changes in their area for their assigned scale. Given that the topic of sociopolitical complexity had previously generated acrimonious debate among some Southwestern archaeologists. Scholars were sought who were perceived to be open minded and who, even if they had been part of the complexity debates, had not been among the most vociferous participants. Once the participants were chosen, attempts were made to assure that the papers dealing with each scale were comparable. Each pair of participants were given a set of questions to address and were asked to work together in formulating their paper outlines.

In many ways, the symposium was a great success. The overall quality of the papers was good and the session was well attended. Personally, however, I found the session to be frustrating in that it did not fully achieve its purpose (i.e., accomplishing comparative analyses of the prehistoric Southwest and Southeast). Each paper focused on just one area, and the session's "interaction" was limited to each author reading his or her paper to the audience.

An alternative forum was needed. A forum in which participants could engage in sustained interaction with the purpose of making systematic comparisons between areas. An ideal alternative was proposed at the SAA meetings by one of the symposium's participants who suggested a week-long seminar. When I approached Anne Woosley, Director of the Amerind Foundation, about sponsoring such a project, her immediate response was enthusiastic and we made plans to seek funding.

Two years after the original SAA symposium, its participants, with Woosley and an additional discussant (Yoffee), reconvened for a week-long seminar at the Amerind. Before meeting, the participants expanded and revised their SAA papers in an effort to make them comparable. The subsequent seminar discussions were both intellectually challenging and substantively productive.

To impose some spatial and temporal limits on the discussions, the Southwest was defined as encompassing the present day states of Arizona, New Mexico, southeast Utah, southwest Colorado, and Northern Mexico (Chihuahua and Sonora; Figures 1 and 2). The Southeast was defined as encompassing the Mississippi River valley, its major tributaries, and the areas east of the Mississippi River and south of the Ohio River (Figures 1 and 3). Temporally, the discussions were restricted to the period between A.D. 900 and European contact, the time known as the Pueblo period in the northern Southwest and the Mississippian period in the Southeast.

The seminar provided an opportunity for sustained discussions about theoretical, methodological, and inter-

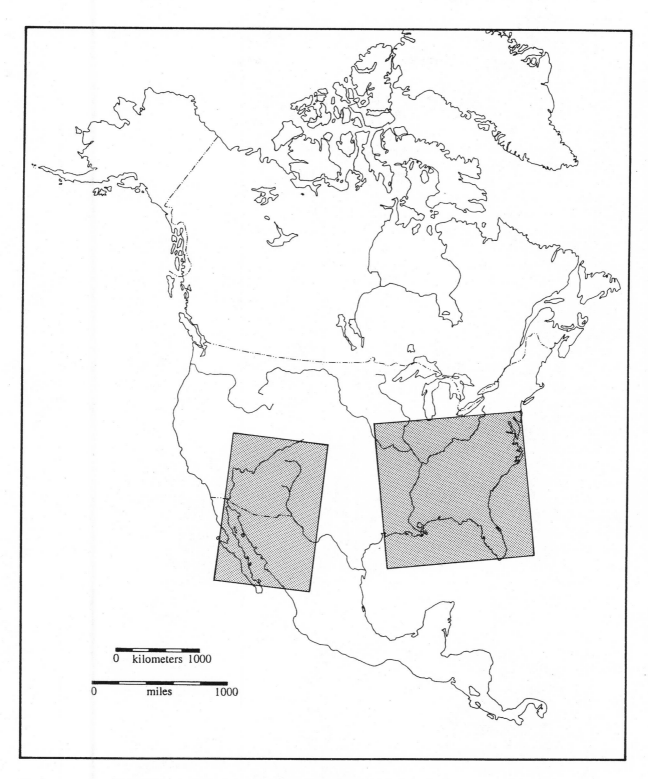

Figure 1.   General location map of the North American Southwest and Southeast.

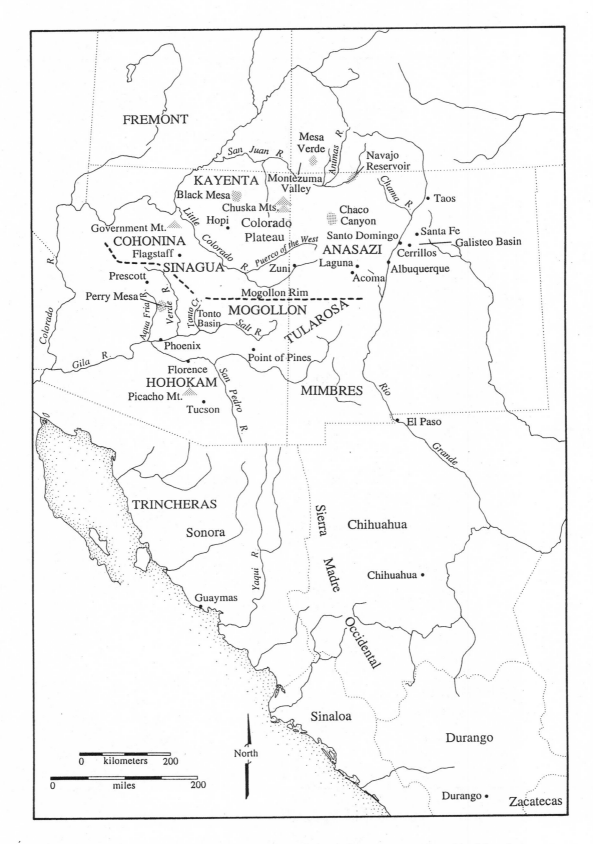

Figure 2.   Map of the North American Southwest showing locations mentioned in this volume.

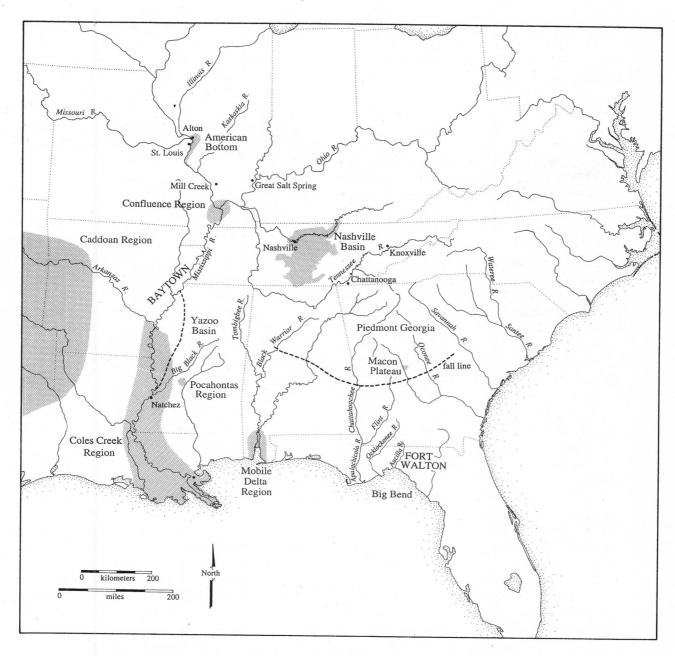

Figure 3. Map of the North American Southeast showing locations mentioned in this volume.

pretive issues that crosscut the Southwestern and Southeastern areas. For both sets of researchers, the questions and comments of outsiders working on similar issues demanded an intellectual rigor not usually required when talking among themselves. Assumptions were challenged, conceptual confusion and sometimes faulty logic were exposed, and alternative interpretations were proposed for consideration.

One issue that dominated the discussions was conceptual. In order for researchers from the two areas to talk with each other, they had to speak the same language. During the seminar, we quickly discovered (to our surprise) that the two groups of researchers often assigned different meanings to the same terms. Consequently, considerable time was spent debating such questions as: Can big sites in the two areas legitimately be called towns? What are communities? What are polities? Can late prehistoric societies in the Southwest and Southeast be called chiefdoms? If not, what should they be called? What is meant by the concept of cultural evolution? How useful is it for explaining change in these societies?

Discussions about these questions were critical for accomplishing the seminar's primary goal of comparison. In order to make systematic comparisons between the Southwest and Southeast, we first had to understand what we were comparing. When we used the same terminology, we had to be certain that we were using it in the same way. Conversely, when we used different terms, we had to decide whether we were speaking about different things or simply applying different labels to the same thing.

During the seminar, each of the six days was allocated for discussions about one spatial scale. In the morning, each paper in the pair under consideration was discussed individually. The afternoon was spent comparing the contents of the two papers to see how the Southwest and Southeast were similar and how they were different. Following the seminar, the participants again revised their papers, incorporating points raised in the group discussions. In addition, each pair of participants jointly wrote a brief summary of the group's comparisons of the Southwest and Southeast for their respective scales of analysis.

This volume is the product of these efforts. Its organization follows that of the Amerind seminar and is intended to facilitate comparisons between areas. With one exception, the chapters are paired, with one chapter dealing with the Southwest and the other with the Southeast. The chapters are ordered by successively larger spatial scales. Considering in turn the characteristics of the two regions' largest sites, the complexity and organization of their associated polities, the links that bound these polities together into macroregions, and the ties that the Southwestern and Southeastern macroregions had with Mesoamerica. Each pair of papers is followed by a brief comparison of the Southwest and Southeast for that particular scale under consideration.

Following the chapters dealing with individual scales are two papers that attempt to integrate the data from multiple scales, first for the Southwest and then for the Southeast. These papers are followed by a comparison of the results of multiscalar analyses. The volume concludes with papers by the seminar's two discussants, who offer the perspectives of archaeologists working with chiefdom and state-level societies in other parts of the world.

Working to make this volume fit the idea as first envisioned has been a struggle. The underlying problem is that comparative research involving multiple investigators is difficult. It requires a constant fight against the natural inclination of individual researchers to focus on the sites and areas that they know best. While comparative research ultimately depends on the knowledge of experts, it requires those involved to look beyond their sites and their areas to search for commonalities and differences. Striving for this comparative perspective has been a challenge throughout the project.

What is the result of this effort? For the first time, sociopolitical developments in the late prehistoric Southwest and Southeast have been systematically compared within a multiscalar framework. This is a task that no one individual could have accomplished alone. It was collaboration, accompanied by the many frustrations that attend collaboration, that was ultimately responsible for the results presented here. We, as a group, hope that our collaborative effort will convince other archaeologists of the value of multiscalar comparative analyses for achieving a better understanding of prehistory.

ACKNOWLEDGMENTS

I thank Anne Woosley and Willett Kempton for their extremely useful comments on earlier drafts of this Introduction. Figures 1–3 were drafted by Julie Barnes Smith.

Great Towns and Regional Polities

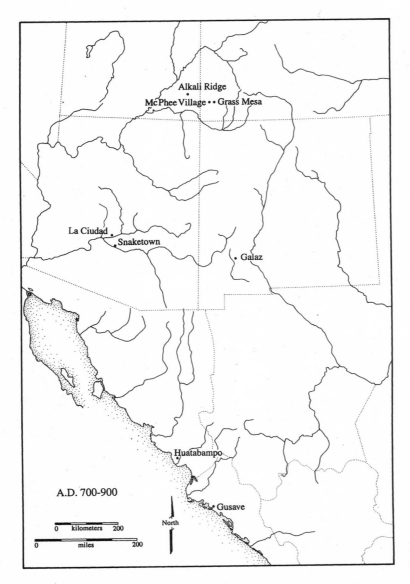

Figure 1.1. Map showing locations of major Southwestern sites, A.D. 700–900.

CHAPTER ONE

Great Towns in the Southwest

Stephen H. Lekson

Wʜᴀᴛ ɪs ᴀ "Gʀᴇᴀᴛ Tᴏᴡɴ" ɪɴ ᴛʜᴇ Nᴏʀᴛʜ Aᴍᴇʀɪᴄᴀɴ Southwest? Although the term is seldom used there (but see Martin and Plog 1973:297), it scans well because it combines two very familiar Southwestern forms: "Great" (great kiva, great house) and "town" (pueblo). In fact, the term "Great Town" translates the old chronological-developmental tag "Great Pueblo" (Roberts 1935), which even today sees occasional use (e.g., Lekson 1984b). However, if by "Great Town" we mean a town hierarchically superior to other towns, the label may be inapplicable to the Southwest. Chaco Canyon and Paquimé are two possible candidates for "greatness" in this hierarchical sense, but many Southwestern archaeologists dispute the existence of settlement hierarchies. Egalitarianism rather than hierarchy continues to dominate much Southwesternist thinking.

In this chapter, I will equate "Great Town" to "large settlement"—or, more accurately, to "big site." By developing the "big site" context, we can more intelligently ask the real "Great Town" question: are these just big sites, or do they represent something qualitatively different from other, smaller sites?

The history of big sites in the Southwest is discussed in five periods: ᴀ.ᴅ. 700–900, ᴀ.ᴅ. 900–1150, ᴀ.ᴅ. 1150–1300, and ᴀ.ᴅ. 1300–1550 (Figures 1.1–1.4). The delineation of these periods should be taken with a plus-or-minus 50 years (cf. Cordell and Gumerman 1989b:6). The big sites in these periods are discussed for the Southwest's three major regions: Anasazi, Hohokam, and Mogollon (but see Lekson 1993 for a reevaluation of Mogollon).

Eʟᴇᴍᴇɴᴛs ᴏꜰ Sᴏᴜᴛʜᴡᴇsᴛᴇʀɴ Tᴏᴡɴs

The basic elements of large Southwestern settlements include: residential structures, public buildings and facilities, and their combination in an overall town plan or landscape.

Residential Structures

The basic residential unit in the Southwest was, until at least ᴀ.ᴅ. 1000, the pit structure: deeper pithouses at higher altitudes in the Anasazi and Mogollon areas, and shallower "houses-in-pits" in the deserts of the Hohokam region. In some areas (e.g., Kayenta Anasazi, upland Mogollon, Hohokam) pithouses continued to be used until the thirteenth century and, indeed, pithouses were used in the early twentieth century at Hopi when a new village site was first developed.

In the Anasazi area, pit structures are usually thought to evolve into kivas prior to ᴀ.ᴅ. 900. There has been some reassessment of the pithouse-kiva transition (e.g.,

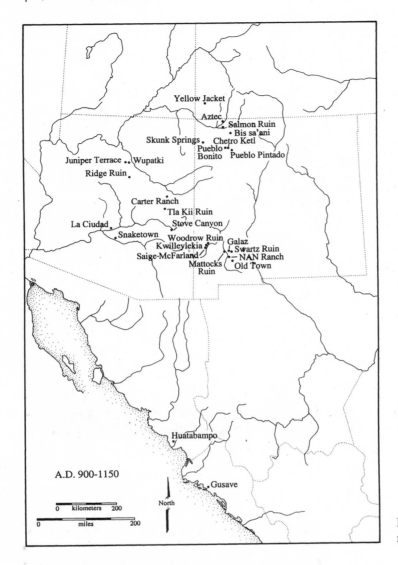

Figure 1.2. Map showing locations of major Southwestern sites, A.D. 900–1150.

Lekson 1988a) and it is possible that pit structures (mislabeled as kivas) continue to be a central element of Anasazi residence until at least A.D. 1300, if not later (for a recent discussion of kivas, see Adams 1991; Lipe and Hegmon 1989).

In the late ninth and tenth centuries, the pit structure (kiva or pithouse) becomes part of a small "unit pueblo," consisting of six to ten rooms in contiguous, flat roofed, masonry roomblocks, with a nearby subterranean pit structure, a clearly defined area ("midden") where post-functional items, including burials, were deposited, and various freestanding "ramada" shades and ephemeral outbuildings. The "unit pueblo" housed a very small group, probably a nuclear or extended family. It was not the huge apartment building we associate with the word "pueblo" today.

Where does the protohistoric and modern Pueblo form—massed, terraced, apartment-style roomblocks around a plaza—come from? It may mirror the largely non-residential Chacoan Great House, with an adaptation of great house form to village use at A.D. 1150–1200 (Fowler and Stein 1992; Lekson 1990d; Lekson and Cameron 1993). Alternately, the Pueblo form may reflect massing around plazas associated with a southern origin of the Kachina cult, at least a century later (Adams 1991). By the mid-A.D. 1200s, many villages were, effectively, single buildings. Roomblocks consisted of contiguous "apartments" of one-room-wide, three-to-five-room deep, and two-to-three-story tall suites, each roughly equivalent to a "unit pueblo"—i.e., nuclear or extended family residences.

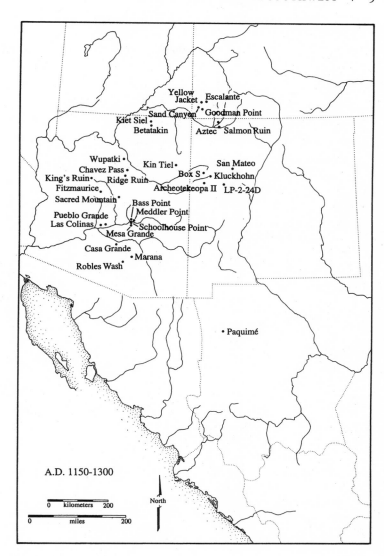

Figure 1.3. Map showing locations of major Southwestern sites, A.D. 1150–1300.

The basic unit of Hohokam domestic architecture was the "courtyard group"—three to six individual pithouses grouped at right angles around a small courtyard or patio. Several courtyard groups were linked in "village segments" sharing a common cemetery, large pit ovens, and trash mound middens (Wilcox 1991d:256).

Beginning about A.D. 1150, Hohokam pithouses, after a developmental sequence of one thousand years, were partially or mostly supplanted by above-grade, flat-roofed, puddled adobe structures in walled compounds. Smaller, earlier compounds probably evolved from Hohokam courtyard groups (Sires 1987), but many later Classic period compounds were much larger than a simple courtyard group, and may reflect the larger "village segment" (Wilcox 1991d:256). Larger compounds may also reflect different uses of architectural space: Doyel (1991:253) argues that compound architecture became more differentiated after A.D. 1300. He notes that at the Escalante site, "90 percent of the roofed space [in pre-A.D. 1300 compounds] was devoted to habitation rooms." In comparison, "less than one-half of the roofed space in the [post-A.D. 1300] Civano phase was devoted to habitation" with the remainder used for storage and ritual (Doyel 1981:65).

Mogollon becomes rather tenuous as a "culture area" after A.D. 1000 (Lekson 1993). A series of variously dated local transitions from pithouse to Pueblo-style architecture may mark the end of Mogollon as a useful taxon. Mimbres is a case in point: at about A.D. 1000, above-

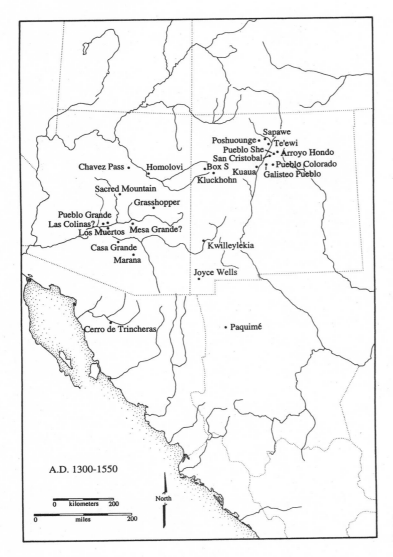

Figure 1.4.   Map showing locations of major Southwestern sites, A.D. 1300–1550.

ground, contiguous, (rarely multi-storied), massed masonry roomblocks replace pithouse villages. There may or may not have been a brief transitional period resembling the Anasazi unit pueblo (LeBlanc 1986; Lekson 1988b; Woosley and McIntyre 1996). In any event, by no later than A.D. 1050 large Pueblo-style masonry villages had replaced the older pithouse settlements. Given the probable non-residential nature of contemporary Chaco Great Houses, Mimbres villages may have been the earliest real "pueblos" in the Southwest. Other upland Mogollon pueblos, beginning in the later A.D. 1100s and early A.D. 1200s, are more usefully considered with southern Anasazi developments. Southern (desert) Mogollon undergoes a similar but more poorly understood transition from pithouses to adobe pueblos at about the same time.

Public Buildings and Facilities

"Public" means non-residential architecture that required construction and maintenance by a group larger than the residential unit (by this definition, the small pre-A.D. 1300 kivas of the Anasazi region and the small Mimbres square kivas are almost certainly not "public" architecture). Public architecture in the Southwest encompasses elements as diverse as plazas, great houses, great kivas, ballcourts, platform mounds, canals, and roads.

Plazas were literally and perhaps conceptually central to almost all Southwestern big sites. Plazas, as central clear areas, appear in very early pithouse villages of the Mogollon and Hohokam regions (e.g., Haury 1976; Lekson 1982). Village plazas were less obvious in early Anasazi pithouse and pre-A.D. 1000 Pueblo settlements, but they are major features of Chaco Great Houses by the A.D. 1020s (Lekson 1984b). Chacoan enclosed plazas were the presumably the idea behind the enclosed plazas that characterized so much of subsequent Pueblo town planning; however, Adams (1991:101–103) presents a well-supported case for a southern (non-Chacoan) origin of the enclosed plaza.

Village plazas (as opposed to compound yards) are less obvious in post-A.D. 1100 Hohokam sites. The compound architecture does not appear to mirror the concentric zoning of earlier Preclassic Hohokam pithouse villages.

Enclosed plazas were present in many later "Mogollon" pueblos, both upland and desert. A case can be made that interior enclosed plazas replace the great kiva with implications for the origin of the Kachina cult (Adams 1991).

"Great Kivas"—very large, round, or rectangular subterranean rooms, almost certainly for community ceremony—characterize the Anasazi and Mogollon areas. It appears that almost every large settlement (aggregated or dispersed) had one. In some sense, the great kiva may have "defined" the town. Conspicuously oversize pit structures began in the earliest agricultural villages and continued at least through the A.D. 1200s in both areas. Until recently, great kivas were all but unknown in the western Pueblo region, but a few examples dating to the twelfth century are now documented, and it seems likely that more will be found, probably dating beyond the A.D. 1200s. Adams (1991:103–110) makes a case for the disappearance of the great kiva and increasing the importance of multiple small rectangular kivas in the western Pueblo area.

Oversize pit structures appear with the earliest Mogollon pithouse villages and develop into large rectangular Mogollon "great kivas" or communal structures (Anyon and LeBlanc 1980; Lekson 1982; Woosley and McIntyre 1996). Rectangular great kivas may not continue beyond about A.D. 1100 in the Mimbres area, presumably being replaced by small enclosed plazas during the Mimbres phase about A.D. 1000 (Anyon and LeBlanc 1980, 1984:115; see Lekson 1992b for a contrary view). Rectangular great kivas continued at Pueblo sites well beyond the thirteenth century in the upland Mogollon areas (Adams 1991:103ff). It is possible that there was a structure much like a rectangular great kiva at post-A.D. 1300 Paquimé (Room 38, Unit 11; Di Peso et al. 1974:508ff).

A possible analogue for Anasazi and Mogollon great kivas is the "large, square communal" or "LSC" house of the earliest Hohokam pithouse villages. LSC houses are not thought to last beyond about A.D. 600 in the Hohokam region (Doyel 1991:246).

Ballcourts in the Southwest appear to form two very distinct traditions: oval courts in the Hohokam region from A.D. 600 to about A.D. 1150 and "I"-shaped courts in the Paquimé region from A.D. 1300 to 1450.

The Hohokam ballcourt is, in some ways, a counterpart to the Anasazi and Mogollon great kiva. While older examples are known, ballcourts appear to become widespread just when Hohokam "LSC" houses are fading from the scene—about A.D. 600, give-or-take a century. Ballcourts served a dual function: they provided a town-focus (much like a great kiva) and signified participation in a larger regional network of ballcourts (Doelle 1988; Wilcox and Sternberg 1983). Oval ballcourts cease to be the major focus of Hohokam public building at about A.D. 1100 or 1150, being "replaced" by platform mounds.

Ballcourts extend north to Wupatki, and co-occur there with a probably post-Chaco great kiva. Intriguingly, the Wupatki and Sinagua ballcourts appear to continue after A.D. 1150. An oval ballcourt co-occurs with a Mogollon great kiva at the Stove Canyon site in the Point-of-Pines area, but this appears to be a remarkable instance (Johnson 1961). There are rumors of Hohokam-style ballcourts in the Mimbres area but, to date, none have been documented. Given the subtlety of many ballcourts (most are far less spectacular than the frequently illustrated Snaketown examples), it is possible that ballcourts will someday be found amid the bewildering berms, depressions, and swales of Mogollon pithouse sites.

Paquimé ballcourts are very different from the oval Hohokam courts. "I"-shaped Paquimé courts have been found at several other sites in Paquimé's immediate geographic sphere, including at least two sites in extreme southwestern New Mexico. Paquimé itself dates to after A.D. 1300. Although both Paquimé and its ballcourts may have an earlier developmental history, "I"-shaped ballcourts appear to postdate Hohokam ballcourts.

Earthen architecture—mounds, berms, platforms, etc.—is best known from the Hohokam and Paquimé area, but recently platform mounds have been described for Chaco Canyon and other Anasazi sites (Lekson 1984b:74; Stein and Lekson 1994).

Mounds are best known from the Hohokam region, where they had a very long history, beginning with oval, rounded mounds formed at least partially of "trash" (Haury 1976). Walled, rectangular platform mounds are a late development in Hohokam earthen architecture (Gregory 1987, Lange and Germick 1992). They replace, in some sense, the older ballcourt as an architectural focus of village identity about A.D. 1100 or 1150. Early Classic period platform mounds address, in their placement, the earlier ballcourts (Gregory 1987:208)—that is, the placement of platform mounds was to some degree fixed by the position of earlier ballcourts. Thus, ballcourts must have continued to have architectural meaning, if not function. Continuity with earlier Hohokam public building is demonstrated even more directly with Classic platform mounds being built over and incorporating earlier pre-A.D. 1150 mounds (as at Las Colinas: Gregory 1987:Figure 3).

There are, however, clear differences between pre- and post-A.D. 1150 Hohokam mounds: pre-A.D. 1150 mounds were built up of trash and soil and then capped or coated with caliche plaster over the mound's rounded mass; and post-A.D. 1150 platform mounds exhibit "a massive rectangular retaining wall of coursed, caliche-rich adobe, with the space defined by the wall filled with some combination of trash and sterile soil, and the whole covered with a plaster cap" (Gregory 1987:188). This shift in technique changed the plan of Hohokam mounds from oval/ovoid to crisp rectangles. It also produced a flat surface for structures atop the mound, which were evidently absent in earlier Hohokam mounds.

Many platform mounds were built as rectangular enclosures with interior cells (e.g., Pueblo Grande, Escalante). These cells have been explained as internal bracing or compartmentalizing of fill (as at the Meddler Point Mound; Craig et al. 1992), but some cells are more complicated than that. Excavations of platform mounds at Tonto Basin sites, constructed about A.D. 1280, show that the cells were at some point functioning rooms (e.g., Rice and Redman 1993). Lindauer (1992) differentiates between purpose-built platforms, like Meddler Point, Bass Point, and Pueblo Grande, and pueblos-turned-mounds, such as Schoolhouse Point in the Tonto Basin. He calls the former "planned" and the latter "organic" (Anasazi archaeologists might be tempted to call some "organic mounds" pueblos).

No earthen structures have been identified in the Mogollon area, but the history of research mirrors that of the Anasazi area: no one has been looking for such structures. Given subsequent developments at Paquimé, it is not unreasonable to expect earthen building in the desert Mogollon area.

Paquimé, the great fourteenth century center in northern Chihuahua, has a wonderful variety of earthen structures. Platform mounds, burial mounds, bird and snake effigy mounds (Di Peso et al. 1974:270ff)—there is nothing else quite like Paquimé in the Southwest. To date, the astonishing range of Paquimé mounds appears to be limited to that site (unlike "I"-shaped ballcourts).

The term "Great House" has been used in at least two senses in the Southwest: the Chacoan Great House and the Casa Grande (or Big House) of the post-A.D. 1300 Hohokam area. Chacoan Great Houses (Fowler and Stein 1992; Lekson 1984b; Vivian 1990) are massively built, large-scale, rigidly geometric masonry buildings that look like pueblos, but probably were not. Hohokam great houses are even more problematic than their Chacoan counterparts. Only one remains with two others, destroyed in historic times, having been documented. The surviving example, Casa Grande in Arizona, is a massively walled adobe building. Wilcox (1991b:268) argues that there may have been as many as five Hohokam great houses and suggests that they may have been astronomical towers "necessary to regulate the calendrical ceremonial system."

Other "public" facilities that shaped "Great Towns" include canal systems in the Hohokam and Mimbres Mogollon regions, and roadways in the Chaco Anasazi area. Huge canal systems "fixed" Hohokam settlement and structured much of Hohokam economy and society (Doyel 1991:247ff; Gregory 1991; Fish and Fish 1991; Wilcox 1991d). Mimbres canals, while much less extensive than their Hohokam counterparts, "fixed" settlement at hydrologically strategic points and no doubt played a role in the early emergence of highly aggregated Pueblo-style villages in the Mimbres region (Lekson 1986a,c; 1993).

Chacoan roads—6 to 8 m wide, straight, engineered roadways—have an extensive literature (see Roney 1992 for a current review) and a contested function. They either connect the huge Chacoan region or represent short segments or ritual entryways to great house communities (Roney 1992; Wicklein 1994). To date only three roads have been systematically studied and all three are continuous (Kincaid 1983; Nials et al. 1987). It is possible that many road segments are just that: short lengths that were "purely local phenomenon . . . one more embellishment of the local integrative structures, complementing earthworks, [berms], great kivas, and the other trappings of these buildings [great houses]" (Roney 1992:130). Either way, roads are a major structural element of Chacoan towns.

Were roads unique to the Chaco Anasazi? Wilcox identifies linear "prehistoric trails" entering the major Sedentary period Hohokam center of Snaketown (Wilcox et al. 1981). The depositional history of the basin-and-range might be far less amenable to the discovery of roads than the soils of the San Juan Basin, although less formal trails are extraordinarily well preserved on some desert surfaces. A possible roadway has recently been identified at the eleventh century Mimbres site of Old Town (Creel 1993). The more we look, no doubt the more we will find.

Plazas, great kivas, great houses, ballcourts, canals, and roads are all "public" architecture, but "public" may not mean "monumental." Labor is one dimension of monumentality. Labor estimates exist for individual Chacoan buildings and for all the Chaco Canyon Great Houses (Lekson 1984b), for Hohokam ballcourts (Neitzel 1991:198ff), and mounds (Craig et al. 1992; Neitzel 1991:201ff). As public works, few of these architectural forms are especially impressive. With two exceptions, Hohokam canals and, perhaps, Chacoan roads, most Southwestern "monumental" building was well within the capacities of the estimated populations of the attendant settlements without undue burdens on the labor force (Lekson 1984b; Neitzel 1991).

Hohokam canals are remarkable on a continental and even global scale. William Doolittle, in a review of prehistoric Mexican irrigation systems, described the Hohokam canals of the Phoenix Basin as "a technological achievement of monumental proportions. In terms of complexity it simply had no rival anywhere in Mexico" (Doolittle 1990:79). Hohokam canals were of "monumental proportions"—but were they monumental? The canals were a necessary tool for subsistence; without them, agricultural life was not possible in the Phoenix Basin. They required massive labor and expertise, but canals did not commemorate kings. Canals were necessary infrastructure, not monuments.

The same could *not* be said for Chacoan roads. Roads were unnecessary, in a practical sense. Even if Chaco was a giant commodities exchange, the tump-line transport technology of its time did not require 8 m wide roads. Roads certainly required a great deal of labor for construction and maintenance, but much less than for an equal length of Hohokam canal. How much labor depends on how long the roads were—an unresolved question discussed above.

Layouts of Southwestern Towns

The residential structures and public facilities and buildings just discussed combined to form the Southwest's large sites. Typical layouts are described for each time period below.

Pre-A.D. 900

The earliest large Mogollon and Anasazi pithouse villages may have shared a common layout: a central clear area (plaza?) with a "great kiva" to one side, separating northern and southern clusters of pithouses (Figure 1.5d) (Wills and Windes 1989; Lekson 1982). The layout of large pre-A.D. 900 Hohokam villages is obscure, but probably included an unusually large "LSC" house, perhaps a "great kiva" counterpart.

By A.D. 700, Anasazi towns consisted of lines of linked rooms fronted by pithouses (e.g., Grass Mesa, Alkali Ridge, McPhee) (Figure 1.5c), perhaps foreshadowing the "street" arrangement of later sites such as Skunk Springs (Figure 1.5b), Yellow Jacket (A.D. 900–1300), and modern Pueblos such as Oriabi and various Rio Grande pueblos (Figure 1.5t).

A.D. 900–1150

The largest Anasazi "Great Town" of A.D. 900–1150 was Chaco (Figure 1.6). Until recently, the many separate buildings of Chaco Canyon were seen as so many separate towns: a cluster of independent, self-sufficient agrarian pueblos, perhaps even of differing ethnic and linguistic traditions, improbably jammed into an inhospitable canyon. The recognition of Chaco Canyon as a "community" incorporating considerable architectural and even ethnic diversity was first articulated in the work of Vivian and Mathews (1964: 108–111, more fully developed by Vivian 1990), but the identification of Chaco as "a coherent settlement, delineated by roads, walls, mounds, and myriad public buildings" (Lekson 1984b) is a product of the last ten years (e.g., Lekson 1991; Stein and Lekson 1992).

The central Chaco settlement covered an area of more than 10 km². There were perhaps eight very large buildings of up to 700 rooms (Figure 1.5g) and hundreds of smaller unit pueblos. A complex net of roadways connected the great houses. Earthen berms and platform mounds lined the roadways and a variety of other above-grade mound construction shared the canyon floor. Great Kivas were located in or near the Great Houses and, in some cases, were freestanding amid the larger community. The plan of individual buildings and the layout of the larger settlement shared a geometry that we are only beginning to decode (Stein and Lekson 1992).

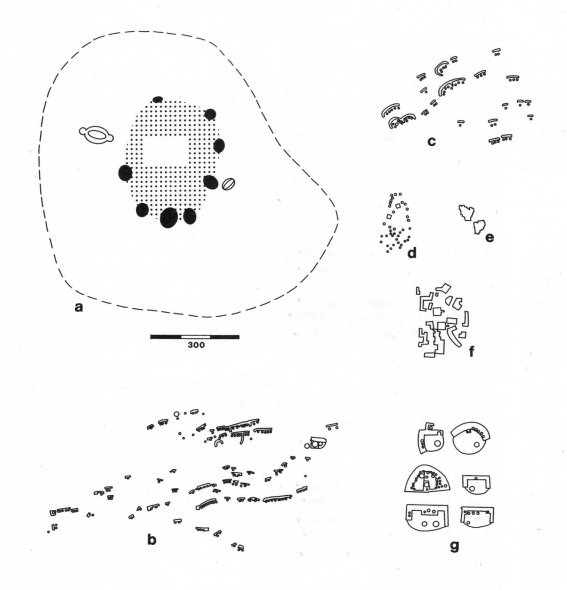

Figure 1.5.   a. Snaketown, Gila River, Arizona, A.D. 975–1150; the inner plaza is surrounded by a zone of dense pithouse residence (stipple), defined by a circle of mounds (solid); an outer zone of more dispersed pithouse settlement (dashed line) also includes two oval ballcourts (after Wilcox 1991:Figure 11.1); b. Skunk Springs, Chuska Valley, New Mexico, A.D. 900–1150 (after Peckham 1969); c. McPhee Village, Dolores Valley, Colorado, A.D. 800–900 (after Kane 1988:Figure 1.13); d. Galaz Ruin, pithouse component, Mimbres Valley, New Mexico, A.D. 700–1000 (after Anyon and LeBlanc 1984:Figure 4.1); e. Swarts Ruin, Mimbres Valley, New Mexico, A.D. 1000–1150 (after Cosgrove and Cosgrove 1932:Plate 238); f. Woodrow Ruin, Gila Valley, New Mexico, A.D. 1000–1150 (after Peckham 1969 and Lekson's unpublished maps); g. Great Houses, Chaco Canyon, New Mexico, A.D. 900–1150; Pueblo Bonito is middle row, left (after Lekson 1986c:Figure 1.2); h. Goodman Point Ruin, Montezuma Valley, Colorado, A.D. 1200–1300 (after Lipe 1989:Figure 3); i. Sand Canyon Pueblo, Montezuma Valley, Colorado, A.D. 1200–1300

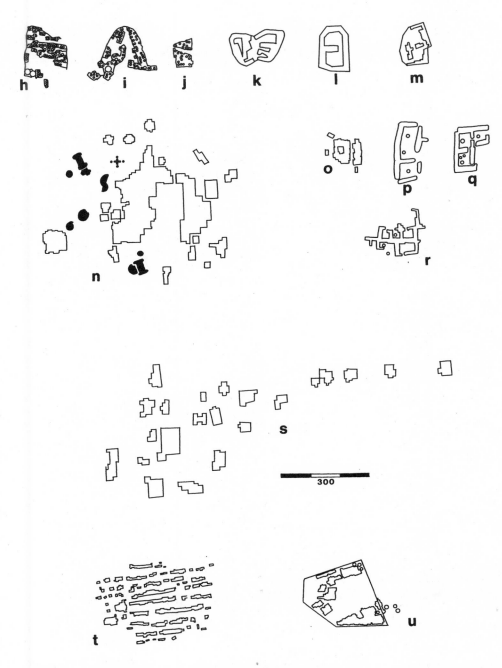

(after Lipe 1989;Figure 2); j. San Mateo site, San Mateo vicinity, New Mexico, A.D. 1200–1300 (after Marshall et al. 1979:196); k. Kin Tiel, Wide Ruins Wash, Arizona, ca. A.D. 1300 (after Mindeleff 1891:Plate LXIII); l. Box S site, Zuni vicinity, New Mexico, A.D. 1200–1300 (after Kintigh 1985:Figure 4.13); m. LP-2–24D, Acoma vicinity, New Mexico, A.D. 1200–1400 (after Dittert 1959); n. Paquimé (Casas Grandes), Chihuahua, Mexico, A.D. 1250–1500, solid forms indicate platform mounds and ballcourts (after Di Peso et al. 1974:Figure 121–4); o. Grasshopper Pueblo, Cibecue vicinity, Arizona, ca. A.D. 1350 (after Longacre and Reid 1974:Figure 7); p. Te-ewi Ruin, Chama Valley, New Mexico, A.D. 1400–1500 (after Wendorf 1953:Figure 9); q. Kuaua, Rio Grande Valley, New Mexico, A.D. 1400–1600 (after Peckham 1969); r. Arroyo Hondo, Santa Fe vicinity, New Mexico, ca. A.D. 1330 (after Creamer 1993b:Figure 1.4); s. Los Muertos, Salt River, Arizona, A.D. 1325–1475 (after Haury 1945a:Figure 2); t. Santo Domingo Pueblo, New Mexico, 1950 (after Stubbs 1950); u. Taos Pueblo, New Mexico, 1950 (after Stubbs 1950). Scale equals 300 meters.

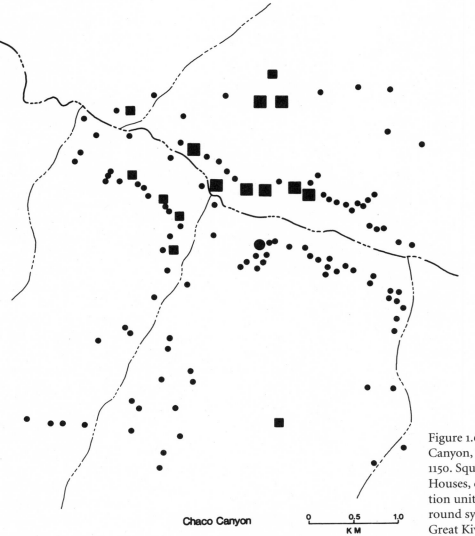

Figure 1.6. "Downtown" Chaco Canyon, New Mexico, ca. A.D. 1150. Squares represent Great Houses, dots represent habitation unit pueblos. The large round symbol represents the Great Kiva at Casa Rinconada.

Chaco Canyon

0   0,5   1,0
K M

After A.D. 1150, Chaco Canyon was greatly diminished and by A.D. 1200, according to conventional wisdom, abandoned. In the early A.D. 1100s, a secondary center mirroring but not quite reaching Chaco's scale evolved to the north along the Animas River (McKenna and Toll 1992). This "epi-Chacoan" Great Town is best known from the Aztec Ruins, but included a remarkable range of building types over a surprisingly large area. Like Chaco, the layout of the Aztec center was elaborately and geometrically formal (McKenna and Toll 1992).

Most Anasazi settlements during the Chaco era and for several decades after Chaco's decline were also multi-structure communities, consisting of a small great house, a great kiva, and a cluster of a dozen or more unit pueblos (Figure 1.5b). At many such settlements, there is evi-

dence of roads passing near the great house. This pattern, which occurs over most of the Anasazi region, has been called a "Chacoan community" (Lekson 1991, following the definition of the Anasazi "community" of Rohn 1977) in reference to its obvious link to Chaco, but the nature of these parallel patterns is not yet clear.

Intriguingly, both Skunk Springs, perhaps the largest Chacoan community (Figure 1.5b), and Yellow Jacket, perhaps the largest Mesa Verde site, share a remarkably formal configuration, with lines of contiguous unit pueblos arrayed in parallel "streets"—almost certainly continuing the linear arrangements of earlier Pueblo I villages (Figure 1.5b). This pattern may be present at other Mesa Verde area Chacoan and post-Chacoan communities (Kane 1993), but it is more noticeable, perhaps, at Yellow Jacket and Skunk Springs because of their remarkable size.

Contemporary Hohokam "big sites" (Doyel 1987, 1991; Fish et al. 1992a; Gregory 1991; Haury 1976) were, in many ways, even more impressive than Chaco. Hohokam sites are architecturally complex, with densely superimposed house remains—a product of the tethering effect of canal systems. They are also huge. For example, the two Sedentary period components at the Marana community covered about 60 and 70 km²; both were later incorporated within a Classic period (A.D. 1150–1350) community of more than 145 km² (S. Fish et al. 1992a). That makes Chaco, at 10 km², look pretty small. The Marana community includes hundreds of separate "sites" and agricultural features and public architecture, but so does Chaco.

Early Hohokam settlements—typified by Snaketown (Figure 1.5a) were structured by concentric architectural zones. At the center was a wide, open plaza (Wilcox and Sternberg 1983; also see Doelle 1988; Doyel 1991; Gregory 1987, 1991). Surrounding the plaza was a dense residential zone of "courtyard groups," with multiple "courtyard groups" forming a discrete "village segment" with an associated cemetery and roasting pits. A ring of earthen mounds marked the outer edge of the residential zone. At the settlement's limits were one or two ballcourts, which symbolized the settlement's place in the larger regional structure (Wilcox and Sternberg 1983; Doelle and Wallace 1991).

Contemporary with Chaco and the Sedentary Hohokam were the Mimbres villages of southwestern New Mexico (Anyon and LeBlanc 1984; LeBlanc 1983; Lekson 1992a,d; Shafer and Taylor 1986). Best known for its artistic pottery, the Classic Mimbres phase (A.D. 1000–1150) is perhaps more significant for its towns (Figure 1.5e). The largest Mimbres ruins include up to 300 rooms tightly massed in irregular roomblocks partially surrounding a central plaza, often with a north-south division of roomblocks on either side of a plaza, perhaps with a great kiva, recalling earlier pithouse village layouts (Lekson 1986c, 1992a,b). Mimbres towns, like Chaco, are thought to have been abandoned about A.D. 1150 (e.g., LeBlanc 1983; see Lekson 1992a,c for a reassessment of Mimbres regional abandonment).

A.D. 1150–1300

There is developing evidence from the Mesa Verde, Zuni, and east-central Arizona regions for a continuation of the great house community pattern after the "fall" of Chaco at about A.D. 1150 (Fowler and Stein 1992; Kintigh 1994; Lekson and Cameron 1993). Post-Chaco great house communities survive for perhaps fifty years after Chaco's "fall" and are replaced by the early to mid-A.D. 1200s by tightly aggregated Pueblo forms. These early pueblos hark back to the massing of the largest Chaco Great Houses (Fowler and Stein 1992; Lekson 1990b, 1992a; Lekson and Cameron 1993).

There is, of course, a great deal of variation in the plan of these aggregated, Pueblo-style settlements over the broad Anasazi region, which, after A.D. 1150, also incorporates the upland Mogollon area. Some settings, such as cliff alcoves and canyon heads, greatly restricted village form (Figure 1.5h). "Open" sites—settings largely free of these restrictions was the rule, not the exception (Figures 1.5i, j); and after A.D. 1200 or 1250, sites in open settings were almost all defined by massed structures around an enclosed plaza (Figure 1.5k, l, m).

Enclosed plazas, surrounded by blocks of rooms, are present in both the Mesa Verde and Zuni-Acoma areas by the mid-A.D. 1200s (Figure 1.5m). Some early Zuni sites completely enclose plazas in formal geometric massings reminiscent of Chaco building: circles or squares, and combinations of circles and squares (Kintigh 1985:42).

As noted above, after A.D. 1150 the northern upland Mogollon area is essentially Anasazi. The southern Mogollon area, in the Chihuahuan desert and its surrounding mountains, goes its own way. Enclosed-plaza, compound, and "street"-like (called "multiple linear") layouts are found in the poorly understood El Paso and related phases (Lekson and Rorex 1987; Marshall 1973). The intriguing variety of compounds, enclosed plazas, and "streets" culminated at about A.D. 1300, in the very Pueblo-like plaza layout of post-A.D. 1300 Paquimé (Figure 1.5n).

The Hohokam region undergoes a very visible transformation at about A.D. 1150, which is the transition between the Sedentary and Classic periods. Settlement locations resemble those of the Sedentary period, since both Sedentary and Classic period sites generally relied upon the same canal systems, but the architectural forms change from courtyard groups to adobe-walled, flat-roofed, rectangular compounds (Figure 1.5s) (for a description of this shift, see Sires 1987). What seem to be new forms of public architecture—rectangular platform mounds and massive multi-storied adobe buildings called great houses—may have older Hohokam roots, but they come into astonishing prominence after A.D. 1150.

Perhaps the best known Hohokam site of this time period is not in the Phoenix Basin, but the Tucson Basin Marana community. Unlike many Classic period settlements, Marana ended prior to A.D. 1300; thus, the confusion and obfuscation of continued, post-A.D. 1300 occupation are not a problem. The Marana community shows a shift, at about A.D. 1150, from ballcourt-centered pithouse settlements to a much larger settlement of adobe compounds clustered around a new style of public architecture, a rectangular platform mound (Fish et al. 1992a). This shift confirms the timing and nature of the sequence interpolated for the Phoenix Basin by drawing a line between pre-A.D. 1150 Snaketown (Haury 1976) and post-A.D. 1300 sites such as Los Muertos (Haury 1945a).

A.D. 1300–1550

Across the whole ancestral Pueblo area (the Anasazi region plus the northern Mogollon), towns from A.D. 1300 to 1400/1450 exhibited two main characteristics: they were very large and they were structured around one or more tightly defined, internal, square or (rarely) circular plazas (Figures 1.5o, p, q, r). As discussed above, the enclosed plaza may recall Chacoan forms (Fowler and Stein 1992; Lekson and Cameron 1993), or it may be a southern development associated with new ceremonial patterns (Adams 1991).

Whatever their history, enclosed plazas form the focus or foci of towns throughout the fourteenth and into the fifteenth century. From Grasshopper (Figure 1.5o) (Reid 1989) to Homol'ovi (Adams and Hays 1991) to the Zuni area (Kintigh 1985) to Arroyo Hondo (Figure 1.5r) (Creamer 1993b), single or multiple enclosed plazas become the dominant town plan throughout the A.D. 1300s (see also Figures 1.5p, q). There appears to be a modal or modular plaza size—something on the scale of 100 m by 100 m—that is carried consistently through towns of varying size. Villages were contiguous multiples of these modular units. In at least some cases, plaza modules at a site were not all contemporary, but so little recent excavation has taken place at the large sites of this period that we do not know whether this was a rule or an exception.

"Great kivas" (or at least single, very large kivas) remain part of a town plan in the Anasazi-Mogollon area, at Zuni sites (e.g., Box S, Kluckhohn; Kintigh 1985) and in the Rio Grande (Cordell 1989b:320) but, perhaps, not in the western Pueblo area. Adams (1991:83ff, 103ff) emphasizes the importance of rectangular kivas in association with enclosed plazas (indicative of new ceremonial

systems) and derives this form from the Mogollon rectangular great kivas. Enclosed-plaza towns continued into the protohistoric period and vestigially to the present at Pueblos such as Zuni and Taos (Figure 1.5u).

Sometime after A.D. 1400, the old "street" village form appears at some Hopi and Rio Grande pueblos (Figure 1.5t). Adams (1991:103) dates the "street-oriented" town plan to A.D. 1400, and argues that it "opened up the village, allowed all households to face the same direction (preferably to the south or southeast), provided more plaza areas for work and ceremony, and allowed physical separation of social groups." As noted above, there is also a thread of continuity in street-type layouts from early sites like Alkali Ridge and McPhee Village (Figure 1.5c), Chaco-era Skunk Springs (Figure 1.5b), and A.D. 1150–1300 Yellow Jacket.

Post-A.D. 1300 Classic Hohokam towns continued and elaborated the pre-A.D. 1300 pattern of adobe compounds. Platform mounds continue, increasing in size, elaboration, and—perhaps—changing function to elite residences (Crown 1991a:151; Doyel 1991:255). A new element in late Classic towns is the big or great house, the only surviving example of which is Casa Grande. As discussed previously, Wilcox has documented three of these massive, multistoried "towers," and suggested that there may have been others (Wilcox 1991d:268).

Large Classic period settlements exhibited a "zoning" of a central core consisting of one or two platform-mound compounds, a central plaza, (very rarely) a great house, and (northeast of the mound compound) a large north-south ballcourt. In an inner zone around this core were the largest residential compounds, surrounded by a second, concentric zone of smaller compounds (Gregory 1987:199ff; Wilcox 1991d:262).

Many post-A.D. 1300 Classic settlements were very large; Los Muertos (one of the largest) covered a little less than 1 km², with at least 35 major compounds (Figure 1.5s). Casa Grande, with its famous great house, was even larger.

Perhaps the largest Southwestern town of its time (A.D. 1300–1450?) was the great center of Paquimé in Chihuahua, Mexico (Figure 1.5n) (Di Peso 1974). Because of its location and its undeniable Mesoamerican features (e.g., "I"-shaped ballcourts), Di Peso interpreted Paquimé as a Mesoamerican-style town. The sampling of Paquimé encouraged this interpretation. Di Peso excavated exterior public and ceremonial precincts and largely exterior portions of the west wing of the huge "U"-shaped roomblock. He only tested the central plaza contained within the "U," and did not approach the eastern roomblocks. Paquimé's domestic architecture (although uniquely elaborate) more closely resembles that of the Pueblo Southwest. Massed, terraced adobe roomblocks form the "U" around a large central plaza (approximately 150 m by 150 m)—much like the modern Pueblo of Taos, which would fit, entire, inside Paquimé's plaza (Figure 1.5u). Outside the residential core of Paquimé lay a bewildering variety of public features, which Di Peso excavated: platform mounds, effigy mounds, burial mounds, ballcourts, communal or commercial roasting pits, domestic water systems, and even a possible Mogollon great kiva (Room 38, Unit 11). Paquimé is a unique site and without question a key link to Mesoamerica; at the same time, it is a profoundly Southwestern site, the largest of all prehistoric pueblos.

POPULATION SIZE AND STRUCTURE

Two key questions for archaeologists studying the Southwest's big sites are how many people lived in these settlements and can any of these people be identified as elites.

A.D. 900–1150

The largest Anasazi towns prior to A.D. 900 rarely exceeded 40 households (Orcutt et al. 1990) or about 200 people. From about A.D. 900 to 1150, Chaco was by far the largest single settlement in the Anasazi area, but how many people actually lived at Chaco (Figure 1.6)? Population estimates peaked early (tens of thousands in the earliest archaeological writings) and have declined ever since. Currently, "safe" archaeological estimates for Chaco hover around 5,000 (e.g., Hayes 1981). I have suggested less, between 2,100 and 2,700 (Lekson 1984b). Other estimates are much lower (Windes 1984a), giving credence to models of a largely empty ceremonial center, periodically occupied by pilgrims.

Most Anasazi communities in the Chacoan region between A.D. 900–1150 were probably about the size of the pre-A.D. 900 towns (e.g., 200 people), but a few grew to impressively large size and could themselves be considered Great Towns. One of the largest was Skunk Springs, in the Chuska Valley (Figure 1.5b). It has never been excavated, but it was comparable to the later site of Yellow Jacket, perhaps the largest of all Anasazi towns before the migrations of the late A.D. 1200s. As discussed in more detail below, Yellow Jacket's population has been estimated between 1,000 and 3,000 people.

How big were the largest Hohokam settlements prior to A.D. 1150? Snaketown is the best known and one of the largest big Preclassic Hohokam sites (Figure 1.5a). Although it is part of a large community, Snaketown proper covers a little less than 1 km² (Haury 1976:9). Haury estimated that it contained 7,000 houses during the nearly 200-year Sedentary period (Haury 1976:75). Wilcox first revised Haury's estimate of houses downward to 1,000, and would "now argue that Snaketown at its height had no more than 300 people" (Wilcox 1991d:261–262). These varying estimates reflect differing projections from sampled data. Fish (1989:48), reviewing these same data, concludes that "it is impossible to arrive at meaningful population estimates for even well excavated samples."

The largest Mimbres pueblos, at about A.D. 1100, had 300 or more rooms (Figure 1.5e). Unlike the Chacoan Great Houses, we can be certain that people actually lived in these rooms, because they are buried in remarkable numbers beneath the floors of Mimbres pueblos—for example, more than 1,000 burials at Swarts Ruin (Figure 1.5e). For the large Galaz site, the excavators estimate a maximum population of 300 (Anyon and LeBlanc 1984:192). LeBlanc (1983:106) notes "the population of any one [Mimbres] village probably never exceeded 300 people"—an estimate that seems very reasonable to me.

A.D. 1150–1300

Yellow Jacket may be the largest post-A.D. 1150 site in the Mesa Verde area (Lange et al. 1986) (Yellow Jacket's attribution to this period, rather than the earlier Chaco era is problematic; see Kane 1993.) Yellow Jacket has a range of population estimates, mostly by Arthur Rohn: 1,200–1,500 (Rohn 1983:Table 1); "2,500 or more" (Rohn 1989:161) and 2,700 with eight outlying villages of "200–250 inhabitants each [and] numerous small hamlets" for a total community in excess of 4,500 people (Ferguson and Rohn 1987:126). Others offer lower estimates. Lange et al. (1986:xi) estimate 1,500–3,000 persons as "realistic" for the Yellow Jacket area."

A score, at least, of large towns in the Montezuma Valley definitely date to this span, and many of these are only slightly smaller than Yellow Jacket (Figures 1.5h, i). Rohn (1977) suggests that none of these towns exceeded 3,000 people. I suspect that the upper limit was less than half that figure. Indeed, a current estimate for the 400 room Sand Canyon site (one of the two or three largest Montezuma Valley sites) is 725 people (Figure 1.5i) (Bradley 1992:95).

The Mesa Verde-Montezuma Valley towns were not the largest Anasazi settlements of the A.D. 1150–1300 span. The sites at Zuni were much larger. Two of the largest Zuni sites (Archeotekopa II, 1412 rooms; and Kluckhohn, 1142 rooms) both pre-date A.D. 1300. Kintigh (1985:Table 5.5) estimates populations of 1,836 and 1,485 people, respectively, assuming 65% occupancy and two persons per room. (Using those same assumptions for Yellow Jacket and Sand Canyon, we arrive at estimates of 700 and 450, respectively.)

In the Hohokam area, the early Classic (A.D. 1150–1300) Marana community includes over 6 km² of "habitation sites" (Fish et al. 1992a:Table 3.1); compare this with Snaketown's size, of about 1 km² (Figure 1.5a). However, Snaketown is a single site, while the Marana community includes more than 50 separate sites. Comparing the single site of Snaketown to the Marana community is comparing not apples and oranges, but an apple to a bag of apples. The central, mound district of Marana may be a more appropriate comparison. Fish et al. (1992a:63) estimate a Marana mound district population of between 400–500 and a maximum of 750 people—larger, perhaps, than the earlier Snaketown, but not by orders of magnitude.

A.D. 1300–1550

After A.D. 1300, pueblos get very large indeed (Figure 1.5o, p, q, r). Many post-A.D. 1300 pueblos ranged from 500 to 700 rooms, and pueblos with 1,000 or more rooms are common. Some of the largest early Rio Grande sites were in the lower Chama River: Poshuouinge had 2,000 rooms, and Sapawe had more than 2,500 rooms built around seven modular plazas. Indeed, Sapawe was one of the largest sites in the ancestral Pueblo region.

Various means of estimating population are based on cross-cultural or historic Pueblo person-per-floor area constants. Sapawe is a suitable example. At 10 m² of roofed space per person (Naroll's 1962 cross-cultural figure that, despite criticisms, has reached rule-of-thumb status) there would have been about 2,270 people. Kintigh's method (described above), gives Sapawe a population of 3,250. Stubbs (1950) used modern Pueblo data to determine an average of three people per room, which gives Sapawe a population of 7,500. These estimates are maximums, since it is unlikely that all of Sapawe's plazas and roomblocks were contemporary.

Post-A.D. 1300 Classic Hohokam settlements were spatially very large, but less dense in population than con-

temporary pueblos. Population estimates for Los Muertos, one of the largest, reach 1,000 (Doyel 1991: 254), although Wilcox (1991d) estimates 520–780 people for Los Muertos, with a "guesstimate" of 600 (Figure 1.5s). At the very large Classic center of Pueblo Grande, recent excavations have suggested a Civano phase (A.D. 1300–1450) peak of 1,500 to 2,000 people (Michael Foster, personal communication). Fish and Fish (1994:Table 10.1) offer some statistics that suggest the maximum population of the average mound community in the Phoenix Basin ranged between 2,100 and 5,300 people. Based on Wilcox and Foster's estimates, I favor the lower end of this range.

One of the largest single settlements in the ancient Southwest was Paquimé (Figure 1.5n). Di Peso (Di Peso et al. 1974:Figure 134–4) estimated a maximum population during the Diablo phase (A.D. 1300–1450, my dates) of about of 4,700, an estimate that seems reasonable (cf. Lekson 1989:183–184).

Population Structure: Elites

During the 1980s, Southwestern archaeologists engaged in considerable debate about whether the organizations of various Southwestern societies were egalitarian or hierarchical. Supporters of both views cited settlement patterns (especially settlement hierarchies), prestige artifact distributions, mortuary analyses, and other lines of evidence. However, there was surprisingly little argument around architecture: where did the purported elites live? I believe this silence reflects a real difficulty in defining elite or even unusual residences in Pueblo-style sites.

Architectural evidence for elites is not nonexistent. Arguments for elites have been mounted concerning Chacoan great houses relative to contemporary unit pueblos (Sebastian 1992), Hohokam residential platform mounds relative to contemporary compounds and pithouses (Lange and Germick 1992; Rice and Redman 1993), and larger relative to smaller Mogollon pithouses (Lightfoot and Feinman 1982). It is my impression that the Mogollon pithouse argument has failed to convince (Wills and Windes 1989:364), while great houses and platform mounds are still the subject of healthy, if inconclusive, debate.

TIMING AND TEMPO

The development of Southwestern towns is a regional contrast in permanence and mobility played over a remarkably large region (Lekson 1990b,d). The Anasazi and Mogollon adaptations were largely mobile (on varying temporal scales) and towns therefore, while sedentary, were not permanent (Lekson 1990d, 1993). An Anasazi site might be used over a long term, but that use was intermittent and noncontinuous. In contrast, Hohokam settlement locations were more-or-less "fixed," because Hohokam agriculture was tied to the fixed infrastructure of canals. Consequently, it is not unusual for a Hohokam site to have many centuries of apparently continuous occupation.

Pre-A.D. 900

Aggregated, short-term (less than 30 years) sedentary villages were present in the Anasazi and Mogollon areas by about A.D. 600, if not earlier. Early Anasazi settlements lasted a generation or less, followed by "short-hop" population movement (probably village-scale relocation) to nearby areas (Orcutt et al. 1990; Wilshusen and Blinman 1992). The Anasazi settlement strategy produced surprisingly large archaeological sites (Figure 1.5c), but these were short-term settlements. Were they "towns"—much less "Great Towns?" Probably not.

In the Hohokam region, sizable permanent communities developed by A.D. 600. Estimating the real size of early Hohokam villages is tricky at best, because the largest Hohokam sites were fully sedentary. Big Hohokam sites, such as Snaketown (Figure 1.5a), were occupied continuously for multiple generations—unlike their Anasazi contemporaries.

Mogollon settlement patterns are less well known than Anasazi and Hohokam, but "mobility" seems the byword of current Mogollon studies. The largest Mogollon pithouse villages before A.D. 900 probably had only a few score people at any one time (Figure 1.5d); and while mobility of the Anasazi was on a generational or 20-year cycle, early Mogollon residential mobility may have been strongly seasonal, as well (Gilman 1991; Lekson 1992a).

A.D. 900–1150

In the Anasazi region, the Chacoan era was marked by a remarkable change from village-level mobility to household mobility; at least, the unit of settlement changes from the contiguous villages of earlier periods to single-family "unit pueblos." In my model of the "Pax Chaco," unit pueblos moved about the landscape between Chacoan communities, each of which was marked by a much more permanent great house (Figure 1.5b) (Lekson 1992c).

Chacoan architecture has a permanence that contradicts this pattern of small-scale, short-term family mobility. Buildings like Pueblo Bonito and Chetro Ketl were built and continuously used (although not for habitation) over several centuries (Figure 1.5g); the fact that Pueblo Bonito was among the first Great Towns excavated and dated led to the erroneous conclusion that Pueblo sites of A.D. 900–1150 were permanent (Lekson 1990b). Only the great houses and public structures were intended to last more than a generation.

Mimbres villages, such as Swarts Ruin and Galaz, show much greater time depth than any non-great house Anasazi site (Figures 1.5d, e). These Mimbres pueblos must have lasted several generations to have produced the impressive number of burials they contain. Moreover, Mimbres pueblos usually overlay sizable pithouse components which, according to most scholars, were transformed rapidly into the Mimbres masonry pueblos about A.D. 1000 (Lekson 1992c; Woosley and McIntyre 1996). In my view, the shift from very high mobility in Mogollon pithouse horizons to significant, canal-based sedentism in the Mimbres towns was sudden and dramatic (Lekson 1992a,c). Large stone-masonry Mimbres pueblos were, unlike the contemporary Chacoan great houses (Figure 1.5g), sedentary residential villages. They may have been the first real "pueblos" in the Southwest (Lekson 1992b). Mimbres is, in many ways, the place where Chaco and Hohokam intersect; that is, where stone masonry architecture joins a modest canal irrigation technology, creating an abbreviated version of Hohokam "deep sedentism" after an earlier history of extreme mobility (Lekson 1992a,b,c, 1993).

Hohokam sites continue to grow and spread along and across the massive canal systems of the Phoenix Basin. In other areas (e.g., the Tucson Basin; Doelle and Wallace 1991) water remains a tether, but the relatively minor investment in canals allows greater freedom to relocate a settlement.

A.D. 1150–1300

Over most of the Pueblo world, the period from A.D. 1150 to 1300 was marked by continued growth and elaboration. Only Chaco Canyon itself was abandoned. Following the "collapse" of Chaco, the great house community continues as an Anasazi town layout for perhaps 50 years (Fowler and Stein 1992, Kintigh 1994). Then, the unit pueblos reaggregate into the visually impressive pueblos and cliff-dwellings familiar from Mesa Verde, Zuni, and

Kayenta (Figure 1.5h, i, j, k). These large pueblos continue the short, generation-scale use-life of prior times (e.g., Creamer 1993b; Dean 1969; Kintigh 1985). Huge pueblos of more than 1,000 rooms were built, used, and abandoned in perhaps 30 years. Presumably, these A.D. 1150–1300 villages also shared the mobility cycle of pre-Chaco times as well. About A.D. 1275–1300, most of the northern Anasazi area is abandoned—an event of great drama for us but perhaps of less importance for the vast majority of communities that continued to grow. Certainly, a different scale of mobility is indicated in the final movements from the Mesa Verde and Kayenta areas, and several thousands of people had to be accommodated in new locales, from the Rio Grande to the Mogollon uplands (Haury 1958).

In the Mogollon uplands, settlement dynamics become indistinguishable from the larger Pueblo patterns. In the Mimbres and desert Mogollon areas, however, A.D. 1150 marks a major departure from prior patterns: in the Mimbres region, this period is remarkably opaque, archaeologically, but it appears that populations shifted architectural and ceramic styles, and moved downstream to lower elevations. There is some disagreement about relative mobility during this span (and, indeed, there are few data). Nelson and LeBlanc (1986) see a trend towards "short-term sedentism" much as I have described for the Anasazi; I have argued for precisely the reverse—that is, sharply increased sedentism in late Mimbres and post-Mimbres villages (Lekson 1992a).

In the Hohokam area, A.D. 1150 marks the transition to the Classic period, and A.D. 1150–1300 the early Classic. Again, we know less that we would like about this span of Hohokam prehistory, but it appears that settlements continue in-place in the Phoenix and Tucson Basins, deeply sedentary and tethered to increasingly large and elaborate canal systems.

A.D. 1300–1550

The Pueblo world after A.D. 1300 was a broad crescent from the upper Rio Grande (on the east) through Zuni and the Mogollon uplands (on the south) and over to the Upper Little Colorado and Hopi (on the west) (see Introduction: Figure 2). In the uplands, "Mogollon" ceases to matter as a culture area. The significance of the extensive desert occupation in formerly Hohokam and desert Mogollon regions is an interesting research question. It is likely that, after A.D. 1300, all these areas were part of the ancestral Pueblo region—that is, all three areas play roles in the evolution of the modern Pueblo peoples.

In the ancestral Pueblo area, the old pattern of short-term, village-level mobility may have continued (with moderate lengthening of the cycle) well into the fifteenth and even sixteenth century. It appears that many villages were short-lived but, surprisingly, we know less about the timing and tempo of Pueblo settlement for this late period than for many earlier stages (see Creamer 1994; Crown and Kohler 1994). Perhaps these longstanding traditions of Pueblo movement might have continued had the Spanish not arrived. Colonization had two effects: first, the in-filling of critical "empty" areas between Pueblos with colonists and, second (and perhaps consequently), increased importance of canal irrigation in the Rio Grande and its drainages, with irrigation's "tethering" of settlement.

After a century of archaeological opacity (A.D. 1150–1250), the southern (desert) Mogollon area is the setting of a remarkable burst of Pueblo-style, adobe villages (Lekson 1992c) and, to an undefined degree, incorporation into the "Salado" horizon (Crown 1994; Lang and Germick 1992; Nelson and LeBlanc 1986)—a ceramic distribution of the late thirteenth and fourteenth centuries that stretched from Phoenix to Paquimé. It is probably no coincidence that the inception of "Salado" occurs at about the same time as the abandonment of the Four Corners area (Crown 1994:203ff). "Salado" alone does not explain the remarkable fluorescence of desert towns in the fourteenth and early fifteenth centuries—or their stunning disappearance, about A.D. 1450, in the Southwest's second great "abandonment." If the details of settlement are obscure, the outlines of this important large-scale movement are completely unknown. The fifteenth century abandonment of the Southwestern deserts is one key theme for future research.

Hohokam sites in the Phoenix Basin continued in place, with increasingly elaborate public architecture (Figure 1.5s), until they were abandoned in the fourteenth or early fifteenth century.

The final, and perhaps most permanent Great Town in this period was Paquimé (Figure 1.5n). The predecessors of Paquimé are obscure. Nevertheless, the Great Town itself was built after A.D. 1300 and lasted until A.D. 1450 or slightly later. The occupation span of Paquimé has been a matter of debate; the best estimates for the city are about A.D. 1300 to the mid—to late-A.D. 1400s (Dean and Ravesloot 1993). It appears that Paquimé was occupied continuously throughout.

HISTORICAL PROCESS

The Southwestern record is comparatively brief, but it is full of incident. Southwesternists have spilled an immoderate amount of ink on wildly differing versions of the region's past. I will not try to compare and contrast those conflicting texts; instead I offer a digest of my own views (Lekson 1990a, 1992a, 1993).

A.D. 900–1150

Between A.D. 900 and 1150, each of the three "cultural" regions of the Southwest was the setting for extraordinarily well-defined archaeological patterns, "strong patterns" that define in some ways the regions themselves: in the Anasazi area, Chaco and its regional network of roads and outliers; in the Hohokam region, the Preclassic climax of the extensive ballcourt system; and in the Mogollon area, the remarkable art and architecture of the Mimbres phase. Chaco and Hohokam—the two big "regional systems"—stood in splendid geographic and taxonomic opposition (Crown and Judge 1991), with an "artsy" Mimbres district off to the southeast.

The three "strong patterns" differed in settlement patterning. Chaco had an obvious center, the complex of buildings at Chaco Canyon. Hohokam and Mimbres did not have a single settlement that represented a clear regional center. Settlement hierarchies were evidently absent among Preclassic Hohokam or Mimbres phase large villages.

Historical processes in the Southwest were, perhaps, more directly tied to large-scale human ecology than many other areas of North America. The Southwest was truly limiting: it was probably one of the least clement environments for a prehistoric agricultural economy. Chaco Anasazi was a rainfall-based agricultural adaptation to the pinyon-juniper and grassland's environment on (and off) the Colorado Plateau. Radiating out from the center at Chaco Canyon, a network of roads linked outlier communities. Under the "Pax Chaco," mobility from community to community was possible on a household level (the unit pueblo). Anasazi settlement reached maximum fluidity.

The majority of Hohokam population lived along the massive canal systems around the confluence of the Salt and Gila Rivers and along smaller streams to the east and southeast. Irrigation, and particularly canal irrigation, was essential to agricultural success in the Hohokam world. This expensive infrastructure fixed settlements in place. Canals severely restrict mobility. A regional system of ballcourts both self-identified and linked communities.

Mimbres looked so much like Anasazi that early archaeologists thought it was a northern intrusion or migration, but the economic base was profoundly non-Anasazi: canal irrigation much smaller in scale than the Hohokam prototype but still quantitatively and qualitatively different from the most elaborate Anasazi water management. Consequently, late Mimbres settlement was far less mobile, and far more sedentary than contemporary Anasazi, and Mimbres pueblos grew to sizes unknown in contemporary Anasazi villages.

A.D. 1150–1300

A.D. 1150 has been recognized as a key "hinge point" of Southwestern history (Cordell and Gumerman 1989b:6). In the Anasazi area, Chaco ceases to be the center. In the Hohokam region, A.D. 1150 marks the beginning of the Classic period. At A.D. 1150, Mimbres ends and "Mogollon" begins to lose meaning as a cultural entity. Indeed, across the old Mogollon area there is remarkable architectural change at A.D. 1150, but no consistency is evident in the nature of the change.

A.D. 1300, the end of this period, marks a number of interesting "events," such as abandonments, phase shifts, and ideological (or at least iconographic) changes. Many things were happening across the Southwest at about A.D. 1300, but those "happenings" were different in different areas.

The end of Chaco by the mid-A.D. 1100s caused the "balkanization" of the Anasazi area into discrete subregional traditions, such as Kayenta, Little Colorado, Zuni, and northern Rio Grande. Initially, the most important configurations were broad, latitudinal ceramic provinces north and south of the old Chaco world. To the north was the Mesa Verde region and to the south was a less-well known but comparably sized Tularosa region, which stretched from the Rio Grande to the Tonto Basin. Along the southern arc of the old Chacoan world, trade and communication continued between subregions, but the Mesa Verde area was effectively cut off. Evidence for long-distance trade at Mesa Verde sites dwindles to almost nothing between A.D. 1150 and 1300. What was once part of a very large regional system fails in the smaller confines of the immediate Four Corners area. After a serious drought in the A.D. 1270s and 1280s, the Mesa Verde area was abandoned. Elsewhere, post-Chacoan public architecture continues for several decades until its functions are replaced, at or after A.D. 1300, by new ceremonial and religious systems.

Although the Anasazi world "contracts" from its greatest western and northern limits, Pueblo-style architecture begins to appear in many parts of the southern and eastern Southwest which had previously been pithouse territory. Because these new "Pueblo" areas were in the old Mogollon and Hohokam regions, we tend to think of a contraction of Anasazi. However, it may be more useful to think of a general shift or "sag" in Pueblo-style settlement, southward and eastward.

This is not to say that every settlement in the A.D. 1150–1300 Southwest was a pueblo (as discussed above, pithouses were always present, even in the Pueblo region). Desert villages early in this period were more compound-like than apartment-like. These are murky times in the archaeology of the deserts: the poorly understood early Classic period in the Hohokam and nearly unknown Animas, Black Mountain, and early El Paso phases in the eastern deserts. In desert areas, lack of archaeological clarity forms a real horizon, which I have described elsewhere as the era of "the people who forgot to paint their pots"—an observation with implications for pre-Paquimé archaeology as well. There probably was no significant depopulation of the New Mexico and Arizona deserts, and the widespread opacity of the record is an important archaeological pattern that we have not yet learned to interpret. In the deserts, nothing ended at A.D. 1300.

A.D. 1300–1550

During the population dislocations of the late thirteenth and early fourteenth century, Pueblo-style towns expanded to or appeared in three areas remarkable for their rich hunting-gathering resources and the prior absence of major agricultural settlement: the Rio Grande Valley, the Mogollon Rim ecotone, and the north and northeast foothills of the Sierra Madre in Mexico. These areas, prior to this time, may have been "preserves" for the large agricultural populations of Chaco, Mimbres, and Hohokam.

The span from A.D. 1300 to 1550 carried the Pueblos over into European history. The Hohokam and Mogollon did not make that transition: the major Hohokam centers in the Phoenix Basin suffered a catastrophic flood about A.D. 1360 and the great center of Paquimé did not survive into the A.D. 1500s. As a result, our thinking is dominated by the Pueblos; but the final Hohokam and Mogollon developments were remarkable achievements.

In the Anasazi region, this period sets the stage for the modern Pueblos. The Four Corners was abandoned by A.D. 1300—an event so dramatic that it has deflected archaeological thinking away from those areas which not only were not abandoned, but also had many times the population of the romantic, but failed, ruins of the Mesa Verde and Kayenta areas. In the Upper Little Colorado (e.g., Adams 1991; Adams and Hays 1991), in the Zuni area (e.g., Kintigh 1985), and in the Rio Grande (Figures 1.5t, u) (e.g., Cordell 1979; Marshall and Walt 1984), things did not end at A.D. 1300. In fact, it could be said that the Rio Grande really started at or just before A.D. 1300.

A key archaeological development, and one with implications for the formation of long-term, highly-aggregated villages, was the first occurrence of recognizable Kachina representations in the southern Pueblo area (Adams 1991; Schaafsma 1994). If Kachina ceremonialism did not arrive deus ex machina, presumably a proto-Kachina iconography is yet to be found (e.g., Schaafsma 1992, 1994). The Kachina religious system would play a key role in the survival of the Pueblos, when Spanish colonization fixed the villages in place on preposterously small land-grants, and ended a thousand years of movement and mobility.

To the south, in the Hohokam region, the Classic period continued canal-based settlement patterns begun 500–600 years earlier. The Classic saw a brief climax from A.D. 1300 to perhaps A.D. 1356, when a huge flood probably destroyed the vital irrigation canals of the Phoenix Basin; if the A.D. 1356 flood did not end the Phoenix Basin Hohokam, equally bad floods in A.D. 1380–1383 finished the job (Gregory 1991:187).

Paquimé, today, is to the archaeology of the fourteenth century what Chaco was, until recently, to the twelfth—extensively excavated, underanalyzed, virtually without context, but clearly the most important single site for understanding its times (Figure 1.5n). The largest areal abandonment and migration in Southwestern history was not the famous Four Corners affair. It was the abandonment of the southern Southwest. Two centuries or more after Pueblo people left Mesa Verde, Paquimé was almost certainly the key to that later, historically more significant displacement. We do not know what Paquimé was, or why it failed. Nevertheless, we do know that Paquimé was the largest, most complex, most cosmopolitan pueblo of its time—and perhaps of any time prior to Spanish colonization. It is simultaneously dismaying and deeply satisfying to state that our understanding of Paquimé and its place in Southwestern history is only beginning (Minnis 1984; Woosley and Ravesloot 1993).

CONCLUDING REMARKS

"Great Towns" are ultimately defined by their hierarchical relationship to other settlements—a topic developed in this volume for the Southwest by Fish (Chapter 4). In this section, I address several topics relevant to the town and the related notion of urbanism.

Chaco has been called "proto-urban" (Lekson 1984b); Rohn (1983) writes of "budding urban centers" of the northern San Juan Anasazi; Paquimé is routinely referred to as a city (Di Peso et al. 1974). "Urban" is in the eye of the beholder: what do we mean by urban? This chapter (and the Southwest) is no place to debate and refine definitions of "city." However, several dimensions of urbanism may be usefully addressed. These are architectural complexity, ethnic diversity, and population thresholds.

All societies use a variety of building types. A basic residence might consist of varied constructions (e.g., in the Southwest: kiva, ramada, roomblock; pithouse, ramada, courtyard). Major non-residential facilities may suggest evolving levels of settlement complexity. Temples, warehouses, palaces, schools, and so forth do not signify the city, but they indicate the beginnings of one aspect of urbanism. In the Southwest, Chaco Canyon, Classic Hohokam settlements, and Paquimé exhibit the most diverse architectural forms, encompassing a variety of non-residential structures and facilities.

"Ethnicity" is a difficult call in prehistory, but claims have been made for dual-ethnic settlements at Chaco (Vivian 1990), a Hakataya "barrio" at the Classic period Hohokam site of Las Colinas (Crown 1991a), and "foreign" enclaves at Paquimé (Di Peso et al. 1974). On some level, modern Pueblos who trace their ancestry to numerous independent clans might also represent "multi-ethnic" communities.

Lekson (1989, 1990b) and Kosse (1990, 1992) have demonstrated cross-cultural thresholds at about 2,500 people for settlements without complex, institutionalized authority structures. Below that number, people just get along; above that number, it's cops, inspectors, and city hall. This threshold arises from internal, cognitive limits on people in groups (for the full argument, see Kosse 1990; Lekson 1989, 1990b). In short, complexity—and specifically, sociopolitical hierarchy—can arise from cognitive social dynamics *within* a town or settlement, unrelated to local or regional settlement systems. We look at geographic frameworks for the recognition and origin of complexity and sociopolitical hierarchy, but important elements of complexity may arise as emergent properties of towns themselves.

Rohn (1977:123ff and elsewhere) has commented on a population "cap" of 2,500–3,000 for prehistoric pueblos: "beyond 2,500 to 3,000 residents, such settlements would need to restructure their society in order to meet the conflicts of larger communities." Historic Pueblos seldom if ever exceeded this level of population.

Both Chaco and Paquimé are prime candidates for complexity: large populations with architectural and ethnic diversity. Individual Classic Hohokam towns were probably not sufficiently large, but the larger irrigation communities may have exceeded 2,500 people. Chaco, Paquimé, and Classic Hohokam irrigation communities all had the attendant regional systems that we customarily associate with hierarchy and complexity; but, it is well to ask, which came first: regional hierarchy or intra-settlement complexity? Population thresholds suggest that *real* Great Towns contained the seeds of their own complexity.

ACKNOWLEDGMENTS

Figures 1.1–1.4 were drafted by Julie Barnes Smith.

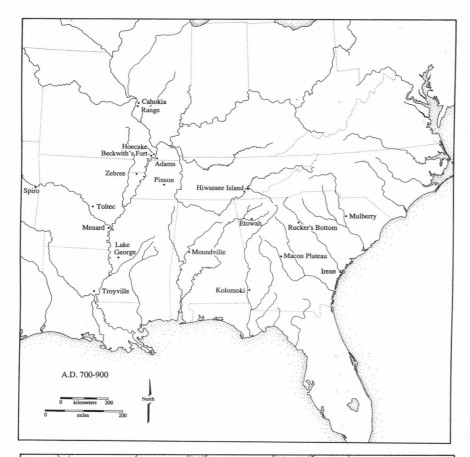

Figure 2.1.   Map showing locations of major South-eastern sites, A.D. 700–900.

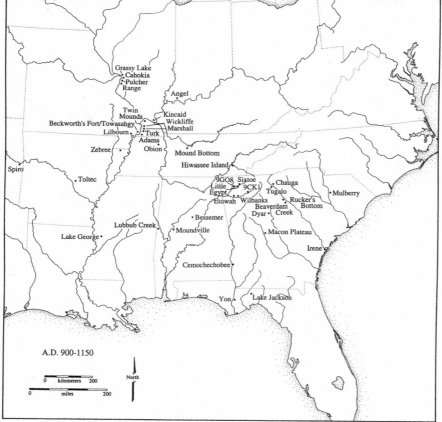

Figure 2.2.   Map showing locations of major South-eastern sites, A.D. 900–1150.

CHAPTER TWO

Late Prehistoric Towns in the Southeast

George R. Holley

IN THE ARCHAEOLOGY OF THE SOUTHEASTERN UNITED States the term "Great Town" is seldom used. Rather the more neutral term "center" is preferred to identify sites with earthen monuments, regardless of time period. Using the criteria of size and pan-Southeastern importance, only two late prehistoric sites, Cahokia and Moundville, would qualify as Great Towns. However, I do not think that these are the only criteria that should be employed. I define Great Town as the seat of a regionally-based chiefdom (Carneiro 1981; Steponaitis 1978; Wright 1984). These towns served as the setting for both communal rituals (e.g., harvest) and those extolling the life-cycle of the chiefly lineage. They emerged within a broader cultural context, identified as Mississippian (A.D. 900–1500), that shared a sedentary lifestyle, a hierarchical social organization (Knight 1990), and a unifying ideology, involving chiefly/warrior and earth/fertility themes and ancestor veneration (Brown 1985; Waring 1968).

Such an inclusive definition renders my identification of the Great Towns equivocal and thus I use both town and center interchangeably. What may have functioned as a Great Town within one region would go unnoticed as a minor player in another; and for a number of regions, multiple sites display roughly the same size. To compare these towns, I chose four variables based on their presumed importance and ease of gathering: town size, number of mounds, height of primary mound, and number of apparent plazas. Town size is a coarse-grained, composite measure of population size and the disposition of occupation across the landscape. The mound variables reflect the relative effort and multiplicity of public construction. I emphasize the main mound (chief's mound) because of its singular importance to the town, regardless of town size. The number of plazas is important, because I assume that the presence of more than one plaza signifies an additional hierarchical level or diversified functions. Towns with high rankings for these variables were undoubtedly important. However, the reverse does not hold.

With these variables I examined a number of towns and chose only 21 to present here (Table 2.1; Figures 2.1–2.4). Three obvious groupings are evident based on size: Mega-center, Large Center, and Small Center. Rank ordering within each group is not as clear cut, nor necessarily desirable. Although all of the largest major sites (in terms of size) are included, a significant number of average sized or smaller towns were not tabulated (I would hazard to guess that the figure is around 100).

Mega-centers, as noted above, comprise only two sites: Cahokia and Moundville (Figures 2.5–2.6). Although these Mega-centers were at the apex of their respective regions, they were not of equivalent scale. The immensity of Cahokia is worth underscoring and for this

Table 2.1. Tabulation of Mississippian Towns by Select Variables.

Site	Size	Number	Height	Plazas
Mega				
Cahokia	1,200	100+	30	Multiple
Moundville	150	20+	16.8	Multiple
Large				
Lake George	21	25	18.4	2
Winterville	20	20+	17	3
Etowah	21	6	20.3	2
Macon Plateau	32	6	15	?
Kincaid	70	19	12	2
Angel	40	11	13	2?
Lake Jackson	26	7	11	2
Small				
Mound Bottom	12	13	11	1
Lilbourn	16	8	8	1
Beckwith's Fort	8	7	7	1
Obion	9	7	7	1
Emerald	3	8	11	1
Menard	8	8	15.2	1
Upper Nodena	6	7	7	1
Shiloh	25	7	4.4	1
Adams	7	7	7	1
Toqua	4	2	7	1
Little Egypt	5	3	3	1
Parkin	7	7	7	1

KEY:

Size — estimated and rounded site size in hectares (of varying accuracy)

Number — number of mounds

Height — height of principal mound

Plazas — frequency of presumptive plazas

Estimates derived from site reports (figures provided or estimated based upon site maps) referenced throughout the paper, except for Shiloh, Menard, Emerald, and Mound Bottom that derived from Morgan (1980).

reason probably deserves singular status. For example, the combined volume of all of the monuments recorded for the Fort Walton area (23 sites and 40 monuments; Scarry and Payne 1986) does not equal the volume of Monks Mound at Cahokia (610,000 m³). Even the second largest town in the Southeast, Moundville, could comfortably fit within the central portion of Cahokia.

Large Centers, of which a few are not included because of incomplete data, are more numerous (Figures 2.7–2.10) and in all examples were prominent regional centers. Note that two excluded examples, the East St. Louis and St. Louis Mound Groups, resided within the Cahokia sphere and were thus second-order centers. The primary mounds at Large Centers ranged in estimated volume from 50,000 to 200,000 m³.

The Small Center in many cases did function as a regional center (Figures 2.11–2.14). Problems arise, however, in deciding which particular center in an area was the most important. For example, the vast floodplain associated with the confluence of the Mississippi and Ohio Rivers contains an impressive number of sites (of which only three are listed here: Lilbourn, Beckwith's Fort, and Adams) that would qualify equally as of paramount importance. Primary mounds at Small Centers ranged in volume from 7,000 to 65,000 m³.

A number of second-order centers, particularly within the Lower Mississippi Valley, would also fall within the parameters of Small Centers. To underscore the variability in town size, many regions lack any nucleated mound grouping within the range of Small Centers (Dickens 1978; Steponaitis 1991).

ELEMENTS OF SOUTHEASTERN TOWNS

Each Southeastern town, regardless of size, was defined by a central focus composed of a mound-plaza configuration. This focality defined and characterized a cultural landscape that embodied the geographical perspective of place and centrality and the cosmological perspective of center of the universe.

Although Mississippian towns are characterized first and foremost by a concentration of mounds, they were more than a constellation of earthen monuments. For too long our understanding of these centers has been based on the study of mounds. Ongoing research at Cahokia (Dalan 1993; Holley et al. 1993) is promoting a new perspective: a view of Mississippian towns as built landscapes. The conclusion that Mississippians trans-

Figure 2.3.   Map showing locations of major Southeastern sites, A.D. 1150–1300.

A.D. 1150-1300

Sites on map (top, Figure 2.3):
Grassy Lake, Mitchell, Cahokia, East St. Louis, St. Louis, Range, Angel, Twin Mounds, Kincaid, Beckworth's Fort/Towasahgy, Wickliffe, Turner/Snodgrass, Marshall, Turk, Lilbourn, Adams, Mound Bottom, Parkin, Nodena, Hiwassee Island, Toqua, Town Creek, Spiro, Shiloh, Little Egypt, Bell Field, Tugalo, Etowah, 9CK4, Rucker's Bottom, Mulberry, Raccoon Creek, Wilbanks, Beaverdam Creek, Free Bridge, Scull Shoals, Dyar, Winterville, Bessemer, Shinholser, Pocahontas, Moundville, Macon Plateau, Lake George, Lubbub Creek, 9TR12, Irene, Roods Landing, Singer-Moye, Emerald, Cemochechobee, Bottle Creek, Yon, Lake Jackson, Borrow Pit, Lake Lafayette

Figure 2.4.   Map showing locations of major Southeastern sites, A.D. 1300–1550.

A.D. 1300-1550

Sites on map (bottom, Figure 2.4):
Horseshoe Lake, Caborn-Welborn, Twin Mounds, Kincaid, Powers Fort, Wickliffe, Turner/Snodgrass, Turk, Lilbourn, Adams, Sassafras Ridge, Lick Creek, Parkin, Upper Nodena, Hiwassee Island, Toqua, Town Creek, Spiro, Shiloh, Citico, 9RA3, Bell Field, Chauga, Little Egypt, 9CK4, Tugalo, King, Freebridge, Rucker's Bottom, Mulberry, Menard, Etowah, Dyar, Scull Shoals, Winterville, Little River, Shoulderbone, Lake George, Moundville, Shinholser, Lubbub Creek, 9TR12, Macon Plateau, Haynes Bluff, Roods Landing, Irene, Singer-Moye, Emerald, Fatherland, San Luis, Lake Jackson, Yon, Borrow Pit, Lake Lafayette

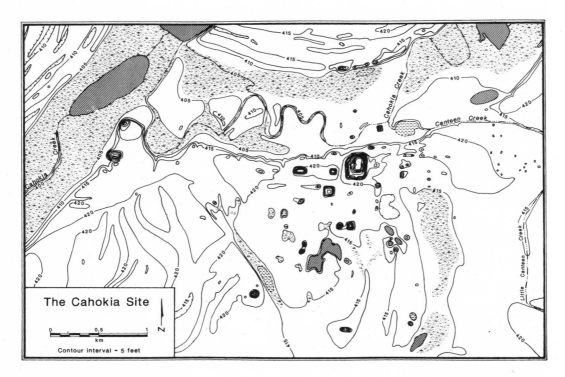

Figure 2.5.   The Cahokia site.

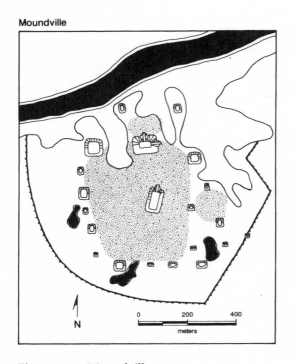

Figure 2.6.   Moundville.

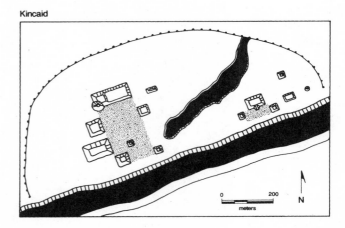

Figure 2.7.   Mississippian large centers—Kincaid (adapted from Cole et al. 1951:Figure 69).

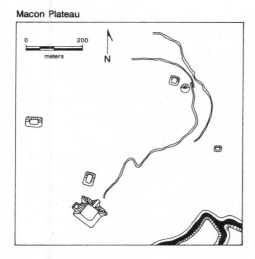

Figure 2.8.   Mississippian large centers—Macon Plateau (adapted from Fairbanks 1946:Figure 2).

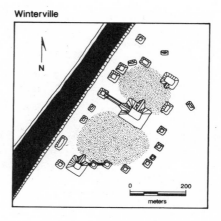

Figure 2.9.   Mississippian large centers—Winterville (adapted from Brain 1989:Figure 12).

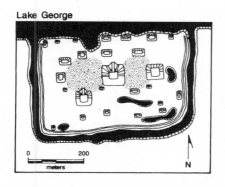

Figure 2.10.   Mississippian large centers—Lake George (adapted from Williams and Brain 1983: Figures 1.2, 2.1).

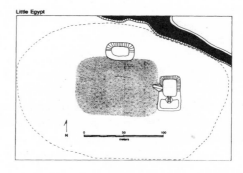

Figure 2.11.   Mississippian small centers—Little Egypt (adapted from Hally et al. 1980:Figure 167).

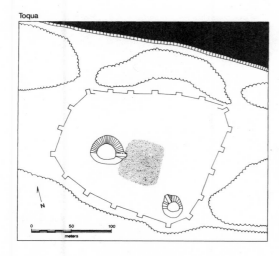

Figure 2.12.   Mississippian small centers—Toqua (adapted from Polhemus et al.1987:Figures 1.3, 3.4).

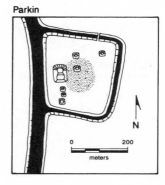

Figure 2.13.   Mississippian small centers—Parkin (adapted from P. Morse 1990:Figure 7.1 and Morgan 1980:67).

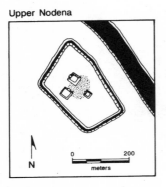

Figure 2.14. Mississippian small centers—Upper Nodena (adapted from D. Morse 1990:Figure 5.1 and Morgan 1980:70).

Chief's Mound

Nearly every town is dominated by a prominent mound, exceeding all other mounds at the site by either volume or elevation (usually on the order of twice the elevation). Opinions vary as to the function of these mounds as either the location of community temples (e.g., Phillips et al. 1951:325) or the chief's mound (Black 1967:504). I interpret these prominent monuments as supporting a chief's compound that encompassed a host of functions. Excavations uniformly document the presence of encircling palisades and large buildings (e.g., Black 1967:357–368; Cole et al. 1951:Figures 24, 27; Garland 1992:50; Williams and Brain 1983:Figure 3.38). The example from the Fourth Terrace of Monks Mound at Cahokia is unique because a large part of the summit building is exposed (Figure 2.15).

formed the natural by borrowing, reclaiming, and manipulating it to mold a symbolically charged landscape is inescapable. The avenues taken vary spatially and temporally and even within the life-cycle of the center. Embedded within rites of renewal and purification (Knight 1981), these alterations created landscapes, the scale of which cannot be ascertained by surficial examination. On a general level, the creation of a plaza, demarcated by the arrangement of mounds, results in a square plan that incorporates a tangible manifestation of the four-quarters world view (Knight 1981:46). Even when mounds ceased to function, this four-quarters perspective was replaced by the historic square-ground.

The mound-plaza configuration created a zone of social distance, contrasting the public-ritual core from the surrounding village. The core of the site contained cleared areas demarcated by mounds and public buildings. Peripheral to this core, with spatial variability, was a packing or scattering of domestic structures. Palisades demarcated either the central precinct or the entire town. I believe that nearly every Mississippian center was fortified in some manner.

Central Area

The elements that comprise the central area of a town include the chief's mound, the temple-mound, a variety of other mounds, and one or more plazas.

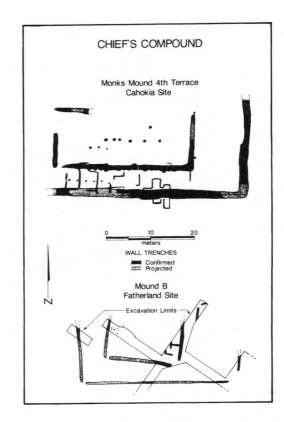

Figure 2.15. Mississippian chief's compound. Monks Mound structure (adapted from Fischer 1972). Fatherland Mound B structures (adapted from Neitzel 1965:Figure 7) and represents an early rendering of buildings on Mound B.

The chief's mound displays features that separate it from the remainder of the mounds: different morphology and mass (such as multi-terraced or elongated with conical additions); larger size; a position that dominated the main plaza; and the summit of which supported the center's largest building, typically a multi-room compound. Internal differentiation and the considerable size of these buildings—more than twice the size of other buildings—indicate that they accommodated a large number of people, such as retainers and select audiences. From an ekistic perspective, these compounds restricted access and visibility.

I suspect that the presence of a single structure on the summit of the chief's mound was confined to only centers that were of paramount significance but not necessarily to just Large Centers. For example, at least two Small Centers that were of primary regional importance during the terminal Mississippian, Fatherland (Figure 2.15) (Neitzel 1965:18) and Little Egypt (Figure 2.11) (Hally et al. 1980:522), had single structures on the summit. Other Small Centers of lesser importance during the same time have yielded evidence for multiple structures on the summit (e.g., DeJarnette and Wimberly 1941; Garland 1992; Lewis and Kneberg 1946; Polhemus et al. 1987; Schnell et al. 1981).

The singular uniqueness of the chief's mound and summit structure implies to me that the chief was superordinate to the constellation of lineage/clan heads that presumably occupied these towns. In contrast, a multiplicity of buildings on the primary mound summit may signify the absence of such a political organization. Although I subscribe to this political interpretation, an alternative view is that multiple structures on the summit reflect regional variation.

Other Mounds

The second primary feature in the Mississippian town is the temple. Temples, also on platform mounds, served charnel and other ritualistic functions. An example of a mortuary complex is clearly evident at the Etowah site (Larson 1971a). Temple buildings are, like the chief's compound, distinguished (often) by two-room partitioning and palisades that limit access. A number of good examples of the temple exist in the archaeological literature (Black 1967:Figure 261; Cole et al. 1951:Figures 15, 18; Larson 1971a:Figure 2; Polhemus et al. 1987:Figure 3.43). Other candidates for temple locations at a number of Mississippian sites have a larger surface area on their summit than the chief's mound.

Elite exclusivity of the charnel house and burial program for towns is unclear within the archaeological record. For example, Mound C at Etowah, which is adjacent to the chief's mound, yielded more than 350 burials (Larson 1971a), a figure that is clearly out-of-line with any reliable estimate of the proportion of elites within any town.

At sites with more than two mounds, the function and use of the remaining mounds varied. I infer their primary functions as elite residences, elite temples, burial chambers, and corporate facilities tethered to formalized kinship divisions. Their presence reflects the contribution of other social units and clans/lineages within the town.

Plazas

Plazas are one of the few monumental features within Mississippian towns that display unlimited access. These open spaces were unequivocally public and were capable of supporting the bulk of the resident population. Events in the plaza objectified and reified the roles and statuses of the social groups. Activities included games, dance, theater, monumental construction, and planting and harvesting ceremonies (Howard 1968; Swanton 1946). The size and frequency of plazas are proportional to town size and the presumed organizational structure. I argue that the number of formal plazas reflects the presence of multiple organizational levels and/or specialized functions.

Plazas, however, were not barren ground. Excavations point to the presence of large posts, post structures, and other features (Chapman et al. 1977; Porter 1974). There is substantial evidence that these plazas were constructed and manipulated to formally set them apart from the village area (Dalan 1993; Holley et al. 1993; Larson 1989; Lewis and Kneberg 1946; Polhemus et al. 1987).

It is a truism in Mississippian archaeology, based on ethnohistoric observations and to a degree archaeological validation, that the area surrounding the mounds and plazas was reserved for elite residence and public buildings. This gives rise to the notion that Mississippian towns were characterized by concentric zones of social distance. However, as detailed below, this model does not map uniformly onto all sites.

Village

The appearance of towns in the Southeast had a profound impact on domestic life. For the first time during Southeastern prehistory we have unambiguous evidence for full-fledged sedentism. At the most obvious, this is evident in residential stability, as seen in the frequent rebuilding of structures in the same location. This longevity of residential space is taken as an indicator of land usufruct. A perusal of household rebuilding from a number of Mississippian towns indicates that from 20 percent to 80 percent of the domestic structures were rebuilt. Here, I use the concept of household to refer to the succession of structures at a given location. At some towns up to nine sequential building episodes have been identified.

For nearly all Mississippian towns, the single family dwelling was the minimal social unit. Most of these structures range in size from 15 to 42 m² on average. Their small size suggests single family residence. These households were probably not independent—their disposition suggests that they formed larger functioning units (Holley et al. 1989; Polhemus 1990:134). At least two forms are indicated: 1) a courtyard group consisting of houses fronting a common space; and 2) right-angle alignments of closely-spaced structures. Regional variation in dwelling size and construction style was pronounced. Material inventories and architectural data indicate an egalitarian aspect to domestic life—there is generally not a marked social differentiation among the commoners. However, differences in lifeways can be recognized in comparing town versus outlying households.

In addition to numerous dwellings, Mississippian towns also had special-purpose buildings, which were distinguished by their shape (circular), size (large), and/or morphology (partitioned). These buildings were, however, numerically insignificant. A rough estimate is that 10 percent of the buildings at Mississippian towns (e.g., Black 1967; Lewis and Kneberg 1946; Holley 1991; O'Brien 1972b; Pauketat 1991) were either outside the size range of domestic structures or had a different morphology. In contrast to domestic structures, these special purpose buildings were seldom rebuilt, indicating their function was singular.

The circular buildings, especially small ones with evidence of burning, are interpreted as sweat baths. At Cahokia, these buildings were often near (or at the future locations of) mounds and other large buildings (Moorehead 1928; Pauketat 1991); but at other sites, they appear intermixed within the village (Black 1967; Chapman et al. 1977:Figure 13). Larger circular buildings, in contrast, appear to conform to the council house (Fairbanks 1946), a poorly understood structure in Mississippian archaeology.

Larger buildings, as a group, are more problematical. They are typically found on top of mounds or at ground level near mounds. Most examples were partitioned in some form and largely free of debris. A variety of functions are indicated: men's house, charnel house, clan/residential grouping, or elite residence.

The impression generated from the Spanish entrada was that Mississippian towns, especially the scores of domestic dwellings, were laid out in a formal manner. That such a pattern is not obvious from the archaeological record is due to frequent rebuilding and flux within village life during centuries of occupation. The short-lived fortified village of the Snodgrass site does support the observations of the Spanish (Price and Griffin 1979).

LAYOUTS OF MISSISSIPPIAN TOWNS

Given these basic features, I will turn to how these are articulated to form variations in town layouts. There are at least three organizational patterns; and since layout is determined by town size, these patterns correspond with the town rankings provided earlier (Table 2.1). However, structural relationships between features are not allometric. That is, an increase in the size of a settlement is likely indicative of a structural change and not simply a proportional increase in the resident population. In other words, the Mega-center, for example, is not simply an enlargement of the Small Center.

The Small Center constitutes the basic pattern identified in the discussion of elements: a single plaza demarcated by mounds. Surrounding this core was a village, the organization of which remains difficult to discern. Formal planning (inferred by alignments of structures) was present as were localized cemeteries (Chapman et al. 1977; D. Morse 1990). Rebuilding of households at Small Centers varied from 50 percent to more than 80 percent. The latter figure is undoubtedly inflated for it refers to only ground level domestic structures with complete data from the Toqua site (Polhemus et al. 1987). Nevertheless, a significant number of the structures at this site were rebuilt. Occupation at many Small Centers was not confined within the palisade (Garland 1992:40–41; Chapman et al. 1977; Morse and Morse 1983:263–264, 285–286). In contrast to Large Centers, nearly all Small Centers are characterized by a relatively dense residential occupation (Hally et al. 1980; Lewis 1986; Polhemus et al. 1987; Walker 1946).

A late variant of this simple layout is the well-known "St. Francis-type" (Morse and Morse 1983; Phillips et al. 1951:329–330). These compact towns had more than 2 m of midden debris accumulate in a relatively short time. All were fortified, but not all had mounds. One of the larger examples, Parkin (Figure 2.13), has a small, two-terraced chief's mound and six additional mounds within only a 6.9 ha palisaded area (Morse and Morse 1983:290–295).

Large Centers represent a transformation by multipli-cation and elaboration. The majority of these sites were much larger than other settlements within their region. All had multiple groupings of mounds and plazas. Two examples are obvious: paired plazas around the central mound (Winterville, Lake George, Lake Jackson, and Etowah) (Figures 2.9, 2.10) and displaced plazas (Kincaid and Angel) (Figures 2.7, 2.16). The paired examples dis-play a bilateral symmetry imbued within Mississippian art and historically documented kinship data (Knight 1990). Such inherent twofold symmetry has given rise to the suggestion that the larger towns manifested oppos-ing clans or moieties, a suggestion supported by some archaeological data (Pebbles 1987a; see also Black 1967:500–501). A twofold division may also suggest ten-sion in the organization of the settlement. However, clans were not exclusively residential units (Knight 1990). The organization of mounds may only reflect the corpo-rate, ceremonial functioning of these groups.

Of all the Large Centers, the Angel site appears to have the greatest density of domestic dwellings and rebuild-ing (roughly estimated at 80 percent). Kincaid is pre-sumed to have had only a modest resident population (Muller 1986a) (Figure 2.7) and Lake George, Winterville, Macon Plateau, and Lake Jackson are characterized as vacant (Brain 1989; Fairbanks 1956:34–35; Williams and Brain 1983; John Scarry personal communication) (Fig-ures 2.8, 2.9, 2.10).

Variability in the formal layout of the Large Center is pronounced. However, all but one (Macon Plateau) have the primary or chief's mound within the approximate center thus confirming the concentric model. Three sites (Winterville, Lake George and Lake Jackson) strike a neat bilateral symmetry in the arrangement of the plaza-mound configuration around the primary mound (Fig-ures 2.9, 2.10). Etowah, although unbalanced in layout, also has all major mounds tethered to the primary mound. Kincaid has a unique disposition of what are essentially two discrete mound-plaza arrangements (Figure 2.7). Angel in contrast is the least formally organized of these Large Centers with a random assortment of mounds displaced away from the chief's mound. The chief's mound is,

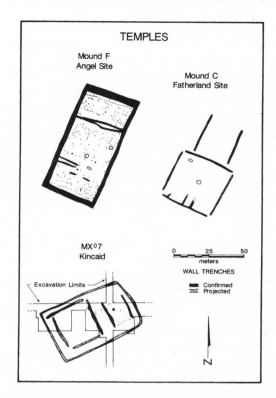

Figure 2.16. Mississippian temples. Angel example (adapted from Black 1967:Figure 14). Fatherland ex-ample of Temple 2 (adapted from Neitzel 1965:Figure 12). Kincaid example (adapted from Cole et al. 1951:Figure 18).

however, roughly located within the geographic center of the town. Finally, Macon Plateau offers an "exploded" perspective, with the major monuments ringing a large rectangular area (Figure 2.8). I agree with Fairbanks' (1956:47) interpretation that the large open center of Macon Plateau was likely not the plaza, but rather each mound complex possessed an individual plaza.

The third layout concerns the two Mega-centers that display both similarities and differences (Figures 2.5–2.6). Both sites are sprawling and defy measurement of both town size and the degree to which dispersed ele-ments were self-contained or interdependent. The prob-lem of town limits remains to be resolved for fortified sites, requiring much more systematic survey than has been done to date.

Moundville and Cahokia differ in the sizes of the areas enclosed by their palisades and in what lies outside these enclosing structures. Moundville's palisade circumscribes a 150 ha area, containing virtually all of the site's major mounds. In contrast, while Cahokia's palisade encloses an area roughly half as small (43 ha), numerous major mounds are located outside this enclosure. The 12 km² figure proposed by several researchers (Fowler 1989; Holley et al. 1989) for the size of Cahokia is based on the distribution of these major monuments; and a sprinkling of mounds continues along nearly all axes from this large area. A similar problem exists for Moundville where artifact scatters stretch outside the fortified zone (Peebles 1978:408).

There may be a disparity as to how both sites are defined. For example, an isolated mound not included within the Moundville site (TU-50) is only .8 km north of the center (Steponaitis 1992), well within the distance to mounds groups that are lumped into the Cahokia site (e.g., the Rattlesnake Mound Group is nearly 1.6 km south of Monks Mound).

Yet, Cahokia departs in terms of the scale of its circum-core mounds, which form groupings and a number of which rank in size with those found enclosed by the palisade. Cahokia's circum-core mound groups are interpreted as representing residential-based subdivisions (Fowler 1989; Holley et al. 1992). These subdivisions, especially those distant from the core, do not replicate all of the integrative features of the core, such as the mound-plaza configuration. Our present reading of these isolated mound groups is that those close to downtown Cahokia have a local orientation along with alignments to the core (Dalan et al. 1994). Moving further away from the core, the local orientation was maintained but pan-site alignment was optional.

Both Cahokia and Moundville manifest elements of the Small and Large Center patterns in the central mound-plaza arrangement and the bilateral division of the core. However, as befitting the presumed multiple hierarchical levels within the settlement, a greater number of large buildings are displaced from the flanks of the mounds than at other towns.

Cahokia and Moundville share another interesting feature in the reduced frequency of domestic structure rebuilding. Comparing two neighborhoods, which were occupied for roughly the same time span at Cahokia (Powell Tract: O'Brien 1972a; the ICT-II: Collins 1990), the percentage of rebuilt houses varies from 44 percent to 52 percent, respectively. For an admittedly small Moundville sample, the figure is 50 percent (Peebles 1971:Figures 7–8, 1978:Figures 13.3–13.5). I interpret this reduced rebuilding as the result of four factors: 1) growth fueled by the incorporation of outlying population; 2) flux caused by vacillations in accrued wealth—fluctuations in relative wealth find expression in a greater number of buildings per household and these buildings would not necessarily be subject to rebuilding; 3) major transformations in the function of town areas; and 4) the large size of these sites that fostered a "spread-out" approach to village organization (Peebles 1978:Figure 13.2).

At Cahokia there was considerable fluctuation in what comprised supra-household groupings. Prior to the Mississippian explosion, the occupation was characterized by small courtyards fronting multiple buildings (Pauketat 1991). Coinciding with the growth of Cahokia was the appearance of larger formulations that gave way to what appear to represent neighborhoods, many of which were centered around mound groups (Collins 1990; Holley et al. 1989; Pauketat 1991). At the termination of Cahokia's occupation, there was a return to the small courtyard grouping.

POPULATION SIZE AND STRUCTURE

Reliable population figures for Mississippian towns are difficult to derive. Intractable problems include sampling and areal exposure, estimates of household size, and estimates of perishable structure longevity (the contemporaneity factor). Another problem is that a number of centers, particularly the Large Centers, were lightly populated, a condition described by the idea of a vacant center.

Initial population figures of 22,500 people for the peak period of occupation at Cahokia (Gregg 1975) perhaps sparked others into the realm of inflated figures. For example, Green and Munson (1978:313) estimated a resident population of 7,400 for the Angel site, considerably greater than the original estimate of 1,000 by Black (1967:547).

When first introduced, the initial population estimates for Cahokia were met with considerable skepticism (e.g., Griffin and Jones 1977). Subsequent estimates, however, have tended to overcompensate such extreme figures. Muller (1978), for example, estimates only 400 people for Kincaid, which seems at odds with a more reliable estimate of 350 people for the modest Snodgrass site (Griffin and Jones 1977). Peebles and Kus (1977:436) estimate a population of 3,000 for Moundville, while

Steponaitis (1993) argues for the smaller figure of 1,000. Other estimates for Small Centers are on the order of hundreds (e.g., Chapman et al. 1977:330). Reasonable estimates project Small Centers as having several hundred people, Large Centers perhaps reached a thousand, and Mega-centers likely housed several thousand.

Milner (1986), applying more exacting controls for farmsteads and villages peripheral to the Cahokia site, derived estimates of 14 to 46 people per km² for rural populations. Using his approach and dividing the Cahokia site into two zones based on projected occupation intensity (high density and low density); I have derived a population range of 3,000 to 12,000 for the site during peak occupation (A.D. 1000–1150) (Holley 1991). Although my estimate considerably inflates the density of people per square kilometer in the center as compared with the outlying populations, it does represent a conservative figure for the site. The Cahokia example serves to underscore the potential population disparity between rural and town settings within the Southeast.

Another perspective of village occupation is the density of households per excavated area. Three relative groupings of occupation density can be identified: sparse, moderate (most sites), and high. A moderate density would be around five to seven structures per 1000 m². However, given that most excavations have been directed toward high-intensity occupation areas (in addition to the other problems discussed above), any population estimates generated by this approach should be regarded as unreliable.

Elites

One question of Mississippian population structure concerns the presence of elites. Our understanding of the hierarchical social structure of Mississippian societies relies on an elite-commoner dichotomy. Elites, to a significant extent are known more for their works (Smith 1992), and excluding mortuary data, are largely unknown themselves. For example, many potential indicators for the identification of elite households have been proposed, including the presence of, or greater number of exotic items, greater proportion of "choice cuts" of deer, and the location or the relative size of dwellings (e.g., Chapman et al. 1977; Pauketat 1991; Schnell et al. 1981; Welch 1991); but the absence of extensive excavation qualifies such assumptions.

Proportional estimates of the elite population are difficult to come by with existing data. Using burial data,

Peebles (1987b) estimates that high-status individuals comprised five percent of the population for Moundville and the same may apply to the Mound 72 burial complex (Fowler 1991); for other hierarchical societies this estimate ranges from 4%–12% (Sanders 1984:Tables 1 and 2). A consideration of structure size at Cahokia (for 144 Mississippian structures) indicates that seven percent of this sample was well beyond the range of typical residences. Of course, this figure includes public buildings as well.

What is poorly understood in the archaeological record for Mississippian towns, and intimately linked to elites, is an administrative architecture such as storehouses and granary bins (Spencer 1987:373). Spanish accounts document the ubiquity of granaries and storehouses, both of which were associated with or were an extension of the chief's household and were used to curate produce, tribute, and trophies. The identification of these features by their relative size and location would assist in disentangling levels of organizational complexity at Mississippian towns. Storage facilities may exist within elite residential groupings at the Kincaid site (Cole et al. 1951:Figure 12) (Figure 2.7), and I assume the odd wall trenches for the chief's compound at Monks Mound were storage facilities (Figure 2.15).

TIMING AND TEMPO OF TOWN GROWTH

Mississippian towns were typically characterized by continuous occupation for at least two centuries. For settlements with longer occupation spans, the period of mound construction appears confined to two centuries. Centers, based on the rates of mound construction, emerged at a phenomenal rate, probably within a century. Settlement histories typically include a period of consolidation and nucleation followed by explosive and continuous growth in both mound construction and resident population before terminating with modest to minimal activity.

What served as the center appears to be established first and this often included the primary plaza of the site (Holley et al. 1993; Peebles 1983; Welch 1990b; Wesler 1991) and the broadest area that could conceivably be considered part of the site. The overall impression is that many centers start as aggregations of domestic villages that fill-in through time and then contract. What follows is a three-stage sequence of development identified from several towns.

Genesis and Take-Off

Most towns had humble beginnings in that occupations predating the explosive emergence were typically mundane, dispersed villages. Mounds were present well before take-off, if they were a component of village life within the region (e.g., Lower Mississippi Valley). Given that towns were established in prime areas such as on landforms with high agricultural potential or proximity to an important water course, every town location should be expected to yield evidence for prior occupation.

In nearly all cases, these village occupants are linked (genetically by inference) to those responsible for the succeeding florescence. An idea inescapable from this reasoning is that of a spiraling relationship between primogeniture and location. Namely, those families favored by location and status were positioned in the future town core. This is perhaps one reason why the concentric social model does not map onto the landscape for some centers. That is, the landscape was never a neutral feature and the center hearth was not necessarily the geographic center of the dispersed village. However, for those sites conforming to the concentric model, the implication is that their growth was different and perhaps more formally planned and/or rapid.

Prior to the appearance of a formal town of regional prominence, relatively dense occupation can be identified. The form of this early occupation varied considerably but always included a nucleated village and/or extensive occupation outstretching the limits of what became the core (Morse and Morse 1983:263–264; Steponaitis 1983:167; Williams and Brain 1983:336). Dense or widespread midden deposits document the intensity of these occupations (e.g., Dalan 1993:97; Polhemus et al. 1987:1217; Steponaitis 1992:10; Williams and Brain 1983:336). Initiation of monumental construction, or transformation of prior construction is also indicated, all of which marked the passage from a passive to an active approach to the landscape.

Fueling the growth of these centers was a profound and very real population explosion (Hally et al. 1980; Holley et al. 1989; Pauketat 1992; Peebles 1987b; Polhemus et al. 1987). It seems unlikely that this growth was the result of increases in fecundity, and there is good evidence for contraction in outlying populations. For Cahokia, this explosive growth in population derived from centripetal processes of absorbing outlying residents (Holley 1993; Woods and Holley 1991).

I interpret two patterns of growth. The first is evident at Cahokia, Beckwith's Fort, and Moundville (Figures 2.5–2.6). These towns emerged from a sprawling village, extending at least over a kilometer. Through time, both occupation and mound construction became more focused in the center. Even Kincaid, with its two plaza configuration appears to have the critical pre-mound occupation at both the central precinct and in the eastern group (Cole et al. 1951:181; Muller 1986a) (Figure 2.7). Kincaid is further distinguished by having residential groupings outside the palisade. The population draw for these sites was within and beyond their kilometer stretches, reaching far into outlying areas. The second pattern is evident at Lake George and Winterville and a host of other sites that appear to grow in isolation and were well-contained towns (Figures 2.9, 2.10). These towns are also splendid examples for the central location of the chief's mound.

That growth was both fast and planned is evident in the rather quick establishment of the central portion of the town, although at Mega-centers, mound construction was quite dispersed spatially as well. Alongside this population influx and transformation from domestic to public, domestic dwelling relocation was a common practice.

Given that all towns emerged within a context of a sufficiently large regional population, supported by maize agriculture, what was the draw of particular towns that allowed them to attain regional prominence? Protection does not seem a likely response, since many sites were not fortified during the initial growth spasm (Chapman et al. 1977; Cole et al. 1951:308; Iseminger et al. 1990; Steponaitis 1992). However, tensions, especially ones caused by competition, may have been severe prior to the ascendancy of a regional center, as witnessed in the massed burials in the Mound 72 mortuary complex at Cahokia (Fowler 1991). Nor does the simple possession or control of prestige goods seem sufficient to transform outlier populations into town residents. Centers of regional importance, wherein seasonal or life-transition ceremonies were undertaken that involved prestige goods, were present before the Mississippian period and did not coincide with a nucleated, resident population. I think that the significance of exotics has been overemphasized in Mississippian archaeology—their negligible presence would support the idea that they were a by-product of the social revolution brought about by town life and not a cause.

Whatever the draw, town growth was characterized by a societal restructuring that included the farming of more distant agricultural fields (Holley 1978; Doolittle

1992), an active approach to landscape modification (Dalan 1993), and the emergence of social hierarchy (Knight 1990). These changes made use of the aggregation of people and the manipulation and objectification of life crises (birth/death and planting/harvesting). Still, given the variability in both town size and the presumed regional impact of town growth, certain individuals had the wherewithal to recognize and manipulate these economic, political, and emotional factors to a greater degree than others.

Climax

The lifespan of a Mississippian Great Town was short-lived—roughly a century. The attainment of regional paramountcy was marked by a flurry of earthen mound construction, unparalleled in previous efforts within and around an already established central area (Brain 1989:105; Dalan 1993; Steponaitis 1983; Wesler 1991; Williams and Brain 1983:338). The erection of a palisade also coincides with this explosive growth. The delay in a palisade emplacement is interpreted as resulting from increased competition within and among these centers after they were established. Although population increases for the Mega-centers were not as dramatic as previously (Pauketat 1991; Peebles 1987; Woods and Holley 1989), they reached the absolute peak attained at any prehistoric Mississippian town at this time.

A marked increase in exotics was also characteristic just prior to or slightly after the attainment of regional paramountcy for the Mega-centers (Pauketat 1991; Peebles 1987). These exotics included not only the standards of shell, minerals, chert, and ceramic vessels but also valued wood species (Lopinot 1991). I believe these towns are best characterized as "grand consumers" as opposed to "grand producers."

Decline

As with their origins, it is a challenge to explain the decline of the Mississippians' towns, although it is a relatively easy task to identify the by-products of their decline. The duration of a center's decline was likely as rapid (in archaeological terms) as its rise. Population loss, and a reduction in monumental construction that was offset by continued revamping of fortifications, are documented at centers from which there is sufficient data (Chapman et al. 1977; Iseminger et al. 1990; Williams and Brain 1983:340). This is seen dramatically at Toqua where the palisaded area downgraded through three stages from 3.9 ha to 1.7 ha (Polhemus et al. 1987) (Figure 2.12).

The chief's mound continued to be important through the end of the occupation of the town (Holley et al. 1989; Williams and Brain 1983:340). I am not sure if this is simply because it was the largest mound, or because the last gasps at control were being attempted. Mound sites continued to have resonance as sacred/important landscape features through the early periods of the European invasion.

For Cahokia, I see its decline beginning during the latter part of the Stirling phase (approximately A.D. 1100) with a gradual decline occurring throughout the succeeding Moorehead phase. It appears that the distribution of exotic goods becomes more equalized (Gums 1993; Pauketat 1992), if smaller in volume, during this decline. Even the spectrum of wood taxa utilized at the site indicates shrinking access to highly desired and exotic species (Lopinot 1991). As the population declined, occupation tended to gravitate toward the core, transforming sacred areas that had originally been residential back again to more mundane uses (Pauketat 1991). Mound construction also appears more concentrated around Monks Mound. Dalan (1993:187) argues that these efforts represent an internalized struggle for power. By the terminal Sand Prairie phase we can speak of a "rump Mississippian" occupying the site (Holley et al. 1989).

Just as Cahokia's earlier population gain had been regional in scope, so was its decline. In the uplands east of Cahokia, there is an influx of people beginning around A.D. 1100 and continuing for another century or so (Holley 1993; Woods and Holley 1989). Profound changes are also evident at other towns. In the Yazoo Basin, the twin Large Centers of Lake George and Winterville gave way to scattered, smaller centers (Brain 1978:352). Moundville downgraded into a "vacant" ceremonial center before disappearing (Steponaitis 1993).

Two major explanations have been proposed to account for the dissipation of individual Great Towns. Some see this decline as a response to the inherent political instability of chiefdoms (e.g., Anderson 1990; Earle 1991:13; Pauketat 1992). Others have cited environmental degradation as being responsible for the decline of Cahokia (Lopinot and Woods 1993) and other Mississippian towns (e.g., Williams and Shapiro 1990), a view that has been forcefully criticized by some champions of the cycling model (Pauketat 1992).

Since I see the emergence of Great Towns as inextricably interwoven with the success of the chiefly institution, I believe that their downfalls parallel that institution's decline. Nevertheless, the workings of this decline should vary from region to region. The diversity in the formal organization and size of centers suggests that no single causal factor can explain their rise or fall.

What is also unclear is the destiny of the Great Towns once the presumed powers of their chiefdoms waned. The emergence of centers that were typically smaller in a nearby locale appears common enough to suggest a simple pattern of spatial relocation and diminution of the capital (Fairbanks 1956; Scarry and Payne 1986; Williams and Shapiro 1990:172). Within the Cahokia area, the emergence of the Mitchell site (Porter 1974) around A.D. 1150, only 10 km north of Cahokia, may be symptomatic of this pattern. For the Natchez region, this pattern ends during historic times with the minuscule Fatherland site (Brain 1978:352).

HISTORICAL PROCESSES

Although valid predecessors to the Mississippian Great Towns stretch far back in time, a few brief comments regarding post-Hopewellian centers (A.D. 700–900) are in order (Figure 2.1). Settlements possessing a central focus (plaza-mound configurations and fortifications) were present, if in limited numbers, throughout the Southeast prior to A.D. 900 (Rolingson 1990a,b). The largest of these (e.g., Toltec, Troyville, and Hoecake) were larger than 40 ha, which is larger than the majority of Mississippian towns. These post-Hopewellian centers differ from their Mississippian successors in their lack of a large resident population. However, the two eras are similar in their absence of large settlements without monuments. Thus, some elements synonymous with Mississippian towns (plaza, mounds) were already present and provided a lexicon for the use of symbolic space, that was reworked and reinvented during the Mississippian period. Here I am referring to the concept of an "invented tradition," by which an attempt was made to identify and legitimize the social order (Hobsbawm 1983).

The late prehistory of the Southeast displays definite pulses in the character of towns. In identifying these pulses I have established three "periods" that are coarse-grained and do not apply equally to all regions. During the first period (A.D. 900–1150), Great Towns were definitely in place (Figure 2.2). The majority of these early examples are difficult to identify from a re-gional perspective because they do not significantly outdistance competitors (Welch 1990a). Examples include Large Centers (Macon Plateau) (Figure 2.8) and Small Centers (Obion). Cahokia was an exception. It dwarfed all of its competitors and successors and probably peaked by the twelfth century (Figure 2.5).

A significant proliferation in mound centers was initiated during the second period (A.D. 1150–1300), and it was during this time that Large Centers climaxed (Figure 2.3). The second largest mound center, Moundville (Figure 2.6), reached its peak during this period and outdistanced, as did Cahokia earlier on, the numerous competitors. Other towns ranged in size from 10 to 70 ha and had from 7 to more than 20 mounds.

The third period, from A.D. 1300–1550 (Figure 2.4), marked a decline in the visibility and therefore the size of the Great Towns. No Large Center was present during this time span and many of these later towns approximate the size of lower order towns during earlier times. All notable towns were less than 10 ha in size, with a range from two to seven mounds.

Although mound construction ended around A.D. 1700, aboriginal towns continued to exist through the eighteenth century. Eighteenth century towns replaced mounds with structures bracketing the plaza, with likely the same, if vestigial, functions. Unfortunately, our perspective of Mississippian towns is molded by these historic towns.

A salient trend in this historical scenario is that town size and efforts directed toward earthen monuments diminished through time. When such reductions are joined with an apparent decline in the presence of superordinate individuals in the mortuary record (Anderson 1990), we are faced with a profound change in the character of Mississippian towns and society.

Scalar reductions in site size and complexity are not atypical for complex societies around the world. For example, in another area with which I am familiar, the Maya, Postclassic centers were miniaturized versions of the Classic period. Many explanations have been offered for this Classic-Postclassic change, and many of them mimic discussions in the Southeast. In the following discussion, I offer several ideas concerning the nature of Mississippian towns and pan-Southeastern processes.

One idea can be discounted, that these late centers were young and therefore not in existence long enough to have erected large monuments or amass a large population. For example, the late centers of Haynes Bluff

(Brain 1988) and Little Egypt (Hudson et al. 1985) (Figure 2.11) both have mounds with four to six construction stages spanning at most 200 years. There is no profound difference in the timing and tempo of mound construction between early and late Mississippian mound centers. Furthermore, these late centers still maintain the focus and distinction of a primary or chief's mound.

Social relationships may provide an answer. The social life brought about by the appearance of Great Towns in the Southeast was unprecedented and involved tensions in newly-defined roles. Thus, the proliferation in ceremonial construction could be argued as sanctifying the emerging ideology (Cherry 1978:429). The multiplicity of mounds in early Mississippian towns can be interpreted as a response to harmonizing nucleated settlements that comprised diverse corporate and kinship units.

Correspondingly, as these tensions were circumvented and assuaged, the need for sanctification declined and the monuments were, accordingly, less impressive. The chief/ancestor ideology was ubiquitous across the Southeast and nearly every region witnessed the emergence of a Great Town prior to the fourteenth century. Subsequent developments saw no need for this display.

One additional factor requiring further investigation concerns the possibility that a greater number of later sites possessed mounds than during earlier times. This proliferation, if indeed valid, would have diluted the signifying value of mounds.

Some have suggested that late Mississippian towns, especially those in the Lower Mississippi Valley, were vacant ceremonial centers (Brain 1989; Brown 1985; Williams and Brain 1983; Williams and Shapiro 1990:172–173). The historic Grand Village of the Natchez, consisting of eight structures, was vacant (Neitzel 1983). However, this site is just one of many within the region, and evidence suggests that not all were vacant. Testing at the Little Egypt site (Hally et al. 1980), the projected seat of the Coosa paramountcy (Hudson et al. 1985), has revealed a high density of estimated households. Spanish entrada accounts, even when read with a skeptical eye, do not suggest that these centers were vacant. Our inability to adequately distinguish occupational variability in Mississippian towns is a glaring problem deserving serious attention.

One perhaps profound difference between early and late towns is that the latter could have been undergoing different and more intensive stress than that witnessed by the earlier. I am referring to the incidence of burned

towns after A.D. 1200 (e.g., Winterville, Toqua, and Snodgrass), the effects of proposed depopulation of large areas (Anderson et al. 1986; Williams 1990), and the proposed environmental instability (Brose 1989). These disruptive factors could have seriously compromised the growth and functioning of large towns and promoted the widespread dissemination of smaller mounds across the Southeast.

DISCUSSION

In this chapter, I have tried to synthesize what would appear to constitute voluminous data relevant to Mississippian towns. Yet the surfeit of data has dwindled in my efforts to make comparisons. Questions about Mississippian towns that arise from a comparative perspective cannot often be answered, because the sites have been investigated using widely varying research designs. As a result, I have relied on a typological approach that has not, I hope, obscured salient aspects of towns and town life.

The durability of the basic elements of Mississippian towns is testimony to a tradition, with antecedent roots, that withstood translation in a variety of environmental settings, regional interpretations, change through time, and perhaps varied attempts at reinvention by Mississippian chiefs. Loosely defined, as are all traditions, the Mississippian tradition included: sedentary lifestyles; concentric zones within settlements tied to a hierarchy; veneration of ancestors; warrior and chiefly rituals. The presence of mounds has served as the sole criterion for inclusion in my discussion of towns. Still, as noted above, during historic times the formal planning of non-mound towns encompassed functions suspected for earlier mound centers. Increasingly, we are finding that villages may contain central plazas bounded by large or unique structures, presumed to represent elite or ceremonial functions (Smith 1978). This argues that mounds served a role that was readily superseded by less monumental symbols.

The number of people attracted to such towns would appear to vary with the "size" of the town. One salient aspect is that nearly all Small Centers were densely occupied, whereas for larger towns, residents were more scattered or tightly clustered in certain areas, or presumably limited to only a small core of elite and retainers (the so-called vacant center). This relationship, if real, implies that there is a threshold (somewhere within the hundreds) to how many people were able to aggregate and remain in the same location for generations. Variation in town size, physically and in terms of resident population, therefore, may inform more about the relative size of the regional population, and the relative success of a chiefdom, than the number of people residing in the town proper.

Large towns and large mounds were a thing of the past by at least the fifteenth century, if not earlier. By this time not only were monuments smaller but they were also less frequent in any one center. The primary centers resembled lower-order examples from earlier times. Besides noting this trend, and speculating on cause and effect, no unequivocal understanding is within grasp. Serious attention in working backwards from historic towns to prehistoric towns seems the most profitable course.

Absent from most of my discussion are regions that lie on the margins, including coastal areas and inland regions such as the Spiro area in Oklahoma, or areas even further north in Illinois, Wisconsin, and Minnesota. These expressions strain, to an extent, the uniformity in towns that I have attempted to synthesize. Interestingly, regardless of how the Southeastern region is drawn, Cahokia lies on its margins as well. My neglect of marginal areas other than Cahokia may have been misguided. Future studies of how towns in these areas interpreted and molded the Mississippian Tradition, as expressed in town layout and history, may prove to be productive for understanding the tradition's genesis and trajectory.

ACKNOWLEDGMENTS

Much of what I have to offer on Mississippian towns grew from experiences gathered from working at the Cahokia site and the Black Bottom. William I. Woods and Jon Muller were instrumental in allowing this to happen. I thank Jill Neitzel for inviting me to participate in a stimulating symposium. Anne I. Woosley and the staff at the Amerind Foundation provided the ideal setting. Rinita A. Dalan offered the most pointed and helpful comments to various drafts. In spite of Steve Lekson's persuasive arguments regarding the importance and scale of the mega-sites, I did not bolt from the overall tone of the symposium that downplayed such a role. The drawings were executed by Mikels Skele, Mike Hemmer, and Julie Harper. Figures 2.1–2.4 were drafted by Julie Barnes Smith.

CHAPTER THREE

Comparing Southwestern and Southeastern Great Towns

George R. Holley

Stephen H. Lekson

THERE WAS A LACK OF UNANIMITY AMONG THE SEMI-
nar participants regarding what term best describes the
large, but varied, prehistoric settlements in the Southwest and Southeast. In this chapter, we employ the term
town, just as the Spanish and English chroniclers described concentrations of domestic dwellings as pueblos
and towns, respectively. Our use of the town concept is
heuristic. We make no inference that the town was,
within the native conceptualization, similar to our own.
Other terms, such as district or community, could
equally apply, but fail to accommodate, in the broadest
sense, characteristics that we wish to distinguish. Here, we
focus on the towns, from which much can be learned, and
leave it to others (see Fish, Chapter 4; Scarry, Chapter 5) to
consider the degree to which Southwestern and Southeastern towns were embedded in broader regional expressions.

One of the primary characteristics associated with
towns is a sense of place. This sense of place gives towns
a longevity or continuity lacking in villages. It also has
implications for the division and usufruct of land and for
the existence of a regional landscape imbued with both
the sacred and profane. Sense of place also plays a role
within towns themselves. All large Southwestern and
Southeastern towns display a focus. Among the Classic
period Hohokam and in the Southeast, this focus is expressed in a concentration of monumental architecture
within a walled compound. Other Southwestern sites
(e.g., Preclassic Hohokam, Chaco) lack physical barriers
but still have a central focus around a plaza or principal
building. This focality gives rise to the notion of concentric zonation that may only superficially resemble geographic models of Western towns and cities.

While there was considerable discussion during the
seminar about the appropriateness of using the term town,
there was general unanimity regarding the poor fit between
prehistoric towns in the Southwest and Southeast and the
ideas of city and urban. Such terms have recently entered
the literature of both Chaco and Cahokia. Lekson finds
merit in a qualified "proto-urban" concept to characterize
Chaco (Figure 3.1); however, Holley finds no solid foundation to warrant comparison of Cahokia (Figure 3.2) with
even qualified Western notions of urbanization.

The crux of the functioning of a town revolves
around the extent to which towns are conceptualized as
the accumulation of smaller, modular (settlement) units
such as the nuclear family or hamlet. Some of the participants felt that towns were simply large versions of
smaller domestic gatherings, with a veneer of ritual trappings. In contrast, we argue that certain of these towns
were more than the sum of their parts. It is our view that
once a threshold of local population was reached, new
organizational forms had to emerge.

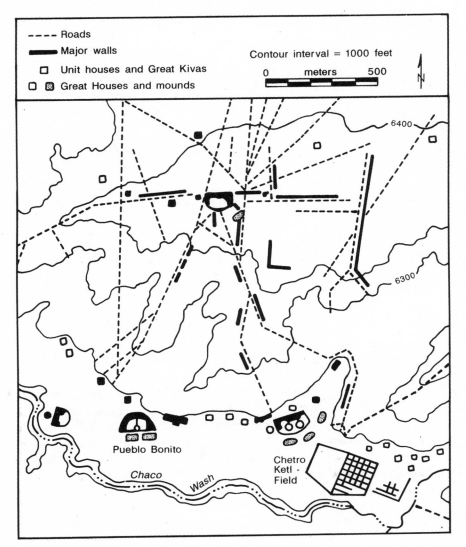

Figure 3.1.
Downtown Chaco.

COMPARING CHACO AND CAHOKIA

The large towns of the Southwest and Southeast shared, in general terms, a number of activities. These include: monumental construction, elite residence, setting for ritual ceremonies, and a concentration of exotic materials and evidence for their manufacture. Comparing the two Brobdingnagian towns in the Southeast and Southwest is illuminating. In spite of the profound differences in the environments and cultural roots that spawned Chaco (Figure 3.1) and Cahokia (Figure 3.2), there are some general similarities between the two.

Timing and Scale

Both Chaco and Cahokia emerged early within their respective regions; and after their decline, no further developments of the same scale occurred. By any comparison, these two towns represent the ultimate concentration of monumental architecture within the boundaries of the present day United States.

Time Span

A maximal three century span, covering early formulations, climax, and decline, characterized both towns.

Population

Population estimates for both, ranging in the thousands, are of the same order of magnitude.

Built Landscape

Active creation of a cultural landscape, which went beyond the simple erection of monuments, characterized both centers.

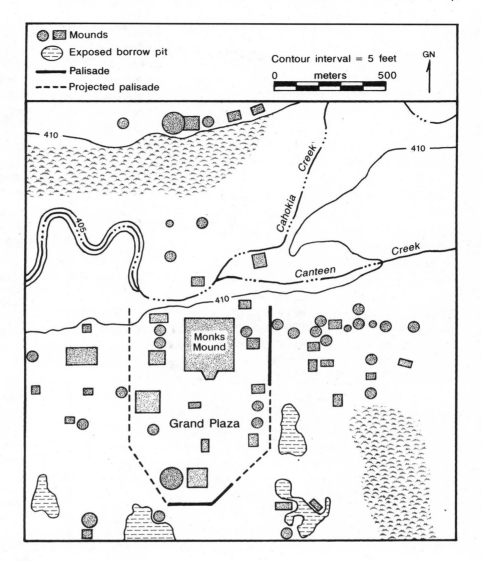

Figure 3.2.
Downtown Cahokia.

Focality

Both Chaco and Cahokia have a strong central focus around truly monumental constructions, the Pueblo Bonito complex and Monks Mound, respectively (Figure 3.1–3.2).

Site Planning

In addition to the central focus, formal alignments of monumental architecture have been suggested for both towns.

Sprawling Nature

Although focality is pronounced at both towns, there is a noticeable spread of monumental architecture from the center. This sprawling feature has given rise to the suggestion of neighborhoods or sub-communities in both.

Unique Monumental Elements

In addition to possessing the largest structures in their respective areas, other unique architectural elements, either in size or shape, appear restricted to these sites.

Circumscription

Both Chaco and Cahokia lie within unique settings. Chaco lay within an oasis of the San Juan Basin, while Cahokia was positioned within a bounded but sufficiently large alluvial flood plain of the American Bottom.

Growth

Both towns emerged from a combination of a local population base and the centripetal movement of peoples from a wider region.

Decline

Both towns exhibit a shift from sacred to profane near the end of the sequence whereby domestic occupation sprouted in previously public areas.

COMPARING HOHOKAM AND MISSISSIPPIAN TOWNS

One observation made during the seminar discussions concerned differences in the amount of variation characterizing Southwestern and Southeastern towns. While the same basic town plan could be applied to Southeastern towns, this was not true for the Southwest. This difference is in large part a function of how the two areas were defined during the seminar. The limits of the Southeast encompassed a single cultural tradition, the Mississippian, with variants (e.g., Spiro) being excluded. In contrast, the Southwest, the smaller of the two areas, was defined as including minimally three major cultural traditions, the Anasazi, Mogollon, and Hohokam.

These differences in numbers of cultural traditions probably reflect the degree of environmental variation in the two areas. However, for purposes of this discussion, it is important to note that comparisons of Southwestern and Southeastern towns must consider not just Chaco and Cahokia but also other Southwestern towns such as those of the Hohokam. To repeat an analogy made earlier by Lekson (Chapter 1), comparisons between Southwestern and Southeastern towns are not comparisons of apples and oranges, but rather a bag of apples to a single apple.

The most notable similarities shared by Hohokam and Mississippian towns include their concentric zonation around plazas and the construction of mounds. In both areas, plazas served as the focal points of towns throughout their occupations; and both Classic period Hohokam and Mississippian towns had mounds displaced around the plazas. For both, the mounds served as the platforms for presumably elite residences and sometimes for burial. Both areas also shared a similar form of domestic structure, which was subterranean and constructed with perishable materials. The areal extent of Classic period Hohokam towns was roughly the same as that of large Mississippian towns. Population estimates for both are of the same order of magnitude.

These similarities are counterbalanced by one significant difference—the "deep sedentism" of Hohokam towns. This deep sedentism produced longer occupation spans for many Hohokam towns than are known for their Mississippian counterparts. In addition, it resulted in an intensive clustering of towns across the landscape and profound changes in town morphology. Both characteristics lie outside the Mississippian experience. The morphological change in Hohokam towns includes the appearance of both platform mounds and walled compounds during the Classic period.

Throughout the prehistoric sequence, Hohokam towns also seem to have had more specialized features than Mississippian towns. This is evident even in the shared architectural feature of the plaza. A variety of activities took place at Mississippian plazas, including the playing of ball games. In contrast, Hohokam ball games took place in specially constructed ballcourts. Similarly, while both Classic period Hohokam and Mississippian towns had walled enclosures, compounds and palisades, respectively, the largest of the Classic period Hohokam towns had multiple, spatially discrete compounds, a multiplication that was foreign to the Southeast. Perhaps as a result of their having more kinds of structures, towns constructed throughout the Hohokam sequence seem to have had a more formalized distribution of these elements than we can discern in Mississippian towns.

FURTHER COMPARISONS

For both the Southeast and the various parts of the Southwest, there is a perceived "boom town" aspect to some towns. Historically, boom towns have been identified by the suddenness of their appearance in which people are drawn primarily by economic motivations and secondarily by social factors. This process of growth is rapid, and the communities formed are short-lived.

In relative terms, the rapidity associated with historic boom towns did not occur in the prehistoric Southwest and Southeast. However, the takeoff in growth expressed at Chaco and Cahokia was rapid in archaeological measurement. We call towns like Chaco and Cahokia "ritual boom towns" to underscore a fundamental difference with their historic counterparts. Though economic and social gains were probably factors in the growth of these centers, so too was ritual, which is evident in site organization and in major labor investments.

This use of the boom town concept raises questions about what happened to the prehistoric towns of both the Southwest and Southeast. What caused oscillations in the relative importance of a town through time? Do some towns represent failed attempts at becoming larger? These questions reinforce our view that documenting variation in the histories of individual towns is integral to understanding the nature of towns in both the Southwest and Southeast.

Another similarity can be seen in the trajectories of Southwestern and Southeastern town development for the post-A.D. 1200 period. At this time more compact towns appeared across the landscape in both areas. As with other seminar participants, we are intrigued by the possibility that the resonance in the fall of Chaco and Cahokia, along with climatic amelioration, may have contributed to this apparently similar reaction.

As a final comparative note, we are impressed by the uniqueness of two towns that lie on the periphery of both regions: Paquimé and Spiro. Although superficially different, each town hybridizes elements of their respective regions in magnified terms: Paquimé with its ritual and economic focus and Spiro with its burial programs.

Despite the significant similarities shared by Southwestern and Southeastern towns, it is important to note that the goings-on of everyday life were profoundly different in the two areas. For the Southwest, most people spent their lives in close proximity with their neighbors. This may have also been true at certain times and in certain parts of Southeastern towns; but we cannot characterize Mississippian social life in general as having such sustained proximity. This fundamental difference may be responsible for the difficulty archaeologists encounter in identifying elites within Southwestern towns and the ease they apparently have in doing so within Southeastern towns. We argue that this singular difference in the mundane character of domestic life may figure prominently in the different configurations of towns within the two regions.

CHAPTER FOUR

How Complex Were the
Southwestern Great Towns' Polities?

Suzanne K. Fish

THE LEVEL OF PREHISTORIC COMPLEXITY IN THE SOUTH-west has been repeatedly contested in recent years (e.g., Cordell and Plog 1979; Cordell and Upham 1989; Graves 1994; Lightfoot and Feinman 1982; Plog 1983, 1985; Reid 1985; Reid et al. 1989; Sullivan 1987; Upham 1982; Upham et al. 1989). The debate has touched a wide variety of archaeological manifestations, but it is at the crux of efforts to understand the polities of the "great towns" that are distinguished by size and elaborated public architecture. Because excavations in the most imposing sites were largely undertaken during the early years of regional archaeology, data for measuring complexity by current standards are non-systematic and inadequate. Knowledge of the settlement systems surrounding great towns also is far from complete. Nevertheless, the debate about complexity does not originate from the fact that different scholars consider disparate sets of archaeological facts or fail to advance explicit criteria. Rather, it arises from the necessity to choose between competing criteria and to defend their significance in a theoretical field with minimal consensus.

The classificatory scheme of bands, tribes, chiefdoms, and states that has dominated North American archaeology since the 1960s offers at best an uneasy fit for the more complex expressions in Southwestern prehistory. A tribal level of organization is embraced by few archae-ologists as a satisfactory interpretive framework for Southwestern great towns. Yet the characteristics of a chiefdom, albeit an evolving concept (Yoffee 1993), also are seldom perceived in the predicted degree or combi-nation—archaeological patterns corresponding to sys-tems of ranked kin, hereditary leaders, and centralized redistribution are not widely recognized. Although com-parisons could be drawn between Southwestern great towns and early configurations in trajectories that cul-minated in states, regional archaeologists seldom refer to the dynamics of cultural evolution to analyze develop-mental sequences lacking similar endpoints. Moreover, ethnographic analogy, the pervasive alternative for inter-preting Southwestern prehistory, is at its weakest in illu-minating the great town polities.

At the outset, a critical contrast between the South-east and Southwest should be drawn in our ability to envision organizational principles and structures of political inclusiveness for the great town polities. The richness of early contact accounts provides a point of entry for understanding Mississippian polities in light of the motivations and machinations of preeminent leaders within observed political frameworks. Although the re-markable ethnographic record of the Southwest reveals continuities into the present, even the earliest Spanish failed to encounter leadership roles and societal milieus that seem commensurate with the prehistorically densest populations, the most intensive subsistence systems, or the hierarchically differentiated settlement patterns containing elaborated centers.

In this paper, I emphasize three geographically separate occurrences of great town polities as embodiments of maximum complexity within the major cultural divisions of Anasazi, Hohokam, and Mogollon. These are, respectively, the fully developed Chaco phenomenon centered in northwestern New Mexico, the Hohokam polities in the Phoenix Basin of southern Arizona during the Classic Period, and Paquimé in northwestern Chihuahua with Southwestern and Mogollon affinities in the broad sense of those terms. In each of these areas, the earliest useful descriptions postdate the Cortes entrada by many decades. By the time of first record, these prehistoric entities were lost from living memory and successor populations exhibited few vestiges of similar aggregation or centralization. Large Puebloan towns were limited to the edges of the post-Chacoan peripheries. Small hamlets of Piman farmers and transient Yavapai hunters and gatherers occupied the Phoenix Basin. The vicinity of Paquimé was inhabited by Jocomes who lived by hunting, gathering, horticulture, and raiding.

Given the absence of ethnohistoric descriptions, my consideration of the polities associated with the Chaco phenomenon, the Classic Period Hohokam in the Phoenix Basin, and Paquimé is necessarily restricted to the archaeological record. I begin by addressing the problem of defining prehistoric Southwestern polities archaeologically. Then, I compare the diversity of the three cases for a series of variables. Finally, I consider several additional dimensions of complexity and their significance for documenting alternative trajectories of organizational change.

A SOUTHWESTERN VERSION OF POLITY

To evaluate the complexity of great town polities in the Southwest, it is necessary first to define what is meant by the term polity. In this chapter, it refers to a territorial and sociopolitical entity with more than one level of settlement hierarchy marked by sites with public architecture. Public architecture in this sense consists of a ritual or political edifice presumed to serve a constituency equivalent to and usually broader than the residents of the settlement in which the feature is located. Such a definition of polity does not reflect a traditional usage. Indeed, Southwestern archaeologists only occasionally apply this term to sociopolitical or territorial configurations.

In the following discussion, a polity is considered a unit of political affiliation for the members of a society. It is the outcome of a political structure through which designated individuals engage in a range of decision making that affects the society as a whole and perform additional activities on behalf of the members. A polity is the sum of political relationships, but it has a spatial expression that generally coincides with the extent of territory to which the member population lays primary claim. Polities have further tangible expression in the remains of integrative institutions and symbols of affiliation.

The very concept of polity conflicts with a strong egalitarian bias in Southwestern interpretation, in large part reflecting the egalitarian ethic highlighted in Puebloan ethnography. The great towns represent the notable and often controversial exceptions. Disagreement revolves around hierarchical supra-site organization and the exercise of centralized power beyond the ethnographically sanctioned consensus of kin group elders or leaders of voluntary organizations. Although egalitarian political interpretation is one consequence of close ethnographic adherence, it also reflects the difficulty of discerning preeminent individuals and roles in the Southwestern archaeological record. The social identity of persons associated with public architecture, political iconography, and differentiated mortuary treatment is not easily resolved through parallels with historic leaders.

Communities

In order to develop a perspective on polity that is appropriate and applicable to Southwestern prehistory, I first turn to the concept of the community, the building block of the more inclusive polity. Unlike "polity," this term has a relatively consistent usage in regional archaeology and recognized correlates in spatial patterns and symbols (e.g., Adler 1996; Doyel and Lekson 1992; Fish and Fish 1994; Lekson 1991; Rohn 1989; Wilcox and Sternberg 1983). A community consists not of a single settlement, but of a set of interrelated sites within a bounded community territory. Such a community contains a center with public architecture that is not duplicated in kind or magnitude in the other community sites. These edifices are the focus of communal events. Architectural forms marking Southwestern community centers are regionally diverse compared to the more standardized erection of mounds throughout the Mississippian realm. Relationships embodied by communal architecture are often the most direct archaeological evidence for the interlinkage of population and settlements composing the community.

Archaeological definition of Southwestern communities is by one of two means. First, boundaries may be indicated by settlement fall off, when a cluster of settlements containing a central site is spatially discrete from other settlement clusters (e.g., Adler 1996; Breternitz et al. 1982; Crown 1987; Fish et al. 1992a). This method necessitates comprehensive settlement data. Alternatively, a community configuration may be recognized through a replication of pattern elements at intervals. The distribution of architecturally differentiated central sites is often considered a proxy for community distributions, whether or not all the associated settlements for each community center have been located (Fish 1996; Fish and Fish 1994; Gregory and Nials 1985; Jewett 1989; Lekson 1991; Lightfoot and Most 1989; Upham 1982; Wilcox and Sternberg 1983).

In some cases, communities are territorially extensive and population is dispersed among a number of residential villages in addition to the community center. Settlements within these communities may be differentiated by such variables as size, architecture, and artifact assemblages. Particularly among late prehistoric pueblos, community population frequently was concentrated in a single large site, accompanied by small and predominantly seasonal outlying sites. The community appears to have been the ultimate political unit throughout most of the Southwest before A.D. 900 and remained so in many times and places thereafter.

The ethnographic record offers some models for prehistoric community patterns. Both in the Puebloan north and in the southern deserts, centrally focused relationships occur among linked sets of sites. Most examples involve the customary return by outlying populations to larger and more continuously occupied settlements for important ceremonial observations. Historic Laguna Pueblo in New Mexico typifies such an arrangement (Eggan 1950:253–254; Parsons 1923:145). Similarly, residents of "daughter" villages formerly returned to a parent settlement for wikita ceremonies among the Tohono O'odham of Arizona (Underhill 1939:58). There are weak analogues for communal architecture in the presence of large plazas and kivas at the main pueblos and specialized communal structures at the central Piman villages. Settlements with such ties also allied (on occasion) for common defense or offense. A particularly significant divergence from prehistoric times is the absence of investment in unique forms of public architecture at a level approaching that of even the modestly elaborated centers of prehistoric communities.

From Communities to Polities

Some general observations can be made about the chronological development of Southwestern communities and more inclusive polities. Incipient community organization is suggested by larger sites within groups of nearby settlements in many parts of the Southwest by A.D. 700. The large sites in these size hierarchies also are distinguished by public architecture in some areas. During Basketmaker III and Pueblo I times in the Four Corners region (the juncture of Arizona, New Mexico, Utah, and Colorado), settlement hierarchies containing sites with great kivas are recognized in a number of locations, including Dolores (Kane 1989), Chaco Canyon (Vivian 1990), and the Navajo Reservoir District (Eddy 1966). Great kivas also mark focal villages in the Mimbres region only slightly later (LeBlanc 1989:182). Among the Hohokam, small caliche capped mounds were constructed about A.D. 600 at Snaketown (Haury 1976). Ballcourts had been constructed in a variety of locations by A.D. 750 (McGuire 1987; Wilcox and Sternberg 1983:193), and distributions at regular intervals along Phoenix canals can be identified within the next two centuries. Around A.D. 1000, instances of aggregated populations, intensified production, and inclusive territorial entities had appeared in regions across the Southwest.

Perception of the complexity of Southwestern communities and polities is unequivocally tied to the elaboration of their centers, a more universal association acknowledged by the great town emphasis of this volume. Monumental architecture is evocative of the strength of centralized functions, communal undertakings, and influence in the contemporary region. The great towns of the Southwest that appear repeatedly in these chapters represent the premier examples of specialized form, massiveness, and diversity in public architecture. It is no accident that a site such as the late prehistoric Sapawe, with a population likely equaling or exceeding that of the more frequently cited great towns, but without similar edifices, figures much less prominently in the discussion. The more impressive community centers as well as the great towns yield disproportionate shares of specialized and high value items and differentiated burial treatments among contemporary settlements.

The inclusiveness of integration is another pivotal factor in the evaluation of complexity. Political and territorial inclusiveness is most frequently attributed to multi-community entities surrounding the architecturally elaborated Southwestern centers, even though it is difficult to specify exact sets of constituent communities and the exact manner of connection among them. Political complexity is judged also by the kind of leadership emanating from the predominant center and the means by which integration is effected. Relatively egalitarian confederacies among prominent settlements have been proposed (e.g., Spielmann 1994), but superordinate relationships have been postulated for Chaco, Paquimé, and Classic Hohokam polities. In these cases, the lower order centers likely served as nodes of polity integration as well as foci for the centralized functions of their individual communities. Again, in contrast to the Southeast, ethnographic analogies for such superordinate relations are elusive.

The Horizontal Dimension

With few exceptions, Southwestern discussions of complexity address the vertical dimension—the degree of centralization in authority. Much less attention has been paid to the horizontal axis, the degree of diversity in the constituent elements that a polity incorporates. Johnson (1989) characterized Southwestern complexity as sequential, in which the integrated whole is composed of the same kind of social subunits. The great town polities are the most convincing candidates for departures from this generalization. Societal complexity increases with the diversity or heterogeneity of integrated parts, a principle that McGuire (1983) has termed segmentation or heterogeneity with reference to social groups. The horizontal axis can also be related to factors traditionally considered in evaluating complexity such as the size of integrated territory and population. For these key variables and others, increases in scale heighten the potential for diversity among components and necessitate greater investment in integrative efforts.

A temporal trend with significance for societal heterogeneity coincides with the rise of great towns and their polities. In later prehistoric times, population became increasingly concentrated in areas capable of supporting intensive agriculture in general and riverine irrigation in particular. The relatively circumscribed distribution at A.D. 1425 is clustered along perennial rivers, and closely parallels the distribution of historic irrigation in the period when gravity-dependent systems were

still comparable to prehistoric technologies. The increasing concentration of population after A.D. 1300 would have resulted in trends toward denser and more heterogeneous membership in communities and polities of given size, greater involvement of cultivators in communal agricultural efforts, heightened interaction along adjacent boundaries, and instances of differing ethnic groups as close neighbors or members of the same territorial entity.

Territorial Size and Diversity

As a factor in complexity, size of integrated territory is often implicitly equated with size of integrated population. However, whether or not substantially more people are involved in areally extensive polities, investment in maintaining communication and coordinating polity-wide functions must be greater. In most parts of the Southwest, topographic variability is pronounced and agricultural water is localized with respect to land forms. Large territories are likely to encompass diversity in agricultural risks, productive technologies, and organizational units reflecting common use of water and land. They are also more liable to offer differential access to raw materials.

The maximum size of integrated territory for great town polities is not a straightforward matter. In some cases there is tangible evidence of association or discrete spatial boundaries for the territory of a single center with public architecture. The numbers and identities of such entities integrated at higher levels is always more speculative.

The wide distribution of Chacoan style public architecture and roads is a recurring topic in Anasazi studies of the last decade. An affinity with developments in Chaco Canyon is unerringly implied for the associated communities. To the extent that these settlements were generally contemporary, the distribution of Chacoan patterns would signify a geographic phenomenon almost as broad as the terms Anasazi, Hohokam, or Mogollon. In fact, scholars of Chacoan developments have acknowledged that in this sense, Chaco intrudes into the Mogollon region and encompasses almost all of the Anasazi world other than the Rio Grande and most of the Kayenta subarea (Doyel 1992; Lekson 1991; Vivian 1990). A growing recognition of the expansiveness of Chacoan patterns of architecture raised questions concerning the political extent of a core containing Chaco Canyon and of potentially competing contemporary or successor polities. Attention is now turning, however, to localized and more precisely argued issues for answers. In this regard, the

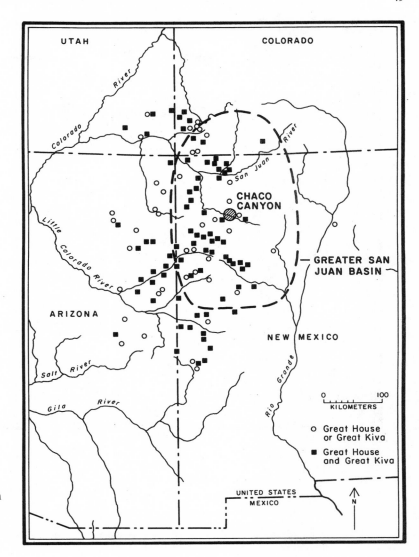

Figure 4.1. Distribution of sites with Chacoan great houses and great kivas (adapted from Doyel and Lekson 1992:17).

scholarly history of the Chacoan phenomenon resembles that of Cahokia.

At the broadest scale, the Chacoan commonality is equated with the distribution of a "community" pattern of smaller residential sites surrounding a center with a Chaco-style great house or great kiva (Figure 4.1). If all of these community replicates are integrated by central functions tied to Chaco Canyon, the size of territory is large indeed at greater than 60,000 km² (Cordell 1984:246; Judge 1991:16) or even 100,000 km² (Doyel 1992:3). However, as Lekson (1991:32) cautions, the Chaco style of public architecture is deduced by equivocal surface indications in some outlying cases, and a direct ritual or economic linkage can be demonstrated only for a smaller subset of communities surrounding the canyon. Furthermore, there is

chronological disjuncture in Chacoan distributions. Chronological resolution is a necessary step in defining communities and teasing out polities.

For analytical purposes, some Chaco scholars such as Toll (1991:78) prefer to deal with a substantially reduced region defined by the San Juan Basin. This boundary appears to account for sources of the vast majority of materials found in Chaco Canyon. Such an economic sphere would encompass an area on the order of 40,000 km². A direct and tangible connection is demonstrated within the area integrated by the famous Chaco roads (Lekson 1991:48). This network is not fully delineated, but a rough outline of known segments would cover about 18,000 km² (Figure 4.1). Whether road-linked centers and their surrounding settlements ever constituted

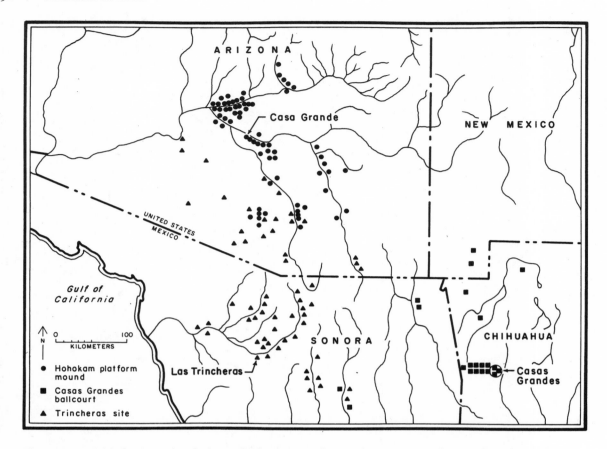

Figure 4.2.   Distribution of Hohokam platform mounds, trincheras sites, and Casas Grandes-style ballcourts (adapted from P. Fish and S. Fish 1994:23).

segments of one polity in a sociopolitical or economic sense rather than a ritual domain is unresolved, but integration in some sense does not seem open to question. At the least, road builders along each stretch had to coordinate adjacent routing and labor, and share the goal of interconnection.

Another recurring idea is that communities with Chacoan public architecture constituted the building blocks of several larger polities, including a major one focused on Pueblo Bonito in Chaco Canyon, and secondary or subsequently established entities organized around preeminent outliers such as Aztec and Salmon Ruin (Neitzel 1989a). Architectural variability in constituent centers likely reflects the diversity in ritual and differential expenditure on public works that was inte-

grated by inclusive Chacoan polities; the degree of diversity again depends on how those units should be grouped at higher levels.

A similar range of possibilities obtains for territorial extent and diversity integrated by the largest polities among the Hohokam. Important contrasts are the absence of a single preeminent center comparable to Pueblo Bonito and the visible demarcation of larger scale linkage provided by roads. The distribution of platform mounds and their surrounding settlements in the Classic Period after about A.D. 1150 is comparable to the distribution of Chacoan communities. Mound centers encompass an area of less than 50,000 km² in southern Arizona (Figure 4.2), although as with Chacoan configurations, not all instances are contemporary.

Territory of the mound communities along massive canals on the Salt and Gila Rivers in the Phoenix Basin roughly averages 40 km^2 (S. Fish and P. Fish 1992). When Thiessen polygons are constructed about centers along Salt River canals, the approximated territories range from less than 20 km^2 to almost 70 km^2 (Fish 1996). The size of communities enclosing mound centers tends to expand away from the Salt and Gila Rivers (Fish 1996:Figure 13.3). In the Tucson area, communities with lesser opportunities for irrigation are both larger and less densely packed. Extensive survey has allowed delineation of three communities that exceed 100 km^2, with two nearing 150 km^2 (Fish 1996).

There have been few suggestions that all Hohokam mounds or even all of the mounds in a geographic sub-area were incorporated by one or a few polities. In the Phoenix Basin, shared canals tangibly link sets of individual mound communities. Doyel (1974) has termed such a set an "irrigation community," a usage different from that of this chapter. Necessarily interactive sets of communities are thus defined, although the centralization of authority with regard to water use and other functions is debated. Several Late Classic sites with the most massive and diverse public architecture such as Casa Grande, Pueblo Grande, and Mesa Grande probably integrated the largest clusters of communities (e.g., Crown 1987; Doyel 1991; Howard 1987).

Overarching polities that integrated mounds along more than one Salt River canal network have been proposed (e.g., Upham and Rice 1980), but lack conclusive means for identifying constituent members. Five mound communities irrigated from the Gila system supplying Casa Grande, the largest and most architecturally impressive center. An overall territory for these five approaches 240 km^2 but includes poorly bounded lateral increments of nonirrigated land (Crown 1987). It has been suggested that Casa Grande also integrated several nearby mound communities that did not share its canals into an even larger entity (Bayman 1994:159–160; Downum and Madsen 1993:141; Wilcox 1988a).

It is particularly difficult to approximate maximum polity size for Paquimé, where investigations outside the site have been limited until recently. An earlier large figure for territorial sway proposed by Di Peso (1974:1:5; Minnis 1989:289) of 85,000 km^2 was derived from the distribution of polychrome ceramics and adobe Pueblo architecture. More recent reconnaissance survey by Minnis and Whalen (1992) has substantially downsized

the area of surrounding settlement with strong ties or relationships to Paquimé. They suggest a 30 km radius (2,800 km^2) based on architecture at secondary centers and the lack of Paquimé elements of ballcourts, stone circles, and macaw breeding at large sites beyond these limits (Figure 4.2); the distribution of polychromes similar to those at Paquimé indicates a slightly larger 3,500 km^2 area of relatively intense interaction (Whalen and Minnis 1996a:177).

Population Size

Population size and diversity for great town polities of the Southwest are highly inferential. Better quantification can be achieved at different scales in different regions. Within Chaco Canyon proper, well integrated by roads, population estimates drawn from room numbers range from 2,500 (Lekson 1984a) to 5,000 (Hayes 1981b; Vivian 1990). In the San Juan Basin, up to 40,000 inhabitants may have been present during the Chacoan peak at approximately A.D. 1075 (Dean et al. 1996). This largest territorial extent is of a scale that would encompass more than one Anasazi branch (a major Anasazi stylistic subdivision based on ceramics, such as Kayenta, Mesa Verde, Winslow, etc.) and several ethnic groups during historic times.

Population estimates range from 500 to several thousand for individual mound communities (e.g., Doyel 1991:266; Fish and Fish 1994:123; Wilcox 1991d:263). Potential polity totals again depend on posited groupings of these units. Population estimates of 20,000 to more than 100,000 have been advanced for all the Phoenix Basin Hohokam in the Classic Period after A.D. 1100. Using recent calculations of irrigable land and Piman land use as a direct analogy, 53,000 to 133,000 people might have been supported by Salt River canal systems (Doyel 1991; Fish and Fish 1991; Haury 1976:356; Schroeder 1940:20). A Yuman enclave at Las Colinas, inferred from stylistically intrusive ceramics in one precinct of this Phoenix site (Beckwith 1988), suggests that extra-local residents may have figured in Phoenix Basin totals.

With excavated data, Di Peso (1974) estimated a peak population of 2,200 at Paquimé. There are as yet no means for calculating population in the reduced hinterland proposed by Whalen and Minnis (1996a) as a more inclusive territory.

Subsistence Diversity

The degree of diversity in subsistence strategies integrated by Southwestern polities can be related to the diffusion of localized risks and to the potential for specialization and exchange. The administration of communal stores and the orchestration of exchange activities are high probability components of leadership roles. In addition, each kind of cooperative venture for water and land use would have created societal subgroups with common interests and the opportunity for leadership roles.

A wide range of subsistence technologies would have existed within the largest suggested spheres of Chacoan influence. Elaborate runoff systems, involving productive coordination, are documented in the Chaco Canyon core (Vivian 1991:68–75). Sebastian (1992) postulates the production of investable food surpluses within the Canyon, while some models postulate a need for provisioning from outside (Judge 1979:903, 1984:10; Marshall et al. 1982; Truell 1986:143). Zones of agricultural production in the Bis sa'ani Community illustrate productive variation according to topography and hydrology in the cluster of settlements surrounding a Chaco outlier (Cully et al. 1982:157–165).

Among the Hohokam, the broad Phoenix Basin is agriculturally homogeneous in the contiguous extent of irrigated land. Nevertheless, differential access to external resources and raw materials characterizes interior and exterior communities in a densely packed array along the Salt River (Figure 4.2). Communities within the narrower valley of the Gila River employed a greater diversity of irrigation and nonirrigation technologies. The greatest topographic and technological diversity within communities occurred in basins without large scale irrigation, such as that surrounding Tucson (Fish 1996).

The full diversity and the spatial arrangement of agricultural technologies are not known for the most recently suggested radius of strong influence about Paquimé. It is clear from available information that different methods were used in proximity to the primary drainages and in the surroundings of large upland sites. Irrigation was practiced near Paquimé and probably other sites along rivers; elaborate stone runoff systems and terraces have been encountered in the vicinity of smaller centers in the surrounding uplands (Di Peso 1984; Herold 1965; Minnis and Whalen 1992).

Diversity in Centralized Activities and Architecture

A diversity of communal architecture within a polity center implies variety in respective rituals and other public functions, each of which in turn entails a body of specialized knowledge, activities, and resources. Pueblo Bonito illustrates the ultimate example of localized diversity in Chaco public facilities. Multiple great houses incorporate plazas, great kivas, small kivas, tower kivas, and shrine rooms (Vivian 1990:265–274). Probable platform mounds are present, and an isolated great kiva seems connected to the complex by a road (G. Vivian, personal communication). Diversity of suggested functions and activities include ritual, residence, communal storage, communal food preparation in large plaza fireboxes (G. Vivian, personal communication), astronomical records and calendrics, necropolis-like burial (Akins 1986:112–128), and a preeminent role in the exchange and consumption of long distance resources.

Architectural diversity at Pueblo Grande in Phoenix is expressed by a plaza, a platform mound with a range of room functions, other structures in the mound compound, a big house, and four ballcourts (Downum and Bostwick 1993). Diversity of functions and activities documented at Pueblo Grande include ritual; residence; communal storage; the stockpiling of crafts such as axes, asbestos, and shell; communal food preparation; calendrics; burial; a prominent role in long distance exchange of resources; manufacture of crafts such as woven textiles and ground stone; and ballgames (Downum and Bostwick 1993). A similar range in public architecture and probably in associated communal activities is present at Casa Grande, which includes a plaza, big house, two platform mounds, a ballcourt, and a series of compounds at the edge of the plaza with specialized ritual functions (Fewkes 1912b; Wilcox and Shenk 1977).

At Paquimé, diversity in the public domain consists of extensive plazas, 18 nonresidential but morphologically distinct platform mounds, three ballcourts, specialized rooms in residential roomblocks, large communal roasting pits, and an elaborate water supply to buildings. Functions and activities include rituals associated with the different mound types, ballgames, communal food preparation, and macaw and turkey breeding (Minnis 1989). Residential roomblocks yield localized evidence of stockpiling and craft manufacture. Di Peso attributed a market function to particular outdoor precincts, although Minnis (1988) questions the strength of such evidence.

The number and diversity of communal activities in centers may approximate a reasonably direct index of centrality and complexity for those cases in which a community constitutes the ultimate political unit. For great town polities encompassing multiple communities, the situation is not so simple. According to comparative studies (Feinman and Neitzel 1984), diversity in the duties of preeminent leaders may decrease after a threshold of hierarchical differentiation, beyond which ancillary functions are delegated to secondary levels of authority. It is therefore also useful to consider how ancillary communal functions that serve to further integrate a polity are distributed throughout smaller centers.

Kowalewski (1990) proposes that the horizontal complexity of an inclusive polity is related to the degree to which secondary central places at the same hierarchical level differ in functional and formal attributes, particularly with regard to functions involving the larger entity. The prehistoric subcenters of Oaxaca, Kowalewski's region of study, exhibit a greater degree of specialization (e.g., primary production, markets, defense, gateway) than might be attributed to those of the Southwest. Nevertheless, this relationship offers a measure for departure from Johnson's (1989) model of sequential hierarchy in which the integrated parts are essentially the same.

A problem in examining the diversity of centers incorporated within great town polities is more basic than a lack of comparable and systematic data for each site. As Kowalewski (1990:39) stipulates, it is first necessary to draw a comprehensive boundary and identify the parts. In spite of the pervasive difficulties of polity definition in the Southwest, his criteria for horizontal complexity are insightful. However it might have been partitioned into centers and communities or bounded as a polity, Chaco Canyon is the prime Southwestern example of locationally differentiated public architecture. The fact that the loci in combination may represent coherence as a ritual landscape (Stein and Lekson 1992) need not diminish the significance of the physical separation of public and ceremonial specialized functions. Improved knowledge of the distribution of residential population and other aspects of a settlement pattern are needed to analyze the implications further.

An appreciation of architectural differences among Classic Hohokam platform mounds and a recognition of additional forms such as towers is emerging as a result of recent archival review (e.g., Downum 1993) and generously funded investigations throughout the central part of southern Arizona. Dating of construction events and mound histories has revealed chronological developments in architectural forms. Numbers of mounds, construction styles, and accompanying public facilities are

clearly varied among centers of the Phoenix Basin. It remains for this variety to be described and evaluated in terms of the contemporary constituent centers of any inclusive polities.

The Tucson Basin Hohokam constructed populous villages on terraced hillside "trincheras" sites within communities that also possessed platform mound centers. Public architecture of a moderate scale may be represented among the structures at these hillside sites (Downum 1993; Downum et al. 1994; Fish et al. 1992a). To the south in northern Sonora, large trincheras sites contain the most massive and specialized constructions (S. Fish and P. Fish 1994). The conjunction of both mound centers and trincheras villages in some Tucson communities may signify the integration of ethnic or ideological elements of southern origin (Figure 4.2). In the Tonto Basin of central Arizona, the contemporary construction of platform mounds at some large sites and Puebloan styles of architecture at others is attributed to ethnic and cultural distinctions among basin inhabitants (e.g., Clark 1995).

The degree to which communal architecture and functions are closely replicated among the larger settlements surrounding Paquimé is under study through regional survey. Preliminary findings (Minnis and Whalen 1992) reveal that settlement patterns include ballcourts with differing attributes and with differing spatial relationships to stone mounds and massive stone circles.

Additional Dimensions of Complexity

In addition to the variability seen in the territorial extent, population size, subsistence practices, and communal architecture of the Southwest's most complex polities, there are several other characteristics that can add to our understanding of their complexity. These include duration, evidence for elites, and developments in the Late Prehistoric period. Together, all of the characteristics discussed in this paper suggest that the traditional cultural evolutionary distinction between tribes and chiefdoms does not account for the trajectories that most prehistoric Southwestern societies followed as they became increasingly complex.

Duration

The duration of Southwestern communities and polities is probably the most complicated issue for the Hohokam.

The productivity of irrigated land in the Phoenix Basin, the investment in huge canals, and the topographic and hydrological limitations on canal location created long-term concentrations of settlement. Snaketown, where the earliest mounds accompany ballcourts, seems to have served as a center for most of its occupation. Although it did not continue into the Classic period, public architecture around the central plaza spans more than 500 years.

Multiple Preclassic ballcourt centers and the later mound centers were tied by common canal networks. The size of both occupations and ballcourts were larger at some of these Preclassic sites than at others, suggesting a potential for preeminence in at least those interactive realms related to ballcourts (Wilcox and Sternberg 1983). Many Classic period mounds were also built at sites with earlier ballcourts. Patterned placement of mounds with regard to the preexisting plazas and ballcourts suggests an uninterrupted transition at some sites (Gregory 1987). Because other Preclassic centers were abandoned and because shifts in the form of public architecture mark the Classic period, it is unclear whether integrative organization and personnel were continuous within persistent centers. Furthermore, the dating of both ballcourt and mound construction is not sufficiently precise at any site to evaluate the periodicity of construction episodes and active use. In terms of locational continuity, however, some community centers conceivably spanned more than 750 years after the inception of ballcourts.

In contrast to this kind of longevity, it is possible to identify realignments of settlement and ballcourt centers within the Preclassic interval in the less densely populated Tucson Basin (Doelle and Wallace 1991). Similarly, several mound-centered Tucson communities seem to have assumed Classic period configurations and then were abandoned in less than 150 years (Fish and Fish 1994). Although Preclassic settlements occur within the later Classic boundaries, community boundaries shifted over time and earlier ballcourt and later mound centers do not coincide. Mound construction, Classic period occupation, and site abandonment proceeded at a similarly more punctuated pace in the Tonto Basin, bordering the eastern extent of the Hohokam domain. These developments were contained within an interval of less than 100 years in one well-documented Tonto case (Craig et al. 1992).

Recent findings distinguish forerunners of the architectural differentiation that culminated in Chacoan public buildings soon after the mid-ninth century in the canyon itself (Windes and Ford 1992). The time span

preceding a demise of vigor in this seminal locality covers less than 300 years. Pulses of construction at existing centers and the appearance of new communities occurred in the canyon during this era of fluorescence, notably at the beginning of the eleventh century (Doyel 1992:4). Although variations on the themes of Chacoan public architecture continued well beyond the major Canyon occupation (Fowler and Stein 1992; McKenna and Toll 1992), the diminution of this foremost node during the twelfth century marks an integrative endpoint; the exact date for significant diminution is not a settled matter (Doyel 1992:4).

The duration of the community containing Paquimé can only be evaluated from chronology at that central site. A reanalysis of tree-ring information has markedly readjusted developments upward in time (Dean and Ravesloot 1993). The revision reflects a review of the incorporation of beams into construction during the Medio period. Construction of the impressive adobe buildings during the Buena Fe phase at Paquimé seems to have begun between A.D. 1200 and 1350. Later beams attributed to the Paquimé phase are compatible with construction until at least A.D. 1400 and possibly into the middle of the fifteenth century. Tree-ring data do not reveal the clearly sequential progression of the phases proposed by Di Peso (1974), but the end of his Diablo phase may be as late as A.D. 1500 (Dean and Ravesloot 1993:96–98). At the outside, the prominence of Paquimé in regional patterns endures less than 300 years; the central Paquimé phase probably began near A.D. 1300 and lasted 150 years or less (Dean and Ravesloot 1993:97).

Although all Southwestern polities, and notably the polity occupying Chaco Canyon, did not continue into the final centuries of the prehistoric period, the organizational modes and solutions underlying aggregated and complex configurations appear to have been shared and cumulative to some degree over time. Successors with Chacoan styles persisted after collapse at Chaco Canyon and mound-centered developments arose among the Hohokam following the demise of the ballcourt system. As noted by Yoffee and Cowgill (1988) in the context of state evolution, successive polities build on the legacy of social innovations and productive technologies of predecessors, whether these predecessors ultimately persisted or not. This premise seems equally applicable to the modest political developments of the Southwest, with fewer indications of hierarchy and linearization (cf. Flannery 1972a,b).

Southwestern Great Town Elites

The identification of Southwestern elites is largely anecdotal due to a dearth of systematic samples for relevant indicators. Hierarchies can be identified at the level of sites in differentiated settlement patterns, but it is difficult to distinguish potential elite residences within centers other than by an association with public architecture. Evidence for differential consumption is largely confined to the documentation of greater proportions of high value and long-distance resources at central sites. However, the extensive body of Southwestern research reveals scanty evidence for attached craft specialists.

Mortuary evidence for privileged treatment often consists of differential placement and may not be correlated with overwhelmingly rich or abundant accompaniments. Among the Classic period Hohokam, unusual attributes associated with status include burial in adobe sarcophagi, in adobe-lined pits, and in mound precincts (Brunson 1989). At Paquimé, distinctive mortuary treatment for potential elites included an urn secondary burial, placement in room subfloor vaults, and rare grave goods such as hand drums (Ravesloot 1988:68–72). Occasional dramatically rich burials have been found such as those of the "Magician" at Ridge Ruin near Flagstaff (McGregor 1943) and interments in Rooms 32 and 33 at Pueblo Bonito (Pepper 1909, 1920). At Pueblo Bonito, one burial contained multiple individuals and approximately 13,000 turquoise objects, five jet inlays, 94 shell bracelets, 3,300 shell beads, a shell trumpet, and many pots and other items (Akins 1986:115). More generally, a contrast is clear between Chaco great house sites where 26% of the burials have turquoise beads and other villages where less than 1% of the interments have associated turquoise (Mathien 1984).

Perhaps the greatest contrast between the Southeast and Southwest with regard to elites lies in the unequal body of evidence for coercive power. Human sacrifice at dedicatory and funerary occasions is tenuous, and rare if ever practiced. Skeletal evidence for armed conflict and other forms of social violence is currently being reevaluated as having been more common in the past than is currently recognized (e.g., Turner and Turner 1990; Wilcox and Haas 1994a,b), but an iconography celebrating warfare and conquest is absent. The limited instances of human trophy materials do occur in conjunction with situations of greatest complexity. For instance, a burial at Pueblo Grande holds an extra skull in the crook of an arm (Downum, n.d.), and skulls, necklaces of phalanges, and a bone rasp were recovered at Paquimé (Di Peso et al. 1974).

If we examine Southwestern situations in which the need for rapid decision-making might make paramount leaders more palatable to their followers, warfare is prominent. For example, upon viewing the "Magician" burial and his accompaniments, various Hopi religious informants independently identified the individual as a military leader (McGregor 1943:295–296). Other contexts in which decisive authority might be critical include massive irrigation canal systems shared by many villages and even large scale runoff systems where water arrives rapidly and departs quickly, such as at Chaco Canyon. In egalitarian societies, the costs of reaching a consensus among equals may become high or inconvenient when time is of the essence and large segments of the population must act together.

Developments in the
Late Prehistoric Period

Beginning after the thirteenth century, very large settlements come to typify both the eastern and western segments of the post-Chacoan Anasazi world. Some of these settlements can only be described as anomalous in the context of prehistoric regional populations. For instance, Sapawe and Poshuouinge on the Chama River have more than 1,800 rooms each. In the Galisteo Basin, Galisteo Pueblo has approximately 1,600 rooms, San Cristobal, 1,650, Pueblo Colorado 1,400, and Pueblo She more than 1,500 rooms (Cordell et al. 1994a). Furthermore, some of these large Pueblo towns are embedded in regional settlement hierarchies defined by site size that include three or more discernible tiers. Clusters of these large pueblos, coinciding with identifiable ceramic constellations and empty zones or "no man's land between clusters," have been the basis for often controversial identification as polities (Lightfoot 1984; Wilcox 1991a; Upham 1982; Upham and Reed 1989). Food redistribution as a risk reduction strategy and warfare or competition between settlement clusters have been cited as factors in polity formation and as mechanisms for the emergence of elite leadership.

Highly flexible alliances or confederacies for the principal purpose of defense or war also have been proposed for some late pueblo clusters (e.g., Spielmann 1994). According to Adams (1991), public architecture in the large late pueblos takes the form of enclosed plazas that serve to crosscut a system of segmentary lineages. He relates the appearance of these plazas to the development of the Katsina cult. The cult provides a mechanism for food redistribution and a means through which town leaders accomplish public works by ritually involving all members of the society. In this scenario, integration does not extend beyond the territory and smaller settlements associated with a single large pueblo.

In significant contrast to architectural expenditure in the "Great Town" polities, these late northern Pueblo instances include no imposing and specialized public edifices that could have served as a locus of polity interactions and a tangible symbol of polity coherence. This lack of architectural correlates for polity-wide interactions makes it difficult to envision or to archaeologically detect linkages among constituent communities that might have surpassed a loose confederacy; the Southwest also lacks early historic observers to delineate such linkages, as was the case for the Coosa polity in the contact-era Southeast. Holley (Chapter 2) suggests that the diminution of mounds in the late prehistoric Southeast reflects the decreasing need to sanctify a chiefly ideology as it became regionally ubiquitous. Perhaps, terminal Anasazi organization should be reexamined in terms of this interesting notion that the routinization of the ideology underlying hierarchy and integration decreases the impetus for architectural display.

In the years between A.D. 1300 and 1450, settlement configurations consistent with community organization can be identified widely within the southern portions of the Greater Southwest. Figure 4.2 shows the distribution of platform mounds, trincheras sites, and Casas Grandes (Paquimé) style ballcourts. Some southern Arizona mound centers were abandoned near the beginning of this late prehistoric interval, indicating a shift in integrative structure. In well-studied cases, it has been shown that settlement was also truncated in the surrounding community (Craig et al. 1992; Downum 1993; S. Fish and Fish 1993b).

This broad geographical trend is accompanied by: 1) increased population densities in centers and communities with greatest irrigation potential (e.g., Doelle and Wallace 1991); 2) an increase in primacy among centers as indicated by the greater size, diversity, and elaboration of public architecture at a few (e.g., Downum 1993; Minnis 1989; Wilcox 1991e); and 3) the replacement of more localized styles of decorated ceramics and architecture with pan-regional polychromes and adobe buildings. The foremost examples of primate sites such as Paquimé in Chihuahua, Casa Grande, Pueblo Grande, and Mesa Grande in south-

ern Arizona, and Las Trincheras in Sonora are roughly contemporary in late prehistoric times.

Where coverage is sufficiently reliable to evaluate settlement trends, simultaneous contraction and aggregation are evident (e.g., Doolittle 1988; Nelson 1993; Whittlesey and Ciolek-Torrello 1992). Population was lost from less agriculturally productive areas, while aggregation correlates largely with irrigable flood plains of major rivers and other settings with potential for productive intensification. Frequency of interaction and occasions necessitating cooperation must have increased among individuals and groups of diverse origin in these situations. Emergent hierarchies, institutions crosscutting social constituencies, and ideologies promoting commonality are among possible and probable resolutions to aggregated conditions. Aside from earlier developments related to Chaco Canyon, most regional archaeologists ascribe greater complexity to variously defined polities in the southern Southwest than in the northern Southwest. Paquimé commonly is cited as foremost in complexity, partly due to Di Peso's (1974) interpretation of the site as a Mesoamerican outpost. His inference that Tula in central Mexico was a distant source of developmental stimuli is not supported by reassessment of chronology (Dean and Ravesloot 1993). Economic centralization at Paquimé (Minnis 1989) and the strength of regional hegemony (Douglas 1992; Minnis and Whalen 1992) are also being questioned in new research and reanalyses.

The Classic period Hohokam of the Phoenix Basin are also usually considered among the foremost examples of Southwestern complexity and hierarchy. Attributes contributing to this perception include dense and permanent populations, construction of the largest prehistoric canal systems north of Peru (Doolittle 1990), and the erection of mounds. Scholars agree on the necessity for coordination in constructing and using canals longer than 24 km. On the other hand, conclusions concerning levels of effort, interconnections between canal systems, the need for centralized control, and the relationship of irrigation networks to political entities show a wide diversity of opinion (e.g., Ackerly 1988; Breternitz 1991; Gregory 1991; Howard 1992; Masse 1991; Nicholas and Feinman 1989).

Alternative Routes to Complexity

The community, consisting of a center with unique public architecture amid surrounding settlements, is the most consensual unit of societal integration in the Southwest. The clustering of communities into encompassing entities or polities is always more controversial, though as at Chaco Canyon, regional scholars have advanced many kinds of inclusive interactions. It is particularly difficult to identify supra-community configurations that embody political integration as distinct from groupings that represent shared canons of style, economic exchange, or adherence to overarching ideologies; the threshold is blurry between what has been defined as a polity in this chapter and the variously defined concept of a regional system.

New ways of perceiving the integrative mechanisms of Southwestern communities may be useful as a starting point for higher order phenomena. Models that derive both from a chiefdom classification and from Puebloan ethnography emphasize pervasive systems of kinship as the primary principle in societal organization and the generation of leadership roles. It is very likely that prehistoric small kivas in the northern Southwest denote the importance of unilineal kin groups as in historic times, but northern great towns also contain distinct and centralized forms of public architecture. In much of the southern Southwest, focal architecture serving kin groups is never present, and ritual artifacts and specialized architecture are highly centralized within communities after A.D. 1150. Moreover, ethnographic kinship among native peoples of the southern Southwest and adjacent Mexico tends to be bilateral, less formally expressed, and less closely coupled with access to land (Fish and Yoffee 1995). Alternatives to kinship therefore should be considered in analyzing the organization and integration of prehistoric Southwestern communities.

One source for envisioning organizational principles other than kinship is the Mexican "comunidad." The comunidad has been a unit of territory and local administration among agrarian and predominantly indigenous populations since early colonial times, with demonstrable continuities from pre-contact patterns in some regions (e.g., Spores 1967; Whitecotton 1977). Comunidades typically incorporate multiple villages, but have a designated administrative center in the largest settlement that also contains the foremost and often the only church. Comunidad boundaries guarantee access to basic resources beyond those available through individual land tenure or membership in a single village. Although kin groups may be strongly involved in political and economic machinations within the framework of the comunidad, locational affiliation is the fundamental principle of integration.

Similarly bounded units of territory and society with a concentration of nonduplicated communal functions in a central site are consistent with the archaeological record of prehistoric Southwestern communities. Such an institutional structure might be more likely to develop and persist where investment in structural improvements was crucial to agricultural success and land was continuously cultivated. To the extent that communal efforts figured in agricultural production, community cohesion might be further strengthened. This factor could change through time with productive intensification. Although the magnitude of communal technologies is not a direct correlate of the magnitude of prehistoric integration, it seems significant that canal networks were shared by the Hohokam and the inhabitants of Paquimé, and that extensive runoff systems conjoined farmers in Chaco Canyon.

An implication of comunidad-like organization is that the architectural symbols of integration are comprehensible within an ideology of community identity and affiliation. The elaboration of centralized symbols communicates the cohesiveness and prominence of the community (probably vis-a-vis neighbors) rather than the preeminence of a leader and his lineage. This sort of ideology is commensurate with Southwestern burial regimes in which the power and status of an individual are reflected more by a locational association with the symbols of community than by displays of kin-based privilege and wealth.

Integrative ideologies that emphasize locational affiliation are not immune to manipulation by competing subgroups within a society, however, including those composed of kin. In fact, if social positions are not comprehensively specified by birth and genealogy is not the sole source of legitimate power, usurpation of central institutions may be more readily achieved. Instances of residence and burial in the precincts of great town public architecture, as at Pueblo Bonito, Paquimé, and Pueblo Grande, likely indicate the establishment of at least briefly sustained successional offices. Centralized functions should be most readily extended from a predominant community to its neighbors where population and communities already formed contiguous distributions. In view of the variety in archaeological expressions, it is probable that multiple routes led to political integration and complexity among the great towns of the Southwest.

Concluding Thoughts

A persisting dilemma in analyzing Southwestern complexity is the uncertainty of polity definition. Settlement data are not presently comprehensive or systematic in the extended surroundings of Chaco, Paquimé, and the preeminent Phoenix Basin sites. More definitive distributions of population in densely settled regional sectors and an improved inventory of the variability in public features of secondary centers are needed. An alternative avenue to the better definition of polities may lie in finely-tuned distributional and stylistic analyses. Studies of material culture, and particularly those of ceramics, have seldom been geared toward questions of polity delineation in the Southwest. While it is risky to assume that economic and stylistically-based distributions are isomorphic with political interactions, carefully selected attributes could provide insights into sets of communities with asymmetrical relationships (e.g., Abbott 1996).

It is doubtful that a uniform cultural concept such as "Mississippian" can ever be similarly applied to the most complex archaeological manifestations across the Southwest. Regional diversity is more pronounced in both the basic fabric of societal organization and the symbols of political integration. A north-south dichotomy is apparent among both the prehistoric and historic cultural configurations of indigenous agricultural groups. Likewise, the social and organizational principles of prehistoric polities on the northern plateaus and in the southern desert basins probably cannot be understood by as singular a model as the ethnohistorically supported "chiefdoms" of the Southeast.

CHAPTER FIVE

How Great Were the Southeastern Polities?

John F. Scarry

Dᴜʀɪɴɢ ᴛʜᴇ Lᴀᴛᴇ Pʀᴇʜɪsᴛᴏʀɪᴄ ᴘᴇʀɪᴏᴅ, ᴄʜɪᴇꜰʟʏ polities emerged and collapsed across the Southeastern United States. This pattern is marked in the archaeological record by the construction and abandonment of mound centers and the occupation and abandonment of large regions (e.g., Anderson 1990, 1996a, 1996b; Hally 1996b; Milner 1986, 1996; Peebles 1986, 1987a, 1987b; J. Scarry 1990a, 1990b, 1996; Williams and Shapiro 1996). However, while individual polities appeared and disappeared, the region as a whole was dominated by Mississippian societies throughout this period.

How great were the native polities of the late prehistoric Southeast? The answer depends. It depends on how greatness is measured. It depends on which polity or polities are looked at. To a very great extent, it depends on who provides the answer.

In this chapter, I consider the question of greatness using the variables of polity size, stability, productivity, and complexity for six well-documented areas in the Southeast (Figure 5.1). The largest Mississippian polities developed in two of these areas: the Cahokia system in the American Bottom and the Moundville system in the Black Warrior River Valley. Three other areas, the Confluence region of the Mississippi River Valley, Piedmont Georgia, and the Big Bend in Florida, were occupied by intermediate to large scale polities. Finally, the Powers phase polity of southeastern Missouri was relatively small and insignificant.

POLITY SIZE IN THE MISSISSIPPIAN WORLD

One measure of greatness is size. Were the Mississippian polities large societies with broad territories inhabited by tens or even hundreds of thousands of people? Or were they small societies whose few thousand people could walk from one end of their territory to the other in a day? Answering these questions requires several kinds of analyses, each with its own methodological difficulties. Political boundaries have to be defined, contemporaneous sites have to be identified, and the populations of households, sites, and regions have to be calculated. When such analyses are done for Mississippian polities, the results indicate that these polities were relatively small both in geographic extent and population.

Geographic Extent

Estimating the extent of Mississippian polities is difficult, because it requires the definition of boundaries. This is not an easy task even where buffer zones are known to have separated polities. Southeastern archaeologists have employed several approaches to boundary

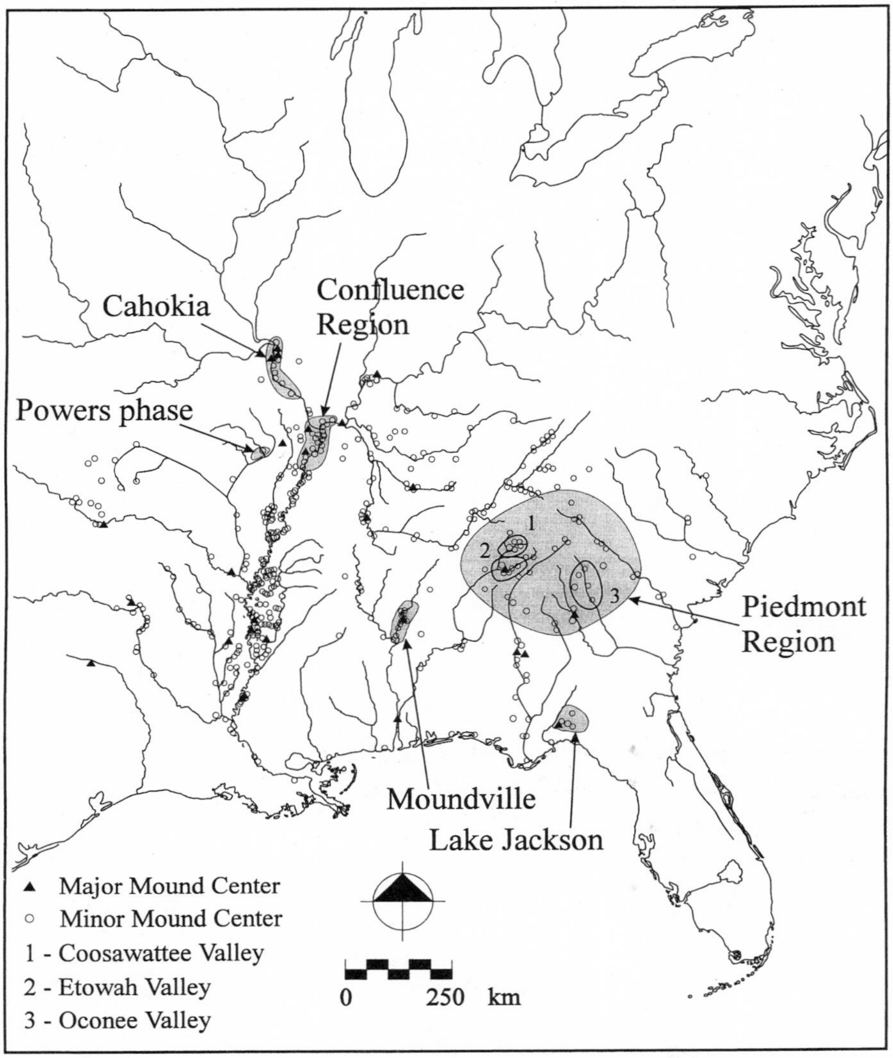
Cahokia
Confluence Region
Powers phase
Piedmont Region
Moundville
Lake Jackson
▲ Major Mound Center
○ Minor Mound Center
1 - Coosawattee Valley
2 - Etowah Valley
3 - Oconee Valley
1
2
3
0 250 km

Figure 5.1. Southeastern United States showing areas and polities discussed in this chapter.

definition, which when applied to the same area have sometimes produced widely varying results. Two approaches rely on the distributions of political centers with mounds. One simply measures and subdivides the distances between these centers (Hally 1993). The other applies various mathematical formulas such as XTENT circles (Scarry and Payne 1986). A third approach expands the data considered to include both mound centers and habitation sites (Smith and Kowalewski 1981; Williams and Shapiro 1996). A final approach relies on historic descriptions by Spanish explorers.

Cahokia

Some have argued that Cahokia, the largest of the Mississippian centers, directly controlled a very large territory and had strong influences on other groups a thousand kilometers away (e.g., Dincauze and Hasenstab 1989). Given the distribution of recognizable Cahokian material culture, however, it is difficult to extend Cahokia's indirect influence even as far as the Iroquois region. To be sure, Cahokia influenced or had some kind of contact with polities considerably distant from the American Bottom, but this influence was limited, and involved no political or economic control. The direct administrative control of the elite of Cahokia probably extended no more than 50–100 km from Monks Mound (Milner 1986). Based on the distribution of distinct ceramic styles and mound centers, Milner (1986:7–9) estimates that the boundaries of the Cahokia polity at its height extended ca. 10–15 km north of Cahokia itself to the Grassy Lake site and approximately 100 km (river distance) south to the mouth of the Kaskaskia River.

Moundville

The political control of Moundville, the second largest Mississippian center, was apparently limited to a segment of the Black Warrior River Valley that extended from the Fall Line to the low, swampy lands south of Moundville. This territory measured approximately 20 km × 50 km (Steponaitis 1983:4). There is evidence for interaction between Moundville and Mississippian polities outside the Black Warrior River Valley in the form of stylistic affinities between pottery types and assemblages. However, there is no evidence that sites outside the Black Warrior River Valley were under the control of Moundville (cf. McKenzie 1966:38; Walthall 1980:228–236).

Confluence

The geographic extent and even the number of polities in the Confluence region is a matter of considerable debate. Based on the absence of clearly demarcated buffer zones between groups of sites, the substantial fortifications at many centers, and the nucleation of populations into those fortified sites, Sussenbach (1993) has suggested that military conflict between centers was frequent and intense and that political boundaries shifted frequently. Given the apparent continuous occupation of many of the centers in the region, Sussenbach suggests that the region was divided into a small number of complex chiefdoms, each consisting of several centers under the domination of a powerful center. In Sussenbach's model, these political entities were temporary entities. Subjugated centers could and did shift allegiance from one paramount to another or achieve independence or positions of domination themselves. Further research is needed to test this model.

Piedmont Georgia

By examining the distribution of Mississippian mound centers in Piedmont Georgia, Hally (1993) argues that the Mississippian chiefdoms in northern Georgia, both those that could be characterized as simple chiefdoms and those that could be described as complex, seldom exceeded 40 km in diameter. The individual polities were separated by roughly 40 km wide buffer zones.

Big Bend

A variety of approaches to estimating polity size have been applied in various parts of the Big Bend area in

Florida. A simulation using the distribution of mound centers and the volume of earthen mound construction produced estimates ranging from 30–100 km in diameter, depending on assumptions about rates of political decline (Scarry and Payne 1986). Especially well studied polities in this region are the prehistoric and protohistoric polities in northwestern Florida (Lake Jackson and Velda phases, respectively). The simulation by Scarry and Payne (1986) indicates that the Lake Jackson Phase polity measured approximately 75 × 75 km. The distribution of both habitation sites and mound centers suggests a core area size of 30 × 30 km (Figure 5.2). The 75 × 75 km area corresponds to the size reported for the succeeding Velda phase polity at contact. However, as in the preceding period, its core area was considerably smaller, as its agriculturally unproductive southern portion was only lightly occupied and used as a wild resource procurement area.

Powers Phase

Data on the distribution of villages and hamlets indicate that the maximal size of the Powers phase polity was roughly .5 × 35 km (Price 1978:209).

Summary

If one assumes that the territories of Mississippian polities were limited to a core area of densest occupation and mound construction, then Hally's (1993) 40 km diameter figure is a reasonable estimate of the size of the majority of these polities. However, many polities claimed, used, and exerted control over considerably larger territories that incorporated lightly occupied, resource procurement areas. In addition, many areas' polities may have claimed and used portions of political and military buffer zones that separated them from their neighbors. Finally, the larger Mississippian polities (e.g., Cahokia) may have had core territories that exceeded the size of Hally's Mississippian module. Even so, it is clear that the Mississippian polities were small by modern standards. Ignoring the possible existence of ephemeral paramount chiefdoms, even the largest Mississippian polities probably did not have maximum dimensions that exceeded 100 km. If we discount Cahokia, the dimensions of individual polities usually did not exceed 40 km.

Regional Systems and Polities

During the Mississippi period, the Southeast can be subdivided into several large regions by significant stylistic differences in ceramic assemblages (Figure 5.3) (see

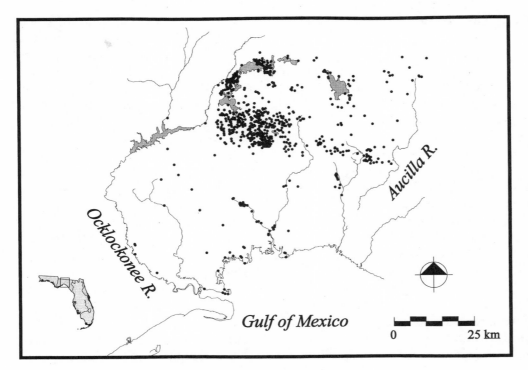

Figure 5.2. Distribution of Lake Jackson phase sites in the Apalachee province.

Chapter 11). Griffin (1967) identified four major variants: Middle Mississippi, Caddoan Mississippian, Plaquemine Mississippian, and South Appalachian Mississippian. Others, such as Fort Walton Mississippian, can also be identified. These large-scale entities are not political units. Rather, they mark multipolity interaction networks whose boundaries were permeable and fluid.

In addition to these extremely large ceramic zones, we can identify smaller areas where sites share many stylistic features, particularly ceramic types (Figure 5.4). I do not believe that these distributions mark independent political entities. Rather, they may signify the spheres of influence of major polities. For example, the distribution of Moundville style pottery extends considerably beyond the limits of Moundville's direct political control. This pottery has been found as far away as the Tennessee River Valley (DeJarnette and Wimberly 1941; Walthall 1980; Webb and DeJarnette 1942; Welch 1994), the Mobile Delta (Brown 1993; Fuller and Brown 1992), and the Big Black River of Mississippi (Steponaitis 1991). Similarly, the Pensacola style zone is centered on the large Bottle Creek center but extends more than 200 km along the Gulf Coast; and the Fort Walton style zone is centered at the Lake Jackson, Roods Landing, and Singer-Moye sites, but extends from the Fall Line down the Chattahoochee-Apalachicola River to the Gulf of Mexico and includes

nearby Mississippian systems outside that drainage (J. Scarry 1985; Schnell et al. 1981).

While I do not believe that the distributions of ceramic assemblages and types are evidence of independent polities, historic documents from the Lower Southeast indicate that large polities (e.g., the Coosa chiefdom) did exist in the Southeast—at least for short periods. Hudson et al. (1985:735) and Hally et al. (1990) call these polities paramount chiefdoms and cite the Coosa chiefdom as an example. Hudson et al. (1985:723) argue that "in de Soto's day the power of the chief of Coosa was felt in a territory that stretched for some 24 travel days from north to south, and the Soto expedition generally traveled about 20 to 24 kilometers per day." As defined by Hudson et al. (1985:735, 1987) and Hally et al. (1990), the Coosa paramount chiefdom subsumed four archaeological phases, Dallas, Mouse Creek, Barnett, and Kymulga, that roughly coincide with political subdivisions of the chiefdom that they established using historical documentation (Figure 5.4).

Hally (1996b) argues that paramount chiefdoms like Coosa were short-lived, weakly integrated, and probably held together by largely symbolic ties between elites (e.g., pledges of loyalty, payment of tribute, intermarriage, and obligations of military support). He sees very little direct involvement by the paramount ruler in the operation of subordinate polities and little coordination of activities

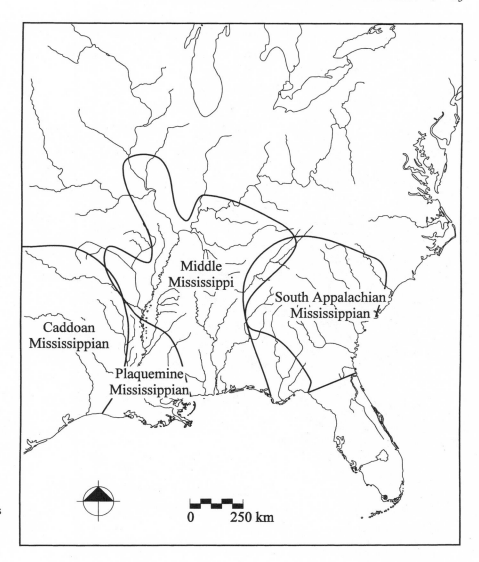

Figure 5.3. Major variants in Mississippian material culture.

among them. According to Hally, paramount chiefdoms formed as a result of one chiefdom incorporating neighboring chiefdoms. Looking at the archaeological data, Hally (1993) suggests that "unoccupied" buffer areas within the Coosa territory mark divides between these previously independent chiefdoms. In the absence of dramatic population growth, and given the weakness of the links between components, there was no need and no incentive to fill buffer zones so they persisted.

It is evident that there were large-scale systems in the eastern United States during the Mississippi period. Some may reflect the existence of multiethnic polities, which we call paramount chiefdoms. Others may reflect the existence of longstanding networks that linked independent polities (Figure 5.5). The large polities were, at best, ephemeral entities whose life spans were probably no more than a single generation in length. The interaction networks, on the other hand, were long-term systems whose life spans probably exceeded those of the individual polities that formed them.

Mississippian Population Size

On a demographic scale, the Mississippian polities were also relatively small. None reached the size of a small modern city. The largest may have had populations that reached the low tens of thousands, while the smaller polities had populations that were less than 10,000. Population estimates, which have been made for three of the areas considered in this chapter, are discussed below together with some historic data.

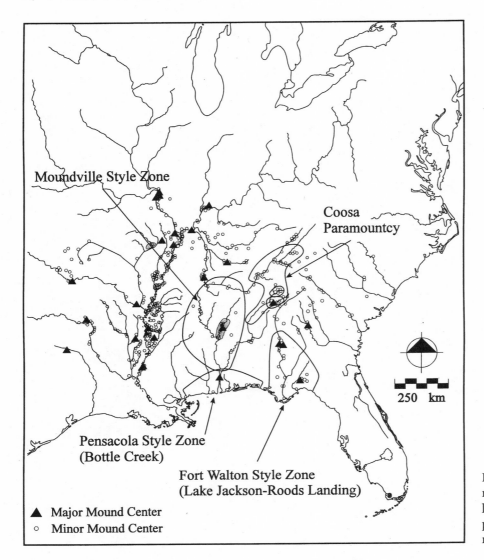

Moundville Style Zone

Coosa
Paramountcy

Pensacola Style Zone
(Bottle Creek)

Fort Walton Style Zone
(Lake Jackson-Roods Landing)

250 km

▲ Major Mound Center
○ Minor Mound Center

Figure 5.4. Regional ceramic style zones in the lower Southeast and the proposed Coosa paramountcy.

Cahokia

Population estimates for the Cahokia polity have focused almost exclusively on the site of Cahokia. Different analytical methods have produced various results. The highest estimate for the Cahokia site of 40,000 people was based on numbers of structures (Fowler 1975a). The same data analyzed with a different formula indicated a center population of 25,500 people (Gregg 1975). Calculations of how much labor would have been necessary to construct the mounds at the Cahokia site produced a figure of 10,000 (Reed et al. 1968). However, analyses of the density of residential architecture and the acreage suitable for habitation suggest that the figure may be even lower, in the 1,000s, not the 10,000s (Milner 1986).

It is this latter approach that Holley (this volume) employed in calculating a population of 3,000–12,000 for the Cahokia site at its peak.

Big Bend

Population estimates for the protohistoric and historic period Apalachee vary considerably. The highest figure, produced by a controversial method of demographic reconstruction, indicates that there were 100,000 Apalachee at the time of contact (Dobyns 1983). A much smaller figure of 6,000 people has been proposed for the Apalachee in the 1590s, roughly 60 years after first contact and 40 years before missions were established in their territory (Swanton 1946). More moderate, and probably more accurate, population estimates have been

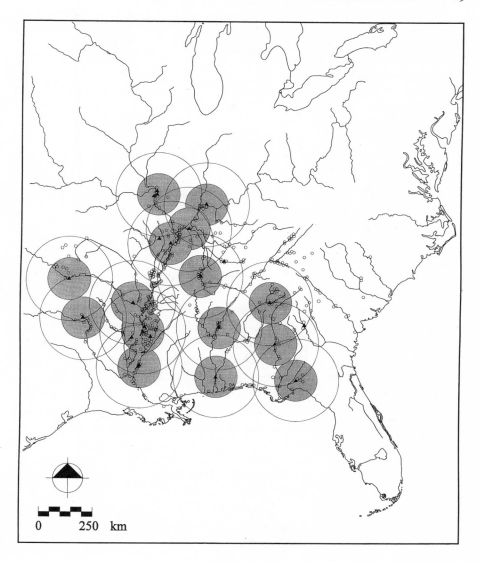

Figure 5.5. Possible spheres of influence of major Mississippian centers.

derived from figures recorded by Spanish colonial and religious officials. These estimates indicate that at the beginning of the seventeenth century the Apalachee had a surprisingly large population of 30,000 people, which underwent a steady decline during the colonial period (Hann 1988).

Powers Phase

Although the Powers phase was a small polity compared to Moundville and Cahokia, it is also one of the most thoroughly investigated of all the Mississippian polities (Price 1978). Assuming that all known Powers phase sites were contemporaneous, their aggregate population would have been approximately 6,000 individuals. However, given Price's (1978) estimate that individual villages

were only occupied for 10 to 20 years, it is unlikely that all sites were occupied at the same time. Consequently, the peak Powers phase population was probably no more than 3,000 people.

Historic data

Muller (1993a) has argued that there was a modal community size among the early historic period descendants of the Mississippian polities. He notes that despite marked population declines, the sizes of individual communities stayed at roughly 1,200 individuals. Muller suggests that communities consolidated in the face of population loss in order to maintain a size sufficient to support the traditional social and political organization. If Muller is correct, and if we can extend his modal size model back in time, then I would expect the population of complex chiefdoms like those centered on Lake Jackson and Moundville to have been in the range of perhaps 15,000 to an outside maximum of 50,000 individuals.

TEMPORAL SCALE:
POLITICAL LONGEVITY AND STABILITY

One measure of how great Mississippian polities were is their longevity. Were they successful, stable societies that lasted for hundreds of years? Or were they unstable, ephemeral systems that arose and collapsed within a few generations? Answering these questions forces us to confront the difficulty of measuring longevity at multiple scales—household, site, as well as polity. However, the life spans of Mississippian polities can be estimated using radiometric dating in conjunction with evidence of mound construction at political centers, site abandonment, and regional depopulation. Taken together, these various kinds of evidence indicate that the life spans of Mississippian polities varied significantly.

Cahokia

Cahokia and the polity it ruled were among the first of the Mississippian societies (Figure 5.6). By roughly A.D. 1000, there were two recognizable Mississippian manifestations in the American Bottom: the Lohmann phase centered on Cahokia and the Lindhorst phase surrounding the Pulcher site 24 km to the south (Kelley 1990a:136–139; Milner 1986:4). These phases may represent two independent political entities. From the burials in Mound 72 at Cahokia (Fowler 1991), it is evident that there were marked status differences among the Lohmann phase peoples and that the leaders of the polity had considerable power and authority. By time of the Stirling phase (A.D. 1050–1150), Cahokia and the polity its leaders ruled had achieved a dominant position in the American Bottom. The Stirling phase was the "climax" of the Cahokia polity. The population at Cahokia appears to have peaked at that time (Milner 1991a:34). Most of the mound construction at the site dates to this phase as well. In the subsequent Moorehead phase (A.D. 1150–1250), the collapse of the Cahokia polity was already underway, although the Cahokia site continued to function as a major center (Milner 1991a:30). The collapse was complete by the end of the Sand Prairie phase (A.D. 1250–1400). Thus, chiefdoms existed in the American Bottom

for roughly 400 years, although the period of Cahokia's greatest power and complexity may have lasted only 150 to 250 years.

Moundville

Our picture of the development of the Moundville chiefdom is now in state of flux. The established picture is as follows (Peebles 1987a,b; Steponaitis 1983; Welch 1990a, 1991). The early part of the Moundville I phase (A.D. 1050–1250) witnessed the emergence of several simple chiefdoms in the Black Warrior Valley. By the end of Moundville I, a single complex chiefdom centered on the Moundville site had subsumed the others and occupied the entire valley. That complex polity lasted through Moundville II (A.D. 1250–1400) and Moundville III (A.D. 1400–1550) times.

It now appears that the emergence and consolidation of the Moundville polity and the construction of the Moundville site took place quickly and at a very early date. Moundville itself appears to have temporal priority over the Moundville I single mound centers. The Great Plaza and all, or nearly all, of the mounds at Moundville were constructed (or initiated) by the end of the Moundville I phase (Knight 1989, 1992, 1993). Moundville had its greatest residential population during this time as well (C. Scarry 1995; Steponaitis 1991, 1993). During the Moundville II phase, the Moundville chiefdom appears to have continued to control a unified Black Warrior River Valley, although the residential population of the site had declined markedly. During the Moundville III phase, the population of the site had decreased even more, and some of the mounds at Moundville itself had fallen into disuse. By the end of the Moundville III phase, the Moundville site was no longer a political center, the Moundville polity had collapsed, and the valley population had largely abandoned the region. Hernando de Soto and his army apparently passed through the Black Warrior River Valley in 1541, but the chroniclers fail to mention a site the size of Moundville (Charles Hudson has suggested that the small chiefdom of Apafayala occupied the valley at that time [Hudson et al. 1990a]). In the Black Warrior River Valley, as in the American Bottom, chiefdoms existed for approximately 400–450 years (Figure 5.6). However, the period during which the valley was united into a single complex polity may have been as long as 300 years—considerably longer than the Cahokia polity.

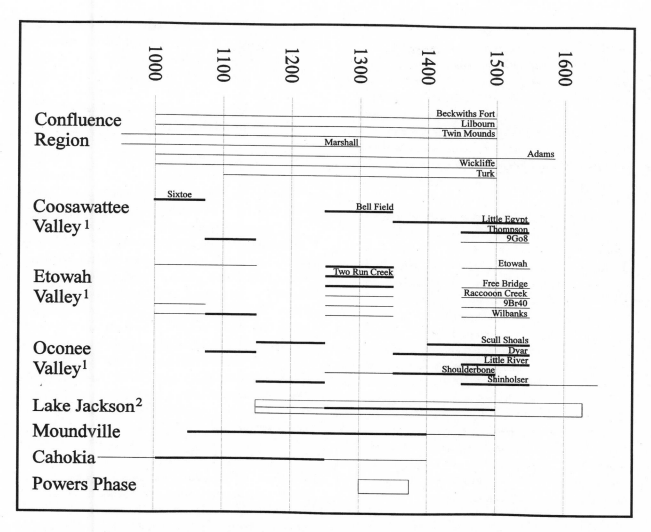

Figure 5.6.   Construction and occupation life spans of selected Mississippian sites and regions. Bold lines show periods of identified mound construction. Lighter lines show dates of possible mound construction and site occupation. Boxes show durations of polities.

[1]Each Piedmont valley was probably occupied by large polities that included several mound centers (e.g., the sixteenth-century Barnett phase Coosa chiefdom in the Coosawattee Valley, the thirteenth to fourteenth-century Wilbanks phase in the Etowah Valley, and the sixteenth-century Ocute chiefdom in the Oconee Valley). It is possible that individual polities lasted for longer periods of time than those reflected in the mound construction episodes at individual sites (this may well be the case for the sequential episodes of mound construction in the Coosawattee Valley), and that some Piedmont sites may have been occupied before or after the securely identified periods of mound construction.

[2]For Lake Jackson, the box encompasses the life span of the Lake Jackson and Velda phase polities.

Confluence

In the Confluence region, Mississippian polities appeared early, although perhaps not as early as in the American Bottom (Lewis 1990; cf. Sussenbach 1993) (Figure 5.6). The initial occupation and mound construction at sites like Marshall occurred by ca. A.D. 900–1100 (Sussenbach and Lewis 1987). By Medley phase times (A.D. 1300–1500), there were numerous Mississippian centers along the bluffs overlooking the east bank of the Mississippi River in western Kentucky and on the lowlands to the west of the Mississippi River in Missouri (Lewis 1990). During this period, most of the Mississippian sites in the region were occupied, and regional population appears to have reached its peak. Individual sites, particularly the nucleated and fortified mound centers of western Kentucky, were intensively occupied during the Medley phase, and rich, deep midden deposits argue for long-term occupations (Sussenbach 1993).

There is disagreement about the dating of the collapse of the Confluence area polities. One view is that the great centers of the Confluence region, as well as those in the Mississippian and Ohio River Valleys upstream, were abandoned and the entire region depopulated by A.D. 1450 (Williams 1990). Another view sees center abandonment and regional depopulation occurring roughly a century later (Lewis 1990). Regardless of which date is used, there appear to have been chiefdoms in the region for at least 450–550 years, although individual centers were probably not all occupied for that entire time span.

Piedmont Georgia

Most of the Piedmont valleys were probably occupied by large polities that included several mound centers. If mound construction is assumed to be an indicator of political activity, then analyses of mound building in northern Georgia indicate that the life spans of most centers and the polities they ruled were relatively short (Hally 1993, 1996b) (Figure 5.6). For more than half the sites, construction was limited to a single period, lasting 75–100 years. In addition, this construction occurred in just a few stages, reinforcing the view of a relatively short life span for the mounds. Some sites did last longer, evidencing construction during two or more sequential or nonsequential periods. Sites with mound construction in nonsequential periods were generally centers within complex chiefdoms and represent either abandoned centers that were reoccupied or centers that had gone into eclipse and then regained political ascendancy.

It is possible that individual polities lasted for longer periods than are reflected in the mound construction episodes at individual sites (this may be the case for the sequential episodes of mound construction in the Coosawattee Valley), and that some Piedmont sites may have been occupied before or after the securely identified periods of mound construction.

Big Bend

I view the Apalachee as an example of the cycling that Wright (1984) believes is characteristic of complex chiefdoms (Figure 5.6). The Lake Jackson phase, which is the prehistoric Apalachee polity, lasted from 250 to 400 years. Ceramic cross-dating and radiocarbon dates suggest that this polity emerged sometime between A.D. 1100 and A.D. 1250; and that its paramount mound center was abandoned around A.D. 1450–1500 (Jones 1982; Payne 1994a; J. Scarry 1990b, 1996). However, in 1540 de Soto found the Apalachee to be a flourishing complex chiefdom. This Velda phase polity lasted roughly 100 years before it was truncated by Spanish colonialism. However, despite their loss of independence in 1633, the Apalachee maintained the structure of a complex chiefdom through the end of the seventeenth century (J. Scarry 1990a, 1992).

Powers Phase

The Powers phase does not appear to have had the lengthy *in situ* developmental sequence that characterizes the Cahokia and Moundville systems (Price 1978; Price and Griffin 1979). In fact, Price has argued that the Powers phase polity was the result of an actual movement of Mississippian peoples into the region. The Powers phase also does not appear to have survived for any great time (Figure 5.6). A suite of radiocarbon dates from excavations at the Turner and Snodgrass sites suggest that the Powers phase chiefdom had a life span of not much more than 50–75 years (Price 1978). During that span, individual villages were constructed and abandoned. Data are lacking on the life span of the major center, the Powers Fort site.

Summary

The life spans of Mississippian polities varied significantly (Figure 5.6). If the Powers phase and Piedmont Georgia chiefdoms are typical, small Mississippian polities had short life spans. At the other end of the Mississippian size-complexity scale, the multiethnic, paramount chiefdoms (Hudson et al. 1985) also appear to have been short-lived, possibly having life spans of no more than a single generation or reign. However, some Southeastern polities survived for much longer periods. Those polities with good evidence of long (i.e., 250+ years) life spans were all large, powerful, and apparently well integrated (e.g., Moundville and Lake Jackson).

ECONOMIC PRODUCTIVITY IN MISSISSIPPIAN SOCIETIES

Another indicator of the greatness of Mississippian polities is their productivity. Were they rich, productive societies whose members were well off and secure? Or, were they poor societies whose members were unhealthy, malnourished, and altogether not well off? Current descriptions of Mississippian economic systems differ markedly (cf. Muller 1984, 1986a, 1987 and Yerkes 1983, 1986, 1989, 1991; or Prentice 1983, 1985, 1987; and Pauketat 1987, 1989). In particular, the descriptions differ in their assessments of the degree of economic specialization in craft production. There are also differences in estimates of the output of Mississippian subsistence economies and their ability to yield either reliable food supplies or consistent surpluses.

Subsistence Economies

Cleared-field agriculture was the basis of Mississippian subsistence economies (C. Scarry 1993b; Lynott et al. 1986; Rose et al. 1991). These economies were complex and varied (C. Scarry 1993a,b, 1994). Numerous crops were grown including chenopodium, maygrass, sumpweed, sunflower, squash, beans, and corn (C. Scarry 1986, 1993a, 1994). The relative importance of these different crops varied from area to area, as did the role of wild resources.

An increased reliance on domesticated crops preceded the emergence of Mississippian societies in many, if not most, areas of the Eastern United States. As seen in the Lower Mississippi River Valley (Rose et al. 1991) and the American Bottom (Johannessen 1984; Milner 1986; C. Scarry 1993b), the initial intensification involved native starchy seeds (e.g., chenopodium) which during Mississippian times were replaced by corn as the dietary staple. In contrast, the intensification of corn agriculture preceded rather than followed the establishment of the Moundville chiefdom. Further evidence for the intensification of agriculture during Mississippian times is the

dramatic increase in chert hoe flakes documented for the Confluence region (Sussenbach 1993).

How productive were the Mississippian farmers? The available evidence suggests that they were very productive. We used to think that Mississippian peoples suffered from their reliance on maize (e.g., they suffered from subsistence stress, anemia, etc. [Goodman and Armelagos 1985; Goodman et al. 1984]); it now appears that in many Mississippian societies the people were well-nourished and healthy. Powell (1988:197) has shown that at Moundville and Etowah, even commoners enjoyed good health and generally escaped major systemic stresses from resource deprivation. In the American Bottom, Milner (1991b) found that Mississippian peoples were as healthy as the people at Moundville.

There is also evidence in at least one area, the Black Warrior River Valley, for both surplus production and the provisioning of elites. The differential distributions of meat cuts, hickory nutshells, and corn kernels and cupules suggest that elites at the center of Moundville were supplied with surplus foodstuffs from outlying rural communities and that they ate better than the residents of those communities. In contrast, Mississippian farmers in the American Bottom apparently did not maximize the productive potential of their catchments, suggesting that elites in this area did not place extremely high tribute demands on them.

Craft Specialization

Much of the literature on craft production in Mississippian societies focuses on the American Bottom and nearby areas in the Lower Ohio River Valley. In particular, the nature of craft production at Cahokia has received considerable attention. Given its size, one might expect that Cahokia's economy was the most complex of Mississippian economies.

Cahokia

Many archaeologists have identified evidence at Cahokia for the specialized production of a variety of craft goods. This evidence includes the fine craftsmanship of some artifacts, the presence of caches, and the localized distributions of certain artifacts (e.g., Esarey and Good 1981; Fowler 1974; Harn 1971; Holley et al. 1989; Mason and Perino 1961; O'Brien 1972a; Porter 1984; Yerkes 1983, 1991). However, the interpretations of this inferred specialization vary widely. The most complex models of Cahokia's economy involve various combinations of such characteristics as a state-level organization, full-time craft specialists working at Cahokia, part-time specialists working at economically differentiated villages, and the possible use of shell beads as money (Prentice 1983, 1985, 1987). In contrast, other models are much simpler (Muller 1984; Pauketat 1987). They reject the possibility of markets at Cahokia, raise the issue of how functional specialization at sites can be confounded with craft specialization, and question the evidence for even part-time specialization for some goods.

Moundville

The other Mississippian case that has seen concerted efforts to examine craft production is the Moundville polity. At the site of Moundville, the presence of spatially restricted craft areas, suggesting the presence of craft specialists, has been argued (Peebles and Kus 1977). Among the goods for which there is some evidence for specialized production at the site of Moundville, but not at secondary mound centers or farmsteads, are burnished pottery, ground stone axes, and mica objects (Hardin 1981; van der Leeuw 1981; Welch 1991).

Paul Welch (1991, 1996) argues that the Moundville polity's subsistence economy was decentralized with most subsistence goods and utilitarian objects being produced by households, primarily for their own use. Some specific foods, such as choice deer parts, shelled corn, and perhaps hickory nut oil, were transferred from households to elite centers, especially the major center of Moundville. In contrast to this decentralized subsistence economy, Welch believes that the economy of exotic and valuable goods was highly centralized. Some artifacts were made only at Moundville, perhaps by specialists. Most imported goods went to Moundville's residents, although small quantities of some kinds of imports were also distributed to outlying settlements.

Summary

At present there is no evidence anywhere in the Mississippian world for occupational specialization or centralized control of production or exchange systems beyond that described by Welch (1991). The only items that appear to be the result of specialized production are elite status markers, items that also circulated through regional prestige networks. The high elite of Mississippian societies were able to extract tribute from their subjects in the form of food and labor for public construction projects and tending of chief's fields. In no case do these tribute demands appear excessive or to have taxed the ability of the populace both to supply the demands of the elite and maintain their own security.

ORGANIZATIONAL COMPLEXITY IN MISSISSIPPIAN SOCIETIES

A final indicator of the greatness of Mississippian polities is their organizational complexity. Were these polities complex societies with marked status differentiation and many specialized economic and political statuses? Or were they simple societies with only limited status differentiation and few specialized positions? Here, I use the two most often cited indicators of complexity, settlement hierarchies and mortuary programs, to answer these questions.

Settlement Hierarchies

The settlement pattern indicators that have been associated with chiefdom-level societies and applied to Mississippian polities include two or three level size hierarchies and the presence of specialized and/or monumental architecture at the largest sites. To an extent, this proposed link between settlement variation and political organization is a reasonable assumption that appears to have wide validity. In most complex societies, the center of political authority is usually the largest settlement (Renfrew and Level 1979). In addition, links between symbol-laden architecture and political-religious authority have also been seen cross-culturally (McGuire and Schiffer 1983). However, we should not presume, as is too often done, that there is a regular and direct correlation between the levels in a settlement hierarchy and the political structure of a society.

Settlement hierarchies can be indicators of complex social and political hierarchies, but they do not necessarily describe those hierarchies. Historic data for the Southeastern United States illustrate this point. Ethnohistoric sources suggest that late prehistoric polities in the Southeast were more complex and differentiated than a two- or three-level settlement hierarchy might suggest. This is not to say that these polities approached the complexity of state-level societies, for I do not believe they did. It does suggest that the common picture of chiefly societies underestimates the internal social and political complexity of such societies.

Cahokia

Although sites in the upper tiers of the Cahokia polity's settlement hierarchy were inordinately large in comparison to other Mississippian centers, the hierarchy itself was not markedly more complex than that of other Mississippian polities. Cahokia's settlement hierarchy can be divided into four tiers, based on site size and architecture (Fowler 1978). The top of the hierarchy, or the first tier, was occupied by Cahokia itself, which covered 13 km² and contained more than 100 mounds (see Holley, Chapter 2, Table 2.1). The second tier included large sites (>50 ha) with multiple mounds (St. Louis, East St. Louis, Mitchell, and Pulcher). Sites of the third tier were considerably smaller than the second tier sites and possessed only a single mound (e.g., Horseshoe Lake; Gregg 1975). The fourth tier consisted of small residential sites (e.g., hamlets, farmsteads) covering only a few hectares.

Moundville

The Moundville polity had a three-tier settlement hierarchy (Peebles 1978; Steponaitis 1978). The Moundville center, with its large size (approximately 100 ha) and 26 mounds, dwarfed the single mound centers that formed the second tier of the hierarchy. At the base of the settlement hierarchy were scattered farmsteads that may have formed discrete dispersed communities (Bozeman 1981).

Big Bend

Three or four distinct levels can be identified for the prehistoric Apalachee (Lake Jackson phase) polity. At the top was the Lake Jackson site, an unfortified, large center with seven mounds and at least one cleared plaza (Griffin 1950; Payne 1994a; Payne and Scarry 1994). Next, there were several smaller sites each containing a single mound that was considerably smaller than the largest mound at Lake Jackson. The third level consisted of hamlets, containing several residential structures and a larger structure that might have been either an elite residence or a public council house (Jones 1990). At the bottom of the settlement hierarchy were small farmsteads of one or two houses, probably linked to hamlets or mound centers. These farmsteads possessed no public architecture, although the two houses at the Velda site did flank a small courtyard.

Powers Phase

The Powers phase polity was, by any measure, the smallest and presumably least complex of the Mississippian polities considered here. Nevertheless, it did possess a clear settlement hierarchy consisting of five distinct size grades (Price 1978). At the top of the hierarchy was the Powers Fort site, the largest, most massively fortified site in the system and the only one with earthen mounds. Below the paramount center were two distinct nucleated village types, which differed in size and nondomestic structures. The third tier in the settlement hierarchy consisted of hamlets that apparently lacked the public facilities, courtyards, and fortifications seen at the village sites. At the bottom of the settlement hierarchy were small farmsteads.

Summary

Mississippian societies were hierarchically structured, and that hierarchical structure is reflected in archaeologically recognizable settlement hierarchies. The complexity of those settlement hierarchies and their exact relationship to political structure is not easily interpretable. The number of levels of distinct mound centers varies from one to three, which fits well with expectations for simple and complex chiefdoms (Peebles and Kus 1977; Steponaitis 1978; Wright 1984). We must remember, however, that these models are based to some considerable degree on Mississippian examples.

Our understanding of the lower levels of Mississippian society and its structure is much less clear. The Powers phase and Apalachee data suggest that there were distinct levels of community size below the mound center level, levels that we have not discerned or not looked for in other Mississippian polities.

Site Complexity

Just as the numbers of levels in Mississippian settlement hierarchies varied, so too did the complexity of the centers of the uppermost levels (see Chapter 2). However, in all cases, the variability seen in site plan and public architecture is consistent with societies at the chiefdom level. Even at Cahokia, while the number of mounds and other public constructions is very large, they form redundant sets of a limited number of elements. Cahokian society was divided into subunits, but those subunits were of similar nature. There is no evidence of the kinds of organizational diversity that marks states. The smaller Mississippian polities show evidence of divisions into elite and commoner segments, public and private spaces, and kin-based segments. Within the elite segment, there is no evidence of more than two or three levels.

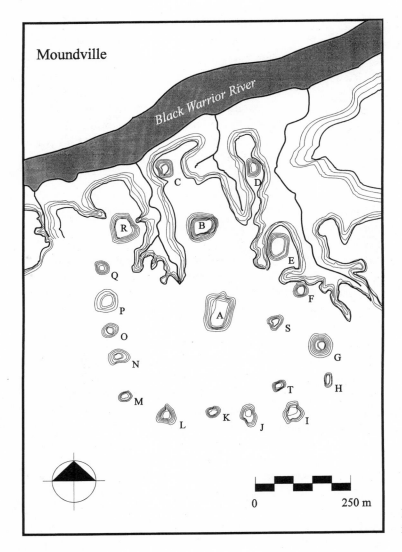

Figure 5.7.   Spatial arrangement of mounds and plazas at Moundville.

Perhaps the most detailed picture of settlement complexity comes from the site of Moundville (Figure 5.7). Fifteen of its 26 mounds define a central plaza with an obvious axis of symmetry. Peebles (1983:190) has argued that the mounds, buildings, and artifact distributions of the two sides of the site mirror one another, providing strong evidence that Moundville was a planned community. All, or nearly all of the mounds were started in the Moundville I phase; and by the end of that phase, the essential layout of Moundville was established.

Knight (1993) has suggested that the spatial organization of Moundville reflects the social organization of Moundville society. The mound pairs (which he suggests supported noble residences and ancestral mortuary temples) were physical manifestations of the primary corporate segments of Moundville society. Knight points to an analogous structure in Speck's (1907) description of the formal arrangement of a Chickasaw camp. In that description, subclans were arranged by social rank around a plaza, with the camp divided symmetrically into two moieties and centered upon a council fire. Knight suggests that the placement of Mound B on Moundville's central axis was a symbolic representation of the transcendent rank of the paramount, above and outside the dual organization. Knight's preliminary account of spatial organization and social organization at Moundville provides a picture of a kin-based society of considerable complexity, but one that is clearly linked to the ethnographically known descendants of the Mississippian peoples.

Mortuary Patterning

Mortuary patterning is probably the most frequently used source of information about the complexity of Mississippian polities (e.g., Brown 1971; Larson 1971b; Peebles 1971). Analyses of variation in grave goods, communal labor investment in graves (Tainter 1978), and burial location (Goldstein 1980) have documented differences between elites and commoners as well as between different levels of elites.

Cahokia

In both the Lohmann and Sterling phase Cahokia polity, the burials of high elites are clearly distinguished from those of commoners on the basis of burial location, form, and grave goods (see Milner 1984). The highest Lohmann phase status level has been documented at Mound 72 at the Cahokia site (Fowler 1991). One elite burial recovered from this mound was a male who was placed within his own submound on a platform covered with shell beads. He had two groups of retainers buried below and alongside him, along with abundant grave goods, including caches of arrows, rolled copper tubes, mica deposits, large conch shell beads, and chunky stones. Another elite burial was buried in a second submound of Mound 72. He was placed over the remains of a presumptive charnel house along with numerous retainers and dedicatory artifact deposits. Another low mound was subsequently constructed over a pit at the geometric center between the two elite submounds. This pit contained the remains of more than 50 young women, with the remains of four men missing their heads and hands placed nearby.

Moundville

Cluster analyses of burial data from Moundville have identified 11 groups (Peebles 1978; Peebles and Kus 1977). Two clusters have been interpreted as representing elite statuses based on their location within or near mounds and special grave goods, including gorgets, axes, stone disks and palettes, pigments, symbols of office, costumes, and beads. Some of these grave goods (e.g., copper axes, celts, gorgets, and stone disks) occurred only with adults, while others (shell beads, pigments) were found with individuals of all ages. Members of the highest status group were all adults who were buried with copper axes and pearl beads in mounds.

The other burial clusters defined at the site are distinguished by the absence of grave goods or by grave goods of a technological nature. The differences among them suggest that the complexity of the lower stratum of Moundville society may have been considerable.

Piedmont Georgia

The Wilbanks phase mortuary complex at the Etowah site provides the best glimpse of sociopolitical status in a complex Piedmont polity (Larson 1971a, 1989). The burials of Etowah's high elite were distinguished by copper artifacts, other valuable raw materials, and objects decorated with iconography of the Southeastern Ceremonial Complex (Galloway 1989). Many of the decorated objects are similar to ones found at other Mississippian centers (e.g., Lake Jackson), located considerable distances from Etowah.

Big Bend

Three status positions have been identified for the Lake Jackson phase, two at Mound 3 at the Lake Jackson site and another at Borrow Pit hamlet. The Borrow Pit burials were found in a large structure, either an elite residence or communal structure, and were interred either without grave goods or else with a very limited set of utilitarian items. These individuals may have been members of the lesser, local elite.

The individuals buried at Mound 3 at the Lake Jackson site represent the highest status group of the society. All of these individuals were adults and were interred with diverse sets of grave goods beneath the floors of structures built on top of the mound. The grave goods included repoussé copper plates, plain copper plates in a variety of forms, shell gorgets, shell and pearl beads, copper and groundstone axes, pigments, pipes with iconographic symbols, badges, costumes, and weapons. Many items found in the graves were of nonlocal origin. The repoussé copper objects were probably manufactured at the Etowah site (Leader 1988). Two ceramic pipes probably came from the Dallas area of the Tennessee River Valley.

Several episodes of elite burial are represented in the mound (Jones 1982; J. Scarry 1990b, 1991, 1992, 1996). Analyses suggest that the earlier stage burials represent two separate status positions, one marked by burial with copper plates and one by burial with stone or copper axes. In the latest burials, the two positions or offices were combined and held by a single individual.

Inferences about the sociopolitical complexity of the Lake Jackson phase can be augmented by seventeenth century Spanish documents as long as these documents are read with caution. We do not know to what extent the Spaniards had caused alterations in Apalachee political structure or misinterpreted the political structure and positions in Apalachee society. Nevertheless, the seventeenth century accounts of Apalachee province paint a picture of political complexity characterized by a wide array of ascribed and achieved political and military positions. Significantly, this complexity is much greater than can be seen in the seventeenth century settlement hierarchy. It seems reasonable to assume that the political complexity of the prehistoric Lake Jackson phase polity was also greater than that evidenced in either its mortuary remains or settlement hierarchy.

Powers Phase

Unfortunately, the top level of the Powers phase sociopolitical hierarchy is not sufficiently represented in the available mortuary data. Only five scattered burials have been recovered from the chiefly center of Fort Powers. However, excavations at the Turner Village site provide a glimpse of the bottom level of the hierarchy, a level poorly known in many other Mississippian polities. Differences in the grave goods buried with individuals at the Turner Village site were quantitative, not qualitative; and the quantitative differences were slight. There are no indications of status differences other than on the basis of age. In other words, the individuals buried at the Turner Village site were apparently egalitarian. However, this does not mean that Powers phase was an egalitarian society, just that rank distinctions were not evident in this village society.

Summary

Members of superordinate groups in Mississippian polities were typically accorded burials that clearly separated them from other people. Not only were high-ranking people buried in special places, their interments were often characterized by conspicuous consumption of valued goods and considerable investments of time and labor.

Most of the people in Mississippian polities did not receive such special treatment at death. The age and sex of individuals appears to account for most of the patterning we see in "commoner" cemeteries. Occasionally, these cemeteries do contain individuals who were buried with high prestige objects or other (disproportionately) rich burial accompaniments. However, where we do find such individuals, other aspects of their interments seem to have been much like those of their peers. Perhaps these people were local community leaders, and their grave goods may have been symbols of their roles as intermediaries between local "commoner" communities and broader social networks that included members of superordinate social groups.

CONCLUSIONS

How great were the native polities of the late prehistoric Southeast? The answer depends on to whom you are comparing these polities. In comparison to the societies that preceded and succeeded them in eastern North America, they were quite great—they were larger, more complex, and influenced other polities over greater distances. However, Mississippian polities pale in comparison to Mesoamerican societies. They were relatively small both geographically and demographically. Economically, they were composed of self sufficient units; and there were no economic classes. While there were individuals and kin groups who had greater access to political authority and perhaps power, Mississippian political offices were neither specialized or particularly diverse. In short, Mississippian polities were chiefdoms.

CHAPTER SIX

How Great Were the Polities of the Southwest and Southeast?

Areas of Comparison and Contrast

Suzanne K. Fish

John F. Scarry

IN ATTEMPTING TO COMPARE THE GREAT TOWN POLITIES of the Southwest and Southeast, we must face the very real problem of just how we can obtain and evaluate measures of "greatness." Clearly what marks these late prehistoric societies of the Southwest and Southeast is the contrast they present to the societies that preceded them, that surrounded them, and that followed them. Compared to those societies, the polities discussed in this volume were more extensive, richer, and more complex—or at least it appears so from the archaeological record. Their most prominent sites are large, architecturally complex, and in many cases visually spectacular. The artifacts they left behind include some of the most evocative art objects recovered from prehistoric contexts in North America.

Quite frequently in Americanist archaeology, characterization of the organizational nature of prehistoric societies is a matter of classification into the neoevolutionary typology of Elman Service (1962): bands, tribes, chiefdoms, and states. This is particularly true in the Southeast where it has been relatively easy to pigeonhole the Mississippian polities as chiefdoms. In the Southwest, this scheme provides a poor depiction of the archaeological record and presumed organization of late prehistoric great town polities. Even casting aside the neoevolutionary baggage associated with the typology,

we simply do not see logical sets of material correlates for the classificatory units in the scheme. Few would argue that the tribe represents a satisfactory description of the most complex Southwestern polities, but the definitive attributes of the chiefdom also provide a poor fit. In the Southwest, identifying archaeological patterns corresponding to ranked kin, hereditary leaders, and centralized distribution is significantly more difficult than in the Southeast.

In drawing this critical contrast, however, we must acknowledge the role of ethnohistoric accounts in our ability to reconstruct Southeastern political structures that are generally compatible with chiefdoms. Although the polities centered on the Southeast's most impressive great towns (such as Cahokia, Moundville, and Etowah) were no longer functioning at the time of contact, early explorers describe the organizational principles and structure of a number of politically preeminent Mississippian societies and some of their neighbors (e.g., Powhatan, Tumucua, Calusa). In contrast, the first Spaniards in the Southwest failed to encounter societies whose political institutions can be related to public architecture and other indications of complexity in late prehistoric polities.

Because the standard evolutionary types do not provide an effective framework for Southwest-Southeast comparison, we have chosen to focus on several dimensions of variability that can be used to assess the late prehistoric societies in question. We have used settlement pattern and mortuary data to look at organizational complexity, and we see marked differences in apparent configurations (structure) of societies in the two regions. We have also considered several scalar measures: geographic extent, population size, and temporal duration. Here, we see greater similarities between the two regions.

Settlement Hierarchies

The Mississippian polities are characterized by clear settlement hierarchies in which there are both quantitative and qualitative differences between sites at various levels. The hierarchies are simple in that they have few levels and there is little diversity among sites at a given level. A typical Mississippian society had a settlement hierarchy of two to three levels (a capital, perhaps a few subordinate centers, and local communities). For the largest and most complex political formations suggested in the Southeast, the paramountcies of Charles Hudson (Hudson et al. 1985), several separate polities would have been incorporated under the paramount chief of one dominant polity. However, given the ephemeral nature of such formations, there is little reason to believe that the capital would have been distinguished from the capitals of the incorporated polities.

Settlement hierarchies can be defined in the Southwest, as in the Southeast, by ranking prominent sites according to size and elaboration of public architecture. Lower levels of hierarchies based on criteria other than public architecture are regionally variable, but numerous scholars have proposed two tiers of centers. Candidates for primacy in such hierarchies of centers are fairly clear-cut in the cases of the largest Classic Hohokam sites, Paquimé, and the largest Chacoan outliers; the architectural differentiation within the uppermost tier in Chaco Canyon presents a more complicated situation. Recent Chaco, Hohokam, and Paquimé research has increased awareness of diversity in the architecture and layout of central sites within each of these cultural spheres, although the significance of such heterogeneity and its precise chronology within individual settlement hierarchies are not yet well understood.

In the Southeast, a consistent pattern marked political centers. The mound and plaza complex, in fact, has served to characterize Mississippian societies in the archaeological record since the days of the Bureau of Ethnology's mound explorations. Much of the variation on this pattern within individual polities and between widely separated ones appears to be largely quantitative: some sites have more or larger mounds, others have fewer or smaller mounds.

There are other differences, however. Some mound centers had significant residential populations and others housed very few people, perhaps only the rulers and their immediate families and retinues. Some centers were tightly nucleated and fortified, others were spread out and open.

Research at Moundville and Cahokia suggests that the obvious replicative patterns of the Mississippian mound centers may conceal considerable complexity (at least at the largest sites). At Moundville, Knight's (1993) research suggests that the organization of the site may be a reflection of the social units that formed Moundville society. The arrangement of the mounds and their relative sizes mirrored the status relationships of the social units associated with them. However, even at Moundville, this complexity still consists of multiples of a basic unit. This unit seems to have consisted of a mound (the substructure for a special building), a burial facility (mound and cemetery), a residential area, and activity areas (plazas and courtyards).

At Cahokia, we may see an exception to this "simple" picture. The multiplicity of mounds, mound types, plazas, interior walls, and other public constructions at Cahokia indicates a structural complexity significantly greater than that seen at other Mississippian centers. Given the scale of Cahokia, perhaps this greater complexity should not be surprising.

One of the more portentous contrasts between the Southeast and the Southwest is the absence of similar uniformity in the components and layout of Southwestern centers, and by inference, in the organizational and integrative rationales of their polities. In the Southwest, there was an enduring north-south dichotomy though boundaries between characteristic patterns shifted over time and intermediate forms or mixtures of regional elements occurred. Great kivas, great houses, and ultimately plazas predominated as Anasazi public architecture, although archaeologists (e.g., Stein and Lekson 1992) have recently recognized an accompaniment of ancillary earthen constructions in Chacoan and post-Chacoan central precincts (including modest-sized mounds in Chaco Canyon). Following a brief and perhaps localized overlap with the final use of ballcourts, platform mounds were erected in the Hohokam domain and along its fringes. Attached and freestanding structures also were enclosed within walled mound compounds. Ballcourts distinct from the earlier Hohokam style were built in public spaces of Paquimé and related large sites mainly to the north and west. Only the inhabitants of Paquimé itself are known to have additionally erected a variety of small mounds, some with effigy shapes. These did not principally serve as platforms for buildings as did the mounds of the Classic period Hohokam, nor do specialized rooms within Paquimé's massive roomblocks resemble kivas of the northern Southwest. In none of these Southwestern configurations do charnel activities or burial appear to have been a primary function of communal edifices.

Populations of many large, late polity centers of the Puebloan pattern were highly nucleated in blocks of contiguous rooms, a characteristic shared by Paquimé and related central sites. The degree of nucleation remains in question for Chaco Canyon, where there is disagreement concerning the exact whereabouts of the resident population among what are otherwise regarded as specialized structures. In late Hohokam centers, there was appreciable space within and between residential compounds. Comprehensive information for even beginning to estimate population magnitudes is available from a limited number of sites. The size of populations inhabiting sites with platform mounds seems quite variable, especially if mounds on the Hohokam peripheries are included. It is unclear how closely population size of centers and investment in public buildings covary with other dimensions of polities.

Quantitatively differentiated modules of the same sort do not account for the layout of public architecture in the large and most elaborate Southwestern centers, and particularly not those with the best claims to strong primate status within polities. Redundant arrangements that appear to represent social units may be identified within these sites (e.g., roomblocks or room clusters associated with small kivas in Puebloan settlements and sets of courtyard groups or residences within compounds that share joint facilities among the Hohokam). Civic-ceremonial constructions are of distinctive form, however. The formal and spatial contexts of Southwestern public architecture at the premier centers are not replicates of the elements of other social and residential units writ large, as at Moundville; in this respect, comparison is closer with the qualitatively differentiated public precincts of Cahokia. Conspicuously absent in the Southwest is a counterpart for the standard Southeastern conjunction of mortuary facilities and a cemetery with each mound complex, implying its symbolic association with a specific social and kin unit.

POLITY LEADERSHIP

Whether elites were generated through a more uniform route of ranked kinship as seems likely in the Southeast or by a more variable and less readily categorized manner as seems likely in the Southwest, the nature of polity leadership is a further question. As combined demonstrations of power and wealth, no Southwestern interments equal the impressiveness of the foremost Southeastern examples such as those in Mound 72 at Cahokia (Fowler 1991). The regalia of Southeastern leadership is ethnohistorically confirmed in some cases, relatively consistent in form, and some styles occur with elite burials in multiple polities over appreciable distances. Similarly, predictable or widespread markers of elite status or badges of office are not as easily identified within the several major Southwestern traditions.

Individuals or limited numbers of persons were buried in the environs of public architecture among the Classic period Hohokam, at Pueblo Bonito and other Chacoan centers, and at Paquimé. These situations do not seem to reflect an association that was institutionalized as broadly or to the same degree as the linkage between cemeteries and Southeastern mounds. The special status of these deceased Southwesterners may more directly reflect the strength of their associations with the symbols of polity than their position within ranked kin groups. Nevertheless, elevated status attached to kin lines and successional principles seem to have operated at times, as indicated by the inclusion of both sexes and infants. The linkage between elite residence and public architecture likewise is more variable in the Southwest. Leaders occupied Hohokam platform mound complexes in much if not all of the Classic period, but elite residence of Chacoan great houses remains disputed, and residences of paramount leaders are not clearly demarcated within the civic-ceremonial complex of Paquimé.

GEOGRAPHIC EXTENT

Sizes of Mississippian and Southwestern polities are difficult to compare, the more so due to the greater lack of consensus in the Southwest on boundaries that encompass multiple central sites and related settlements. Mississippian societies are geographically much more widespread across eastern North America and collectively involve greater numbers of settlements than the stylistically more diverse Southwestern configurations. Expectably, there would be a greater range in the size of Southeastern political and territorial aggregates. The circumscription of contiguous expanses of arable land also must have influenced polity extent and spacing in the arid Southwest.

Where there is relatively good distributional data for segments of the Hohokam domain, estimates for territory assignable to single centers ranges from less than 20 km^2 in the densely packed and massively irrigated Phoenix Basin to about 150 km^2 in less agriculturally favored locales (Fish 1996). Most currently posited higher political groupings of these centers cover no more than 250 km^2, with a debatable maximum near 1,000 km^2 (e.g., Bayman 1996; Fish 1996).

The direct influence of Paquimé is presently being refined within previous expansive stylistic boundaries that were drawn in conjunction with very fragmentary distributional information. Even so, a newly reduced estimate near 3,500 km^2 (Whalen and Minnis 1996) exceeds the largest integrative entities proposed for the Hohokam.

The Chacoan situation is complicated for geographic estimates. One well-studied Chacoan great house outside Chaco Canyon and its surrounding settlements cover about 10 km^2 (Breternitz 1982:454). Clusters of related centers have been noted inside the canyon and in outlying areas, but in general, Chacoan archaeologists have not focused on delineating, analyzing, and comparing territories affiliated with individual central sites or closely allied subgroups. A rough outline of road segments approaches 20,000 km^2 (Lekson 1991). Beyond this, various means of defining a Chacoan sphere are based on more politically tenuous relationships and merge with various criteria for regional systems.

Even small and simple Mississippian polities are larger than some Southwestern examples incorporating several centers. The Powers phase polity with a single mound center and relatively well settled core of 250 km^2 would enclose settlements surrounding from two to six Hohokam mound sites. David Hally (1993) concluded that in Georgia polity cores seldom exceeded 1,250 km^2; total polity area including sparsely occupied buffers rarely exceeded 5,000 km^2. These parameters are generally compatible with several other Southeast calculations.

The upper inclusive size of about 5,000 km^2 for Mississippian polities is greater than recent estimates for immediate Paquimé influence, but lower by several magnitudes than the outline of Chacoan roads. The largest reconstructions of the territorial sway of Cahokia, representing maxima for proposed polity size, have been challenged. Recent careful estimates place the limit of direct political control within a 50 to 100 km radius. These dimensions surpass any currently posited spheres of political relationship in the Southwest with the exception of the variably defined and more doubtfully political spheres centered on Chaco Canyon. The largest Chacoan roads extend as far as 50 km from Canyon centers, however, in the most tangible North American demonstration of relationships that mobilized joint labor at such scales.

In both the Southeast and the Southwest, it can be questioned whether the archaeological attributes invoked to support the most far-flung dominion do indeed track the sorts of relationships usually ascribed to polities. Even so, asymmetrical political relations at comparably large scales derive greater credence in the Southeast from ethnohistorical accounts that are explicitly cast in these terms. For example, the early historic Coosa paramountcy and the prehistoric Classic Hohokam domain both encompass several tens of thousands of square kilometers and both are composed of several contiguous sets of divisible settlement hierarchies and ceramic variants. The Coosa paramountcy may have been short-lived and weakly integrated, but even the most attenuated political sway of an equivalent scale has not been broached for the broadly parallel Hohokam pattern.

POPULATION SIZE

Population size is the most tentative realm of comparison. There are few instances in either region with adequate bases for estimating population at encompassing scales. The most frequently attempted calculations, for the size of population at major centers, have produced notably divergent figures. Such estimates are significant for overall polity population only if there is justification for assuming that a large proportion of overall population resided in the centers, an unconfirmed assumption even for many of the more strongly primate settlement hierarchies such as that of Paquimé in the Southwest. It bears reiterating that population is unresolvable where meaningful boundaries remain in dispute, as for the Chaco "phenomenon."

At the low end of the integrative scale, broadly comparable population numbers are cited for Southwestern and Mississippian entities. The Powers phase polity, consisting of a single mound center and related settlements, appears to have included between 3,000 and 6,000 persons (see Scarry, Chapter 5). Jon Muller (1993a) has suggested a modal size near 1,200 for communities reflecting Mississippian organization in the early historic period. Estimates for Hohokam communities surrounding individual mound sites range between 500 and several thousand. These Hohokam estimates that include centers and multiple settlements overlap with projected totals for Paquimé, Moundville, or all of Chaco Canyon, however, and do not approach the middle range of the most conservative and downsized population figures for the Cahokia center.

At more inclusive levels, data underlying estimates are much more fragmentary, and equivalent configurations for comparison are less clear. Using Muller's ethnographically derived estimate of 1,200 per community, the polities of Lake Jackson and Moundville might have had populations from 15,000 to 50,000. Southwestern comparisons could be the entire San Juan Basin containing Chaco Canyon, perhaps 40,000 (Dean et al. 1996), or all the Hohokam communities in the Phoenix Basin, perhaps 25,000 to 150,000 (Fish and Fish 1991). On the other hand, it might be more appropriate to compare these large Southeastern polities with the population of the six Hohokam communities along the canal network of the preeminent Casa Grande, a total of 9,000 persons if an average of 1,500 is assumed for each. According to current regional trends in interpretation, the maximum numbers of people integrated by relationships of an explicitly political nature would be much higher in the Southeast than the Southwest.

TEMPORAL DURATION

Longevity is primarily judged in both the Southeast and Southwest by the persistence of polity centers, the seats of integrative power. Building episodes at mounds have been examined in the Southeast to refine intervals of active ascendancy (usually less than 100 years, but some-

times recurring) by David Hally (1996b), a technique and interpretive framework not yet considered for the episodically enlarged mounds in the Southwest. In both areas, relatively simple configurations with single centers can be circumscribed within a century. Preeminent Hohokam centers and those of Chaco Canyon arise in the midst of previous patterns with centralization and public architecture, although the background of Paquimé is less clear. This also seems to be the case for more complex Mississippian configurations such as Moundville and Cahokia. About 400 years appears to be the maximum for Mississippian polities with a continuously prominent center, but intervals of greatest influence and unification may be significantly shorter. Major centers in Chaco Canyon and the site of Paquimé probably were ascendant in their regions for less than 300 years.

Some Hohokam sites served as centers for more than 500 years, as indicated by the erection of ballcourts and then platform mounds. Thus, these centers span two integrative ideologies. Quite possibly, they experienced intervals of greater and lesser influence and discontinuities in leadership lines and rationales. Other centers were less persistent, even where irrigation networks similarly tethered population distributions over many centuries. These situations may represent an anomalous organizational longevity among complex North American configurations. Alternatively, they may be comparable to the persistence of transformed Chacoan architecture and institutions over much of the Anasazi world following the demise of Chaco Canyon or to the persistence of the historic Velda phase chiefdom in the Apalachee area after the demise of the prehistoric Lake Jackson polity.

FURTHER COMPARISONS

One of the fundamental contrasts between Southeastern and Southwestern polities stems from the way that archaeologists approach them. There may be disagreement about the magnitude and boundaries of outlier cases such as Cahokia, but the identity of most polities is not at issue. In the Southwest, there are few instances of consensus on the outline and constituents of political entities encompassing multiple centers. Ethnohistoric accounts of the Southeast provide a model of political integration that is consonant with the archaeological record, and the ultimate examples outstrip in scale any political configurations that are currently accepted in the Southwest. At the lower end of the integrative scale, convergences can be found in such parameters as estimated population.

Contrasts between settlement pattern hierarchies, one of the basic archaeological measures of complexity, are not a primary source of the difference in regional perceptions of integrative modes. Rather, the attributes of communal constructions and their arrangement in centers reveals an organizational divergence. Additionally, there is evidence for a degree of coercion in the Southeast that is missing from both the ethnographic and archaeological records of the Southwest. Finally, there is a striking contrast in the uniformity of integrative styles. Although Mississippian patterns encompassed a vaster demographic and geographic array, diversity of form is greater in the Southwest. Likewise, the cycling of Southeastern chiefdoms appears to have been a more predictable dynamic than the emergence and demise of Southwestern polities.

CHAPTER SEVEN

How Were Precolumbian
Southwestern Polities Organized?

Linda S. Cordell

THE VAST MAJORITY OF ARCHAEOLOGISTS WORKING in the Southwest today, I suspect, would use the term "tribe" to refer to the organization of communities encountered by the Spaniards when they ventured into the region beginning in A.D. 1540. The word "tribe" would be applied in a way that is closer to its use in the general lexicon of American English, than to the technical and narrow use of the term in anthropology. The term "tribe" is commonly used despite the fact that, for example, the Navajo refer to themselves as the Navajo Nation or that Pueblo historian Joe Sando (1992) entitled his most recent book, *Pueblo Nations*. In both cases, "tribe" is rejected because it signals the kind of relationship colonial countries have with indigenous governments.

Descriptions of the ways in which societies are organized include the composition and function of various groups of people. These may be groups that are coresident, such as a matrilocal extended family responsible for child raising. They may be special task groups, such as a matrilineage that cares for ritual information or a curing society that heals the sick. Characterizations of organization include identifying different roles important to interactions within the society, such as war chief or shaman, and describing how individuals are selected to fill these roles, perhaps by primogeniture or ritual capture. Most organizational features are not directly observable in archaeological contexts and various sources must serve as bases of inference. How one describes, in the absence of written records, the way in which past societies were organized depends on anthropological models about the organization of human groups and archaeological notions about how social behavior may be extracted from archaeological contexts. Both the anthropological models and ideas linking these to archaeological data are highly contested problems.

In general anthropology, there has been a rejection of studies of "social organization" in favor of work that focuses on the dynamics of interaction at various levels (person to person, group to group, etc.) and on the creative manipulation of relationships and symbols. As Wolf (1990:591) has remarked, "We structure and are structured, we play out metaphors, but the whole question of organization has fallen into abeyance." Organization "types" viewed as a series or set of forms and as end products are too static to be useful in understanding either real interactions among interests or processes of evolutionary change.

Southwestern archaeologists have proposed widely varying interpretations of the forms of organization represented in the Southwest between A.D. 900 and 1540. Ancient southwestern societies have been classified in categories ranging from egalitarian "tribes" (Vivian

1990) to "empires" (Wilcox 1991a). Population estimates for the same multivillage communities, such as eleventh century Chaco Canyon, differ by orders of magnitude from thousands to hundreds of thousands. Some Southwestern archaeologists argue that at specific periods in the past, a few indigenous groups were hierarchically organized resembling the "Big Man" societies of Melanesia or the chiefdoms of Central America or Polynesia (see Lightfoot 1987; Lightfoot and Feinman 1982; Upham 1982, 1983). Other archaeologists commonly insert the words "egalitarian society" in titles of works dealing with fourteenth and fifteenth century Pueblos (i.e., Spielmann 1982). Still others write about changes in the form of archaeological settlements or stylistic distributions of artifacts as evidence of a process of "tribalization" (Braun and Plog 1982) or the formation of "complex tribes" (Habicht-Mauche 1993) or confederacies (Spielmann 1994).

My goal here is not to resolve these different perspectives or to suggest how they might somehow be reconciled. I intend to explore the development of, and some of the reasons for, inconsistencies among Southwestern archaeologists and to offer what I view as productive avenues that might be pursued in the future. At the outset, I caution that I will not conclude with arguments for adopting a particular taxonomic label for the societies of the past. Rather, my intention is to clarify the debate.

A BRIEF HISTORY OF
ARCHAEOLOGICAL RECONSTRUCTIONS OF
SOCIOPOLITICAL ORGANIZATION IN THE SOUTHWEST

Those writing about histories of archaeology note that such works may be contextualized either internally, by reference to the development of archaeology and anthropology, or externally, by reference to events and the general social and intellectual background of the time (Hinsley 1989; Dyson 1989). Most often, histories written by archaeologists, rather than those by historians or philosophers of science, are internally contextualized, and this is the case in the remarks I offer here.

As I have noted elsewhere (Cordell 1984:50–51; 1989a), early discussions of the Precolumbian Southwest are essentially atemporal, relying on the modern Pueblos, especially Zuni and Hopi, for interpretation of archaeological remains (Hinsley 1983). An overriding concern of the Mindeleff brothers, Bandelier, Cushing, Fewkes, and even Morgan was to establish continuity between the ancient ruins and the modern Pueblo Indians. Without this crucial continuity, the ancient remains could be "invested with a halo of romantic antiquity, and regarded as remarkable achievements in civilization by a vanished and once powerful race." (Mindeleff 1891:224–225).

With their emphasis on continuity and their use of a simplified, uniform model of Pueblo society, these nineteenth century chroniclers of southwestern ruins were counteracting the excesses of the romantic school of Donnelly, Le Plongeon, and others who imagined lost continents, lost worlds, ancient voyagers, and cataclysmic events as forces responsible for precolumbian sites. If anthropology were to be established as a "science" of human culture, then "methodologically, continuity was critical. Like geology, a scientific anthropology could not admit discontinuities and cataclysms in the record. There were not wide gulfs between naturalism and the world of artifice" (Hinsley 1981:89–90).

Not having done much excavation, and lacking methods to determine the age of remains, most of what the late nineteenth and early twentieth century explorer-archaeologists observed were structures that looked remarkably like the pueblos. These structures included the great houses of Chaco Canyon and the northern San Juan Basin as well as the Mesa Verde cliff dwellings, which are currently classified within the Anasazi/Pueblo continuum. They also included the adobe great houses of Casa Grande and Pueblo Grande, which are now considered Hohokam; the fallen masonry walls of the Swartz Ruin, now classified as Mogollon; and the multistoried marled adobe of Paquimé, which is difficult to classify. When variants were encountered, as of course they were, these were generally attributed to the migrations of clans before the major villages were established.

Although one can find statements in these early writings that can be used to support a view that Pueblo society was stratified (i.e., Cushing 1888), or that it was clan based and egalitarian (i.e., Morgan 1878 in White 1942:24), the authors do not offer procedures appropriate for evaluating discrepancies among alternatives. The statements were written in the context of arguments very far from our interests today. Yet, there are legacies of the early work that are worth remembering. One is a tendency to diminish the influence of the Spaniards. During the late 1800s, anthropologists spent time with the Pueblos making ethnographic observations as well as doing archaeology. Despite this, there is little systematic discussion of the impact of nearly three hundred years of

Spanish domination of the Southwest. This neglect was maintained and used by some later Boasian scholars who recorded memory ethnographies as though they were windows into very ancient Pueblo times (see Cordell 1989a; Hinsley 1981).

Unlike most of his contemporaries, Bandelier (1890, 1892) made extensive use of Spanish documents and archives and might have been in a position to lay the foundations for a strongly ethnohistoric archaeology in the Southwest. Such a tradition did not develop, and Bandelier's use of historic records was criticized. How useful ethnohistoric documents might have been, however, is not clear because as Fish (Chapter 4) reminds us, even the earliest Spanish chroniclers were not witness to southwestern peoples when they were at the height of their population densities, building their most elaborate architecture, or practicing their most intensive forms of agriculture.

The amount and importance of archaeological work conducted in the Southwest between 1930 and 1960 is astounding (see Cordell 1991; Martin and Plog 1973; Willey and Sabloff 1980). While this is not the place to review that epoch in any detail, a few of the major accomplishments were the introduction of stratigraphic excavation techniques, development and application of tree-ring and radiocarbon dating, and the discovery and acceptance of Pleistocene antiquity for Native American settlement of the Southwest. Extensive programs of regional survey were conducted. The subregional southwestern cultural variants (Anasazi, Hohokam, Mogollon, etc.) were defined, and excavation projects took place at major sites in each subregion.

The principal concerns of southwestern archaeology between 1930 and 1960 were establishing cultural boundaries and regional chronologies and inferring cultural relationships. In my view, the primary organizing strategy of American archaeology of this time was to ascribe nearly all variation in archaeological data exclusively to variation in culture, with culture itself viewed in normative terms—as shared ideas and behavior. For example, when the spatial limits of Hohokam pottery were traced in sherd surveys and a neighboring red-brown pottery discovered, the newly described pottery became the basis for differentiating Mogollon culture. When late Hohokam settlements were found to contain inhumations whereas the burial norm in older Hohokam sites was predominantly cremation, an intrusive culture was deemed responsible for instituting the new form. Variation in house style, burial type, and painted pottery at Hohokam

sites dating to the A.D. 1200s, was attributed to the peaceful coexistence, in the same settlements, of two different cultural groups. There are many other examples. Perhaps the normative view in the Southwest is at its most excessive in discussions of the Salado culture, an entire "culture" defined on the basis of two pottery types, i.e., Gila and Tonto Polychromes (Cordell 1984; Crown 1994; Le Blanc and Nelson 1976).

Although today we suggest that there may be other reasons for the variety in pottery, house types, burial practices, and other material remains, normative archaeological recognition of geographic and cultural variation in the otherwise monotypically-described Pueblo Southwest was a valuable contribution and not an easy one. In 1931, when Haury proposed the nomenclature that added the Hohokam to the Southwestern cultural repertory, Roberts quietly commented, "That's a lot of hokum," (in Woodbury 1991:32), and at the 1947 publication of Wormington's summary of Southwestern archaeology, the jury was still out on the existence of the Mogollon (Wormington 1947).

Whether or not we view the results of processual archaeological research in the Southwest as useful, significant changes were introduced in the 1970s and 1980s. Processualists argued that describing only norms requires ignoring patterned variation that could help us understand more about the ways in which ancient southwestern societies were organized and how they may have changed over time. For example, the normative view of sites of different sizes with different tool assemblages but sharing some tool types was that they were the settlements of culturally different groups who either traded some tools or influenced each other in their ideas about a few classes of tools. An alternative, processual interpretation was that these sites might represent seasonally differentiated activities among the same group of people (Goodyear 1975). Similarly, as a result of processual influences, a variety of factors other than shared cultural norms began to be recognized as potential explanations for differences in the sizes and shapes of rooms within a pueblo as well as in the material remains found in those rooms. Proposed explanations included differences in room function, the presence of different descent groups (actually reflecting cultural norms but at a smaller scale), the presence of individuals with access to different social networks, different behaviors at abandonment, and different modes of excavation or archaeological analysis (Hill 1970a,b; Longacre 1970a,b; S. Plog 1980; Schiffer 1976).

Another significant impact of processual archaeology on Southwestern archaeology was its zealous endorsement of science. For processual archaeologists, scientific method allows ideas, models, and hypotheses to be checked, shown to be erroneous, and either modified or discarded on that basis (Cordell 1994a; Cordell et al. 1994b). It is unfortunate from my perspective that the "battle lines" between processual and post-processual southwestern archaeologists seem to have been drawn in reference to whether or not there were social hierarchies in the Precolumbian Southwest rather than about how ideas about the past, including those related to social hierarchies, are evaluated. In fact, it is through the application of the normal scientific procedures of evaluation that the statement that there were social hierarchies in the past can be refuted.

For many who are critical of processual archaeology, there has been an explicit retreat from science sometimes accompanied by movement toward Marxism and/or other contextual approaches (see Cordell et al. 1994b). McGuire (1992b) and McGuire and Saitta (1996) clarify the Marxist view far better than can I. In my opinion, Marxists studies provide detailed reconstructions that are tremendously interesting and provocative in suggesting lines of inquiry that seem to be worth pursuing. Yet, because I accept science as an appropriate model for the evaluation of archaeological ideas, I am generally discouraged when a Marxist argument goes no further than stipulating causes of social change. I, of course, want the cause (or causes) and the particular area (or areas) of social conflict somehow to be evaluated and tested in scientific terms.

During the late 1970s and continuing into the 1980s, processual archaeology itself underwent internal evaluation as well as external criticism. Binford's earlier archaeological proscriptions and prescriptions had focused on elaborating a systemic view of culture—one in which archaeologists could address issues of a social or ideological nature—and on elaborating methods by which models and propositions could be evaluated and hypotheses tested. Neither of these general perspectives prevented processual archaeologists from making potentially ambiguous or "untestable" assumptions about the past (see Binford 1983, 1989:16–19). Binford (1983) addressed this problem in his call for "middle range theory," which would link the statics of the contemporary archaeological record with the dynamics of behavior that archaeologists are interested in studying. Whereas general anthropological theory that

relates to behavior, change, and evolution could be borrowed from other disciplines, Binford argued that middle range theory had to be constructed to serve archaeology—it had to be strictly archaeological theory. Further, the only way that such a theory could be built was from observations archaeologists make in the world of their experience, including experiments, ethnoarchaeology, and the use of historic documents (see Binford 1989 for references).

It is of considerable interest to me that the directions Fred Plog took in the late 1980s eschewed normative archaeology, "neo" evolutionist thought (see Yoffee 1993 for discussion of the nuances involved in "neo"), and middle range theory in Binford's terms. In conversations with me and certainly with others, Plog acknowledged that while constructing middle range theory might be necessary, it was not of interest to him. He remained interested in the big questions of general anthropology, particularly those of evolutionary change. I return to some of his later ideas at the end of this discussion.

Today, I think that there has been a retreat from some of the more grandiose notions of some processual archaeologists about how ancient Southwestern societies were organized and how they changed over time. Some former positions have been abandoned as the result of their systematic evaluation in light of both new arguments and new data. In the remainder of this chapter I provide a brief sketch of what I believe are currently defensible interpretations of the organization of ancient southwestern societies. The discussion focuses on current work that contradicts processualist judgments of the late 1970s and early 1980s. In some cases, the new data offer what for me are well-supported inferences about past organization. Other cases are less clear, indicating that more work is needed. I conclude the chapter with a consideration of topics of contention and possible directions for exploring them.

DOWN-SIZING, RIGHT-SIZING OR SOMETHING ELSE?

In the Southwest, there is acknowledged continuity from the Mid to Late Archaic (about 4,000 to 2,000 B.C.) to the later Anasazi, Hohokam and Mogollon developments beginning in the first millennium A.D. and extending to A.D. 1500. The continuity spans the acceptance of maize agriculture virtually throughout the region at 1500 B.C.; but unlike the Southeast and East, there appears not to have been supra-local entities comparable to those of the Adena and Hopewell prior to the Early and Late Mississippian.

From a normative perspective, settlements throughout the Southwest, between ca. A.D. 200 and 500, consisted of circular or subrectangular pithouses. Although the term village has often been used to refer to these communities (e.g., Cordell 1984:215–240; Cordell and Plog 1979:414–415), the terms farmstead, hamlet, or settlement are more appropriate. Many of these sites consist of four or five houses, which even if they were occupied simultaneously, indicate populations of 25–30 people. This is surely below the numbers anyone would consider a village. Some of these sites had oversize pit structures, some with special features. These structures have been variously interpreted as communal houses associated with group-level control or as households of village leaders (Lightfoot and Feinman 1982). However, others make a convincing case for attributing formal differences among sites to contrasting patterns of group mobility rather than to functional or social differentiation (Camilli 1983; Wills and Windes 1989). This alternative view sees Mogollon and Anasazi sites before A.D. 700 as examples of compounds (see Flannery 1972a) that were not occupied year round on a continuing basis (Wills 1988a,b; Wills and Windes 1989). Camilli (1983) also provides a convincing argument that differences in site sizes and some assemblage characteristics noted in site survey data, reflect reuse rather than functional or social differentiation. On a regional basis, early Anasazi and Mogollon settlement sizes do not suggest hierarchical organization. Instead, big sites may have been reused more often than other sites (see Camilli 1983; Wills and Windes 1989).

In the Hohokam region, Pioneer period houses were arranged in clusters of two to four structures facing a courtyard area. House clusters appear to have been very stable social and economic units throughout the Hohokam tradition. They are associated with distinct burial, trash disposal and work areas. At Snaketown, three "oversize" houses were arranged around a central area and may have been used for ceremonies or other special activities (Crown 1990a:232). Although the Pioneer period Hohokam were farming, it is not at all clear that irrigation canals were in use before the end of the period (Crown 1990a:232).

Throughout the Hohokam area before A.D. 750, settlements manifest a two level hierarchy in size (exclusive of seasonally used field houses). Farmstead sites consist of a single house or a single house cluster with material assemblages that indicate a complete annual round of activities. Hamlets consist of a number of houses or house clusters, which were also occupied year-round by populations of less than 100. Given the extreme localization of settings in which crops can be grown through floodwater, runoff, or rainfall farming in the lower Sonoran Desert, it seems reasonable that an important settlement strategy may have involved establishing settlements to claim rights to land (and water). The only craft items that were marked by a production peak during the Pioneer period are figurines, which were not produced by specialists and whose function may have been to enhance agricultural productivity (Neitzel 1991:190, 193).

In sum, before A.D. 750, settlements in the Southwest do not appear to be functionally differentiated. Groups in the three major traditions of this time varied in the degree to which they were seasonally mobile and in their reliance on agriculture. Anasazi and Mogollon groups seem to have been more mobile than the Hohokam; and although agriculture was practiced by groups in all three traditions, it seems to have been more influential with respect to residential stability among the Hohokam. For none of the traditions is there evidence of either craft specialization, status differences, or formalized exchange patterns at this time. Oversize structures may well have served for community rituals. Even the irrigation canals that the Hohokam built along perennial and semi-perennial streams about A.D. 700 provide no evidence for organizational complexity. These canals did not require a large, well-organized labor force either to build or operate; and they were not linked in ways that would have required an integrated decision-making structure.

Between A.D. 775 and 1150 (Colonial and Sedentary periods), the Hohokam tradition developed some characteristics of institutional differentiation and specialization. There is apparent functional differentiation among settlements beyond that of size. The largest Hohokam sites of this time housed more than 100 people and included facilities, such as ballcourts, that were absent from smaller sites and farmsteads. Although these large sites can be further subdivided based on the number and sizes of both ballcourts and platform mounds, these divisions apparently did not relate to differences in function. Canal construction increased substantially during this time, enough Neitzel (1991:196) believes to have necessitated both a large labor force and some sort of formalized leadership for the coordination and supervision of that labor. The canals did not serve a hierarchy of settlements and no hierarchical decision-making structure was needed to allocate water among settlements.

Hohokam ballcourts likely had multiple functions. They probably not only served as an institution for economic and social interaction but according to Wilcox (1991e) also reflected basic elements of the Hohokam world view. Ballcourts were open to public view, indicating that both this ideology and access to the court itself were open to the community at large.

The functional differentiation of Hohokam sites during this period is matched by some evidence for specialization, probably part-time, in the production of ritual objects such as palettes, censers, and serrated projectile points (Neitzel 1991). While none of these objects were associated with status differences, Neitzel (1991) proposes that shell jewelry which was not made in the Hohokam core area until after A.D. 975, was.

Overall, while there was distributional differentiation and specialization among the Hohokam during this period, it was not pronounced. Supporting this view is the size of one of the largest Hohokam sites of this time, Snaketown, which Wilcox (1991d) thinks probably had a simultaneous population of no more than 300 individuals. This seems to be below a number that might have supported a hierarchical decision-making organization on a continuing basis. Nevertheless, it is high enough to have provided the largest labor crew estimated to have been necessary to construct both Pioneer and Colonial period irrigation canals (Neitzel 1991).

From about A.D. 1000/1040 to 1150, much of the northern Southwest is thought to have been tied to or influenced by events centered in Chaco Canyon and that may have begun there by about A.D. 900. There is scholarly disagreement in interpreting how the Chacoan system was organized and how it functioned. Everything from a nonhierarchical, moiety structure (Vivian 1990) to an empire extracting tribute (Wilcox 1991d) has been suggested. Elements of the Chacoan organization that are most often debated include: 1) the size of the population resident in Chaco Canyon; 2) the number of individuals needed to build Chacoan structures; 3) differential distributions of some goods—turquoise, cylindrical vessels, burials with elaborate grave goods; 4) the significance of the distribution of great kivas and elevated kivas; 5) the amount of coordinated labor required for an agricultural system that involved irrigation channeling runoff water

on the north side of Chaco Canyon; 6) a lack of noticeable differences in diet, stature, or pathologies between populations buried at the Chacoan great houses and those at contemporary villages; and 7) a lack of apparent differences in most material culture items among the settlement types described. In order to evaluate each of these points, one would have to write volumes. In fact, there are volumes on most of them.

The size of the Chacoan system outside the canyon, the function or functions of the outliers, and the relationships among outliers, local populations, and the canyon proper require more information than is currently available. At present, we do not know whether outliers were built and/or inhabited by people from Chaco Canyon itself or by local people emulating Chaco. It is likely that outliers differed among themselves in this regard (Doyel 1992; Eddy 1993). It cannot be assumed that those Chacoan outliers that are surrounded by local communities were functionally equivalent to those that were isolated. Further, just as Chacoan outliers were probably not functionally equivalent, there were likely to have been differences among them in function over time.

As Lekson (1991) states, it is the road system that gives coherence to what the Chacoan system was and to the probability that there was a system at all. The system is not well documented through distributional analyses of goods, raw materials, or surrogate measures of information exchange and interaction (Toll 1991). Some (i.e., Wheat 1983) are reluctant to define a system at all for this reason. There are different assessments of the number of levels and institutions in the hierarchy. For example, it is possible to count all households as one level, all Great Houses as one level and all villages as another level for a total of three levels. It is equally possible to rank order the Great Houses into three or four distinct levels and to rank villages inside the canyon as one level and those outside the canyon as another level, for a total of six levels (Doyel 1992; Judge 1991).

Clearly, it is important to our understanding of whatever Chaco was in the past, that it be described today in terms of interactions and organization rather than formal characteristics of architecture. Until that is done, I offer the following as plausible. The Chaco system did unite a region at least in being able to bring labor into the canyon. Despite Lekson's often cited and thoughtful comment that "a 30-person crew could cut and transport beams for about 1–1.2 months a year over a 6-year period, . . . and build the single largest construction event in the

Chacoan record" (Lekson 1984a:262), there is no way that the variety of concurrent construction episodes could have taken place without requiring more labor than was available in the canyon and some degree of institutional leadership of that labor (Sebastian 1991).

It is not yet possible at present to determine the sources within the San Juan Basin of raw materials that were imported into the canyon. However, the Chuskas seem to have been the source area for much of the imported Chacoan ceramics found in the central canyon and possibly for much of the timber used for construction (Dean and Warren 1983; Windes 1977). The Chuska slopes and Narbona Pass also provided lithic raw materials brought into the canyon. Since Chaco Canyon lacked significant wood resources during the height of its occupation, it seems reasonable that ceramic production, that requires wood for firing, should have been done routinely at a remote location with abundant wood, such as the Chuskas. Obtaining timber for building and cherts for stone tools, making pottery, and hunting may have been activities imbedded in structured interactions with community's resident in the Chuska area.

In an earlier paper, Cordell and Plog (1979) argued that reciprocal exchange, which is characteristic of egalitarian societies, could not have accounted for the enormous quantities of ceramics traded throughout the Pueblo Southwest during both Chacoan times and later during the fourteenth century. I now think that argument should be modified. What has changed? One general change has been a growing dissatisfaction with cultural evolutionary typologies—both with the use of stages to classify societies (e.g., egalitarian *vs.* ranked) and with the use of substantive categories of exchange (e.g., reciprocity *vs.* redistribution) as markers of particular levels of sociocultural integration.

Another change has been a greater appreciation for variability in how the large scale movement of goods occurs in ethnographic contexts. I use an example rather than an analysis of cross-cultural examples. Ethnographically documented exchange networks in Melanesia exhibit three characteristics that should be kept in mind when interpreting the relative complexity of Chacoan ceramic exchange, even when the use of boats for transport in the Pacific is considered. First, there is a virtual monopoly of specialist pottery production that operates over long distances on a regular basis. Secondly, Melanesian island communities that greatly exceed their carrying capacities can exchange pottery for food. Finally, both of the latter

two characteristics occur in the absence of a hierarchial social organization (Kirch 1991).

There is evidence that turquoise was worked in several different settings in Chaco Canyon. Its most likely source was the Cerrillos mines. However, the quantity of the material does not require a connection to the Cerrillos mines, similar to that to the Chuskas (Toll 1991). Neither Chacoan turquoise, nor cylindrical vessels, suggest more than part-time specialists (Mathien 1984). The difficulties in sorting out whether or not there were high status, "elite" individuals at Chaco underscores the likelihood that social difference among the people, as well as internal organizational differentiation and interdependence of Chacoan groups, were not marked.

Recent literature suggests that before A.D. 1200/1250, both the Hohokam and the Chacoan Anasazi were able to recruit labor from beyond a single local settlement. Hohokam settlements are more stable through time than are their Anasazi counterparts, in large part because agriculture cannot be practiced everywhere in the Hohokam area and irrigation canals are not easily moved. Both Hohokam and Anasazi seem to have used architectural features (ballcourts, great kivas, great houses) to express extra-settlement group identity or ideological unity. During this time, there is no evidence that access to architectural structures or features was restricted to particular groups or classes of individuals. There are craft items among both Hohokam and Anasazi, but these do not seem to have required more than part-time specialists to produce.

The period between A.D. 1250 and 1450 was one of dramatic change throughout the Southwest. Among the Hohokam, irrigation canals reached their maximum extent between about A.D. 1150 and 1400, and it was at this time that communities along a single canal would have had to cooperate in order to allocate water and maintain the canals. Settlements interacting in these ways have been termed "irrigation communities," at least 17 of which have been documented (Masse 1991; Wilcox 1991e). Most of the 206 ballcourts, at 165 sites, were in use around A.D. 1100–1150, but after about A.D. 1300, no new ballcourts were built (Wilcox 1991e). Large, rectangular platform mounds were built at more than 40 sites between about A.D. 1150 and 1300. In the mid-A.D. 1200s, at the very end of the Hohokam sequence, houses were constructed on platform mounds and access to these houses was impeded by walls (Gregory 1991; Fish, Chapter 4). Overall, Hohokam sites reflect a shift in architecture and organization. A dispersed settlement pattern continued at some sites but at other sites rectangular compounds enclosed several households and open plaza work areas and were associated with a community cemetery as well. Architectural patterns therefore are interpreted as suggesting that greater emphasis was placed on group cooperation and integration above the household level.

As the increase of irrigation canals suggests, Hohokam agriculture expanded during this period. New types of spindle whorls, which allowed spinning of very fine threads, suggest that cotton textiles may also have become a commodity produced by specialists. Neitzel (1991:195) suggests that while the specialist-produced ritual items of previous periods were no longer made, specialized production of utilitarian objects (textiles, tabular knives, and ground stone axes) and status symbols (shell and stone jewelry) occurred at sites with platform mounds, possibly "under the auspices" of high-status individuals. Evidence for village-level specialization has been recovered at the early Classic Marana community of the Tucson Basin (P. Fish et al. 1992a). Some sites within the Marana community seem to have specialized in the production of corn, others in agave, and some in agave, saguaro, and cholla. It has been suggested that the tabular knives used to process agave were produced by craft specialists (Neitzel 1991).

South of the Hohokam area, the period between A.D. 1250 and 1450 was marked by the development of a major center at Paquimé in Chihuahua. At its height in the fourteenth century (Dean and Ravesloot 1993), the site contained more than 2,000 habitation rooms, elaborate public buildings (including effigy mounds, ballcourts, and a possible market area), and a covered ditch system that may have provided for the distribution of water throughout the settlement (see Lekson, Chapter 1). Some archaeologists who are reluctant to consider social hierarchies in the context of ancestral Pueblos, accept the possibility of such institutions at Paquimé. Recent studies of burial ritual and human remains from Paquimé support interpretations for the existence of hereditary classes (Ravesloot 1988).

Paquimé is spectacularly different from most Anasazi and Mogollon sites. Di Peso (1974) concluded that Paquimé was a city involved in the production of goods for regional and long distance trade. In his view Paquimé was an outpost of a Mesoamerican mercantile system with roots far to the south in the Basin of Mexico. In later writing, Di Peso (1983) modified his opinion about the di-

rect influence of central Mexico, suggesting that Paquimé functioned in a network of complex regional interactions between Mesoamerica and the Greater Southwest.

As a regional center, Paquimé distributed scarlet macaws, turquoise, copper, shell, and pottery. More than 300 scarlet macaw skeletons were recovered at Paquimé from parts of the site that contained pens with egg shell, perches, and grain, suggesting that macaws were bred there. Most scarlet macaw skeletons from southwestern sites probably came from Paquimé. It is also likely that the birds were used by the residents of Paquimé itself, perhaps for feathers (Minnis 1984). Like scarlet macaws, Minnis (1984) thinks that the turquoise jewelry and copper recovered from Paquimé were used at the site itself and not for export. Although turquoise is not as abundant as other minerals at the site, 2.2 kg were recovered there. Paquimé is the northernmost site in north and west Mexico where copper was produced. The 688 recovered copper artifacts were made by a variety of techniques, including cold hammering and lost wax casting.

Fitting with his model of Paquimé as a mercantile center, Di Peso (1974) inferred that the rooms containing turquoise, copper artifacts, and shell served as warehouses. More recently, Minnis (1984) has suggested that these contexts could represent hoarding by a high status group or individual. In either case, the amount of shell artifacts, 4,000,000 artifacts weighing 1,324.5 kg, is impressive.

The other major trade good identified by Di Peso (1974) was Ramos Polychrome pottery, which he thought was produced at Paquimé and then widely distributed. This view may be only partially true. Recent compositional studies indicate that the Ramos Polychrome made at Paquimé was distributed to communities only within a radius of 75 km (Woosley and Olinger 1993). The type was probably made at other sites as well.

Archaeologists may well debate the mercantile nature of Paquimé for years as more is learned about the ways in which resources were procured and distributed from the site. The current view is that Paquimé developed as an enormous and significant center whose influence derived from its economic and political status. Its importance has not been interpreted as being primarily ceremonial. Thus, it has not been identified as the source of any of the religious belief systems thought to have been integrating forces among refugees from recently abandoned districts to the north.

In the Mogollon and Anasazi areas, the period between A.D. 1250 and 1450 was marked by the processes of regional abandonment and population aggregation. The reason for the increased instability of settlement systems is still not clearly understood; but the relationship between the two processes of abandonment and aggregation has been succinctly described by Adams (1991:151):

> The possible settlement decisions stemming from a large-scale immigration into an area where resources are dwindling due to moderate drought and where populations have grown to near-carrying capacity are basically two: join the indigenous population in new or existent settlements or build and maintain separate settlements.. . . The archaeological data clearly point to the aggregation option as the one selected.

Recent studies have attempted to explain these processes of regional abandonment and population aggregation using various models of organizational change (as did Cordell and Plog 1979). Among the variables discussed in these models are hereditary leadership, peer polity interaction, "cults," and the relationship between agricultural intensification, specialization, and exchange. In the Pueblo world, there was an initial aggregation in the A.D. 1150s to 1280s, which was often facilitated by the institution of the great kiva. Adams (1991) and others suggest that at some very large villages, the organizational structures included the development of leadership and the establishment of hereditary status differences. In other areas, such as Mesa Verde and Zuni, this may not have occurred. At Zuni, Kintigh (1994:134) sees no region-wide political subordination at Zuni after A.D. 1150. Consequently, he finds the concept of peer polity interaction, with its emphasis on the processes of competitive emulation and symbolic entrainment (see Renfrew and Cherry 1986), to be relevant for understanding post-Chacoan aggregation in the Zuni area and possibly elsewhere in the Chaco "extended core."

In any case, much more extensive population aggregation occurs after A.D. 1275. Over much of the Pueblo world, this aggregation is "synchronous with the disappearance of the great kiva, the appearance of rectangular kivas in the plaza.. . . The crystallization of this new village layout and the cooperative system it fostered was the fertile soil in which the katsina cult sprouted" (Adams 1991:154).

Adams (1991) sees katsina beliefs and ceremony as a way of integrating people of divergent backgrounds and varied beliefs. Katsina rituals involved mechanisms of social control, craft and resource specialization at the village level, and trade between Pueblo groups. He suggests the belief system came together in the upper Little Colorado area, but shared iconographic elements with the Salado region below the Mogollon Rim. Similarly, Crown (1994) argues that the designs/icons of the "Salado" polychromes represent a "regional cult" among heterogeneously organized groups. In her view, "regional cults" are neither the kinship-based, ancestor cults of tribal societies nor are they the "universal religions" of nation states. "Regional cults" emphasize shared values and concern with earth and fertility. The "cults" are capable of uniting people of diverse ethnic and linguistic backgrounds and would have been highly advantageous among ethnically heterogeneous villagers of the post-A.D. 1300s abandonment Southwest.

These descriptions of the katsina and Salado belief systems highlight the need to document craft specialization and exchange. Crown's (1994) analyses have shown that despite considerable uniformity in ceramic technology and iconography, the Salado types were produced locally over broad areas. Nevertheless, the distribution pattern does not support the normative appellation of Salado Culture. Adams (1991) suggests that among Pueblo groups, specialized production included the Hopi Mesa Pueblos making yellow wares, the Homol'ovi site cluster specializing in cotton production, and settlements at Chavez Pass/Anderson Mesa specializing in obsidian from Government Mountain.

In an earlier paper Fred Plog and I interpreted the evidence for craft specialization in the Puebloan Southwest between A.D. 1000–1425 as part of a shift in productive strategies. We argued that by A.D. 1000 continued population growth within the context of normal fluctuations in agricultural production could no longer be handled by either the expansion of storage facilities or community fissioning. In our view the new productive strategy involved the intensification of agriculture and the reorganization of specialized production and exchange. This reorganization involved increased specialization and the formation of "elaborated exchange networks coordinated by elites in systems characterized by differential access to status and authority" (Cordell and Plog 1979:420).

To support this interpretation, we cited Chavez Pass Pueblo, a site that we thought stood at the apex of a settlement hierarchy and was inhabited by elite individuals who controlled access to certain redware and polychrome pottery types. At a minimum, this argument depends on demonstrating the contemporaneity of Chavez Pass Pueblo with surrounding, smaller settlements that contain primarily black-on-white pottery. In 1979 the evidence for simultaneous occupation was from unpublished and only partially analyzed excavation data from Chavez Pass Pueblo. A decade later, Upham and Bockley (1989) published a candid review of why Upham used mean ceramic dates to date the site, how he inferred the simultaneous use of types found together in arbitrary 10 cm levels dug in a midden deposit, and how he then applied his chronology to the small sites comprising the rest of the "Chavez pass settlement system."

I do not find Upham and Bockley's (1989) argument for the simultaneous use of ceramic types to be compelling. Therefore, it is difficult for me to arrive at the conclusion that Chavez Pass Pueblo was at the top of a local settlement hierarchy in which sites constituting the base of the hierarchy lacked access to prestigious black-on-red (or orange) and polychrome pottery. Rather, it appears to me as though the area around Chavez Pass was like many other fourteenth and fifteenth century southwestern regions in that once aggregation occurred, it was complete. As there were no contemporary small settlements left in the vicinity, there is no evidence that elites at Chavez Pass were controlling small settlements or access to land or status goods. This reinterpretation of Chavez Pass demonstrates how accurate and precise dating can provide a powerful technique for evaluating statements about how prehistoric Southwestern societies were organized.

ESCAPING THE CONFINES OF CORDELL AND PLOG

In my own discussions, I have assiduously avoided using the term "chiefdom" with reference either to Chaco Canyon or to the thirteenth and fourteenth century aggregated settlements in the northern Southwest. Further, I intend not to use the term in the future. There are two reasons for this "omission." One relates to chiefdoms and economic redistribution, the other to chiefdoms and colonial governments. First, although the term "chiefdom" implies the existence of a set of characteristics (e.g., the existence of a chief, rules of chiefly succession, sumptuary rules, authority expressed through religious sanctions and taboos rather than the use of force, kinship organization

based on ramages or conical clans, and others), the redistribution of resources is central to the way chiefdoms work. In his classic statement, Service (1962:144) wrote:

> Specialization in production and redistribution occur sporadically and ephemerally in both bands and tribes. The great change at the chiefdom level is that specialization and redistribution are no longer merely adjunctive to a few particular endeavors, but continuously characterize a large part of the activity of the society. Chiefdoms are *redistributional societies* with a permanent central agency of coordination (emphasis in original).

Service (1962) maintained that chiefdoms arose in areas of relatively high topographic diversity and high population density. Such characteristics would preclude groups of people from moving from one resource to another for food. In such circumstances, the local chiefs could exhort their followers to produce (or gather or fish) a surplus of food that could be collected and exchanged for food products from different areas that had also been centralized by other local chiefs. This model of chiefdoms and redistribution seemed to fit Sahlins' (1958) portrayal of the "classic" cases of Polynesian high islands, and was tremendously influential to some archaeological versions of cultural evolution in the Americas (i.e., Flannery 1968; Sanders 1972; Sanders and Price 1968; see Yoffee 1993 for further discussion).

As ethnographers and archaeologists conducted fieldwork in Polynesia and elsewhere, and as they reviewed ethnohistoric literature, it became apparent that redistribution was not a typical model of exchange among societies identified as chiefdoms. Further, the chief himself might not amass any surplus from his followers (Earle 1977, 1991a,b; Kirch 1984; Sahlins 1972, 1976, 1985; Trigger 1985). Consequently, it is problematic for me to use a term that has been defined largely with reference to a particular kind of exchange, when the kind of exchange is rare to nonexistent even among cases once regarded as "classic."

For archaeologists, documenting the variety in kinds of production and exchange is more useful than applying the chiefdom label. Characteristics of "chiefdoms" do not necessarily co-occur. Just because there was some productive specialization does not automatically mean that there was redistribution, and vice versa. For the characteristic of redistribution, archaeologists have developed a number of indices of how it can be recognized in ancient contexts (see Renfrew 1977; Renfrew and

Cherry 1986). In the Southwest, despite expectations for its occurrence in the Chacoan regional system, little evidence has been found (Toll 1991). On the other hand, specialization in both food production and in crafts, perhaps at the village level, appears to have been important among some Hohokam communities (Fish et al. 1992a), perhaps among the fourteenth and fifteenth century Anderson Mesa and Middle Little Colorado settlements (Adams 1991; Upham 1982), and among the late fifteenth century Rio Grande region pueblos, particularly those along the Chama and in the Galisteo Basin (Anscheutz 1995; Shepard 1942; Spielmann 1994; Warren 1979). If archaeologists do identify redistributive networks, that alone is far more informative than labeling one or more multisettlement region as a chiefdom.

The second problem that I have with the term chiefdom relates to chiefdoms and colonial governments. Structuralists writing in ethnology and critical writing in ethnology and archaeology develop persuasive arguments that both chiefdoms and tribes are artifacts of colonial expansion rather than stages along a trajectory to political complexity (see Fried 1975; Sahlins 1976; Trigger 1985; Wolf 1982; Yoffee and Sheratt 1993). Fried (1975) has shown that entities that have been called tribes are not homogeneous with respect to language, nor do they form closed breeding populations or have single names for themselves as entities. They operate neither as bounded economic units nor as political groups. Fried concluded that "tribes" do not constitute a stage in political evolution but that they develop as secondary phenomenon to the expansion of nation states. Fried's (1975) discussion is particularly useful, in my opinion, because he explicitly recognizes that the nation states that have caused the secondary development of tribes need not be Western European colonialist states. Rather, the expansion of China and of various indigenous African states also generated secondary formation of tribes.

> Secondary tribalism takes different forms and appears in various guises in the political processes of states new and old. It may parallel the development of political parties or manifest itself in bloc politics. It is obviously related to the phenomenon of ethnic group formation, sometimes substituting for it, at other times forming a portion of a larger process (Fried 1975:104).

In the Southwest, typological debates about whether particular societies were tribes or chiefdoms seem to have led to a dead-end in terms of understanding how those societies were organized and how they changed through time. By 1989, Fred Plog (1989:108) had gotten to the point of writing that "continua such as band-tribe-chiefdom-state have never had clear empirical referents. They break down . . . over criteria of internal consistency."

I see three promising alternatives to relying on typological labels for understanding prehistoric organization and change. One proposed by Plog (1979) lies in the realm of general anthropological theory. Inspired by research by John Casti and others on the relationships among artificial life, artificial intelligence, cognitive science, and evolution (see Casti 1994; Gell-Mann 1990; Gumerman and Gell-Mann 1993), Plog attempted to redefine complexity and cultural evolution. His scheme, which is not fully developed in his published record, was based on the idea that the organizational features of societies can be viewed as occupying different quadrats of Cartesian space rather than points along continua. The quadrats were defined by three dimensions: scale (or size), stability (or the investment in buffering mechanisms), and complexity, defined following Casti, as diversity and nonpredictability of societal behavior.

There are two minor problems in Plog's notions of complexity and cultural evolution, which may hinder archaeological efforts to investigate them further. One is Plog's lack of interest in developing middle range theory to link his ideas to the peculiar perspective of the archaeological record. The second is the lack of fit between Plog's theoretical notions and his ideas about environmental variability. However, overall, I believe that Plog's insights are worth pursuing, although I suspect that those continuing on with them will be cognitive scientists or those working with Artificial Life models rather than archaeologists.

Another approach to studying past organization and change is more grounded in middle range theory. As exemplified by the work of Adler (1990) and a few others (e.g., Wilshusen and Blinman 1992), this approach begins with initial hypotheses, which can be derived from any scientific perspective, about causal relationships between specific organizational variables. Only those variables that have material correlates which therefore can be studied by the archaeologist are considered. By providing both a warranting argument for examining particular variables and an expectation that the selected variables are related in certain ways, this initial hypothesis insures that any correlations discovered are not the result of "mindless" pattern searches. The testing of the hypotheses proceeds in three stages. The first is to see if there is a strong fit among those variables as expressed in an appropriately broad range of ethnographies. If such a fit is found, or if the ethnographic descriptions require only some modifications of the variables, the second step is to see if other ethnographically documented variables, also ones with material expression, are also strongly correlated. The third step is to examine the archaeological record for evidence of strong patterning in the same variables.

By first examining the ethnographic literature, this approach develops links between behavior and the archaeological record, thus satisfying some requirements of middle range research. The approach seems appropriately cautious since in no single case is the archaeological record examined for one or two "traits" from which a great deal of social behavior is extrapolated. For example, one might want to evaluate a hypothesis that specified a causal relationship between redistribution of some kinds of items and sumptuary mortuary rituals. The ethnographic record would be examined to see if there was a strong pattern between redistribution of specified materials and sumptuary behavior reflected in mortuary activities and, if so, perhaps additional associations of potentially archaeologically observable characteristics. If that were true, then the specific variables that do strongly correlate would be examined in the archaeological record. The value of this approach is that it allows falsification of suggested causal relationships. It is also valuable in encouraging archaeologists to become familiar with the vagaries of ethnographic reporting and more sensitive to the lack of specificity in archaeological data.

If we are interested in evolutionary and organizational change, we should be concerned that there are inherent limitations in any ethnographic data, ethnoarchaeology, or work with cross-cultural materials (i.e., HRAF). This is especially true when we acknowledge that the ways of life of all modern peoples have been changed by contact with colonial peoples and governments. Binford's work among the Nunamuit and his observations of the Alyawara must be open to the same criticism leveled at others: their behavior does not take place in an environment isolated from the industrial world. Does Nunamuit mobility and hunting strategy remain unaffected by the fact that the Numamuit have access to an air strip and cargo flights? Does the fact that Alyawara use motor vehicles have no implications for their hunting methods? Yet, Binford and other archaeolo-

gists using contemporary ethnographic data obviously do so with care. They have more confidence in generalizing about those observations that relate to the most constant elements of the environment such as the number of bones in a particular species of animal and its weight at different times of year or the fracturing quality of rocks of various sorts. As we move away from such non-human qualities, there is greater risk in generalizing. I am not sure what kinds of strategies hunters pursued when they occupied the most productive environments on earth and never interacted with others who were not also hunters.

An approach, similar to Adler's (1990), that I advocate and find useful (Cordell 1994a) is to look at patterns that we can document archaeologically, describe the results, and examine changes in those patterns that can be documented archaeologically. With this approach, we should expect to find situations that do not occur ethnographically and should learn a great deal when this is the case. In applying this approach, I argue that we should limit our attention to material outcomes that depend largely upon natural rather than behavioral processes. The reason for this restriction is that I think we can control the former much better than the latter. For example, in the Southwest it appears that there was more locally specialized production over large areas after A.D. 1200 than there had been previously. Further, this specialization occurs in the context of no readily apparent functional differentiation or hierarchy of settlements. This situation is not described in the ethnographic record of Pueblo peoples and is of interest for this reason alone.

CONCLUSION

If we suspect that tribes and chiefdoms are secondary creations of states, how do we begin to understand cultural evolution? One beneficial approach, perhaps best left to ethnographers, is to use the historic colonial documents and compare the trajectories of indigenous peoples when they interact with the expansionist mode of diverse states—ancient and modern, European, African, Asian, and American. We may learn that what Fried (1975:103) suggested long ago is generally true; that secondary tribes are often stratified with different classes seeking different goals. To better understand the context in which this occurs, Spielmann's (1994) comparison between the fifteenth century Pueblos and the Iroquois confederacy takes on considerable meaning.

The approaches to studying ancient organization and change discussed in this paper highlight the difficulty imposed by the limited repertory of cases that we generally examine through our evolutionist writings. Relatively non-specialized forms of organization are difficult to detect archaeologically. Further, there is undoubtedly much greater variety among these systems than our understanding of comparative cultural evolution would lead us to believe. Our data base is not wide enough to capture all the kinds of examples to which we might turn. We do not have a comparative archaeology of the development of organizational forms that includes examples from sub-Saharan African, Southeast Asian, Eastern European, Western European, Central Asian, East Asian, North African, Andean, and Mesoamerican states, and the kinds of societies they interacted with and that preceded them; but we might make a positive step toward achieving such a comparative base.

CHAPTER EIGHT

Mississippian Sociopolitical Systems

George R. Milner

Sissel Schroeder

SOCIETIES OFTEN REFERRED TO AS CHIEFDOMS WERE scattered unevenly across the Southeast and southern Midwest from about a millennium ago to shortly after initial European contact. They conformed largely, but not exactly, to the distribution of archaeological complexes called Mississippian. Over the past two decades, a rapid accumulation of information from reasonably well-dated sites in many places has made it possible to address questions about the structure, function, growth, and decline of these late prehistoric societies.

MISSISSIPPIAN

The definition of what is meant by Mississippian has changed over time. Throughout much of this century, Southeastern archaeologists concentrated on the classification of materials, the identification of regions distinguished by particular kinds of artifacts, and the excavation of large mound centers where wonderful objects were likely to be found. As a result of this work, the Mississippian label was applied to a complex of traits, particularly shell-tempered pottery, wall-trench houses, and flat-topped rectangular mounds. Artifacts and, to a lesser extent, architecture were also used to characterize a number of regional variants whose names are often still employed.

Archaeologists have gradually switched from an emphasis on classifying artifacts and sites to investigating how people once lived. Interests in the subsistence and sociopolitical dimensions of life were prompted by discipline-wide shifts in research objectives and a dramatic increase in contract archaeology projects that have provided unprecedented opportunities for new fieldwork and analyses of a wider range of materials. It has been established that these people relied heavily on the cultivation of several crops, including maize, and favored resource-rich riverine settings, although different solutions to the demands of food acquisition and group protection were adopted in various natural and social environments (Griffin 1967; Smith 1978b). They lived in what were for the most part ranked societies (Anderson 1996b; Peebles and Kus 1977; Smith 1985a; Steponaitis 1986; after Fried 1967). The rapid accumulation of information about how these societies were organized has stemmed mostly from studies of mortuary contexts and settlement characteristics in conjunction with work that juxtaposes early historic descriptions and archaeological data (Brown 1975; Hally et al. 1990; Hudson et al. 1985, 1990a,b; Peebles 1971; Peebles and Kus 1977; Smith 1987). While some skepticism about the perceptiveness and veracity of the European chroniclers is warranted, from a comparative perspective much of what they said about the sociopolitical relations among the people they met rings true.

The label Mississippian, therefore, now refers to late prehistoric societies that shared certain similarities in artifact content and style, architectural features, subsistence practices, and sociopolitical organization. Because of the different weights researchers attach to the various characteristics that define Mississippian, there is no agreement over what should, and should not, be included within this archaeological category (Muller and Stephens 1991). Classification imbroglios aside, the term typically is applied to sedentary agriculturalists who lived in ranked societies scattered across much, but not all, of the Southeast and southern Midwest during late prehistoric and early historic times. The Mississippian archaeological category, however, does not encompass all chiefdoms that existed in the southern Eastern Woodlands (Potter 1993; Rountree 1989; Widmer 1988). Early seventeenth century Virginia tidewater societies occasionally are mentioned in this paper to flesh out the picture of life in eastern chiefdoms.

Organization

Mississippian societies are generally called chiefdoms (Anderson 1996b; Blitz 1993; Johnson and Earle 1987; Smith 1985a; Steponaitis 1978, 1986, 1991; after Service 1971, 1975). Some of these societies, however, appear to have had a structure more closely approximating sociopolitical formations commonly referred to as tribes (Smith 1985a; Steponaitis 1991). Several archaeologists also believe for rather unconvincing reasons that a few Mississippian societies, particularly Cahokia in Illinois, were full-blown states with all that such a label implies about population size, internal functions, and foreign relations (Conrad 1989; Gibbon 1974; O'Brien 1989, 1991; Sears 1968). All archaeologists, however, would agree that some Mississippian systems were large and powerful, whereas others were not (see Scarry, Chapter 5).

The use of a term such as chiefdom does not mean that an archaeologist's job is done when the best fit is found between archaeological remains and categories defined by ethnographically or historically known societies. The imposition of altogether too restrictive and static cultural categories on archaeological materials has been roundly criticized, and these objections need not be repeated here. Comparative materials, however, still play a central role in making sense out of prehistoric remains, particularly if some cultural continuity can be established (Spencer 1987). These ethnographic and historical data provide a basis for models that can be evaluated for their goodness of fit with archaeological evidence, and they establish general boundary conditions for societies that share gross similarities in size, technology, ways of life, and environmental settings.

Many researchers frequently use modifiers such as simple, complex, and paramount when referring to Eastern Woodlands chiefdoms. These labels underscore poorly understood variability in the organizational structure, geographical scale, and population size of roughly contemporaneous societies that shared certain similarities in artifact inventories, settlement characteristics, and diets. The various categories used here for Mississippian sociopolitical systems are deliberately simplified approximations of the ways these societies were organized. Site distributions are emphasized because settlement data are abundant, although existing information is flawed by uneven sampling, differential preservation and visibility, loose chronological controls, and inadequate knowledge of past environmental settings.

Documented variation in the best known Mississippian societies, from the smallest to the largest, can be accommodated by simple models consisting of similarly constituted units (e.g., Anderson 1996b; Butler 1977; Steponaitis 1978) (Figure 8.1). Small outlying sites were linked together under the umbrella of a locally important settlement where a chief resided and where there were often one or more mounds. These mounds supported houses for highly ranked people, charnel structures for their ancestors' bones, or atypical buildings where leaders met and deliberated (Anderson 1996b; Griffin 1967; Smith 1985a; Steponaitis 1986). Where mounds were lacking, locally important sites had centrally located open areas flanked by large buildings and domestic structures (Hally 1988; Santure 1981; Sullivan 1987). Many of these community constellations were politically autonomous. Others formed quasi-distinct districts within geographically larger systems dominated by one of the mound centers. These simple models are consistent with existing information, and it is not at all clear that even the largest Mississippian societies that encompassed several mound centers, such as the Cahokia sociopolitical system, were anything other than bigger versions of their smaller counterparts.

Simple Chiefdom

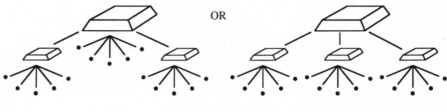

OR

Complex Chiefdom

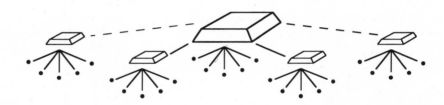

Paramount Chiefdom

Figure 8.1. Large and small sites in simple, complex, and paramount chiefdoms.

– – – – Ties Across Unoccupied Areas   ▱ Mound Center

——————— Ties Among Local Communities   • Outlying Site

Presumptive and Simple Chiefdoms

Many site complexes classified as Mississippian on the basis of physical remains—artifacts, features, and the like—fall in the low end of the organizational complexity spectrum. To use common but not entirely satisfactory labels, these societies approximated tribal and big-man systems, as well as simple chiefdoms (Smith 1985a; Steponaitis 1991). In this context, the low end of this spectrum of societies can be viewed as presumptive chiefdoms—multicommunity societies with largely merit-based and situationally determined positions of authority. Simple chiefdoms were ranked sociopolitical formations with fixed, inherited leadership positions with limited authority.

Short-lived presumptive chiefdoms were undoubtedly part of highly volatile sociopolitical settings where competitors sought to forge, enlarge, and solidify constellations of kin-based support populations. Time and again ambitious people along with their close supporters, principally kinfolk, must have found themselves involved in struggles to quash potential rivals; appropriate social functions augmenting their prestige and authority; recruit more followers; legitimize claims to high status; and keep positions of influence, trade partnerships, and key resources within narrowly defined genealogical groups. All such actions would have been aimed at embedding chiefly positions in the fabric of these societies.

Balanced precariously on the cusp between success and failure, only the most adroit and situationally advantaged aspirants to power would have found it possible to expand the scope of their positions to the point where there was a reasonable chance that their commands would be regularly obeyed and an ideal successional progression frequently followed. Even in groups where inherited leadership positions were firmly entrenched, chiefs had to be unusually capable people. To maintain or enhance their positions, high-ranking people must have been continually engaged in manipulating alliances, giving gifts to foster indebtedness, and invoking customary obligations and ritual sanctions to inveigle or intimidate their followers, potential supporters, and rival groups.

Archaeologically speaking, these societies consisted of scattered settlements dominated by a nearby community where important people lived (Anderson 1996b; Milner 1986; Muller 1986a; Peebles 1987; Steponaitis 1978, 1991; Welch 1991) (Figure 8.1). Principal settlements are identifiable by mounds, special architecture, or both. Smaller sites, which are more difficult to detect archaeologically, surrounded locally preeminent settlements.

Complex and Paramount Chiefdoms

The upper end of the Mississippian organizational spectrum has attracted considerable attention in recent years. The labels complex and paramount, when applied to chiefdoms, are often used interchangeably. It is useful, however, to draw a distinction between them when describing structural variability in societies at the high end of the range of organizational complexity, particularly in terms of their spatial dimensions.

Several archaeologists have argued that large Mississippian societies consisted of multiple similarly structured components with one, for a time, emerging as more important than the others (Anderson 1996b; Butler 1977; Hally 1993; Hally et al. 1990; Milner 1986; Peebles 1987a; Steponaitis 1978, 1986, 1991; Welch 1991). The principal distinction between large and small societies was the existence in the former of several organizationally similar, politically quasi-autonomous, and economically self-sufficient units that, crudely speaking, could be likened to a series of simple chiefdoms. This building block model, in one form or another, is probably applicable to all organizationally complex Mississippian systems.

Complex chiefdoms consisted of a series of districts made up of large and small settlements where only one principal site was preeminent (Figure 8.1). The linkages between high-ranking and low-born people in these societies are not completely understood. Current models highlight uncertainty over the nature of relations among chiefs at the principal center and subsidiary sites (Anderson 1996b; Milner 1986; Peebles 1987a; Steponaitis 1978, 1991; Welch 1991). In some scenarios, leading people in principal places are seen as interacting with less important chiefs at intermediate nodes in a settlement hierarchy. Subordinate chiefs, in turn, communicated with the bulk of the population living in outlying communities. We prefer a somewhat different means of linking principal chiefs with their primary followers. The principal leader exercised direct control over his or her own supporters, including many low-status people. This person also communicated with subsidiary chiefs who had their own self-sufficient constituencies at their disposal. Lesser chiefs acted as articulation points between the people of their districts and the principal chief. Thus, the superordinate leader directly dominated his or her own support population, and that person also maintained ties with subsidiary chiefs who exercised control over their own followers.

Complex chiefdoms are identifiable archaeologically as spatially discrete clusters of contemporaneous settlements that include two or more sites marked by special forms of architecture, especially mounds (Hally 1993). Although the identification of such sociopolitical systems might seem straightforward, archaeologists face great difficulties caused by the conflation into one horizon of sites with distinct occupational histories. The presence of two or more mound centers within one cluster of sites could be interpreted as either a complex chiefdom with multiple principal places where leaders once resided or a series of sequential simple chiefdoms, each with one site that was for a time more important than the others (cf. Hally 1993; Williams and Shapiro 1990).

The use of the term paramount chiefdom stems largely from recent work on mid-sixteenth century societies encountered by Spanish adventurers who penetrated deep into the interior of the Southeast (Hally et al. 1990; Hudson et al. 1990). In some places these Spaniards found sociopolitical formations composed of spatially separate population aggregates, one of which was dominated by a principal chief and the others by subordinate leaders (Elvas in Smith 1968:65–84; de la Vega in Varner and Varner 1951:129, 271–347) (Figure 8.1). Unoccupied areas of variable dimensions lay between the separate components of these regional systems.

From an archaeological perspective, large-scale paramount chiefdoms consisting of spatially discrete constellations of sites would be difficult, if not impossible, to

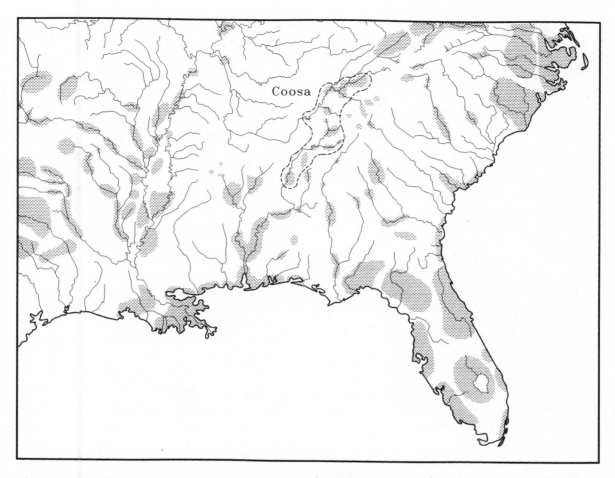

Figure 8.2.   Early sixteenth century archaeological phases and site concentrations in the Southeast, including the approximate dimensions of the paramount chiefdom of Coosa encountered by de Soto.

detect (Hally et al. 1990; also see Scarry, Chapter 5). In the Coosa example, thought to be roughly 400 km long, groups of sites were separated from other such clusters by uninhabited areas, and material inventories are distinct enough that they have been given several separate phase designations (Hally et al. 1990; Hudson et al. 1985; Smith 1987) (Figure 8.2). The individual site clusters each have the archaeological signature of simple or complex chiefdoms; that is, they encompass small and large settlements, including preeminent places marked by special architecture and concentrations of prestige-denoting artifacts in certain contexts.

In some circumstances, subsidiary chiefs in large-scale chiefdoms retained considerable autonomy, as the Spaniards discovered. A tendency for geographically and socially segmented regional systems to fission along existing cleavage planes is illustrated by the Coosa paramount chiefdom described by the de Soto and Luna adventurers and studied by several archaeologists (Hally et al. 1990; Hudson et al. 1985, 1990; Smith 1987). All things being equal, the ability of the principal leader to influence neighboring peoples decayed as distance from the core of the chiefdom increased (de la Vega in Varner and Varner 1951:346). In fact, members of the Luna expedition were persuaded to help the principal leaders of Coosa reestablish control over a distant group, the Napochies, who had refused to make their customary payments of goods (Davilla Padilla in Swanton 1922:231–239).

Less than a century later, English settlers in tidewater Virginia encountered a structurally similar situation where loosely aligned, and not always obedient, groups—characterized by Rountree (1989:14) as an "ethnic fringe"—were located some distance from the groups most closely allied with Powhatan, the principal chief. The potential for independent action by local chiefs was not lost on the English, who found they could use latent dissension to their own advantage.

> There is a king in this land called great Pawatah, vnder whose dominions are at least 20ty severall kingdoms, yet each king potent as a prince in his owne territory (Anonymous in Barbour 1969:102).

CHIEFLY AFFAIRS

The affairs of important people are emphasized in discussions of the centripetal forces that held these kinship-based societies together because it is the presence of ranked social positions that differentiates late prehistoric chiefdoms from their antecedents. These chiefs and other leading people have been portrayed in dramatically different ways by archaeologists, although exchanges for political rather than strictly economic ends are for good reasons increasingly being emphasized.

Benign Managers

At one time chiefdoms were defined as redistribution systems in which a formally recognized and regularly conducted society-wide movement of large amounts of goods leveled out resource disparities among sometimes specialized communities, thereby ensuring group survival (Sahlins 1958; Service 1971, 1975). Perspectives on these societies have changed over the past few decades, and it is now widely recognized that redistribution among such communities is not a defining characteristic of chiefdoms (Earle 1977; Peebles and Kus 1977; Steponaitis 1978; Taylor 1974).

It has been argued recently, however, that there was a high degree of economic interdependence among sites in the Cahokia area (O'Brien 1989, 1991). The major components of this argument are as follows: nodes at each level in a multi-tiered site hierarchy displayed different suites of functions; various goods that included bulk commodities needed to sustain life were passed up and down the hierarchy; residents of important places depended on surpluses of food produced by the inhabitants of lower ranked settlements; and the entire system was closely regulated by an experienced bureaucracy. Solid evidence has not been presented to support this argument, nor are we aware of any that could be used for this purpose (Milner 1986; Muller 1987).

Nevertheless, some items certainly moved among different communities in Mississippian chiefdoms, and members of the superordinate social stratum seem to have had a heavy hand in many exchanges within and between these societies (see Scarry, Chapter 5; Muller, Chapter 11). Highly valued nonperishable artifacts made of nonlocal materials are concentrated in contexts associated with important people (Milner 1984; Peebles 1987a; Peebles and Kus 1977; Steponaitis 1991). There is some evidence for the movement of meat, particularly choice cuts, to mound centers, and this food was presumably used for occasionally occurring and socially significant feasts that augmented the prestige of leading people (Blitz 1993:125; Rolingson 1990b; Welch 1991:179). Such exchanges of limited amounts of goods were conducted primarily for political ends. They were not part of a frequent large-scale movement of goods that balanced out surpluses and deficits of unevenly distributed critical resources among specialized communities (Brown et al. 1990; Milner 1986; Muller 1987; Steponaitis 1991).

Commerce Regulators

Some models of Mississippian intergroup relations emphasize the long-distance shipment of bulk commodities on a frequent basis. Leading figures in these societies played a major part in promoting centrally-controlled trade among distant peoples.

Such scenarios primarily pertain to Cahokia and its domination of economic connections among societies scattered widely across the midcontinent. It has been argued that Cahokia was strategically placed as a gateway between a Mississippian heartland and the wide-open spaces of the upper Midwest and eastern Plains (Kelly 1991). Several archaeologists believe that Cahokia's leaders were behind far-flung trading ventures among dissimilar societies spread over an enormous part of the continental interior (Dincauze and Hasenstab 1989; Goodman and Armelagos 1985; Kelly 1991; Little 1987; O'Brien 1991; Peregrine 1992; Tiffany 1991). The site's central position within a transportation network encompassing much of the Mississippi drainage made the control of the movement of highly valued items and bulk goods possible. In several respects, these ideas are updated versions of an earlier characterization of Cahokia's superordinate social stratum as a "merchant class" likened to Aztec pochteca who profited from economic relations imposed on widespread peoples held in thrall by their insatiable lust for mystical ceremonies and fine goods (Porter 1969; 1974:28–29, 176, 186).

Vast quantities of essential bulk commodities, including maize, meat, and hides, are said to have been transported on a regular basis across hundreds of kilometers in heavily laden and presumably well-protected canoes, eventually reaching Cahokia (e.g., Dincauze and Hasenstab 1989). In return, finished products were shipped to far-off places to satisfy the cravings of hinterland folk for these items. It has been argued that people 200 km away from Cahokia were deprived of so much food that their skeletons showed signs of the deleterious effects of malnutrition and associated infectious diseases (Goodman and Armelagos 1985). This scenario implies that Cahokia's leaders wielded enormous power, enabling them to wrest food from the hungry mouths of people in distant lands.

Despite gaining some acceptance, these center-driven trade models feature temporal inconsistencies and do not make sense considering what is known about late prehistoric midcontinental societies (Griffin 1993; Milner 1986). No empirical evidence supports models featuring a highly centralized Cahokia that had the capacity or need to pursue an economically driven agenda involving the domination of far-flung trading relations, an exploitation of distant peoples, and the routine and safe shipment of enormous amounts of goods across great distances.

Desperate Competitors

Competition and its counterpart, cooperation, are increasingly being emphasized in portrayals of relations among political factions both within these chiefdoms and between separate societies (Anderson 1996a,b; DePratter 1991; Milner 1986; Steponaitis 1991). These models incorporate rivalry and alliance formation among kin-based groups, uneven distributions of prime resources, intergroup exchanges to further political ambitions, and a need to establish coalitions for mutual defense. High-ranking people and their lineages are seen as actively engaged in efforts to expand the size of support populations, increase the amount of goods and labor expected of them, and eliminate the threat of usurpers from within and interlopers from afar. Limited amounts of prestige-enhancing goods were exchanged, well-placed marriages arranged, and established positions of importance appropriated, all of which were

calculated to advance the aims of particular people and their close kinfolk.

Valued objects would have been hoarded by both high and low-status people, and exchanged to fulfill social obligations. Most of these items were concentrated in the hands of the highest ranked people, as were the finest quality objects and those indicative of exalted positions (see Scarry, Chapter 5). In places such as Cahokia, valued goods were distributed unequally, evidently by social position, among various superordinate groups (Milner 1984). These items presumably were used to put people in positions of indebtedness so that their goods and labor could be called upon in times of need. Low-born people who managed to hoard smaller amounts of these objects probably used them in meeting various social obligations and, in so doing, were able to exert some influence over their neighbors. In the Cahokia area, such items included hoes from nonlocal chert and marine shell beads mostly of mediocre quality.

Some highly prized objects were fashioned by practiced hands, but the great majority of them, such as most marine shell beads, did not require any special skills to produce (see Scarry, Chapter 5). Concentrations of tools and debris in certain parts of large centers such as Cahokia and Moundville indicate that highly valued items from exotic raw materials were made at important sites (Milner 1986; Steponaitis 1991; Welch 1991). Yet even the occupants of outlying communities in the Cahokia area, and presumably elsewhere as well, enjoyed access to nonlocal materials used to fashion items such as beads that were important in discharging social responsibilities (Milner 1986).

For highly ranked people, carefully planned marriages would have expanded close kin ties, increasing the size and cohesion of support groups and facilitating access to needed resources and prized positions of ritual or social import. In fact, powerful chiefs at the time of European contact found it advantageous to have close relatives in positions of authority (Laudonniere in Bennett 1975:42, 76, 80; Rountree 1989:117; Elvas in Smith 1968:71; de la Vega in Varner and Varner 1951:129, 273). On occasion such individuals could represent indisposed chiefs who were temporarily unable to conduct their own affairs (Barlowe in Quinn 1955:98–100).

Aspirants to power probably took any opportunity to arrogate to themselves existing social and ceremonial functions that could be used to buttress their positions. In so doing, they manipulated customs to meet the requirements of new conditions, with an emphasis on their own needs (see the maneuvering two centuries ago among the Omaha [Thorne 1993]). A clever redefinition of malleable traditions would have reinforced the often times tenuous grip of Mississippian chiefs on positions of authority.

One example of high-ranking people insinuating themselves into the everyday concerns of common people is their involvement with a competitive game known as chunkey. In historic times, chunkey was played to demonstrate athletic prowess, and some gaming stones, or discoidals, were treasured possessions of individual communities (Hudson 1976:421–425; Swanton 1946:547–548, 682–684). Important people in at least some prehistoric chiefdoms maintained a close and highly visible association with the game. An elite-related burial episode in Mound 72 at Cahokia included a cache of discoidals along with other valued objects, and several examples of Mississippian artwork depict chunkey players (Brown 1985; Fowler 1975b).

The seeming naturalness of social inequalities would have been legitimized by widely shared beliefs that added an aura of sanctity to leading figures, particularly chiefs. Judging from early historic accounts, key members of superordinate groups promoted self-aggrandizing rituals and required deferential behavior from their followers (Laudonniere in Bennett 1975; Ranjel in Bourne 1904; Rountree 1989; Elvas and Biedma in Smith 1968; du Pratz in Tregle 1975; de la Vega in Varner and Varner 1951). Appropriate genealogical credentials and the weight of custom, however, would not have been sufficient to maintain leaders in exalted positions when faced with challenges from assertive subordinates or antagonistic neighbors. Chiefs had to be quite adept, even ruthless, in the pursuit of their own political ends. For example, in the early historic period aspiring men schemed to put themselves in favorable positions before the deaths of their predecessors. The sixteenth century Spaniards found that one such person ruled on behalf of an old chief whose faculties were failing (Ranjel in Bourne 1904:91). A century later, one of Powhatan's successors, an ambitious and capable man, acted as principal chief for a number of years before eventually ascending to that position (Potter 1993:184–185; Rountree 1989:118). Yet the conduct of these chiefs was constrained by commonly held understandings of acceptable behavior. High-handed actions, even if successful over the short run, were likely to result in smoldering resentments that could flare into outright defiance at any sign of weakness.

Skillful maneuvering among initially more-or-less equivalent social groups was driven by demographic imperatives: to recruit new followers, to solidify existing constellations of kin groups, and to prevent an erosion of supporters through the calving off of loosely aligned factions. Poor relations between two groups, the Coosa and Napochies, during the mid-sixteenth century underscores the central role of maintaining a numerical advantage and the ability to deploy it effectively.

In ancient times the Napochies were tributaries of the Coza people, because this place [Coza] was always recognized as head of the kingdom and its lord was considered to stand above the one of the Napochies. Then the people from Coza began to decrease while the Napochies were increasing until they refused to be their vassals, finding themselves strong enough to maintain their liberty which they abused. Then those of Coza took to arms to reduce the rebels to their former servitude, but the most victories were on the side of the Napochies. Those from Coza remained greatly affronted as well from seeing their ancient tribute broken off, as because they found themselves without strength to restore it (Davilla Padilla in Swanton 1922:232).

Recent archaeological discussions of rivalries among political factions focus on canny scheming by important people to secure greater access to labor, resources, or trading relationships, as well as a deliberate broadening of social relations to ensure self preservation. Jockeying for advantageous positions by self-sufficient groups took place in contexts where people relied on unevenly distributed, spatially fixed, highly productive, reliable, and readily storable foodstuffs. In such situations there is a great potential for conflict over access to prime land where resources were concentrated and regularly available.

It appears that the weight of large numbers was all important to the formation, expansion, and maintenance of chiefdoms in the late prehistoric southern Eastern Woodlands. Many people were needed to assemble goods for great displays and to provide the warriors needed to ensure the compliance of affiliated groups who might otherwise ignore the demands of leaders. A threatening posture seems to have been essential for the persistence of these chiefdoms. Great numbers of reliable supporters would have enabled emerging or existing chiefs to outmaneuver rivals attempting to seize high leadership positions. They also would have been useful in keeping at bay more distant adversaries who could attract the allegiance of loosely aligned outlying groups. For example, one subsidiary chief upon seeing the de Soto expedition considered severing existing relations with a dominant neighbor and allying himself with this new, and obviously powerful, presence in his world (Ranjel in Bourne 1904:90). Contentious neighbors used any opportunity that might present itself, including the surprising arrival of European soldiers, to advance their own positions (Laudonniere in Bennett 1975:91, 117–120; Elvas in Smith 1968:110–115; Davilla Padilla in Swanton 1922:231–239; de la Vega in Varner and Varner 1951:277–278, 434–445). Intimidation seems to have been a particularly effective tactic in early seventeenth century Virginia. Powhatan's opponents were roughly handled whenever sufficient support was available to pursue military solutions to problems posed by obstreperous groups both within his geographically large chiefdom and around its borders (Rountree 1989:118–121).

TEMPORAL PERSPECTIVE

Archaeologists are only beginning to define the individual trajectories of Mississippian chiefdoms that rose and fell at different times over several centuries. While much remains to be learned about these sociopolitical systems, the broad outline of what happened to them has been established.

Stability

From a multi-generational perspective, the southern Eastern Woodlands was a scene of constantly shifting sociopolitical relations and population distributions (Anderson 1996a,b; Milner 1986; Peebles 1987a; Steponaitis 1991; Smith 1985a). Individual chiefdoms experienced periods of formation, florescence, and fragmentation, a process increasingly being referred to as "cycling" (Anderson 1996a,b) (Figure 8.3). Recognition of this general pattern did not originate with Mississippian archaeologists—indeed, Service (1975:151) identified "cycles of centralization-decentralization"—and the pattern has been identified in other parts of the world (Wright 1984). It should be emphasized that the use of the term cycling does not mean that there was some intrinsic force that drove cultural trajectories through phases of development and senescence in an inevitable sequence with a fixed amplitude and frequency.

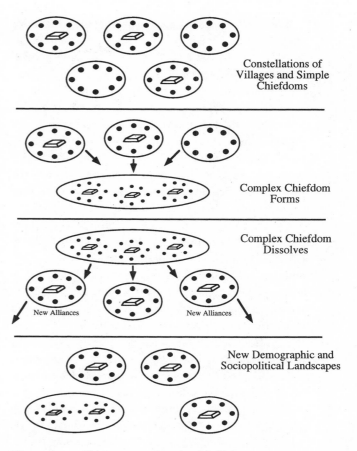

Figure 8.3.   Change over time in chiefdoms.

Inequalities among small-scale, sedentary societies in kin-group strength, intergroup contacts, and access to prime environmental settings provided a context where situationally based leadership eventually became transformed into more permanent positions of broader authority. The leading figures of these simple chiefdoms were differentiated to varying degrees from their followers by signs of high rank, including distinctive architecture indicative of an ability to mobilize labor for their own aggrandizement. Centralized decision making invested in a chief was not an all or nothing affair. Leadership positions were attained through some variable mix of fixed descent rules and individual, or group-based, competition favoring the strongest and most capable aspirants to power.

In the right circumstances, some simple chiefdoms coalesced to form complex chiefdoms, a development that occurred when one of a number of roughly equivalent societies gained ascendancy over its peers. Once numerical dominance was achieved, expansion could be rapid through the addition of easily cowed neighbors. Warfare, or the threat of it, shifted from inconclusive fighting to the subordination of ever more groups, especially those that found it difficult to move to other places. Outward expansion would have continued until the principal chief could no longer project his or her power consistently and effectively. A high degree of social and geographical segmentation was retained by even the most impressive of these chiefdoms, including Cahokia (Milner 1986). The problems of dampening divisiveness among allied groups close to home would have eventually acquired a higher priority than growth through the incorporation of new groups. Nevertheless, established custom and numerical supremacy would have bolstered the positions of existing leaders. Despite inherent weaknesses in the structure of large-scale chiefdoms, it was still an uphill battle for usurpers to topple holders of high office and for enemies to gain ascendancy over them.

Complex and paramount chiefdoms, no matter how powerful they might become, contained within them the seeds of their own destruction. Gravitation towards centers of power increased the risk of resource shortfalls that caused hardship for local populations and undermined the sense of efficaciousness chiefs strove to cultivate. Rifts between geographically and socially separable units that were economically self sufficient, politically quasi-autonomous, and only situationally aligned with a principal chief were weak points in regional systems. Principal chiefs must have experienced difficulties dominating distant subordinates, all of whom were potential rivals skilled at manipulating social relations to their own advantage. Paramount chiefdoms consisting of far-flung and quasi-independent population aggregates would have been especially difficult to hold together with the relatively weak means available to chiefs, including appeals to honor customary obligations and threats of sanctions that could not be backed consistently by overwhelming numbers of warriors.

The likelihood of potentially destructive disputes would have increased during the inter-generational transfer of exalted positions. At such junctures, aggressive internal and external rivals backed by their own followers were presented with opportunities to promote their own political agendas by putting forward acceptable genealogical rationales to validate disruptions of ideal successional sequences.

The dissolution of large-scale chiefdoms was accompanied by a restructuring of sociopolitical and demographic landscapes in response to new political realities. In areas where temporally precise spatial information is available it is apparent that the locations of population aggregates and the most powerful chiefdoms changed from one time horizon to the next (Anderson 1996a,b; Brain 1988). The distribution of people was constrained by the disposition of the best land, but not all prime areas were occupied at any particular time in the past. Reasonably well-defined clusters of roughly contemporaneous sites yielding stylistically similar pottery tend to be elongated because they often correspond to river valleys. Survey coverages, while flawed, are sufficient to indicate that the lengths of these site concentrations range from no more than a few tens of kilometers to just over 100 km (Brain 1988:266–272; Hally 1993; Hally et al. 1990; Milner 1986; D. Morse 1990; P. Morse 1990; Morse and Morse 1983:270).

Warfare

Warfare leading to considerable mortality in certain times and places undoubtedly influenced late prehistoric population spacing and served as an incentive for the aggregation of people. The archaeological record, imperfect as it is, indicates that the intensity of fighting changed over time and varied from one place to another.

Judging from published osteological reports, lethal intergroup conflicts increased in frequency late in the first millennium A.D. prior to the development of societies classified as Mississippian. Several centuries later the mutilation of slain enemies became more common. Disfiguring corpses and taking trophies presumably demonstrated prowess in war and intimidated potential antagonists. The demoralizing effect on enemies of body-part displays was apparent to sixteenth century Spaniards (see Davilla Padilla in Swanton 1922:236–237).

Fortifications, including ditch-and-embankment defensive works, massive log walls with bastions, and simple pole constructions, became common shortly after A.D. 1000. Variation in defensive structures must have been a function of site longevity, community size, and perceived threat. One outcome of warfare was the forging of alliances among formerly discrete constellations of villages for mutual defense. Larger and more varied groups brought together under the threat from neighbors required new means of social integration and provided more latitude for particularly successful warriors to further their ambitions and those of their kin groups.

An association between high status, ferocity in war, and daring leadership is shown by warlike themes in Mississippian artwork (Brown 1975, 1985). Successful chiefs would have attracted people who could find sanctuary in their domains. Generations-long enmities and dangerous unoccupied zones between population aggregates allowed chiefs to extend the scope of their authority over the affairs of people who were unwilling to move to more remote places. The risks of leaving the safety of an established chiefdom outweighed the problems of accommodating the demands of chiefs, at least as long as these obligations were perceived as reasonable.

While gaining numerical superiority was undoubtedly of great importance, the chiefs also had to have an effective means of wielding it. Trusted lieutenants who could be counted on to pursue a chief's bidding in matters of war seem to have been encountered by sixteenth century Spaniards (de la Vega in Varner and Varner 1951:277–278). Skilled war leaders in highly developed chiefdoms would have enhanced the chances of success in raids by stiffening the resolve of men engaged in hazardous undertakings (Reyna 1994). At the very least, success in war was an important means of elevating one's social status in several early historic Southeastern societies (Hudson 1976:325–327; Rountree 1989:101).

Unoccupied buffer zones formed between hostile societies as people gravitated toward powerful and successful chiefs (Anderson 1996a,b; DePratter 1991). For example, early in the sixteenth century, Spanish adventurers found that the Savannah River Valley was located between two antagonistic chiefdoms, Ocute and Cofitachequi, that were centered on major rivers to the south and north, respectively. Only a few generations earlier, this area was home to many people living in numerous large and small settlements (Anderson 1996a,b; also see Anderson, Chapter 15).

It is possible that a wide spacing of population aggregates, new and larger constellations of previously separate groups, and a deflection of the energies of high-spirited warriors towards distant enemies diminished the likelihood of violent death among the inhabitants of some Mississippian societies. In at least two places—Cahokia and Moundville—the development of more centralized sociopolitical systems was accompanied by the appearance of dispersed patterns of settlement in areas dominated by major mound centers (Milner 1986; Steponaitis

1991). Near Cahokia, this dispersal was an energetically efficient response of individual families to the spatial structure of valley floor environmental settings. Once a balance between the opposing demands of defense and food acquisition was tilted by a dampening of intergroup tensions, the settlement of the floodplain surrounding Cahokia shifted from an emphasis on small, compact villages to isolated, single-family farmsteads.

Mississippian Trajectories

While temporal controls are far from adequate, it seems that the widespread development of societies featuring archaeologically obvious signs of pervasive social and political inequalities was preceded in the late first millennium A.D. by an increase in intergroup violence. Hazardous social settings contributed to great suffering among hard-pressed groups and presumably restricted options for movement to places held or claimed by other peoples. Ambitious leaders of political factions backed by many supporters, especially those controlling areas with rich and reliable resources, were thereby presented with opportunities to increase the numbers of their subordinates by attracting groups forced to seek close affiliation for self preservation. Movement toward powerful chiefs contributed to the formation of broad buffer zones that included both high and low-productivity land.

Chiefdoms appeared early in the central and lower Mississippi River Valley and its principal tributaries. Jockeying among political factions was played out in social and environmental settings that, when taken together, were unusual for the southern Eastern Woodlands. Relatively large populations that possessed the means of producing surpluses from field and stream were scattered across a broad valley where the kinds of resources, their productivity, and the risks of harvest shortfalls were unevenly distributed. Variability in the yield and reliability of needed resources meant that some areas were more desirable than others and could support more people. Some emerging chiefdoms possessed a greater potential for gaining numerical advantage over their neighbors than their counterparts in less advantageous places. Growth outward was limited by the capacity of a principal chief to project his or her authority across increasingly large areas and by the presence of rival and similarly expanding systems.

Complex chiefdoms wherever they occurred in the southern Eastern Woodlands seem to have developed when one of a number of roughly equivalent groups surged to regional prominence, reaching a position of ascendancy over its similarly structured counterparts. The rise of mound centers to preeminent positions within their respective regions appears to have occurred rather suddenly in at least two instances: Cahokia and Moundville (Milner 1986; Pauketat 1992; Steponaitis 1991). Rapid development, once the process of agglomeration got underway, probably owed much to the relative ease their leaders experienced in gaining a decisive advantage over smaller neighboring groups, none of which were located a great distance from the principal centers.

Following their initial emergence, chiefdoms proliferated throughout much of the southern Eastern Woodlands. The early development of chiefdoms in some areas influenced life in other places. It is possible that disaffected factions calved off already internally segmented systems, resulting in the appearance of chiefdoms elsewhere (Emerson 1991; Scarry 1990b). Structurally similar sociopolitical formations developed around the peripheries of expanding chiefdoms, primarily for reasons of self defense (Clark and Rountree 1993; Potter 1993:169–170; Welch 1990a). Strong chiefdoms also arose at the periphery of geographically large regional systems when these internally segmented societies broke apart (Milner 1986).

Once strong Mississippian chiefdoms were established, their leaders tried to add a measure of stability to threatening social arenas by forging alliances with potential rivals. Exchanges of highly valued symbol-laden objects accompanied efforts to establish amicable social relations among independent chiefs, to signify submission to regionally powerful leaders, or to reward subordinates who had their own supporters at their disposal. Widely recognized tokens of mutual esteem included some Southeastern Ceremonial Complex items that were broadly disseminated among the leading people of different societies. Many of these objects display motifs that highlight the importance to high-ranking people of success in war and of ancestor veneration to legitimize the exalted status of leading figures and their close kin (Brown 1975, 1985).

Even the largest chiefdoms did not remain strong for many generations. Only several centuries spanned the rise, florescence, and decline of the most powerful of these sociopolitical systems (Milner 1986; Pauketat 1992; Peebles 1987b; Steponaitis 1991; also see Scarry, Chapter 5). Much like Dorian Gray's portrait, decay set in long before the facade maintained by the superordinate social stratum crumbled. For example, mound construction at Cahokia continued long after a stout defensive palisade was built around the core of the site and a depopulation of the valley was well underway (Milner 1986).

Chiefdoms formed and collapsed in the Southeast throughout the Late Prehistoric period. A return to the conditions of earlier times was not possible in this highly charged atmosphere of intergroup tensions and inconclusive standoffs between often similarly sized societies, many of which were separated by long stretches of land that were too hazardous to use regularly. Nonetheless, the development of truly stratified sociopolitical systems was inhibited by the internal workings of geographically and socially segmented, kinship-based societies scattered across a landscape that to the end still provided opportunities for population movement, despite quarrels over prime land. Chiefdoms would disappear only after the sixteenth century arrival of Europeans when native numbers declined dramatically and the survivors became embroiled in the economic and political affairs of the newcomers to North America.

The northernmost Mississippian chiefdoms, however, had all but disappeared by the fifteenth century. The reasons behind their demise are not understood, although population movement from valleys to upland settings and the appearance of new groups of people have been documented for some parts of the Midwest (Milner 1986; Santure et al. 1990; Woods and Holley 1991). Later societies in these areas had comparatively more egalitarian social structures. Much like their counterparts to the south, intergroup fighting was a conspicuous part of these people's lives (Milner et al. 1991). Retaliatory attacks sometimes escalated into situations producing large numbers of fatalities and great hardship for villagers tormented by their adversaries. For these groups the lethality of small-scale hit-and-run attacks punctuated by massacres of large numbers of people was every bit as high as that known for conflict-prone, kin-based societies from other parts of the world that have been described in historical and ethnographic accounts.

CONCLUSION

The findings of recent ethnohistoric and archaeological work on the late prehistoric Southeast complement research on chiefdom-level societies elsewhere in the world (e.g., Drennan and Uribe 1987; Earle 1991; Yoffee 1993).

Large and small chiefdoms were organized along similar lines, with the largest being repetitive structures consisting of multiple similarly constituted elements.

The archaeological coverage of the southern Eastern Woodlands is spotty, but enough is known to say that people and powerful chiefdoms were unevenly distributed geographically and temporally. Outright warfare was an ever-present threat that, at times, led to great mortality, group dislocation from prime areas, population gravitation towards strong protectors, intergroup alliances forged for mutual defense, and within-group elaboration of status positions. Political factions constantly sought advantageous positions in heterogeneous social and natural environments, and struggles for domination within and among these societies were the normal state of affairs.

Acknowledgments

We appreciate the comments of Jon Muller, Claire McHale Milner, and Jill Neitzel on a draft of this paper, and the stimulating questions and ideas of the Amerind seminar participants.

CHAPTER NINE

The Organization of Late Precolumbian Societies in the Southwest and Southeast

Linda S. Cordell

George R. Milner

THE ENVIRONMENTS OF THE SOUTHWEST AND SOUTHERN Eastern Woodlands differ greatly, as did the accommodations Precolumbian people made to them. Efforts at comparisons that go beyond obvious differences in natural settings and cultural remains are complicated further by distinct histories of archaeological investigation. They are different enough that most researchers can only view efforts in the "other" area with a sense of bemused detachment. Yet for many of us there remains a nagging worry that questions demanding so much attention elsewhere might be important to work in our own area.

One such topic concerns the nature of the societies that arose late in the Precolumbian era and that were responsible for the construction of large sites and impressive architecture. The label Mississippian is applied to most of these societies in the Midwest and Southeast. In the Southwest, there is no single designation for the diverse archaeological entities known as Chacoan Anasazi, Classic period Hohokam, fourteenth century Western Pueblo, and Paquimé.

Only a few similarities and differences in Precolumbian ways of life and current outlooks on research cropped up repeatedly in the Amerind seminar sessions. In this overview, we highlight several points raised about spatial and temporal variability in the distributions of these peoples, how their societies may have been organized, and the ways historical and ethnographic information influence current interpretations of life in Precolumbian times.

NATURAL ENVIRONMENT

The environments of the Southwest and Southeast differ greatly. As a natural region, the Southwest is united by an arid or semi-arid climate. Temperature, precipitation, and hence biotic zones vary greatly, particularly with elevation. Precipitation, which is the limiting factor for crops, not only is low but fluctuates greatly from one year to the next.

From a Southwesterner's perspective, the Eastern Woodlands, of which the Southeast is a part, appears homogeneously green and incomparably rich in both natural edible resources and well watered, fertile soil. In the East, latitudinal and longitudinal gradients in temperature and precipitation, respectively, exert a strong influence on plant and animal distributions. As a result of these gradients, the Eastern Woodlands are not as homogeneous as they might first appear to Southwesterners. Rather, there is variability among areas in resource richness, yield, and reliability, which would have had a significant effect on ancient human land use patterns. Nevertheless, the Eastern Woodlands supported higher Precolumbian population densities overall than the harsher environment of the Southwest.

SETTLEMENT DISTRIBUTIONS

Late Precolumbian settlement distributions in both the Southwest and Southeast were determined primarily by the availability of water and other resources associated with its presence. The two areas differ, however, in the numbers and broader environmental contexts of desirable places to live. In the Southwest, well-watered locations occur infrequently across a relatively inhospitable, semi-arid landscape. In contrast, such places are not only much more numerous in the Southeast, but they are surrounded by a richer, woodland environment.

Settlement location in the Southeast was also affected by social factors. While late precolumbian peoples preferred to live in the Southeast's major river valleys where resources were abundant and productive, at least in good years (Smith 1978), not all rich locations were equally occupied. Antagonisms discouraged settlement between hostile groups, producing vast areas that were, at best, sparsely occupied and frequently used only as hunting territories.

Both the Southwest and Southeast were marked by major changes in settlement distributions through time. A recurring theme in southwestern archaeology is the large scale abandonment of particular areas that occurred between A.D. 1150 and 1500. These regional abandonments have been attributed to many causes, including conflicts with nomads, internecine warfare among agriculturalists, factionalism that led to community fissioning and population dispersal, epidemic diseases, "cultural proclivities," drought, gradual lowering of water tables, changes in the seasonal distribution of rainfall, flooding of major rivers, and resource depletion (see Cordell 1981, 1984, 1994; Douglass 1929; Gumerman 1988; Upham 1984).

Centers of population likewise shifted over time in the Southeast, although for the most part they are not as well-delineated archaeologically as the large-scale abandonments of the Southwest. In the Midwest, organizationally complex and densely populated Mississippian societies, including Cahokia, disappeared several hundred years after their origin. These shifts in sociopolitical organization and population distribution occurred for as yet unknown reasons during a time when Mississippian chiefdoms to the south continued to thrive. Throughout their geographical distribution, however, individual Missis-

sippian societies seem to have lasted anywhere from a few generations to several centuries (see Scarry, Chapter 5). Thus from an archaeological perspective, both the Southwest and Southeast were highly dynamic demographic landscapes, although the causes of settlement instability were most likely quite different.

CULTURAL DIVISIONS

The Late Precolumbian Southwest and Southeast differ in the cultural divisions which archaeologists have applied to them. In both the Southeast and Midwest, the single label of Mississippian has been applied, implying at least some degree of cultural similarity over an extremely broad territory. In the Southwest by contrast, there is no single designation for the diverse archaeological entities known as Chacoan Anasazi, Classic period Hohokam, fourteenth century Western Pueblos, and Paquimé. These differences in cultural labeling are not just the product of different archaeological research traditions. They reflect, in large part, differences in cultural adaptations to different natural environments.

One other cultural difference characterizes the Southwest and Southeast—that is the kind of development that preceded the Late Precolumbian period. Unlike the Southeast, later developments in the Southwest were not preceded by supralocal entities comparable to those of Adena and Hopewell. There is no reason to believe, however, that there was any direct connection between what are sometimes misleadingly referred to as cultural climaxes in the Eastern Woodlands.

ARCHAEOLOGICAL RESEARCH TRADITIONS

While both Southwestern and Southeastern archaeologists share an overriding interest in how intermediate level societies in their respective areas were organized, they differ markedly in the ease with which they classify these societies as chiefdoms. While this label is applied routinely by Southeastern archaeologists, it is used infrequently and with much controversy in the Southwest. Much of the discussion in the Amerind seminar focused on the extent to which these differences in terminology reflect different archaeological research traditions versus real differences in how Late Precolumbian societies in the two areas were organized.

The Southwest and Southeast represent two different intellectual traditions in archaeology, the former having been greatly influenced by ethnographic data and the latter by historic accounts. Until recently, ethnographic descriptions of Pueblo life were uniformly accepted as appropriate analogs for all Late Precolumbian southwestern societies, in large part because the modern Pueblo Indians of Arizona and New Mexico are recognized descendants of the archaeological Anasazi and Mogollon traditions. The rich ethnographic information about modern Pueblos has been central to archaeological interpretations of ancient southwestern groups, including the apparently non-Puebloan Hohokam.

In contrast to the use of ethnohistoric data in the Southeast, early written sources are underutilized in the Southwest. In most instances, the routes of the earliest chroniclers are well known, and the communities observed at contact are still either inhabited today or they are part of traditional histories actively maintained by indigenous peoples. Continuity since the sixteenth century is far greater in the Southwest than in the Southeast.

Unfortunately, ethnohistoric descriptions of the social and political organization of Southwestern peoples are vague or contradictory (Fish, Chapter 4; Riley 1987; Upham 1986). Riley (1987), one of the few Southwestern scholars who has compiled pertinent ethnohistoric information, found accounts of certain aspects of indigenous societies, including population size, to be unreliable, and others, such as the nature of settlements, poorly described. For these reasons, most archaeologists simply ignore early sources and rely instead on ethnographic findings that uniformly present Pueblos as politically and socially independent communities featuring a nonhierarchical social organization (Upham et al. 1994).

One reason why early explorer chronicles loom so large in current Southeastern research is the success archaeologists have had in tracing the paths of early historic period adventurers and in linking clusters of sites and sometimes specific settlements with the places they visited (Hally et al. 1990; Hudson et al. 1985, 1990). These accounts describe, however obliquely, architecture, site layouts, settlement patterns, and various cultural practices, particularly those having to do with high-ranking people, that are consistent with the archaeological record. Early historic commentaries on vibrant societies, buttressed by solid archaeological data, highlight the extent to which some of these sociopolitical systems changed in the few centuries following a sustained European presence in North America. The inadequacies of information gathered by early ethnographers from numerically diminished and displaced peoples serve as a powerful impetus behind recent work that tackles the formidable problems of collecting useful tidbits from early historic chronicles, evaluating them with other evidence, and synthesizing documentary information and archaeological findings to form a coherent picture of life in earlier times.

Interpreting the Evidence for Ranking

Similar evidence can be used to conclude that Late Precolumbian societies in both the Southwest and Southeast were characterized by an intermediate level of complexity. In both areas, large scale architecture requiring great effort to build and serving as centerpieces of settlement layouts are conspicuous features of many, but not all, sites. Such architecture, coupled with the presence of both large and small sites, implies the existence of multicommunity societies that depended on effective food production strategies and incorporated substantial numbers of people, although archaeologists disagree over the sizes of populations and the specific compositions of their diets. However, further comparisons of these architectural and settlement pattern data, especially when considered in light of the results of mortuary analyses, point to significant differences in how Late Precolumbian Southwestern and Southeastern societies were organized, differences that are not just a function of differing research traditions.

The Southwest

Archaeologists now acknowledge that in some times and places, Southwestern societies encompassed more than one settlement (Cordell 1984; Lekson 1989). The recognition of multicommunity societies is a major departure from ethnographic dogma. Whether or not these particular societies also featured hierarchies of individuals or lineages with differential access to certain kinds of goods and fixed leadership roles is far less clear.

In most examples of Southwestern societies, including those consisting of multiple communities, there is little indication that specific groups of people either lived or were buried any differently than others. The lack of obvious social and economic differentiation among peoples within the same communities (even in large fourteenth century villages) is so marked that one key proponent for the existence of status hierarchies described elite individuals as controlling sacred information rather than goods indicative of differential wealth (Upham 1982; Upham and Plog 1986).

There is little evidence that the large scale structures built in the Late Precolumbian Southwest were used as elite residences. The Great Houses of Chaco Canyon and the Chacoan outliers were not palaces. They are most often considered examples of public architecture used for purposes other than, and in addition to, ordinary domestic tasks and were not restricted to only a few high-status people and their immediate households (Judge 1989; Marshall et al. 1979; Powers et al. 1983). Similarly, access to Anasazi great kivas is also thought to have been open to community members (Marshall et al. 1979; Vivian and Reiter 1965). The large fourteenth century villages of New Mexico and Arizona, as well as Paquimé in Chihuahua, seem to have lacked special elite residential precincts (Minnis 1984). The sole exception to this pattern is among the Classic period Hohokam. During the Soho phase (ca. A.D. 1150–1300), houses were built on top of platform mounds, and the mounds were surrounded by adobe walls and compounds (Fish 1989).

In the Southwest, there is also little indication that high rank for any particular group was acknowledged in late precolumbian funerary proceedings. People who lived in large and long lasting settlements that were the principal sites of multicommunity societies did tend to be buried with more materials from more distant sources than contemporaneous villages elsewhere (Mathien 1993; Ravesloot 1988). There is a handful of exceptionally rich burials that are remarkable precisely because they are so atypical for the region (Frisbie 1978; Reyman 1978). There are also instances in which people belonging to roughly equivalent social groups were marked by distinctive mortuary treatment, as at Grasshopper Pueblo (Reid 1989).

Paquimé is exceptional in this respect, as it is in so many other ways. There, elite people were interred as secondary urn burials, with specific, rare grave goods, and they were buried in areas of the site that were not locations of the burials of ordinary people (Ravesloot 1988:68–72). The multiple interments in Room 33 at Pueblo Bonito and the buildings on Classic period Hohokam platform mounds may indicate the sporadic appearance of an ambitious leader or a short period during which high-status people exercised authority within a small geographic area (Akins 1986:115; Fish 1989). It is true that Southwestern archaeologists have rarely examined burial populations in such a way that clearly demonstrates either the presence or

absence of groups of elite individuals (Plog 1985; Upham and Plog 1986). However, if exalted positions were indicated by robust patterns sustained over long periods of time and broad geographical regions, it is likely that they would have been identified by now.

The Southeast

It is generally accepted that ranked societies, or chiefdoms, existed in the Southeast. There is solid archaeological evidence for access by a few people to disproportionately large amounts of labor and goods, particularly fancy prestige-denoting objects. This evidence is consistent with sixteenth century and later commentaries on social relations within native societies. While the term chiefdom is associated with entirely too much unwanted baggage, it is evocative of societies where leaders held, however tenuously, inherited positions of authority in more-or-less well-defined, generally small areas and exercised some control over their followers through custom, persuasion, and intimidation.

Mississippian societies have long been recognized as consisting of numerous large and small contemporaneous settlements, some of which were politically more important than others (Smith 1978). It is generally assumed that well-delineated site concentrations yielding stylistically uniform artifact inventories are archaeologically visible manifestations of the disposition of people who maintained reasonably frequent interaction with each other. In several better known regions, site clusters assumed to be crude approximations of Mississippian chiefdoms are reasonably consistent with the writings of early historic adventurers who passed through these areas (Hally 1993; Hally et al. 1990; Hudson et al. 1985, 1990).

Unlike the largest of the Late Prehistoric societies in the Southwest, Mississippian societies clearly distinguished high ranking from ordinary people. These distinctions were readily visible and were a pervasive part of everyday affairs. They were repeated continuously during life and with great fanfare at death in numerous societies, both large and small, distributed across a broad geographical area through many centuries.

Archaeologically ostentatious structures and community layouts underscored a clear separation of space used for various purposes by peoples of different ranks. The dwellings of leaders and their close kin were distinguished by their size, placement on mounds, and central position adjacent to public space used for various community functions (Anderson 1996b). High status people were also distinguished by their appearance. In many places, they possessed certain kinds of symbols and artifacts, such as falcon-related regalia and monolithic axes, which legitimized their high status positions by emphasizing their prowess in war and affiliation with venerable ancestors (Brown 1975, 1985). These distinctions between certain members of leading lineages and commoners were so noticeable that sixteenth and seventeenth century Europeans often called attention to the special dress of important people and the ways their followers acted toward them (De Pratter 1991).

Just as Mississippian elites were distinguished by highly visible and redundant accouterments of their special status throughout their lives, so too were they distinguished at death (Brown 1975, 1985; Larson 1971a; Milner 1984; Peebles and Kus 1977). This status related differentiation is so striking that it was recognized by Southeastern archaeologists long before the development of sophisticated mortuary analyses. Early excavators soon discovered that elite burials could be found with large quantities of valued goods in mounds at large sites.

Mississippian mortuary practices differed from those in the Late Precolumbian Southwest not only by the obvious special treatment of highly ranked people but also in their prior history. The institutionalization of social inequality evident in differential burial treatment had a long history in the Eastern Woodlands. In many places during Middle Woodland times—and even earlier in the Adena mounds of the central Ohio River Valley—a few individuals were singled out for special burial in mounds and with treasured objects (Brown 1978; Webb and Snow 1945).

What distinguishes Mississippian societies from their predecessors is that the differentiation between high and low ranking people evidenced in mortuary treatment was also a pervasive part of everyday life. In Mississippian societies, high status positions were constantly being legitimized, largely because attainment and maintenance of these positions were a function of the combined roles of ability and descent. Perhaps because accouterments of high rank and architecture associated with important people played such an integral part in legitimizing inequalities in social standing, there was greater homogeneity in their expression in Mississippian societies than among their Southwestern counterparts.

CONCLUSION

The strong orientation toward social ranking in the Southeast as opposed to the more egalitarian emphasis in the Southwest presumably had much to do with differences in resource productivity and reliability. In the Southeast, ambitious leaders of favorably positioned social groups were often presented with occasions to accumulate surpluses through hard work, to recruit more followers, and to mobilize the labor at hand for their own benefit. When shortfalls occurred, these people typically had a broader array of choices for alternative foods than Southwestern villagers, although some privation was still likely to accompany failures in the harvests of dietary staples.

The Southwest was a less productive and more uncertain environment. Priority seems to have been placed on social strategies to distribute risks among more-or-less equivalent social groups within and between settlements. Ambitious leaders arose for short periods in several places, but they were not able to destroy the social leveling mechanisms and egalitarian ethos that for good survival reasons dominated Southwestern societies (see Sebastian 1992).

Much remains to be learned about variation in the structure, scale, longevity, and positioning of sociopolitical systems within both the Southwest and Southeast, but as a whole the Southwestern societies differed greatly from their southeastern counterparts. Aspiring leaders in Mississippian societies seem to have employed any means at their disposal to reinforce and legitimize individual or lineage power, including the use of highly visible and always present reminders of distinctions in social rank. The messages sent about the social standing of certain people, the distinction between them and their followers, and the legitimacy of their exalted positions was neither ambiguous nor subtle. In the Southwest, considerable effort was taken to conceal nascent hierarchical distinctions and to dampen the development of differential prestige and influence. While Southwestern societies seem to have had elaborate mechanisms of within and between community integration, these forms of sociopolitical organization were different from those of the Southeastern chiefdoms where the high rank of a small number of people was emphasized repeatedly.

CHAPTER TEN

A Peregrine View of Macroregional Systems in the North American Southwest, A.D. 750–1250

David R. Wilcox

THE NOTION OF A SOUTHWESTERN "MACROREGION" has its origins in the culture area concept of the early twentieth century (e.g., Wissler 1914). Beginning with A. V. Kidder's (1924) "An Introduction to the Study of Southwestern Archaeology," which quickly achieved a consensus in the first Pecos Conference (Kidder 1927), subsequent scholars have generally assumed that the practice of maize horticulture and pottery-making served to differentiate a set of "Southwestern" cultures from their neighbors in California, the Great Basin, the Rockies, and the western Plains. Without pausing to think much about the "external" boundaries, or what made the Southwestern culture area distinctive, workers in this field almost immediately began dismembering it into six material-culture classifications regarded as "cultural traditions" (Colton 1939; Gladwin et al. 1937; Hawley 1936; Haury 1936; Jennings 1978; Kidder 1936; Kroeber 1928; Morss 1931; Roberts 1937; Rudy 1953; Steward 1933; Willey and Phillips 1958). Hence we have the Western and Eastern Anasazi, Fremont, Mogollon, Patayan, and Hohokam concepts.

This division into six cultural traditions did not wholly inhibit discussion of macroregional interaction among them, or between them and their non-Southwestern neighbors. However, in keeping with the categorical thinking of the cultural-historical approach, what was usually measured was "influence" of one cultural tradition on another.

Today, the "cultural-historical" calculus devised during the first surge of Southwestern studies remains central to the way most people working in this field still choose to talk about what they are doing and what they are finding. It is, however, under attack (Speth 1988; Tainter and Plog 1994); and as more and more archaeologists begin to address organizational issues, with the objective of understanding behavior and history and not simply material-culture patterning, new ways of talking about archaeological data will probably have to be devised.

As a transitional strategy, I have advocated efforts to redefine some traditional categories, suggesting the concept of a "regional system" as a more meaningful way to understand sets of neighboring populations who clearly were interacting with one another (Wilcox 1979a, 1980, 1987a). The distribution of red-on-buff pottery, for example, does indicate such interaction and "Hohokam" can be redefined as a "regional system," thus shifting the referent from artifacts to people (see Chang 1961). But there are conceptual pitfalls in this approach as well, as McGuire (1991) and Gregory (1991) have made clear. If we think of a Hohokam regional system in terms of the ceremonial exchange network indicated by ballcourt distributions (Wilcox 1987a; Wilcox and Sternberg 1983), how should we refer to the peoples in the Tucson Basin once they stopped using ballcourts after A.D. 1000 (Doelle and Wallace 1991)? If we invoke the economic concept of dependency in such a definition (Crown and Judge 1991:1), then the Hohokam "regional" system would have to be drawn much smaller, especially after A.D. 1000 (see Altschul 1993; Gregory 1991:188, 190–191; Wilcox 1991b). A "macroregional" concept seems necessary.

It has also become popular to refer to the Chacoan and Mimbres "regional systems" (Crown and Judge 1991; Lekson 1986c, 1991, 1992a; Wilcox 1988a). I would argue that there were dependency relationships in the Chacoan case, as the idea of "outliers" suggests (see Wilcox 1993, 1995), but *not* on the scale now seen in great house distributions (Toll 1991; cf. Lekson 1992a). To the contrary, in the Chacoan case, a set of contiguous regions formed a larger, *macroregional* system of interaction (Wilcox 1995) analogous to what has been called "peer polity interaction" (Renfrew and Cherry 1986).

Three other examples of "peer polity" interaction in the Southwest, but differently structured from one another and from the Chacoan case, are the Salado macroregion (McGuire 1991:262, 268; Wilcox and Sternberg 1983:244), the Paquimé regional or macroregional system (McGuire 1991; Minnis 1989; Wilcox 1991a) and the protohistoric Pueblos (Ford et al. 1972; Kintigh 1994; Schroeder 1979; Wilcox 1991a). I will thus use the concept of a "macroregion" in two senses: 1) for the whole Southwest and beyond; and 2) for smaller-scale interaction spheres where the "region" is tightly defined in economic, political, or ideological terms.

The systematics of Southwestern archaeology is thus in a transitional period. This makes it difficult to talk about the assignment of this chapter, macroregional interactions and their implications. Nor is there space to talk about all aspects of these problems in the detail they demand (see also McGuire et al. 1994). What I have chosen to do, therefore, is to focus on the Hohokam and Chacoan cases. To set the stage for these discussions, I first take a critical look at the traditional models of long-distance exchange in the Southwest, thus defining several basic spatial parameters of the discussion that follows. I then turn to a critical reassessment of several key chronological parameters. After briefly discussing several useful theoretical concepts, I analyze the structure and history of the macroregional systems characterized by Hohokam ballcourts and Chacoan great houses. Several significant ways that interaction occurred between these systems are also identified. I conclude by briefly outlining some of the research that is needed in other related

domains of macroregional interaction as we pursue the task of reconceptualizing Southwestern archaeology.

SPATIAL PARAMETERS OF LONG-DISTANCE EXCHANGE

Not all archaeologists in the 1930s were anthropologists. Some of them were trained in geography or zoology, and they used studies of artifacts to understand behavior or population dynamics (Brand 1935, 1938; Colton 1918, 1941, 1960; Sauer and Brand 1931). They thus pioneered attempts to identify economic behavior and to define patterns of long-distance exchange. Their maps were the first models of macroregional interaction in the Southwest (for example, see Figure 10.1). Together with the later work of Tower (1945; Figure 10.2), their work has, until recently, been accepted uncritically as definitive. New data, however, today require a fundamental revision of these models, and thus necessitate a general rethinking of the structure of macroregional interaction in the Southwest.

Here, I confine myself to only one positive and one critical comment. Based on his extensive knowledge of Sonoran and Chihuahuan archaeology, Brand (1938) shows a shell-procurement route along the Yaqui River, linking the Guaymas area to the Mimbres and Paquimé areas (see Figure 10.1). Di Peso's discovery of nearly four million shells at Paquimé, most of which were *Nassarius* (formerly called *Alectrion*), led him to postulate a Yaqui River route of access (Di Peso et al. 1974:vol. 6). Although, to my knowledge, there are no archaeological data from either the Guaymas coast or the Yaqui valleys to confirm such a route, two other facts seem to lend additional support. First, many of the fish designs on Mimbres Classic Black-on-white pots portray an assemblage of marine fish found in the Guaymas area (Jett and Moyle 1986). Such accurate renderings also suggest that the potters would have had to see the fish. Second, *Nassarius* shells are present in Classic Mimbres sites (Bradfield 1931:62; Cosgrove and Cosgrove 1932:Plate 77) at a time before they are common in the Tucson and Phoenix basins (McGuire and Howard 1987). Thus, it appears that after A.D. 1000, when Hohokam elements generally drop out of Mimbres assemblages (LeBlanc 1983; Minnis 1985, Woosley and McIntyre 1996), the Mimbres villagers had discovered their own access corridor to shell valuables, independent of the Hohokam. This corridor was also used later by the polity of Paquimé.

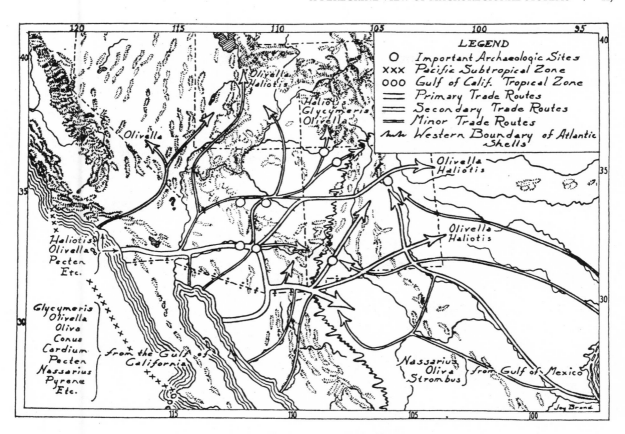

Figure 10.1.   Brand's (1938) long-distance shell exchange map of the Southwest.

The greatest error in Brand's (1938) model is the over-emphasis on a route from San Diego to Yuma and the Hohokam area (along today's Interstate 8; see Figure 10.1). If such a connection existed, it could have brought *Haliotis* and *Olivella* into the Hohokam area from the Pacific; and the Hohokam could have then passed these shells on to the Anasazi and Mogollon further north and east. Haury (1937) in fact did advocate this concept of the Hohokam as "middlemen" in a pan-Southwestern long-distance exchange system, and Brand (1938) supported this view. Tower (1945:40; see also Malouf 1940) also thought this must be the case (Figure 10.2).

In fact, there are alternative routes for bringing Pacific shells into the Southwest, which bypass the Hohokam. One is a pedestrian route across the northern Colorado Plateau; today it is called the "Old Spanish Trail" (Hafen and Hafen 1954; Figure 10.3). There are other alternatives as well, including a Mohave trail or La Paz route. Equally important is the fact that there is no evidence in the lower Colorado River area to support the claim of a major shell connection to the west prior to the Protohistoric period (Rogers 1941; Vokes 1984; Warren 1984). These findings greatly diminish the probability that the Hohokam were the suppliers of shell to the Anasazi, a conclusion that Haury (1976:305, 321), too, had begun to accept. This is not to say, however, that there were not patterns of connectivity at certain times that did facilitate a movement of some Hohokam-style shell bracelets into Anasazi sites (e.g., see Lightfoot and Etzkorn 1993:191).

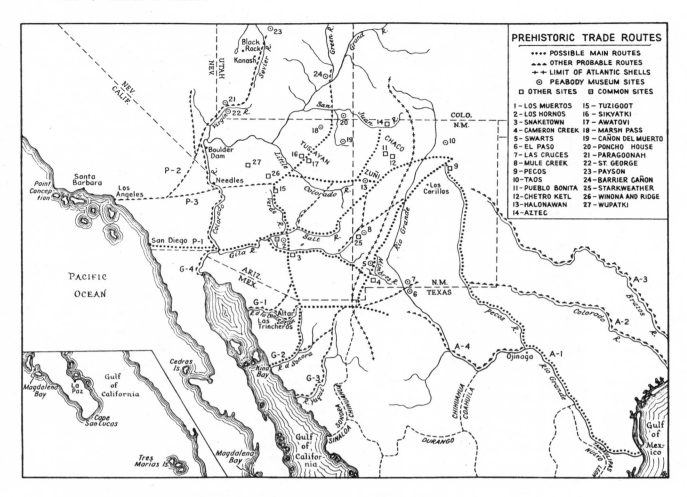

Figure 10.2.   Tower's (1945) map of long-distance shell exchange routes.

Two important points can be made by comparing Brand's (1938) model with Colton's (1941) later one. The discovery of the so-called "magician" burial at Ridge Ruin (McGregor 1943) with its whole *Haliotis* shell with the holes plugged up with asphaltum, its *Haliotis* fish-hook blanks used as ear bobs, and its cap of *Dentalium* shell (all from the Pacific coast) led Colton (1941) to propose an eastern extension of the Mohave trail (Farmer 1935), which went from Santa Barbara and San Bernardino via Cahon Pass past Victorville and the eastern edge of Antelope Valley to the Mohave Valley (Figure 10.3). Colton (1941) thought that this trail would have followed Route 66 (today's Interstate 40) from the Mohave Valley across the Cohonina area to Flagstaff. Further support for this idea is provided by the facts that great quantities

of *Olivella* have been found in the Flagstaff area (Museum of Northern Arizona collections), the Verde Valley (Caywood and Spicer 1935), and the Prescott area (Barnett 1974), some of which has been identified as *O. baetica* (M. W. Knapp in Barnett 1974, 1978). The second major point is that the "magician" burial and many other shell assemblages in the Flagstaff area include *mixtures* of *Glycymeris, Laevicardium* and other Gulf of California shells with Pacific shells (Colton 1941; McGregor 1943; Stanislawski 1963).

Some Hohokam painted pottery has been found in the greater Los Angeles area (Moratto 1984:359, 390–391) and at Bouse (Harner 1958), suggesting at least one of the ways that some *Haliotis* and *Olivella* reached the Hohokam (Gross 1990). Hohokam-style shell beads

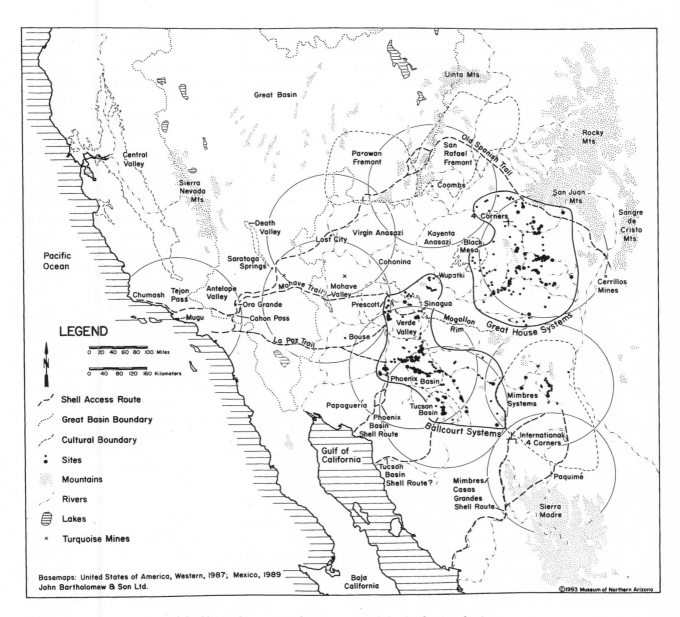

Figure 10.3. A current model of long-distance exchange connectivity in the Southwest.

119

made from *Glycymeris* have also been found at the Oro Grande site near Victorville, California (King 1983; Warren 1984), so the Mohave trail may also have facilitated such connectivity. Logically, we might also suppose that *O. dama* might have moved northward along the Colorado River corridor via the Mohave Valley to sites such as Main Ridge (a.k.a Lost City)—where it is found (Lyneis et al. 1989:69–71)—and thence eastward. The chief implication that may be drawn is that the Hohokam were probably not the great "middlemen" of pan-Southwestern shell exchange as previously thought.

Claims have also been made for the Hohokam as the great purveyors of cotton textiles (Haury 1950; Kent 1957), but the fact that the Anasazi fancy weaves contrast with those predominant in Hohokam assemblages (Kent 1957) suggests that such textiles may not have moved across very great distances (Wilcox 1987b). As with shell, however, the Flagstaff area is exceptional, being a place where Hohokam-style cotton textiles were produced and did accumulate in large quantities (Stanislawski 1963). At Wupatki, which lies at the edge of both the Anasazi and Hohokam worlds, we also find a conjunction of a Hohokam-style ballcourt (the only one made with sandstone masonry), a great kiva-like "amphitheater," and a Chacoan-like great house (though one with rectangular room-kivas and not circular kivas embedded in the front of the roomblock). To explain these facts, and at the same time to construct for the North American Southwest a new, comprehensive model of macroregional interaction in the A.D. 750–1250 period, are the central tasks of this paper. To do so it is first necessary, however, to address several key chronological issues and then to consider several comparative, theoretical possibilities.

SEVERAL KEY CHRONOLOGICAL PARAMETERS

Southwestern archaeologists can be justly proud of the progress that has been made in constructing cultural chronologies. The exact information afforded by tree-ring dates is often little short of miraculous, although a general understanding of the complexities of translating the information from tree-ring dates into an inference about the date of a target event is still woefully inadequate (see Dean 1978). Radiocarbon and archaeomagnetic dating have also proved helpful, though the problems of their interpretation are even more difficult and puzzling (Berry 1982; Dean 1978; Eighmy and

Sternberg 1990; Schiffer 1982; Smiley 1985). Ceramic seriation and ceramic cross-dating are both well developed techniques in the Southwest, although the calendar calibration of these findings depends on tree-ring and other "independent" methods and thus is also subject to similar interpretive difficulties (Ambler 1985; Downum 1988; Fairley and Geib 1989). All chronologies are necessarily inferential constructs. Sound chronologies, however, are the first requirement of any historical model (Bloch 1953), and this is most true when we attempt to correlate chronologies on a macroregional scale where small errors at a local or regional level can be magnified into major misconceptions. In the hope of identifying such pitfalls it is necessary to review several current, widely-held assumptions about Southwestern chronologies.

Hohokam

Criticisms of the original Snaketown chronology led Haury (1976) to seek new data and then to propose some modest revisions. Beginning with my dissertation (Wilcox and Shenk 1977:176–180), his new chronological model was promptly attacked on many grounds, later causing Haury (1987:249) to remark that "modifying the Snaketown chronology has become a national sport." The most recent attempt to bring order to this seeming chaos has been by Dean (1991) who chose to leave archaeological judgments about associations and phase assignments to others. In my view, some of these phase assignments are clearly wrong (e.g., dates from Los Solares [a.k.a. La Ciudad]). As a result, I think that Dean's Hohokam chronology is skewed, particularly in the temporal correlations for the so-called Colonial and Sedentary periods. Further work, with better controlled data, is necessary before the Hohokam chronology can be reliably used for comparative purposes. In what follows I employ the chronology that I have discussed elsewhere (Wilcox 1979a, 1991d).

Chaco

Based as it is on tree-ring dating, the Chaco chronology is less prone to fundamental disputes. One parameter is problematic, however: the end of the occupation in the canyon (Dean 1992; Judge 1989). The latest tree-ring date is often said to be A.D. 1132, forgetting the 1178v date from a piece of charcoal in secondary refuse in Kin Kletso (Vivian and Matthews 1964:171). The 1132 date is best viewed as a construction date, unrelated to the question of abandonment (Wilcox 1975). Already in 1960, stratigraphic data from Chetro Ketl—and the late Kin Kletso date—led Vivian and Reiter (1960:50) to suggest that, "This was the period after 1100 when there was little new construction in the community—a period of probably slow decline, but which could have lasted into the last quarter of the century." A great deal of other stratigraphic data (Wilcox 1993) further supports this view, implying that occupation in Chaco Canyon great houses was continuous up to the time that Mesa Verde Black-on-white pottery was introduced sometime after A. D. 1175–1200 (Breternitz et al. 1974; Blinman and Wilson 1989; Morris 1939). Similar continuity is also being advocated for great houses in the Animas drainage (McKenna and Toll 1992; Stein and McKenna 1988).

It now can be shown that ceramic evidence strongly supports the inference of continuity in the occupation of Pueblo del Arroyo, Pueblo Bonito, Kin Kletso, and probably other Chacoan great houses throughout the twelfth century. Pottery recovered in the 1920s excavation of Pueblo del Arroyo was recently restudied by Windes (1985), who defined a "Chaco-McElmo" type that was predominant at both that site and in Pueblo Bonito's latest deposits. Citing multiple tree-ring (construction) dates and one archaeomagnetic date, Windes suggested A.D. 1100–1150 as the age of the Chaco-McElmo type. As he recognized, much of it has Sosi-style designs, but several of the sherds illustrated (Windes 1985; Windes and McKenna 1989) are clearly in the later Flagstaff Black-on-white style (Phil Geib, personal communication; see Windes 1985:Figure 3a:rows 2:3 and 4:1, Figure 4:row 4:1, Figure 5:row 4:4). Flagstaff Black-on-white, which is predominant at Wupatki Pueblo and in Elden phase sites such as Ridge Ruin, is well dated between A.D. 1150 and 1250 (Anderson 1980; Ambler 1985; Downum 1988; Fairley and Geib 1989). Blinman and Wilson (1989) also recognize the Flagstaff Black-on-white connections of McElmo and Chaco-McElmo, stating that these types have their period of greatest predominance in the A.D. 1150–1200 period.

When, then, did the "decline" of the Chaco Canyon great houses and the system linked to them occur? Judge (1989) and others (Dean 1992; Vivian 1990) have suggested that its decline was well under way by 1150. Some support for this view is apparent in the crudeness of the latest construction in Chetro Ketl great kivas (Vivian and Reiter 1960) and Bryan's (1954) dating of arroyo cutting in the canyon. However, Lekson (1984a:271–272) has aptly pointed out that much of the most exotic of

Chacoan valuables (macaws, turquoise, shell) occurs on the uppermost floors—a conclusion supported by data in Pepper (1920) and Judd (1964). I believe this evidence indicates that the Chacoan polity continued to be a major power throughout the twelfth century. A corollary of this conclusion is that Chaco was therefore a contemporary of Wupatki (which began in the middle A.D. 1100s and lasted to perhaps A.D. 1250 [Burchett 1990]). Thus, the cultural likenesses of the Wupatki data to things Chacoan (Stanislawski 1963), including the presence of 41 macaws (Hargrave 1970), copper bells, and turquoise, very likely indicates some kind of connectivity with Chaco Canyon.

Mimbres and Paquimé

It was once argued that the Classic Mimbres phase lasted to about A.D. 1200 (Danson 1957; Graybill 1975; Wheat 1955), but a decade or so ago a revision of the Mimbres sequence was proposed that would place abandonment of these sites around A.D. 1130 or 1150 (Anyon et al. 1981; LeBlanc 1983; LeBlanc and Whalen 1980). This argument, which appeared to fit the data then available, is tied to an evaluation of ceramic connections of the subsequent Black Mountain phase to the Medio period material at Paquimé, which LeBlanc (1980:803) argued fell into the period A.D. 1150–1300. Furthermore, "the later Cliff phase sites no longer show any close resemblance to Casas Grandes, indicating that the Casas Grandes interactive sphere was no longer in existence by the Cliff phase."

Many more data are available today that force a profound revision of LeBlanc's Mimbres and Medio period models. Local tree-ring sequences have been developed that tie the Mimbres-Paquimé areas into the Southwestern master tree-ring chronology (Dean and Ravesloot 1993). Scott's (1966) Paquimé chronology has been upheld, but not Di Peso's (1974) interpretation of it, nor that suggested by LeBlanc (1980). Reexamination of the wood specimens from Paquimé (Dean and Ravesloot 1993) has shown that all or most sapwood rings are missing, and a retrodiction that considers this results in a Medio period chronology of A.D. 1250–1500, with the greatest period of fluorescence at the site falling in the later A.D. 1300s. Paquimé thus was contemporaneous with Kwilleylekia (A.D. 1380: Dean, personal communication), other Cliff phase sites (Nelson and LeBlanc 1986), and the Joyce Well site (A.D. 1390:DeAtley 1980).

Current tree-ring data from the Mattocks Ruin, NAN Ranch, and Saige-MacFarland sites suggest construction continued in these sites into the A.D. 1120s (Dean, personal communication). Unlike the Chacoan great houses, where the tree-ring dates come from lower-story rooms, and thus may not be representative of the latest construction events in the upper stories (which were the first to erode), the Mimbres dates derive from burned rooms (Dean, personal communication). Even so, the question of abandonment of these sites is better addressed by looking at the ceramic cross-dating of the latest assemblages found in them. That was the procedure of those earlier workers who suggested occupation to about A.D. 1200. As for the Black Mountain phase, the tentative date of A.D. 1179 (LeBlanc 1980:803; LeBlanc and Whalen 1980:532) for the Montoya site is not credible (Dean and Ravesloot 1993:101). The dates that are credible (LeBlanc and Whalen 1980) fall into the A.D. 1200s, and the ceramic cross-dating fits that time frame too (see also Creel 1994). These Black Mountain components may thus have been contemporaneous with the beginnings of the Medio period in the middle A.D. 1200s.

Discussion

Recent attempts to correlate Southwestern cultural sequences have focused on A.D. 1150 as a "hinge point" of general significance (Cordell and Gumerman 1989a; Lekson 1993). The Hohokam, Chacoan, and Mimbres "regional systems" are all thus presumed to have "collapsed" at that time. The present analysis suggests otherwise. True, the Chacoan and Mimbres systems do still appear to disappear about the *same* time, but those processes probably occurred in the early-to-middle A.D. 1200s, not around A.D. 1150. The Hohokam ballcourt network significantly shrank about A.D. 1000—at the beginning of the Classic Mimbres phase—expanded northward in the A.D. 1000s, experienced a major internal reorganization about A.D. 1100 with the abandonment of Snaketown and certain other sites (Gregory 1991; Gregory and Huckleberry 1994), and was again transformed in the middle A.D. 1200s, "collapsing" about a century later, just before the Paquimé macroregional system began to reach its apogee (Wilcox 1995). About A.D. 1150 there was not a collapse *but a coming together* of a Southwestern-wide macroregional system that then experienced massive disintegration and reorganization in the middle A.D. 1200s. These conclusions contrast with some of my own earlier positions (see Wilcox and Sternberg 1983; Wilcox 1987a), but I believe they best fit current facts. While continued testing of these propositions is needed, they can

properly serve here as a set of assumptions needed to construct a new macroregional conception of Southwestern prehistory.

SOME THEORETICAL CONSIDERATIONS

Unlike the Southeast, where a broad consensus has formed that one or another conception of chiefdom organization best characterizes the kinds of social complexity found there, no such agreement has been achieved in the Southwest (Wilcox 1991c; Whittlesey and Ciolek-Torrello 1992). Ethnographically, the issue is moot (Wilcox 1981a), and no analyses have attempted to trace the transformations of socioceremonial and kinship organizations of Southwestern societies, as has been done in the Southeast (e.g., Knight 1981). Several reasons for this lack of agreement are that: 1) few exceptionally "high status" burials have been found in the Southwest, and nothing like the spectacular deposits found at Cahokia's Mound 72 (Fowler 1974); 2) the evidence for "attached specialists" or craft-specialization is everywhere quite weak in the Southwest (Cordell and Gumerman 1989a; Crown and Judge 1991); 3) the evidence for violence or warfare has, until recently, remained scattered and poorly known (but see Turner 1993; Wilcox and Haas 1994a,b); and 4) among the protohistoric Pueblos few individuals stand out, leading even those sympathetic to the hypothesis of social complexity to postulate "councils" and "ethnic alliances" rather than "chiefdoms" (Wilcox 1981a, 1991c). Where, then, is the evidence for "chiefs?" It has seemed quite reasonable to many archaeologists to conclude with Toll (1985) that, if there were chiefs at Pueblo Bonito, Pepper (1909) found both of them a century ago—and one died violently!

Another reason that the nature of Southwestern political organization has remained uncertain is that appropriate bodies of theory have not been brought to bear to interpret these data. A paper by Blanton et al. (1996) points to a 20 year old theoretical distinction by Renfrew (1974) between individualizing and group-oriented chiefdoms (Table 10.1) as a point of departure for moving forward. These distinctions seem particularly apt in comparing the Southwest and Southeast.

Clearly, in the Southwest, the evidence for individualizing chiefdoms is generally lacking in those places we have most often looked for it, the biggest sites and larg-

Table 10.1. Renfrew's (1974) Comparison of Individualizing and Group-Oriented Chiefdoms

Group-Oriented	Individualizing
Low wealth contrasts	High wealth contrasts
Leaders difficult to identify	Leaders easy to identify
Modesty	Snobbery
Only part-time craft specialists	Evident craft specialization
Internal peace	Warfare/fortifications
Low level of technology	High level of technology
Low ecological diversity	High ecological diversity
Periodic redistribution (communal)	Permanent redistribution (prestige)
Impressive group monuments	Monuments individualized
Emphasize group activities	De-emphasize group activities

est "regional systems." But the criteria for identifying group-oriented, or corporately structured, chiefdoms in which a council or assembly of corporate leaders governed, are readily documentable in the Phoenix Basin, Chaco Canyon, and the protohistoric Pueblos. The proposal of Blanton et al. (1996) that a "dual-processual" approach should be taken also has much to recommend it to Southwestern archaeologists. In Mesoamerica, they find that the ruling arrangements at Teotihuacan and Tenochtitlán, for example, were "corporate," while in peripheral areas away from these centers individualizing organizations emphasizing a "network" strategy are to be expected. Such a pattern may also be identified in the Southwest.

Another conceptual model that may prove helpful in the analysis of Southwestern macroregional organizations is Southall's (1956, 1988a, 1991) notion of a "segmentary state." He defines this type of organization "as one in which the spheres of ritual suzerainty and political sovereignty do not coincide. The former extends widely towards a flexible, changing periphery. The latter is confined to the central, core domain" (Southall 1988b:52). Originally developed to account for the Alur society in Africa (Southall 1956), this model has now been fruitfully extended to a variety of societies in India (Southall 1988a), and I shall argue that it has even wider applica-

bility. The brilliant analysis by Fowler and Stein (1992) of the Chacoan system is, in fact, a model of ritual suzerainty whose political implications they sensed but did not develop. Southall's (1988a, 1991) perspective can help to draw out the political implications of their ideas.

A segmentary state can be organized either corporately or as an individualizing polity (Southall 1988a). It is thus a cross-cutting conceptual model to that of Renfrew (1974) and Blanton et al. (1996). Furthermore, both approaches open up ways to understand the increase or decrease in social complexity as changes in the mode of production (Southall 1988a,b) or in the ideology of social and religious integration (Blanton et al. 1996; Zantwijk 1985) are brought about.

Finally, the archaeological methods developed by Paynter (1982) to measure social stratification can help us to evaluate several aspects of the Chacoan macroregional system. Like Wolf (1966), Paynter defines surpluses in terms of a set of funds, such as a seed replacement fund, a ceremonial fund, or a fund of rent. Following Harvey (1973), Paynter recognizes two other basic funds: a settlement fund of "crystallized surplus" and a transportation fund. Paynter's (1982:33) dramatic insight identifies the components of settlement pattern both: 1) as outcomes produced by the mobilization of labor and the production of surpluses to create them and; 2) as places that regulate subsequent circulation of social surpluses, thus reproducing the relations of social order.

The accumulation of surplus involves a transportation cost. Paynter (1982:38) argues that the way an elite addresses this problem is to pass the cost on to others. To reduce the cost of moving police (warriors) between fixed resources, the resources can be concentrated, thus reducing the elite's transportation costs. In that way, "fewer police [warriors] could protect more resources with less movement and thus reduce elites' indirect transport costs" (Paynter 1982:33). I shall argue that the fixed resources of massive Chacoan great houses and Hohokam platform mounds represent just such a pattern. As for smaller, outlying elite centers, Paynter (1982) sees them as "entrepots" (Casagrande et al. 1964) that facilitated the flow of surplus from the peripheries to the core area. The fixed resources of entrepots permit them to bulk up surpluses accumulated from client "frontier towns" and then to efficiently transport them to the core, skimming off a portion of the surpluses for the entrepot's use.

One of Paynter's examples is particularly interesting when thinking about how the Chaco system may have worked. Suppose the core and entrepot elites were able to stimulate infrequent interactions with outlying communities involving periodic labor services (or pilgrimages) to the core or the entrepot. To solve the problem of increasing the flow of food to the elite, "smaller order entrepots [can be deployed]. These more specialized, lower order entrepots include both military outposts to physically coerce flows of surplus along with provision of more benignly extracted goods-services" (Paynter 1982:139).

How are we to decide if a system such as this was operative? Firstly, Paynter (1982:155) concludes that, "If one system dominates the others, this results in a single settlement system in the study area, approximated by the rank size rule." Fortunately, there are sufficient data from the Chacoan case to at least begin this kind of analysis (see also Neitzel 1989a). Secondly, he expects that the economic landscape around a core area will be differentiated into production zones à la the German economic geographer Von Tunen (Paynter 1982; see also Chisolm 1979). Such zonation has been documented in the Phoenix and Tucson basins during the Classic period (Crown 1987; Wilcox 1988b; S. Fish et al. 1984), and perhaps the Chaco Canyon irrigation systems (Vivian 1974, 1990, 1991) qualify as such a zone at the center of that core area.

THE HOHOKAM MACROREGIONAL BALLCOURT SYSTEM

In 1979, I proposed that the culture-area conception of the Hohokam should be redefined as a "regional system" (Wilcox 1979a, 1980). Based on a distributional study of oval, earthen features that arguably were ballcourts where fertility rituals were performed, I later proposed the model of a regional ceremonial exchange system centered on the Phoenix Basin (Wilcox 1987a; Wilcox and Sternberg 1983). While some Hohokam sites are larger than others, and about twenty percent of the ballcourts are twice as large as the rest, both types of court are widely distributed and the general picture is one of redundancy (Wilcox 1987a, 1991b). The distribution of ballcourt sites is markedly linear along the river valleys where irrigation was practiced, and there is a convergence in the Phoenix Basin that could have provided populations there with a net economic advantage from ceremonial exchanges (Wilcox 1987a), but I know of no evidence that they exercised any political or even economic control (see Upham et al. 1994).

New data developed by Doelle and Wallace (1991) on the age of ballcourts in the Tucson Basin, by Dart (personal communication) in the lower San Pedro Valley, and by recent work in the greater Flagstaff area (Wilcox et al. n.d; Downum, personal communication) has allowed a revision of the rather static image of ballcourt distributions previously published (Figures 10.4 and 10.5). Beginning about the same time that large scale irrigation was implemented in the Phoenix Basin—at the end of the Pioneer period (Cable and Doyel 1987; Wilcox and Shenk 1977:180–181; Wilcox et al. 1990)—a distinctive Hohokam religion began to emerge. Initial evidence for this religion is seen in a new style of rock art (Wallace and Holmlund 1986) and ceramic designs. These designs soon became quite elaborate during the Gila Butte phase when ballcourts were introduced, cremation death ritual became general, and a wide variety of ritual paraphernalia (e.g., palettes, carved stone bowls, carved shell) as well as the pottery designs and rock art expressed the iconography of the new Hohokam religion (Haury 1976; Wallace 1994; Wilcox 1991d). A "ritual suzerainty" thus rapidly came about that by the late A.D. 800s was accepted across an area over 800 km east to west and 400 km north to south (Figure 10.4; see also Upham et al. 1994). Snaketown (Gladwin et al. 1937; Haury 1976; Wilcox et al. 1981) is the best known of these sites, has the largest of all Hohokam ballcourts, and is surely one of the most complex sites. Yet I still see no good way to argue that it was preeminent in a "segmentary state," and, if it was, it had no coercive power that is measurable today.

At the Stove Canyon hamlet in the Point of Pines area, a Hohokam-style ballcourt was proximate to a square great kiva (Neely 1974), the only case of this known. In general, however, it appears that the cremation death beliefs and the associated ritual paraphernalia co-occur with the ballcourts prior to A.D. 1000. Not so afterwards (Figure 10.5), when the presence of ballcourts in the middle Verde and the Cohonina and Sinagua areas looks like local people of different beliefs interacting with the remaining Hohokam in ceremonial exchanges somehow differently conceived than before. Cremation was adopted as a death treatment for some people in the Cohonina and Sinagua areas at about the time ballcourts were adopted, and in the Cohonina area "walled plaza" sites came about, suggesting a community-wide form of political integration (Wilcox et al. 1996). In the late A.D. 1100s, ballcourts were built or used at the middle Verde Valley site of Sacred Mountain, the Sinagua site of Ridge

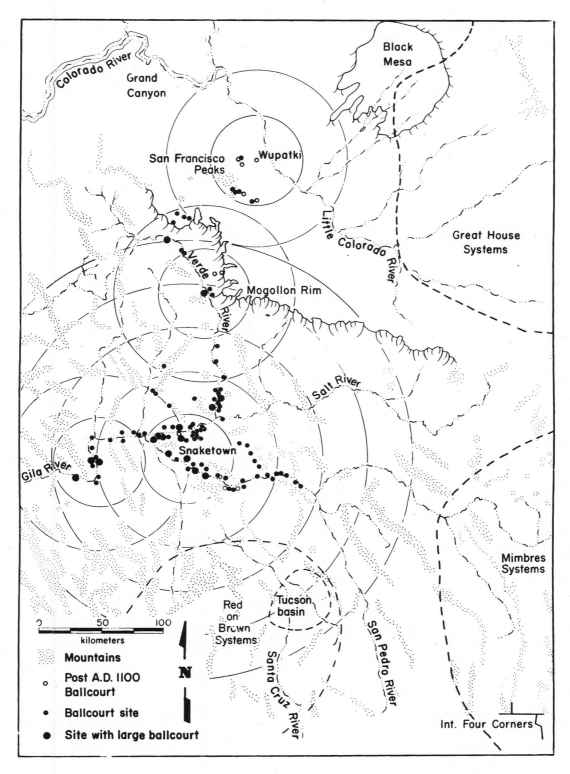

Figure 10.4.   Hohokam ballcourt distribution before A.D. 1000 (the 36 km circles represent a day's travel on foot) (Drennan 1984).

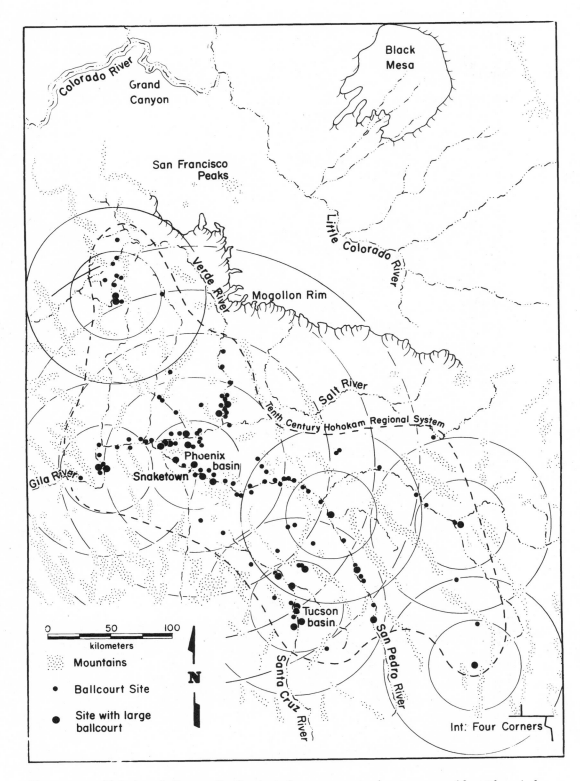

Figure 10.5. Hohokam ballcourt distribution after A.D. 1000 to about A.D. 1250 (the 36 km circles represent a day's travel on foot) (Drennan 1984).

126

Ruin, the Cohonina walled-plaza site of Juniper Terrace, and the southern Kayenta site of Wupatki. In all four cases these ballcourts are located well away from the nuclear occupation zone; and closely associated with each habitation zone is a distinct form of ceremonial architecture, different in all four cases. I infer that these ballcourts facilitated ceremonial exchanges among very different "ethnic" groups, none of whom were politically controlled by another, and none of whom were economically dependent on another. Thus, it seems that the ballcourt network at this time—when, in the Phoenix Basin, platform mounds without structures on top coexisted with ballcourts as public architecture (the Santan phase), and pottery from northern Arizona was still reaching the Salt River Valley (Abbott et al. 1988:199–256; Wilcox 1987b:64)—might best be called a "macroregional" system.

The Chacoan Macroregional System

Prior to A.D. 890, Chaco Canyon was a distant oasis in the middle of the San Juan Basin, a place on the far periphery of where the action was during Pueblo I times (Vivian 1990; Windes and Ford 1992). Along the eastern flanks of the Chuskas and in the Puerco of the West village networks apparently existed with villages of a hundred people or more, but none of them is yet excavated (Vivian 1990; Anyon, personal communication). Many more data are available in the northern San Juan, where several Pueblo I village networks in the greater Mesa Verde area had begun to experiment with corporate forms of kinship and ritual organization (Kane 1989; Wilshusen 1990). Room suites composed of a circular pit room and a surface roomblock consisting of four back rooms and two front rooms were the module of household domains (Kane 1989). Suprahousehold domains of these modules were arranged in arc shapes and formed the social elements of villages, some just starting out, and others a mature expression of the domestic cycle of these groups. The complex of ceremonial facilities in the floors of the circular rooms is more elaborate in some of them (Wilshusen 1989), and only the larger suprahousehold domains have an elaborate one. These data support the inference that these domains were corporately integrated, with one household designated as leader of the group. Ritual feasting (Blinman's [1989] "potlucks") also apparently occurred among the suprahouseholds.

About A.D. 880, the northern villages were suddenly abandoned, and perhaps as one consequence of the result-

ing diaspora of these ritually sophisticated people, new beginnings were made in several places, including Chaco Canyon (Wilcox 1993). Vivian (1990) and Varien et al. (1996) have argued persuasively that a *dual* culture pattern then came about in Chaco Canyon, with one "ethnic" group building planned, arc-shaped great houses, and the other continuing to live in expediently built small houses. These are precisely the conditions and expectations that Southall (1988a) suggests created a two-class system among the Alur:

> [W]hen the Atyak ancestors arrived in the [Alur] country, they consisted of a small, relatively homogeneous group of members of various lineages. They recognized a ritual leader, or recognized several, all of them being senior members of their lineage segments, but probably one of them somewhat above the rest, credited with a superior ability to make rain and ensure the fertility of plants, animals, and women but having no coercive political power (Southall 1988a:57).

The local people in Chaco Canyon may have invited the northerners to come there, particularly if they believed that their rain-making ability was great, and they would therefore also have been willing to provide the newcomers with ritual services in return.

Quite possibly other aristocratic lineages claiming rain-making ability took root elsewhere in the San Juan Basin about A.D. 900, but current data of their existence are sketchy at best (McKenna and Toll 1992:134; Windes and Ford 1992; Wilshusen, personal communication). Once the seeds of inequality were planted in Chaco Canyon, however, it proved to be a fruitful place for their increase. Sebastian (1992) has postulated a model that explains how the generosity of the great house lineages could have brought about their greater prosperity during the A.D. 900s. Southall's (1988a) concept of "hiving off" whereby "troublesome sons" of the ritual leaders were sent off to found their own great houses, or where other sons were "kidnapped" to help outlying communities, also nicely explains the seeming proliferation of great houses in the San Juan Basin during the A.D. 890–1040 period (Figure 10.6; Windes and Ford 1992) and thereafter. Each of these new great houses would thus represent a localized segment of the aristocratic lineage. Thus, a "segmentary state" system would have come about in which a ritual suzerainty was established that was centered on Chaco Canyon. Based on current data, the fact that Pueblo Bonito was the first great house arc

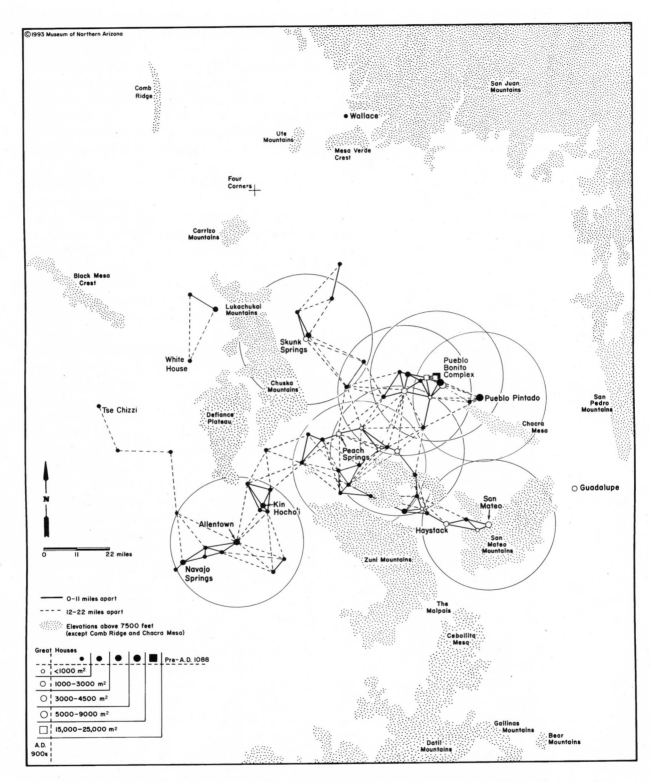

Figure 10.6. Chacoan great house distribution prior to A.D. 1088 (the 36 km circles represent a day's travel on foot) (Wilcox 1993, Drennan 1984).

to be built in Chaco Canyon, the next one coming a generation or more later (Lekson 1984a; Sebastian 1992; Windes and Ford 1992), all of these Chacoan lineages may derive from one, founding segment, which can thus be called the "Bonito lineage." The greatest concentration of the great houses of this core lineage was in Chaco Canyon.

A radical disjunction in the gradual evolutionary history of the Chacoan system occurred in the late A.D. 1030s. Consider the following conjunction of changes:

1. A great increase of trachyte-tempered pottery and Washington Pass chert from the Chuska area 70 km west of the canyon began (Cameron 1984; Toll 1985).

2. A rapid change from Red Mesa to Gallup Black-on-white style in pottery took place (Toll 1985; Windes 1984b:108).

3. Over 5,000 wooden beams from high mountain sources (such as the Chuska Mountains afford) were brought to the canyon and Chetro Ketl was rapidly built (Dean and Warren 1983; Tainter 1988).

4. Two adult men in full, glorious regalia of turquoise and shell were buried, one above the other, beneath the floor of Room 33 in the oldest part of Pueblo Bonito (Akins 1986; Judd 1954; Pepper 1909).

In the generation that followed these remarkable events, from the A.D. 1040s to the A.D. 1070s, huge building programs occurred, first in the construction of Pueblo Alto and then the massive additions to Pueblo Bonito and Chetro Ketl, though the Una Vida and Hungo Pavi great houses also experienced huge increases too (Lekson 1984a; Figure 10.7). Much of this roofed space was most clearly for storage, probably of cultigens

as well as ritual goods (Judd 1954; Pepper 1920). In addition to huge quantities of pottery and wood coming into the canyon from sources 1–3 days away, great quantities of meat also reached the canyon from the distant woodland zones during this period, including a great increase of deer meat compared to the earlier period (Akins 1984; Toll 1985).

The conjunction of events in the late A.D. 1030s, and the subsequent enormous increase of fixed resources in storage warehouses in Chaco Canyon, are most parsimoniously explained as a transformation of the internal structure of the Chacoan segmentary state from one organized in terms of a kinship mode of production (like the Alur: Southall 1956, 1988a,b) to one organized according to a tributary mode (Southall 1988a; Wolf 1982). A tributary mode requires higher net productivity, greater extractable surplus, and improved means of enforcement. Southall (1988a:76) suggests that the transition from a kinship to a tributary mode occurs when the elite become parasitic consumers of surplus extracted from the direct producers. "The direct producers remain in autonomous communities, but the ruler and his close family, kin, and retainers become a ruling class of parasitic consumers" (Southall 1988a:76). Consolidation of political sovereignty in the Chaco Canyon community in the 1130s and perhaps its conquest of the Chuska area may be events that precipitated this change.

Figure 10.8 details the distribution of episodes of mass violence currently known in the area of Chacoan or Chacoan-like great houses in the period A.D. 900–1150. Over 30 cases of mass graves are known that are now reasonably interpreted as resulting from humans being eaten like animals (Fagan 1994; Turner 1993; White 1992).

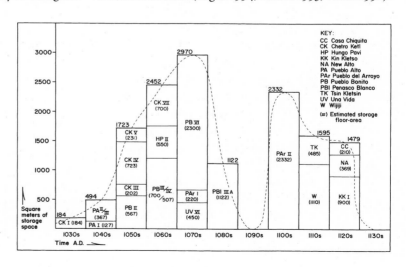

Figure 10.7. The bimodal pattern of large scale construction of crystallized storage in Chaco Canyon from A.D. 1037–1132 (data from Lekson 1984a).

The patterning of the distribution of these episodes has led Turner (1993:434) to infer that, "Under orders from their religious and war chiefs, [Chacoan] Anasazi warriors might have committed example-setting acts of extraordinary violence against tribute- or politically-resisting individuals or entire communities." On the other hand, the relative absence of such data from inside the 2.5 day Chacoan polity may suggest a "Pax Chaco" (see Lekson Chapter 1 and 1992c) there (though the comparability of samples from different areas remains an open question).

The two men with all that turquoise buried below Room 33 in Pueblo Bonito are also of great interest to the hypothesis of an A.D. 1030s conquest of the Chuska population. They have many of the same elements that the much later "magician" burial in Ridge Ruin had (McGregor 1943), and that man was regarded as a war leader by Hopi elders. So, too, may the Chaco men have been. The presence of cut marks and puncture wounds on one of them fits this hypothesis (Akins 1986:116). That there are two of them may also be significant. Duality is a pervasive characteristic of the ritual organization of Chaco great houses (Vivian 1990), and Zantwijk (1985:71) sees dual rulership as a general feature of Mesoamerican polities. Upon the death of one of these Mesoamerican rulers, the other was sometimes killed to be buried at the same time (Weigand, personal communication). Two other pairs of sub-floor burials of fully adult men are also reported from Pueblo Bonito, though neither of them had the elaborate regalia of those below Room 33 (Akins 1986).

What I suspect happened in Chaco Canyon in the early A.D. 1000s is that an individualizing dual chieftainship emerged that separated the Bonito lineage into an uppermost level of supreme power. Having first consolidated their sovereignty within the Chaco Canyon community, they proceeded to take the plundering of their San Juan Basin neighbors to a new level. The success of this venture was invested in new fixed resources in what I shall call the "Chetro Ketl complex," the administrative center of the Chacoan segmentary state. In so doing, they also greatly increased their claims to ritual sanctity and power. For it was in this same period, from A.D. 1040 to 1080, that the sophisticated knowledge of the cosmos that recent analyses have shown is expressed in Chacoan architectural arrangements was manifested (Fritz 1978; Reyman 1976; Stein and Lekson 1992; Williamson 1984). Fritz (1978) also showed that the *axis mundi* of this ritual landscape is sited in the oldest part of Pueblo Bonito, directly above the burial of the two men below the floor of Room 33.

Figure 10.9 shows the currently known distribution of all Chacoan or Chacoan-like great houses. The numbers indicate the rank-order of each great house (based on its total estimated roofed floor area plus the area of all enclosed plazas; see Powers et al. 1983; Schelberg 1984; Wilcox 1993; Wilcox and Weigand 1993). The cluster of extra-large great houses (shown as squares) in and next to Chaco Canyon is evident. It has previously been noted in the concepts of a "Chaco halo" (Doyel et al. 1984), a "macrocommunity" (Vivian 1991), and is what Weigand et al. (1977:22) suggested was a "primitive city." I shall call it the "Chaco Core Community."

At the center of the Chacoan Core Community is a dense aggregate that Lekson (1984b:70–71), too, has recognized as "nearly urban." Vivian (1990; see also Cooper 1992) has shown that the set of buildings in this center, comprised principally of Chetro Ketl, Pueblo Bonito, Pueblo Alto, and Pueblo del Arroyo, are a functionally integrated whole. They are the administrative "downtown" or city center of the Chacoan Core Community. Contrary to the view of Judd (1964) these great houses are not "towns" analogous to the historic Pueblos (see Lekson, Chapter 1).

There are two reasons why I think the Chacoan polity became group oriented. The first is the fact that great houses *outside* the central complex (Hungo Pavi and Una Vida) also benefited from input of "crystallized" surplus in the middle 1000s. The second is the absence of strong evidence for either high status burials or craft specialization. I suggest that the group-oriented polity was governed by an assembly of the lineage heads of the extra large great houses that were part of the Chaco Core Community. This is where political sovereignty resided.

Figure 10.8. *(Facing page)* The distribution of documented episodes of violence in the domain of Chacoan great houses, A.D. 900–1150 (data from Turner 1993; plotted by Christy Turner). 1. Rattlesnake Ruin; 2. Alkali Ridge; 3. Comb Wash; 4. St. Christopher; 5. Monument Valley; 6. Charnel House Tower; 7. Yellow Jacket; 8. Marshview hamlet; 9. Grinnel; 10. Snider's Well; 11. Coyote Village; 12. Aztec Wash; 13. Hanson Pueblo; 14. Teec Nos Pos; 15. Mancos Canyon; 16. La Plata 23; 17. La Plata 41; 18. La Plata Highway; 19. Aztec Ruin; 20. Salmon Ruin; 21. Huerfano Mesa and Alkali Springs; 22. Largo-Gallina sites; 23. Penasco Blanco; 24. Ram Mesa I, II; 25. Leroux Wash; 26. Canyon Butte #3; 27. Fence Lake.

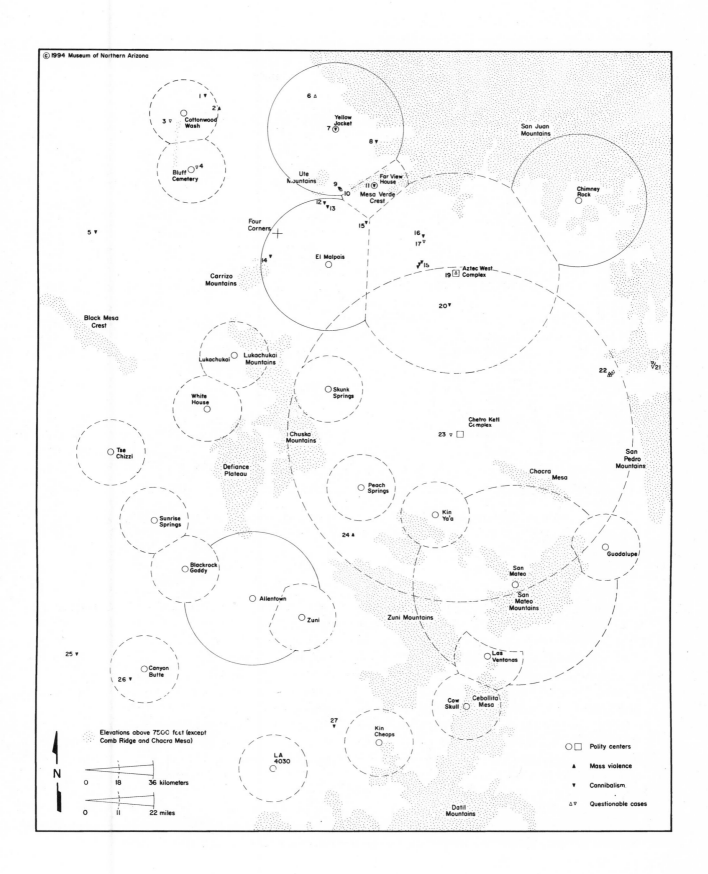

1 ▼
2 ▲
3 ▽
○ Cottonwood Wash
Bluff Cemetery ○ ▽4

6 △
Yellow Jacket
7 ▼
8 ▼
San Juan Mountains

Ute Mountains
9 ▼
10 ○
Far View House
11 ▼
Mesa Verde Crest
Chimney Rock ○

12 ▼ ▼13

5 ▼

Four Corners
15 ▼
16 ▼
17 ▽

El Malpais ○
14 ▼
18 ▼
Carrizo Mountains
19 △ Aztec West Complex

20 ▼

Black Mesa Crest

Lukachukai ○
Lukachukai Mountains

White House ○

Skunk Springs ○

22 ▲▼
▼21

San Pedro Mountains

Tse Chizzi ○

Defiance Plateau

Chuska Mountains

Chetro Ketl Complex
23 ▽ □

Peach Springs ○

Chacra Mesa

Sunrise Springs ○

Kin Ya'a ○

Guadalupe ○

Blackrock Gaddy ○

24 ▲

San Mateo ○
San Mateo Mountains

Allentown ○

Zuni ○

Zuni Mountains

25 ▼

Las Ventanas ○

26 ▼ Canyon Butte ○

Cow Skull ○ Cebollita Mesa

27 ▼
Kin Cheops ○

LA 4030 ○

Elevations above 7500 feet (except Comb Ridge and Chacra Mesa)

N

| 0 | 18 | 36 kilometers |
| 0 | 11 | 22 miles |

Datil Mountains

○ □ Polity centers

▲ Mass violence

▼ Cannibalism

△ ▽ Questionable cases

131

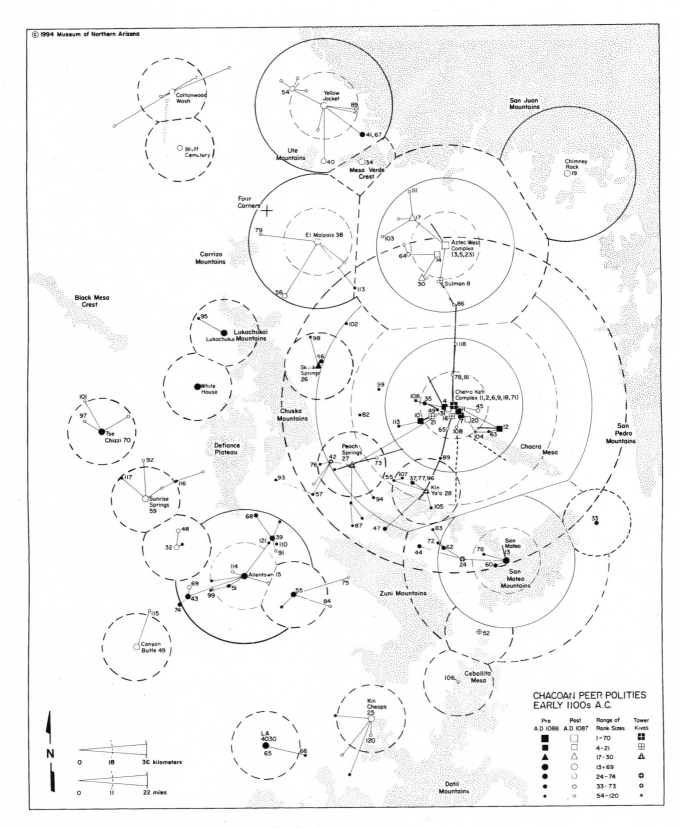

Figure 10.9.   The Chacoan great house distribution, A.D. 890–1150.

I further suggest that the occupants of outlying great houses (Figure 10.6) were lesser ranked segments of the Bonito lineage who looked to the center for support and in some cases owed tribute to it, but otherwise were largely autonomous.

A second pattern apparent in Figure 10.9 is that while the size of great houses generally becomes smaller and smaller as one moves out from the canyon (like a dendritic system: Kelly 1976; Paynter 1982), there are a series of extra-large great houses 2.5 to 4 days out that also have their own site hierarchies. To investigate this pattern further, a series of rank-size graphs was constructed (Figures 10.10, 10.11). Many interesting patterns were discovered.

1. The set of all great houses is remarkably close to a rank-size curve (Figures 10.10–10.15). This suggests a considerable degree of integration (Paynter 1982). Given that much of the San Juan Basin is open country with gently rolling topography, it is likely that communication among neighboring settlements was quite easy (see Figure 10.6), and this factor may partially explain this pattern.

2. If, however, we lump together the Chetro Ketl complex as a single entity, or the whole Chaco Core Community, then a rank-size or concave curve, respectively, appears. The numbers we are using are not population estimates—though great houses may be a good proxy for them (Schelberg 1984). They are estimates of the net settlement fund (Paynter 1982) invested in particular places. The rank-size and primate patterns are thus another way of expressing the tribute hypothesis.

3. I have argued elsewhere that the site hierarchies located two or more days out from Chaco represent "peer polities" that broke away from the Chacoan polity at various times in the late A.D. 1000s or 1100s (Wilcox 1993). This possibility appears to receive support from the rank-size curves documented for the San Mateo (Figure 10.16) and Allentown systems (Figure 10.17). The convex pattern of the Aztec curve (Figures 10.18, 10.19) is more interesting. It might indicate that the study area chosen includes a pooling of independent systems, and Morris 41 at the upper end of the La Plata might then be a separate center (McKenna and Toll 1992). Convex rank-size curves also occur in situations of dependency where an area is being exploited by an outside center (Johnson

1980; Paynter 1982). The "Chaco Polity II" rank-size curve (Figure 10.15) includes the Aztec-polity sites, suggesting that—at the time of construction—it was integrated with Chaco Canyon.

4. Figure 10.12 graphically illustrates the tiering effect of two sets of great houses within the San Juan Basin. This image brings into focus two probable equivalence classes of differently functioning great houses: 1) the set of elite Bonito lineage segments occupying Hungo Pavi, Una Vida, Kin Bineola, and Salmon, with Pueblo Pintado being a close runner up to membership in this class; and 2) the set outside the Chaco Core Community formed by Skunk Springs, Peach Springs, and Kin Ya'a. The latter two (and Salmon Ruin) have a tower kiva and Skunk Springs is on a high ridge with good line of sight toward Chaco Canyon. All four of these sites were connected to the canyon by the best attested of the long-distance Chacoan roads (Stein 1989; Roney 1992; Wicklein 1994). However, contrary to Lekson's expectations, Roney (1992) has shown that roads quite possibly do not connect all great houses to downtown Chaco.

Salmon, built rapidly from A.D. 1088 to 1094 (Ahlstrom 1985), is thus seen to be the first of the core community's elite lineages to be established outside of that community. Its construction followed a decision not to enlarge Pueblo Bonito further (Lekson 1984a:116, 136–137), and may indicate a policy shift to incorporate the Animas-La Plata area into the Chacoan tributary state. Irwin-Williams' (1983) conception of Salmon as a Chacoan colony fits this hypothesis. So does the likelihood that Salmon was the first great house built in the Animas-La Plata area (Figure 10.9). Even more decisive is the pattern of massive building programs in the Chaco Core Community: it is *bimodal* (Figure 10.7), the low point coming in the very decades when core-community investment in fixed resources had shifted to Salmon and other Animas-La Plata great houses. The tribute payoff came in the early A.D. 1100s, beginning with the massive addition in A.D. 1103 of vast new storage warehouses onto Pueblo del Arroyo in the Chetro Ketl Complex (see Lekson 1984a).

Kin Ya'a was built in A.D. 1106 (Bannister et al. 1970:25). Ceramic data from Peach Springs (Powers et al. 1983:68) and Skunk Springs (Marshall et al. 1979:111) indicate that tenth century great houses at these sites were built up into large structures with tower kivas or road associa-

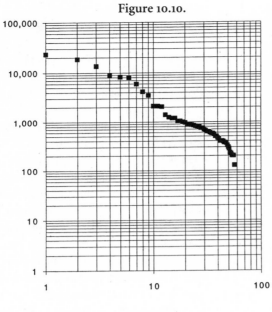

Figure 10.10.

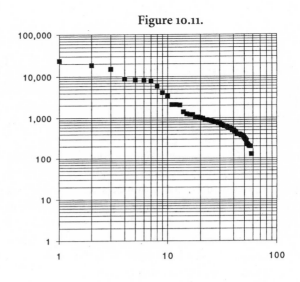

Figure 10.11.

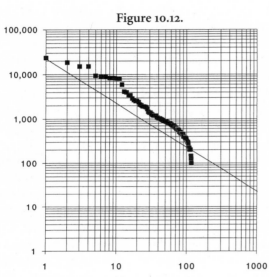

Figure 10.12.

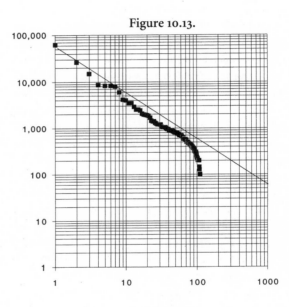

Figure 10.13.

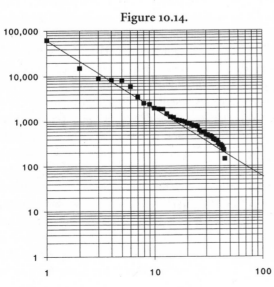

Figure 10.14.

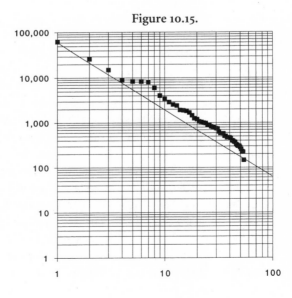

Figure 10.15.

Figure 10.16.

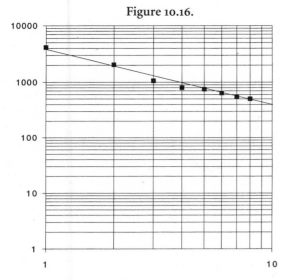

Figure 10.17.

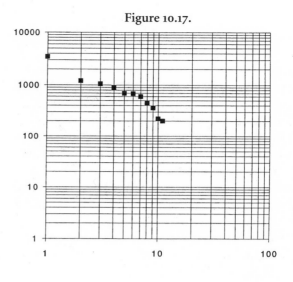

Figure 10.18.

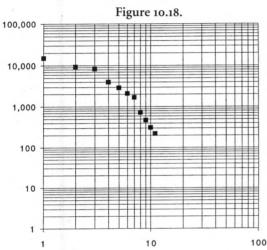

Figure 10.19.

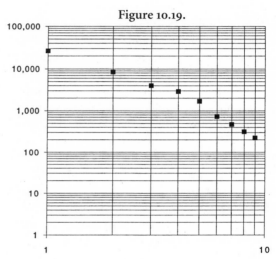

Figure 10.10. Comparison of rank size curves for Chacoan great houses at three stages in their history —before A.D. 1088.

Figure 10.11. Comparison of rank size curves for Chacoan great houses at three stages in their history —ca. A.D. 1088.

Figure 10.12. Comparison of rank size curves for Chacoan great houses at three stages in their history —total Chaco system.

Figure 10.13. Comparison of rank size curves for Chacoan great houses at three stages in their history —total Chaco system (lumped).

Figure 10.14. Comparison of rank size curves for Chacoan great houses at three stages in their history —Chaco polity I.

Figure 10.15. Comparison of rank size curves for Chacoan great houses at three stages in their history —Chaco polity II.

Figure 10.16. Comparison of rank size curves for three peer polities of the Chaco polity—San Mateo.

Figure 10.17. Comparison of rank size curves for three peer polities of the Chaco polity—Allentown (Puerco).

Figure 10.18. Comparison of rank size curves for three peer polities of the Chaco polity—Aztec.

Figure 10.19. Comparison of rank size curves for three peer polities of the Chaco polity—Aztec (lumped).

tions in the early A.D. 1100s. Red Willow, which also has a tower kiva (Fowler et al. 1987), may be another building in this class. At the edge of the Chaco Core Community, tower kivas at Kin Klizhin and Tsin Kletsin appear to articulate with Kin Ya'a and Peach Springs, respectively, thus binding these unusual sites tightly to the core polity (see Lekson 1984a:231). Kin Bineola was also massively enlarged at that time and reconfigured (Marshall et al. 1979:59–60), perhaps serving new administrative functions vis-à-vis the Kin Ya'a-Red Willow sector.

The inference I would make that coherently explains these data is that a new form of more centralized political integration was being imposed by the Chaco Core Community onto its segmentary clients. Kin Ya'a, Peach Springs, Red Willow, and Skunk Springs may thus have become a set of fortresses and administrative entrepots (cf. Paynter 1982:139) that facilitated the efficient flow of tribute to the center of the polity. They would also have served to tighten the core's "span of control" (see Johnson 1987), but could also have served as bases for protecting client communities from raiding launched from the "peer polities" farther out. At the same time, from A.D. 1110 to 1130 (Ahlstrom 1985), the Aztec complex was built in the lower Animas. Originally, it was probably intended as an administrative center—second only to the Chetro Ketl Complex in sophistication and authority—from which to manage the new estates of the Animas-La Plata. Its position in the lower Animas both guarded the northern frontier and had ready access to Morris 41, the largest great house on the La Plata.

We can now reject the idea that the Chaco Core Community moved bag and baggage to Aztec (Toll et al. 1980) and the long-held belief that Chaco was abandoned or even went into an instant decline immediately after the Aztec complex was completed. Initially, Aztec was probably a major dependency of the Chaco core polity, as the rank-size curve found in Figure 10.15 seems to imply. The internal structure of the Aztec Complex replicates more closely and fully than any other Anasazi site the complexity of the Chetro Ketl Complex (Wilcox and Weigand 1993). However, it may soon have become independent of the Chacoan polity and established its own segmentary state. Ceramic data from Salmon indicate a sharp reduction of connectivity with Chaco Canyon and, in general, after A.D. 1125, "there appears to be a generalized decline in long-distance exchange volume, whereas local exchange remains relatively constant through the Northern Anasazi area" (Blinman and Wilson 1993:83). Equally

interesting is the fact that innovation in ritual expressions was vigorously pursued at the Aztec Complex, as the several tri-wall structures attest (Reyman 1985; Stein and McKenna 1988; Vivian 1959). Thus Aztec may have been seeking to attain *ritual equality* with the Chetro Ketl Complex, even if it were not as powerful politically. A tri-wall structure was later added to Pueblo del Arroyo, but later yet was razed (Judd 1959; Vivian 1959).

While major construction may have stopped in Chaco Canyon following the rise of Aztec, the canyon polity remained powerful throughout the twelfth century. In the early A.D. 1100s, defensive front walls were added to many of the elite great house structures in Chaco Canyon (Judd 1959; Lekson 1984a). In the A.D. 1140s or 1150s, the fortress of Bis sa'ani was built to guard the northeastern flank of the Core Community (cf. Doyel et al. 1984). The emergence of "peer polities" hemming in the Chacoan tributary state would probably have placed a premium on highly exotic prestige goods, such as copper bells and macaw feathers for ritual garments (cf. Renfrew and Cherry 1986). The famous Mesoamerican hall of columns (Ferdon 1955) was probably added to Chetro Ketl in the early A.D. 1100s (Lekson 1984a:192), and this also appears to be the time that the Chacoans somehow made contact directly or indirectly with one or more polities of West Mexico, exchanging turquoise for macaws and copper bells (Weigand and Harbottle 1993).

The appearance of Chacoan-like great houses in the Zuni area and southward to Quemado (Fowler et al. 1987; Figure 10.9) may have established some long-distance exchange links in this process. Both copper bells and macaws occur in Classic Mimbres sites (Minnis 1985). The fact that macaws are often pictured on Mimbres pottery as young birds sitting on carrying baskets or in cages (Creel and McKusick 1994; Wilcox 1993), may indicate that these people became "middlemen" in such a long-distance exchange network. If there were Mimbres people penetrating into the Guaymas area (Jett and Moyle 1986), this would have positioned them close to networks extending southward through Sinaloa to Nayarit (see also Bentley 1987). The presence of *Nassarius* shells at Kin Kletso, Bis sa'ani and Pueblo Bonito (Mathien 1993:52) confirms the hypothesized Mimbres connection.

Wider Macroregional Implications

From an economic perspective, the model of an evolving Chacoan segmentary state implies that the great house landscape (Figure 10.9) constituted a complex, evolving *macroregional* system (Wilcox 1996a). And its ripple effects should be expected to have affected the organization of peoples far beyond the edges of the great house distribution (see Tainter and Plog 1994). This model thus has the potential to explain many otherwise largely inexplicable and disconnected facts of Southwestern prehistory. Only a few points can be briefly explored here.

1. South and west of Navajo Springs is an extensive twelfth century archaeological zone in the middle Little Colorado River Valley characterized by circular great kivas, associated hamlet-scale room blocks, a predominance of Cibola White Ware as decorated pottery and local plainwares (Fowler and Stein 1992). Carter Ranch Pueblo (Longacre 1970a), Tla Kii (Haury 1985), and the "smaller ruin near Linden" (Hough 1903) are among the best known of these sites. They form a periphery of the great-house peer polity system, and the network of great kivas in this area may have facilitated prestige-good and possibly commodity flows (hides?) into and out of the great-house systems.

2. In the late A.D. 1000s (Gilpin 1989), Kayenta Anasazi people living along the southeastern flanks of Black Mesa built great houses and a great kiva at Tse Chizzi and other sites (Figure 10.9). The rest of the Kayenta people successfully resisted incorporation into the expanding great-house network, and little or no Chacoan pottery is known in those sites (Gumerman and Dean 1989). In a systemic sense does this mean they were "unaffected" by the rapid incorporation of their eastern neighbors into the great-house network? I say "no," for suddenly in the middle A.D. 1000s the Kayenta began vigorously advancing northward and westward, filling up previous no-man's lands (Lipe 1970; Matson et al. 1988), and moving into close proximity with new neighbors: Mesa Verde, Southern San Rafael Fremont, Parowan Fremont, Upland Virgin Anasazi, and Cohonina (Effland et al. 1982; Geib 1993; Lister 1964; Lyneis 1984). New kinds of exchange flows between the Kayenta and these new neighbors and allies would be expected and are supported by existing data (Lyneis 1984).

3. Wupatki was founded in the middle A.D. 1100s, rapidly becoming the largest habitation locus in the Flagstaff area and stimulating a significant restructuring of Sinagua and Cohonina settlements in this area (Wilcox 1986a, 1996c). I interpret Wupatki as an outpost of the Chacoan macroregional system, built by southern Kayenta people coming westward from the northern drainages of the Little Colorado River Valley. It was a gateway (Hirth 1978) between that system and the Hohokam macroregional ballcourt network. It clearly is on the periphery of both of these systems (Figure 10.4), and its leadership, like that of the neighboring Sinagua, Cohonina, Verde Valley and Prescott peoples, has a distinctly individualized character (Renfrew 1974), best known in this area from the "magician" burial at Ridge Ruin (McGregor 1943). Similar personages are known from King's Ruin (Spicer and Caywood 1936) and Fitzmaurice Ruin (Barnett 1974) in the Prescott area, and in other burials from the Flagstaff area (Babbitt Collection, Museum of Northern Arizona). These data indicate the kind of widespread contacts expected in individualizing chiefdoms (Blanton et al. 1996; Renfrew 1974). The large number of sophisticated cotton textiles from Wupatki, and the solid evidence for local production (Stanislawski 1963), are good evidence for at least part-time craft specialists. Cotton textiles were found in Pueblo Bonito (Judd 1954:69) and they quite possibly reached there from Wupatki. Shell is also more frequent in the latest Chacoan assemblages (Akins 1986:104).

4. Emblems of ritual and political office, which probably derive their inspiration from Chacoan models, were adopted in the Flagstaff-Verde Valley-Prescott area in the A.D. 1150–1250 period. They consist of the turquoise-encrusted raptorial bird symbol (present in the "magician" burial: McGregor 1943) and the turquoise-encrusted toad (present in burials at King's Ruin, Fitzmaurice Ruin, and Tuzigoot: Barnett 1974; Caywood and Spicer 1935; Spicer and Caywood 1936). Noseplugs of red argillite and other fancy stones also appear at this time. The frequency of the smaller ones suggests that all male adults (or all adults?) may have worn one, while the largest and most elaborate was found with the "magician" war leader (McGregor 1943). A little later, the raptorial bird and toad emblems, and the nose plugs, were

adopted by the Hohokam in the Phoenix Basin, the peoples of the Tonto Basin, and many other peoples involved in the fourteenth century Salado macroregional system (Billideau 1986; Di Peso et al. 1974:vol.6:459; Wilcox 1987b, 1996b;). What this evidence suggests is that a Chacoan dualistic ideology of earth and sky, transformed, perhaps, by the individualizing ideology of the Wupatkians and their neighbors, was taken up by the Phoenix Basin Hohokam and used to help restructure their society. The time these emblems were adopted coincides with the moment when large structures began to be built on top of the Hohokam platform mounds (Gregory et al. 1988:48).

SOME DIRECTIONS FOR FURTHER RESEARCH

Beginning in the Santan phase, no-man's lands began to separate the Phoenix Basin-Picacho Mountain area from its neighbors to the north, northeast, east, south, and west (Figure 10.20). The abandonment of ballcourt communities in the lower Verde and the Buttes area along the Gila east of Florence came about at least by the twelfth century (Canouts 1975; Debowski et al. 1976). South of the Picachos, the Robles and Marana platform mound communities have no Gila Polychrome on them and thus appear to have been abandoned by about A.D. 1300 (Downum 1993; P. Fish et al. 1992a). The large area between Gila Bend and the junction of the Salt and Agua Fria Rivers was largely abandoned by the early Classic (Antieau 1981). North of the Phoenix Basin, a string of defensive hilltop sites appear to be counter-threat attempts by people related to the populations aggregated in small fortified villages on Perry Mesa (Ahlstrom and Roberts 1994; Spoerl 1984; van Warden 1984). Similar fortified hilltop sites occur south of the Picachos (Wilcox 1979b). The compound walls surrounding Phoenix Basin suprahousehold groups would have made their internal security much greater than earlier. It thus has long appeared that the Classic period was characterized by conditions of region-wide warfare (Ahlstrom and Roberts 1994; Doelle and Wallace 1991; Wilcox 1979b, 1989; Wilcox and Haas 1994a,b; Wilcox and Sternberg 1983; but see Downum et al. 1994).

If so, and if the Phoenix Basin was able to become politically integrated, it would unquestionably have been the greatest threat to all of its neighbors, all of whom were now a relatively safe distance away. Many resource zones of great importance to the Hohokam lie outside the Phoenix Basin; there they would have had to go to get piñon nuts, deer meat and hides, saguaro fruit, and mineral resources, for example (Wood 1985). Their neighbors either occupied those zones or had competing demands for them. These neighbors would have had to organize themselves for mutual protection against a threat from the Phoenix Basin polity in order to resist its plundering raids or tribute demands. Population estimates for any archaeological context are notoriously difficult to make with any confidence. Whether we argue for 10,000 (Doelle et al. 1992) or 24,000 (Wilcox 1991b:263), or more (Fish and Fish 1991; J. Howard 1993), the Phoenix Basin net population was proportionately two to five or more times larger than the net population anyone can credibly estimate for the Perry Mesa area, the Tonto Basin, the lower San Pedro River Valley, or the Tucson Basin, where most estimates range from about 2,000 to 5,000 (Doelle et al. 1992). In fact, these differences are so great that, to meet a threat from a united Phoenix Basin polity, its neighbors would have had not only to unite internally, but they would quite probably have had to form outside alliances as well.

The early Salado polychromes cross-cut these sociopolitical relationships. Crown (1994) argues that they are not associated with a death cult or ancestor worship, proposing instead that they are the manifestation of an earth/fertility cult. The further suggestion that such a cult served to maintain peaceful relationships among neighboring populations, however, does not square with the extensive evidence for no-man's lands (Jewett 1989) and widespread warfare in this area in the late A.D. 1200s and later (McKusick 1992; Wilcox and Haas 1994a,b). The contextual distributions of the polychromes indicate that the Salado cult, like the Kachina cult, was for every man. Such an organizational ideology would have facilitated the mobilization of whole communities, overcoming the partitioning engendered by segmentary organization or differences of ethnic background. Just as one of the principal functions of the aboriginal Kachina cult may have been warfare/defense (Plog and Solomento 1995), so too the Salado cult may have served similar objectives.

What makes the Salado polychromes especially interesting is the strong iconographic relationships they bear to both the White Mountain redwares (Crown 1994) and to the Chihuahuan polychromes (Di Peso et al. 1974:vols.6, 8).

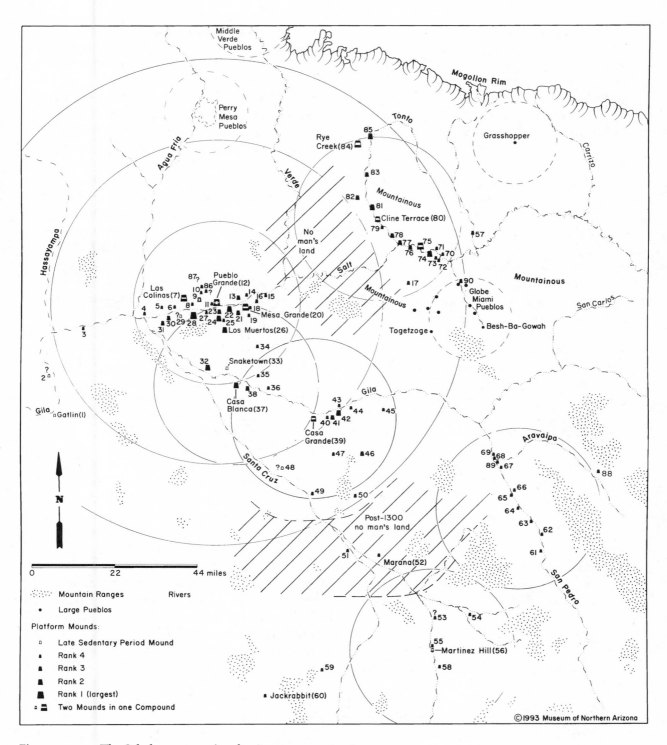

Figure 10.20.   The Salado macroregional system, A.D. 1250–1360.

Whittlesey (1993) and Crown (1994) have recently done much to clarify this picture. They argue that the Salado polychromes originated from the White Mountain Redware tradition, but that later on, after Tonto Polychrome appeared, probably in the middle of the fourteenth century, the designs exhibit much greater similarity to the Chihuahuan polychromes. As we have seen above, the hegemony of Paquimé reached its apogee in the mid to late A.D. 1300s, apparently after the power of the Phoenix Basin was broken. In the subsequent Polvorón phase, there is a greater frequency of Salado polychromes than there had been in the Civano phase, and Hopi Yellow Wares also appear (Crown 1989:406). These data probably indicate a major restructuring of the macroregional system after the Phoenix Basin polity collapsed, with at least the Tonto Creek sites entering into connections with Chavez Pass (Upham 1982) and the Homol'ovi sites (Adams 1991).

I am thus led to propose that we need to construct models of at least *two successive* macroregional systems: 1) a Salado macroregion during the period of about A.D. 1250 to, say 1360; and 2) a Casas Grandes macroregion from approximately A.D. 1350 to 1450 (see Douglas 1992; Minnis 1989; Whalen and Minnis 1996a; Wilcox 1991c).

The Hohokam area was not the only part of the Southwest to experience a major reorganization in the middle A.D. 1200s. On the Colorado Plateau that was also the time when from one end to the other there was a general redeployment into what Fowler et al. (1987) have aptly called "walled towns." In Kiet Siel and Betatakin, true kivas were located "down front" in a separate precinct and probably now became spaces dedicated to ceremonial activity (Dean 1969). Where earlier small-house settlements had only a few families at most in them, now several hundred people nucleated into a single plaza-centered village with high outside walls and controlled access became the norm. A qualitatively new kind of community organization had thus come about (Lipe 1989), and probably because of this, the whole northern Rio Grande area suddenly became a target of opportunity for large-scale human exploitation.

The Rio Chama, for example, had virtually no visible occupation for millennia (Beal 1987). Suddenly, in the late A.D. 1200s a string of small walled-town sites appeared that established a defensive perimeter along the river. The design of these settlements is well suited to defense (Peckham 1981), and plentiful evidence of death and mayhem has been found in them (Reed 1948, 1953). Within two or three generations, the success of this "tak-ing" of the Rio Chama is apparent in the truly huge "great towns" at Sapawe and many other sites in the valley systems (Beal 1987). What had kept Pueblo people out of here for so long?

North of the Rio Chama are the southern Rockies, home of hunter-gatherers from Paleoindian times. Black (1991) recognizes a "Mountain tradition" in this area that is distinguished by its own rock art styles and subsistence technologies. Could it be that the Rio Chama was to the people of the Mountain tradition what the upper Gila River was to the White Mountain Apache (Goodwin 1942)—a place to winter where it was both warmer and there were suitable resources? Ute Indians whose range extended well northward into the Rockies did occupy parts of the Rio Chama in the eighteenth and nineteenth centuries—in association with Jicarilla Apache (Stewart 1966).

This example is enough to raise the general point that I wish to make. On all sides of the North American Southwest, except, perhaps in Sinaloa and southwestern Chihuahua, the neighbors of the Southwestern farming populations were primarily hunter-gatherers. What was the history of interactions between these various hunter-gatherers and their agricultural neighbors? Astonishingly little research has been conducted on this macroregional question. The greatest attention, in this regard, has been paid to the initiation of the "dog-nomad" trade between early Apacheans and Teya on the southern Plains and the protohistoric Pueblos (Baugh 1986; Gunnerson 1956; Kelley 1952a,b, 1986b; Spielmann 1991; Wilcox 1981b). The long-standing fascination with the entry of Numic speakers into the Southwest is another example (Ambler and Sutton 1989). But, as the Rio Chama case may indicate, there are many more loci of potentially fruitful research that can and should be investigated along this perimeter (see McGuire et al. 1994).

In conclusion, this paper has explored many ways in which a macroregional scale of analysis in the North American Southwest has been and can be investigated. My objective has been to demonstrate not only the fruitfulness of such studies, but also the necessity of them. The interplay of internal versus external processes is vital in the explanation of the history of any open system (cf. McGuire et al. 1994). In recent years, with the enormous growth of knowledge, Southwestern archaeologists have become increasingly specialized, setting their sights on increasingly narrow research domains. If the discipline is to move forward, however, ways must be found to overcome this handicap.

ACKNOWLEDGMENTS

Many, many people over the last 25 years have helped me in the research that now culminates in this paper. Special thanks goes to Jodi Griffith, Museum of Northern Arizona Exhibits Department, for drafting the original figures, her assistance in plotting the locations of sites mentioned in this chapter, and putting up with endless changes as my ideas evolved. My thanks extend to illustrator Julie Barnes Smith for adding sites I have discussed to Figures 2, and 1.1–1.4. Stephen Kowalewski graciously prepared the rank-size graphs and provided many other valuable insights. Phil Geib, Navajo Nation Archaeology Department, provided critical information on ceramic identifications. I also owe a great debt of thanks to Phil Weigand, Jerry Howard, Jeffrey Dean, Steven LeBlanc, Henry Wallace, Alan Dart, William Doelle, David Abbott, David Phillips, Todd Bostwick, David Gregory, Owen Lindauer, David Jacobs, Jonathan Reyman and Douglas Craig. For any errors or faulty interpretation, I alone am responsible.

CHAPTER ELEVEN

Southeastern Interaction and Integration

Jon Muller

IN THIS PAPER, EMERGENCE OF TRANS-REGIONAL INtegration in the Southeast is summarized first in terms of exchange and interaction. The second part of the paper deals with integration on three scales: integration of localities within a region, integration of regions to each other, and relationships of these regions to those outside the Southeast proper. Finally, issues of production and exchange are briefly discussed as aspects of a political economy of Mississippian times.

THE AMERICAN SOUTHEAST THROUGH TIME

Such "macroregional" integration as there was in the Southeast did not fully emerge until complex political economies developed near the end of the first millennium of the current era. The Southeast by that time became no less than a culture-historical "culture area," at least in the sense that its peoples were biologically, socially, culturally, and historically linked. Development did not occur in complete isolation, but Southeastern local and regional development was not marked by obvious external influences. The absence of any evidence of direct exchange with Mesoamerica is especially striking (see Cobb et al. Chapter 13).

Culture historians of the East have emphasized a first "climax" in the years around 1000 B.C. to A.D. 300, often subdivided into early ("Adena") and late ("Hopewellian") periods. A second culture-historical "climax" was the development of Mississippian and related complexes, beginning around A.D. 700 and continuing until historic times, with a major "climax" circa A.D. 1100–1200 (cf. Hall 1980). The supposed gap between these climaxes is present only from a Northern perspective, however, as societies in the Gulf Coastal Plain and in the Lower Mississippi River valley show continuity throughout the A.D. 400–1000 period. In the North, virtual—if not complete—abandonment of "temple mound" centers began after A.D. 1250, but Late Mississippian complexes persisted in the South. Late Mississippian societies are seen as being simpler and smaller than earlier Mississippian, but the evidence for differences is not so great as often assumed. The size of many political entities continued at high levels into the Historic period, although there were indisputable reductions in both the number of polities and the number of towns (see Muller 1993b, 1995).

Movement of raw materials and some finished goods occurred from Late Middle Archaic times (ca. 3000 B.C.) through the Historic period. Raw materials formed the bulk of exchanges. Early exchange goods included marine whelk shell and native copper, linking regions from the Gulf Coast to Lake Superior.

Slightly more finished goods were exchanged in Adena times in the North, but this system had little impact on the Southeast proper. The "Hopewellian Interaction Sphere" (ca. 200 B.C. to A.D. 300) of the upper Ohio Valley and the Illinois River valley involved the Southeast as a marginal supplier of raw materials, and a few "Hopewellian" complexes occur in the Southeast proper, the most striking of which is Marksville in the lower Mississippi River valley. Copper, mica, and galena were dispersed over very great distances. The sources for some small quantities of obsidian are in Wyoming, over 1800 km away. South Atlantic marine shell was found 1600 km away from the coasts. Most known goods were still "raw materials," but exchange in finished items such as fancy ceramics became more common among different Hopewellian societies.

Between A.D. 400 and 700, exchange of both finished and raw goods in (archaeologically surviving) media declined considerably in the East. This "Late Woodland" time in the Northeast is where the idea of a "decline" from the earlier Hopewellian originated. In the Southeast, however, complexes such as Troyville, Baytown, and Weeden Island show continuation of elaborate mortuary ritual and the continuing transformation of burial platforms into substructure mounds. Such complexes formed the base out of which complex Late Prehistoric societies developed.

The final period of prehistoric intensive interregional exchange, as measured by finished goods and exotic raw materials, intensified before A.D. 900 and continued at higher levels until after A.D. 1250. Long-distance exchange in both raw materials and finished goods was still relatively rare, but a few distinctive themes such as the so-called "long-nosed god" motif occur over a wide area by the end of this time (Muller 1989; Williams and Goggin 1956). The best known period of widespread interaction in archaeologically known materials is the so-called Southeastern Ceremonial Complex around A.D. 1250. This "Southern Cult" period had very widespread, but brief, exchange of raw materials and finished goods. After A.D. 1250, exchange intensity declined, with a secondary peak at A.D. 1450 in the Nashville Basin and the eastern Tennessee River valley. Thus, interaction—shown by surviving materials, as always—increased and decreased through time, with several more or less distinct periods of relatively high interaction.

A dispute continues over what role widespread systems of exchange played in creating area-wide unity. Arguments can be made that many similarities were the result of development in similar environments from similar political-economic bases. Similarity of such general characteristics, per se, cannot be assumed to be solely a result of "interaction" with other societies. Recent assessments of various shared cultural and social elements of the area still wrestle with the problem (see the wide diversity of opinion in Emerson and Lewis 1991 and Galloway 1989). Widespread exchange systems certainly linked much of the East, but the surviving archaeological traces of these exchanges are an objectively tiny total of goods. One important question is whether these few objects represent "tokens of exchange" in a larger-scale system involving movement of more "utilitarian" goods.

SCALES OF INTEGRATION

A number of scales of integration have to be considered. The first is local integration. How large were communities and how did they deal with their neighbors? In turn, how were groups of communities in regions linked to other regions? What larger scale channels of communication tied regions and areas together?

Two major arguments against continuity of scale in the East between prehistoric and historic times have been depopulation and a supposed concomitant decrease in scale of later political integration. These arguments have been based on data on depopulation as a result of introduced European diseases and on a decline in public works such as mound construction. In the northern areas of the East, at least, there was a decline in population after the mid-thirteenth century. Naturally, mound building also declined in those areas. However, I question whether the scale of depopulation justifies a conclusion that the political systems of the Late Prehistoric Southeast "collapsed" (Muller 1993b). As discussed in the next section, the scale of mound construction fell off after the thirteenth century; but mound construction never ceased. Historic depopulation as a result of the introduction of European diseases and military methods is certainly well documented, but it should not be forgotten that there were still many historic political entities in the East whose population exceeded 20,000 persons. The supposed "disappearance" of Native Americans was a convenient historical justification for the appropriation of their lands, but a number of large and complex societies managed to survive the impact of European invasion.

Local and Regional Integration

Southeastern town size was relatively stable in Mississippian times, but the number of towns in each polity seems to have declined after the mid-thirteenth century. In historic times, *tribal* population oscillated in relation to events such as various wars, but consistency to *town* population size reflected both the political and economic importance of the "standard" historic town. Towns had social, economic, and political "purposes" that could be served only if local population continued at certain minimal levels. For example, frontier settlements often needed to concentrate within the protection of palisades. At the same time, the data on the Creek and other historic "Mississippian" peoples suggest that the importance of a town in political and economic terms depended on a number of variables, among which size was only one. Finally, the historic data show that "size" is sometimes difficult to determine, since the aboriginal definition of a "town" might be much larger (or even smaller) than "towns" recognized by Europeans.

A French copy of an aboriginal map of the Chickasaw towns shows one, apparently widespread, aboriginal way of viewing community structure (Figure 11.1). In maps of these sorts, the scale of the circle was proportional to the size of the community (see Waselkov 1989). A map such as Figure 11.1 indicates the structure of communities as links of individual smaller units, each with considerable autonomy, but each tied by interactions along established routes. Such maps show a view of "towns" (the common English word applied to these communities by contemporaries) that are linked by "paths." The towns themselves were either dispersed or aggregated according to economic and military conditions at a particular time. Named towns often persisted through time, but were sometimes spread out over the landscape or tightly packed into fortified communities. Romans (1775:62–63) noted such changes in the Chickasaw settlements a half century later than the map:

> They have in this field what might be called one town, or rather an assemblage of hutts, of the length of about one mile and a half, and very narrow and irregular; this however they divide into seven, by the names of Metattaw (i.e.) hat and feather, Chatelaw (i.e.) copper town, Chukafalaya (i.e.) long town, Hikihaw (i.e.) stand still, Chucalissa (i.e.) great town, Tuckahaw (i.e.) a certain weed, and Ashuck hooma (i.e.) red grass; this was formerly enclosed in palisadoes, and thus well fortified

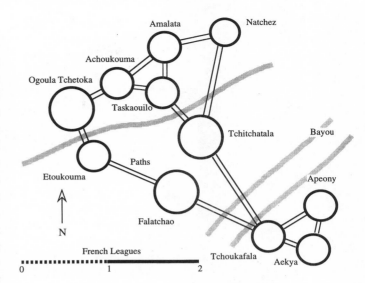

Figure 11.1. A Native American map of Chickasaw Villages in 1737.

against the attacks of small arms, but it now lays open; a second Artaguette [the French commander who attacked the Chickasaw for sheltering Natchez refugees], a little more prudent than the first, would now find them an easy prey.

The data on town size indicate, as I have argued elsewhere (Muller 1993a,b), that there is little justification for making a distinction of *kind* between historic and prehistoric towns in the Southeast (see Muller 1993a,b). There were *fewer* towns in the historic period, but most of them were about the same size as early historic and prehistoric towns.

Mound building is often taken as a measure of complexity. Figure 11.2 illustrates the large scale of the largest mound constructions from A.D. 800 to 1600, but it also shows that substantial mound construction continued later. Although no other mound construction approached the scale of the Cahokia site (the largest bar on the chart), the biggest of the late mounds are quite large by world standards.

Analysis of the labor investment represented by mound construction (Figure 11.3) shows that it represents activities that would have been quite feasible for any of the larger historic polities, many of whom were much larger than the examples of 5,000 and 10,000 people shown in the figure.

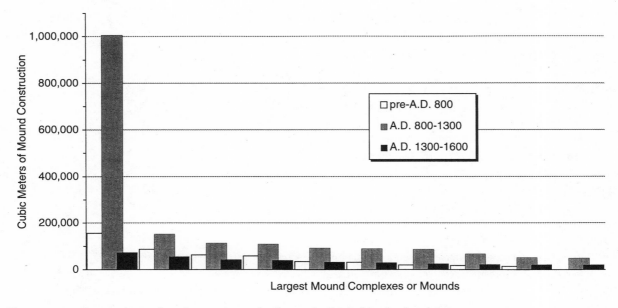

Figure 11.2.   Comparison of ten largest mound volumes by period in the Southeast.

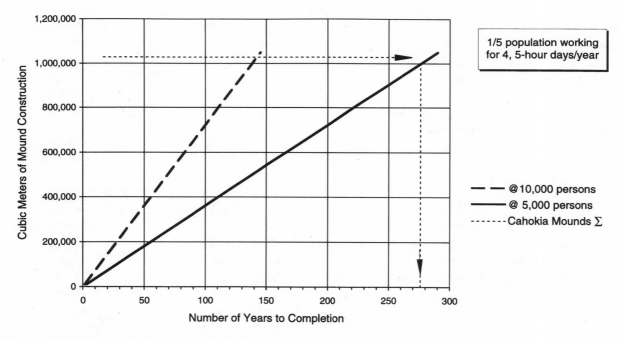

Figure 11.3.   Labor costs of construction at large Mississippian sites.

Moundbuilding is an expression of social dominance (if not *necessarily* domination), but it is easy to forget what relatively small numbers of well-organized workers can do (also see Muller 1986a:200ff.).

In moundbuilding, the regular and steady diversion of one person's labor from each five-person household (out of 1,250 people in the immediate locality) to public works for only four days a year could accumulate the site total at Kincaid of 93,000 m³ in only 46 to 103 years (cf. higher figures in Muller 1986a:203). This estimate assumes that each day's work (i.e., five hours) would allow excavation, transport, and spreading of between 0.6 to 1.1 m³ of clay fill per person. This is, overall, a very conservative estimate, as workers with elan could accomplish much more.

If one forgets how much moundbuilding relatively small numbers of workers could accomplish, then it is also easy to forget that a decline in such activities should not automatically be interpreted as due to political devolution. Historic Eastern Native Americans had much of their energies directed elsewhere by warfare accompanying the European invasions.

Marvin Smith (1987:89) has argued that the decline in scale and particularly the "loss" of secondary mound centers indicates loss of political control. However, we are coming to see that smaller mound sites near larger ones may indicate local autonomy rather than subordination (as also suggested for the American Bottom by Milner 1986, 1991a). If this is so, decline in regional population and aggregation of the survivors at surviving larger centers would not imply the loss of a political "control" that the large centers may never have had. As M. Smith (1987:142) also observes: "depopulation and decentralization of sixteenth century chiefdoms . . . led to increasing recombinations of refugee groups."

Indeed, such "recombinations" were these societies' best efforts to maintain as much centralization and complexity as they could. The village map (Figure 11.1), for example, shows the incorporation of refugee Natchez as a distinct settlement within the Chickasaw chiefdom. There is every reason to see the same processes occurring before European contact. It is in this context of relative autonomy and sometime linkages of political fealty and economic interdependence that both historic and prehistoric social interactions need to be understood.

Far from eliminating historic political organizations from comparison because of their supposed "degeneracy," we may even have to exercise caution in historic-

prehistoric comparisons in quite a different way than is usually proposed: we should recognize that some historic societies were enhancing political power for war chiefs under external military pressures (see Gearing 1962, analysis of Cherokee priests and warriors; also Adair 1775, on leadership; and Hawkins 1848 and Milfort 1802, on changes in military authority). In the historic cases, local levels were composed of semi-autonomous units, each with its own leadership, paralleling the structure, as we shall see, of the polity as a whole. There is really no reason to doubt that the same kind of "modularity" characterized prehistoric Mississippian local and regional organization.

Macroregional Integration

Figure 11.4 is re-oriented from a 1737 French redrawing of aboriginal, area-wide map of the peoples surrounding the Chickasaw—drawn at the same time as Figure 11.1, probably from the same, likely Alabama, sources. Note that the larger communities in Figure 11.4 (which are indeed "polities" as the word has been used in English since the sixteenth century; v. OED) are connected in the same way as the towns in Figure 11.1. On this map, war paths (considered to be "red") are distinguished from the "white" paths of peaceful relations. Other historic representations show similar means of symbolically representing the social and political relations (see Waselkov 1989). Lafferty (1994) has offered the intriguing speculation that one engraved shell cup from Spiro (Phillips and Brown 1975–82 (Volume III):Plate 122.3) may be a similar representation of social entities.

Linkages among political entities on Figure 11.4 and similar maps are "paths" of several sorts, including rivers (see Myer 1928). The size of the symbols, as in Figure 11.1, is roughly proportional to the importance of the group. Non-riverine linkages are now difficult to identify in the East since these ancient paths grew into modern highway systems. In a few places like the Natchez Trace, the ancient roads are still easily visible today, and other traces still can be found (e.g., Morrow and McCorvie 1983). In any case, the evidence suggests that the rivers played the most important part in the movement of heavy and bulky goods. While lighter, finished goods could have followed other paths, even the distribution of these suggests the importance of water transportation.

The evidence of exchange relationships across the Southeast, by its nature, does not give much information about the limits of political entities in the area. Normal

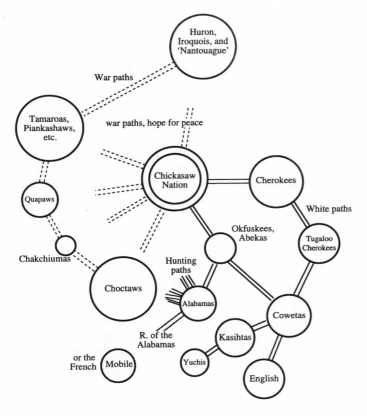

Figure 11.4. The Chickasaw world in 1737.

Although it has been mentioned only indirectly in this paper, the phenomenon of warfare was endemic in the East in historic times. Kroeber (1939:148), for example, saw warfare in the area as the most direct "social factor" explaining low population density. Most certainly historical warfare played an important part in defining the "no-man's lands" that existed between polities. These zones partly reflected areas where residence was too risky, but they also often reflected areas that were unattractive for settlement for environmental reasons. Given the indisputable aggressiveness of European slave raiding and military invasion, it is not surprising that the European view of native Easterners was focused on war. What is less certain is whether prehistoric peoples engaged in these practices to the same degree as in historic times. Was one of the causes of the supposed thirteenth and fourteenth century "decline" of Mississippian an increase in regional conflict? Perhaps, but there were other factors operating as well. Shortening of the growing season probably had the same effect of increasing the distance between polities. Consequently, abandonment, and probably aggregation, decreased the number of polities in the Southeast even before European invasion.

Relations to Other Areas

Some years ago, it seemed likely that "influences" from outside were implemented by "trade" with either Mesoamerica directly or by indirect contact through the Southwest. However, as discussed by Cobb et al. in Chapter 13 of this volume, there is a complete absence of evidence supporting any direct exchange relations between the Southeast and Mesoamerica. As for the Southwest, a good argument can be made for contacts across the Great Plains. Unfortunately for any idea that this was a channel for early external stimulus, these contacts through the valleys of the Arkansas and Canadian Rivers in the southern Plains (see Krieger 1947a,b) only show up after the middle of the fifteenth century—far too late to have played any role in the development of Southeastern social formations.

Of course, one has to be struck by the apparent synchrony of later Southwestern and Southeastern "climaxes" around the A.D. 1000 to 1200 period; but the fact that cathedral building in Europe also peaks at this time is a compelling argument that factors other than direct contact may be involved in these developmental coincidences. In general, the Southeast cannot be thought of as totally isolated from other North American and Carib-

archaeological data on distributions of phases and most especially the gaps between zones of occupation are probably better indications of boundaries. However, it should be noted that style boundaries for such media as engraved shell are noticeably different from the boundaries defined from ceramic styles—the normal criteria used to define archaeological phases. In some cases, the distribution of so-called prestige items may mark larger scale integration of local communities, as suggested for the Citico gorget style and the Coosa paramount chiefdom (although I doubt the correctness of that particular attribution, cf. M. Smith 1989). By their very nature, so-called prestige goods are also desirable items for exchange or even for capture as trophies, so distribution outside their zone of origin is to be expected.

bean societies, but there is little reason to see any such links as playing important historical roles in the Southeast. The only Southeastern society that would have possibly been of such power and magnificence that it could have sought to control exchange in the area would have been Cahokia. Recent views of the localities and regions surrounding Cahokia, however, can find little evidence that Cahokia's hegemony extended very far out of the American Bottom around modern-day St. Louis (e.g., Milner 1986, 1991a, 1993), despite efforts to see Cahokia as the center of a "world system" (Dincauze and Hasenstaub 1989; Peregrine 1991, 1992).

Interpretation

We do not know precisely which predecessors of historic groups were part of the most extensive prehistoric interaction systems. The impact of Old World diseases and European invasion was so great that the situation could hardly be otherwise (see Jennings 1975). Certainly many of the historic Muskhogean and Caddoan-speaking groups of the Southeast had ancestors who participated in these wide-spread interregional events.

But what was the nature of the social and political entities that were so involved? In the 1960s, in line with the positivist paradigms then current in archaeology, the functionalist-evolutionary models of Service (1962, 1975) and Fried (1967) were applied to the area, especially in the form of the concept of chiefdom. Changes in archaeological theoretical positions have resonated, if in a somewhat muted way, in Southeastern archaeology (e.g., Barker and Pauketat 1992). However, Lee's (1992) summary of the current state of hunter-gatherer studies arguing for the continuing usefulness of that concept could apply equally well to "chiefdom studies," (a point anticipated in some ways by Johnson and Earle 1987).

Notwithstanding unpleasant appurtenances to the term chiefdom, there really is little alternative to using some halfway descriptive word for societies that have relatively little general social differentiation (i.e., are still classless in the strict sense) yet have leaders who are somehow much more than mere headmen. In discussion of these issues during the symposium upon which this volume is based, "duck" was jokingly suggested as a term in place of chiefdom that was free from baggage of unilineal evolution. While this suggestion has a certain daffy attractiveness, the issue here is a documented form of social formation seen in historic records of the East, not one derived from the evolutionary stages of theoretical works.

Paradoxes abound in the nature of Eastern chiefdoms. They lacked classes, but had elites. They lacked true economic differentiation (i.e., specialization), but had production of fancy goods. They had economies that were still largely communal, but they had property symbolizing differences in power. How and why free persons gave up some of their freedom and became enmeshed, even weakly, in relations of subordination to these chiefs is by no means simply or easily answered. In general, the social separation of the chiefs may be tolerated because of the social benefits both from their "princely" generosity (noblesse oblige) and from their taking on "administrative" tasks. Of course, some diversion of goods surely occurred as they passed through the chief's hands. Personal relationships to the chiefs served as "insurance" for periods of shortages. In the historic East, at least, these relationships were mirrored in the relationship of one's own town chief to the "paramount" chief.

The data suggest that the most successful historic groups maintained a scale of life in both town and polity size that was essentially the same as in the heyday of Mississippian. The conceptual structure of the local map and the area-wide map of Figures 11.1 and 11.4 are the same. "Centers" of one kind or another are linked by paths of communication. Historically, and very probably prehistorically, regional political integration was maintained by a complex series of local alliances and exchange between local authorities (town chiefs) and their regional leaders (paramount chiefs). These relationships define a modular structure of authority by settlement, by localities, and by regions. Towns were linked together in confederacies (so-called paramount chiefdoms) of considerable political sophistication. These alliances had both military and economic dimensions, but were ultimately based on household economies with little social or economic differentiation.

If every person could not be a chief, historically there were still many potential chiefs among the elite members of each community. Kin leaders, town chiefs, and paramount chiefs all had parallel political and social roles, each on their own scale. The physical and social layout of the hamlet is magnified into the town, and even the region. The implication of such a political economy would be that exchange and other forms of "macroregional integration" would as often be individually or kinship mediated, as centrally controlled (again, compare the Kula Ring; e.g., Weiner 1976).

Historic Creek and Choctaw polities were surely as large as those present in places like Cahokia and Moundville. Moreover, the site plan of the huge site of Cahokia is very similar to the layout of smaller sites, both contemporary and historic, except that substructure mound construction extends down to what would be non-mound residences at smaller mound centers. There is no question that scalar, quantitative change of this kind can represent qualitative differences in social-political organization. However, the question is whether these particular scalar differences *were* actually qualitatively different. I believe that the scale of documented, historic groups shows that qualitative differences (such as state formation) are not *required* to explain the organization of even the most exaggerated populations proposed for sites like Cahokia. In my view, most Mississippian societies were low-level chiefdoms, while a few notable cases such as Cahokia were more complex but not to the degree that they could be called anything more than complex chiefdoms (cf. Muller 1987:11 to Stoltman 1991:352 for a misrepresentation of my views on this topic).

INTEGRATION AND POLITICAL ECONOMY

The structure of integration in the Southeast was then not necessarily so different from the Historic period societies as some have thought. The same may be said for the character of the economic systems that produced and exchanged the goods that we know archaeologically. The vast majority of accounts on production and exchange that we have from the Historic period clearly illustrate the domestic character of production, distribution, and consumption in the East. In the sections that follow, a brief look will be taken at the conditions, so far as we can know them, of the character of, first, production, then exchange, and, finally, the reproduction of the system.

Production and Social Context

Late Prehistoric Southeastern societies, like those of the preceding and succeeding periods, produced almost all goods domestically. Little, if any, real specialization of production was present (e.g., Cobb 1988; Muller 1984), although there were clearly differences of skill. Chiefs expressed differences of status and rank by symbolic means, probably using the so-called "prestige goods" characteristic of their regions. The production of items of this kind may be a path by which elites sometimes come to dominate some segments of production (e.g., Earle 1978, 1987b; Johnson and Earle 1987). However, I

remain very skeptical that producers north of Mexico went very far down this path.

Too often the argument for the identification of "prestige" goods has been circular. While many "prestige goods" discussed here are found in greatest quantity in "elite" contexts such as charnel temple mounds, it is wrong to assume that strong sumptuary taboos existed in the Southeast. Elaborate "prestige" goods often occur in small sites where they are sometimes the *only* evidence of supposed "elite" rank. Even more compellingly, production debris shows that so-called prestige goods were made at large and small sites alike. The idea of elite regards to followers is not so compelling as to mean that we are not first obliged to consider the simpler alternatives that these goods were *not* elite controlled. Elites probably had somewhat greater access to such goods, but hardly monopolized them.

The Kula Ring of Melanesia needs to be considered more closely by Eastern archaeologists as a carefully studied real example of how distribution of prestige goods can work without involving much "control." Malinowski's functionalist explanations of the Kula Ring in Melanesia (1932) outlined the operation of such systems, but without addressing evolutionary implications of these behaviors. Exchange in desirable "prestige goods" can encourage more socially necessary, but less exciting exchange of other kinds of goods. Recent analyses (Weiner 1976) have furthered a kind of dialectic of these exchanges, involving the contradictions between private and public benefit.

One striking paradox for the "prestige economy" model in the East is that the distribution of "prestige goods" peaks among "core" and "peripheries" at the very point that the supposed "center" of Cahokia is fading away. The A.D. 1250 "Southern Cult" is really too late to be the "state religion" of the so-called Ramey state. Perhaps, just perhaps, the wide-spread growth of exchange indicates that the factors that seem to have caused the decline in northern Mississippian centers were at the same time increasing the social need for macroregional integration.

The forms and character of goods produced in the Southeast show both talent and ability. However, complex items of great artistic and social value can be created by artisans who do not make their living by these means and who are not alienated from their products by great "lords." I think that we may reasonably conclude from both archaeological and historical evidence that patronage rather than domination, of production is a more likely role for Eastern elites.

Goods and Exchange

Many kinds of goods are known to have been exchanged in Mississippian times. Some of the finished goods had considerable symbolic content, although the meaning of this symbolism is difficult to approach. Procrustean attempts to force these motifs into Mesoamerican ideology are unconvincing (see Cobb et al. Chapter 13). Like other aspects of Eastern life, the best examples for understanding prehistoric symbolism would be careful historical, comparative study of this area. Analysis of the distribution of symbolic archaeological remains has been approached in a number of ways. Various artistic styles were defined in the late 1960s and later (e.g., Muller 1966a,b, 1979, 1986b; Phillips and Brown 1975, 1984), and revisions and amendments to these interpretations have been proposed (e.g., Brown 1989).

Another way that exchange items may suggest something of their distribution systems is through careful study of their spatial dispersal. Identifiable exchange items may show fall-off in density of archaeological occurrence proportional to the square of the distance from known sources. This pattern is usually taken to indicate goods passed along from person to person (i.e., "down-the-line;" Renfrew 1969).

Intermediate community control of exchange might be expected to produce concentration of items at these sites, with secondary fall-off from those locations. If used cautiously, fall-off curves have value as an investigatory approach, even where they may be weak "proof" of the kinds of exchange relationships. Of course, quantities reflect intensity of archaeological work as well as prehistoric interactions, and this needs to be taken into account.

Recently, Brown et al. (1990) have used such an examination of patterns of dispersal for stone hoes made from the relatively distinctive Mill Creek chert, probably mostly from Union County, Illinois. In their analysis of stone hoe distribution, they present data on distribution in "fall-off" curves by distance from the presumed source. They further relate these data to gravity models that analyze the "attractions" between two locations in terms of the "mass" of population in each area in a manner derived from Newtonian physics (e.g., Hodder and Orton 1976:188). They also suggest some interesting possibilities for using this approach to assess relative population (Brown et al. 1990:269).

Figure 11.5 shows the number of Mill Creek hoes north of Union County, Illinois plotted against distance

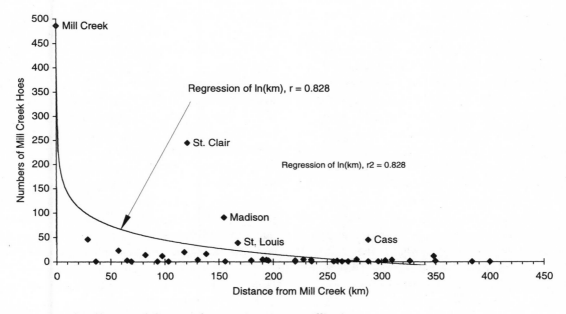

Figure 11.5.   Finds of hoes and distance from Union County, Illinois.

from Union County, together with a regression curve of number of hoes against the logarithm of distance. The product-moment correlation between number of hoes and logarithm of distance for all hoes in *all* directions from Union County is 0.0732 (the adjusted r^2 is 0.532 with p<.0001). A logarithmic correlation is, of course, desirable because the *distribution* of finds is by *area* not by distance.

The correlations of distance and number of hoes for the northern distributions only, as shown in Figure 11.5, is better(r=0.83; the adjusted r^2 is about 0.68), and the removal of Cahokia in the computations improves the correlation somewhat (the r increases to 0.898 with the adjusted r^2=0.802, significant at $\propto$=.01 with p<.0001). These statistics suggest that the overall distribution in this "Northern Mississippi" drainage category of Brown et al. (1990) shows no important, non-local effect of the Cahokia site.

A line graph connecting the hoe findspots (compare Brown et al. 1990:Figure 87) misleads the eye into seeing a surrounding "influence" around the "peak" at Cahokia. Brown et al. recognized this and presented a second chart with averaged numbers (Brown et al. 1990:Figure 88). After eliminating Union County distributions, they concluded that Cahokia "does not explain the hoe numbers to the south" (Brown et al. 1990:268). I suggest further that the distributions actually falsify a *major* effect for Cahokia in "redistributing" or "controlling" Mill Creek hoe distributions in *any* direction. In my view, the number of hoes at the Cahokia locality should be taken as indicative of the "attraction" of that center. Removal of the Cahokia outlier shows that the distributions better fit the curve of "down-the-line" distributions from Union County than could be the case if Cahokia were mediating the distribution of stone hoes to other locations. This is merely to say that it is difficult to justify an interpretation of Cahokia as controlling "trade" in hoes when it has so little effect on distributions outside its immediate locality.

As far as production at the source areas is concerned, Cobb's work at the Union County quarries has shown likely small-scale production (Cobb 1988, 1989, 1991, personal communication). Certainly, the evidence from the hoe production sites and other sites in Union County make it difficult to agree that "a substantial amount of the trade in Mill Creek hoes was carried out by one or more Union County centers" insofar as that statement implies even local elite control of exchange (Brown et al. 1990:269). The nature of the hoe exchange process remains to be understood in its social and economic context, but the present evidence is as consistent with the idea of production by transients coming to the source areas during off seasons as it is with any idea of controlled, organized production and "trade." Although we cannot see salt exchange in the archaeological record in the same way as chert, ten years of work at the Great Salt Spring saltern in Gallatin County, Illinois, has shown transient, domestic salt production, not specialized production (Muller 1984, 1992); and there is no reason to suppose that distribution was controlled while production was not.

In general, well-documented exchange of utilitarian goods in the Southeast does not require more complex models than "person-to-person" movement of goods. This has even been acknowledged by some arguing for strong degrees of control of "wealth" by elites (Stoltman 1991:352). However, the situation is not much different even when we look at elaborate "prestige" artifacts. As we shall see, these show patterns like those seen in more practical goods, although their rarity makes their study subject to bias.

Engraved shell is one of the best of the supposed prestige items for archaeological study simply because these items are complex in form and are relatively common, even though their manufacture represented a substantial labor investment (see Lawson 1709:193–194). Stylistic analysis of engraved shell items in the form of shell cups and gorgets has allowed a detailed appreciation of their chronology, likely origins, and distributions (e.g., Galloway 1989; Muller 1966a,b, 1979, 1989; Phillips and Brown 1975–82). Illustrations of these styles and discussions of their character may be found in several papers in Galloway (1989). The content and themes of these styles are of less interest here than their distributions, so the reader should simply note that each of the following named "prestige" goods styles is known from relatively broad areas (see further discussion of these issues in Muller 1997).

In Figures 11.6 and 11.7, the size of each symbol is proportional to the number of items at a given coordinate, the largest being around 20 objects at a single site. This form of presentation parallels the eighteenth century aboriginal maps of the area in Figures 11.1 and 11.4. Figure 11.6 graphically presents the locations (by degrees longitude and latitude) and numbers of gorgets in different styles during the Southern Cult horizon at A.D. 1200–1450. If the Spiro cups were shown here, they would indicate a very large triangle for the Braden style (similar to Eddyville gorgets) at that location (roughly 95°W, 35°N) as well as another large symbol for the Craig style.

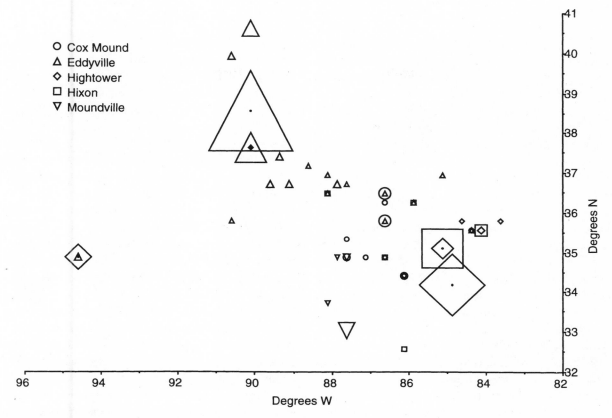

Figure 11.6.   Southern Cult and derived gorget style distributions, ca. A.D. 1200–1450.

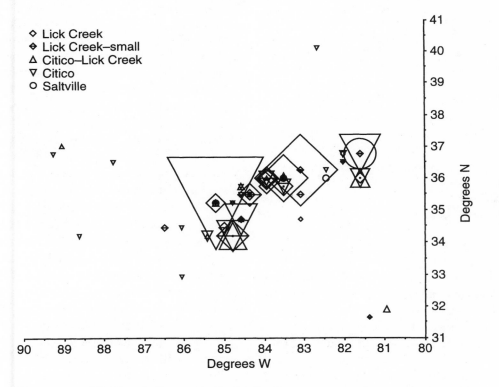

Figure 11.7.   "Rattlesnake" gorget style distributions, A.D. 1450–1650.

The thirteenth century styles plotted in Figure 11.6 are Eddyville (anthropomorphic and spider themes from the Mississippi-Ohio confluence), Hightower (anthropomorphic and zoomorphic themes from the upper Tennessee), Moundville (anthropomorphic gorgets from the central Southeast), and Cox Mound ("woodpecker" gorgets in the central Southeast, related to the Moundville style). The later Hixon style (ca. A.D. 1450) derived from Hightower is also shown. Spiro styles as defined by Phillips and Brown (1972–1985)—constituting the largest single collection of engraved shell art from the Southeast—are not shown; but they have distributions that are essentially limited to the Caddo archaeological area around the furthest west symbols on the map. The Braden A style on engraved cups at Spiro is essentially the same as the gorgets identified as Eddyville style by me (Muller 1966b). The Craig style at Spiro is largely limited to the Caddo region. Spiro is important because some items found there were almost certainly executed by the artisans who made items found in the Mississippi and Tennessee River valleys, documenting long-distance dispersal of finished items. It is these widely dispersed thirteenth century styles and their associations in other media that constitute the real core of the "Southern Cult" or "Southeastern Ceremonial Complex."

Thirteenth century "centers" such as Etowah and Moundville had large numbers of gorgets; but such items were *not* limited to central, elite contexts. For example, research in the Kincaid locality has shown that small sites have about the same *percentages* of "prestige goods" as the largest sites, but lack other evidence of social differentiation. The distributions shown in Figure 11.6 are partly based on the communication channels provided by major river systems. Each of the styles had a fairly clear regional affiliation (leaving aside the complex issue of the Braden style at Spiro and its relationship to the Eddyville style of the Mississippi-Ohio confluence, see Brown 1989; Muller 1989; I do not accept Brain's [Brain and Phillips 1996] revisionist late dates for these objects).

Styles not plotted here, such as the fifteenth century and later Williams Island gorgets, are often associated with likely Creek and Apalachee historical associations. The Williams Island and Hixon styles, apparently derived from Hightower, are more likely associations of the Coosa chiefdom and its neighbors than is the Citico style. Lick Creek and Saltville date to the fifteenth century and Citico dates from post-A.D. 1550 into the contact period.

Figure 11.7 shows the distribution of the fifteenth to eighteenth century so-called "rattlesnake" (perhaps the Cherokee Uktena) gorget styles most often associated with proto-Cherokee and historical Cherokee contexts. One style, Saltville, appears to be a protohistoric Piedmont Siouan style. These objects are most common in the eastern Tennessee River valley, but single items in these styles have been found as far away as southern Canada.

In these figures, it can be seen that more long-distance dispersal of finished goods occurred before A.D. 1300 than after. Nonetheless, the "rattlesnake" gorgets were sometimes moved over very long distances, and they often occur in association with gorgets from either the South Atlantic Coast or from the Nashville locality, as well as with other contemporary "rattlesnake" styles. In all time periods, trying to explain these artifact distributions in terms of the "attraction" of centers alone seriously biases our understanding.

As in the case of the stone hoes, we may examine dispersal patterns for the shell gorgets in terms of distance from hypothetical "origins." In Figure 11.8, the Eddyville pattern is measured from the oft-used "view from the summit of Monks Mound at Cahokia." Admittedly, Cahokia was on its last legs then, but there is some evidence of "Southern Cult" associations for the site and locality. Again, the Spiro Braden A materials related to the Eddyville style are not included here, although some of the Braden artifacts may have come from eastern sources. The distances between the Spiro people and those in the Missouri-Mississippi-Ohio confluences are great and much remains to be explained about their relationships. The intraregional relationship of the American Bottom to other locations where Eddyville gorgets have been recovered is also obscure. The Cahokia count in the chart is inflated by a number of small fragments.

The correlation of number to log-distance is surprisingly good, given that these gorgets certainly do *not* have a single source at Cahokia (adjusted $r^2 = .207$; $p = .0087$). Eddyville style items were made over an area from the American Bottom to the Mississippi-Ohio-Tennessee confluence localities, as suggested by variability in numbers along the x axis out to the 300 km limits of the area in which the gorgets were produced. In any case, it is clearly impossible to argue that Cahokia controlled the distribution of these prestige goods.

Figure 11.9 shows the pattern for the fifteenth century "rattlesnake" Lick Creek style, which has a relatively restricted distribution in the source areas of the Tennessee Valley above Knoxville. This is the earliest of the "rattlesnake" gorget forms, although small gorgets in essentially

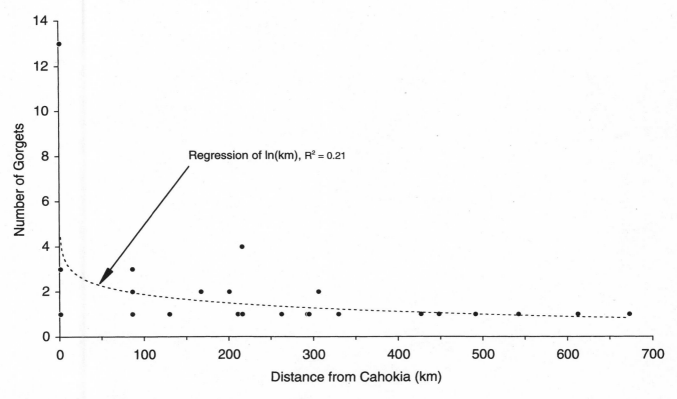

Figure 11.8.   Eddyville gorgets and distance from Cahokia.

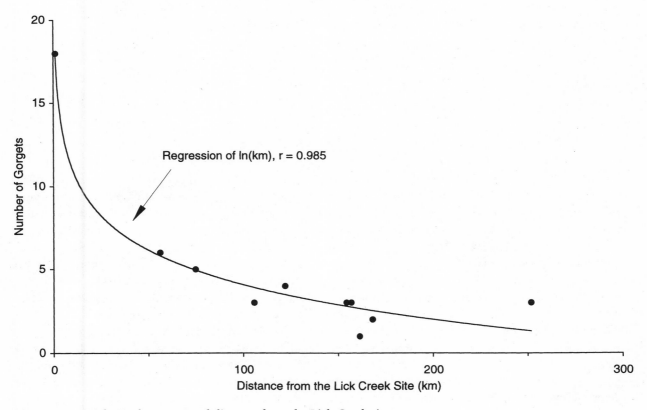

Figure 11.9.   Lick Creek gorgets and distance from the Lick Creek site.

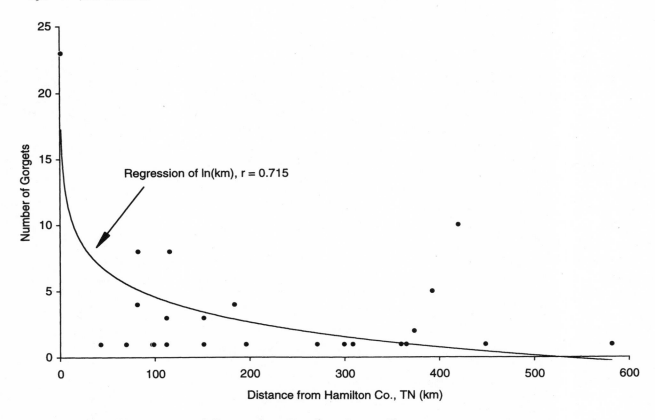

Figure 11.10.   Citico gorgets and distance from Hamilton County, Tennessee.

this style persisted. Grave lot associations suggest fairly close relationships with the Nashville Basin to the west, and down to the South Atlantic Coast. Also note that these gorgets are found no more than 250 km from the Lick Creek site. Here the pattern of dispersal clearly suggests down-the-line movement of goods from a relatively localized origin.

Figure 11.10 shows the Citico style gorgets of the seventeenth century as plotted from Hamilton County, Tennessee, where the largest numbers have been found. The distribution suggests widely scattered places of manufacture, rather than localization. Indeed, one would conclude from stylistic evidence alone that the Citico style gorgets were made in many different locations in the Tennessee Valley and its tributaries and exchanged among different producing localities (Muller 1966a,

1979). Nonetheless, the overall fit to a gravity fall-off model is better than one would expect from the graph.

The secondary peak at 450 km is in extreme western Virginia, close to the earlier locations of Lick Creek gorget manufacture. Late Citico gorgets are usually associated with protohistoric and early historic Cherokee contexts (not Creek). Lick Creek and Citico are stylistically closely related. Citico represents, in some senses, a later style phase of the same style represented in Lick Creek gorgets, with structural as well as morphological changes (Muller 1966b, 1979). The transition from Lick Creek to Citico styles is associated with the spread of the theme in the sixteenth century from the upper reaches of the eastern Tennessee River valley into the Chattanooga locality and south. It is, of course, tempting to see this as possibly representing the period of expansion of Cherokee territory sometimes proposed (e.g., Swanton 1946:14; cf. Sears 1955).

These analyses indicate the similarity of patterns of interaction in many kinds of goods in the prehistoric Southeast. These cases, and others not presented here, all indicate the general adequacy of a person-to-person model of movement of goods over the entire area and through time. Those who seek to explain the distributions of these objects in terms of the power and influence of powerful elites at central sites will have to present more cogent arguments in place of their assertions of that supposed influence.

While some have even suggested that "trade" was a specialized profession in the prehistoric Southeast (e.g., Porter 1969), few who have actually worked with objective data can hold this view today. Exchange of goods in the prehistoric Southeast, to the contrary, appears similar to the patterns documented in the historical literature. "Interlinear" and direct reading of these accounts indicates that "traders" encountered by European narrators were visitors from other societies, or—in some accounts—occupying a new status created by the Europeans (as Nuñez Cabeza de Vaca [1542] did on first contact in Texas).

Historically, "ordinary" persons seem to have visited other groups as a part of their domestic and kinship-based economies and obligations. There is no solid historic evidence, moreover, for any special social status of trader in this area *before* the establishment of European trade (Myer 1928). Again, we have to remember that exchange can occur without traders in any meaningful sense of that term. Even in contexts in which European-established trade reached levels far exceeding anything we can see in the archaeological evidence, there is nothing in the historic record that resembles the kind of elite control of exchange seen by some at Cahokia (e.g., Stoltman 1991:352). To judge from historic records in the Southeast, both elite *and* non-elite exchanges were important, and households and kin groups had more to do with "trade" than did chiefs.

Reproduction

Reproduction of a society and its relationships takes place alongside biological reproduction. Economic reproduction takes place by producing subsistence goods and then distributing these goods so that they may be consumed in the productive cycle (e.g., Meillassoux 1981:51). Simple reproduction simply implies the need to produce enough to support the producer and her fam-

ily. However, in risky floodplain environments, normal and rational planning will result in the regular production of surplus subsistence goods, in order to plan for short-term threats such as 10-year flood dangers. Such surplus goods present social dangers, as well as benefits. If too much of this normal "surplus" is reinvested in biological reproduction, the "contradiction" of population expansion—new mouths to feed—results. On the other hand, such short-term surpluses can be shared, as they typically are even in very simple societies, to subsidize public events that further cement social obligations owed by one family to another, thus assisting social reproduction. In such circumstances, elaborate items of exchange can serve as a stimulus both to surplus production and to exchange with persons external to the domestic production unit, as well as "markers" with which to keep "score." One historical source even called shell gorgets "money" and indicated that finished gorgets ranged in value from "three or four Buck-Skins ready drest" to much cheaper (Lawson 1709:193). While this account reflects economic circumstances created by the developing trade with Europeans in deer skins, it does suggest the high value placed on gorgets, perhaps even for potential exchange conversion into more practical goods.

Conclusions

Neither the scale of public works, nor population density, nor the size of towns, nor the extension of political power over large regions suggest that the so-called "lords" of the Southeast exercised more power than the most important of the many chiefs and war chiefs described in the historic record for the area. Neither conquest nor domination of the sort that exists in class societies is a legitimate explanation for integration of localities and of regions in the Southeast. The scale of the patterns of exchange in the area suggests that the development of political power took place in the give and take of the relations among communities, town chiefs, councils, and the leaders to whom they owed fealty, rather than within the conflicts of even emergent classes. Relations with external elites provided additional prestige for local leaders who had somewhat easier access to valued goods. However, the patterns suggest that leaders exercised no monopoly on external relations and exchanges. Most long-distance exchange relations in the Southeast are reasonably modeled by simple person-to-person movements of goods from their diverse and often dispersed centers of production. It is necessary to see more explicit arguments and evidence for "control" of production and exchange before proposing that such institutions are *necessary* to explain these data. I am not arguing that "control" never existed, but rather that it certainly cannot be *assumed*.

Comparison between historic and prehistoric town sizes suggests that depopulation in the Historic period may have had more to do with the reduced number of towns rather than town size. Moreover, though we have less evidence, it seems that the number of distinct polities, rather than the size of polities, is most affected by historic depopulation. Where depopulation, in combination with other factors, might otherwise have led to a breakup of political-economic entities, the pressures of European trade and military action may have more than compensated for these centrifugal forces. Not least of these pressures is the indirect effect of depopulation in increasing wild food resources.

Mound construction was used as one measure of the level of public commitment commanded by "chiefs." The evidence suggests that public works were of such scale that chiefly societies in the historical "normal" size range of from 2,500 to 35,000 people could have supported such activities, if they had been allowed to do so in the strife-torn Historic period.

In short, it is reasonable to look to historic political economies for analogies and homologies with prehistoric Eastern societies and their systems of integration. Archaeological evidence from the Southeast shows little, if anything, that could not have been accomplished with the populations *and* organizations of the Historic period. Overall, we may conclude that the Historic period was more complex than usually recognized and that the prehistoric Southeast was probably comparable in its organization and character. Both political and economic development in eastern North America were probably greater than anywhere else north of Mexico. However, the roots of the "Great Towns" in the Southeast were in the small villages that still possessed many of the characteristics of the tribal communities that preceded them.

The examples given here illustrate a general pattern of exchange and interaction in the Southeast that is consistent with what we know about the character of production and political economy in developing chiefdom-level societies. Full-time, craft specialization (in the strict sense, see Muller 1984, 1992) is absent; production of every kind of goods and raw materials was profoundly domestic. Southeastern economies were still at almost a tribal level. Even so, politically there were emergent groups of persons who acquired central administrative roles managing risk through allocation of stored resources, through their ability to stimulate fealty from their followers, and through developing alliances with external leaders. The nature of exchange and "macroregional interaction" in the Southeast does not, however, lend much support to models of elite *development* that emphasize features, such as power and exploitation, that exist primarily in already developed class societies.

Acknowledgments

This paper is part of an ongoing project on Mississippian political economy. Some graphics and data are similar to those published elsewhere (Muller 1993a, 1995). I want to thank James Brown for making Howard Winter's data on hoe distribution by county available to me.

CHAPTER TWELVE

Powhatan's Mantle as Metaphor:

Comparing Macroregional Integration in the Southwest and Southeast

Jon Muller

David R. Wilcox

IN THE SOUTHEAST, THE ETHNOGRAPHIC ARTIFACT known as Powhatan's mantle can be viewed as a metaphor in several ways. This deerskin cloak is thought to have belonged to Powhatan, ruler of the Powhatan confederacy during the early seventeenth century (Waselkov 1989:306–308). It is decorated with numerous shell beads depicting a human figure, two animals, and 34 spirally formed circles (Figure 12.1). The mantle has been interpreted as a symbol of Powhatan's power, with the 34 circles representing the districts under his control and influence. By the late seventeenth century the mantle had become part of the Ashmolean Museum of Oxford University. Thus, the cloak can also be viewed as a metaphor for the political autonomy, as well as everything else, that European intruders took from Native American populations during the contact period.

For archaeologists interested in comparing macroregional integration in the Southwest and Southeast, Powhatan's mantle can also be used as a metaphor for how such integration can be conceptualized. In both areas, the same kind of structure as that illustrated in Powhatan's mantle can be discerned. This structure con-

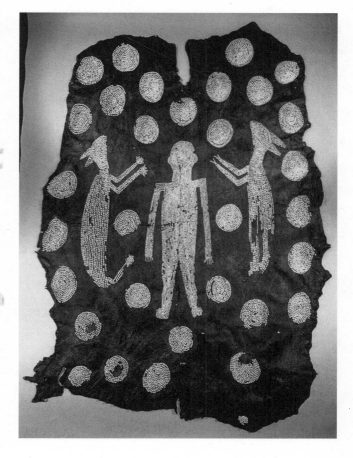

Figure 12.1. Powhatan's mantle (photograph courtesy of the Ashmolean Museum, Oxford).

sists of replicated units connected by paths. Wilcox's maps (Figure 10.6, 10.9) of Chacoan great houses evidence this pattern. It can be seen even more clearly in Muller's two historic maps of Chickasaw villages and territory (Figures 11.1, 11.4). The Chickasaw maps are basically graphs of relationships. They show scaled circles, which represent political entities, and lines, which represent paths connecting the entities. As seen in a number of examples published by Waselkov (1989) for the Colonial period, such maps seem to have been the common Indian way of symbolizing and representing the structure of relationships among towns and peoples in the East.

These maps, including Powhatan's mantle (Figure 12.1), represent how we have come to see both the Southwest and Southeast. In both areas, relatively small and simple settlements form the building blocks for the "Great Towns," however large and complex. Similar political structures are replicated at each level, but with increasing complexity or "promotion" as the area and number of people increase. Sahlins' (1972:Figure 5.1) model of reciprocity and kinship residential sectors represents a local, segmentary view of the lower levels of such social units. However, according to Sahlins, these lower level units were also part of other kinds of social formations, which were hierarchical, even imperial, in scope. In these broader systems, powerful elites could exercise rigid control over goods, exchange, interaction, and even people. One of the key issues in understanding both the prehistoric Southwest and Southeast is to discern the relationships among local, regional, and "macroregional" levels of integration. In both areas, "Great Towns" were foci of interaction within and among different regions, groups, and peoples.

In an advanced seminar setting, segmentary opposition throws the assumptions of one's own camp into a relief that would not be so obvious in any other setting. The issues that continue to stir controversy in one area are illuminated by comparison to the parallel arguments in the other. Many of us came to Amerind with fairly firm views on the reasonableness of the application of such terms as state, specialization, and chiefdom. While fundamental differences remain, agreement was reached on the character of some questions that need to be settled. These issues include whether the Southeast and Southwest can or should be described within the same models of political or economic integration. In this chapter, we compare first the temporal and spatial scale over which macroregional interaction occurred in the

prehistoric Southwest and Southeast and then the developments which occurred in the two areas in different time periods.

COMPARATIVE SCALES

The relationships briefly described below for the Southeast are the result of over 4,000 years of widespread exchange linking areas that are thousands of kilometers apart. The structure of aboriginal political discourse in the East—certainly in historic times—reveals competitive, even warlike, relations among the various levels of political power. Individual power, both political and spiritual, was obtained by achievement rather than ascription. The paradox of politics and power in the East lies in the dynamic balance between public affairs and private glory. For all the difficulties in interpretation, prestige goods are linked, whether as amulets or as emblems, to these public-private contradictions. They are commonly associated with persons whose relative power was likely great, but their distribution throughout the Late Prehistoric East is consistent with their movement through face-to-face contact, either through exchange or as trophies.

In contrast, chiefs are hard to identify in the Southwest, and even the interpretation of a chiefdom level of organization remains controversial. The flaunting of private glory was not the Southwestern mode of political action. To the contrary, corporate structures seem much more evident empirically, and this is leading some Southwesternists to suggest group-oriented chiefdom organizations (see Wilcox, Chapter 10). Religious ideologies that fostered cooperation within and among corporate groups may have afforded the greatest adaptive advantages to such groups in the arid Southwest. Even so, increasingly complex structures of political and economic organization were constructed, and archaeologists are just beginning to learn how to recognize their hallmarks and to understand their workings. Just as in the Southeast, where we may raise questions about the scale over which political power was exercised in different places and periods, so too in the Southwest such questions legitimately arise. Even if the scales were arguably comparable in the two areas, how people managed power probably rested on quite different social and political arrangements.

Empirically, this issue comes down to whether the apparent strata of large and small sites represent hierarchical organizations combining domination and subordination of second and third level sites (such as "secondary mound centers" in the Southeast, or "outliers" in the Chacoan system). Alternative views have inferred the autonomy of the supposed second and third levels of the so-called hierarchies and have suggested spheres of influence, rather than domination. Studies of the distribution of goods and exchange relationships have not completely settled these issues, but clearly can be of substantial assistance. One of us (Muller) feels at present that the balance has tilted in the direction of influence rather than domination, both in the Southeast and Southwest. The other (Wilcox) suspects that in some cases in both areas domination had the upper hand for various periods of time. We join in hoping these differences of view will be a basis for continuing dialogue, the common ground being the shared quest for new data that may resolve these differences.

At the Amerind symposium, differences of archaeological systematics also loomed large in our attempts at comparison. The largest scale of interaction in the Southeast is huge. Goods moved thousands of kilometers from the Gulf Coast to the Great Lakes, from Wyoming and even the Southwest to the Atlantic Coast. Cultural similarities throughout the area have led many to emphasize a single macroregion, the Southeast, and to think of neighboring regions (Caddoan, Oneota, Iroquoia) in relation to it.

In the Southwest, six different "cultural traditions" have been defined, and there archaeologists tend to think separately of each; thus we have the Hohokam, Mogollon (Mimbres), Eastern Anasazi (Chacoan), Western Anasazi, Fremont and Patayan. Long-distance exchange of shell and other valuables also occurred in the Southwest, however, cross-cutting the "cultural traditions." Exchange connectivity with West Mexico is also documented, and debate about the cultural significance of those relationships still rages, while in the Southeast it is now generally accepted that no direct connections with Mesoamerica are documented (see Cobb et al. Chapter 13).

Is the tendency to think of the Southwest in multiple terms only a matter of emphasis, a function of perception rather than substance? Perhaps not: we note that Southwestern environments are in fact more diverse than those in the Southeast, and the Southwestern "cultural traditions" correlate well with those differences. Should, then, the whole Southwest be compared to the whole Southeast, or is the Southeast, processually, more akin to, say, the Chacoan "macroregional" system or the Hohokam "macroregional" system? While we believe the latter approach has merit, in the summaries presented below we seek commonalties or differences of process by comparing both areas as wholes.

Temporally, there is a similar scale difference, the Southeasternists tending to think of the whole period from A.D. 700 to 1450 as a single unit, albeit with a succession of changes experienced throughout the whole area. Traditional Southwestern systematics have stressed the sequences of change within each "cultural tradition," differences of terminology deliberately emphasizing the independence of temporal processes. In recent years efforts have been made to identify "hinge" points, moments of pan-Southwestern change linked to environmental processes. While Wilcox takes issue with several of these claims, he too argues that there are some broad commonalties. For purposes of comparison between the Southeast and Southwest, we have selected a series of six dates or periods to structure our discussion.

ANTECEDENTS

One of the chief differences between the Southwest and Southeast is revealed by a comparison of antecedent social systems in the two areas before A.D. 800. In the Southeast, the antecedents of Mississippian complexes were already reasonably complex societies with massive public works such as the great Hopewellian geometric embankments of southern Ohio or the mounds and earthwork rings of Poverty Point, Louisiana. Once thought to have been strongly hierarchical, these societies are now seen as occupying a kind of ambiguous position that does not fit well into typological categories such as "tribe" or "chiefdom." Certainly, the burial evidence supports the conclusion that social rank in many Hopewellian societies was achieved, rather than ascribed. The idea of a "dark age" following A.D. 400 in the East is true only for the more northern areas, and there is considerable evidence for continuity of development in the Southeast proper during the times between Hopewellian and Mississippian. This is not to deny the strong, local and regional character of specific developments, but merely to recognize that there is a kind of area-wide unity and continuity that is less clear for the Southwest.

Until maize was adopted in the Southwest three millennia ago, there is little sign of anything but small-scale hunter-gatherers who shared a widespread technocomplex of tool types and an abstract style of rock art. With maize, hamlets appeared, and long-distance shell exchange began. The earliest large pre-ceramic settlement is the newly discovered Vacas Muertas site under modern Tucson that dates to 400 to 200 B.C. It had over 150 small pithouses without hearths but with numerous storage pits, a high maize ubiquity, and much shell (Jonathan Mabry, personal communication). It was another 800 or more years, however, before the implementation of large-scale irrigation in southern Arizona led to the general appearance of networks of true year-round villages. Concurrently, "suprahousehold" residence groups appeared, and new forms of public architecture (ballcourts). Interestingly, in the northern Southwest networks of villages with 100 people or more also appeared about this time, though they were based on dry farming, not irrigation. "Suprahousehold" groups also formed the basic building blocks of those "Pueblo I" villages, and "great kivas" served as public architecture. Little or no evidence of social rank is apparent anywhere in the Southwest before A.D. 800, except, perhaps, some Basketmaker burials in Canyon de Chelly. By the A.D. 800s, however, clear differences in both material culture and ideological expression indicate the differentiation of several distinct "cultural traditions."

A.D. 1000

In the period between A.D. 800 and 1000, a number of locations in the Southeast saw the emergence of complex political and economic structures that clearly were more hierarchical than those of earlier times. Maize became the staple crop nearly everywhere by A.D. 1000, but large public works sometimes preceded the introduction of maize. Cahokia, especially, presents a scale of construction and organization that dwarfs any other public works in the East. South and east of Cahokia, other early Late Prehistoric complexes are simpler, but still show considerable evidence of the "emergence" of at least modest levels of rank. A major contradiction in Mississippian society was the inconsistency between the economic roles and interests of the "chiefs" and an overall economy that remained fundamentally domestic.

By A.D. 1000 in the Southwest, three distinct "macroregional" cultural networks are apparent, one just beginning to shrink only to expand in a new way (Hohokam),

and two others beginning to expand (Chaco and Mimbres). All are marked by a distinctly expressed ideology or ritual suzerainty, but only the Chacoan case is arguably hierarchical, becoming more so during the eleventh century. Each of these systems had its own access to valuables, the Hohokam and Mimbres emphasizing shell and the Chacoans turquoise. The complex of great houses constructed in Chaco Canyon and its immediate environs is the first Southwestern "great town." If we equate Cahokian mounds and Chacoan great houses, supposing they are the seats of elite residential kin groups, then many interesting comparisons can be suggested (see Holley and Lekson, Chapter 3). Most striking are the differences, Cahokia showing more emphasis on individual rank and production of "prestige goods," while Chaco appears much more group oriented and lacks much evidence for craft specialization.

A.D. 1150

By A.D. 1150, Cahokia had reached its peak population and, probably, power. Even at this time, however, the "hegemony" of Cahokia arguably did not extend very far beyond its large and productive bottomlands near modern St. Louis. Recent reviews of the localities and regions surrounding Cahokia can find little hard evidence for dependency on Cahokia (Milner 1986, 1991a, 1993), despite efforts to see them as "hinterlands" in a Cahokian "world system" (Dincauze and Hasenstaub 1989; Peregrine 1991, 1992). One may suggest that, given the economic and political structures of this period in the Southeast, political power for specific chiefs rarely extended beyond a few hundred kilometers, and then probably only briefly. Even in this peak period (in the northern localities, at least), most polities seem to have controlled only their immediate bottomlands and hinterlands. As noted in one historic source, "extensive and puissant Indian American empires" seem unlikely in any period in the east (Adair 1775:427). Considerable quantities of raw materials and "utilitarian" goods such as quality chert seem to have been exchanged from one locality to another; but the exchange of fancy, high labor-value "prestige goods" was quite limited.

In the Southwest, challenging decades of standard opinion, Wilcox (Chapter 10) argues that by A. D. 1150 the Chaco, Mimbres, and Hohokam systems had not "collapsed" but were becoming knit together along a fragile series of connections that resulted in the flow of "prestige goods" from West Mexico to the Southwest. A pan-Southwestern macroregional system thus briefly emerged that facilitated a transfer of ideas and a syncretism that soon resulted in massive reorganizations of all its constituent sub-systems. The apogee of Chacoan power in the early A.D. 1100s, and political reactions to it, may have stimulated the formation of this large-scale connectivity, but the extent of Chaco's direct hegemony probably lay within 100 km of the Canyon. Its ritual suzerainty, however, apparently extended much farther, to as much as 225 km.

A.D. 1250

By the middle A.D. 1200s in the Southeast, the "Southern Cult," or the "Southeastern Ceremonial Complex," was a fairly large-scale, but short-lived, episode of widespread exchange of finished goods as well as valued raw materials. Although there were still communities in the American Bottom around Cahokia, these appear to have become reduced in scale to a level at which Cahokia was merely another large Mississippian center of perhaps a few thousand people. In other areas, such as the Lower Ohio River valley, this may actually have been the period of peak occupation. In both the twelfth and thirteenth centuries, however, even the largest polities were probably not much, if at all, larger than the historic Choctaw, for example.

The middle A.D. 1200s in the Southwest were a time of general systemic reorganization and long-distance population movements that resulted in the abandonment of the whole northern Southwest and the peopling of what had been "backwater" areas: the northern Rio Grande River valley, the Mogollon Rim country in Arizona, and northwestern Chihuahua. By the late A.D. 1200s, ceramic and rock-art data indicate the emergence of religious cults in both the middle and southern Southwest that spread rapidly east and west. Unlike the Southern Cult, however, the long-distance exchange of cult objects is not apparent. Nucleated "walled towns" replaced the earlier loosely aggregated villages, and average settlement size increased sharply. In the Hohokam area, platform mounds surrounded by high compound walls became the center of still loosely aggregated irrigation communities. The coalescence of groupings whose identities in many (but not all) cases were maintained into the historic period was now taking place.

A.D. 1450

This is the period of the so-called "Attenuated Cult" of the Southeast, but that name reflects a tendency by archaeologists to collapse all Late Prehistoric fancy goods into one or two taxonomic categories. The reality is that some of the very late prehistoric centers of production were related to styles and local organizations that were probably descended from earlier local social formulations. Others, like the so-called rattlesnake gorget styles, seem to have emerged from contexts that do not suggest strong ties to any of the "centers" of production and exchange in earlier times. There clearly is some process of fragmentation going on in the East at this time, but this is by no means the same thing as a "collapse" and should not be interpreted as one. If anything, actual interaction may have increased, although there are some hints that these interactions may have been becoming more often hostile than formerly.

The balkanization of the Southwestern political landscape apparent in no-man's lands and site clusters (polities), just as in the Southeast, suggests that warfare and a narrowing of the pool of economic resources had much to do with the political collapse indicated by regional abandonments in the fifteenth century. By the beginning of the Protohistoric period, the large centers and great towns of the southern Southwest (Hohokam, Paquimé) had begun to fall into ruins. Just as in the northern Southwest, an ecological replacement then took place when hunter-gatherers and small-scale agriculturists moved in from the peripheries to establish residence. That left the middle, which also shrank with the abandonment of the Mogollon Rim country, and a little later, the Chama River valley in the northern Rio Grande. Beginning about A.D. 1450, the commencement of a new kind of multiethnic exchange between Plains bison hunters and Pueblo farmers became an important factor to the survival of the Pueblos (Wilcox 1984). This new long-distance exchange network extended across the Plains into the Caddoan area, thus linking the Southwest and Southeast for the first time into an inter-related macroregional system (Krieger 1947a,b; Wilcox 1991b). Glimpses of the operation of this system are provided by the earliest Spanish entradas ca. A.D. 1540.

EARLY HISTORIC PERIOD

Although the Southeast lacked large deposits of precious metals, some trade items, such as deerskins, and later beaver, became much sought after by Europeans. The transition to a hide-trading economy occurred largely out of sight, so far as the written record is concerned, so that many of our best historic sources describe systems of exchange that were substantially affected by the presence of European trading agents. Thus, the historic Eastern Native Americans entered the "European World System." There is a strong argument during this period for a devolution of political structures in conditions of widespread and deadly Old World diseases. At the same time, however, there is other evidence that suggests that groups such as the Choctaw, Iroquois, and Creek managed not only to maintain themselves in population, but actually started what is arguably a process of promotion of their institutions into state-level social organizations. The scale and complexity of these historic groups have consistently been underestimated in terms of their attempts to pursue "macroregional integration" and in terms of their levels of exchange and political sophistication.

Sixty years after the first abortive entrada to the Southwest, the profits of silver mining in nearby Zacatecas and Durango resulted in the successful incorporation of New Mexico into the Spanish empire. The Puebloan macroregional economy was quickly reorganized to serve as a supplier of food, textiles, and slaves to the mining zone. Of no strategic importance to the Spanish Crown until the late eighteenth century (when French and Americans threatened on the east and Russians on the California coast), New Mexico became a poor outpost of empire where priests sought souls and squabbled for pitiful resources with corrupt government officials. Disillusioned after their initial enthusiasm for colonization by the ravages of repeated epidemic disease and unfair judicial treatment, the Pueblos rose in a proud but futile revolt in 1680. Economic chaos resulted, and twelve years later they grudgingly began to rejoin the empire. Their aboriginal lifeway was forever gone.

CONCLUSION

Macroregional interaction was an important component of the sociopolitical landscape in both the late prehistoric Southeast and Southwest. In both areas, important foci for this interaction were "Great Towns," and it involved the movement of valuables over great distances. However, on closer examination, the differences in Southeastern and Southwestern macroregional interaction outnumber the similarities. Late macroregional interaction in the Southeast encompassed for the most part one broad cultural tradition. In the Southwest, it crossed multiple cultural traditions, each with its own independent chronological sequence. The goods which were traded included both status and "cult" items in the Southeast but only the former in the Southwest. In addition, late prehistoric status differentiation and macroregional interaction had deep antecedents in the Southeast but not in the Southwest. Finally, the social and political arrangements for managing power relations were quite different in the Southeast and Southwest. Southeastern power relations were characteristic of individualizing chiefdoms (Renfrew 1974) and network-based political-economic strategies (Feinman 1995). In contrast, Southwestern power relations were characteristic of group-oriented chiefdoms (Renfrew 1974) and corporate-based political-economic strategies (Feinman 1995). Together, these differences reinforce the unifying theme of all the chapters in this volume—that despite their apparent similarities, developments in the late prehistoric Southeast and Southwest differed in some very fundamental ways.

CHAPTER THIRTEEN

Feathered, Horned, and Antlered Serpents:

Mesoamerican Connections with the Southwest and Southeast

Charles R. Cobb

Jeffrey Maymon

Randall H. McGuire

THE WIDESPREAD SIMILARITIES BETWEEN MESO-american cultures and the late prehistoric cultures of Southwestern and Southeastern North America have long fascinated archaeologists. Both North American culture areas have a lengthy history of investigations into the extent of the similarities and the implications of those similarities for interaction with Mesoamerica. Here we place these issues into a comparative framework. By contrasting the nature of the evidence from both the Southwest and Southeast, we are able to systematically consider the kinds and strengths of ties with Mesoamerica. Although Mesoamerican similarities appear strongest during the late prehistoric era, we adopt a longer time-frame that allows us to explore the possibility of indigenous origins.

GEOGRAPHY AND CULTURE AREAS

A foremost issue in the question of long-distance ties between Mesoamerica and the North American Southwest and Southeast is geography. A glance at a map quickly shows that straight-line distances between the two northern regions traverse very different surface areas—an arid and rugged terrain in the case of the Southwest and the Gulf of Mexico in the Southeast (Figure 13.1). These geographi-cal conditions alone presuppose that the nature of the interaction between the two North American regions and Mesoamerica was probably quite different. Moreover, the Southwest is closer to Mesoamerica and, not unexpectedly, demonstrates clearer evidence for Mesoamerican ties.

Just as important as distance and topography between regions are local geography and internal relations. Both the Southwest and Southeast constitute large regions which are culturally and physically heterogeneous. Mesoamerica, in turn, is also composed of a great range of cultures and environments. Hence, the nature of long-distance ties transcends the issue of border to border contacts. Traits or objects may have originated from different points in Mesoamerica and then filtered differentially throughout the Southwest and Southeast. Their dispersal was ultimately subject to geographical constraints as well as the dynamically changing landscape of social alliances and ties in North America.

Because of the importance of geography and the human landscape, we use these topics to frame our discussion of long-distance interaction with Mesoamerica. We believe that one cannot compare a homogenous body of Southwestern-Mesoamerican traits with a homogeneous body of Southeastern-Mesoamerican traits. There is important internal synchronic and diachronic variation within each region which must be considered.

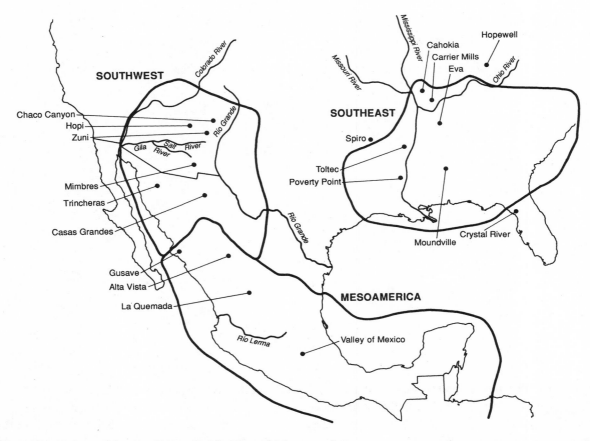

Figure 13.1.   Map of the Southwest, Southeast, and Mesoamerica.

The Southwest

The Southwestern culture area, as usually defined, extends from southern Utah and Colorado on the north to the Mexican states of Chihuahua and Sonora on the south (Figure 13.1). The distance between these northern and southern boundaries is about 1300 km. The southern boundary abuts the upper frontier of Mesoamerica, roughly along the northern borders of Sinaloa and Durango (Kirchoff 1943); and it is roughly 1500 km from the Southwest's southern boundary to the Basin of Mexico. Evidence for contact between the Southwest and the Basin of Mexico is slight. The vast majority of objects of definite Mesoamerican origin found in the Southwest come from western Mexico (Jalisco, Durango, Sinaloa, and Nayarit) at

distances of less than 1,000 km from the Southwest culture area's southern boundary (McGuire 1980:27–28).

There are, however, serious problems in treating the Southwest and Mesoamerica as units defined by the boundary that separates them (McGuire et al. 1994). Such a view implies that the cultural stuff of each area was spread evenly from boundary to boundary, like the colors on a culture area map. There is also a tendency to project the boundary back into time periods long before the cultural patterns it separates existed.

The boundary defined above existed from about A.D. 950 to 1350. It is during these 400 years that the upper frontier of Mesoamerica reached the northern borders of Durango and Sinaloa. In both the Southwest and Mesoamerica the frequency and density of population and regional centers (or towns) declines as the boundary is approached (McGuire et al. 1994). In Mesoamerica, a dense concentration of regional centers, usually called city states, existed in the Basin of Mexico; north of the Lerma-Santiago drainage, however, the density drops off. The northernmost Mesoamerican regional centers, such as La Quemada and Alta Vista, were islands of town development separated from each other by 150 to 200 km and surrounded by vast expanses of land inhabited by small scale agriculturalists or hunter-gathers. In contrast, the gaps between Southwestern towns were filled by culturally variable but basically similar agriculturalists. The major regional centers, Chaco Canyon, the Hohokam, Paquimé, and the Pueblo IV pueblos, were elaborated expressions of larger surrounding cultural patterns. No towns and little evidence for villages have been reported in either southern Sonora or southern Chihuahua, suggesting a marked break in the distribution of Southwestern and Mesoamerican regional centers.

For the roughly 300 years before A.D. 950, the northern boundary of Mesoamerica lay much further south and it is not clear into which cultural area, if either, the modern states of Durango and Sinaloa should be placed. Before A.D. 600 the Southwest is not clearly separable from other cultural developments north of the Basin of Mexico, so no boundary should be defined.

Throughout the prehistoric period, the physiography of northern Mexico shaped contacts between the Southwest and Mesoamerica. The Sierra Madre Occidental rises at the United States-Mexico border and runs south, dividing Sonora from Chihuahua. This mountainous spine defined two corridors linking the Southwest and Mesoamerica (Haury 1945b). One ran along the eastern flanks of the mountains and the second ran up the coast on the west side of the mountains.

In historic times the Southwest was linguistically connected to Mesoamerica. The Uto-Aztecan language family extends from points north of the Southwest to central Mexico. One language in this family, Tepiman, includes Pima, Tepehuan, and Tepecano speakers who extend from southern Arizona to Durango. Wilcox (1986b) has suggested that this distribution was established with the spread of agriculture and that the Tepiman language group was the major conduit for Mesoamerican traits into the Southwest before A.D. 1000–1150.

The Southeast

As Smith (1985a) has observed, the boundaries of the Southeast vary depending upon whom one reads. From a historic perspective, the Muskhogean-speaking groups form a generally agreed-upon Southeastern "core." As one moves back into the Late Prehistoric period, however, archaeologists tend to delimit the Southeast as including groups traditionally defined as Mississippian as well as some of their immediate neighbors. Some of the key edge areas over which archaeologists dicker include the Tidewater areas of North Carolina and Virginia and the Caddoan region that is centered in eastern Oklahoma and western Arkansas.

At its greatest extent, the Southeast during the Late Prehistoric period extends from the Caddoan area to the west and the Atlantic Ocean to the east, spanning about 1,400 km (Figure 13.1). The northern boundary loosely follows the lower Ohio River Valley while the Gulf of Mexico marks its southern edge. The distance between them is about 900 km. Southeastern archaeologists tend to agree that central and southern Florida followed a distinctive culture history in both prehistoric and historic times and do not include those regions in the Mississippian culture area.

Like the Southwest, the boundaries of the Southeast shift as one moves further back in time. The Late Woodland period (A.D. 400–900) is ironically known best for what it lacks rather than what it represents, particularly the mound-building, long-distance exchange, and elaborate mortuary practices that characterized the preceding Middle Woodland and following Mississippian periods (Brown 1991). Except for the Coles Creek mound centers in the Lower Mississippi Valley, the Late Woodland period does not yield any strong traditions that clearly distinguish the Southeast from the adjoining Midwest and Middle Atlantic regions.

During the preceding Middle Woodland period (A.D. 0–400), the Southeast participated in the Hopewellian interaction sphere. At that time, there emerged a number of distinctive regional traditions, such as Marksville in the Lower Mississippi River Valley and Copena in northern Alabama. No strong continuities have been documented between Middle Woodland and Mississippian traditions—an absence which is not surprising given the characteristics of the intervening Late Woodland period.

One potentially important geographic difference in comparing Mesoamerican ties with the Southwest and Southeast is the number of directions from which ideas and traits may have filtered into the Southeast. In the Southwest, Mesoamerican influences appear to derive from northwest Mexico. The southwestern border of the

Southeast in eastern Texas is not that much further from the major Mexican city states than is the Southwest, around 900 to 1,000 km following the Gulf Coast shoreline. Yet the Mesoamerican frontier does not seem to have reached as far into northeast Mexico as it did in western Mexico, in part because the terrain in northeastern Mexico is particularly inhospitable. Several corridors of diffusion were still possible through the area, which was inhabited by Coahuiltecan hunting and gathering groups at the time of European contact (Kelley 1952a,b). However, the lack of Mississippian sites at the northern end of this route (southeast Texas and western Louisiana) further reinforces the idea that if Mesoamerican goods did travel this way, the process was more down-the-line than point-to-point contact between Mesoamerican and Southeastern sites (Griffin 1980).

Traveling straight-line by water, the Yucatan Peninsula is slightly closer to the Southeast than central Mexico. A distance only slightly over 800 km separates the northern tip of the Yucatan from New Orleans. It is thus perhaps not surprising that some Mesoamerican-Southeastern parallels seem Mayan in character. The Southeast region's extensive Gulf coastline has also led some to argue for seaborne contact with Mesoamerica or the Caribbean region (e.g., McMichael 1964; Sears 1977).

Mesoamerican ties with the Southeast have been pushed back into the Archaic period by some researchers. However, it is Mississippian sites that have demonstrated the strongest links. As the previous chapters in this volume have demonstrated, Mississippian centers, villages, and hamlets were dispersed widely across the Southeast, even into upland zones not usually associated with the riverine orientation of late prehistoric settlements. Similarly, the traits that are suggestive of Mesoamerican ties cluster at the large, well-known centers, but have a fairly wide dispersal. It is noteworthy that most of the "classic" Mississippian sites that have been cited in the Mesoamerican-Southeastern interaction literature are located in the interior riverine Southeast. They are not found along the Gulf Coast or in the Lower Mississippi River Valley where, based on distance, one might expect the strongest ties. Perhaps significantly, although Mississippian influences were strongly felt along the Gulf Coast and in the Lower Mississippi River Valley, both of these areas experienced histories somewhat different than the usual Mississippian trajectory.

MESOAMERICA AND THE SOUTHWEST

There can be little question that prehistoric cultural developments in the Southwest and Mesoamerica were connected in profound and important ways. The two regions shared a common, dynamic boundary that originated with the establishment of agricultural societies in each area. The agricultural complex upon which Southwestern cultural developments were based clearly originated in Mesoamerica. Hundreds of objects of obvious Mesoamerican origin have been found in Southwestern sites and a host of Southwestern cultural "traits" clearly derive from Mesoamerica. Finally, aboriginal Southwestern cosmologies, religions, beliefs, and rituals show striking similarities with Mesoamerican counterparts. The similarities between the two regions are so great that current researchers debate whether the Southwestern region should be considered a separate region or the northernmost extension of Mesoamerica.

Southwestern archaeologists have traditionally talked about Mesoamerican contacts in terms of two distinct waves of influence (Haury 1945b; Schroeder 1965, 1966). The first of these was pre-A.D. 1 and brought the basic components of Southwestern village life—corn, beans, squash, ceramics, and pithouses. The second occurred after A.D. 600 and brought a host of Mesoamerican objects and traits to the Southwest. It is now apparent that this two-part division is far too simple and episodic— Southwestern-Mesoamerican interactions were continuous but with varying intensity throughout prehistory.

Early Prehistoric Period

We now know that the three major components of village life entered the Southwest at different times from the south. The first corn appears at about 1,000 B.C., but it does not lead immediately to settled life (Wills 1988a). Small pithouses appear between 200 B.C. and A.D. 200, but ceramics and a sedentary farming lifeway do not become widespread until A.D. 200 to 300. Pottery seems to spread over most of the Southwest very quickly when it does come on the scene (Leblanc 1982).

From A.D. 200 to 600 the incipient agricultural tradition of the Southwest looks like the northern extension of the Chupícuaro tradition of the Bajío in Mexico (Braniff 1974; Kelley 1966). This tradition begins by 200 B.C. and spreads northward along the east flanks of the Sierra Madre Occidental into Guanajuato, Jalisco, Zacatecas, Durango, and then leaps over an arid southern

Chihuahua into Arizona and New Mexico. In addition to the economic components of this tradition, there also exist stylistic similarities. From Guanajuato to Arizona the earliest pottery is a brown or greyware with reddish paint and quartered designs.

Starting about A.D. 300, regional distinctions begin to appear in this widespread agricultural tradition differentiating both the Southwest from Mesoamerica and regional traditions within the Southwest. An Anasazi tradition emerges on the Colorado Plateau, a Mogollon tradition in the mountains, and a Hohokam tradition in the deserts. Each of these traditions manifests itself as a relatively uniform pattern of ceramic style, architecture, subsistence, ritual, and social organization spread over a large area. By A.D. 600 these traditions are clearly distinct from each other, yet together they form a larger cultural development separable from Mesoamerica.

The Hohokam of southern Arizona exhibit the strongest evidence of Mesoamerican contacts in the period between A.D. 600 and 1150. The Mesoamerican flavor of the Hohokam has led several authors to suggest that they must have migrated from Mesoamerica (Di Peso 1956; Haury 1976). The evidence includes actual Mesoamerican artifacts, architectural features, stylistic attributes, and inferred similarities in beliefs and religion.

The total number of Mesoamerican items recovered from Colonial and Sedentary period (A.D. 750 to 1150) Hohokam sites comes to several hundred pieces (Nelson 1981). The most common Mesoamerican artifacts are copper bells with over 150 examples found principally in mortuary or ritual contexts at larger village sites (Figure 13.2). These same contexts have yielded 75 to 80 iron pyrite mirrors and a handful of scarlet macaws. Mesoamerican ceramics are relatively rare with only about a dozen sherds and one tripod vessel reported in the literature (Nelson 1981).

Numerous architectural parallels can be seen with Mesoamerica. The basic unit of Hohokam settlement was the courtyard group which consisted of a group of two to six houses facing a common courtyard (Fish and Fish 1991). These courtyard groups were scattered around central plazas to form larger villages. At the largest such village, Snaketown, adobe capped platform mounds ringed the central plaza (Haury 1976). A version of the Mesoamerican ballgame was apparently played by the Hohokam, but their ballcourts were oval, not rectangular or "I"-shaped as in Mesoamerica (Wilcox and Sternberg 1983).

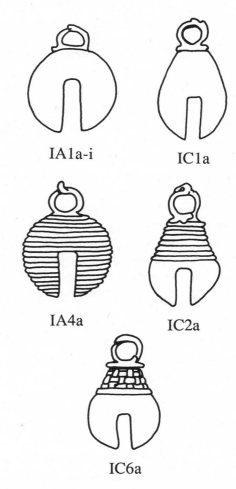

IA1a-i   IC1a

IA4a   IC2a

IC6a

Figure 13.2.   Some copper bell types from the Southwest with type designations (from Pendergast 1960).

Hohokam irrigation agriculture has often been seen as a Mesoamerican introduction (Di Peso 1974; Haury 1976). The general assumption is that since Mesoamerica had agriculture earlier and was more "advanced" than the Southwest, irrigation must have originated there. In reality, however, irrigation technology was much more highly developed in the Southwest than in Mesoamerica (Feinman 1991:465).

Haury (1976:345–348) identifies a number of Hohokam stylistic attributes as deriving from Mesoamerica. These include motifs like the bird-snake, the burden carrier, feathered head dress, cipactli, intertwined snakes, and human effigies, executed on pottery and shell jewelry. They also encompass various ceramic vessel forms such as censers, effigy vessels, and legged vessels. Hohokam aesthetic expression was distinctly different from that of Mogollon and Anasazi groups, with a greater flamboyance, whimsy, and use of human and animal motifs. Researchers have ascribed this uniqueness to a Mesoamerican origin.

A number of scholars have attempted to infer Hohokam cosmology and religion and link these aspects of Hohokam culture to Mesoamerica. In a series of articles Wilcox (1987a; Wilcox and Sternberg 1983) attributes various facets of Hohokam cosmology, including color directional symbolism, certain astronomical beliefs and orientations, and beliefs associated with the ball game, to a Mesoamerican fount. Di Peso (1979:94) derives Hohokam cosmology from the central Mexican Tezcatlipoca cult.

Much of the uniqueness of the Hohokam, which has led to theories of migrations from Mesoamerica, melts away when the Hohokam are compared to the other prehistoric cultures of the Sonoran desert. These cultures include the Trincheras in northern Sonora and the Huatabampo in southern Sonora (Alvarez 1985). From A.D. 700 to 1000, both of these cultures produced settlements, figurines, and ceramic vessel forms similar to the Hohokam. All three produced a distinctive marine shell jewelry that is stylistically similar from northern Sinaloa to central Arizona. Thus, the uniqueness of the Hohokam in comparison to the Anasazi and Mogollon appears to derive from the cultures of Sonora and northern Sinaloa; and only the southernmost edge of these latter cultures is generally considered part of Mesoamerica, and even then not until after A.D. 1000.

Late Prehistoric Period

Starting in the tenth century A.D., the northern frontier of Mesoamerica moved north to the modern states of Sinaloa and Durango. In northern Sinaloa, the Gusave tradition with its Mixteca-Puebla inspired style replaces the Huatabampo. On the other side of the Sierra Madre Occidental, the Chalchihuities tradition expands northward in Durango almost to the Chihuahuan border. It is also at this time that evidence of Mesoamerican goods and contacts first appears in non-Hohokam, Southwestern sites in both the Mimbres River Valley and Chaco Canyon. Kelley (1986a) has suggested that the exchange of Southwestern turquoise into Mesoamerica starts in this period, if not earlier.

From A.D. 1000 to 1150 a distinctive Mimbres tradition emerged out of a Mogollon cultural base in southwestern New Mexico. A handful of copper bells has been found in the larger sites of this tradition (Sprague and

Signori 1963). Some archaeologists have interpreted the anthropomorphic designs on Mimbres Classic Black-on-white pottery as indicative of Mesoamerican introduced cosmology and religious ritual. These designs are the earliest evidence for a Southwestern Kachina cult with its masked dancers and dancing for rain (Carlson 1982). Mimbres sites also commonly contain shell jewelry made in the Sonoran style with various Mesoamerican derived motifs.

Perhaps the most dramatic development in Southwestern prehistory between A.D. 950 and 1150 was the growth of a regional center at Chaco Canyon. Evidence for Mesoamerican connections at Chaco Canyon is not nearly as great as among the Hohokam. Items from Mesoamerica include almost 50 copper bells, over 30 macaws, and a handful of pseudo-cloisonné artifacts. They occur in several great house sites in the canyon with most coming from the largest ruin, Pueblo Bonito (Toll 1991:84). Lister (1978) lists 30 Mesoamerican traits at Chaco Canyon during this time. Of these traits only eight, such as the colonnade at Chetro Ketl, are definitely of Mesoamerican origin or do not occur earlier than A.D. 900 in the Southwest (McGuire 1980:7–10).

The one hundred years from A.D. 1150 to 1250 saw major reorganizations in Southwestern cultural developments. The Chaco and Mimbres regional systems collapse and the Hohokam regional system breaks down. Out of this confusion in the late thirteenth and early fourteenth centuries arise a plethora of regional centers in the Phoenix Basin, the mountains of Arizona and New Mexico, along the Little Colorado River in Arizona, and along the Rio Grande River in New Mexico. One of the most impressive of these late centers is the town of Paquimé in northwest Chihuahua.

The Medio period at Paquimé dates from about A.D. 1250 to the late fifteenth century (Dean and Ravesloot 1993). During this period, the site grew to contain two massive roomblocks of several thousand rooms with an adjacent ceremonial precinct including two "I"-shaped ballcourts, a rectangular ballcourt, an elite tomb complex, and seven platform mounds. The site contained large quantities of marine shell (over 3,000,000 pieces) and other exotic trade goods, leading its excavator to conclude that it was a trade outpost of a Mesoamerican state (Di Peso 1968, 1974, 1983). This view has been contested by a number of archaeologists who argue that the site should be seen as a regional center in its own right and not as an extension of a Mesoamerican state (McGuire 1980; Minnis 1989).

Paquimé yielded an ample number of items of probable Mesoamerican origin. Di Peso (1974) reports 32 sherds of Mesoamerican pottery originating from Durango, Jalisco, and Nayarit in the site collection. He also recovered six spindle whorls, probably from Durango, and a ceramic hand drum that he sources to an unidentified locale in west Mexico. In addition to the ceramics Di Peso found two pieces of obsidian from Durango.

Of greater importance than these imports was evidence recovered from Paquimé for the production of objects whose only source in earlier time periods had been Mesoamerica. This local production included the crafting of copper artifacts and the raising of scarlet macaws. The site yielded 39.6 kg of almost pure copper ore and pieces of copper metal along with 688 copper artifacts. One hundred and fifteen of these objects were bells. At least four of the domestic compounds in the town contained macaw nesting boxes, some with the macaw egg shells in them and the bones of young macaws (Figure 13.3). In total, the excavators recovered the remains of 322 scarlet macaws and another 100 individual macaws that could not be typed to species.

Architectural parallels to Mesoamerica were numerous at Paquimé. The most obvious are the two "I"-shaped ballcourts and the various platform mounds associated with them. Nine of the large apartment complexes included colonnades. Di Peso (1974:637) argues that the occupants of Paquimé also buried human sacrifices as dedication offerings for many of the town's major architectural features.

Di Peso (1974) found many stylistic attributes at Paquimé that he ascribes to Mesoamerica. These include trophy skulls, a rasp made out of a human femur that he identifies with the Aztec Xipe Tótec cult, feathered serpents that he links to the cult of Quetzalcoatl, and round-eyed images that he attributes to the Tlaloc cult. There is little question that most of the symbolism that Di Peso recognizes is ultimately of Mesoamerican origin, but other researchers have questioned the presence of specific Mesoamerican cults at the town. They argue that Mesoamerican beliefs and symbols were transformed into distinctively Southwestern religions (Adams 1991; McGuire 1980).

Contemporary with the Medio period at Paquimé is the spread of Mesoamerican goods in towns throughout the eastern half of Arizona and the western half of New Mexico. Between 60 to 70 scarlet macaws and more than 100 copper bells have been recovered from these sites. It

Figure 13.3.   Ramos Polychrome effigy vessel from Paquimé representing a macaw in its breeding pen.

is likely that these items did not originate in Mesoamerica but instead derived from Paquimé.

The presence of Mesoamerican goods in the Southwest raises the question of what was being traded south for them. A wide variety of things have been suggested, including slaves, hides, feathers, peyote, ceramics, and turquoise (Di Peso 1983). Of these items, only ceramics and turquoise are routinely found in archaeological sites. Archaeologists have found no more than a few dozen Southwestern ceramic sherds or vessels in Mesoamerica. The record for turquoise, which Mesoamerican crafts persons used to make elaborate mosaics, is, however, much more impressive. Weigand and Harbottle (1993) estimate that between 500,000 and 1,000,000 pieces of turquoise have been found in Mesoamerica. Turquoise appears in Mesoamerican sites as early as A.D. 400 and increases in frequency through the post-Classic period (A.D. 900–1521) when it outstripped jade in importance for highland Mesoamerican peoples.

All of the turquoise in Mesoamerica came either from the Sierra Queretaro and Chalchihuities areas of northwestern Mesoamerica, or from the Southwest (Weigand and Harbottle 1993). Turquoise mining begins in the Chalchihuities area by the Classic period (A.D. 300–900), and archaeologists have identified over 800 mines in this region. In the Southwest, where turquoise was widely used after A.D. 900, Weigand and Harbottle (1993) have identified 175 prehistoric turquoise mines. Trace element analyses indicate that Southwestern miners extracted turquoise to meet regional demand and that some of their product also went south to Mesoamerica.

Around A.D. 1350 there is a retraction of the northern frontier of Mesoamerica as regional centers such as Gusave in Sinaloa and La Quemada in Zacatecas were abandoned. By the time the Spanish arrive in the early sixteenth century, only mobile hunters and gatherers lived in what had been the northern reaches of Mesoamerica.

Historic Southwestern cosmology, religion, and ritual exhibit many striking parallels with Mesoamerican beliefs and practices. Anyone familiar with the mythology of the Pueblos, Navajos, O'odham, and Cahitas is struck by the similarities with the Quiche Mayan Popul Vuh, especially the spider women and warrior twins of that myth. Other common elements in many Southwestern and Mesoamerican belief systems include the new fire ceremony, the notion of a multitiered universe, color directional symbolism, and origin tales of the cyclic destruction and creation of the world. The only major element of Mesoamerican religion missing from the Southwest is the idea of blood sacrifice that dominated so much of post-Classic Mesoamerican belief. Feinman (1991) has argued that the ubiquity of bone awls in Southwestern sites may indicate the presence of blood sacrifice in the prehistoric Southwest.

MESOAMERICA AND THE SOUTHEAST

One of the more enduring and seemingly intractable issues in the Southeast is the question of long-distance ties with Mesoamerica. On the one hand, there are numerous examples of intriguing similarities in artifact styles, monumental architecture, and site configurations that have been remarked upon as far back as the works of Moore (1907:346) and Holmes (1903). On the other hand, we have yet to see a convincing cluster of these traits at any one Southeastern site or region that would argue for a sustained, intensive interaction with Mesoamerica. Nor is there the occasional copper bell or macaw burial to support the possibility of sporadic, direct movements of Mesoamerican goods into the Southeast. Nevertheless, the combined weight of the similarities has long fascinated Southeastern archaeologists. While it is not possible at this time to add new substantive data that

would seriously revise past interpretations, a comparison with the Southwest provides an opportunity to reconsider Mesoamerican and Southeastern ties as a scalar process at a continental level.

Early Prehistoric Period

At least partially sedentary sites occur in the Southeast as far back as the Middle Archaic period (ca. 6,000–3,000 B.C.). Substantial sites such as Carrier Mills and Eva display evidence for relatively affluent hunters and gatherers who left large mortuary populations (Jefferies and Butler 1982; Lewis and Lewis 1961). Burial items indicate that these groups did participate in long-distance exchange networks, although all of the recovered non-comestible items are of Eastern Woodlands origin. Domesticated cucurbits do appear on some Middle Archaic sites, but their Mesoamerican origin is now open to question (Fritz 1990).

The first substantial earthwork site in the Southeast is Poverty Point in northeastern Louisiana, an impressive array of radial mounds and a bird-effigy mound encompassing an area of some 200 ha. Current dates for the Poverty Point site place it at the terminal Late Archaic, or 1700–700 B.C. The genesis and function of this mound complex are still debated by Southeastern archaeologists. Early hypotheses laid the origins of the Poverty Point site to Olmec influences (Webb 1968), but most archaeologists today disagree with that assessment.

The first substantial wave of earthwork construction at a regional scale occurs with the Adena phenomenon (1000–200 B.C.) and continues into Hopewellian times (200 B.C.–A.D. 400). Strictly speaking, both of these traditions are more Midwestern than Southeastern, but influences from both, particularly Hopewell, were strongly felt in the South. The monumental scale of many Adena and Hopewell earthworks may seem to speak to Mesoamerican influence, but their configurations do not resemble the temple and plaza arrangement associated with central Mexican and Mayan sites. Instead one finds sacred circles, geometric arrays, and isolated tumuli in various combinations.

The first coalescence of settled village life with a dependence on cultigens occurs during the Hopewell period, with the best subsistence evidence coming from the Illinois River Valley (Asch and Asch 1985). Indigenous starchy and oily seeds rather than tropical imports represent the important cultigens in Hopewell subsistence. Maize rarely appears on Hopewell sites and seems to have been a very minor constituent of the diet (Fritz 1990).

The first appearance of artifacts with strong echoes of Mesoamerican influence occurs on Hopewell sites. One of the more intriguing examples is an ivory figurine from the Hopewell Mound group in Ohio. Beneath its chin are possible bar-and-dot glyphs, which according to Hall (1989:266–267) could be interpreted as Thirteen Cimi, the Mayan god of long-distance traders, death, and the underworld. Another interesting Hopewellian specimen is a shell gorget depicting a large feline. The gorget was recovered from Missouri and has traditionally been associated with Hopewell, although a few have argued for a Mississippian context (Chapman 1980; Howard 1968). The cat on the gorget clearly looks like a jaguar, and its rendering is strongly reminiscent of classic Mesoamerican styles, particularly the tongue protruding from the mouth in a manner stylistically similar to voice glyphs (Figure 13.4a, c).

Examples such as these are extremely rare, however. There is also little redundancy in the artifact types and symbolism that are thought to reflect Mesoamerican influences during the Hopewell period. If Mesoamerican influences were being felt during this time, they were as isolated ideas and artifacts rather than as artifact or symbolic complexes. Nevertheless, it cannot be ignored that some Hopewellian individuals or interest groups were spectacularly successfully in amassing quantities of raw materials from distant sources. Particularly notable are grizzly bear canines and obsidian from the West, a distance from the core Hopewellian region comparable to that of Mesoamerica.

Most of the Southeast experienced a hiatus between the archaeologically ostentatious Middle Woodland and Mississippian periods. However, Coles Creek sites (A.D. 600–1000) in the Lower Mississippi River Valley are note-worthy for a continuation of mound-building. Toltec Mounds in central Arkansas, a Coles Creek related site, witnessed the development of a large complex of earthworks, including an encircling embankment, a large platform mound, and mounds arranged around plazas (Nassaney 1991; Rolingson 1990a,b). Despite its name and its pre-Mississippian development of a temple mound complex, Toltec Mounds has yielded no hard evidence of Mesoamerican ties, nor has any Coles Creek center.

Late Prehistoric Period

Sometime around A.D. 800 the Mississippian phenomenon began to sweep across the Southeast. Current evidence indicates that there is no single hearth—external or internal—from whence the central Mississippian traits derived (Smith 1984). Despite the dearth of hard evidence for direct Mesoamerican ties, it is nonetheless intriguing that many of the same traits used to define Mississippian also comprise the arguments for Mesoamerican influences. These parallels fall into three general categories: 1) the temple mound complex, 2) motifs and symbols, and 3) cultigens. The similarities found in these categories has spawned a long-term interest in the Mesoamerican connection by many of the key figures in Southeastern archaeology (e.g., Bennett 1944; Griffin 1966; Krieger 1945; Phillips 1940).

Temple-Mound Complex

Mississippian period temple mounds are the most obvious examples of possible links between Mesoamerica and the Southeast (Covarrubias 1954; Phillips 1940; Wicke 1965). In particular, the arrangement of Mississippian mounds around plazas and the association of structures

Figure 13.4.   Comparison of feline representations from; A) Mesoamerica, B) the Southwest, and C) the Southeast.

with the tops of platform mounds have strong parallels with Mesoamerican sites. However, it is now recognized that platform mounds are found in the Southeast during the Middle Woodland period (Mainfort 1986; Toth 1975), frequently without structures and unrelated to plaza arrangements. While this does not rule out Mesoamerican influences for platform mounds, it does suggest that the constellation of platform mounds, structures, and plazas could be an indigenous phenomenon.

Motifs and Symbols

The bulk of the evidence for Mesoamerican-Southeastern ties derives from a wide array of similar motifs and symbols. In particular, attention has focused on the possible Mesoamerican origins for the various symbols and styles associated with the so-called Southern Cult or Southeastern Ceremonial Complex (SECC), which dates to the Mississippian period (Brown 1976; Galloway 1989; Howard 1968; Waring and Holder 1945).

There are no unassailable Mesoamerican imports represented in the SECC on the order of copper bells or pyrite mirrors in the Southwest. Instead, there is an admittedly impressive list of circumstantial evidence, consisting of design elements that are strikingly similar to Mesoamerican motifs. It must be emphasized that the similarities in these motifs are not the occasional find; in many cases they are widespread in both Mesoamerican and Southeastern contexts. Some of the more common elements include the guilloche cross (Phillips 1940:353–354), the solar disk (Webb 1989), and a number of copper objects such as double bell copper earspools and cutouts (Bennett 1944). A particularly striking parallel is the unusual eye-in-hand motif (Figure 13.5), which occurs in Southeastern, Aztec, and Classic Maya iconography (Rands 1957). Rands (1957) also points out its widespread occurrence in Northwest Coast material culture, which could be used to argue both for and against Mesoamerican origins.

Another stylistic parallel occurs on "long-nosed" god maskettes which have a strong similarity to the merchant gods of Mesoamerica (Hall 1989). Renderings in shell and copper of a face with a very long nose appear early in the Late Prehistoric period and have a fairly wide distribution throughout the Eastern Woodlands (Brown et al. 1990; Williams and Goggin 1956). These objects are usually manufactured in copper to the south and marine shell to the north, "representing the principal exotic material in the place of deposition" (Brown et al. 1990:264).

Individuals wearing bird costumes represent one of the more famous SECC images (Figure 13.6). This design is executed in a number of media, including copper, shell, ceramics, and sandstone, and depicts individuals wearing regalia of raptorial birds. Phillips (1940:356) observes that bird-men, as well as other figures depicted in SECC art, often exhibit sprightly dance-like attitudes that were similar to some Mesoamerican styles. The bird-men frequently strike militaristic poses, holding weapons and severed heads in their hands. Not surprisingly, bird-men are presumed to represent warriors or military leaders. In Mesoamerica, there is a lengthy history of representations of individuals wearing bird costumes, extending from Formative times to the Contact period codices. Strong (1989) proposes that this symbolism reflects a widespread belief that the costume embodies protection or guidance by higher powers, but he does not argue for a direct Mesoamerican influence for the manifestation of bird-men in the Southeast.

In many cases Mesoamerican-appearing symbols in the Southeast occur as intriguing, yet isolated, elements. That is, they do not occur within larger thematic sets with which one might associate religious or mythical meanings well-established in Mesoamerican cosmology. There are, however, some apparent exceptions to this rule. The eye-in-hand motif does seem to demonstrate some recurring association with symbols connected with death in both Mesoamerica and the Southeast (Rands 1957). Webb (1989) has defined several conceptual clusters in the Southeast for which there are Mesoamerican analogues. These include an earth-water-sky reptile associated with fertility and regeneration, large felines associated with force or leadership, and raptorial birds associated with astral phenomena and conflict.

Figure 13.5.   Eye-in-hand symbol on a stone disc from near Carthage, Alabama.

Figure 13.6.   A bird man with a severed head (on a copper sheet from Etowah).

Perhaps the best candidate for an obvious ceremonially-charged Mesoamerican symbol is the feathered or flying serpent (Figure 13.7). Serpents with wings or feathers are widely found as motifs on media ranging from gorgets (Prentice 1986) to engraved shell cups (Howard 1968; Phillips and Brown 1975). It is noteworthy that the association of the eye with the elbow that is seen in depictions of Queztalcoatl is represented in Spiro art (Rands 1957:249). Although destruction of the famous Piasa in Alton, Illinois makes reconstructions of that petroglyph questionable, the recent description of another petro-

glyph Piasa in Illinois shows bird-like wings on the back of a serpent. Unfortunately, the Piasa as a motif in the Southeast is such an unpredictable mixture of human, feline, deer, bird, serpent, and other characteristics that it is difficult to equate it with the well-known Quetzacoatl representation (see Phillips and Brown 1975:140). Many of the serpents, such as rattlesnakes occurring on shell gorgets, are obviously native to the Southeast. The snakes frequently have antlers, which also seems to be unique to the Southeast (Howard 1968).

The problem with all of these similarities is the well-documented fact that SECC styles and artifact frequencies display extreme variation across space and through time (Muller 1986c, 1989). Thus, whatever is being shared across the Southeast as reflected in the SECC was greatly modified into a number of local and regional variants. Furthermore, many of the elements seem to have a great time-depth. For example, Rands (1957) sees possible antecedents of the eye-in-hand motif on Adena tablets; and Hall (1989) also traces early indigenous roots for the long-nosed god. Krieger (1945:505) astutely observed that art technology as well as styles had a long history in the Southeast—cold-hammering of copper and incising of marine shell began at least as early as Hopewell times.

Further weakening arguments for a direct Mesoamerican-Southeast connection is the fact that Mesoamerican traits in Southeastern art appear in juxtaposition with elements that are completely alien to the central Mexican and Mayan regions. Common SECC motifs such as the beaded forelock, bi-lobed arrow, and bellows-shaped apron have no Mesoamerican parallels. Recognition of the spatio-temporal diversity of SECC objects and styles, combined with the out-of-context presentation of Mesoamerican appearing

Figure 13.7.   Serpent motifs from; A) Mesoamerica, B) the Southwest, and C) the Southeast.

symbols, has led researchers away from any notion of a core area in the Southeast from whence the Southern Cult sprung (Webb 1989). It has also dampened enthusiasm for the idea that SECC motifs represent the direct movement of Mesoamerican objects or ideas into the Southeast.

Other assorted Mesoamerican-like items occur throughout the Southeast. Arguments for two Mexican-influenced stelae near a platform mound have been made for the Crystal River site in the Florida panhandle (Bullen 1966). One limestone slab was plain, but the top of the second was shaped by pecking into an upper torso and head. Bullen argues that concentrations of food and debitage at the base of the anthropomorphic stela parallel stelae votive deposits in the Maya area. The lack of glyphs on the stelae, combined with a lack of other Mayan traits on the site, make it difficult to interpret this find, which is unique to the Southeast.

Tripod pots have been recovered at a number of sites in the Central Mississippi River Valley. Yet the range of experimentation seen in various Southeastern compound and zoomorphic vessels suggests that the idea of creating a pot with three legs was an innovation entirely within the realm of indigenous developments. Rocker stamping is an unusual ceramic surface technique found in both the Southeast and Mexico (Griffin 1980; Phillips 1940), but again, it appears to be a relatively mundane decoration that might be expected to occur within the context of a wide experimentation in decorative treatments.

Cultigens

The one category of unquestionable Mesoamerican imports into the Southeast is cultigens. However, the prior presence of tropical cultigens in the Southwest raises the possibility that the plants did not enter the Eastern Woodlands directly from Mexico but from the Southwest instead. Another alternative argument sees maize entering the Southeast by way of the Antilles (Lathrap 1987; Sears 1977).

Current early dates for maize place it in the Midsouth and Midwest during the Middle Woodland period (Chapman and Crites 1987). Following a very slow increase during the Late Woodland period, its use exploded with the onset of the Mississippian period. Beans do not appear in the Southeastern archaeological record until Mississippian times (Ford 1985). The case for cucurbits is still unsettled. Apparent domesticated varieties occur in eastern North America as early as the Middle Archaic period, but there is an ongoing debate as to whether they represent either tropical imports or an independent episode of domestication (see Fritz 1990).

There is little question that future research will alter the dating of the introduction of tropical cultigens into the Southeast. But given the disparity of the best documented early dates for maize, beans, and squash, it seems unlikely that they entered the Southeast as a complex. It seems more probable that they slowly diffused into the region in several pulses, and may have arrived via the Southwest. Thus, even the only unambiguous Mesoamerican imports into the Southeast do not necessarily imply direct connections between the two regions.

SOUTHWEST-SOUTHEAST COMPARISONS

Both the Southwest and Southeast share a number of parallels with Mesoamerica. In some cases, the similarities overlap. In other cases, particularly in the realm of actual imports, there are distinct differences. In this section, a systematic comparison is made between the Southwest and Southeast in terms of their respective parallels with Mesoamerican cultigens, architecture, iconography, and cosmology. The section ends by contrasting the models that have been proposed to account for Mesoamerican connections in the Southwest and Southeast.

Cultigens

The earliest evidence of North American ties to Mesoamerica is the appearance of non-indigenous cultigens such as maize, squash, and beans. These tropical domesticates were not adopted as a set, but rather accumulated over many years in both the Southeast and Southwest. Nor did adoptions of domesticates in one region parallel the other. This unevenness in the timing and kinds of Mesoamerican plants adopted in North America reflects the differing climatic and social conditions of the Southwest and Southeast, as well as the different nature of the ties each region had with Mesoamerica.

Architecture and Site Configuration

Many features of the monumental architecture and community plans of the two North American regions parallel those of Mesoamerica. Ballcourts in the Southwest and platform mounds in the Southeast are frequently cited as examples of Mesoamerican influence. However, Hohokam ballcourts differed from their Mesoamerican counterparts, and the Mississippian arrangement of mounds around a plaza had precedents in the Middle Woodland site of Toltec. Similarities in Southwestern and Southeastern community plans, especially the arrangement of structures around a plaza, could be construed as evidence of either Mesoamerican influence or connections between the Southwest and Southeast. The fact that plazas appear in both the Southwest and Southeast prior to the construction of platform mounds would seem to weaken arguments that the mound-plaza arrangement was imported as a coherent entity to either the Southwest or Southeast from Mesoamerica.

Iconographic Motifs and Symbols

The Southwest and Southeast share several motifs, symbols, and iconographic themes with Mesoamerica. Although their representations differ somewhat, serpents, large felines, and large predatory birds (raptors) are found on prehistoric materials and were important figures in the cosmologies of ethnographic groups in all three regions. Other Mesoamerican-looking motifs such as the eye-in-hand, solar disk, and long nosed gods are present only in the Southeast, whereas the bird-snake, burden carrier, feathered headdress, and cipactli are present only in the Southwest.

Serpent Iconography

In the Southeast, Brown (1985), Prentice (1986), and Emerson (1989) have noted a close association of serpent iconography with water-agricultural-fertility symbolism (Figure 13.7). Emerson (1989) and Prentice (1986) convincingly argue that many female figurines, including two from the BBB Motor site in the American Bottom, were dominated by such symbolism. Nearly all other Mississippian-period female (non-mortuary) figurines and pipes show women processing grain or seed foods with burden baskets on their backs. Most researchers associate this iconography with inclusive, communal cults (Brown 1985; Emerson 1989). Brown (1985) argues that Piasas, the combination of felines, serpents and other animals, also have a fertility connotation given their similarity to the Birger serpent and depictions of the underwater panther which "... retains a mythic association with fertility among Great Lakes Indians today" (Brown 1985:127).

Serpent iconography in the Southwest has similar connotations. Giant feathered serpents (Zuni = Ko'loowisi/ Hopi = Pa'lülükoña), appear during Zuni and Hopi Kachina rituals bringing life-giving moisture to begin the growing season (see figure in Stevenson 1904:Plate XIV). In prehistoric kiva murals rain is commonly associated

with plumed or horned serpents as well as stepped rain cloud/altars, some birds, and offerings (for Kuaua Ruin see Dutton 1963:Plate XIII). Similar horned and plumed serpents are also found in Jornada style rock art; and Schaafsma (1980:217) has suggested that these serpents are symbolic of the Mexican-derived Quetzalcoatl, though only a few have anthropomorphic attributes.

The pan-Mesoamerican feathered serpent deity, Quetzalcoatl, was both a creator deity and a symbol of kingship (Carrasco 1982). While he participated in the creation of human life, corn, and pulque, he was also closely associated with the rulership. The major drawback to equating North American snakes with Mesoamerican gods is the lack of an organized Southeastern or Southwestern religion with central deities. It cannot be denied that the idea of the feathered serpent may have moved northward, but if so, it is clear that its meaning changed dramatically as it was incorporated into Southeastern and Southwestern belief systems.

Birds, Jaguars, and Other Felines

In Mesoamerican and Mississippian iconography, large raptors appear to be associated with warfare and rulership. The eagle is a prominent symbol of warfare and ferocity in Mexican iconography. Likewise, falcon iconography appears to be associated with the elite and probably with warfare in the Southeast (Brown 1985; Knight 1986; Strong 1989). In the Southwest, and indeed much of North America, eagles have great symbolic power and their feathers are sought for use in rituals. However, they do not have the same recurrent iconographic association with warfare seen in the Southeast and Mesoamerica.

The jaguar is prominent in the iconography of rulership in Mesoamerica, especially among the Maya (Figure 13.4). During the Mississippian period in the Southeast, large felines also seem to have elite connotations as evidenced by their depiction on mortuary artifacts. In the Southwest, large felines, particularly the mountain lion, are symbolically important to the Zuni and other Puebloan groups. Mountain lions are associated with the north and become beast priests with the power to heal upon their death. Representations of jaguars themselves appear in late Kachina iconography where they do not appear to be associated with rulership. In the Southeast, the puma/panther is associated with the underwater/ underworld which according to some has the ability to control the weather and also possesses medicinal qualities (Howard 1968).

Variation in the veneration of large felines between the three regions, in conjunction with the ceremonial importance of cats throughout the Americas, makes it difficult to use these animals as a strong link between Mesoamerica and North America. The same holds true for raptors and other birds.

Cosmology

Late Prehistoric and contemporary cultures in the Southeast and Southwest also share a number of basic elements of their cosmologies and ritual beliefs with Mesoamerican cultures. Some of these are commonplace throughout the New World. Others, such as the multitiered conception of the universe and new fire or renewal ceremonies, are less widespread, yet are common to the three regions considered here.

Directional Symbolism and Multitiered Cosmos

The Aztec, Maya, and other Precolumbian Mesoamerican peoples believed that the world in which they lived was one in a cyclical sequence of creation and destruction. This world was multitiered and divided into quarters following the cardinal directions, each of which was associated with certain qualities, colors, and deities. The Aztec and Maya envisioned 13 heavenly layers above the earth and nine below, each presided over by its own deity and attributes. The earth, which floated on the waters, was divided into four quarters such that for the Maya the East was associated with the color red, west with black, north with white, south with yellow, and the center with blue-green (Marcus et al. 1983; Morley et al. 1983). The Mixtec and Aztec used the same colors but associated them with different directions (Berdan 1982: Table 6–2; Marcus et al. 1983).

Puebloan cultures and their antecedents in the Southwest shared this conception of the cosmos with their Mesoamerican neighbors, as did the Cherokee and Creek peoples of the Southeast. According to the Cherokee, the world that humans occupy is a place between the upper world above the sky and the under world beneath the land and waters. Legendary creatures and "gods" live in these places which have the general connotations of good, purity, and order (the upper world) and danger, disorder, and change (the under world), respectively. The Zuni envision a similar world in which they occupy the middle world, surrounded by water, between the four levels of the upper world and the four of the under world (Tedlock 1979). Ceramic designs, iconography, and the organization of space in archaeological sites suggests that this quadrilateral organization may have been important at least as early as Pueblo I and Mississippian times.

New Fire Ceremonies

The indigenous people of each of these regions believe that they have an important role in ritually maintaining or preserving the world in its present state. The Aztec and Maya practiced blood sacrifice, made extensive calendrical and astrological observations, and conducted periodic ceremonies to ritually cleanse and renew the earthly world. Once every 52 years all fires were extinguished and household idols discarded, as were cooking implements and hearth stones. In the darkness priests started a new fire—in the open chest cavity of a sacrificed captive in the case of the Aztec—which was dispersed to every household in the community. During this ceremony, every man, woman, and child bled their ears both in penance and to "feed the sun," which would keep the forces of darkness from ending the world. If the fire did not light and the ceremony failed, everyone knew that the end of the present sun, and therefore of the present world, was at hand (Berdan 1982:119).

Some version of the new fire ceremony is common in Southwestern Pueblo groups. At Hopi in the Wuwuchim ceremony, adolescent boys are initiated into the men's societies. At this time a new fire is lit as a symbol of renewal. At Zuni in the Shalako ceremony, one of the key participants is the Fire God who lights new fires in the kivas.

The Creek and other Southeastern groups practiced a yearly ceremony of renewal and purification commonly called the Green Corn ceremony or the Busk. Held when the late corn was ripe, this four day ceremony was the single most important of the year. Beginning with a cleaning, plastering, and painting of public and private spaces, it culminated in the extinguishing of all fires in the village and the rekindling of a new, ritually-pure one. The fire, which serves as the earthly symbol of the sun, is thus rekindled and renewed and the earthly world ritually purified. Hudson (1976) and Howard (1968) argue that many traits of the Southeast Ceremonial Complex may have been the product of the Green Corn ceremonies. These traits include the rebuilding of mounds and mound structures, cross-in-circle motifs, and conch shell cups. However, during the Historic period of the Eastern Woodlands, there was great variation in Green Corn ceremonies, which has led Witthoft (1949) to doubt their derivation from the Southwest or Mexico.

Models of Long-Distance Interaction

The widespread traits, symbols, and belief systems shared by Mesoamerica, the Southwest, and the Southeast readily bring to mind a picture of long-maintained and far-reaching connections. Some of the traits, such as color-related world quarters and Heroic Twin myths, are so widespread in North, Middle, and South America that they may betray the common Pleistocene ancestry of their peoples. In this vein, it has been argued that the parallels spring from an ancient nuclear belief system (Covarrubias 1954; Webb 1989).

At the same time, there is little question that ideas and goods continued to move northward out of Mesoamerica long after the peopling of the New World. Thus, arguments among Southwestern and Southeastern archaeologists about this long-distance interaction have focused on three topics: 1) documenting the material culture similarities, which have been summarized previously in this chapter; 2) identifying the mechanism by which this continental scale interaction may have occurred; and 3) assessing the impacts this interaction had on developments in both the Southwest and Southeast.

Attempts to account for the Mesoamerican influences in the Southwest tend to be highly polarized (Wilcox 1986a). Some individuals view the Southwest as little more than the northernmost extension of Mesoamerica (Di Peso 1983; Kelley 1986a), while others argue that the Southwest was removed from Mesoamerica and developed separately with only infrequent borrowings (Haury 1976; Schroeder 1981). In the 1970s and 1980s these two views manifested themselves in an isolationist versus imperialist debate. The imperialists, led by Di Peso (1968, 1974, 1983) and Kelley (Kelley and Kelley 1975), argued that a pre-Aztec pochteca-like guild entered the Southwest and set up the major centers such as Chaco Canyon and Paquimé.

Isolationists largely dismissed any notion of direct Mesoamerican influence on the region (citations in McGuire 1980). Numerous critiques of the pochteca theory have generally led to its abandonment; and the isolationist position has been shown not to be viable either (McGuire 1980; Mathien and McGuire 1986; Plog et al. 1982; Schroeder 1981).

The debate about Mesoamerican influence on the Southwest remains highly charged and polarized. Some researchers, who by and large work in the frontier area of Mesoamerica, still argue that Mesoamerican-based groups or individuals entered the Southwest and directly affected the development of the region (Di Peso 1983; Kelley 1986a; Weigand and Harbottle 1993). Others, who primarily work in the Southwest, argue for more indirect but still significant connections through mechanisms such as elite exchange networks (McGuire 1989; Minnis 1989; Nelson 1990). A recent survey of external connections to the Southwest concludes that the social systems of Mesoamerica and the Southwest are analogous to two families of languages with some cognates but different deep structures (McGuire et al. 1994).

In contrast to the hard evidence from the Southwest, evidence for Southeast-Mesoamerica ties is circumstantial. If we are willing to at least entertain the notion of Mesoamerican-Southeastern links, the evidence points more strongly to a steady drip of goods and ideas moving into the Southeast than to a flood or even a single unit-intrusion. For that reason, most Southeastern archaeologists seem to have arrived at a tacit consensus that down-the-line movement perhaps best describes the mechanism of broad scale interaction between the two regions and that direct Mesoamerican influence was slight (Griffin 1980). Obvious routes of interaction include northeastern Mexico and Texas, the Gulf of Mexico, and Florida via the Antilles.

Recognition of the nebulous and long-term movement of goods and ideas into the Southeast from Mesoamerica has made Southeastern archaeologists extremely cautious about postulating formal models of long-distance trade. Thus, notions of world systems, prestige goods economies, and the like have not seriously entered the discussion for Mesoamerican-Southeastern interaction as they have for the Southwest. Further complicating the picture of Mesoamerican-Southeastern connections is the possibility that many of the parallel traits have a lengthy history in the Southeast and appear to exhibit an in situ evolution over time. Consequently, despite the possibility of influential surges of innovation from Mesoamerica, particularly in the realm of cultigens, historical transformations in the Southeast are viewed as largely indigenous phenomena.

It is interesting that with all of the historical emphasis on Mesoamerican connections with the Southwest and Southeast, so little attention has been paid to the possible long-range connections between these two North American areas themselves. Perhaps this neglect is due to the fact that the two culture areas do not look very similar—which may be saying something important about the strength (or weakness) of their Mesoamerican ties.

Although Southwestern items are extremely rare on the westernmost margin of the Mississippian world, they still outnumber Mesoamerican objects, which stand at nil. Cotton cloth, which must have come from the Southwest at least indirectly, has been recovered from Spiro (King and Gardner 1981). Phillips and Brown's (1975:203) Spiro study found at least one engraved shell figure that looked Southwestern: a bird man with a cloud terrace motif that looks very similar to a Zuni Knife-wing Being. Despite the 500 year difference between the two figures, Phillips and Brown rightly point out that iconographic comparisons between the Southwest and Southeast is a sorely neglected and potentially fascinating avenue of research.

GEOGRAPHY AND CULTURE AREAS REVISITED

Before closing this chapter we return to the topics of geography and culture areas. Beyond the very different nature of their Mesoamerican ties, one of the major difficulties encountered in comparing the Southwest and Southeast is typological. In other words, scholars in the two North American regions have developed different approaches toward defining their late prehistoric culture areas, and it is worth considering briefly how this may bear on the issue of Mesoamerican ties.

Both the Southwest and Southeast witnessed the emergence of strong regional traditions during the late prehistoric interval of immediate interest to this volume, ca. A.D. 900–1400. Yet there are some interesting differences as well. For one, despite the strong regionalization, Southeasterners recognize a much wider pan-regional phenomenon uniting the various traditions that are labelled "Mississippian." While most of the Southeastern contributors to the volume would probably agree with this statement, they still would have a difficult time providing their Southwestern colleagues with a unanimous consensus on what constitutes "Mississippian." At the least, it would include a sedentary lifestyle greatly dependent upon maize agriculture and the building of temple mound complexes. From a neo-evolutionary perspective, Mississippian groups are also considered to represent a broad spectrum of chiefdoms (Peebles and Kus 1977; Smith 1978).

Another important contrast between the Southwest and Southeast is the duration of Mississippian versus the major Late Prehistoric Southwestern traditions. The large, Late Prehistoric centers at Paquimé, in the Phoenix Basin, and in the Salado and Western Pueblo areas appear

to have declined around A.D. 1450, whereas at the time of the Spanish entrada in the Southeast, explorers such as De Soto described thriving chiefdoms that could comfortably be categorized as Mississippian.

But here we begin to see some of the archaeologically-imposed difficulties in comparing the Southeast and Southwest as culture areas. If one were to use, for example, agricultural, sedentary societies with Puebloan architecture as an archaeological culture type, then there was a larger Southwestern tradition that, like Mississippian, was thriving and widespread at the arrival of the Spanish. Conversely, if one looks at individual Mississippian regions closely, there is a strong pattern of coalescence, collapse, and abandonment (often with a later re-coalescence) that is reminiscent of the Southwest.

At the grand scale then, our differing classificatory schemes may be masking some interesting structural similarities between the two regions, similarities which in fact form one of the key themes of this volume. But if we think in terms of agency and history, then the issue of Mesoamerican ties is not only useful as a contrast and comparison between the Southwest and Southeast as grand entities—it is also a point of departure for addressing variability within those regions as well. In other words, we believe that the issue of Mesoamerican connections is not merely a question of one culture area influencing another culture area—it is also a question of how smaller traditions within larger cultural areas reacted to the importation of new objects and ideas. Indeed, except for cultigens, it seems likely that Mesoamerican influences had little impact on the broad structural trends in the Southeast and Southwest. At a much smaller scale, however, Mesoamerican influences on the day-to-day experiences of different times and places may have been very important.

Barring the discovery of a Mayan stela or pochteca burial in North America, if there are any new worlds to conquer in the topic of Mesoamerican connections, especially in the case of the Southeast, they would appear to lie in the detailed study of regional diversity in the content and spread of Mesoamerican traits. Is there systematic variation in the treatment of pyrite mirrors within and between Southwestern regional traditions? Is the eye-in-hand motif regularly depicted in different media and in different contexts through space and time in the Southeast? Can we move from these patterns to indigenous perceptions of these symbols and objects? Such questions allow us to move beyond merely comparing the nature of contact between homogenized culture areas to considering the nature of and variability in the indigenous acceptance of outside influences.

The initial impetus for the early studies of Mesoamerican ties was to evaluate the impact of the diffusion of traits from the Mesoamerican "high" cultures to their less advanced neighbors to the north. With an increased data base, more sophisticated technologies, and changes in theoretical outlook, we now have the opportunity to address the dynamics of external influences. We can consider how the integration and modification of these influences was a function of the historical trajectories of specific regional traditions in both the Southwest and Southeast.

Conclusions

In both the Southwest and Southeast, the ties to Mesoamerica appear most pronounced during the Late Prehistoric period. It is at this time that architectural and iconographic similarities are clearest and belief systems appearing to incorporate Mesoamerican concepts are definable. It is apparent that the ties are not simply the result of an intrusion of Mesoamerican peoples into these regions. Rather, they are the result of complex historical processes involving some degree of commonly held conceptual ancestry, indirect transmission of iconography (with or without their original meanings), and in the case of the Southwest, limited contact with northern Mesoamerican cultures through elite exchange networks or other mechanisms. Lying at the conceptual base of the amalgam of such regional traditions such as the Mississippian, Hohokam, Pueblo, Toltec, and Aztec was a set of widely held ways of conceptualizing and symbolizing significant aspects of reality. Regional manifestations of these themes were the result of the unique historical, social, and environmental conditions of each area.

CHAPTER FOURTEEN

Examining Societal Organization in the Southwest:

An Application of Multiscalar Analysis

Jill E. Neitzel

W HILE THE AMERICAN SOUTHWEST HAS ALWAYS BEEN an exciting place for archaeologists to work, this has been especially true over the past three decades. During this time, the question of how prehistoric Southwestern societies were organized has become an overriding research issue. This question has not only framed an unprecedented surge of fieldwork and analysis, which has resulted in large part from contract funded projects. It has also provoked vigorous and sustained debates about how research should be conducted and interpreted. Southwestern archaeologists are in the enviable position of having lots of colleagues working in some way or other on the problem of prehistoric organization, lots of data available on this topic, much of it with relatively fine-grained chronological control, and lots of interpretations, many of them conflicting, about what the data mean.

In my view, Southwestern archaeology is currently entering a new phase in its studies of prehistoric organization. The focus of much research and debate over the past decade or so has been on determining whether or not various prehistoric societies should be labeled as "complex." The very nature of this question, which seemingly requires a yes or no answer, has contributed to polarizing and often acrimonious debates. Thankfully, this intellectual environment now seems to be shifting. In part, this shift is due to an increasing appreciation for the organiza-

tional diversity that characterized prehistoric Southwestern societies with the realization that labeling particular cases as complex does not really help (and may in fact impede) our understanding of this diversity.

Critical for accomplishing the tasks of documenting and explaining organization diversity is comparative analysis. For particular cases, comparisons need to be made between different variables, such as population, subsistence intensification, and hierarchy development. Individual cases in turn need to be compared with one another to identify similarities and differences in the patterns of change characterizing specific variables and in the interrelationships among variables. While the comparative method has been an integral part of Southwestern archaeology since its inception (e.g., Kidder 1927), discussions about prehistoric organization have brought a renewed appreciation for its value, as evidenced by a series of recent publications comparing prehistoric developments in different parts of the Southwest (e.g., Cordell and Gumerman 1989b; Crown and Judge 1991; Gumerman 1988, 1994; Gumerman and Gell-Mann 1993).

The major point of this paper is that the value of the comparative method could be enhanced if Southwestern archaeologists incorporated a multiscalar perspective in their research. With a few notable exceptions (e.g., Lipe and Hegmon 1989; Minnis 1989; Neitzel 1989a,b), scale is a topic that Southwestern archaeologists have paid relatively little attention. The focus of most research has generally been on developments at a single scale of analysis, such as the site, locality, or region. Questions about how developments at different scales may have affected one another have for the most part not been raised. Interpretive models derived from one scale have generally been assumed to apply to other scales as well.

This paper is intended to illustrate the value of applying a multiscalar perspective to the problem of how prehistoric Southwestern societies were organized. The discussion is divided into three parts. First, multiscalar analyses are performed for two of the Southwest's best documented cases, the Hohokam and Chacoan. Next, an overview of how a greater array of key variables changed at multiple scales is presented for a larger sample of Southwestern cases. Finally, questions about the complexity and organizational diversity of prehistoric Southwestern societies are considered.

MULTISCALAR ANALYSES OF TWO CASE STUDIES

The multiscalar perspective emphasizes the importance of scale and context in studies of social groups (see Adams 1977; Arensberg 1961; Blanton 1976; Flannery 1976; Johnson 1977). From this view, groups can be conceptualized as forming an embedded hierarchy with smaller groups combining to form larger groups. Thus, for example, households are part of villages, which are part of localities, which are part of regions, which are part of macroregions, which are finally part of world systems.

The major implication of this embedded hierarchy is that the study of any specific group cannot focus on that group alone. Instead, its component groups, and the larger groups of which it is a part, must also be considered. This embedded hierarchy not only defines a group's characteristics at any single point in time but also how these characteristics change. From the bottom of the hierarchy looking up, the temporal patterns at any one level represent in large part the aggregate of patterns exhibited among its components. From the opposite perspective, the temporal patterns at any one level may be affected by those of the larger scale units of which it is a part.

The significance of these temporal interrelationships is that an understanding of change at any level can be achieved only if the smaller and larger levels are also considered. Not only can the range of variables that cause change operate at many levels or scales simultaneously, but the measurable effects of any one variable may vary appreciably depending upon the scale selected for analysis. These temporal interrelationships among levels raise the possibility that different explanatory models may be applicable to different scales. For example, some variables or intervariable relationships may be more significant for explaining change within households or villages, while others may be more significant for explaining change in localities, regions, or macroregions.

In the Southwest, two of the best documented prehistoric societies can be used to illustrate the value of applying a multiscalar perspective. Both of these cases, the Hohokam and Chacoan, have been the subject of intensive study concerning the question of how they were organized. Although they are both frequently cited as two of the Southwest's three most complex societies (with Paquimé being the third), this view is not universally held and has been the subject of debate. The multiscalar perspective can offer new insights into Hohokam and Chacoan organization as well as a greater appreciation for the ways in which these two societies were similar and how they differed.

The Hohokam Case

Over the past two decades, there has been a virtual explosion in the amount of Hohokam research being done (Gumerman 1991). It has included both surveys and excavations, financed for the most part by cultural resource management contracts. These investigations have been done at a variety of scales with a unifying theme being the question of how the Hohokam were organized. Three variables for which multiscalar analyses can be performed for the Hohokam case are organization, demography, and agricultural intensification. In the discussion that follows, these variables are first considered individually and then are compared with one another.

Organization

Until the 1980s, the prevailing view of Hohokam sociopolitical organization was that it was egalitarian, a conclusion derived from analogy with the historic Pima (Haury 1976; Woodbury 1961). Subsequent settlement pattern and mortuary analyses has reversed this traditional view. The Classic period Hohokam are now generally interpreted as having had a hierarchical sociopolitical organization, and the possibility of some degree of hierarchy development has been raised for the preceding Sedentary period as well (see Fish, Chapter 4).

Data from a variety of scales reveal a pattern of increasing complexity throughout the Hohokam sequence (Table 14.1). Through time, burials exhibit more status levels (Haury 1976; McGuire 1992a; Wasley and Johnson 1965) and sites comprise a more hierarchical settlement system. Greater administrative complexity is also evidenced by the interconnectedness of the Lower Salt River Valley's irrigation canals during the Classic period (Nicholas and Neitzel 1984). At the regional level, the rank-size data indicate that the Hohokam were never a single, unified sociopolitical entity. Instead, throughout its duration, Hohokam society contained a number of independent systems that were apparently linked by ceremonialism, trade, and other aspects of culture (see Wilcox 1979a).

Although the overall trend is toward greater complexity, the Hohokam sequence is also characterized by a qualitative organizational shift between the Sedentary and Classic periods (Doyel 1980). This shift is marked by the replacement of ballcourts by platform mounds as the major architectural feature at large sites (Gregory 1987; Wilcox and Sternberg 1983). Both features had ceremonial functions, but platform mounds also served as elite residences (Doyel 1974; Hammack and Hammack 1981). This double function suggests the ceremonial legitimization of elite status during the Classic period (Neitzel 1991).

Demography

Comparisons of Hohokam demographic trends can be made for a number of scales, which are represented by data of varying temporal coverage and precision. Excavated pithouses at two sites, La Ciudad (Henderson 1986) and Snaketown (Wilcox et al. 1981), can be used to reconstruct how household size changed during the Preclassic period (Figure 14.1). The shifts are marked at Snaketown and more subtle at La Ciudad. At Snaketown, the largest pithouses are the earliest, after which pithouse size declined markedly and then remained relatively constant through time. At La Ciudad, median pithouse size is relatively constant with a slight decline occurring at the beginning of the site's occupation and a slight increase occurring at the end. Both sites have larger pithouses during their later occupations, which suggest the possibility of social differentiation among households.

At a larger scale, pithouses were often arranged in groups or courtyards. At La Ciudad, courtyards were constructed in stages, beginning with a single pithouse, which was usually the largest (Figure 14.2). The timing of when new pithouses were added to a courtyard probably reflects the domestic cycling of families (Henderson 1986).

At an even higher level, courtyards were sometimes part of groupings of courtyards. At La Ciudad, there was apparently a limit on how many pithouses could be added to a courtyard. One way for a courtyard to cope with extra people was to establish a new courtyard nearby. Whether or not a courtyard ultimately had other courtyards established around it, seems to have been related to how quickly it reached it maximum size (Table 14.2). Figure 14.3 shows the growth of one of La Ciudad's courtyard groups, which grew around one of the courtyards shown in Figure 14.2.

Together, changes in the numbers of people living in households, courtyards, and courtyard groups at La Ciudad and Snaketown produced the population changes seen at the sites as a whole (Figure 14.4). La Ciudad reached its

Table 14.1. Organizational Trends at Different Spatial Scales for the Hohokam Case

Period	Burial Levels	Sites	Salt Valley	Region Levels	Region Rank Size
Pioneer	1	No special features	Independent, linear canals	1	Convex
Colonial	1–2	Some have ballcourts	Independent, linear canals	2	Convex
Sedentary	2–3	Some have ballcourts; a few have mounds	Independent, branching canals	3	Convex
Classic	3	Some have mounds	Interconnected, branching canals; sites served by multiple canals	3–4	Convex

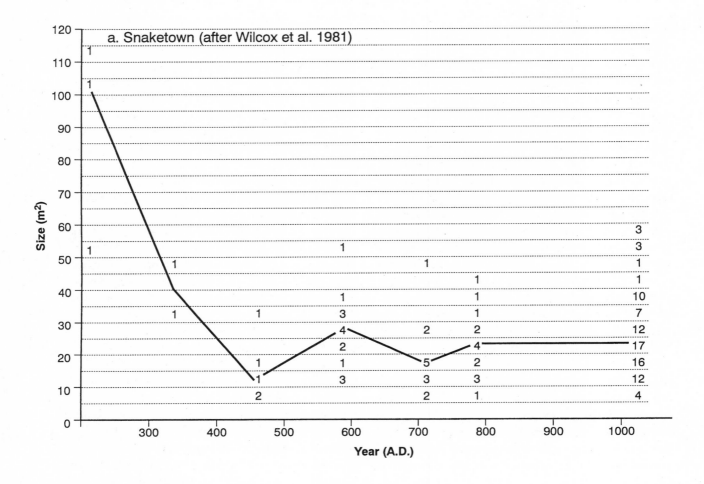

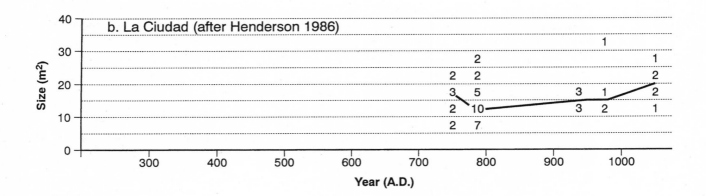

- indicates the number of pithouses in that 5-m² increment

—— - indicates median number of pithouses in 5-m² increment

Figure 14.1.　Household population at two Preclassic Hohokam sites.

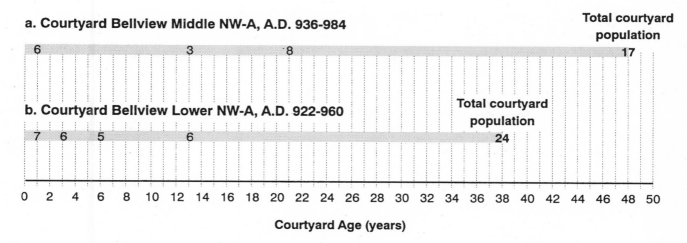

a. Courtyard Bellview Middle NW-A, A.D. 936-984

Total courtyard population

6   3   8   17

b. Courtyard Bellview Lower NW-A, A.D. 922-960

Total courtyard population

7 6 5   6   24

0 2 4 6 8 10 12 14 16 18 20 22 24 26 28 30 32 34 36 38 40 42 44 46 48 50

Courtyard Age (years)

\# - indicates pithouse population

Figure 14.2.   Timing and sizes of pithouses added to courtyards at La Ciudad (from Henderson 1986).

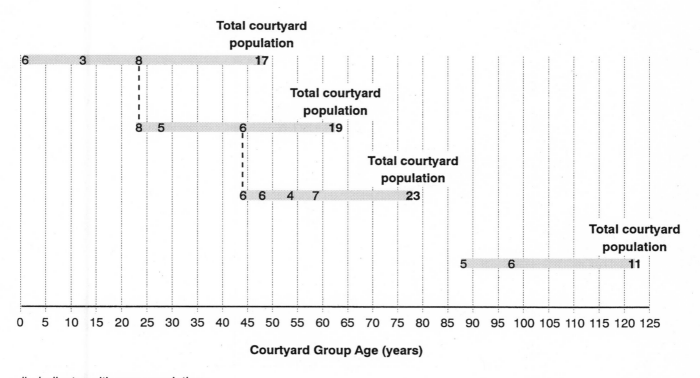

Total courtyard population

6   3   8   17

Total courtyard population

8 5   6   19

Total courtyard population

6 6 4 7   23

Total courtyard population

5   6   11

0 5 10 15 20 25 30 35 40 45 50 55 60 65 70 75 80 85 90 95 100 105 110 115 120 125

Courtyard Group Age (years)

\# - indicates pithouse population

Figure 14.3.   Timing of courtyards added to Bellview Middle northwest courtyard group at La Ciudad, A.D. 936–1058 (from Henderson 1986).

187

Table 14.2. The Growth of Courtyard Groups at La Ciudad (after Henderson 1986)

	Courtyard reached maximum size in ≤ 10 years	Courtyard reached maximum size in ≥ 10 years
Remained single courtyard	4	2
Expanded to courtyard group	3	5

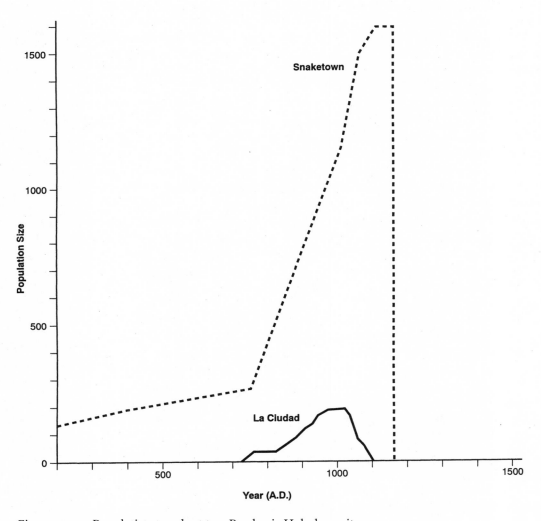

Figure 14.4. Population trends at two Preclassic Hohokam sites.

peak of approximately 150 people between A.D. 950–1025 (Henderson 1986:209). Snaketown, which was always substantially larger than La Ciudad, reached its peak of approximately 1,250 people roughly 100 years later (A.D. 1150) (Wilcox et al. 1990).

A major gap in Hohokam intrasettlement population reconstructions occurs after A.D. 1150. Information is available on the overall structure of the largest Classic period sites (Gregory 1987) and in two cases on how this structure changed through time (Brunson 1989). However, two critical sets of information are lacking. One is how the smaller scale units comprising Classic period sites (e.g., households and the compounds of which they were a part) changed through time. The other is what physical changes at all levels suggest about population size. Thus, while maximum population estimates of 1,000–2,500 people have been proposed for the largest Classic period sites (see Lekson, Chapter 1), the intra-settlement demographic trends that produced these figures are unknown.

Together, the aggregate population changes of individual settlements produced the demographic trends of larger spatial scales, such as the Lower Salt and Middle Gila River Valleys, the entire Phoenix Basin (or Hohokam core area), and the Hohokam region as a whole. Given that only two Hohokam sites have reliable population estimates, calculating numbers of people for larger spatial scales is an extremely speculative endeavor. However, various proxies, such as aggregate site size and number of sites, can be used to look at relative trends through time (without specifying a vertical scale of actual numbers of people) (Figure 14.5). The major conclusion that can be drawn from these graphs is that the embedded levels exhibit very similar patterns of growth. However, data from La Ciudad, Snaketown, and the Middle Gila River Valley show that this growth was not uniform. La Ciudad and Snaketown were abandoned before the peaks in Figure 14.5; and growth in the Middle Gila River Valley slowed during the Classic period (and perhaps even declined, as indicated when adjustments are made for varying time period length). These variable patterns at different spatial scales highlight the importance of employing a multiscalar perspective in Hohokam demographic studies.

Agricultural Intensification

Evidence from multiple scales suggests that the process of agricultural intensification among the Hohokam was complicated and varied. Plant remains from individual sites indicate that corn was an important crop from the start of the Hohokam sequence (Gasser and Kwiatkowski 1991). The only plant for which there is direct evidence of increasing reliance through time is agave in the northern Tucson Basin (Fish et al. 1985). However, there is indirect evidence (e.g., spindle whorls) which suggests that cotton may have become a key crop during the Classic period.

Changes and variation in the process of agricultural intensification are best seen in multiscalar comparisons of canal construction in the Lower Salt River Valley. For the valley as a whole, various measures are not consistent in identifying when intensification reached its peak. Two measures indicate that the peak occurred during the Classic period (Figures 14.6a-b), while another indicates the Sedentary period (Figure 14.6c).

The picture becomes even more complicated when smaller scales are considered. For example, while the percentage length of new canal construction devoted to laterals in the valley as a whole was greatest during the Classic period (Figure 14.7a), its peak in the southern part of the valley was during the Colonial period (Figure 14.7b). Individual canal lines within this southern area exhibit diverse temporal patterns (Figure 14.7c). Another measure, volume of dirt excavated for new canals, exhibits less temporal diversity at these same spatial scales (Figures 14.8). Clearly, the lesson to be learned from these various measures is that the process of agricultural intensification among the Hohokam was neither steady nor uniform. It proceeded at varying rates and to varying degrees in different areas and at different scales. Again, a multiscalar perspective, as well a reliance on a variety of measures, is essential for documenting these varied patterns.

Comparing Variables

For the Hohokam, comparisons of the variables of organization, demography, and intensification can best be made at the largest spatial scales. As Hohokam society became increasingly complex, the populations of its core area and region grew. Within the Lower Salt River Valley, increases in complexity and population were positively correlated with the expansion of canal irrigation.

What is missing from these comparisons is a sense of what was going on at smaller spatial scales. The variable represented at the most scales, intensification, exhibits diverse temporal patterns. A question for future investigation is how this diversity in intensification compares with demographic and organizational changes at similar scales.

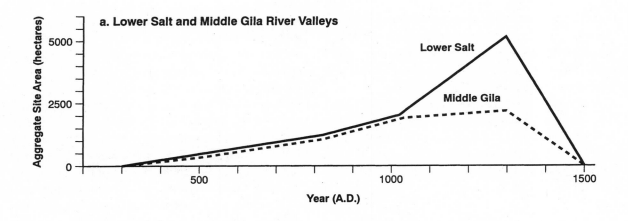

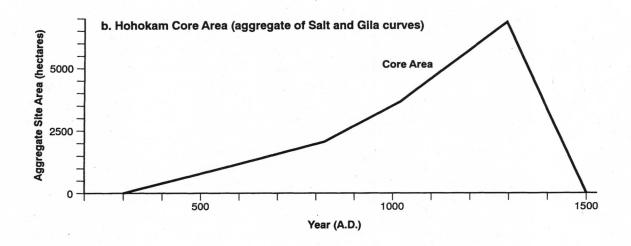

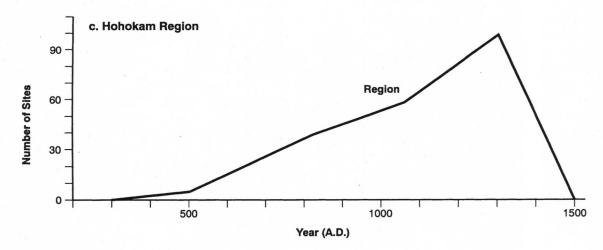

Figure 14.5.   Hohokam relative population curves.

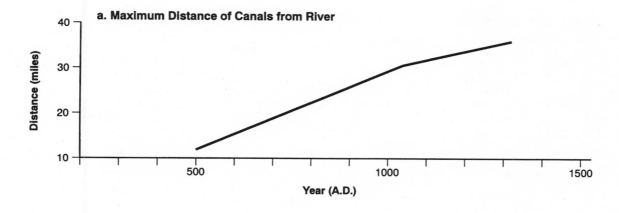

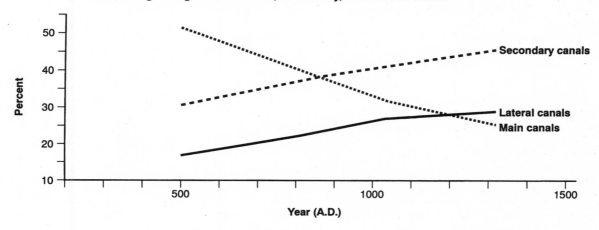

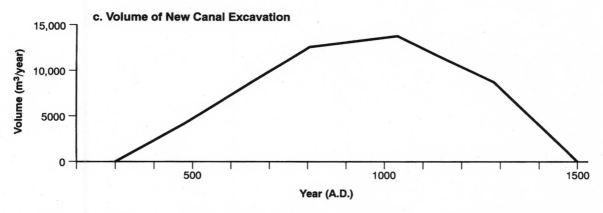

Figure 14.6. Measures of agricultural intensification in the Lower Salt River Valley (derived from Nicholas and Feinman 1989).

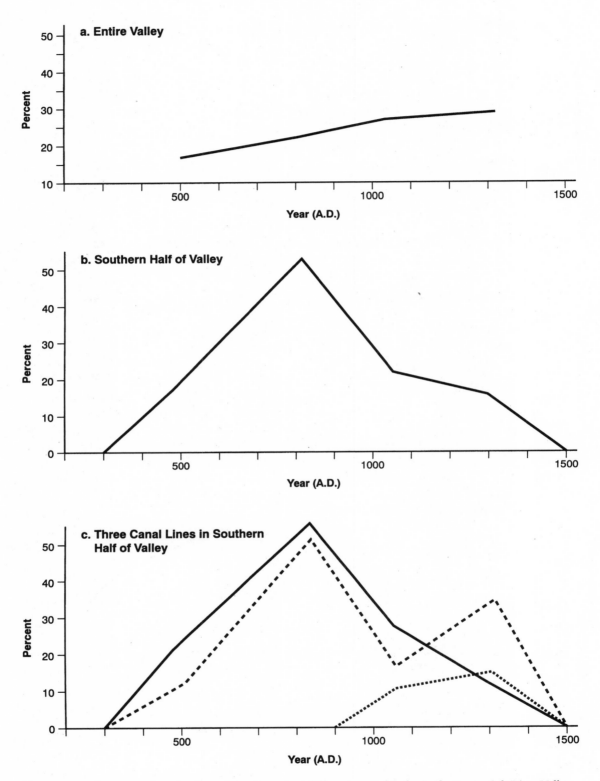

Figure 14.7.   Percentage length of new lateral canals at different spatial scales in the Lower Salt River Valley.

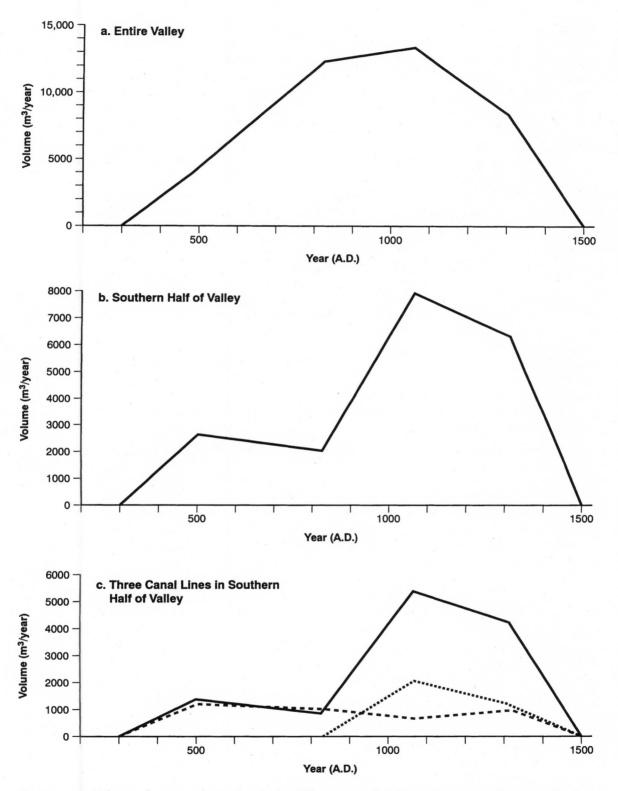

Figure 14.8.   Volume of new canal construction at different spatial scales in the Lower Salt River Valley.

For Hohokam research, the multiscalar perspective can make two major contributions. First, it can structure analyses so that trends at different scales are compared and their effects on one another considered. Secondly, it can highlight scales that are poorly documented and for which further data collection is necessary.

The Chacoan Case

Our current understanding of Chacoan prehistory is derived in large part from research undertaken by the National Park Service's Chaco Project from 1971 to 1986 (e.g., Hayes et al. 1981; Judge and Schelberg 1984; Powers et al. 1983). A major goal of this large scale, multidisciplinary project was to investigate how Chacoan populations were organized, a question addressed at multiple scales using both survey and excavation data. In the discussion that follows, the multiscalar data available for the same variables considered for the Hohokam case, organization, demography, and agricultural intensification, are presented and then compared with one another.

Organization

How Chacoan society was organized continues to be a topic of considerable debate among Southwestern archaeologists. The traditional view derived from ethnographic analogy with historic Puebloan groups was that the Chacoans were egalitarian, with the occupants of town and village sites representing different moieties (Vivian 1990). While some continue to argue for egalitarianism (Vivian 1990), the prevailing view at present is that Chacoan society was hierarchically organized (Neitzel 1989a,b; Sebastian 1992). However, among proponents of this view there is considerable debate about the number of levels in the organizational hierarchy, the kind of control that this hierarchical structure exerted, and the areal extent of Chacoan society as opposed to Chacoan influence.

Chacoan mortuary and settlement pattern data indicate that, like the Hohokam, Chacoan society became increasingly complex through time (Table 14.3). Burials exhibit more status levels (Akins 1986) and sites comprise a more hierarchical system (Neitzel 1989a,b; Powers et al. 1983). Throughout the sequence, the physical marker of the Chacoan society was always the great house, a combination elite residence and ceremonial structure (Lekson 1984c, 1991). This combination of functions suggests that differences in sociopolitical power were being legitimized from the start.

Regardless of how one defines the extent of Chacoan society, rank-size data suggest that its organization changed through time. Whether one defines Chacoan society as encompassing all known great houses, only those great houses in the San Juan Basin, or only those great houses within the area defined by the maximum extent of roads radiating from Chaco Canyon, the organizational shifts indicated by rank-size graphs are the same. The data indicate that the organization of Chacoan society shifted from several independent entities, to a well integrated, unified system, and then to a primate system dominated by the Pueblo Bonito complex (Neitzel 1989a,b; cf. Schelberg 1984). In the final period, Chacoan society fragmented and was again characterized by a number of independent entities.

Demography

In some ways, the problem of demographic reconstruction may be a much more straightforward task for the Chacoan case than for the Hohokam. After all, most

Table 14.3. Organizational Trends at Different Spatial Scales for the Chacoan Case

Period Size	Burial Levels	Sites	Chaco Canyon	Region Levels	Region Rank
Early Pueblo 2	1	First small great houses	Three local systems	1–2	Convex
Late Pueblo 2	2?	More and larger great houses	Canyon unified under Pueblo Bonito	3	Linear
Early Pueblo 3	3	More and larger great houses	Canyon dominated by Pueblo Bonito complex	4	Concave
Late Pueblo 3	?	No new great houses	Pueblo Bonito complex and canyon abandoned	3	Convex

major Chacoan sites have published room counts and approximate ceramic dates, and many have tree-ring dates as well. In addition, considerable research has been conducted at prehistoric and historic Puebloan sites on converting room counts to population estimates.

However, these advantages are counterbalanced by the proposal that the primary function of Chacoan great houses was not residential (e.g., Judge 1989). It has been suggested that these structures served ceremonial/storage purposes and were occupied by relatively small numbers of individuals who supervised these tasks. Thus, according to this view, the procedure of converting room counts to population estimates, as has been done for other Puebloan sites, inflates, perhaps grossly, the number of occupants of Chacoan great houses.

Much more research is necessary to resolve the question of how many people lived at great houses. Here, to look at population trends at Pueblo Bonito and in the canyon, I rely on the traditional conversion procedure, recognizing that the resulting figures should be viewed as maximums since they may be inflated to some yet to be determined degree.

Demographic trends at the household level can be compared for the major Chacoan site, Pueblo Bonito. Here, the first households were the largest (Figure 14.9). In succeeding periods, household size declined and then increased again. During two of these intervals, there were larger rooms, which suggest the possibility of social differentiation among households.

For Pueblo Bonito as a whole, initial construction was followed by a 100 year lull (Figure 14.10a). Then, the site grew steadily to a peak population of 700 to 950 people before declining.

At a larger scale, Pueblo Bonito was part of a dispersed urban center, referred to here as the Pueblo Bonito complex, which consisted of a cluster of nine structures at the center of Chaco Canyon (Lekson 1984c; Neitzel 1989a,b). Although none of the complex's other structures ever attained the size of Pueblo Bonito, their growth trends were quite similar. Consequently, the growth of the Pueblo Bonito complex mirrors that of Pueblo Bonito alone. Its peak population was probably just under 2,000 people (Figure 14.10b).

Chacoan demographic trends can also be monitored at higher levels (Figure 14.11). At the locality level, Chaco

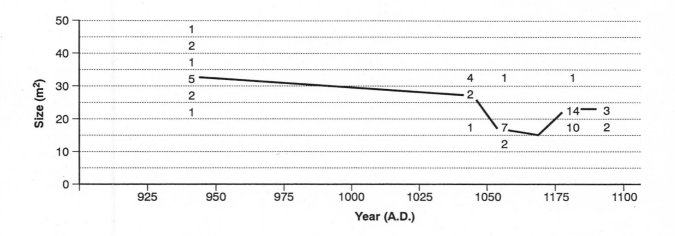

\# - indicates the number of ground floor habitation rooms in that 5-m² increment
— - indicates median number of ground floor habitation rooms in 5-m² increment

Figure 14.9.   Household population at Pueblo Bonito.

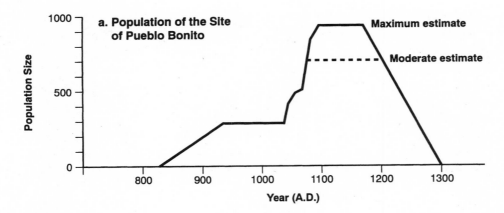

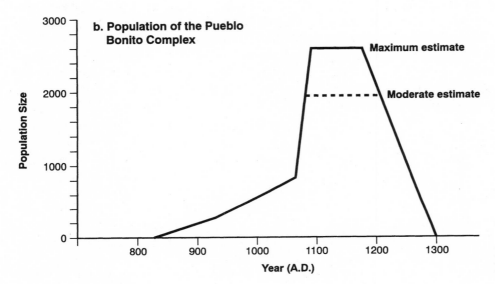

Figure 14.10. Pueblo Bonito population size.

Canyon's demographic trends mirror those of both Pueblo Bonito and the Pueblo Bonito complex (Figure 14.11a). A similar pattern of growth and decline also occurred at the regional level (Figure 14.11b). In comparing Chacoan demographic trends at different spatial scales, the most noticeable observation is the correspondence between the growth and subsequent decline of Pueblo Bonito, the Pueblo Bonito complex, Chaco Canyon, and the Chacoan region as a whole.

Intensification

Only rudimentary multiscalar comparisons can be carried out on the process of Chacoan agricultural intensification. At the site level, the only indication of change in Chacoan plant use comes from a single large canyon site,

Pueblo Alto (M. Toll 1984). Its latest occupation was marked by an increase in smaller sized corn and wild grasses and a decrease in squash, beans, and wild plant foods in general.

The best evidence for Chacoan intensification comes from elaborate water control systems constructed on the north side of Chaco Canyon (Vivian 1974). These systems consisted of diversion dams, ditches, and head gates, which directed water off the top of the canyon walls to a series of gridded gardens and collecting pools on the canyon floor. Because dating these features is extremely difficult, it is only possible at present to discern gross trends for the canyon as a whole. According to Vivian (1990), some rudimentary water control features may have been in operation between A.D. 920–1020. However,

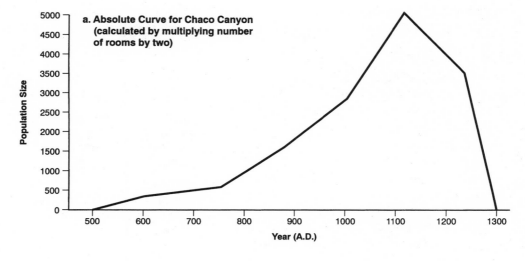

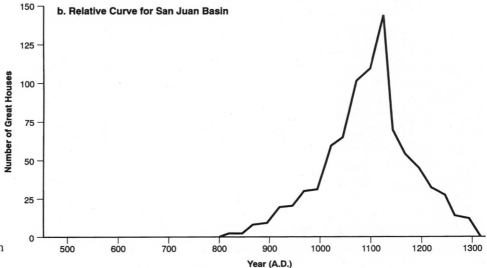

Figure 14.11.   Chacoan population curves.

Vivian believes that most of the agricultural features were built in the following century. After A.D. 1120, construction ceased but existing systems probably continued to be used.

Comparing Variables

The Chacoan case is like the Hohokam in that comparisons of the variables of organization, demography, and intensification can best be made at the largest spatial scales. As Chacoan society became increasingly complex, the populations of its core area and region grew. Within Chaco Canyon, the interval with the greatest complexity and population coincided with the time of the most agricultural intensification. Like the Hohokam case, what is missing from these comparisons is a sense of what was going on at smaller spatial scales.

This consideration of organizational, demographic, and subsistence change for the Chacoan case should illustrate how the multiscalar perspective offers the same advantages for Chacoan research as it did for the Hohokam. First, it structures analyses so that trends at different scales can be compared and their effects on one another considered. Secondly, it can highlight scales that are poorly documented and for which further data collection is necessary.

Comparing Hohokam and Chaco

Systematic comparisons among cases are necessary both for documenting the organizational diversity of prehistoric Southwestern societies and for explaining why these societies developed the way they did. Here, the organizational, demographic, and agricultural trends of the Hohokam and Chacoan cases are compared.

Organizational Trends

In comparing organizational trends, the most striking similarity of the Hohokam and Chacoan cases is that each exhibits a consistent trend toward increasing complexity at all documented scales and that this complexity is greatest in a centrally located area. The two cases also exhibit similar trends in archaeological interpretations about their organizations. For both, the longstanding view derived from ethnographic analogy was that they were egalitarian (e.g., Haury 1976; Vivian 1990). However, as more research has been done and as archaeologists have turned to other models besides the ethnographic present, the prevailing interpretation has shifted to the view that their organizations were nonegalitarian or hierarchical. Similarly, more research has produced a reconceptualization of what the terms Hohokam and Chacoan mean. In the past, they were seen as cultural designations. Today, archaeologists use them to refer to regional systems of interaction (e.g., Judge 1991; Wilcox 1979a).

These similarities are matched by differences. One is how long they lasted, almost a thousand years for the Hohokam and several hundred years for the Chacoan. Another difference is the characteristics of their core areas. For as long as Chaco Canyon was the Chacoan system's geographic and cultural center, Pueblo Bonito was the canyon's preeminent site. In contrast, despite proposals concerning the importance of several sites (e.g., Snaketown in the Preclassic period; Los Muertos and Pueblo Grande in the Classic period), no single settlement obviously dominated the Hohokam core area during any one period, let alone the entire duration of the Hohokam regional system. These differences in their respective core areas in turn affected the overall unity of Hohokam and Chacoan society. While the Hohokam were always a collection of independent polities, Chacoan populations may have been unified by a single sociopolitical organization.

The role of ceremonialism also differs. Throughout the Chacoan sequence, elites and ceremonialism were visibly joined in the specialized architectural feature of the great house. This association does not occur among the Hohokam until the construction of platform mounds during the Classic period. While elites may have been present during earlier periods, their special status was manifested in ways other than being publicly associated with ceremonial architecture (Neitzel 1991).

Demographic Trends

In comparing Hohokam and Chacoan demographic trends, there are several similarities and one major difference. In both, the largest documented households were the earliest and there is suggestive evidence for social differentiation among households. In both, the maximum populations of the largest sites were approximately 2,000 people. In both, the populations of their core areas increased steadily, declined at a faster pace, and were finally abandoned. At the regional level, the demographic trends for both systems mirror those of their core areas. One major difference between the two areas is the peak population of their core areas, which may have been as much as 20 times larger for the Phoenix Basin (approximately 100,000) than for Chaco Canyon (approximately 5,000).

Agricultural Trends

The Hohokam and Chacoans were both intensive agriculturalists, and their greatest intensification occurred in their respective core areas. However, while both core areas offered considerable agricultural potential, this potential was much greater for the Phoenix Basin than Chaco Canyon. In addition, the Phoenix Basin was clearly the area with the greatest agricultural potential in all of its surrounding region. In contrast, while Chaco Canyon did have greater potential for agricultural intensification than the immediate surrounding area, this potential was less than the San Juan River Valley to the north. So other factors besides agricultural potential alone probably contributed to sociopolitical development in Chaco Canyon.

Only rudimentary comparisons of Hohokam and Chacoan subsistence intensification can be made due to the absence of diachronic and multiscalar data for the Chacoan case. At present, the most that can be said is that there is evidence of substantial intensification in both, with the overall trend being an increase through time followed by a decline.

Comparing Variables

Comparing the processes of change in the Hohokam and Chacoan cases reveals both similarities and differences. There are two similarities, neither of which is insignificant. The first is classificatory. On a scale of cultural evolutionary development, both cases could reasonably be labeled as middle-range or intermediate level. Their organizations were more complex or hierarchical than egalitarian tribes but less complex or hierarchical than states. Typologically, this "in-betweenness" suggests that both the Hohokam and Chacoan cases should be classified as chiefdoms. However, this is a designation that, for a variety of reasons, is problematical for many Southwestern archaeologists and thus is not widely used for either case (see Fish, Chapter 4; Cordell, Chapter 7).

The second similarity between the Hohokam and Chacoan cases is processual. For those scales and variables for which comparisons can be made, the two cases are characterized by similar increases in organizational complexity, population growth, and agricultural intensification. For both cases, the three variables considered here were positively correlated, with greater complexity being associated with higher populations and more intensification.

Counterbalancing these very general classificatory and processual similarities of the Hohokam and Chacoan cases are some truly significant differences. That these two cases differ should not be surprising given the tremendous variation that has been found to characterize middle-range societies cross-culturally (Feinman and Neitzel 1984). However, as Southwestern archaeologists have focused their debates about prehistoric organization on the issue of complexity, the Hohokam and Chacoan cases have tended to be lumped together as examples of so-called "complex societies." It has only been recently that the differences between them have begun to be systematically considered (Crown and Judge 1991).

The differences are numerous. They include duration, the populations of their core areas, the numbers of major settlements, their means of agricultural intensification, changes in their regional organization, and the linkage between elites and ceremonialism. These differences underscore a major question for future studies of prehistoric Southwestern social organization: Why did these differences exist? Do they represent adaptations to different environmental conditions? Are they products of unique historical trajectories? Or, are they the result of some combination of factors? Explaining the variation that characterized two of the prehistoric Southwest's most complex societies is an important first step in explaining the organizational diversity that characterized late prehistoric Southwestern societies in general.

The consideration of these two cases should have demonstrated the value of employing a multiscalar perspective to explain organizational diversity in prehistoric societies. The Chacoan case revealed how changes at different levels can sometimes mirror one another. The Hohokam case illustrated how this is not always so. Instead, diachronic trends at higher levels can mask variation in trends at lower levels. The diversity of the lower level changes in Hohokam demography and intensification suggests that the interrelationships among variables may be more complex than we might assume based on higher level comparisons alone. Employing a multiscalar perspective forces us to compare trends at different scales and to consider their effects on one another.

The conclusion that can be drawn from comparing the Hohokam and Chacoan cases within a multiscalar format is that the two of the prehistoric Southwest's best documented cases are characterized by critical gaps in their data bases. The absence of information on how key variables changed at multiple scales has three consequences. First, it precludes a full understanding of how either Hohokam or Chacoan society was organized through time. Second, it limits the comparisons that can be made between the two cases, causing any generalizations about organizational diversity and change to be tentative. Finally, the data gaps highlight where more research needs to be done.

OVERVIEW OF TRENDS

If the picture gained from comparing the variables of organization, demography, and agricultural intensification in the Hohokam and Chacoan cases is one of variation in societies with an intermediate level of complexity, the degree of variation is multiplied when the picture is broadened to include comparisons of more variables and more cases. In this section, I attempt to present this broader picture with the aid of a series of tables. The cases considered here were included because they met several criteria: they contain some of the Southwest's biggest sites and thus are the most likely candidates for organizational complexity; they have been the subject of relatively intensive investigations; and archaeologists working with them were gracious enough to share their expert knowledge with me.

The variables considered are those that have been emphasized in discussions about how prehistoric Southwestern societies were organized. They include not only the variables of sociopolitical organization, population, and agricultural intensification, but also those of craft specialization, prestige goods exchange, and warfare. In the discussion that follows, these variables are first considered individually and are then compared with one another.

Sociopolitical Organization

Recent debates about the complexity of societies in the late prehistoric Southwest have generally focused on the question of whether or not the sociopolitical systems of these societies were egalitarian or hierarchical. In other words, were they complex or not (see McGuire and Saitta 1996; Nelson et al. 1994)? As was done previously for the Hohokam and Chacoan cases, the number of hierarchical levels (or the absence of them) can be monitored using both settlement pattern and mortuary data (see Peebles and Kus 1977). These two measures are usually positively correlated. However, they do not always indicate the same number of levels.

For the cases in Tables 14.3 and 4.4, the number of levels in the organizational hierarchy ranges from a low of one, suggesting an egalitarian society (or no hierarchy at all), to a high of four, indicating the presence of what in typological terms could be considered a complex chiefdom (Steponaitis 1983). Thus, in terms of their sociopolitical organizations, late prehistoric societies containing some of the Southwest's largest sites were quite diverse, exhibiting a much greater variety than was seen in the previous consideration of just the Hohokam and Chacoan cases.

Two other observations, one chronological and the other geographic, can be made of the data presented in Table 14.4. First, not all of the listed cases were contemporaneous. Instead, at different points in time, societies emerged, developed to varying degrees of sociopolitical complexity, and then disappeared. At any one time, a subset of cases representing all stages of this evolutionary process were present. For the most complex cases, probably no more than 2 to 3 were ever contemporaneous. Through time, there was no overall pattern of increasing complexity. In fact, two of the most hierarchical societies in the table, the Phoenix Basin Hohokam and the Chacoan, were among the earliest. Some of those apparently lacking a hierarchy, such as the Rio Grande pueblos, were the latest.

The second observation to be drawn from Table 14.4 is that no clear geographic trends can be seen in where the cases were located. Throughout the Late Prehistoric period, societies with varying degrees of complexity developed in different parts of the Southwest where agricultural intensification was possible. However, while there is no obvious temporal pattern in where these societies were founded, there may have been a pattern in their collapse. For the northern Southwest, Upham (1982) has argued that the polities in existence immediately before contact collapsed from the geographic center outward. Thus, only the most peripheral polities (and apparently among the least complex), such as Zuni and the northern Rio Grande pueblos, were the ones that survived into the protohistoric period.

Demography

Table 14.5 presents the population/demographic data for the cases considered here. Available household estimates are fairly consistent. However, considerable variation can be seen in the sizes of large sites and their associated polities. The largest sites have maximum population estimates of approximately 2,000 people. Polity population estimates are more problematical due to the difficulty in defining polity boundaries. The highest numbers come from the Phoenix Basin where more than 100,000 people may have lived in its northern half, the Lower Salt River Valley. However, Hohokam archaeologists disagree about how many polities are represented by these numbers.

Table 14.5 reveals no overall demographic trends through time. Some of the largest sites and polities and the densest populations occurred early. Also, there appears to be no consistent relationship between maximum site size and polity size. During the protohistoric period in the Upper Rio Grande River Valley, there were some extremely large sites, but their associated polities may not have been that much bigger. In other words, population was extremely aggregated with site size approximating polity size.

Subsistence

Table 14.6 documents how all of the cases considered here depended on intensive agriculture for the bulk of their subsistence. Throughout the Southwest, the major plant food was corn with beans and squash being of secondary importance. Among the Hohokam, agave and cotton were also important crops. In all cases, agriculture was supplemented to varying degrees by wild plant gathering and hunting.

All of the cases intensified their practice of agriculture with the aid of various constructions. These facilities included canals, rock piles, terraces, check dams, and gridded gardens. The type of feature emphasized in an area varied depending on local topographic and hydrologic conditions (Fish and Fish 1984; Plog and Garrett 1972).

For specific cases, intensification of agriculture can be seen through time, and for the Southwest as a whole from the Archaic through the Late Prehistoric period, the overall trend is one of increasing reliance on agriculture. However, within the Late Prehistoric period itself, no trend of increasing intensification can be discerned. The most compelling argument against such a trend is that the two cases with the greatest intensification, the Phoenix Basin Hohokam and the Chacoan, were also among the earliest.

Craft Specialization

Craft specialization does not seem to have been widespread in the late prehistoric Southwest (Table 14.7). Where specialists have been documented, they are usually associated with the production of prestige goods at large sites. With the possible exception of Paquimé (cf. Minnis 1989), these crafts people worked part time at their crafts. No clear temporal trends exist, with part-time craft specialists being documented for two of the earliest cases, the Phoenix Basin Hohokam and Chacoan.

Prestige Goods Exchange

By moving status markers throughout the Southwest, prestige goods exchange linked the residents of big sites, or at least some subset of their residents (e.g., elites) to one another both directly and indirectly (Table 14.8). While this exchange was important throughout the Late Prehistoric period, its structure shifted as different sites controlling different goods emerged as dominant players and then declined in importance (Neitzel 1989a,b). For example, turquoise was always a valued trade good, but the quantities traded were greatest when Chaco was at its peak. Similarly, the organization of the shell trade shifted as the major centers for this material shifted from the Phoenix Basin Hohokam to Paquimé.

Warfare

Recent efforts to synthesize the evidence for conflict have revealed variation in time and space (Table 14.9). Temporal variation has been documented previously by Wilcox and Haas (1994a,b). For example, in the La Plata/Animas area of the northern San Juan Basin, burned sites are widespread in the Basketmaker 3 to Pueblo 1 periods, absent in the Pueblo 2 to early Pueblo 3 periods, and recur in the late Pueblo 3 period. At a broader scale, Wilcox and Haas (1994a,b) have shown how the evidence for increased conflict during the late Pueblo 3 period occurs throughout the Anasazi area and correlates with population aggregation.

The evidence of conflict also varies spatially in amount and kind (Table 14.9). For example, in comparing the Chaco and Hohokam cases, Chacoan society has skeletal and architectural evidence (e.g., signal towers), while Hohokam society has architectural evidence (hillside retreats) and no man's lands but little skeletal evidence.

Several conclusions can be drawn about conflict in the late prehistoric Southwest (Table 14.9; see Wilcox and Haas 1994a,b). First, warfare was not an endemic part of late prehistoric Southwestern societies. It occurred in some times and some places, but not everywhere all of the time. Second, the reasons for the conflict that did occur and the forms this conflict took probably varied. In addition, conflict probably also varied in its duration, intensity, and its participants (e.g., internecine vs. intertribal). Finally, as noted by Wilcox and Haas (1994a,b), even low level conflict could have had significant effects on peoples' behavior as they sought to minimize its negative effects.

A question for future research is what kinds of models are most appropriate for interpreting the evidence for conflict in various late prehistoric Southwestern societies. Wilcox and Haas (1994a,b) derive their interpretations primarily from ethnographic descriptions of tribal warfare. This use of ethnographic analogy not only seems logically justified for the prehistoric Southwest's tribal-level societies, but it also seems to fit well the archaeological evidence cited by Wilcox and Haas. However, the applicability of ethnographically derived models of tribal warfare to the prehistoric Southwest's most complex societies, societies that were clearly not tribal (e.g., Chaco, Hohokam, Paquimé), requires closer consideration. If future comparisons reveal no significant differences in the incidence of conflict within and among prehistoric Southwestern societies with varying degrees of complexity, then the tribal model may apply to all. However, if there are differences, then other models, such as ones derived from ethnographic descriptions of chiefdoms, may be more appropriate for the Southwest's most complex cases.

General Comparisons

Comparisons of the variables in Tables 14.4–14.9 reveal some positive correlations. The cases with the greatest complexity, as measured by the number of hierarchical levels, are the ones with the highest populations and greatest subsistence intensification. They are also the ones with the most clear-cut evidence of part-time craft specialization and the greatest participation in prestige goods exchange. However, the interrelationships among variables are not as straightforward for the less complex cases. Some have very large sites and substantial intensification but relatively small polities, no specialization, and limited participation in prestige goods exchange. One other observation to be drawn from comparing Tables 14.1–14.9 is that positive correlations among variables exist for individual cases and is not an overall trend for the late prehistoric Southwest as a whole.

Organizing Tables 14.4–14.9 within a multiscalar format is a useful exercise in several ways. First, for myself and those who shared their data with me, it forced us to grapple with the difficulties of defining meaningful scales (e.g., household, site, polity, interpolity region) and of synthesizing the data relevant to those scales. Second, the numerous empty cells in the resulting tables highlighted how even the best documented of the Southwestern areas containing big sites are characterized by critical gaps in their data bases. Clearly, more data are needed. How the multiscalar perspective can aid in this process of data collection is to focus attention on those variables and scales for which the gaps are most glaring. Finally, the multiscalar perspective provides the opportunity for examining how developments at different scales affected one another. As more data are collected and the gaps in Tables 14.4–14.9 are filled in, multiscalar comparisons similar to those done previously for the Hohokam and Chacoan cases can be performed on a greater range of cases. Such comparisons will provide a more comprehensive picture of the variation that characterized Southwestern societies during the Late Prehistoric period.

DEVELOPING EXPLANATORY MODELS

The concept of complexity has dominated most efforts to characterize how late prehistoric Southwestern societies were organized. This concept has proven to be useful in some ways and limiting in others. Its utility stems from its being somewhat ill-defined, vague, and elastic in meaning. Its limitation lies in the fact that, until recently, its usage has been basically typological.

Why are Southwestern archaeologists more comfortable talking about complexity than tribes and chiefdoms, the traditional typological labels which are most commonly applied to societies, such as those in the Southwest, which are organizationally intermediate between egalitarian bands and bureaucratic states? Many South-

western archaeologists do apply the tribal designation to egalitarian-looking societies with big sites, but the chiefdom label is rarely applied to societies that appear to be nonegalitarian. Instead, such societies are usually described as complex.

There are several major reasons why Southwestern archaeologists discuss complexity rather than chiefdoms. Some are historical. First, the earliest and strongest proponents of the view that some late prehistoric Southwestern societies were nonegalitarian were processualists (e.g., Cordell and Plog 1979), whose criticisms of culture historical approaches could apply equally well to traditional cultural evolutionary typologies. In addition, these early discussions about nonegalitarian sociopolitical organizations occurred at a time when the chiefdom concept itself was being reevaluated in the anthropological literature (see Feinman and Neitzel 1984). One advantage of describing nonegalitarian societies in the late prehistoric Southwest as complex was that it avoided all of the controversies associated with defining what a chiefdom is.

Another reason nonegalitarian societies in the late prehistoric Southwest have generally been described as complex rather than as chiefdoms lies in the characteristics of the societies themselves. While cases such as the Phoenix Basin Hohokam, Chaco, and Paquimé are clearly not tribes, they do not neatly fit either the traditional chiefdom definition or its subsequent modifications and subdivisions. If they are neither tribes nor chiefdoms, then what are they?

The complexity concept offers a partial escape from this classificatory conundrum. When Southwestern archaeologists say that a particular prehistoric society was complex, they usually mean that it was not egalitarian, but in what way is (perhaps purposely) not clear. Possible synonyms include nonegalitarian, hierarchical, or even complicated, which do not necessarily mean the same thing. By being ambiguous, the complexity concept glosses these definitional problems. In doing so, it offers archaeologists a means for dealing with the fact prehistoric Southwestern societies are often difficult to classify.

Despite its vagueness, the complexity concept has not eliminated classificatory difficulties from discussions about how prehistoric Southwestern societies were organized. In fact, the use of the complexity concept has become in many ways typological. In traditional cultural evolutionary thinking, key questions might be: Is this case a tribe? Or, is it a chiefdom? If it is a chiefdom, is it a simple or complex chiefdom? With their reliance on the complexity concept, Southwestern archaeologists have replaced these classificatory questions with another: Is this case complex or not?

There are three major problems with this question. One is that it implies a yes or no answer, which virtually guarantees that any disagreements will be polarized as they have often been (see McGuire and Saitta 1996; Upham et al. 1989). Another is that even if a consensus could be reached about whether the answer is yes or no, that would not really add much to our understanding of the case under consideration. Finally, by lumping all cases into just two categories, the yes/no complexity question obscures variation to an even greater degree than the three part division of tribes, simple chiefdoms, and complex chiefdoms.

Although the complexity concept shares problems inherent in any typology, several recent publications have identified ways in which the concept may still have value for Southwestern archaeologists. The most promising research direction lies not so much in defining more precisely what the term means (e.g., Gumerman and Gell-Mann 1993). Rather, it involves disentangling, monitoring, and then comparing the different dimensions of complexity. With this approach, the typological question of whether or not a specific prehistoric society was complex is replaced by a more multifaceted question: In what ways was this society complex (Nelson et al. 1994)? Implicit in this latter question is the recognition that individual societies may be complex (or nonegalitarian or hierarchical) in some ways but not others (McGuire and Saitta 1996; Plog and Solomento 1995) and thus that different societies may be complex in different ways.

This more nuanced conceptualization of complexity should enable archaeologists to do the kinds of intra- and intersocietal comparisons necessary for documenting and explaining the organizational diversity that characterized the Late Prehistoric Southwest. Three major issues should be the focus of attention. They are: 1) how and why did nonegalitarian societies appear in the Southwest in the first place; 2) why did some of these societies continue to develop into more complex forms; and 3) why did virtually all of these societies ultimately collapse? Some general observations related to each of these issues are briefly presented below.

The Emergence of Complexity

The question of the initial emergence of complexity in the Late Prehistoric Southwest requires a contrast be-

tween those areas where some degree of social differentiation did appear and those areas whose populations remained egalitarian. The differences between these two sets of areas are still poorly understood. Factors that may have contributed to the two alternative trajectories of change include population dynamics, agricultural potential, proximity to trade networks, conflict, as well as the abilities of individual leaders (see Lightfoot and Feinman 1982; Plog and Solomento 1995; Upham 1990).

Comparisons of the Hohokam and Chacoan cases quickly make it obvious that the task of explaining why complex societies developed in the prehistoric Southwest will not be easy. These cases do exhibit some similarities in their beginnings. Both emerged from an earlier cultural base of simple, agricultural villages. Both were located in environments where the intensification of agriculture was possible. What makes the task of explanation difficult is not only are these similarities few, but they are also shared by many Southwestern societies that never developed the degree of complexity seen in the Chacoan and Hohokam cases. Other factors, such as access to valuable trade goods, may explain why complexity evolved in the Hohokam and Chacoan cases and not elsewhere. However, while both were major players in long-distance exchange networks, whether this was a cause or a consequence of increasing complexity, or both, is not clear at present.

INCREASING COMPLEXITY

Once social differentiation began to emerge in various parts of the Southwest, another question to be answered is why did some societies continue to develop, becoming increasingly complex through time, while others did not. Was it that the conditions and processes of change leading to the initial emergence of social differentiation continued to operate or occurred to a greater degree in some areas than others? Or, were other factors, such as ameliorating climatic conditions (Gumerman 1988; Jorde 1977; Slatter 1979) or conflict (Wilcox and Haas 1994a,b), also important?

Further complicating efforts to understand why some societies became increasingly complex through time is the diversity of the Southwest's most complex societies. Thus, even if similar variables are found to have been responsible for the evolution of these societies, the result was not always the same. The differences were not just ones of greater or lesser complexity. There were also differences in form. Thus, for example, there were structural differences in the organizations of Hohokam and Chacoan societies and probably between them and Paquimé as well. The reasons for this diversity is another problem requiring explanation if we are to understand why prehistoric Southwestern societies were organized the way they were.

The Decline of Complexity

With several notable exceptions, one characteristic shared by all Southwestern areas that had big sites and thus for which the question of complexity can be raised is that these big sites were ultimately abandoned. The exceptions to this pattern were the Rio Grande pueblos, Hopi, Acoma, and Zuni; and a variety of answers have been proposed to the question of why their major settlements continued to be inhabited through the Historic period (e.g., Upham 1984). However, for most Southwestern societies with big sites, whatever their degree of sociopolitical complexity, this complexity could not be sustained. At some point for each case, the big sites were abandoned and their associated polities disintegrated. This process is what Southwestern archaeologists have traditionally referred to as abandonment.

Studies of abandonment have a long history in Southwestern archaeology (see Cordell 1984). Initially, researchers saw abandonment as occurring throughout the Southwest in the thirteenth century. Most explanations sought to identify a single cause, such as drought, disease, factionalism, or warfare, for what was presumed to be a single event (e.g., Colton 1960; Davis 1965; Schoenwetter and Dittert 1968). When tested, each of these prime mover explanations is inadequate.

With more research, Southwestern archaeologists have recognized that abandonment was a complicated process (Cordell 1984; Lekson and Cameron 1993). It was marked by variation in timing and location and occurred at multiple spatial scales. This variation strongly suggests that no one factor can account for why all sites, localities, and regions in the late prehistoric Southwest were abandoned. Different combinations of factors were probably operating at different scales and at different places and times.

One potentially important variable that has not received much attention by Southwestern archaeologists is chiefly cycling (see Drennan 1991; Earle 1987a,b; Goldman 1970; Sahlins 1963; Wright 1984, 1986). Cross-cultural research on chiefdoms has revealed how such societies are characterized by a structural limit on how large and stratified they can become without undergoing a major reorganization. As a result of this limit, chiefdoms often follow a historical trajectory of emergence, further development, and then collapse. This cycling process seems to be most obvious among complex chiefdoms that develop within a regional landscape of simple chiefdoms (Anderson 1994). While the chiefdom concept is problematical for many Southwestern archaeologists, the idea that there may be structural reasons for why societies collapse may be relevant to explaining the abandonment of the prehistoric Southwest's largest sites and most complex polities.

CONCLUSION

An underlying theme of this paper has been that Southwestern archaeologists need to shift their conceptual focus in their studies of prehistoric organization. Instead of trying to determine whether particular cases were complex, researchers need to document and explain organizational diversity.

Traditional typological distinctions, such as tribes *vs.* chiefdoms, simple chiefdoms *vs.* complex chiefdoms, or egalitarian societies *vs.* complex societies, are not that useful, and may in fact be counterproductive, for documenting and explaining this organizational diversity. The value of the labels is that they provide a convenient shorthand for saying that some prehistoric Southwestern societies were organizationally intermediate between egalitarian bands and bureaucratic states. The problem with the labels is that they obscure the tremendous variation that characterized these intermediate level societies. Yet it is this variation that we seek to understand.

A more useful research strategy is to monitor and compare different societal characteristics through time. For individual cases, such comparisons can produce an understanding of how they were organized at any one point in time and how they got to be that way. Then, by comparing the insights gained from individual cases to one another, investigators can begin to address questions central to explaining the organizational diversity that characterized the Late Prehistoric Southwest.

There are a series of questions that should be addressed. For example, do prehistoric Southwestern societies exhibit continuous or qualitative differences in their organizations? If the variation is continuous, does it occur along one or several lines? In the latter case, the resulting societies might be roughly equal in overall complexity but different in form. If the variation is qualitative, can groups of cases be ranked in any way using single or multiple criteria? If multiple criteria are used, do the rankings obtained from different measures coincide? Finally, how do the processes of change characterizing different societies compare? Did the various Southwestern cases experience similar or different processes? And did these similar or different processes result in similar or different organizational forms? It is by focusing on questions such as these that we can begin to explain the organizational diversity of prehistoric Southwestern societies.

This paper has also emphasized the importance of considering scale. Scale is critical to studies of prehistoric organization, because social life exists at many levels, which mutually affect one another. While it is usually beyond the ability of archaeology to examine the lowest unit of analysis, the individual (cf. Hill and Gunn 1977), that person's decisions affect activities at the successively larger scales of the household, household group, site, locality, region, and macroregion. The aggregate behavior exhibited at one scale produces the pattern observed at the next. From the opposite perspective, the patterns at higher scales may affect behaviors and decisions at lower scales.

In some sense, reconstructing how prehistoric societies were organized is a three-dimensional jigsaw puzzle. We must fit together the pieces at different scales and then see how these different scales interrelate to one another. Adding the dimension of time makes the puzzle even more complicated. Nevertheless, that may be what we need to appreciate if we are to move closer to our goal of explaining how societies were organized and how they came to be that way. Societal change is complicated and multiscalar models provide the tool for making the complicated manageable and ultimately understandable.

In the Southwest, the value of multiscalar analyses for studying organizational diversity and change is just beginning to be explored. Our understanding of causal relations among variables is inadequate, and the gaps in the available data for many areas are numerous. However, a multiscalar perspective not only serves to highlight where data collection and analyses need to be done, but also forces us to do the kinds of diachronic comparisons among variables, scales, and cases that are necessary for accomplishing our goal of explanation.

ACKNOWLEDGMENTS

Many individuals helped me at various stages in writing this paper. Mike Adler, Bruce Anderson, Winifred Creamer, Suzy Fish, Steve Lekson, Jeff Reid, and Glen Rice generously shared their time and expertise in preparing Tables 14.4–14.9. Discussions with David Anderson helped me focus and structure my discussion. Various drafts of the paper were read by Gary Feinman, Randy McGuire, Steve Plog, Willett Kempton, and Anne Woosley. Their comments have vastly improved its content and presentation.

See following pages for Tables 14.4–14.9.

Table 14.4. Evidence for Organizational Change at Different Spatial Scales in the Late Prehistoric Southwest

	Household	Community	Polity	Interpolity Region
Mimbres[1]	Shift from pithouse to stone masonry ca. A.D. 1000 to adobe pueblos ca. A.D. 1150.	Settlement pattern always nucleated, public structures include great kivas and plaza; formal layout of north and south roomblocks separated by a plaza.	No site hierarchy.	Influenced by both Hohokam and Chaco.
Chaco[2]	At Pueblo Bonito, some extra large, possibly residential rooms; at end of Chacoan sequence, some great house rooms subdivided into residences.	Public architecture includes great houses and great kivas; ceremonial vs. storage vs. residential functions of great houses debated; also mounds, berms, roads.	3 tier hierarchy defined for limited mortuary data from canyon; 4 tier settlement hierarchy in San Juan Basin; some roads connect outlying great houses to canyon; other roads are great house entryways.	Number of polities occupying San Juan Basin at Chaco's peak under debate with estimates ranging from one to many.
Wupatki[3]			No site hierarchy; rather a number of focal sites of which Wupatki is the largest.	
Hohokam-Phoenix Basin[4]	Shift from Preclassic period pithouses to Classic period above ground rooms in compounds.	Preclassic primary public architecture of ballcourts; also some mounds; Snaketown has formal layout; limited evidence for mortuary differentiation; Classic period primary public architecture of platform mounds; formal layout of mounds at multi-mound sites; evidence for mortuary differentiation more pronounced and prevalent.	At least 3 tier site hierarchy can be defined for Classic period based on site size and public architecture.	Number of polities in Phoenix Basin during Classic period under debate; estimates range from several to many; never unified into a single polity.
Hohokam-Tucson Basin[5]	Mound houses similar to residential ones; mound house walls more massive.	Classic period public structure of platform mounds; no mortuary data from Marana; Marana is only site in its community with platform mound.	3 tier habitation site size hierarchy; 100,000 m² pithouse architecture 78%, 100,000–400,000 m² adobe and dry laid masonry compounds 15%, >500,000 m² compounds 7%; site of Marana with only platform mound in its community is in the largest category.	Marana polity is one of many; mound centered compounds continuously distributed from Tucson Basin into Papagueria and Phoenix Basin.
Salado-Tonto Basin[6]		Classic period public structure of platform mounds; in early Classic (A.D. 1150–1320), burial hierarchy; at Schoolhouse mound, important individuals are both male and female; distinguished by high number and special grave goods; also family burial plots and ranked crypts.	Hierarchy of platform mound sites.	Tonto Basin contained a number of polities, each centered around a platform mound site; after A.D. 1320, reduction in number of mounds, but those remaining grew larger.
Paquimé[7]		Paquimé exhibits greatest diversity of public structures of any site in Southwest; 18 mounds of diverse shapes, 3 ballcourts, massive multistory roomblocks, water distribution system; burial differentiation suggests ranked society with ascribed status.	Site of Paquimé was center of one of most highly centralized Southwestern polities; 3 tier site size hierarchy; sites linked by fire communication system.	

Table 14.4.   *(continued)*

	Household	Community	Polity	Interpolity Region
Grasshopper[8]		Enclosed plazas found at most sites with 30+ rooms; great kiva at Grasshopper is only one in region; status differentiation in mortuary remains based on age, gender, kinship, sodality membership, and ethnic affiliation.	4 tier site size hierarchy; 30–35, 60–70, 120–140, 500 rooms with size being a function of length of occupation prior to abandonment; Grasshopper is only site in largest size category and only one with great kiva.	Pan-Pueblo ceremonialism evident in small kivas, great kivas, and plazas; also pan-Puebloan ceramic similarities; external influences primarily due to movement of people.
Arroyo Hondo[9]	Shift from masonry to puddled adobe construction associated with depletion of local andesite slabs for masonry.	Pre-A.D. 1350 public architecture includes 4 kivas and 1 great kiva; post-A.D. 1350 public architecture includes 1 kiva; roomblocks arranged around plazas; some evidence for age/status grading in mortuary data.	Pre-A.D. 1350, Arroyo Hondo with 750 ground floor rooms was largest and the 1 major center in region; site hierarchy can be defined based on size and great kivas; post-A.D. 1350, Arroyo Hondo with 200 ground floor rooms was large but not unusually so as multiple centers grew with increasing aggregation.	Throughout sequence Santa Fe area probably contained multiple polities.
Galisteo Basin[10]		Public structures of kivas; also shrines within roomblocks and separated from rest of site; most roomblocks orientated along compass points; no mortuary data.	No apparent site hierarchy based on site size or public architecture.	Pre-A.D. 1680, Basin contained either 1 or 8 polities; unified into single polity A.D. 1680–1692.
Taos[11]	Sedentary pithouse settlements appear A.D. 1000–1075; shift to small unit pueblo surface rooms in A.D. 1100s.	Dispersed community structure present from A.D. 1000s on; small kivas present by A.D. 1150; large aggregated communities (50+ rooms) are post A.D. 1250; post-A.D. 1250 public structures of kivas and great kivas; formal layout of multiple roomblocks each with small plaza and kiva and all arranged around large open plaza with great kiva; no mortuary differentiation.	2 tier site hierarchy can be defined based on presence of small vs. large kivas; but no other evidence of sociopolitical complexity; most people lived at 3 large sites of Pot Creek, Taos, and Picuris; may have also been some small sites occupied in intervening areas.	Area contained multiple communities but not multi-community polities; share pan-Anasazi ceremonialism.

Notes for Tables 14.4–14.9

[1]Anyon and LeBlanc 1984; Blake et al. 1986; Bradfield 1931; Cosgrove and Cosgrove 1932; Findlow and DeAtley 1978; Herrington 1982; LeBlanc 1983; Lekson 1984c, 1986b, 1990c; Minnis 1985; Nelson and LeBlanc 1986; B. K. Nelson 1977; M. Nelson 1993; Woosley and McIntyre 1996

[2]Lekson, Chapter 1; Fish, Chapter 4; Wilcox, Chapter 10; Neitzel, Chapter 14; Akins 1986; Crown and Judge 1991; Doyel 1992; Irwin-Williams and Shelley 1980; Judge and Schelberg 1984; Judge et al. 1981; Kantner n.d.; Lekson 1986c; Marshall et al. 1979; Neitzel 1989a, 1989b, 1994; Neitzel and Bishop 1990; Powers et al. 1983; Sebastian 1992; Toll 1985; Vivian 1990; Wilcox and Haas 1994a; Windes 1993

[3]K. Anderson 1980; Colton 1946; King 1949; W. Smith 1952

[4]Lekson, Chapter 1; Fish, Chapter 4; Wilcox, Chapter 10; Neitzel, Chapter 14; Crown 1990a; Crown and Judge 1991; Doyel 1979, 1987; Doyel and Plog 1980; Fish 1989; Fish and Fish 1989; Gumerman 1991; Haury 1976; Henderson 1986; McGuire and Howard 1987; Nicholas and Feinman 1989; Wilcox and Haas 1994a; Wilcox et al. 1981; Wilcox and Sternberg 1983

[5]Bayman 1993, 1994; Downum et al. 1994; Fish and Fish 1989; P. Fish et al. 1992a; P. Fish et al. 1992b; S. Fish and Donaldson 1991; S. Fish and P. Fish 1990; S. Fish et al. 1989, 1990, 1992; S. Fish et al. 1984

[6]Jacobs 1994, n.d.; Lindauer 1995, n.d. a, n.d. b; Oliver, n.d.; Oliver and Jacobs, n.d.

[7]Lekson, Chapter 1; Fish, Chapter 4, Di Peso 1974; Di Peso et al. 1974; Minnis 1989; Reyman 1995; Ravesloot 1988; Whalen and Minnis 1996a, 1996b; Woosley and Ravesloot 1993

[8]Clark 1967; Crown 1981; Graves 1987; Graves et al. 1982; Griffin 1967; Longacre et al. 1982; McGuire and Saitta 1996; Plog 1985; Reid 1973, 1978, 1984, 1985, 1989; Reid and Whittlesey 1982, 1990; Sullivan 1980; Triadan 1994; Tuggle 1970; Tuggle et al. 1984; Upham and Plog 1986; Whittlesey 1978, 1984; Zedeno 1991

[9]Creamer and Habicht-Mauche 1989, 1993b; Dickson 1980; Habicht-Mauche, 1993, n.d.; Kelley 1979; Palkovich 1980; Rose et al. 1981; Wetterstrom 1986

[10]Creamer 1990, 1991, 1992a, 1992b, 1993a, 1994; Creamer and Renken 1994; Creamer et al. 1992; Hamlen 1993; Lang 1988; Nelson 1914; L. Reed 1990; P. Reed 1990

[11]Crown 1990b, 1991b; Crown and Kohler 1994; Dick 1965, 1980; Green 1976; Jeancon 1929; Loose 1974; Ottaway 1975; Wendorf and Reed 1955; Wetherington 1968; Woosley 1980, 1986

Table 14.5.   Evidence for Population Trends at Different Spatial Scales in the Late Prehistoric Southwest

	Household	Community	Polity	Interpolity Region
Mimbres[1]		Maximum site size of 100–150 aggregated rooms with estimated population of 300 people.	Estimated peak population of 4,000 people in Mimbres Valley (A.D. 1000–1150).	
Chaco[2]	At Pueblo Bonito, first households are largest; habitations at some outlying communities have larger rooms.	Much debate about population of Pueblo Bonito; maximum estimate of 950 people but probably much less; maximum estimate for Pueblo Bonito complex 2,000 people but probably much less; other great houses and their associated communities vary greatly in size.	Estimates for peak population of Chaco Canyon range from 2,500–5,000 people.	About A.D. 1075, there may have been as many as 40,000 people in San Juan Basin.
Wupatki[3]		Wupatki has approximately 100 rooms.		
Hohokam-Phoenix Basin[4]	At Preclassic period La Ciudad, pithouses of 2–8 people grouped into courtyards of 10–27 people, which sometimes in turn part of courtyard groups of 30–70 people; variation in population and degree of grouping reflects domestic cycling and recruitment.	One of largest sites (Snaketown) had peak population of 1,250 people; population of Classic period mound communities ranged from 500–2,500 people; mound communities contain multiple compounds.	In some cases, a community may have been a polity; in other cases, multiple communities may have comprised a polity.	Population estimated for Phoenix Basin during Classic period range from 20,000–100,000 people.
Hohokam-Tucson Basin[5]	2–4 houses/house group; 4–5 house groups/compound; if 2 people/house, then 4–8 people/house group and 16–40 people/compound.	Marana consists of 20–25 compounds with total population of 400–500 people.	Marana polity has 1,000–2,000 people.	
Salado-Tonto Basin[6]	Compounds consist of 3–5 rooms inhabited by one family.	Later multisite communities consist of groups of compounds; e.g., Cline Terrace has 50 rooms at mound and 250 rooms in community.		Agricultural land in Tonto Basin could support 2,700–6,500 people; room counts indicate Classic period population of 5,000–5,800 people.
Paquimé[7]		Estimated peak population of site of Paquimé 2,200 people.		
Grasshopper[8]	Households vary; some occupy multiple rooms for habitation, storage, and manufacturing; others occupy single, generalized habitation room; variability in size due to different stages in development cycle of domestic groups.	500 aggregated rooms comprising 180 households.	± 2,000 rooms dated to 1300s.	
Arroyo Hondo[9]	Pre-A.D. 1350, average room size 6 m² with 1–14 rooms/room group and room groups covering 6–624 m²; post-A.D. 1350, rooms slightly smaller and only 1–2 rooms/room group covering 6–12 m².	Pre-A.D. 1350, 750 ground floor rooms and 250 second story rooms with estimated population of 400–1200 people; post-A.D. 1350, 200 ground floor rooms with estimated population of 75–350 people.		At A.D. 1330 Arroyo Hondo is largest site in region; by A.D. 1400 there are other sites of similar size.

Table 14.5. *(continued)*

	Household	Community	Polity	Interpolity Region
Galisteo Basin[10]	Pueblo Blanco has 1 or more aggregated rooms/household.	Population highly aggregated; at Pueblo Blanco, increasing population between A.D. 1350–1450 and then steady; site has 1450 rooms, but probably only 40% contemporaneous; estimated population of 580–1500 people.		Besides Pueblo Blanco, population of other sites varies from 200–800 people/site; 8 other sites are roughly the same size as Pueblo Blanco and all increase in size from A.D. 1350–1450; from A.D. 1450–1600, 5 of 8 sites abandoned; from A.D. 1600–1680, number of sites stable but overall population declining.
Taos[11]	Pre-A.D. 1200, pithouses 20–40 m² with 3–5 people/pithouse; post-A.D. 1200, average surface room 12 m² with 2–3 rooms/room suite and 3–5 people/suite.	Pre-A.D. 1200, 1–4 dispersed pithouses/site with 5–20 people/site; post-A.D. 1200, shift to aggregated rooms; Pot Creek Pueblo has 300–400 rooms and 300+ people.		

[1-11]See notes for Table 14.4

Table 14.6. Evidence for Agricultural Intensification at Different Spatial Scales in the Late Prehistoric Southwest

	Household	Community	Polity	Interpolity Region
Mimbres[1]	Corn, beans, squash, wild plants, hunted animals, and possibly agave.	Canal irrigation along major creeks; upland check dams, terraces.		
Chaco[2]	Diet of corn, wild plants, and hunted animals.	Elaborate run-off diversion and field systems in canyon.		
Wupatki[3]	Grew corn and probably cotton.	Check dams, cleared areas, waffle and gridded gardens, trincheras.		
Hohokam-Phoenix Basin[4]	Diet of full range of domesticated crops, and desert plants and mammals; corn most important.	Progressive but uneven expansion of irrigation canals; also dry farming features such as terraces, rock piles.		
Hohokam-Tucson Basin[5]	Diet of full range of domesticated crops and desert plants and animals; corn most important.	Large scale rockpile fields for agave production.		
Salado-Tonto Basin[6]	Diet of corn (major crop), agave, wild plants and animals.	Canals, rock piles; after A.D. 1320 expanded and reorganized canals to maximize length.		
Paquimé[7]	Diet of corn, agave.	The site of Paquimé had sophisticated water distribution.		
Grasshopper[8]	Pre-A.D. 1325, diverse diet of wild plants, cultigens, deer, rabbit, turkey; post-A.D. 1325, greater reliance on corn, less on wild plants, less hunting.	Check dams, linear borders; no evidence of technological intensification; rather expanded by cultivating new and marginal lands.		
Arroyo Hondo[9]	Diet of corn (most important), beans, squash, wild plants and animals.	No agricultual features identified.		
Galisteo Basin[10]	Diet of corn, beans, squash, rabbit, deer.	Numerous agricultural/water control features surrounding each site; e.g., check dams, bordered gardens, reservoirs.		
Taos[11]	Diet of domesticates and large and small wild mammals.	Check dams, bordered gardens, and possibly gravel-mulch fields; intensification appears to be post-A.D. 1200; but Greisers (based on Taos land data) have irrigation in A.D. 1000s; claims for canals debatable.		

[1-11]See notes for Table 14.4

Table 14.7. Evidence for Craft Specialization at Different Spatial Scales in the Late Prehistoric Southwest

	Household	Community	Polity	Interpolity Region
Mimbres[1]	Unresolved debates about ceramic specialization.	Unresolved debates about ceramic specialization.		
Chaco[2]	Some household specialization in turquoise jewelry production at village sites.	Possible specialized production of cylinder vessels at Pueblo Bonito; turquoise specialization at both canyon villages and great houses; lithic specialization at Pueblo Bonito.		Specialized production of ceramics in Chuska Valley; specialized lithic production at outlying great house of Salmon Ruin.
Wupatki[3]		Currently no evidence but very limited excavation data; possibly specialization in cotton textiles.		
Hohokam-Phoenix Basin[4]	In Preclassic Snaketown, household specialization in ceramics and shell ornaments; in Preclassic La Ciudad, specialized production of projectile points in single courtyard.	At some sites possible specialized production of Red-on-Buff and Gila Polychrome pottery; may be specialized production of cotton textiles, tabular knives, axes, shell ornaments, serrated projectile points at mound centers.		In Preclassic, specialized production of shell ornaments in Papagueria.
Hohokam-Tucson Basin[5]	Part-time specialization in diverse crafts, including shell ornaments, agave and cotton fiber, projectile points.	Agave production at Marana mound center for use in fiber goods and probably food.		Neutron activation suggests Tanque Verde Red-on-Brown exported to Phoenix Basin.
Salado-Tonto Basin[6]		Possible specialized production of polychrome ceramics.		
Paquimé[7]		Part-time specialization in shell jewelry, parrots, agave, turkeys.		
Grasshopper[8]	One roomblock of 2–3 households specialized in production of turquoise pendants and Four Mile Polychrome.			
Arroyo Hondo[9]		Some culinary and decorated pottery made at site; any specialization part-time; fewer ceramics made at site and more obtained through trade after A.D. 1350.		
Galisteo Basin[10]	Probably part-time specialization in ceramics, which may have increased from 14th–15th century; kilns discovered at San Lazaro.	Village specialization in both turquoise and ceramics at San Marcos.	Probably all big sites in basin made and traded glaze pottery; but some sites may have specialized in its production.	Rio Grande glaze wares traded out to Salinas Pueblos (S), Chama areas (N), Jemez Mts. (W), Plains (E).
Taos[11]	None prior to protohistoric, but evidence mostly poor.	By A.D. 1400s, only some communities may have been making ceramics probably on part-time basis.		

[1-11]See notes for Table 14.4

Table 14.8. Evidence for Prestige Goods Exchange at Different Spatial Scales in the Late Prehistoric Southwest

	Household	Community	Polity	Interpolity Region
Mimbres[1]		Many sites have lots of shell and some sites have parrots and copper bells.		
Chaco[2]		Pueblo Bonito has the most turquoise of any Southwestern site.		Chaco Canyon importing large quantities of turquoise from Cerrillos and elsewhere, ceramics from Chuska valley; also shell from Gulf of California and Pacific Coast; small numbers of macaws and copper bells from north Mexico.
Wupatki[3]		The site of Wupatki has more macaws/parrots than any other Southwestern site except Paquimé; other prestige goods include shell, cotton textiles, copper bells, turquoise.		Site of Wupatki located along main trading route.
Hohokam-Phoenix Basin[4]		Exotics include shell, imported ceramics, turquoise, obsidian, nonlocal chert.		May have been major supplier for shell for Southwest; may have also exported cotton textiles.
Hohokam-Tucson Basin[5]		Marana had better access to exotics than other sites in its community; e.g., shell, imported ceramics, obsidian, nonlocal cherts.		
Salado-Tonto Basin[6]		Some sites trading Gila Polychromes.		
Paquimé[7]		The site of Paquimé imported small amounts of turquoise and exported macaws, copper, and shell.		Exporting shell, copper, macaws; importing small quantities of turquoise.
Grasshopper[8]	Larger, older households have proportionately more tools and equipment than small households.	Hawks, macaws, shell, turquoise found as burials or with burials.		Minimal participation in long-distance exchange networks; importing macaws and copper bells from Chihuahua, shell from Gulf of California, a few ceramics from Colorado Plateau.
Arroyo Hondo[9]		Some shell, jet, turquoise.		Participation in long-distance trade rare; macaw possibly from north Mexico.
Galisteo Basin[10]	Enigmatic collections of concretions, chert eccentrics, fluorite and quartz crystals, animal claws, shaped stones/effigies.	All sites have some regionally exchanged exotics, including turquoise, obsidian, fibrolite axes, travertine, pedernal chert, bison hides, marine shells, feathers.		Importing food and skins from Plains, occasional macaw and copper bell from north Mexico; historic documents suggest they also imported basketry, textiles, leather, drums, rattles, and medicinal plants; exporting ceramics and perhaps some turquoise and other lithics.
Taos[11]	Not yet quantified.	Some sites have small quantities of turquoise and White Mountain redwares; also some obsidian from Jemez area; lithics and ceramics indicate more exchange prior to 13th century.		Probably also exchanged bison robes and cotton cloth, but archeological evidence is rare; bison phalanges and femur head abraders present, coming from Plains.

[1-11] See notes for Table 14.4

Table 14.9. Evidence for Warfare at Different Spatial Scales in the Late Prehistoric Southwest

	Household	Community	Polity	Interpolity Region
Mimbres[1]	Pottery designs depict weapons, body armor, arrows embedded in human figures; burned pithouses.	Skull burials.	Early pithouses A.D. 300–500 in defensive locations and possibly fortified.	
Chaco[2]		Skull burials; burials at Pueblo Bonito, Aztec, Yellow Jacket evidence violent death; cannibalism at Penasco Blanco; warrior grave at Aztec; some great houses may be fortified; ritual human sacrifice at Pueblo Bonito.	Signaling towers; some great houses act as guard villages.	More evidence of violence further from canyon; no man's land between Gallina area.
Wupatki[3]		Decapitated burials and other skeletal evidence for violence; possible fortifications.		
Hohokam-Phoenix Basin[4]		Skull burials; burials evidencing violent death in Classic period platform mounds at Las Colinas; La Ciudad; compound walls may have been defensive.		No man's land in Classic period.
Hohokam-Tucson Basin[5]	Most houses at Marana site purposefully burned probably for ritual purposes.		Hilltop trincheras sites possibly for defense.	Uninhabited buffer zones in Classic period, but may not be defensive in nature.
Salado-Tonto Basin[6]		Post-A.D. 1320 abandoned and burned sites with intact floor assemblages and dismembered bodies in rooms.		
Paquimé[7]	Trophy skulls.			
Grasshopper[8]	Burned rooms pre-1300 A.D.	Evidence of scalping; site of Chodistaas burned but probably for ritual purposes.	Small sites located in defensive locations; evidence for site destruction A.D. 1250–1300, but not after A.D. 1300.	Possible buffer zones during A.D. 1300s.
Arroyo Hondo[9]	Burned rooms.	Few ground floor doorways or doors to exterior; 5 individuals evidence violent death.		Buffer zones.
Galisteo Basin[10]	1 burned room at Pueblo Blanco.	No first story doors at Pueblo Blanco; possible site destruction at Pueblo Blanco about A.D. 1526; individuals burned in Te'ewi kiva located 50 mi. north of Galisteo Basin in Chama River valley.		Buffer zones; destruction of several sites by Pueblo/non-Pueblo warfare.
Taos[11]	Burned households both pre- and post-A.D. 1200.	Pre-A.D. 1200, burned pithouses; post-A.D. 1200, as many as 50% of rooms at Pot Creek Pueblo show evidence of burning; but no full roomblocks burned in toto; probably the burn rate is more in 20–30% range; pre- and post-A.D. 1200, a few examples of major skull traumas.		Post-A.D. 1200, possible buffer zones.

[1-11]See notes for Table 14.4

CHAPTER FIFTEEN

Examining Chiefdoms in the Southeast:

An Application of Multiscalar Analysis

David G. Anderson

Multiscalar analysis is a powerful tool for studying long-term change in the archaeological record. In this chapter, I use this approach to evaluate the importance of variables traditionally used to explore culture change in the Late Prehistoric Southeast. My analyses rely on data for a series of geographic scales from a number of Mississippian societies. My goal is to help develop a better understanding of the emergence and subsequent development of the region's chiefdoms.

Chiefdoms were present throughout the Southeast less than half a millennium ago. Thus, unlike those parts of the world where the first states arose, their archaeological remains are comparatively recent, relatively well preserved, and only rarely covered by subsequent occupations, although they are seriously threatened by our own civilization's growth. In addition, an extensive ethnohistoric record describing these societies survives from the period of initial European contact.

The Southeast's archaeological data base is truly massive, and thanks to more than a century of near-continuous investigation, the region has one of the best documented archaeological records in the world from which to examine the evolution of chiefdom societies. Through 1994, for example, more than 180,000 archaeological sites were recorded in the lower Southeast, and of these almost 20,000 had components dating to the Late Prehistoric and initial contact era between ca. A.D. 800 to 1600. Hundreds of these late period sites have had at least some level of excavation, and dozens have been extensively excavated and reported. Particularly intensive bursts of fieldwork occurred during three periods: during the 1880s and early 1890s when some 2,000 mounds were examined by the Mound Division of the Bureau of Ethnology; during the public works era of the 1930s and early 1940s when dozens of large village and mound sites were completely excavated; and during the past quarter century, when tens of thousands of sites have been recorded and many hundreds intensively examined as a result of federally-mandated cultural resource management activity (Anderson 1997a; Bense 1994). This massive data base and long history of research have made the construction of fine-grained cultural sequences possible in many areas, permitting us to monitor closely changes that occurred as chiefdoms emerged and evolved.

How can this record be used to achieve the objectives of this paper? Multiscalar analyses proceed by examining at different geographic scales the effects of single (isolated) and multiple (interrelated) variables on individual societies and across multiple societies. Calls for the adoption of such a perspective in exploring chiefdom political changes are beginning to appear in the Southeast (e.g., Smith 1990:3, 8), as in other parts of the world (e.g.,

Earle 1991:4,13; Upham 1990:97). Applications in the Southeast have most typically examined evidence for prestige-goods exchange, status differentiation, warfare, or settlement variation (e.g., Blitz 1993; Hally 1993; Hally et al. 1990; Steponaitis 1991, Welch 1990a).

In this paper, I build on this previous work by presenting three examples of multiscalar analysis. First, a brief examination of the Mississippian occupations within a single drainage, the Savannah River basin, is provided to show how the archaeological record from individual sites and within given localities can only be understood by employing data from a number of geographic scales. Second, data from a number of Southeastern societies are compared to illustrate the insights that can be gained from a broad, general application of the multiscalar approach. Finally, the approach is used to evaluate and refine models of culture change surrounding Mississippian emergence, expansion, and collapse. My overall objective is to show that the adoption of multiscalar analysis is essential and ideally suited to the formulation and testing of models of long-term societal change.

EXPLORING CHANGE IN A SPECIFIC LOCALITY

Research in the Savannah River basin of Georgia and South Carolina illustrates how use of a multiscalar perspective can elucidate the causes of culture change. To date, more than 500 Mississippian components have been identified in the basin, and extensive excavations have occurred at more than two dozen sites, including most of the known mound centers (Anderson 1990, 1994, 1996a; Anderson et al. 1986). Cultural sequences are detailed enough to permit the dating of components to within roughly 100 years. This degree of chronological control, in combination with the extensive survey and excavation data, makes it possible to examine culture change from a number of scales of analysis.

The Savannah River Basin Chiefdoms

Simple and complex chiefdoms rose and fell in the Savannah River basin over a span of four centuries. The initial appearance of simple chiefdoms is evidenced by the first Mississippian ceremonial centers sometime between A.D. 1100 and 1150 (Figure 15.1). By approximately A.D. 1200, simple chiefdoms were centered around sites with one or two mounds scattered throughout the basin. By A.D. 1350 (Figure 15.2), however, the political landscape changed

dramatically. Most of the small centers were abandoned, and two major multimound centers, presumably the ceremonial and political foci of complex chiefdoms, were present in the central part of the basin. By A.D. 1400 or so (Figure 15.3), only one of these large centers was left in the central basin. Soon after A.D. 1450, it too collapsed and the central and lower basin was abandoned. Further upriver, small mound centers not only continued but may in fact have expanded, possibly as the result of population movement from lower in the basin.

The pattern of the lower portions of the basin being abandoned before those further upriver may have been linked to variation in the basin's size and productivity. The lower Savannah basin is quite narrow. It has few well-defined terraces along its margins and extensive pine forests in the interriverine area. In contrast, the upper Savannah basin is characterized by pronounced relief, better defined terraces, and a richer deciduous canopy. Thus, chiefdoms lower in the basin may have relied on a less productive resource base, making them more vulnerable to stress than their neighbors upstream.

THE BROADER CONTEXT OF THE SAVANNAH RIVER BASIN CHIEFDOMS

Turning to a larger geographic scale, the Savannah River basin is comparatively small, and Mississippian societies occupying it may have been at something of a disadvantage in competition with groups occupying the much larger Oconee and Santee/Wateree basins to the north and south, respectively. In the sixteenth century these larger basins were occupied by powerful chiefdoms, which the Spanish described as the provinces of Ocute and Cofitachequi. De Soto expedition chroniclers amply document relations between the Ocute and Cofitachequi during the early historic era as being characterized by rivalry and enmity. This competition probably had a long history and may have taken place at the expense of the elites and commoners in the Savannah River chiefdoms who were caught in the middle.

Coupled with these broad scales, political conditions, the period between the late fourteenth through late fifteenth centuries was a time of moderate environmental deterioration, which would have placed the agriculturally-based Savannah River basin chiefdoms under considerable stress. Rainfall reconstructions derived from bald cypress tree-ring data indicate that growing season precipitation was below average over much of this inter-

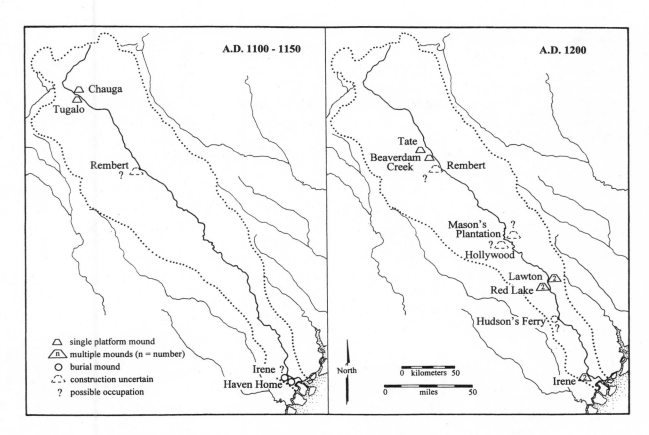

Figure 15.1. Political change in the Savannah River basin, A.D. 1100–1150 and A.D. 1200.

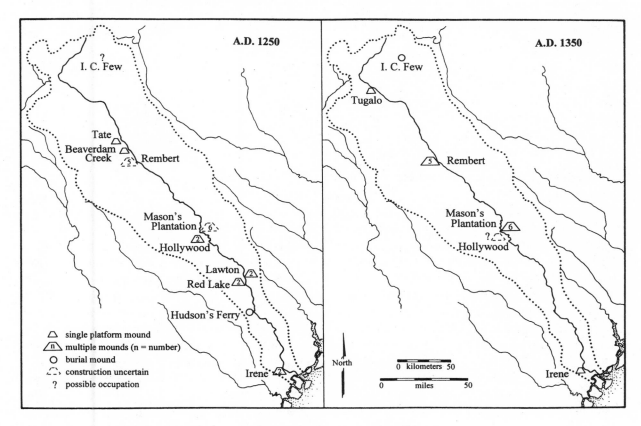

Figure 15.2. Political change in the Savannah River basin—A.D. 1250 and A.D. 1350.

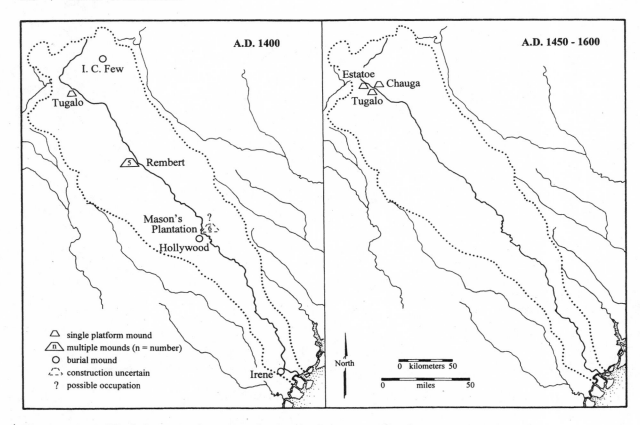

Figure 15.3.   Political change in the Savannah River basin—A.D. 1400 and A.D. 1450–1600.

val (Anderson et al. 1995). Declining harvests would have hampered the ability of elites to mobilize tribute and may have forced an increased reliance on wild plant and animal resources from the interriverine buffer zones. However, this wild resource exploitation may have been difficult due to the presence of the powerful Ocute and Cofitahequi chiefdoms on the opposite sides of the buffer zones. The ultimate abandonment of the Savannah River basin suggests that the local chiefly elites failed to respond effectively to these broader scale, political and environmental challenges.

Site Types

At a smaller scale of analysis, five major site types can currently be identified in the Savannah River basin at one time or another over the Mississippian period. These include: 1) "vacant" ceremonial centers or chiefly compounds (after Williams 1996) where little evidence has been found for permanent occupation by more than a few people, yet where large numbers of people apparently came together for short intervals for collective ceremonial activities; 2) permanently occupied ceremonial centers with large residential populations present year round; 3) organized villages occupied for extended periods; 4) isolated hamlets, also occupied for extended periods; and 5) short-term, presumably nonresidential sites where hunting, collecting, or other specialized activities occurred.

To make sense of events documented for any one of these site types requires that comparisons be made with the other site types as well. For example, shifts in the locations of both villages and hamlets can be linked to the location and stability of regional ceremonial centers and to climatic conditions. When political conditions were stable and polities were at relative peace, and when the climate was favorable to the production of agricultural surpluses, people appear to have dispersed into a series of unfortified villages and hamlets, congregating periodically at otherwise "vacant" ceremonial centers. In contrast, when hostilities were pronounced, or when climatic conditions were unfavorable, population nucleation into larger fortified communities occurred.

While the need to compare developments at different site types, which represent embedded scales of interaction, may seem obvious, interpreting the results of such comparisons can be difficult. Take, for example, the case of hamlets that were common in parts of the basin whose distributional shifts have been linked, as noted previously, to the location and stability of ceremonial centers. However, the nature of this linkage is unclear. In the lower basin, early Mississippian hamlets were located both along and away from the river, while Middle Mississippian hamlets (from the period just prior to the abandonment of the lower basin) were located almost exclusively away from the main channel. This locational shift may have been a defensive measure—an attempt literally to hide from raiding groups, who favored the major transportation arteries. Alternatively, given that complex chiefdoms had emerged in the central basin during the Middle Mississippian, some of the observed population relocation may have been an attempt by local populations to avoid or lower their tribute burden.

Rucker's Bottom

Changes in the political landscape can be seen at a still smaller scale at Rucker's Bottom, the basin's one Mississippian village that has been intensively studied (Anderson and Schuldenrein 1985). Located in the central basin, this village was small throughout its occupation, never exceeding a hectare in size and with a population on the order of 90 to 150 people. These occupants were commoners, and skeletal analyses indicate that they were subject to considerable disease stress. This village was a part of a larger chiefdom, and the villagers were undoubtedly subservient to the elites ruling this society. However, the presence of communal buildings in both the early and later occupations of Rucker's Bottom indicates that at least some decision-making was under local control.

The archaeological record of Rucker's Bottom appears to reflect conditions in the larger polity and interpolity region. Changes in the larger political landscape are indicated in a number of ways. Settlement shifted from an open, roughly circular arrangement of houses around a central plaza during the twelfth and thirteenth centuries to a similar arrangement of structures around a plaza in the north-central part of the terrace during the fourteenth and early fifteenth centuries. This later community was fortified, first by a semicircular enclosure and later by a rectangular ditched and stockaded enclosure. During this time, Rucker's Bottom also grew larger, suggesting the increasing concentration or nucleation of local populations, perhaps as a defensive measure. The appearance and increasing complexity of the fortifications suggest that hostilities were occurring during the century before the abandonment of the central and lower basin. The causes of these hostilities were probably the broader scale political and environmental conditions discussed previously.

Analyses of a range of data categories at a still smaller scale, the household or feature level, help us to understand how and why something as dramatic as the abandonment of much of a river basin could have occurred. Paleosubsistence analyses undertaken at the Rucker's Bottom site suggest an increase in land clearing and a greater use of acorns in the years immediately before abandonment (Moore 1905). As climate was deteriorating locally and warfare was increasing, the villagers' response appears to have been to increase farming activity and the gathering of wild plant resources like acorns, probably to make up for harvest shortfalls or surpluses lost to raiding.

During most of Rucker's Bottom's history, maize storage is assumed to have been in aboveground facilities, or barbacoas, like those reported by the early Spanish explorers. Many small circular and rectangular post arrangements have been excavated and interpreted as possible storage sheds or corn cribs (Judge 1991). In the last village occupation prior to site abandonment, these structures were located in prominent positions in the village, adjacent to the probable council house and near the rectangular palisade wall. Anyone accessing these facilities would have been clearly visible, something that may have facilitated their defense from raiders. What appear to be massive subterranean storage features were also constructed at the site during its final occupation, suggesting a desire to hide food supplies or restrict their use.

Summary

Elsewhere I have argued that the dramatic changes observed in the late prehistoric archaeological sequence of the Savannah River basin were caused by a complex array of factors (Anderson 1994, 1996a,b). These include: 1) weaknesses inherent to chiefdom organizational forms in general, such as divisive factional competition centered on chiefly succession and the allocation of wealth and power; 2) shifts in the structure of the local and regional political organization; and 3) short- and long-term changes in climate, and their effects on local and regional patterns of resource availability.

While my explanations require additional testing, what I have presented here should illustrate how investigating the causes of culture change can proceed at many different scales and with many kinds of data. In fact, accurately interpreting the local archaeological record in the Savannah River basin would probably not be possible without a multiscalar perspective.

EXPLORING CULTURE CHANGE AT THE REGIONAL LEVEL

Comparative analyses of Mississippian chiefdoms can be productive in two ways. First, by placing individual chiefdoms in their broader contexts, such analyses can make developments within those chiefdoms more understandable, as in the Savannah River basin. Secondly, by revealing the similarities and differences among Mississippian chiefdoms, such analyses can provide the basis for formulating explanatory models of culture change for the Southeast in general. In this section, comparative data on a series of Mississippian chiefdoms are presented in a multiscalar format. The following section uses these data to consider the problem of formulating models of culture change.

The data considered here consists of qualitative summary information on organizational change, agricultural intensification, population/demographic trends, prestige-goods exchange, craft specialization, and warfare for a dozen localities selected to maximize geographical and organization diversity across the Southeast (Figure 15.4). The scales or levels of analysis encompass the household, community, chiefly polity, and interpolity regions (see Earle 1991:4).

Qualitative summary data rather than quantitative values are used because this is the kind of information most typically available in the published literature. While a number of exceptional analytical studies exist that have explored some of these variables quantitatively, they have typically focused on small samples or on only one or a few localities, rendering comparative analyses difficult. Thus, for example, while population estimates and settlement spacing have been calculated for every known center and village within the Coosa polity (Hally et al. 1990), this kind of data remains to be developed elsewhere in the Southeast. Fortunately, detailed quantitatively-based analyses are appearing with increased incidence, offering great hope for the future. Examples of such studies include analyses of site size or mound volume across the region (e.g., Holley, Chapter 2; Muller, Chapter 11), of mound center longevity and spacing (e.g., Scarry, Chapter 5; Hally 1993, 1996b), and of prestige grave-good incidence over time (e.g., Anderson 1994; Steponaitis 1991; Welch 1991). The value of the qualitative data considered here is that it permits comparisons of multiple variables, cases, and scales. Even the simplest comparisons reveal important trends, which currently cannot be discerned in more focused, quantitatively-based studies.

Organization

Evidence for organizational change has received intensive study across the region, and a number of attributes have been associated with the emergence, expansion, and collapse of chiefly polities (Table 15.1). Architectural correlates of chiefdom emergence in the Southeast include, for example, the disappearance of council houses and the appearance of elite residences both atop and away from mounds, presumably reflecting changes from collective/egalitarian to hierarchical/elite decision-making apparatuses. In contrast, chiefdom collapse is correlated with the disappearance of elite residences and sometimes with the reappearance of council houses.

Fortifications, besides signaling periods when conflict was widespread (such as during the Late Mississippian period), are also observed when chiefdoms first appear in some areas (i.e., in northeast Arkansas at the Zebree site, at several centers along the Savannah River, and at Town Creek in North Carolina). This suggests that Mississippian emergence was not an altogether peaceful development and, at least in some areas, involved competition or conflict between groups.

The occurrence of fortifications also provides clues about regional political relationships later in the Missis-

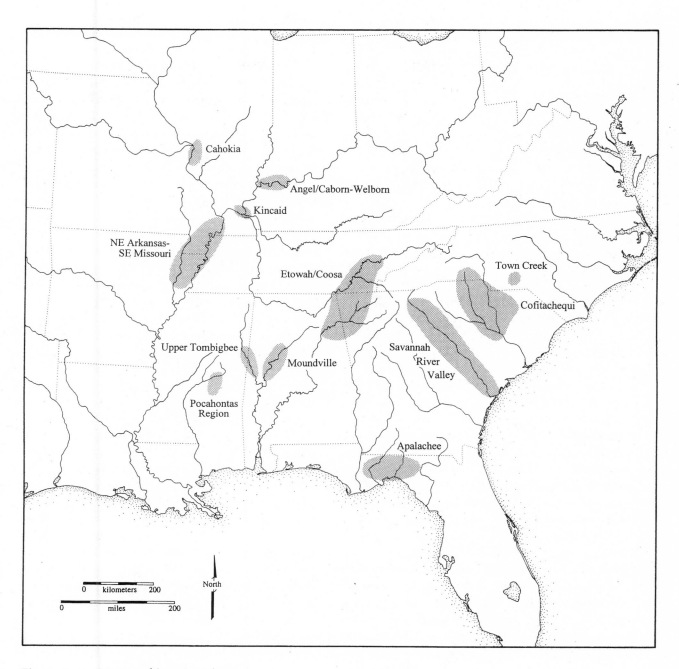

Figure 15.4.   Areas used in comparisons.

sippian era. The expansion of the complex chiefdom at Moundville, for example, appears linked to the disappearance of fortifications at centers in nearby areas (i.e., at Lubbub Creek along the Tombigbee), and the outright disappearance of societies from other areas (Welch 1990b, 1991). This suppression of potential rivals seems to have been a common strategy by elites in complex Mississippian chiefdoms.

Individual construction stages in Southeastern mounds are commonly thought to reflect successional episodes, specifically demarcating the replacement of one chief by another. Taken collectively, periods when mound stages were being added without interruption are viewed as probable measures of polity duration, or the lifespan of politically successful chiefly lineages at a given center. Mound stage construction appears to have occurred about once a generation or so at many sites. Since more than four to six successive stages are only rarely present without major interruption, some researchers have suggested that Southeastern chiefdoms usually did not last more than 50 to 150 years (Anderson 1994; Hally 1993, 1996b).

Just as centers were occupied, abandoned, and sometimes reoccupied, so too were much larger parts of the region at various times during the Mississippian era. The abandonment of chiefdoms over large parts of the central Mississippi Valley and along the central and lower Savannah River in the Late Mississippian period are among the most dramatic examples of sweeping organizational change known from the region (Anderson 1994, 1996a,c; Williams 1990).

Demography

While little firm data exists as to the actual numbers of people present in various parts of the Southeast, evidence about settlement distributions is on secure footing in many areas (Table 15.2). During the period of Mississippian emergence appreciable demographic variability is evident across the region, with little evidence for uniformity in either settlement change or population growth. In some areas, for example, small villages were replaced by a dispersed hamlet/center settlement pattern (i.e., in the American Bottom around Cahokia and in western Alabama around Moundville), while in other localities dispersed populations aggregated into larger villages and centers, at least for portions of the year (i.e., in southwestern Indiana around Angel and along the upper Tombigbee in Mississippi near Lubbub Creek). While population growth may have been occurring at this time,

population reorganization is what stands out in the archaeological record.

Comparable settlement variability likewise characterizes localities where chiefdoms have time-depth. In parts of the region the only settlements away from major centers are small farmsteads and hamlets, while in other areas hamlets and villages, or just villages may occur away from the centers. The larger polities in terms of numbers of people are typically the most complex organizationally, a pattern characteristic of pre-state societies throughout the New World (Feinman and Neitzel 1984).

Major population change unquestionably occurred during the Mississippian era, with particularly dramatic examples including large scale abandonments like those noted previously or the dramatic expansion in the size of some centers (i.e., at Moundville and Cahokia). Whether these large scale changes reflect actual population growth or decline within the larger region, or merely population relocation or reorganization, is unknown.

Subsistence

Agricultural intensification is clearly associated, on a broad level, with the emergence of chiefdoms across the region (Table 15.3). Examining specific cases, however, it appears that the adoption of intensive maize agriculture preceded the Mississippian emergence in some areas (i.e., along the upper Tombigbee, in northern Florida), paced it in others (i.e., in the American Bottom, in the Savannah River Valley), and did not occur until appreciably later in still other areas (i.e., in northeast Arkansas). The adoption of intensive maize agriculture appears to have spread across the region faster than Mississippian political organization itself. However, in areas unusually rich in wild food resources, maize did not become a major element of the diet until after Mississippian emergence, even in areas where Mississippian political organization arose early, as in the central Mississippi Valley (i.e., in northeast Arkansas at Zebree).

Subsistence resource procurement likewise tended to be highly diversified in unusually rich locales, while in other areas it became increasingly focused over time (i.e., directed to a few crops and game species). A possible reason for this contrast is that the labor requirements associated with agricultural intensification may have forced a restriction of hunting effort to one or a few species offering a high rate of return (Speth and Scott 1985). Interestingly, when complex Mississippian societies collapsed, use of maize may have declined as well. This is clearly the case at the Irene site along the lower Savannah River (Larsen et al. 1992), although the pattern is by no means universal. Over the region it appears that the appearance of intensive agriculture may be more closely linked to major patterns of population growth than to the emergence of chiefdom organization.

Population skeletal health, a direct measure of the effectiveness of provisioning systems, appears closely tied to organizational complexity across the region. Population health for all segments of Mississippian society was generally better in the most complex chiefdoms than it was in simpler societies, unless the less-complex chiefdoms were located in resource-rich areas (e.g., Hatch 1987; Powell 1988). This patterning also appears related to societal stability and longevity. Typically, the largest chiefdoms were among the longest-lived, indicating that they had developed highly successful strategies for reducing subsistence-related stress. These strategies were most likely tied to maximizing production of and control over subsistence surpluses. Finally, more than maize was involved in the subsistence tributary base of the Mississippian political economy. Evidence for the provisioning of elites with choice game such as deer meat has been recovered in some areas (i.e., Savannah River Valley, upper Tombigbee drainage) (Jackson and Scott 1995).

Prestige Goods Exchange

Prestige goods exchange and use varied appreciably over the region (Table 15.4). Distributions of specific goods indicate that interaction spheres existed and varied in size, and that regional political geography shaped the flow of goods. The larger centers appear to have constrained the use or even the receipt of prestige goods by populations at smaller centers, both in areas under their direct control and in adjoining polities. Thus, the emergence of the presumed Moundville paramount chiefdom after A.D. 1200 is tied to a diminution in prestige-good incidence in smaller societies to the west, along the Tombigbee and in the Pocahontas region of Mississippi (Blitz 1993; Steponaitis 1991). Prestige goods flowed to major centers of power where they would have proven useful to the elites. How these exchange systems actually operated, however, is poorly known at the present.

An interesting consequence of the apparent centralization of control over long distance exchange was that extralocal materials or "prestige goods" came to be viewed differently in societies of differing levels of complexity. Elites in the more complex Mississippian chiefdoms exercised considerable control over the use of prestige goods in their own societies, often restricting the use of specific goods to particular social segments. In these societies prestige goods were used to signal status, with specific goods or items viewed as insignia of rank. In contrast, prestige goods in less complex chiefdoms tended to occur (if they occurred at all) more widely over all segments of society and were viewed as wealth items.

The maintenance of prestige goods exchange networks across the region does not appear to have been crucial to the successful operation of many Mississippian chiefdoms. Exchange waxed and waned over time and was quite important during some periods and less so during others. From a pronounced peak in the thirteenth century, when the Southeastern Ceremonial Complex was at its height (Muller 1989), evidence for long-distance exchange declined markedly in the fifteenth and sixteenth centuries. However, even given this decline, many chiefdoms both large and small continued to function in the Late Mississippian period. Even during earlier periods there is evidence from a number of areas that ceremonial centers continued to be occupied, and mound stages continued to be added, well after a major decline in prestige goods incidence occurred (Anderson 1994; Steponaitis 1991; Welch 1991).

Craft Specialization

Evidence for the existence of full-time craft specialists, something often advanced as a hallmark of fairly complex society, is ambiguous over the region (Table 15.5). There is little doubt, however, that the specialized manufacture of a wide range of goods by small segments of the population occurred in a number of Southeastern societies. In most cases, however, this production appears to have been a part-time affair conducted as one part of everyday life. Evidence for the existence of full-time craft specialists supported by an elite is not obvious, although an extensive and sometimes quite impassioned debate does admittedly exist on the subject. Modifying a "rule" advanced by Yoffee (1993:69) to encompass similar arguments about whether or not states are present in an area. I suggest that since we can argue heatedly about whether or not craft specialization occurred, it probably did not at any level of importance (that is, if it occurred enough to matter, the evidence would be clear cut). The comparative data does indicate that considerable variation occurred in the production and use of specialized goods over the region. In some polities these goods were apparently produced by elites, or at least made at elite centers, while in other societies they were more widely produced at farmsteads, villages, and centers, possibly by elites and commoners alike.

Warfare

Mississippian chiefdoms appear to have both constrained warfare and given it reign in new forms over the region (Table 15.6). The Mississippian emergence witnessed a decline in warfare compared with the preceding Late Woodland period in some areas (i.e., at Moundville and along the Tombigbee), while in other areas it was accompanied by the appearance of fortifications around sites, suggesting disagreements with local or nearby groups.

Differing solutions to perceived threats were adopted throughout the Mississippian era. In some areas populations nucleated. In others they remained dispersed, yet converged on fortified centers during periods of conflict. Additionally, in some areas attempts were apparently made to conceal stored food reserves during periods of unusual stress.

There appear to have been periods when warfare occurred with greater or lesser intensity across the region as a whole. The Late Mississippian in particular appears to have been a time of increased strife across the region. Settlement nucleation, improved fortifications, and an increased incidence of weapons trauma on skeletal remains has been observed at this time in a number of areas, suggesting increased frequency or intensity of conflict. This is probably directly tied to the decline of the region-wide prestige goods exchange network that occurred following the Middle Mississippian period. This network would have facilitated interaction and alliance formation between elites in differing polities, fostering cooperation rather than conflict. A decline in mound building also occurs during the Late Mississippian period, and it has been suggested that societal energies were increasingly directed to defense rather than to ceremonialism.

EVALUATING MODELS OF CULTURE CHANGE IN THE SOUTHEAST

The data presented in the preceding section provide a basis for developing explanatory models for culture change in the Southeast, models that may offer insights for archaeologists working in other parts of the world as well. In the Southeast, the three questions that have been the focus of efforts to formulate explanatory models all pertain to the general topic of chiefdoms. First, how and why did such societies evolve in the Southeast? Second, once chiefdoms appeared, how and why did they spread? Finally, how and why did these societies collapse, individually and collectively? Each of these questions is considered below.

Models of Chiefdom Emergence

In the introduction to a volume addressing the problem of how and why chiefdoms arose in the Southeast, Smith (1990:1–2) noted that the major frameworks advanced to explain the Mississippian emergence comprised a seeming polar opposition, what he called the homology/analogy dilemma. The homology or "historical relatedness" position sees the emergence of chiefdoms across the region as due to the movement of people or innovations from a central core area, with their survival or selection due to the adaptive advantage of new organizational forms. The alternative, analogy or "process" position views the Mississippian emergence as "independent and isolated cultural responses to similar challenges" (Smith 1990:2). Although the record of Mississippian emergence is superbly documented in many localities, Smith (1990:1–2) has observed that it is "far from clear to what degree this broadly similar process of cultural transformation was due to developmental interaction between river valley societies in transition, as opposed to their independent response to similar developmental constraints and opportunities." Explanatory mechanisms or frameworks are not well worked out, although the role of a few key variables have been explored, such as the use of maize or other domesticates (i.e., the impact of agricultural intensification), demography (i.e., the impact of population growth and pressure), and trade (i.e., the importance of elite/prestige goods exchange). Recognizing that "there is no single, simple, all encompassing and comforting theoretical explanation for the Mississippian emergence" (Smith 1990:2–3), Smith has argued that the best way to identify and evaluate the factors that led to the Mississippian emergence is through the adoption of a multiscalar analytical approach that:

> . . . seeks out and accommodates information from the full range of nested levels, ranging from basic economic unit households up through regional systems . . . [we] need to simultaneously consider and pursue explanations of Mississippian origins on a number of nested levels [employing] multiple, if partial, explanations from a variety of theoretical perspectives (Smith 1990:3,8).

Whatever brought about the emergence of chiefdoms across the Southeast, the simple comparison of developments in a number of localities highlights the inadequacy of prime-movers, or single causal factors (Table 15.1–15.6). Patterns of organizational change varied appreciably during the period of Mississippian emergence. In some areas such as the American Bottom, small villages were replaced by a center-hamlet dichotomy, while in other areas such as along the Savannah River, hamlets were replaced by nucleated villages and centers (Table 15.1). Population distributions appear to have varied widely over the region, rendering it difficult to accept that any one trajectory or critical threshold was required before chiefdoms could emerge (Table 15.2). Likewise, agricultural intensification, leading to either population growth and pressure or storable surpluses promoting elite prestige goods exchange, has been suggested as a factor in the emergence of chiefdoms. However, comparative analysis makes it clear that in differing areas the adoption of intensive agriculture preceded, was contemporaneous, or even postdated the Mississippian emergence (Table 15.3). Arguments linking the Mississippian emergence to agricultural intensification or population pressure—usually focusing on the control of subsistence-generating resources like prime agricultural soils or hunting territories—are particularly hard to accept since large portions of the region remained unoccupied even after intensive agriculture was widely adopted and chiefdoms were present over much of the landscape. Settlement distributions appear to have been shaped as much as by political as by environmental conditions.

The importance of prestige goods exchange likewise appears to have varied greatly over the region (Table 15.4). The data clearly indicate, however, that the growth of political centralization and the development of prestige goods exchange networks in the Southeast were closely linked. Accordingly, the purpose of exchange may not have been merely to promote alliance formation (e.g., Brown et al. 1990:253), but also to facilitate the accumulation of wealth and power in the hands of individuals and lineages. It is possible that demand for prestige goods may have contributed to agricultural intensification and organizational changes by generating increased requirements on subsistence production (i.e., to generate and control the surpluses needed to acquire prestige goods). While trade was indeed "an instrument of political activity" (Brown et al. 1990:255), its result was the accumulation of power, which was maintained for its own sake. However, once chiefdoms were in place, and elite power was centralized

and reasonably secure, the importance of trade goods for the maintenance of elite authority declined. As Drennan (1991:281) has it, once chiefdoms are in place, long-distance trade "provided the plumes of the chiefly peacock, not its basic diet." The decline of the Southeastern Ceremonial Complex after ca. A.D. 1250 may reflect such a broad-scale evolutionary process.

The variable of prestige goods exchange illustrates how the timing and interrelationships between many variables need to be considered to understand Mississippian emergence. At Emergent Mississippian sites like Range in the American Bottom (Kelly 1990a), shifts in community plan over time evidence increasing social differentiation, including the probable emergence of ranked population subsets. A recently favored explanation for this emergent ranking has been elite competition and associated prestige goods exchange, leading to the accumulation of wealth and power and the development of permanent status differences within privileged lineages. However, this explanation has little empirical support, since the documented occurrence of elite/prestige goods in emergent Mississippian settings is minimal. Extensive elite exchange did occur throughout the region by early Mississippian times (ca. A.D. 1000–1100), peaked by ca. A.D. 1200 or so, and declined after that. Thus, while prestige goods exchange apparently was not the cause for the emergence of chiefdoms, it may have played an important role in their subsequent development.

The Spread of Mississippian: Timing and Precursors

While chiefdoms emerged across the Southeast within no more than 300 years, from ca. A.D. 900 to 1150 or so, there is an apparent time-transgressive west to east spread of the adaptation in the region (Table 15.7; Figure 15.5). Chiefdom societies are present after ca. A.D. 900 in the central Mississippi River Valley, but do not appear in places like Moundville until ca. A.D. 1050, and only after ca. A.D. 1100–1150 in the Carolinas. While few now believe that waves of chiefly elites moved out of a central/lower Mississippi River Valley heartland, it may be that chiefdom organizational forms in the late prehistoric era did indeed first arise in this area, and spread through a process of both competitive emulation and defensive reaction (Anderson 1997b).

Given the scarcity of evidence for chiefdom organizational spread through migration (something now suggested in only a few areas such as at Macon Plateau in central

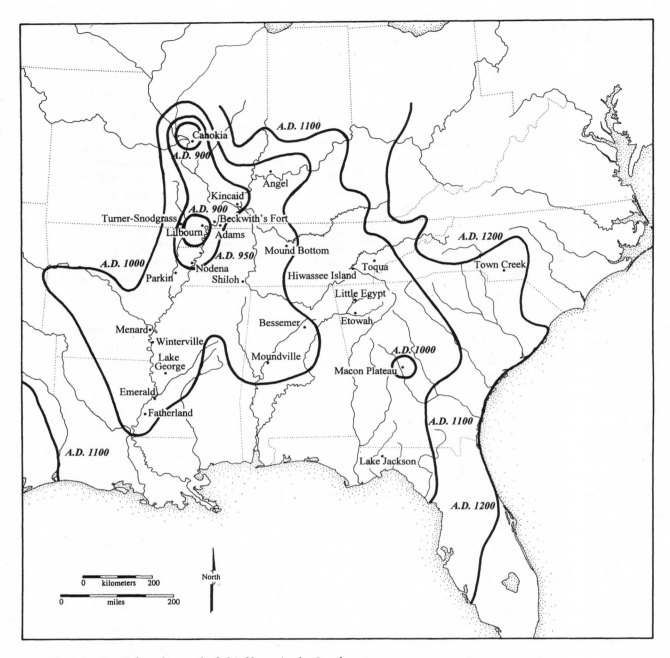

Figure 15.5.   Inferred spread of chiefdoms in the Southeast.

Georgia or at the Zebree site in northeast Arkansas) and the fairly clear indication for in situ development in many areas, a direct movement of people as the primary cause of the Mississippian emergence over the region is unlikely. Instead, the spread of chiefly organization was more likely something of a reactive process. Following arguments by Carneiro (1970, 1981), if the first chiefdoms were predatory, chiefdoms may have emerged across the region as a defensive reaction. Alternatively or additionally, they developed to allow privileged lineages to participate more effectively in expanding trade and status-based, power-enhancing games through a process of competitive emulation.

We need to look very carefully at preexisting conditions, the long historical trajectories leading to the critical two centuries when the Mississippian emergence occurred. Until quite recently there has been an unfortunate tendency for researchers to simplify Middle and Late Woodland organizational complexity (but see Nassaney and Cobb 1991), with the result that the Mississippian emergence appears all the more impressive and disjunctive. However, many of the largest mound and other earthen constructions and some of the most elaborately furnished burials in the region occur well before the Mississippian era at Middle or Late Woodland centers like Pinson, Kolomoki, Lake George, and Toltec. We need to consider the kinds of organizational forms that could have produced these remains, and how their existence shaped subsequent developments.

Likewise, care must be taken to differentiate between the evolution and spread of chiefdom organizational forms over the region and the spread of Mississippian ideology (Pauketat and Emerson 1997). The former (i.e., chiefdom-like societies) appears to have emerged in the ninth and tenth centuries, if not before, in some areas. The latter (i.e., Mississippian ideology and religion) appears to have developed or crystallized in the tenth and eleventh centuries, after chiefdoms themselves had emerged in a number of areas, and Cahokia seems to have been the primary center where this took place. "Mississippian" increasingly is thus coming to be recognized as an ideological/religious system that a number of the region's chiefdoms participated in, and whose origin and spread owe a great deal to the early and dramatic emergence of Cahokia (Anderson 1997b; Emerson 1997; Knight 1986; Pauketat 1994, 1997; Pauketat and Emerson 1997).

Models of Chiefdom Development and Decline

By ca. A.D. 1100 or shortly thereafter the Southeast was dotted with simple and complex chiefdoms from east

Texas and Louisiana to the Carolinas and north to the Ohio River. Over the next four centuries complex chiefdoms rose and fell over the region, with Moundville, Cahokia, Spiro, and Etowah being four of the better-known societies that collapsed well before contact. Elsewhere I have argued that cycling—the emergence and collapse of complex chiefdoms amid a regional landscape of simple chiefdoms—is an inherent property of chiefdoms (Anderson 1990, 1996a; 1997b). David Hally (1996b:124–125), in an important extension of research on chiefdom emergence and collapse and cycling theory, has shown with a large archaeological sample from the Georgia area that simple chiefdoms, like complex chiefdoms, are also extremely fragile and short lived, and themselves "'cycled' between birth and death." We are now at the point where we can examine and compare the historical trajectories of a large number of chiefdoms in the region, to understand better how processes like cycling operate to produce cultural change (e.g., Drennan 1991; Earle 1991:4; Upham 1990:97; Wright 1986).

Why one or more Mississippian societies in the Eastern Woodlands never developed into state-level polities is also a question of some interest, since chiefdoms elsewhere in the New World made this transition. Comparative studies have shown that state formation does not automatically occur when a threshold population size/density is reached (Upham 1990). More typically, the response is system collapse and downward cycling. Thus, thresholds of population size/density were reached repeatedly throughout prehistory; but only rarely and in a few parts of the world did successful organizational responses occur. These selection events, however, never happened in the Southeast.

The societies of the Eastern Woodlands apparently developed in isolation, with little or no direct contact with other New World states, precluding the likelihood of secondary state formation. The nearest state-level societies were in central Mexico at a considerable distance and separated by major geographic barriers. Currently no conclusive evidence of any kind has been found for direct or regular contact between the Middle American states and the Mississippian or pre-Mississippian societies of the Eastern Woodlands (see Cobb et al. Chapter 13). The only Latin American artifacts reaching the Eastern Woodlands were domesticates such as corn and beans, and they apparently spread gradually from group to group.

The development of increasingly complex societies may have been hindered in many parts of the Eastern

Woodlands by their physiographic and resource structure. Although the area occupied by Mississippian chiefdoms was quite large, larger in fact than nuclear Mesoamerica, comparatively small portions of this broad area were suitable for the emergence and development of agricultural/ game-based chiefdoms. These portions were (typically) river floodplains, most of which were not only narrow but also widely spaced.

Both of these characteristics would have discouraged state formation. Narrow valleys could not contain multiple, densely packed, complex chiefdoms, a condition favorable for state formation. Also, the distances between individual chiefly societies would have made the formation of stable, multipolity aggregates difficult. It is true that some Mississippian chiefdoms apparently exerted influence over considerable areas. However, their direct administrative control appears to have been within fairly small areas.

Mississippian chiefdoms did exhibit one characteristic that comparative studies have identified as conducive to state formation—the prevalence of warfare often involving the unification of a number of chiefdom-level societies through conquest and subsequent administrative reorganization (Wright 1986). Among Mississippian chiefdoms, low intensity warfare, which occasionally gave way to major episodes of apparent conquest or extermination, was a way of life. Some have suggested in fact that increasing competition and conflict among chiefly centers occurred over the course of the Mississippian period. If true, it may be that European contact truncated trends that otherwise would have led to state formation.

Two other trends observed among Mississippian chiefdoms could also be suggested as precursors of state formation. One is the apparent gradual change from sacred, cooperatively base forms of political control to secular, more authoritarian forms. The other is settlement nucleation, which may have been related to the apparent pattern of increased warfare.

I think that if European contact had not occurred, it is probable that conquest-based states would have eventually emerged in at least some parts of the Eastern Woodlands. In my view, the most likely location would have been the central and lower Mississippi River Valley, one of the largest and most ecologically rich areas in the Southeast where large numbers of complex chiefdoms were closely packed together in the landscape. Elsewhere, the wide spacing of chiefdoms would have made conquest difficult and state formation much less likely.

Unfortunately for Mississippian populations, European contact did occur and within a century chiefdom level society had ended across much of the Southeast. It has traditionally been thought that Mississippian chiefdoms underwent a general collapse or "devolution" prior to contact, a view largely shaped by the abandonments observed at such major centers as Cahokia, Etowah, and Moundville. This regional decline has been variously attributed to the collapse of interregional exchange networks, climatic changes such as the onset of the Little Ice Age, or even population pressure. Such views are no longer widely held. We now know, for example, that the chiefdoms observed in the interior by the Spanish at the time of initial contact in the mid-sixteenth century, such as Cofitachequi or Coosa, were likely as large and as powerful as almost any that existed previously in the region. Very real changes did occur over the Southeast in the centuries before contact, such as a decline in mound construction and long-distance exchange and an increase in warfare and settlement nucleation. However, these trends are better explained as the long-term consequences of chiefly cycling than as the result of evolutionary collapse.

The post-contact Mississippian collapse cannot be fully understood through reference to the chiefdom organizational systems existing previously. The native social systems were simply overwhelmed by the combined effects of a variety of external forces, including introduced diseases and unavoidable competition with foreign populations possessing adaptationally advantageous technological, organizational, and ideological systems. Any long-term developmental trends among Mississippian chiefdoms, wherever these trends may have been headed, were truncated by European contact.

CONCLUSIONS

An excellent series of articles outlining the theoretical and methodological approaches brought to the study of Mississippian societies was published in a recent issue of *Southeastern Archaeology,* celebrating the fiftieth anniversary of the Southeastern Archaeological Conference. As Peebles (1990:25) noted in an article devoted exclusively to work on the Mississippian period, there has been "a sustained development of models of the Mississippian" in the region. These approaches have included the development of ecological/adaptationist models helping us to understand why certain locations within the landscape were repeatedly selected (e.g., Griffin 1967; Larson 1972; Smith 1978); analyses of population health, trauma, and demography, indicating the effects of organizational change on the lives of the inhabitants of these cultural systems (e.g., Hatch 1987; Milner et al. 1991; Powell 1988); and evaluations of the role of iconography and ritual in the maintenance of authority structures (e.g., Brown 1985; Knight 1986; Sears 1961, 1973). In the same issue Watson (1990:43–50) and Dunnell (1990:18–19) recounted some of the research themes and accomplishments of Southeastern archaeology, which have included advances in areas as diverse yet interrelated as artifact classification and chronology, cultural historical reconstruction, trade and exchange (particularly raw material sourcing studies), paleoclimatic reconstruction, and the reconstruction of prehistoric lifeways and subsistence systems.

The contributions of Southeastern archaeology to anthropological theory, particularly the exploration of cultural evolution, however, were not viewed as profound. For example, Dunnell (1990:19) described research on the subject of the origins of cultural complexity in the region as "little more than searching for surrogates to warrant calling one or another units a tribe, chiefdom, or state" with "no new paradigm on the horizon." As I have attempted to demonstrate in this paper, and as the other Southeastern papers in this volume make clear, this assessment is simply not correct, at least as far as the contemporary research picture is concerned.

Southeastern archaeologists are currently taking full advantage of the exceptional opportunities offered by the Mississippian archaeological record to explain political change in chiefdom-level societies. They are performing sophisticated analyses of extensive survey and excavation assemblages, with fine-grained cultural chronologies, and with detailed paleoenvironmental data. The results of this work indicate that the emergence, development, and collapse of chiefdoms within the Southeast were due to a variety of factors, of which climate, regional resource structure and physiography, and local and regional political conditions all appear to have played a part.

The question now confronting Southeastern archaeologists is where do we go from here? In this paper, I have attempted to show how the study of cultural complexity, particularly long-term change in chiefdom societies, can proceed. To model political change in the Late Prehis-

toric Southeast, we need to control for the effects of many variables at many scales of analysis. In applying the multiscalar approach, we must of necessity be multidisciplinary and diachronic.

From the topics briefly explored in this paper, we have seen that any explanatory model of Mississippian emergence and subsequent development must incorporate a wide range of variables. Some of these variables are the physical environment, including climate and regional physiographic and resource structure; demography, including the question of whether threshold values triggering change exist; subsistence, particularly the relationship between agricultural production and surplus mobilization; the nature of local and regional sociopolitical organization, including long-term historical or developmental trajectories; and internal and external exchange networks, particularly the location and operation of prestige-based systems.

We need to look at the big picture and the small, and let our observations from each analytical level inform our research on the other levels. Multiscalar analyses highlight the fact that the causes of culture change in chiefdom society are multifaceted and multivariate. That is, change comes about through the action of a wide range of factors operating at many levels or scales simultaneously, and whose measurable effects vary appreciably depending upon the scale selected for analysis. While some variables admittedly play a greater role than others, it is becoming clear that only rarely do single causal mechanisms bring about change. Accordingly, our analyses—and, ultimately, the theoretical models built from them—must encompass multiple causal mechanisms (i.e., independent as well as interrelated variables and lines of evidence) and at the same time be plausible, logical, and verifiable.

The Southeast is an ideal region for investigating long-term change in chiefdom level societies. If present work is any guide, it is clear that in the years ahead Southeastern archaeologists will be offering increasingly well grounded explanations of how and why the region's complex prestate societies evolved.

ACKNOWLEDGMENTS

My thanks to illustrator Julie Barnes Smith for drafting Figures 15.1–15.5.

See following pages for Tables 15.1–15.7.

Table 15.1. Evidence for Organizational Change at Different Spatial Scales in the Late Prehistoric Southeast

Archaeological Culture Area/ Locality	Household	Community	Chiefly Polity	Interpolity Region
American Bottom (including Cahokia and FAI 270 Project area)[1]	Replacement of small villages with dispersed households upon onset of Early Mississippian.	Increasingly formalized arrangements of houses around plazas, centralized storage facilities over course of the Emergent Mississippian (data from Range).	Main polity in place for ca. 250 years; outlying centers exhibit varied (often volatile) occupational histories. Residential areas replace ceremonial precincts prior to Cahokia abandonment. Population peaks in Stirling phase, but moundbuilding/ palisade construction continues if not increases prior to collapse.	Threat zone/symbolic tribute likely exacted from immense area (far beyond the area under direct control of the chiefdom). Elite social stratum developed early, in the Lohmann phase, w/ marked social differentiation (i.e., Mound 72).
Zebree/Parkin/ Nodena NE Arkansas/SE Missouri[2]	Small Late Woodland hamlets and villages replaced with nucleated villages in Emergent Mississippian.	Nucleated villages replaced by villages and dispersed hamlets in Middle Mississippian.	Direct placement of Late Woodland Community at Zebree site. Appearance of fortified nucleated towns and centers in Late Mississippian.	
Kincaid Southern Illinois[3]	Numerous dispersed farmsteads.		No secondary centers (perhaps suppressed by primary center).	
Angel/Caborn-Welborn Southwest Indiana[4]			Replacement of center/village settlement hierarchy with separate(?) villages.	
Pocahontas Region Mississippi[5]			Contemporaneous, contrasting mound burial patterns (mounds w/primary burials and few grave goods vs. mounds w/mostly isolated skulls and elaborate grave goods) suggest distinct social groups or segmentary organization.	Stability throughout sequence indicated; persistence of simple chiefdoms. Many small centers, no paramountcies.
Upper Tombigbee Chiefdoms Northeast Mississippi[6]	Most people live in dispersed farmsteads for much of the year. Population concentrations at local center infrequent, probably for ceremonial/ social functions, or during warfare.		Food storage/feasting at local center in vicinity of mound. Paired ceremonial(?) structures replaced by low platform mound/plaza complex in Early Mississippian (Summerville I). Stability throughout sequence indicated; persistence of simple chiefdoms.	Intensive interaction w/Moundville indicated in Summerville II/ III (extensive Moundville Engraved pottery, suppression(?) of fortifications). Area abandoned ca. A.D. 1600.
Moundville Western Alabama[7]	Nucleated Late Woodland (West Jefferson phase) villages replaced by dispersed farmsteads in Early Mississippian (Moundville I phase). Nucleated villages reappear in Late Mississippian (Moundville IV) following Moundville collapse.	Burial population at Moundville increases markedly as residential population declines from Moundville I to Moundville III. Burial population declines in late Moundville III times, coupled w/an expansion of cemeteries at outlying centers.	Occupation at paramount center declines markedly after Moundville I. (Dense residential zone about small center replaced by large, planned civic-ceremonial precinct). Superordinate segment of population apparently increases from ca. 1-2% to 5% between Moundville I and III.	Paramount chiefdom apparently stable for ca. 250 years. Threat zone likely over large area (far beyond the area under direct control of the chiefdom).

Table 15.1.   (continued)

Archaeological Culture Area/ Locality	Household	Community	Chiefly Polity	Interpolity Region
Etowah/Coosa Northwest Georgia[8]		Earth-embanked structures (council houses?) replaced by platform mound/plaza complex in Early Mississippian. Organized communities (houses around plazas) characterize Late Mississippian.	Mound centers <17 km or >31 km apart in Coosa polity. Centers rarely occupied for more than 100-150 years.	Occupation at Etowah interrupted twice (before and after Wilbanks phase complex chiefdom).
Savannah River Chiefdoms Georgia/South Carolina[9]	Household shape changes from round to square between Early and Middle Mississippian times.	Earth-embanked structures (council houses?) replaced by platform mound/plaza complex in Early Mississippian. Council houses present in villages in both simple and complex chiefdoms (data from Rucker's Bottom).	Council house replaces platform mound following chiefdom collapse (data from Irene). Major occupational shifts sometimes signaled by pronounced mound construction activity (i.e., placement of rock or shell coverings).	Rise and fall of complex chiefdoms evident over the course of the Mississippian. Much of basin abandoned after ca. A.D. 1450.
Lake Jackson/ Apalachee Northern Florida[10]		Council houses evident in both historic and late prehistoric period.	Simple chiefdoms in Early Mississippian, replaced by complex chiefdoms ca. A.D. 1200. No precursor Late Woodland groups; polity derived from Chattahoochee River area?	Main polity in place for ca. 300 years. Centers shifted location and some were abandoned in Lake Jackson Velda phase transition.
Cofitachequi Central South Carolina[11]			Historic 16th polity very complex in 1540, may have declined appreciably by 1566-1568 (De Soto, Pardo expeditions).	Contraction of polity in 15th and 16th centuries. Tributary/threat zone immense in A.D. 1540 (>300 km).
Town Creek Central North Carolina[12]			Vacant fortified center throughout period of occupation used for ceremony and protection?	Mississippian organization disappears after ca. A.D. 1400.

Notes for Tables 15.1–15.7

[1]Kelley 1990a; Milner 1986, 1990; Pauketat 1994; Pauketat and Emerson 1997

[2]Morse and Morse 1983

[3]Muller 1978, 1986a

[4]Green and Munson 1978; Muller 1986a

[5]Steponaitis 1991

[6]Blitz 1993; Steponaitis 1991:208–209

[7]Peebles 1986, 1987a,b; Powell 1988; Scarry 1986; Steponaitis 1991; Welch 1990a, 1996

[8]Hally and Rudolph 1986; Hally et al. 1990; King 1991; Smith 1987

[9]Anderson 1994b; Anderson et al. 1986; Anderson et al. 1995

[10]Scarry 1990a,b; 1996; Chapter 5

[11]DePratter 1991; Hudson 1990

[12]Coe 1995

Table 15.2. Evidence for Population Trends at Different Spatial Scales in the Late Prehistoric Southeast

Archaeological Culture Area/ Locality	Household	Community	Chiefly Polity	Interpolity Region
American Bottom (including Cahokia and FAI 270 Project area)[1]	House size increases over time, size increase dramatic in later Mississippian (date from Range).	Village size increases over course of Emergent Mississippian (data from Range). Villages replaced by center/ hamlet dichotomy in Lohmann phase.	Populations increasing through Early Mississippian, followed by (apparent) gradual decline; area largely depopulated after Sand Prairie Phase.	Largest population levels in Eastern Woodlands at peak? Area largely depopulated after ca. A.D. 1350–1400.
Zebree/Parkin/ Nodena NE Arkansas/SE Missouri[2]	Villages/hamlets centers in Early and Middle Mississippian.	Village size increases over the course of the Mississippian from ca. 150 to several hundred or more.	Nucleated towns replace dispersed villages/hamlets in Late Mississippian.	Dramatic abandonment of SE Missouri and much of NE Arkansas's western lowlands after ca. A.D. 1450.
Kincaid Southern Illinois[3]	Hamlets of from 1–3 houses each widespread.	Groups of 8–15 houses comprise small hamlets or villages.	Polity population ca. 4,000?	
Angel/Caborn-Welborn Southwest Indiana[4]	Hamlets, small villages (1 ha) in Late Woodland.	Center, large and small villages in Angel phase replaced by discrete villages in Caborn-Welborn phase.	Angel center ca. 1,000 people; large village ca. 350 people; small 25-75 people; hamlets 10-15 people.	Caborn-Welborn phase large and small villages replace Angel phase central town/dispersed settlement system.
Pocahontas Region Mississippi[5]	Most population lives in small hamlets 0.1 to 0.8 ha in extent.		Small numbers of people lived near mound centers.	No evidence for Late Woodland or Contact era settlement.
Upper Tombigbee Chiefdoms Northeast Mississippi[6]	Movement between farmstead/local centers fluid. Farmsteads evince lesser degree of site permanence than local centers.	No villages.	Population at local center (Lubbub Creek) very low (Summerville I: 5-30 people) (Summerville II/III: 25-90 people) (Summerville IV: 10-35 people).	
Moundville Western Alabama[7]	Dispersed households become widespread and replace small nucleated villages with Mississippian emergence.	Nucleated villages reappear in late Moundville III, as Moundville center declines.	Moundville resident population declines markedly after Moundville I (based on sheet midden debris). Moundville burial population increases markedly after Moundville I.	Depopulation of areas to north and northeast w/emergence of Moundville complex chiefdom.
Etowah/Coosa Northwest Georgia[8]		Most towns had between 200–300 people present.	Individual chiefdoms composed of 4-7 towns in Coosa paramountcy. Paramount chiefdom composed of ca. seven simple/ complex chiefdoms.	Individual chiefdoms of the Coosa paramountcy occupied by up to ca. 5,000 people.
Savannah River Chiefdoms Georgia/South Carolina[9]	Hamlets throughout drainage during Early/Middle Mississippian era.	Villages ca. 1 ha., 120–150 people (data from Rucker's Bottom). Village size increased ca. 25% over course of Middle Mississippian (data from Rucker's Bottom).	Minor centers ca. 1-2 ha in extent; major centers ca. 2-5 ha in extent.	Growth in number of sites and centers from Early to Middle Mississippian in drainage, marked decline thereafter.
Lake Jackson/ Apalachee Northern Florida[10]	Appreciable population living in dispersed farmsteads.	Numerous scattered settlements tied to major town/ ceremonial centrals.	Total polity population estimated at between ca. 10,000 and 30,000.	Gradual population increase over time.

Table 15.2.   (continued)

Archaeological Culture Area/ Locality	Household	Community	Chiefly Polity	Interpolity Region
Cofitachequi Central South Carolina[11]	Poor data, dispersed farmsteads suggested in some periods.	Poor data; small (1–2 ha) villages observed near major centers.	Large central towns (up to 20 ha).	Population contraction during Late Mississippian, abandonment of outlying centers and areas.
Town Creek Central North Carolina[12]		Small (1–2 ha) villages away from local center.	Small local center (ca. 2 ha).	Chiefdom/area abandoned after Middle Mississippian.

[1-12]See notes for Table 15.1

Table 15.3. Evidence for Agricultural Intensification at Different Spatial Scales in the Late Prehistoric Southeast

Archaeological Culture Area/ Locality	Household	Community	Chiefly Polity	Interpolity Region
American Bottom (including Cahokia and FAI 270 Project area)[1]	Increasing use of starchy seeds in Late Woodland. Maize use increases markedly after ca. A.D. 750.		Intensified maize production paces Mississippian Emergence.	
Zebree/Parkin/ Nodena NE Arkansas/SE Missouri[2]	Increased species diversity evident in Emergent Mississippian sites.	Corn evident in Emergent Mississippian but not a major dietary constituent until Middle Mississippian times (trace element data).	Population skeletal health better in Emergent Mississippian populations than in later times.	
Kincaid Southern Illinois[3]	Hamlets occupied much of the year with evidence for highly diversified resource exploitation.			
Angel/Caborn-Welborn Southwest Indiana[4]				
Pocahontas Region Mississippi[5]			Agricultural intensification assumed to accompany chiefdom emergence.	
Upper Tombigbee Chiefdoms Northeast Mississippi[6]	Maize intensification begins in Late Woodland (Miller III), becomes marked in Early Mississippian (Summerville I). Maize use declines, nut use increases Late Mississippian (Summerville IV). Late Woodland food resources diversified, procurement becomes more focused in Early Mississippian.	No villages.	Late Woodland populations evince greater dietary stress than Early Mississippian populations. Population skeletal health good over all Mississippian phases. Hamlet/local center faunal data (deer element distributions) indicate provisioning of elites(?) at centers.	
Moundville Western Alabama[7]	Maize common at hamlets.	Faunal data from Moundville and farmsteads (deer element distributions) indicate provisioning of elites at centers. Trace element evidence suggests elites may have eaten more meat than commoners.	Population skeletal health good over all Mississippian phases (over both elites and commoners). Considerable dietary stress indicated following collapse of Moundville polity (Alabama River Phase).	
Etowah/Coosa Northwest Georgia[8]			Population skeletal health good over all Mississippian phases (over both elites and commoners).	
Savannah River Chiefdoms Georgia/South Carolina[9]	Maize intensification appears with Mississippian. Maize is not present in any quantity in the Late Woodland.	Increasingly focused procurement of game over course of Mississippian (data from Rucker's Bottom). Maize use decline, nut use increases over course of Mississippian (data from Rucker's Bottom).	Maize use declines at Irene with organizational decentralization. Commoner population skeletal health improves w/emergence of complex chiefdom (data from Rucker's Bottom).	Spring rainfall variation apparently linked to crop yields/political stability of local societies. Evidence for forest clearing indicated through pollen, wood charcoal diversity data (data from Beaverdam Creek).

Table 15.3. *(continued)*

Archaeological Culture Area/ Locality	Household	Community	Chiefly Polity	Interpolity Region
		Maize use paces Mississippian emergence, declines w/collapse (data from Irene).	Commoner population skeletal health poor compared with elites at nearby center (data from Rucker's Bottom, Beaverdam Creek).	
Lake Jackson/ Apalachee Northern Florida[10]			Maize use appears in Late Woodland, but does not become important until Early Mississippian.	
Cofitachequi Central South Carolina[11]			Maize common in Middle and Late Mississippian contexts at major center (data from Mulberry).	
Town Creek Central North Carolina[12]			Maize evident at most site types.	

[1-12]See notes for Table 15.1

Table 15.4.   Evidence for Prestige Goods Exchange at Different Spatial Scales in the Late Prehistoric Southeast

Archaeological Culture Area/ Locality	Household	Community	Chiefly Polity	Interpolity Region
American Bottom (including Cahokia and FAI 270 Project area)[1]		Extralocal pottery and other materials found at large and small sites through later Mississippian periods.	Elite burials characterized by elaborate grave goods, many of extralocal raw materials.	Ramey Incised pottery found in low incidence over a large area. Greatest interaction in Emergent Mississippian and Stirling phases.
Zebree/Parkin/ Nodena NE Arkansas/SE Missouri[2]			Extensive shell bead blanket found on elite burial at Zebree.	
Kincaid Southern Illinois[3]				
Angel/Caborn-Welborn Southwest Indiana[4]				
Pocahontas Region Mississippi[5]			Extralocal material incidence and diversity greatest in Early Mississippian; marked decline after ca. A.D. 1200.	Rise of Moundville to east and Lake George and Anna to west may have constrained prestige goods exchange.
Upper Tombigbee Chiefdoms Northeast Mississippi[6]	Shell beads are mostly of local shell in Late Woodland, majority are of marine shell in Early Mississippian Finewares (and rarely, extralocal wares) occur at both hamlets and local center.	No villages.	Prestige goods treated as wealth items in Early Mississippian, do not appear restricted to superordinate segment. Prestige goods incidence in burials declines after Early Mississippian at both farmsteads and local center.	Rise of Moundville to east appears to have constrained prestige goods exchange.
Moundville Western Alabama[7]	Prestige good use appears restricted exclusively to centers.	Extralocal shell and greenstone use increases just prior to emergence of single mound sites; prestige goods found at these sites during the Early Missippian. Extralocal pottery incidence declines after Moundville I.	Prestige goods incidence in burials increases during Early Mississippian; peaks at Moundville I/II transition; declines during Moundville II/III; gone by Moundville IV. Elaborate prestige goods serve as insignia of rank (i.e., copper).	Nonlocal pottery minimal from east, suggesting major cultural boundary; nonlocal pottery more common from areas to west and lower midwest. Rise of Moundville tied to reduction in prestige goods exchange in smaller surrounding chiefdoms.
Etowah/Coosa Northwest Georgia[8]			Elaborate prestige goods serve as insignia of rank (i.e., copper).	Moundville pottery nonexistent, suggesting major cultural boundary. Etowah ceramics earliest Mississippian evidence at many sites over South Appalachian area.
Savannah River Chiefdoms Georgia/South Carolina[9]		Shell beads, copper artifacts found with elites at centers; shell beads, more mundane items found with commoner burials at villages and hamlets.	Additional mound stages constructed at several centers following a marked decline in prestige goods incidence in burials (data from Hollywood, Chauga, Beaverdam Creek).	Pottery from western Southeast found with Hollywood burials.
Lake Jackson/ Apalachee Northern Florida[10]			Increasing number and diversity of extralocal goods in burials evident at Lake Jackson	Interregional trade in prestige goods prominent ca. A.D. 1100-1200, trade disrupted ca. A.D. 1400.

Table 15.4.   (continued)

Archaeological Culture Area/ Locality	Household	Community	Chiefly Polity	Interpolity Region
			in Middle Mississippian, suggesting increasing elite power.	
Cofitachequi Central South Carolina[11]			Elaborate carved mica artifacts found at major center (data from Mulberry).	
Town Creek Central North Carolina[12]				

[1-12]See notes for Table 15.1

Table 15.5.   Evidence for Craft Specialization at Different Spatial Scales in the Late Prehistoric Southeast

Archaeological Culture Area/ Locality	Household	Community	Chiefly Polity	Interpolity Region
American Bottom (including Cahokia and FAI 270 Project area)[1]	Part-time household production of specialized craft goods indicated, including use of extralocal materials.		Ambiguous evidence for specialized production at centers.	Major regional center/node for prestige goods exchange.
Zebree/Parkin/ Nodena NE Arkansas/SE Missouri[2]		Bead manufacture restricted to areas within communities (data from Zebree).	Communities might produce specialized products (i.e., salt collection).	
Kincaid Southern Illinois[3]				
Angel/Caborn-Welborn Southwest Indiana[4]				
Pocahontas Region Mississippi[5]				
Upper Tombigbee Chiefdoms Northeast Mississippi[6]	Household production of chunky stones indicated.	No villages.	Fineware, greenstone, and shell bead manufacture appears restricted top local center.	
Moundville Western Alabama[7]	Household manufacture of shell beads widespread in Late Woodland (as suggested by microdrill occurrence).	Extralocal goods processed at centers (greenstone, copper, mica, and graphite).	Engraved vessels may be made solely at major center; most specialized production restricted to major center in Moundville II/III phases.	Major regional center/node for prestige goods exchange.
Etowah/Coosa Northwest Georgia[8]		Citico gorget co-extensive w/ Coosa; may indicate extent of marriage/alliance network.	Manufacture of copper prestige goods at major center indicated.	Major regional center/node in prestige goods exchange network?
Savannah River Chiefdoms Georgia/South Carolina[9]	No evidence for craft specialization.	No evidence for craft specialization (local manufacture of pottery, stone tools indicated).	Production of carved soapstone pipes appears restricted to local center (data from Beaverdam Creek).	
Lake Jackson/ Apalachee Northern Florida[10]			No evidence for standardized production of shell beads.	
Cofitachequi Central South Carolina[11]			Evidence for mica processing found to be highly restricted in central community (data from Mulberry).	Major regional center/node in prestige goods exchange network.
Town Creek Central North Carolina[12]				

[1-12]See notes for Table 15.1

238

Table 15.6. Evidence for Warfare at Different Spatial Scales in the Late Prehistoric Southeast

Archaeological Culture Area/ Locality	Household	Community	Chiefly Polity	Interpolity Region
American Bottom (including Cahokia and FAI 270 Project area)[1]			Cahokia center proper fortified throughout much of its existence.	Extent of Cahokia domination over surrounding macroregion uncertain; likely cast a long "threat" shadow.
Zebree/Parkin/ Nodena NE Arkansas/SE Missouri[2]		Fortifications around earliest Mississippian community; suggestion that replacement of Late Woodland populations/ organizations occurred (data from Zebree).	Fortifications (ditch and stockade lines) around major Late Mississippian communities.	Intensive competition between centers documented ethnohistorically.
Kincaid Southern Illinois[3]		Storage in underground pits in Early Mississippian (concealed?).	Main site palisaded.	Indication that household populations converge on main center during periods of conflict (large area at center defended, more than the small resident population would need).
Angel/Caborn-Welborn Southwest Indiana[4]			Angel site palisaded; no clear evidence for fortification in Caborn-Welborn?	Outlying populations converge on center during periods of conflict?
Pocahontas Region Mississippi[5]				Complex chiefdom formation constrained by other such societies?
Upper Tombigbee Chiefdoms Northeast Mississippi[6]	Late Woodland burials exhibit high incidence of trauma (parry fractures, embedded points); much lower in Early Mississippian.	No villages.	Local center had a bastioned palisade in Summerville I, this disappeared in the Summerville II/III; fortifications reappear in Summerville IV. Miller III (Late Woodland) storage in concealed pits; Summerville I (Early Mississippian) storage in aboveground corn cribs.	Outlying populations converage on center during periods of conflict?
Moundville Western Alabama[7]	Late Woodland burials exhibit high incidence of trauma; this decreased in Moundville I through early Moundville III, then increased again.	Elite burials exhibit less evidence for trauma (injury) than nonelites at Moundville.	Moundville extensively fortified from Moundville I through III phases. Nucleated villages reappear in late Moundville III, possibly for defense.	Moundville appears to have dominated polities (i.e., had a large threat zone) over an appreciable area; suppression of nearby societies indicated.
Etowah/Coosa Northwest Georgia[8]		Fortifications around 16th century towns (data from King Site).	Etowah center massively fortified with ditch and bastioned stockade.	Rivalry with Alabama chiefdoms documented ethnohistorically.
Savannah River Chiefdoms Georgia/South Carolina[9]	Hamlets in lower/central Savannah relocated away from major drainages w/rise of complex chiefdoms nearby.	Fortifications appear, become more elaborate at previously unfortified village prior to its abandonment (data from Rucker's Bottom).	Fortifications at local centers noted early, late in occupational histories (data from Irene, Chauga, Tugalo).	Abandonment of central, lower basin after A.D. 1450

(continues on overleaf)

Table 15.6. *(continued)*

Archaeological Culture Area/ Locality	Household	Community	Chiefly Polity	Interpolity Region
		Storage concealed in underground pits prior to site abandonment (data from Rucker's Bottom).	Evidence for increased incidence of trauma prior to abandonment of Irene.	
Lake Jackson/ Apalachee Northern Florida[10]	Dispersed, unfortified hamlets.	Violent factional competition between members of the nobility documented ethnohistorically.	Major centers were unfortified.	Chiefdom was feared and respected over a wide area in the 16th century, as documented ethnohistorically.
Cofitachequi Central South Carolina[11]		Suggestion for fortifications around local villages (data from Ferry Landing).	Fortification ditch at major center (data from Mulberry).	Rivalry with chiefdoms in central Georgia (Ocute) documented ethnohistorically.
Town Creek Central North Carolina[12]		Fortifications around outlying villages.	Fortifications around local center.	Furthest expansion of Mississippian to the north along the Atlantic Slope.

[1-12]See notes for Table 15.1

Table 15.7. The Emergence and Collapse of Mississippian Chiefdom Organizational Forms in the Late Prehistoric Southeast

Archaeological Culture	Date of Initial Chiefdom Appearance	Date of Ultimate Collapse/Abandonment
Cahokia (including FAI 270 Project)[1]	ca. A.D. 850–900 (American Bottom Area)	ca. A.D. 1300 (Cahokia proper)
Zebree/Parkin/Nodena NE Arkansas/SE Missouri[2]	ca. A.D. 900–950 (Zebree)	Post Contact (16th century?) (Parkin/Nodena)
Kincaid Southern Illinois[3]	ca. A.D. 900–1000	ca. A.D. 1500
Angel/Caborn-Welborn Southwest Indiana[4]	ca. A.D. 1950 (Angel)	ca. A.D. 1700 (Caborn-Welborn)
Pocahontas Region Mississippi[5]	ca. A.D. 1000	ca. A.D. 1500?
Upper Tombigbee Chiefdoms Northeast Mississippi[6]	ca. A.D. 1000–1050	European Contact?
Moundville Western Alabama[7]	ca. A.D. 1000 (Black Warrior drainage)	ca. A.D. 1500 (Moundville)
Etowah/Coosa Northwest Georgia[8]	ca. A.D. 1100–1150	ca. A.D. 1350 (Etowah) ca. A.D. 1565–1600 (Coosa)
Savannah River Chiefdoms Georgia/South Carolina[9]	ca. A.D. 1100–1150	ca. A.D. 1450 (central and lower basin)
Lake Jackson/Apalachee Northern Florida[10]	ca. A.D. 1050–1100	ca. A.D. 1450 (paramount center)
Cofitachequi Central South Carolina[11]	ca. A.D. 1150–1200	ca. A.D. 1600? (Cofitachequi)
Town Creek Central North Carolina[12]	ca. A.D. 1150–1200	ca. A.D. 1400

[1-12]See notes for Table 15.1

CHAPTER SIXTEEN

Multiscalar Analyses of Middle-Range Societies:
Comparing the Late Prehistoric Southwest and Southeast

Jill E. Neitzel

David G. Anderson

Iɴ ᴡʜᴀᴛ ᴡᴀʏꜱ ᴡᴇʀᴇ ꜱᴏᴄɪᴏᴘᴏʟɪᴛɪᴄᴀʟ ᴅᴇᴠᴇʟᴏᴘᴍᴇɴᴛꜱ in the Late Prehistoric U.S. Southwest and Southeast similar? In what ways were they different? Addressing these two questions has been a primary goal of this volume. Another goal has been to demonstrate how a multiscalar analytical approach can be used to address such questions. The results, as seen in the various papers in this volume, are significant not only for what they tell us about the prehistories of the Southwest and Southeast, respectively. They are also significant for what they reveal about the regularities and diversity of middle-range societies and the process of cultural evolution.

This chapter summarizes the results of the Southwest-Southeast comparisons presented in the preceding chapters and considers the broader implications of those results. It begins by contrasting the two areas' archaeological research traditions. Next, the cultural similarities and differences evident at different spatial scales are summarized. Then, the possible effects of the two areas' environmental characteristics are considered. Finally, the implications that Southwest-Southeast comparisons have for the study of middle-range societies and cultural evolution in general are discussed.

Archaeological Research Traditions

Southwestern and Southeastern archaeology share several general similarities in their historical development. For both, the first century of research was dominated initially by the collection of museum specimens and then by culture historical concerns. Throughout this time, field-work in both areas was directed primarily to the biggest, most spectacular ruins, an emphasis that hindered recognition and interpretation of cultural variability. Consequently, the kinds of sites where most prehistoric peoples lived (e.g., hamlets and villages) were ignored. On those rare occasions when sociopolitical organization was considered, early researchers in both areas generally saw late prehistoric societies as being similar to contemporaneous indigenous societies—that is, egalitarian.

The past two decades of research in both the Southwest and Southeast have seen increased emphasis on the investigation of sociopolitical organization, an effort facilitated by the vast amount of new fieldwork that has occurred over this interval. In both areas this interest has prompted a reevaluation of earlier conclusions about egalitarianism and a greater concern for intra- and intersocietal variation. As a result, both Southwestern and Southeastern archaeologists have been able to identify evidence of organizational complexity in their respective areas. The existence of chiefdoms in many parts of the Southeast is now almost universally accepted, and the presence of similarly elaborate organizational forms has been inferred for some parts of the Southwest. More recently, the most extreme claims for complexity in both areas (i.e., for state-like organizational forms) have themselves begun to be reevaluated, as seen in current work at Chaco and Cahokia.

While they share these general similarities, Southwestern and Southeastern archaeological research traditions differ in two significant ways. The first concerns their reliance on ethnography *vs.* ethnohistory. The second involves culture area systematics.

Ethnography vs. Ethnohistory

Early interpretations about the supposed egalitarianism of Late Prehistoric Southwestern societies were derived primarily from ethnographic analogy. The justification for this use of analogy was the egalitarian architectural continuity observed in the northern Southwest between the Prehistoric and Historic periods. The assumption was made that this architectural continuity reflected organizational continuity as well. Thus, ethnographic descriptions of modern Southwestern groups as living in socially and politically independent communities with an egalitarian organization were thought to apply to prehistoric groups as well. However, as Southwestern archaeologists have become increasingly interested in prehistoric sociopolitical organization, the validity of this assumption has been questioned. A primary reason has been the recognition of archaeological evidence for complexity, such as site hierarchies, burial differentiation, high population densities, intensive agricultural systems, and specialized forms of public architecture, all of which are lacking ethnographically.

Whereas ethnographic studies have had a significant impact on Southwestern archaeology, ethnohistoric studies have not. In fact, it has only been recently that Southwestern archaeologists have begun systematically to examine early historic accounts of indigenous peoples. Unfortunately, these documents are often vague and contradictory with key variables of interest to archaeologists being poorly described. In addition, they share with Southwestern ethnographic accounts the inadequacy of dealing with societies that were significantly less complex than some evidenced archaeologically.

Unlike the Southwest, the role of ethnography in archaeological interpretations of the late prehistoric Southeast has until quite recently been virtually nonexistent. The reason is that even the earliest ethnographies were typically done of displaced peoples whose cultures had been drastically altered by several centuries of Euroamerican domination, extermination, and removal. These alterations undoubtedly contributed to the absence of any obvious continuity, architectural or otherwise, between prehistoric groups and those studied by ethnographers.

While Southeastern archaeologists have virtually ignored ethnography, they have relied heavily on ethnohistory. In marked contrast with the Southwest, the Southeast's ethnohistoric record is enviably rich with extensive accounts dating back in some areas to the period of initial European contact in the sixteenth century. Early ethnohistoric studies, as exemplified by the writings of John R. Swanton (e.g., 1911, 1922, 1946), tended to conflate several centuries of accounts. They concluded that, with the notable exception of unusual cases like the Natchez, Southeastern societies at contact were egalitarian. However, as interest in sociopolitical organization has grown and archaeological evidence for organizational complexity has accumulated, researchers have begun to study the available ethnohistoric documents more systematically and critically.

The picture of a more complex sociopolitical organization drawn from the Southeast's earliest ethnohistoric accounts has been consistent with the archaeological record but with the added advantage of containing information about individuals and activities impossible to detect archaeologically. Thus, for example, the Southeastern ethnohistoric record has provided insights into such topics as the motivations and machinations of preeminent leaders and how polities sometimes joined to form everything from loose confederations to complex/paramount chiefdoms. This kind of information has given Southeastern archaeologists a much more detailed understanding of late prehistoric sociopolitical organization than their Southwestern counterparts who, at least for their most complex societies, must rely on the archaeological record alone.

Culture Area Systematics

Another significant difference in Southwestern and Southeastern archaeological research traditions concerns the definition of culture areas. Late Prehistoric period societies occupying the geographic entity of the U.S. Southeast have typically been given one cultural designation—Mississippian. While some cultural variation has been documented, the most notable cases occur on the margins of the region (e.g., Caddoan, Calusa, Timucua, Siouan-Algonkian), and have not (except perhaps the Caddo) been considered part of the Mississippian phenomenon. Thus, Southeastern archaeologists often use the terms Mississippian and Late Prehistoric Southeast interchangeably.

For the geographic entity of the Southwest, in contrast, no single cultural designation has been applied, and the same is true for the area's most complex societies. Instead, archaeologists have subdivided the Southwest into a number of discrete culture areas or traditions, of which the Anasazi, Mogollon, and Hohokam are the best known.

This difference in classification raises a series of related questions. Does it reflect fundamental differences in prehistoric culture, including sociopolitical organization, within different parts of the Southwest? Or is it simply the product of different archaeological research traditions? If the difference in classification does in fact reflect prehistoric behavior, then why did late prehistoric Southwestern cultural traditions never attain the same geographic extent as the Mississippian cultural tradition in the Southeast? This question is especially pertinent to the underlying structure and objectives of this volume, because it suggests that the most informative macroscale for Southwest-Southeast comparisons may not be between the Southwest as a whole and the Southeast as a whole but rather between individual Southwestern cultural traditions and the entire Southeast.

Multiscalar Comparisons

The multiscalar comparisons of the preceding chapters have revealed some general similarities and several fundamental differences in the societies of the late prehistoric Southwest and Southeast. These similarities and differences are summarized here for the range of scales considered in this volume: the great town, the polity, the macroregion, and beyond.

Great Towns

Big sites in both the Late Prehistoric Southwest and Southeast had large scale public architecture that would have required the mobilization of group labor to build. In both areas, these structures, or the empty space formed by them, served as the centerpieces of settlement layout, giving all big sites a central focus. These structures also created a cultural landscape within which sociopolitical and ceremonial activities occurred. As discussed by Holley and Lekson (Chapter 3), further similarities also characterize both Mississippian and Classic period Hohokam sites as well as the Pueblo Bonito complex and Cahokia.

Together these similarities are balanced by two fundamental differences. The first concerns spatial and temporal variation. Throughout the Southeast during the entire Late Prehistoric period, an essentially similar site plan of mounds erected around a plaza was duplicated at all major settlements. The only marked variation was in various aspects of size—sites varied in their physical extent, numbers of mounds, sizes of mounds, and numbers of occupants.

In contrast, the Late Prehistoric Southwest was never characterized by a single site plan. There were instead regionally distinct architectural forms and layouts whose distributions generally correlated with the Southwest's major environmental subdivisions. Furthermore, shifts in architecture and layout occurred through time, with the most dramatic example being the transition from the Sedentary to Classic period Hohokam.

The second difference in Southwestern and Southeastern big sites lies in the function of their large scale public architecture. Throughout the Southwest, the function was social. Ballcourts, plazas, kivas, great kivas, and even perhaps great houses all served as arenas of communal ritual. Except for Classic period platform mounds, unambiguous evidence for residential differentiation was generally absent. In contrast, the focus of public architecture throughout the Southeast was elite individuals, and there is substantial evidence for residential differentiation. The layout of platform temple and mortuary mounds around plazas was intended to highlight the position of the elite both in life and death.

Polities

The big sites in both the Southwest and Southeast were part of multi-site organizational systems that in this volume have been called polities. These were the maximal independent sociopolitical units to which people belonged. The similarities in studying Southwestern and Southeastern polities are both methodological and substantive. Methodologically, archaeologists in both regions confront similar difficulties in interpreting site hierarchies and defining polity boundaries. Substantively, researchers have documented several similarities in the two regions' polities. Economically, polities in both areas depended primarily on intensive agriculture, involving the same nonindigenous cultigens of corn, beans, and squash; local domesticates, while assuming greater importance in some areas, do not appear to have been critical to the provisioning of these societies. In both areas, significant labor investments were made in constructing public architecture. In both, craft production seems to have been at most a part-time activity, producing both sumptuary and utilitarian goods. Finally, in both, the polities that arose during the Late Prehistoric period did not last. Rather, they emerged, existed for some length of time, and then declined until they ultimately disappeared.

Underlying these general similarities are three significant differences: one involves the differential emphasis in social ranking, another relates to variation in basic polity organization; and the last concerns the reasons for polity collapse.

Evidence for ranking

The social relationships underlying Southeastern polities were characterized by a pronounced emphasis on ranking, and in the Southwest they were not. Consequently, the node at which the polity was expressed differed. In the Southeast, it was through the office of the chief; in the Southwest it was through allegiance to places or communities and was reinforced through collective ceremonials. These differences can be viewed as those between polities and ritualities, labels that highlight how the primary integrating mechanisms in the two regions differed.

In the Southeast, the archaeological evidence for social ranking is highly visible, pervasive, and redundant. High status individuals and their families were obviously and repeatedly distinguished from commoners in where they lived, what they wore, and how they were buried. As mentioned in the preceding great town comparisons, public space and architecture at Southeastern centers were clearly associated with elites, serving to highlight their special position both in life and death. Typically, these individuals and their families resided on or near temple/domiciliary mounds and were interred in elaborate mortuary facilities (i.e., mounds, temples, or special cemetery areas) along with a variety of status markers and consistent symbols of leadership. Such mortuary differentiation had a long tradition in the prehistoric Southeast, with perhaps the best-known precedents being Hopewellian and Adena burial practices.

The archaeological evidence for social ranking in the late prehistoric Southeast has been corroborated by ethnohistoric research, which has also documented a high degree of competition for political power among contact-era Mississippian elites. While power and status were to varying degrees ascribed to certain family lines, who actually assumed preeminent positions among those eligible was determined in large part by achievement. The power of successful leaders was considerable—they could mobilize labor, control agricultural surplus, live sumptuously, and even (in some societies) enforce or oversee human sacrifice in special circumstances. These powers made leadership positions highly desirable, and provided the motivation for intense competition.

In stark contrast with the Southeast, evidence for social differentiation in the Southwest is infrequent, inconsistent, and relatively hard to discern archaeologically. Only a few cases (e.g., Chaco, the Classic period Hohokam, and Paquimé) exhibit any clear evidence for ranking and this evidence is usually not redundant. As was described previously, most Southwestern public architecture had a community orientation rather than the obvious and widespread association with elites as in the Southeast. The only Southwestern case with clearly identified elite residences is the Classic period Hohokam. Archaeologists disagree about whether or not Chacoan great houses were elite residences; similarly the evidence from Paquimé is ambiguous.

While there are a few high status burials in the Southwest, they are notable because they are rare. Only at Paquimé is there a robust pattern of ascribed status. The few rich burials at Classic period Hohokam sites, Chaco, and Paquimé are associated with public architecture, but because they are so few, the association does not seem to have been as institutionalized as in the Southeast. None of the Southwestern cases exhibit consistent status markers and symbols of leadership as seen throughout the Southeast.

In general, marked social differentiation in the late prehistoric Southwest seems to have been rare and relatively short-lived. When it did occur, there is varying evidence for control of agricultural surplus and the ability to mobilize labor. The evidence for human sacrifice is significantly less than in the Southeast. While the overall emphasis seems to have been egalitarian, competition for power probably did occur but apparently more infrequently and to a lesser degree than in the Southeast.

Polity organization

Southwestern and Southeastern polities also differed in the extent to which their basic organization varied. Because of the common site plan found throughout the Southeast, archaeologists have been able to apply one model of polity organization throughout the area. This building block model has as its basic unit a center and its surrounding villages and hamlets. It varies primarily in how multiples of the basic unit are combined. Simple polities consisted only of the basic unit—the center and its surrounding sites. In more complex polities, one of the basic units dominated others through a vertically-organized administrative and social hierarchy.

A building block model, employing centers and their surrounding villages and hamlets, can also be applied to polities throughout the Southwest. However, in the Southwest, the model is characterized by two kinds of variation not evident in the Southeast—one in the content of the basic building blocks and the other in the way building blocks combine to form polities. Due to the previously discussed variation in Southwestern site plans, the basic unit of the building block model differs depending on location and time period. In addition, unlike the Southeast, clear evidence for vertically organized, administrative and social hierarchies occurs infrequently. The more common pattern is what Johnson (1980) has called a sequential hierarchy in which power and control relations are spread horizontally. This difference in vertical *vs.* horizontal power relations is clearly related to the differential emphasis on social ranking in the two regions.

Polity collapse

In both the Late Prehistoric Southwest and Southeast, polities emerged, existed for some length of time, and then declined until they ultimately disappeared. The ranges of polity duration in the two areas varied. In the Southeast, durations range from roughly 100 to 400 years. A relatively simple polity oriented around a single mound center might last just a few generations. At the other extreme, the most complex polities, which encompassed a hierarchy of mound centers, sometimes lasted several centuries.

In the Southwest, the range of polity duration was greater. The minimum duration was probably less than in the Southeast, lasting perhaps only a generation or two. For the most complex polities, the minimum spans of less than 300 years proposed for Chaco and Paquimé fall within the high end of the range defined for Southeastern polities. However, some Hohokam centers, and probably their associated polities, have documented spans of 500 or more years, which exceed the maximum duration of the most complex Southeastern polities. The longevity of these Hohokam polities can probably be attributed to their deep sedentism, resulting from the tethering of irrigation canals.

Southwestern and Southeastern archaeologists have used different labels and proposed different explanations for polity collapse, and associated population shifts, in their respective areas. Southwestern archaeologists have used the term abandonment to characterize the depopulation of various sites, localities, and regions in the post-A.D. 1150 period. Proposed explanations cite various combinations of interrelated variables, such as climate change, resource exhaustion, and population and organizational growth beyond the minimal carrying capacity of highly variable environments.

Southeastern archaeologists have generally characterized polity collapse and its associated population shifts as the result of chiefly cycling. According to this explanation, centers and polities emerged, grew, and declined for a variety of (largely) interrelated reasons, of which the most important was elite competition for power. This competition within and among chiefly factions in the region's centers and polities is thought to have occurred throughout the Southeast.

Is Southwestern abandonment the same as Southeastern chiefly cycling? We would say for the most part no. In the Southwest, the greater emphasis on group solidarity rather than on individual competition for power together with the very few clear instances of complex polities would have made cycling, such as seen in the Southeast, less likely. This is not to say that cycling never occurred. Again, the issue is scale. While chiefly cycling was probably not a macroregional process characterizing the Southwest as a whole, it may have been an important component of change in areas associated with complex polities with multiple centers, such as Chaco and the Classic period Hohokam.

Macroregional Interaction

Macroregional interaction in the Southeast was qualitatively different from that in the Southwest in both its geographic extent, intensity, and historical precedents. The Late Prehistoric Southeast comprised a single, large macroregion that contained numerous, clearly hierarchical polities whose proximity with one another and resulting interactions created a politically complex and dynamic cultural landscape. Not only was this macroregion extensive, but the interactions comprising it were redundant. There was cultural unity as evidenced by common architectural plans and artifactual styles, there was religious unity provided by Mississippian ceremonialism and iconography (as exemplified by the Southeastern Ceremonial Complex), and there was long-distance exchange of both status and religious goods. Within this widespread pattern, competition and conflict added a dimension of volatility to the interactions among polities. Intensive and extensive macroregional interaction had a long history in the Southeast, dating as far back as Middle Archaic times (8,000–6,000 B.P.), with pronounced peaks during the Poverty Point, Hopewellian, and Mississippian eras.

In comparison to the Southeast, macroregional ties at the scale of the Southwest as a whole were weaker and more tenuous. Only one kind of linkage, the long-distance exchange of status goods, seems to have been operating throughout the Southwest, and only some of this interaction appears shaped by members of the region's small number of more complex polities. Unlike the Southeast, these pan-Southwestern exchange networks of the Late Prehistoric period had a short history. They were not in place until the first millennium A.D. and had no earlier precedents.

It is only when one considers particular areas within the Southwest, rather than the Southwest as a whole, that evidence for more intensive and redundant interactions can be seen. It is at this smaller scale that the cultural uniformity that characterized the Mississippian world existed and that cults developed. If polity boundaries are defined conservatively, it is at this scale that regular interactions among at least a moderate number of polities can be seen. For example, if great houses were the centers of independent polities, rather than components in a unified Chacoan system, then their close proximity may have made interactions among them quite dynamic and volatile. The same may be true of relations between the Hohokam platform mound sites of the Phoenix Basin.

Beyond the Southwest and Southeast

Some polities participating in the Late Prehistoric Southwestern and Southeastern macroregions had more distant ties as well. These broader connections consisted almost entirely of long-distance exchange. Various Southwestern polities traded with populations in northwest Mexico, California, the Great Basin, and the western Plains. In the Southeast, various Mississippian polities traded with groups in south-central Florida, the south Atlantic seaboard, the upper Midwest, and the eastern Plains.

The area that had the greatest and most long lived influence on the Southwest was Mesoamerica. The earliest direct evidence of these broader ties is the introduction of Mesoamerican cultigens before 1000 B.C., and continued contacts of varying duration and intensity occurred throughout the following millennia resulting in a list of Southwestern-Mesoamerican similarities (artifactual, architectural, stylistic, religious, and hundreds of Mesoamerican trade goods) that is so impressive that some have questioned whether the Southwest should in fact be considered part of Mesoamerica.

Unlike the Southwest, no outside area seems to have significantly affected the prehistory of the Southeast. Developments at all spatial scales have generally been viewed by Southwestern archaeologists as local rather than something stimulated by events or peoples coming from outside the region. In marked contrast with the Southwest, there is no time in Southeastern prehistory for which there is indisputable evidence for trade or other influences from Mesoamerica. There are vague similarities in artifacts, architecture, site plan, and iconography, but these are best explained as the product of a common cultural ancestry, and intermittent and clinal (i.e., down-the-line) interaction perhaps extending as far back as Paleoindian times, which was diluted and/or elaborated to varying degrees in different areas. While some of the Late Prehistoric Southeast's major cultigens, such as maize probably did ultimately originate in Mesoamerica, their adoption appears to have been a gradual process, perhaps even via contacts with Southwestern groups.

The issue of Southwestern-Southeastern contacts remains to be fully addressed. We know that late prehistoric polities in the eastern ranges of the Southwest and the western margins of the Southeast both maintained trading relationships with nomadic groups in the intermediate Plains area. Whether or not this trade resulted in any direct or indirect contacts between Southwestern and Southeastern groups is unknown at present. What does seem certain is that if such interaction did occur, it had little significant, archaeologically obvious impacts on sociopolitical developments in either area.

The World-Wide Scale

Both the Late Prehistoric Southwest and Southeast were characterized by two sets of roughly contemporaneous developments that suggest that archaeologists need to consider even broader spatial scales in their research on these two areas. The first is the emergence of the two areas' largest, most primate centers, Chaco and Cahokia, at roughly the same time. The decline of these two centers and their respective polities may be roughly contemporaneous. These corresponding developments coincided with the beginning and end of a period of generally favorable climate worldwide. Lasting from roughly A.D. 850–1250, this Medieval Optimum or Neo-Atlantic period was followed by a deterioration in global climate variously called the Pacific/Neo-Boreal or "Little Ice Age" (e.g., Bryson 1988; Bryson and Murray 1977; Wendlund and Bryson 1974).

Another global scale process that affected both areas at approximately the same time and with the same consequences was a cultural one: the arrival of Europeans to North America. In both the Southwest and Southeast, European contact brought population decimation and massive culture change.

Comparing Scales

The goal of multiscalar analysis is to compare developments at different scales with one another to see how they may have been interrelated. In both the Late Prehistoric Southwest and Southeast, there are clear linkages between the characteristics of great towns, polities, and the macroregion. The sizes of big sites were correlated with the preeminence of their associated polities. The kinds of public architecture constructed at big sites reflected the relative importance of social ranking *vs.* group solidarity within the broader polity. The emphasis on social ranking within polities, with the number and complexity of those polities, in turn affected macroregional interaction. Thus, developments had different scales and were highly interdependent. The lesson for archaeologists is that to get as complete a picture as possible of a particular prehistoric society, whether it is in the Southwest, Southeast, or elsewhere, all scales need to be studied and then compared.

EXPLAINING THE DIFFERENCES

The preceding multiscalar comparisons of Late Prehistoric Southwestern and Southeastern societies have re-vealed two fundamental differences: one in the relative emphasis on social ranking in the two areas and the other in the extent and intensity of macroregional interaction. Both differences can be explained largely by differences in the two areas' natural environments. However, environmental characteristics alone do not explain everything. The effects of these characteristics are to impose constraints and offer opportunities. It is the interactions of social variables within the context of these constraints and opportunities that ultimately produce the trajectories of change evident in different areas.

Environmental Comparisons

The natural environments of the Late Prehistoric Southwest and Southeast shared two similarities. First, as mentioned previously, both experienced the relatively favorable climatic conditions associated with the Medieval Optimum or Neo-Atlantic period and the deterioration of global climate that began around A.D. 1250. Second, in both environments water was a critical environmental variable determining where prehistoric populations lived and in what numbers.

Counterbalancing these similarities were several important differences in water availability, physiographic structure, and relative diversity. The Southwest is a harsher, less productive, and riskier environment than the Southeast. Its climate is arid, and precipitation is not only low but highly variable. Consequently, although prehistoric agriculture could be very successful in good times, it was not consistently a reliable subsistence strategy. In contrast, the Southeast is characterized by a moist temperate climate, which makes agriculture both a highly productive and (for the most part) a fairly reliable subsistence strategy.

The Southwest and Southeast also differ in physiographic structure, as created by and reflected in their respective river systems. In the Southwest, the major rivers are few, not very interconnected, and often intermittent in their flow. Thus, the best places to live prehistorically were small in number and widely scattered across a relatively inhospitable landscape. In contrast, the Southeast is spanned by a highly interconnected network of large permanent rivers and their tributaries. Consequently, the best places to live there prehistorically were numerous, closely spaced in a relatively hospitable natural landscape, and linked by easy routes of communication and transportation.

The Southwest and Southeast also differ in the relative diversity of their natural environments. The Southwest can be subdivided into several major zones, most notably the desert, plateau, and mountain, whose differences in elevation are in turn correlated with pronounced differences in temperature, rainfall, and vegetation. Biomass of use to human populations throughout the Southwest is quite varied and in some areas minimal. In comparison, the Southeast is a relatively homogeneous environment, with consistently higher biomass. While latitudinal and longitudinal variation can be defined based on temperature and precipitation, respectively, this variation is fairly continuous. Relatively distinctive macroenvironmental zones, with pronounced differences in biota, such as those seen in the Southwest, are absent.

The Environment and Social Ranking

Differences in the availability of water and biomass of use to humans in the Southwest and Southeast undoubtedly affected the relative emphasis on social ranking in both areas during the Late Prehistoric period. In the harsh, unpredictable, and less productive environment of the Southwest, subsistence would have been a constant concern. Consequently, the most adaptive social strategies would have been those that emphasized cooperation within (and to a lesser extent between) groups in order to even out risks of food shortage. In fact, these are the kinds of strategies that are most evident archaeologically. Throughout the Southwest, the emphasis on polity formation and functioning was the corporate group, not the individual, and the primary ties were ceremonial, fostering cooperation within and between groups. Surplus production would have been possible at some times in some locations, making social ranking possible at some places in the short term. However, ranking was never widespread and where it occurred apparently could not be sustained. Thus, the Southwest's environmental characteristics apparently contributed to an overall pattern of egalitarianism marked by just a few notable examples of ranking, examples whose archaeological indicators are not as clear-cut or consistent as those in the Southeast.

In contrast with the Southwest, the Southeast's rich, productive, and reliable environment not only made subsistence not an overriding concern from early on but offered a high potential for consistent surplus production. This potential would have provided individuals with seemingly ideal opportunities to enhance their social position through competition. As a result, there was a sustained and widespread emphasis on social ranking in the Southeast; and the focus of polity formation and functioning was the chief and proximate elites whose positions were generated through competition within and between ranked kinship lines. This competition contributed to the late prehistoric Southeast's political landscape being much more dynamic than that of the Southwest.

The Environment and Macroregional Interaction

Both the relative diversity and physiographic structure of the Southwestern and Southeastern environments affected macroregional interaction in the Late Prehistoric period. In both areas, macroregional interaction, as evidenced by the limits of major cultural traditions, corresponded to environmental zones. In the Southwest, there were several such zones, each with its associated cultural tradition. In the Southeast, similar environmental divisions were absent, and intensive macroregional interaction, as evidenced by the Mississippian cultural tradition, were pan-Southeastern.

Contributing to these differences was the two areas' physiographic structure, which hindered broad scale macroregional interaction in the Southwest and promoted it in the Southeast. The Southwest's relatively few, not very interconnected, and often intermittent rivers provided few really good places to live and made travel and communication by water difficult. As a result, complex polities were few and widely spaced. Interaction among them was less intense and less extensive than that seen among Southeastern polities. In addition, there was less conflict, which made the overall social landscape less volatile and dynamic than in the Southeast.

In contrast, the Southeast's highly interconnected network of large permanent rivers provided many good places to live, which were closely spaced and linked by easy routes of communication. As a result, there were numerous complex polities, and macroregional interaction was both far-flung and intensive. In addition, the frequency of conflict made the overall social landscape volatile and dynamic.

The Limits of Environmental Determinism

Environmental characteristics clearly contributed to the differential emphasis on social ranking and the different patterns of macroregional interaction in the Late Prehistoric Southwest and Southeast. However, we would reject purely environmental explanations for these differences. While environmental differences explain a lot, the effects of social variables are also critical in both the Southwest and Southeast. Environmental conditions set the stage, offering possibilities and imposing constraints. However, it was the interaction of social variables that determined whether the possibilities were realized.

Three brief examples, one from the Southwest, one from the Southeast, and one that applies to both areas, illustrate our point. First, the longer duration of those Southwestern polities that practiced large scale irrigation was due in part to environmental conditions (e.g., water flow, appropriate expanses of arable land) which made canal irrigation possible. In addition, corporate-solidarity enhancing mechanisms, such as the ball game, could have helped channel intra- and interpolity individual and factional competition into socially desirable (and therefore less destabilizing) ends.

A second example is the greater volatility and dynamism of the Late Prehistoric Southeast's cultural landscape. These characteristics were the product of not only the region's environmental characteristics but also of the interaction of the region's emphasis on social ranking, the reliance on competition for achieving high rank, and the proximity of numerous complex polities.

A last example of the inadequacy of environmental determinism is the effects that global climate change had on cultural developments in both the Late Prehistoric Southwest and Southeast. As was mentioned previously, the roughly simultaneous emergence and decline of Chaco and Cahokia coincided with two major climate shifts, the first to favorable conditions and the second to more difficult conditions. The fact that these correlations occur at both Chaco and Cahokia suggest the possibility that climate was a factor in their developmental histories. Yet while climate may answer questions about timing, it cannot account for why Chaco and Cahokia were located where they were. Environmental factors other than climate may have been responsible, or some kinds of social variables, or the interaction between environmental characteristics and social variables.

There are also other questions about the rise of Chaco and Cahokia that cannot be explained by climate change alone. For example, why were Chaco and Cahokia qualitatively different from preceding and succeeding large sites in size, complexity, and impact on the regional landscape? After Chaco and Cahokia had peaked and gone into decline, what came after—even if possessing similar organizational properties—never approached these primate centers in size and architectural elaboration. Were Chaco and Cahokia as large as they were because

they were the first? This may not be a question that can be answered by referring to climate change alone.

In both the Southwest and Southeast, the collapse of Chaco and Cahokia was followed by the spread of regional and macroregional cults. These cults may have been a response either to deteriorating climatic conditions or to the leadership and spiritual vacuum created by the disappearance from the cultural landscape of Chaco and Cahokia, both of which seem to have been ideological and political centers.

These examples demonstrate that while environmental characteristics are important, and may in some cases be very important, they alone cannot provide a complete explanation for why the Late Prehistoric Southwest and Southeast were similar and different in the ways they were. Social variables, or more specifically the interactions among them, were also critical. Simple environmental determinism is inadequate. Instead, we strongly advocate a multi-variate systemic model that incorporates both environmental and social factors and focuses on the interactions among them all.

BROADER IMPLICATIONS

The differences characterizing the Late Prehistoric Southwest and Southeast have implications for studies of middle-range societies and the process of cultural evolution in general. Traditionally, both ethnographers and archaeologists have approached the task of explaining societal variation and change by classifying societies in a sequence of cultural evolutionary stages. However, the polities of the Late Prehistoric Southwest and Southeast illustrate the inadequacy of such stages for understanding middle-range societies and reinforce the need for alternative approaches to the study of cultural evolution.

The Problem of Classification

In the most widely used cultural evolutionary typology (Service 1962), middle-range societies encompass the societal types of tribe and chiefdom. The differential emphasis on social ranking in the Late Prehistoric Southwest and Southeast highlights a significant problem with using such categories. Namely they constrain our recognition of differing organizational systems and our understanding of how they formed and operated (see Blanton et al. 1996; Earle 1987a, 1991; Feinman and Neitzel 1984:40–45; Spencer 1987:379–383, 1990).

This problem is not so obvious in the Late Prehistoric Southeast. Among Southeastern archaeologists there is an almost universal consensus that most if not all of the late prehistoric societies of their area were chiefdoms. The diagnostic characteristics of chiefdoms, as traditionally defined, are readily apparent, including the obviousness and persistence of ranked kin groups and ascribed leadership. This classificatory success has had the beneficial effect of minimizing typological arguments, and has helped direct research to questions such as how these societies were constituted, interacted, and changed or evolved over time.

However, problems with cultural evolutionary typologies are readily apparent in the Late Prehistoric Southwest. Here, the chiefdom label is used infrequently and with much controversy, primarily because of the absence of clear-cut and sustained evidence for social ranking. While the designation of tribe seems applicable to many Late Prehistoric Southwestern societies, it is clearly inadequate for the area's most complex polities such as those of Chaco, Paquimé, and the Classic period Hohokam. Thus, traditional cultural evolutionary categories cannot accommodate the Southwest's most complex cases—they are neither tribes nor chiefdoms, if chiefdoms are defined as having ranked kin and ascribed leadership.

This difficulty is analogous to the classification difficulties that Southeastern archaeologists have encountered in their studies of societies dating to earlier periods. For example, a number of Hopewellian sites have public architecture and elaborate burials, but as in the Southwest, there is no clear-cut evidence for ranked kin or ascribed leadership. Consequently, as in the late prehistoric Southwest, neither the designation of tribe nor chiefdom seems to accommodate adequately what is known about Hopewellian societies.

These classificatory difficulties can be remedied using a typological subdivision of chiefdoms originally proposed by Renfrew (1974). For Renfrew, individualizing chiefdoms have pronounced kin-based social ranking, which is at least partially ascribed. In group-oriented chiefdoms, group cohesion rather than individual rank is emphasized. This distinction seems to correspond well to the differences observed between Late Prehistoric Southeastern and Southwestern polities as well as between Mississippian and Hopewellian polities.

However, while subdividing the chiefdom category remedies the classificatory difficulties created by the tribe/chiefdom dichotomy, it does not resolve the central task of understanding how Southwestern and Southeast-

ern polities were organized and how they changed. The problem remains one of accommodating variation. In the Southeast, polities seem to fit neatly under the designation of individualizing chiefdom with the primary axes of variation being in their size and degree of complexity. In the Southwest, many Late Prehistoric societies fit neatly into the designation of tribes and the most complex under the designation of group-oriented chiefdoms. These societies, like those in the Southeast, vary in their degree of complexity, and in addition, the group-oriented chiefdoms also vary in their basic structure. Thus, the category of group-oriented chiefdoms suffers on a smaller scale from the same problem of the broader chiefdom category—the problem of not being able to accommodate the variation evident in how prehistoric societies were organized.

A modern, and to date highly productive, resolution to this dilemma of classificatory ambiguity, has been to focus instead on delimiting the range of variation in middle-level societies (e.g., Feinman and Neitzel 1984) and on developing typologies based on explanations as to how and why such variation occurs. Thus, Johnson (1982) has examined how information flow and control mechanisms operate, offering the concepts of simultaneous and sequential hierarchies to describe how decision-making occurs in societies that are vertically as opposed to horizontally integrated; these administrative classifications conform nicely to those in individualizing vs. group-oriented (or Southeastern and Southwestern) societies, respectively.

Likewise Feinman (1995) and his colleagues (Blanton et al. 1996) have argued for a societal classification based on political economy, specifically the kinds of individual behavior that produce two kinds of middle-range societies. When individual actors engage in "network" strategies, the resulting polities are characterized by individual-centered and externally directed hierarchies with power relations predicated on exchange and status enhancement. In contrast, when individual actors engage in "corporate" strategies, the resulting polities are group-focused and internally-directed, promoting group solidarity and relative egalitarianism, and suppressing self-aggrandizing behaviors. These corporate and network strategies, not surprisingly, clearly correspond to Renfrew's group-oriented and individualizing chiefdoms, and Johnson's sequential and simultaneous administrative hierarchies.

Together, variation in the kinds of societies that made up the Late Prehistoric Southwest and Southeast strongly reinforces the idea that middle-range societies are quite varied. As Yoffee (1993) has noted, complexity can take many forms. Comparisons of Southwestern and Southeastern polities highlight the need to develop alternative approaches that explain rather than obscure our understanding of this variation.

Studying Change

The Late Prehistoric Southwest and Southeast not only illustrate alternative approaches to social existence but they can also be viewed as laboratories for the exploration of cultural evolution. If traditional cultural evolutionary typologies cannot accommodate the variation characterizing middle-range societies, then alternatives to unilineal evolutionary theory, from which these typologies were derived, need to be developed.

One major conclusion that can be drawn from the comparisons presented in this volume is that cultural evolution is not a unilineal process. The variation evident in the Late Prehistoric societies of the Southwest and Southeast suggests that there may be several trajectories middle-range societies can follow.

One problem that confronts anthropologists in any discussions of cultural evolution is determining when in fact evolution has occurred. This determination has been complicated in the past by the ambiguous definition of the terms change and evolution, terms which are sometimes given different meanings and sometimes used interchangeably. We feel that this conceptual confusion can best be remedied by viewing change and evolution as synonymous and as a scalar process that occurs along a continuum of magnitude. Change at the low end of this continuum is microevolution, involving simply oscillations around a norm. Change at the high end is macroevolution, involving fundamental structural change and the emergence of new forms. Between the two extremes is a continuum with no clear division between where microevolution ends and macroevolution begins. This continuum can take the form of embedded scales with microevolution occurring within the context of macroevolution, and lower-scale macroevolution occurring within the context of higher scale macroevolution. An example of the latter is the process of chiefly cycling which can be directional in the long run.

We would argue that evolution along the continuum from macro- to microevolution is a multiscalar process is another way too. Time, like space, can be studied at different analytical levels. There are changes that occur over short intervals, those that take more time, and those that occur over even longer periods. These temporal units can be viewed as forming an embedded hierarchy, just as the spatial units do. The relevance of this temporal hierarchy for explaining change is that short term changes need to be considered with reference to the long term trends of which they are a part and vice versa.

It is macroevolution with which traditional cultural evolutionary research has been concerned in its conception of cultural evolution as a ladder-like progression through societal stages or types. As we have discussed, societal comparisons of the late prehistoric Southwest and Southeast reveal the inadequacies of this approach. We would argue that the Late Prehistoric Southwest and Southeast demonstrates macroevolution as a multilineal process, leading to a wide range of social forms. It is analogous to a branching tree with the branches extending in many directions (see Yoffee 1993).

Thus, the approach we advocate for studying macroevolution as a multiscalar, multilineal process is to document how specific variables relating to settlement, subsistence, political economy, social ranking, ideology, agency, the natural environment and other factors change over time; to compare the respective trends at multiple spatial and diachronic scales within societies; and finally to compare their interrelationships between societies.

In developing explanatory models for societal variation and change, our approach must be multivariate, multilineal, and multiscalar both in space and time. The result of such research may in fact reveal that different explanatory models are appropriate for micro- vs. macroevolution, for different time frames (a short term vs. a long term), and for different spatial scales. However, it will only be through research that accommodates all of these different perspectives that we will discover whether this is so.

CONCLUSION

The multiscalar perspective offers a powerful tool for disentangling the interrelated processes that produced the similarities and differences characterizing Late Prehistoric Southwest and Southeast polities. By requiring a consideration of the effects of scale, this perspective imposes a much needed degree of systematization on comparisons between both variables and cases and in turn offers an analytical framework for considering how developments at different scales may have affected one another. The studies by Neitzel (Chapter 14) and Anderson (Chapter 15), and comparisons of the chapters that preceded them, have shown how developments at different scales in the Southwest and Southeast were interrelated, but sometimes in complex ways. Recognition of this fact highlights the importance of adopting a diachronic cross-cultural multiscalar approach to the analysis of archaeological data, with the goal of advancing our understanding of individual societies (past and present) and anthropological theory in general. Multiscalar analyses, in a very real sense, thus reflects an approach to archaeology capable of answering the kinds of questions appropriate to archaeological data, questions dealing with broad socioenvironmental processes operating over large areas and extended time spans.

As for our understanding of middle-range or intermediate level societies, the analyses presented here have two major implications. The first is that such societies are quite varied. They can vary in their size and degree of complexity, as is evident in Southeastern polities. They can vary in their basic structure or form as is seen both in the Southwestern polities and in comparisons of Southwestern and Southeastern polities.

The second implication for middle-range societies is a consequence of the first—that societal types are not very useful for understanding these societies. Instead, documenting and comparing variation is critical; by masking variation, typologies, however precisely defined, hinder efforts to accomplish this goal.

One final conclusion that can be drawn from the comparisons presented in this volume is that cultural evolution is clearly a multilineal process, leading to a wide range of social forms—a branching tree rather than a ladder, and going in many directions rather than in a simple progression. This conclusion raises several questions. For example, what combinations of environmental and social factors were responsible for determining which trajectory a particular society took? Another question is which of these trajectories, if any, offered the greatest potential for the emergence of state-level societies? Given time, for example, would any Southeastern polities have broken the pattern of chiefly cycling and evolved into even more complex forms? If so, what conditions and/or processes would have made this possible? Multiscalar analysis, involving comparisons among variables, among scales, and among cases, is an essential approach for answering these kinds of questions in order to achieve a better understanding of both middle-range societies and cultural evolution.

ACKNOWLEDGMENTS

We are grateful to Gary Feinman for his detailed and incisive comments on an earlier version of this paper and to Tom Rocek for his thought provoking questions about the limits of environmental determinism and the relationship between change and evolution.

CHAPTER SEVENTEEN

Analytical Scales, Building Blocks, and Comparisons

Robert D. Drennan

THE MULTISCALAR APPROACH TO ANALYZING AND COM-paring the prehistoric societies of the Southeastern and Southwestern United States that has been adopted as the organizing principle of this volume derives from the notion of social building blocks that are put together into larger entities that become, in turn, the constituent units of yet larger scale social phenomena. As Neitzel (Chapter 14) notes, such an analytical approach derives part of its strength from focusing clearly on just what is being compared at different scales. It is natural to begin with the smaller scale phenomena and proceed "upward" toward the larger scale ones, and that is the path taken in the preceding chapters. Such a course to some extent recapitulates the developmental trajectories taken by human societies in the Southeast and the Southwest.

The individuals and apparently nuclear family units that formed the most elemental social building blocks in both the Southwest and the Southeast have received relatively little attention here; the comparative analysis began working its way up from a starting point already at a larger scale than that of the family. In this context, though, it is worth noting that, despite the architectural differences between Mississippian houses, unit pueblos, and pithouses, there is apparently considerable similarity between these fundamental social units in the Southeast and the Southwest. The nature of these family units also appears to change little through time in either the

Southeast or the Southwest. Such changes as do occur in the numerous regional sequences that make up these two large areas, then, are principally changes that occur at larger social scales—scales at which the basic building blocks are put together into larger shapes.

Even to begin the comparative consideration in this way makes it clear that it is social phenomena rather than archaeological phenomena, strictly speaking, that are to be compared. Archaeology has a long tradition of comparative analysis, but it has traditionally focused on such narrowly defined archaeological units of comparison as artifact types, sites, phases, components, cultures, culture areas, and the like. Sometimes these serve reasonably well as proxies for the human activities and organizations that we wish to study and sometimes they do not. Indeed there is considerable diversity among the preceding chapters in regard to terminology and to the correspondences that are assumed between archaeological and sociological units of analysis as we move to scales larger than that of the family or household. To pick just three of the most vivid terms applied in this volume to the very next larger unit into which families combined themselves, we have hamlets, villages, and towns. These three terms, of course, imply groupings of rather different scales and characters. They do not necessarily all exist in any one regional system, but they can. Attention in this volume moves quite quickly to the larger variety of local agglomeration of families, the town. The town has a pretty good correspondence to an archaeological unit, the site, or as Lekson (Chapter 1) points out the "big site."

Settlements we are willing to call towns, however, usually coexist in a landscape with smaller settlements. These may be villages or hamlets, and, although these are not terms that are universally used in the Southwest, such smaller settlements do exist in many regions. For a number of parts of the Southeast, however, settlement patterns are so dispersed that it is not always easy to identify the archaeological entities that correspond to such local groups. The contrast between the formation of compact small settlements and broader dispersal of family units across the landscape is worth pursuing further in the context of multiscalar approaches to comparison. A fairly compact town located in a region of highly dispersed rural settlement seems a fundamentally different kind of phenomenon from the smaller co-residential units that surround it, whereas a town in a landscape of hamlets or villages seems a more direct outgrowth of the next smaller-scale settlement units.

As already mentioned, the kind of multiscalar analytical approach advocated in this volume can become a characterization of developmental trajectories. This requires emphasizing the different scales as building blocks rather than simply different scales at which quite possibly contrasting analyses might be carried out. Towns, for example, are built up of smaller units chronologically as well as analytically; their growth involves the progressive addition of larger numbers of smaller units and the emergence of the probably novel patterns of organization that bind these smaller units together. Comparison of trajectories of social change is much more difficult than comparison of static social units, but a multiscalar approach can facilitate it. As one moves from smaller to larger and larger units of analysis, one can think of the similar nature of the trajectory of development of these larger units as they were progressively built up through time. The emergence of towns, regardless of the precise nature of the smaller settlements in their regions (which may themselves change in character as larger units emerge), can be expected to be accompanied by the emergence of new kinds of relationships between settlements in a region. These relationships create a regional entity with novel cultural, social, economic, and political characteristics, and we arrive at a still larger scale of analysis.

At this scale we begin to have more difficulty identifying (or agreeing on) the archaeological entity that corresponds to the relevant entity in human behavioral terms. Holley

(Chapter 2), Scarry (Chapter 5), Milner and Schroeder (Chapter 8), Muller (Chapter 11), and Anderson (Chapter 15) all find it easy to speak of Mississippian regional polities because settlement distribution, stylistic phenomena, and ethnohistoric descriptions seem to converge nicely. Fish (Chapter 4) calls Hohokam entities of roughly similar scale "communities," however, in part to emphasize some of the uncertainties involved in specifying their political nature. Considerable disagreement exists in the Anasazi world about the nature (and extent) of such regional entities. This is a point of departure for discussion of one of the most fundamental issues to arise in any consideration of Southeastern and Southwestern societies: the nature of political leadership and social hierarchy. These two fundamental and interrelated phenomena have occupied a great deal of the attention that social scientists have paid to the glue that holds smaller building blocks together in larger-scale social constructions, and concern with them is not absent from any of the preceding chapters (although it takes a number of different forms).

Elites have always been as conspicuous in the archaeological record for the Southeast as they have been elusive in the Southwest. There is certainly room for argument over the nature of prehistoric political leadership and social hierarchy in the Southwest (and wherever there is room for argument in archaeology we can be sure that it will be filled with archaeologists arguing). The occasional Southwestern examples of familiar kinds of archaeological evidence for elites, however, serve largely to make two points. First, the kind of non-perishable evidence we customarily and readily interpret as an indication of social hierarchy does, indeed, occur; it is not somehow obviated by particular cultural norms that systematically rendered social hierarchy archaeologically invisible in the Southwest. Differences in wealth or prestige, when present, can indeed put in their appearance in precisely the ways we are accustomed to seeing them in the archaeological record. This leads us directly to the second point: as archaeologists have observed ever since they began working in these two regions, such evidence is far more abundant in the Southeast than in the Southwest. Whether Hohokam or Anasazi groups can be classified as egalitarian or not, elite personages played a far less central social role than they did in Mississippian societies.

Mississippian regional polities were integrated to a large extent by the centripetal forces exerted by political leaders who had a great deal of personal prestige, considerable sacred power, and (at least by some accounts) substantial personal wealth. Whether such centripetal forces exerted by political leaders even existed in the Southwest has been questioned; the conclusion that they were far weaker than in the Southeast is inescapable in virtually all the preceding chapters. The forces that held Hohokam and Anasazi societies together at the regional scale would seem to be principally those at play in the rituals conducted at such archaeologically visible structures as ballcourts, platform mounds, and kivas. Such rituals are generally taken to be ones that, among other things, tended to affirm cultural identity and social solidarity on a much more nearly egalitarian or communal basis than the elite-focused rituals that took place in Mississippian centers. It is worth underscoring that the observation made here is not that Mississippian societies lacked rituals or that Hohokam or Anasazi societies entirely lacked elites or political leaders. It is rather that the balance of centripetal, integrative forces appears to have differed between the Southeast and the Southwest.

As Wilcox (Chapter 10) points out, this parallels the distinction made by Renfrew (1974) between individualizing and group-oriented chiefdoms. At this point we risk getting diverted into a futile argument over the definition of chiefdom. For those who see strongly developed social hierarchy and hereditary political leadership as central features in chiefdom organization, Renfrew's group-oriented chiefdoms (and probably Hohokam and Anasazi societies) are not chiefdoms. So be it. The labels we attach to these societies are of interest only insofar as they increase our comprehension of their operation and development. The interesting point here is that in the Southwest and in the Southeast there developed societies of regional scale incorporating populations numbering into the thousands and with some degree of territorial control over scores of square kilometers. These regional societies appear to have been constructed of similar smaller-scale building blocks, but the integrative glue that held them together differed substantially. It is easy to attach the label *polity* to this scale of integration for Mississippian, because politics seems to be the arena in which the leaders who integrated these entities emerged. Politics, in the broadest sense at least, are probably not entirely absent from any human society, but they seem remarkably undeveloped in Hohokam and Anasazi societies. It is tempting to call Hohokam and Anasazi entities at this scale *ritualities* or *communalities* (to exaggerate Fish's [Chapter 4] use of *communities* for Hohokam regional societies), thereby emphasizing the ritual, communal, group solidarity on which these entities were founded.

In regard to economics, Southwestern and Southeastern regional polities and the towns on which they were focused seem more alike than different. In both areas, these towns seem remarkably lacking in one of the principal features usually taken to set towns off from villages. Southwestern and Southeastern towns set themselves off from smaller communities in their regions by larger populations and larger-scale architecture, but in neither region do towns seem to owe their existence much to the production and distribution of goods. Craft specialization, while demonstrably present, is not highly developed, especially insofar as goods of daily use by large segments of the population are concerned. Goods, probably largely agricultural staples, surely flowed from the countryside into these towns to support the special activities that occurred there, but there is little indication that the countryside was supplied with very much from the towns. It is in this aspect, perhaps, that application of the term town to these settlements is least appropriate. The economic (or even commercial) implications of the term, although justified for some archaeologically-known areas in the world, do not seem applicable to Hohokam or Anasazi or Mississippian settlements.

The next larger scale of analysis is more difficult to work with. It is clear that some towns (Cahokia, Moundville, Pueblo Bonito, Snaketown, etc.) were larger than others. For the Southeast, the notion of paramount chiefdoms seems applicable and worthy of further archaeological exploration. Paramountcies are normally taken to emerge from competition between chiefs of neighboring polities with eventual subordination of some chiefly centers by other chiefly centers, whose chiefs consequently gain prestige, power, and wealth. Such a dynamic, however, is difficult to graft onto the patterns of societal integration most strongly suggested by the Southwestern archaeological record. In this light, the Southwest poses a challenge to those who would see competition for wealth, power, and prestige as the central driving force in the development of complex societies. Mississippian societies are extremely easy to interpret in these terms, but the scheme does not lend itself nearly so directly to the apparent nature and course of development of societies of similar scale and degree of complexity in the Southwest. It is certainly possible to imagine larger-scale entities centered on Snaketown or Pueblo Bonito whose integrative forces derived from the same kind of ritual base important at smaller scales of integration, but there is not such a readily available and directly connected ethnohistoric or ethnographic analogue as there is for Southeastern paramountcies.

This should not discourage us from exploring the idea, though, as important as it is to archaeologists to make effective use of the ethnographic and ethnohistoric records. If we refuse to accept the possibility of documenting archaeologically societies that differ significantly from those known ethnographically or ethnohistorically, why should we bother with such a difficult, time-consuming, and, yes, tedious chore as archaeology? Only if we think that the range of human societies is not fully documented ethnohistorically or ethnographically can archaeology add to our social scientific knowledge, as opposed to being a derivative application to prehistory of understandings achieved by ethnographers.

These larger-scale entities in the Southeast and the Southwest are more difficult to study and compare because we are less certain of their nature in the Southwest. In both areas, however, they seem to have been relatively fragile. Not many such larger-scale entities emerged, and those that emerged did not attain much permanence. This is sometimes attributed to a failure to establish the effective and durable integrative mechanisms that characterize states. It is also interesting to consider whether the fragility of these larger-scale sociopolitical entities resulted from weakness or lack of rigidity of the building blocks of which they were made rather than from lack of appropriate glue. Even aside from the formation of larger-scale entities, the regional polities of the Southeast and the "ritualities" of the Southwest do not seem to have had great staying power. They waxed and waned; population built up in some regions, then declined precipitously; and so on. If, indeed, the principal integrative forces of these societies in the Southeast and the Southwest differed, they nevertheless seem to have had quite similar limitations.

As usual, broadly comparative studies bring us emphatically to the issue of what forces drive social change, and in this case in particular, of what forces produce larger-scale and more complex patterns of social organization. Also as usual, the explanatory power of some simple models quickly proves inadequate to the task. If hierarchy based on control over critical resources is the be-all and end-all of complex societal development, the irrigation systems of the desert Southwest would seem to offer an opportunity unmatched in any other part of the Southwest or Southeast; but Hohokam society does not stand out for vigorous hierarchical development. If management of agricultural risk is handled much more suc-

cessfully by larger-scale integration, then Chaco Canyon seems an ideal seedbed for cultivating such integration; but the "Chaco phenomenon" was at least as transitory as other such large-scale organizations in the Southwest and the Southeast.

At even larger scales of analysis, we are on shakier ground. Concreteness in the multiscalar approach around which this volume is structured comes from considering the entities at one scale as the constituent units of which the entities at next larger scale are made up. At the macroregional scale, however, it is not at all clear just how to do this. In short, just what kind of thing is Mississippian, as a whole? Or Hohokam? Or the Southwest? None of the authors in this volume seems entirely content with the traditional approach to such things as archaeological cultures or culture areas, and the call to move beyond them to concepts that have more reality in human behavioral terms is by no means new. Muller finds exchange and interaction a useful framework in which to view integration on this scale, although he sees this less as elite control or corporate action by regional polities than as a plethora of individual actions. Wilcox finds shifting from culture area notions to regional and macroregional systems an improvement, but finally is dissatisfied with a variety of existing approaches. As he notes, at this scale, the actions that comprise integration are external to the maximal sociopolitical units. These units are not building blocks of which anything larger is built up—at least not in the same sense that they are themselves made up of smaller and smaller nested social units.

At this level the questions are ones essentially of "foreign" relations. How did the maximal regional polities (or "ritualities") interact with each other? Were relations equal or unequal? Were there ways in which these units threatened each other? Cooperated with each other? Did their relationships encourage or discourage the development of more such units in neighboring regions? To what extent were relationships conducted between the polities as corporate or collective activities, as opposed to by elites or by ordinary individuals acting on their own across "borders?"

This conceptual quandary is even more vexing for the consideration of relationships on a still larger scale. Cobb, Maymon, and McGuire (Chapter 13) attempt to get beyond the conceptually bankrupt diffusionist approaches to relationships between the Southwest and the Southeast and especially Mesoamerica. Their focus on the ways in which the scattered individual Mesoamerican items and traits that were adopted in the Southwest or the Southeast were utilized in different regional polities brings us back to those regional entities. The Southeast, the Southwest, and Mesoamerica simply were not entities with enough self-consciousness to be, themselves, the actors in interaction with each other. Regional polities (or "ritualities") or individuals in these different regions might conceivably have interacted, directly or indirectly, but the fact is they simply do not seem to have done so very much. It is worth questioning whether there is really anything much to say about relationships between the Southwest, the Southeast, and Mesoamerica that is different from what can be said about relationships between the maximal sociopolitical entities within those regions at much shorter distances.

Most of the "Mesoamerican" objects and traits that appear in the Southeast and the Southwest would seem as foreign in the central and southern Mexican highlands, where I have worked, as they do in the Southeast and the Southwest. The "Southwest," of course is not limited to the United States, but is part of a good old-fashioned culture area that extends a considerable distance south of the border between the United States and Mexico, where its neighbor is the "Mesoamerican" region of West Mexico. It can be argued that West Mexico has as much in common with the greater Southwest as it does with the Central Mexican highlands, and considerably more than it does with the Maya area. In terms of forms of social organization and trajectories of development, the Southeast lends itself much more readily to comparison with the Caribbean, Central America, and northern South America. Whatever it is that may be shared at such a large geographic scale, then, it is with these regions that the Southeast seems to share it more than with Mesoamerica. It is at this scale, however, that our conceptual advances beyond diffusionism are least impressive.

So—where has all this comparative analysis gotten us? And where do we go from here? As Neitzel promised in the Introduction (wise move), this volume has not provided a full explanation of all the similarities and differences between the various trajectories of sociopolitical development in the Southeast and the Southwest. A cynic would compare archaeologists in both of these regions to the six blind men describing an elephant by feeling alternatively its tusk, its trunk, its ear, its leg, its tail, etc., and might question whether twelve blind men with two elephants were any better off. Since neither set of blind men really has much comprehension of what their elephant is like, perhaps they need to do a good deal more data collection before attempting to compare. This, however, is a prescription for never arriving at meaningful or interesting conclusions. If we do not now have enough data for the Southeast and the Southwest—two of the world's most intensively studied archaeological regions—to attempt some comparisons, those of us who work in many other parts of the world truly have cause for despair. It should be particularly enlightening, for example, for those Andeanists who think that all our problems will be solved once we establish chronologies with periods not more than two or three centuries long to examine some of the incredibly detailed regional chronological frameworks that exist in both the Southeast and the Southwest and to recognize the additional confusion and doubt introduced by such chronological precision.

More data does not necessarily produce greater understanding. Indeed, comparing the intensity of archaeological research and the level of dispute over conclusions in the Southeast or the Southwest with that in most of the rest of the world leads one to the opposite conclusion: the more we know the less we understand. If we take comparative study of human societies in different parts of the world as one of our ultimate aims, then we cannot afford to put it off until we are "finished" knowing about each of the regions we want to compare. By attempting comparisons, premature though they may be, we can continually correct our aim in regional studies, defining what, exactly, it is that we need to know and what disputes we really may not need to resolve (at least not in the ways they are currently framed).

As a closing example of this last point, the presence, nature, or extent of social hierarchy continues to be one debate in Southwestern archaeology, even though many archaeologists already have their minds firmly made up (at both extremes). This debate cannot simply be wished away as a question of whether we view the glass as half-full or half-empty. It really is a question of how much water there is in the glass. Compared explicitly to the social hierarchy glass in the Southeast, however, it seems quite clear that the Southwestern glass has considerably less water. It may be less important ultimately to determine absolutely how much water it does contain than to recognize that Southwestern societies do seem to be rather different from Southeastern ones in this regard. Comparative analyses, then, are worth attempting, even if only to make us confront forcefully just how good (or bad) our answers are to some regional questions and just how important it is (or is not) to answer them in the way we have framed them.

CHAPTER EIGHTEEN

Comunidades, Ritualities, Chiefdoms:

Social Evolution in the American Southwest and Southeast

Norman Yoffee

Suzanne K. Fish

George R. Milner

THIS TRIOLOGUE DOES NOT PRETEND TO SUMMARIZE THE proceedings of the "Great Towns, Regional Polities . . ." conference, but it does reflect the spirit of discussion that took place in Dragoon. By means of point and counterpoint, we illustrate several main lines of debate in the interpretation of Southwestern (hereafter SW) and Southeastern (hereafter SE) prehistory. We also delineate some of the merits—and difficulties—of comparing social organizations and evolutionary trajectories between the two regions. In this way we intend to clarify positions and to determine what, if anything, we can claim to know about (and how we can represent) the past and what are the explanatory mechanisms we can use to resolve rival claims to knowledge.

Our separate interests dictate the structure of this chapter, and our different expertise ensures a measure of control over—or at least a healthy skepticism about—the rich data and complex literature of SW and SE archaeology. Yoffee (1993) among others has argued that not all prehistoric societies lie on a single evolutionary trajectory that leads to statehood. Thus, evolving social systems in the SW and SE, regions where states did not appear (in our view), might be interesting examples of alternate social evolutionary trajectories (Yoffee 1993:72, Figure 6.6). This perspective undermines a sacred tenet for many SW archaeologists, namely that the region

serves as a laboratory of wide-ranging evolutionary investigations (e.g., Wills 1994), because of the amount of work done, the degree of chronological precision afforded by tree-ring dating, and the judicious, but invaluable application of the "direct historical method" (ethnographic analogies). By exploring whether SW social systems represent exceptions to the "rule" of unilinear evolution, higher purposes for SW archaeological research may be discovered (Johnson 1989). The ongoing debate on the nature of "complexity" (Yoffee 1994) in the SW has been discussed earlier by Fish and Yoffee (1995) and we resume that debate here.

In contrasting the nature of elites, aggregation and abandonment of sites, economic and ritual power in the SW, Milner's perspectives from the SE provide important comparative data on the political organization of big sites and the significance of impressive monuments and artifacts. In the SE there are also new ideas about the nature of societies and social change that we discuss in comparative perspective. We focus on the concept of the "cycling" of chiefdoms, advanced by Service (1971:142–143), developed by Wright (1971, 1984), and elaborated more recently by Earle (1991) and Anderson (1996a) among others. The possibility of constraints in social evolutionary trajectories is the thread that links SE and SW examples in this essay.

THE STATE OF HOHOKAM

"Yoffee's Rule" (1993:69)—"if you can argue whether a society is a state or isn't, then it isn't"—entails an important corollary and considerable problematization in the case of Hohokam (Fish and Yoffee 1995). Since, in our view, the Hohokam cannot be characterized as a "tribe" or a "chiefdom," the typologically-minded might be obligated, if limited to the canonical neo-evolutionary nomenclature, to conclude by default that the Hohokam were a "state." Labeling the Hohokam as a "middle-range" society—big but not too big, complex but not too complex—is no great improvement. More to the point, Hohokam societies are not simply intermediate between small-scale societies referred to as bands and those much larger and internally differentiated ones conveniently called states. In rejecting essentialist and unilinear thinking altogether, we reconsider the meaning of Hohokam in social evolutionary theory. We present here a digest of Hohokam social organization and a way out of the typological cul de sac.

Several lines of evidence point to the Classic period Hohokam (after A.D. 1100) as a society or group of societies in which certain socioeconomic roles and administrative structures were not prescribed by the kinship system. First, there is little evidence for unilineal kinship as the overriding principle of economic and political organization in Hohokam societies, although residential patterns suggest some form of extended family social structure (P. Fish and S. Fish 1991:159–160; Wilcox 1991d:255–258). Logically, the persons inhabiting the adobe-walled compounds of the Classic period were grouped according to kinship ties and were accordingly identified with respect to other such groups. Similarly, cemeteries often coincide with residential units or serve only segments of a village (McGuire 1992a:17–40). It is likely that these patterns reflect households of related persons and the local structure of kinship.

The imprint of kinship on residential layout and as the unique framework for social prestige and power, however, is not necessarily synonymous with a ramage, conical clan, or any other such idealized social structure described in the ethnographic literature. Familial shrines and the veneration of lineal ancestors have not been found, even in Preclassic period times when ritual artifacts included portable items with relatively widespread distributions within and among sites (but see Wilcox and Sternberg [1983:229] for a proposed use of figurines in conjunction with an ancestor cult during the initial Pioneer phase). An iconography of clans is likewise unknown.

Perhaps most significant by comparison with Puebloan neighbors (whom we can't even pretend formed states), is the absence in the Hohokam archaeological record of any functional equivalent for small kivas. Associated with delimited sets of domestic structures, small kivas (at least those that are not simply pithouses) are commonly interpreted as the architectural indicators of kin-based ritual and political structures analogous to those of historic clans (Lipe and Hegmon 1989). Evidence for kin-based ceremonial activity, other than possibly crematory rituals, is virtually absent in Hohokam society during the Classic period. Instead, with its focus on platform mounds in large sites, Hohokam ritual seems strongly "centralized," overarching local kin-groups. This ritual focus on mounds in large sites also occurs in the SE, but with an important difference—in the SE, different highly ranked kin-groups had their own charnel structures on mounds. Although linkage between kinship groups and ritual in Hohokam communities is likely, access to and the function of sacral leadership roles seems not to be ascribed and limited. This situation stands in contrast to the case of the historical pueblos of the northern SW (and to the prehistoric SE). Indeed, if the "SW" is a useful concept in sociopolitical terms, it must be broken down into its particular regions and histories, as many insist and we can only adumbrate in the two SW sections of this chapter. The contrast with a much less differentiated "SE" is also explored below.

If we turn to economic behavior, further sources of non-kin organizational principles can be suggested. Analogies from the rancheria peoples of the low southern deserts of the southwestern United States and northwestern Mexico are more relevant to the Hohokam than Puebloan comparisons. In these societies, kinship tends to be more flexible and bilateral than among the pueblos (Beals 1943; Crumrine 1977; Underhill 1939). Locational affiliation can be of importance in that village approval as well as kinship rights determine access to agricultural land. For example, participation in the initial construction of canals was the mechanism for obtaining rights to irrigated land among the Pima, who succeeded the Hohokam (Castetter and Bell 1942:126; Russell 1975:88). This sort of land tenure for the Hohokam is consonant with Netting's observation (1993:157–188) that there is a tendency toward direct control by farmers over cultivated land in situations of intensive production and high investment in agricultural improvements. Under such systems of tenure that are normally outside the "moral economy of kinship," advantages in land quality or productive capacity were the bases upon which economic power could be built.

In early states, societal (or ideological) power (see Runciman 1982, 1989; Yoffee 1985, 1993; compare Mann 1986) was typically exercised by persons who manipulated, maintained, and reproduced the symbols by which groups with different cultural orientations were integrated within a larger societal umbrella. For many early states, that territorial boundary is the city-state (Yoffee 1996). Mesopotamian city-states, for example, were independent, usually walled, cities that dominated an agricultural hinterland of villages. They encompassed political, economic, social, and ideological elites (whose roles were to a degree separate, although leaders sought to achieve power over their rivals) as well as large populations of contracted and unfree laborers, dependent and independent craftspeople, landholders, merchants, and local community structures of power and authority (see Postgate 1992).

Ideological elites derived their status, wealth, and leadership from their control of specialized information. They normally stood at the apex of a hierarchy of dependent personnel, for example, of priests, craft specialists, and agricultural laborers on temple estates. Understanding the evolution of these ideological elites requires tracing the development of: 1) interacting but differently constituted social units; 2) the nature of the symbols that integrated them; and 3) the social and economic power of people who created and managed these symbols.

Among the Classic period Hohokam, there were no city-states, of course, but there were "communities" ("comunidades" in the rancheria model) which consisted of central sites with public architecture and surrounding interrelated villages and special purpose sites (see Fish, Chapter 4; Crown 1987; Doyel 1974; P. Fish and S. Fish 1991:162–166; Wilcox and Sternberg 1983).

The creation of symbols of cultural and political commonality, conspicuously the platform mounds for Hohokam communities, bestowed special status on the officiants of ceremonies of social incorporation. Although such officials might have legitimately amassed and controlled local resources on behalf of the community, the display of great individual wealth is not apparent. This is an indication that societal power exercised through Hohokam public architecture and an ideology

of centralization probably was not legitimized through the exalted status of individuals or as a consequence of their superordinate place in the genealogical system. Nevertheless, communal edifices (especially in the Classic period) and their residents did link socially diverse and geographically widespread Hohokam populations, as attested by burials of all ages and both sexes in platform mound precincts.

In the rise of many early states, the founding of new sites is an important process through which political power can be disembedded from the structures of kinship and other, traditional organizational formations. Whereas kin-groups certainly do not disappear in early states, offices are created in new capitals over which kin-group leaders and other powerful individuals can legitimately compete. Familiar examples of new capitals include the founding of Monte Alban (Blanton 1983), Akkade (Liverani 1993), various Middle Assyrian and Neo-Assyrian cities (Saggs 1984), Jerusalem of King David (Ahlstrom 1993), and An-yang and other Shang dynasty cities (Chang 1980). Such relocations of the royal court also provided the opportunity for new systems of land tenure and control of other basic means of production to be regulated by kings and other political leaders.

The Hohokam Classic period is marked by a change from an ideology that focused on ballcourts to one of platform mounds, with a concomitant increase in the exclusivity of ritual space and the number of elite celebrants (P. Fish 1989; Gregory 1991). Some locational shifting of centers and reorganization within persisting ones (Gregory 1987:182–183; Wilcox and Sternberg 1983:242–243) occurs particularly in the areas where massive investment in canals restricted population movement. However, in areas of mixed agriculture, new mound centers were systematically established at locations distinct from prior ballcourt sites, and mound centers were founded in regions that previously had no ballcourts (Doelle and Wallace 1991; S. Fish et al. 1992). This discontinuity of centers and in the architecture characteristic of the new central sites of communities represented an opportunity for the development of new bases of societal power.

The trajectory of development in emerging states includes an interplay among various and often competing sources of power in society (Yoffee 1993). Furthermore, such interaction means that those who held status and wealth by means of their control of certain valued resources and dependent labor characteristically tried to accrue power generated from the control of other resources and the kinds of behavior needed to produce them.

Performers of centralized ritual functions associated with Hohokam platform mounds are the obvious candidates to convert ideological power into economic gain, partly by negotiating between other sectors of interest and influence in society. Heads of kin-groups are also political actors and, in a time of demographic aggregation, one expects they would intensify their leadership roles in the association of groups with differing geographic and/or ethnic origins (P. Fish et al. 1994; S. Fish and P. Fish 1993). Especially important leadership activities in the Classic period were the maintenance of large canals and the coordination of water availability in irrigation and other modes of agricultural joint use (Crown 1987; Gregory and Nials 1985; Nicholas and Feinman 1989). Differential distributions of high value items, exotic goods, and manufacturing activities between mound sites and other kinds of settlements reflect limited zones of distinctive interests, influence, and perhaps the coordination of aspects of production and exchange (Howard 1987; Teague 1984; Bayman 1992; Wilcox 1987a,c).

Whereas we have not argued that the Classic period Hohokam were in reality anything like ancient states—economically driven, managed by bureaucrats with distinct offices, with mercantile elites, private landowners, and subjugated masses, we have sought to emphasize those aspects of Hohokam society that do not easily fit the category of "chiefdom." (Of course, we also could have satisfied some criteria that apply to chiefdoms, and perhaps we could have found a few attributes for "tribes").

Our goal is to show that the traditional neo-evolutionary conception forces the archaeologist to choose among a small number of idealized types arranged neatly in a row, as if in natural progression. It both structures the question and dictates the answer, for the archaeologist must ask, "Is this extinct society a tribe or chiefdom (or type of chiefdom) or state?" The answer must be, "Yes, it is a tribe or chiefdom or state because it best fits those defining criteria and is therefore at the corresponding evolutionary stage." While an understanding of sorts about the archaeological record is achieved in this manner, if left at that point the method necessarily diminishes any concern over variability within a particular "type," and little progress can be made in ascertaining why or how a society might, or might not, evolve from one type to another.

Moreover, the small set of neo-evolutionary types are packages of attributes from a limited number of ethnographic examples (Feinman and Neitzel 1984; McGuire 1983; Paynter 1989). Because particular social institutions are characteristic of a type, all must change in tandem in order to reach the next stage. This scheme cannot accommodate mixes of attributes thought to characterize different stages, and it cannot measure different rates of change in institutions. In studies of the collapse of ancient states and civilizations, however, it has been shown that some institutions can fail, while others survive or become stronger (Yoffee and Cowgill 1988), and the same is true of the smaller scale ranked societies typically called chiefdoms (Milner 1986). The various social agents and environmental conditions causing cultural change and their significance at different points along an evolutionary sequence are undervalued in a model that perceives change as occurring in a lockstep fashion. In fact, much of the debate over whether a particular society fits within one or another type stems from different emphases on the various attributes considered to be defining characteristics of so very few cultural categories.

An alternative to the typological approach to social evolution in archaeology must break down the components of organizations and identify the distinctive and empirically evident features of change. It involves comparison of real sequences of change in the archaeological record, rather than reliance on an artificial sequence of stages abstracted from ethnographically contemporary societies. It is in this spirit that new questions can be posed about the structure of Hohokam societies and the nature and meaning of change in them.

DEBATING THE HOHOKAM

If trends toward increasing social differentiation, stratification, and political centralization are probable in post-Pleistocene societies (Yoffee 1996), social evolutionary theory must also explain why some societies did not become states. For the Hohokam, two rival interpretations of evolutionary change can be considered. In the first, the difficulty of obtaining reliable and storable agricultural surpluses in harsh and unstable environmental conditions leads to the constraints on the kinds and quantities of economic specializations that characterize the Hohokam (Yoffee 1994). The terminal prehistoric Hohokam collapse that is the region-wide abandonment of large sites and irrigation systems and the disaggregation of communities, implies that political centralization was maladaptive. Societies dependent on intensive irrigation agriculture, in conflict for scarce resources (Wilcox and Haas 1994a,b), and vulnerable to prolonged droughts and severe episodes of riverine down-cutting (Graybill and Nials 1989) disaggregated so as to manage resources more flexibly. In doing so, they channeled social behavior from individualized economic gain toward risk-sharing, and they structured social institutions predominantly through the medium of kinship.

In this explanation, the evolutionary trajectory of Hohokam communities implies no failure to "progress" along a normative evolutionary trajectory to states. It does insist, however, that Hohokam societies cannot be used as direct analogies for the pre-state levels of social organization in societies that did become states. This explanation further requires that comparisons of the Hohokam be made with other societies that did not become states, perhaps Amazonian Brazil (e.g., Roosevelt 1991) or the SE.

The second explanation of the evolutionary significance of Hohokam societies objects to the teleological nature of trajectories to states since what defines these pathways is the end product. In this explanation, the previous description of terminal Hohokam development as a "collapse" is inappropriate. Rather, this period might represent an interval between the first sedentary, domestic economies and territorial "comunidades" which might have then regrouped into larger and more centralized polities with increased amounts of economic and social stratification. From the earliest agriculture in the Hohokam area to the Spanish entrada was about 2,500 years; in Western Asia the first states appeared about 5,000 years after the first villages based on domesticated crops.

This second explanation does not find the Hohokam to have been environmentally challenged, unable to produce reliable surpluses in a desert subject to decades-long droughts and riverine down-cutting. The approximately 500 km of main canal lines in the Phoenix area (Masse 1981) represent a more massive irrigation system than in Mesoamerica or any other part of the New World north of Peru (Doolittle 1990:79–81) and one that persisted for nearly 1000 years. Moreover, the Hohokam in some regions practiced a variety of successful agricultural technologies (Fish and Nabhan 1991). An historic Pima population that was much reduced from its prehistoric levels in the same area, after refurbishing a minor fraction of the prehistoric Hohokam canal system (Russell 1975:90), was able to produce an exchangeable annual crop of about 204,100 kg (or 450,000 lb.) of wheat as well as other cultigens.

These two alternate explanations both turn from the received neo-evolutionist types and toward comparisons based in the archaeological record. While we debate the meaning of collapse/desegregation in Hohokam societies, whether there are ceilings on evolutionary growth, and the (im)probability of resurgence after collapse, we can begin to narrow the choices among these perspectives and so help build improved explanations within an expanded social evolutionary theory.

SW RITUALITIES

In a recent paper comparing societies at Chaco Canyon, New Mexico, and La Quemada, Zacatecas, Ben Nelson (1994) insists that "complexity needs to be dimensionalized." The La Quemada site, in Nelson's analysis, has much less population than Chaco Canyon, its road system connects military outposts rather than settlements, and it is a fraction of the size of the Chacoan system. Nevertheless, at La Quemada political elites were able to compel dependent labor to construct monumental terraces, elite residences, "causeways, staircases, pyramids, altars, ballcourts, and a huge palisade-like wall encompassing the core of the site." There were at La Quemada overt signs, even public demonstrations, of orchestrated violence of a sort unknown at Chaco. At Chaco Canyon circular kivas are usually interpreted as focal points of prayerful, consultative action, and they contrast with the ceremonial and social restrictiveness of La Quemada's pyramids. In sum, Nelson asks not "how complex" were the two sites, but "how were they complex."

Nelson's perspective is important in our own reflections on the terms "great towns" and "polities" that appear in the title of this volume and which are meant to indicate a certain level of complexity in the SW. In Dragoon discussants indicated there were problems with both terms. The former implies a scale of settlements in which the "towns" provide functions, especially economic services, to a hinterland of thereby interconnected villages and rural sites, more or less conforming to a model of Western urban places. "Polities" also carries its own baggage, being derived from a concept of urbanism and a set of behaviors that are thus "political." To obviate some of these problems, and especially to describe the supposedly non-townish and not really political nature of

Chaco, Dick Drennan proposed the term "rituality" to refer to its "ritual boomtown" nature. This neologism is attractive to us, since it is not borrowed from the extensive Western literature on urban geography, and it must be unpacked and explained in its own context.

The term Chacoan "rituality," of course, suggests that the fundamental component of the existence of Chaco and of the Chacoan network was its elaborate ritual apparatus. While we cannot forget that there were important aspects of economic and political behavior at Chaco and its outliers, the ritual nature of Chaco cannot be reduced to its being the handmaiden of economic and/or political institutions. The term "rituality" also implies that Chacoan society (or societies) cannot readily be typed in neo-evolutionary terms as being somewhere on its way to statehood.

In A.D. 850, Chaco was much like everywhere else in the Anasazi world. Located in the San Juan basin, Chaco does not seem the foremost candidate on environmental grounds for the spectacular social transformations that made it the center of the Anasazi world from ca. A.D. 900–1150 (or a little later). Summers were short and hot, winters long and bitterly cold, edible plants and animals were few, and firewood was limited. There was not much land to cultivate, and the water for irrigation was inadequate (Lekson 1994). A consensus seems to be that the growth of Chaco and the nature of the Chacoan system cannot be explained by economic or political means. Chaco was not the center of trade in turquoise, and its leaders were not marked by large amounts of wealth from their power as redistributors of goods.

The principle arguments for the Chacoan rituality can be summarized as follows: 1) "great houses" were not much like pueblos in that they were not massive residential complexes but were ceremonial monuments; 2) population of the entire canyon was modest, perhaps not larger than a single large pueblo of the Pueblo IV period, and it was perhaps seasonal (Nelson [1994] estimates 2,985 people); 3) the system of roads connected an area that was perhaps 112,500 km^2 (Kohler 1993:254). These roads, up to 10 m wide in the canyon, connected the larger buildings into a "downtown Chaco." Through the extent of the Chacoan system, utilitarian goods were transported to Chaco and may have been redistributed there. The roadways were not merely utilitarian, however, since they are too finely built and too broad in parts simply to be used to transport crops and logs. In one segment between Chaco and Salmon Ruin, the road splits into four parallel segments.

Entering the canyon, the sight of Chacoan grandeur was awe-inspiring. An Anasazi, who had never seen a structure larger than a few unit-houses, was confronted by a "ritual landscape that functioned as the ceremonial/political center for a vast region" (Stein and Lekson 1994:58); 4) the quantity and design of the architecture, which went far beyond the size and number of buildings, was unprecedented in the Anasazi world. The great houses themselves "confront and balance the earth shapes" (Scully, quoted in Stein and Lekson 1994:52); trash mounds were themselves monumental constructions, scenes of ritual destructions; paths between these mounds created routes and lines of sight to other monumental structures; great kivas, shrines, ramadas, and ramps were integrated in the ritual landscape.

The major centers of Chaco Canyon did not themselves form a "community" in the sense in which Fish (Chapter 4) has defined individual communities for the Hohokam (although some archaeologists describe clusters of settlements around Aztec Ruin and other sites as communities). They were visually not the scenes of village life and were unique in the Anasazi world, central in time and space, the fulcrum of ceremonies that created and legitimized the economic and political interactions among Anasazi. Chaco's collapse, presumably the effect of a humongous drought, decisively shaped subsequent Puebloan prehistory. No such aggregation of ritual architecture ever again appeared, and native Puebloan histories warn of the ultimate perils of that previously splendid, but dangerously hubristic world. On the other hand, settlement patterns containing sites with smaller scale but Chaco-like public architecture proliferated widely in the latter period of Canyon developments and persisted beyond its demise.

If the status of Chaco Canyon as a series of settlements whose position and architecture were influenced decisively by ritual concern, as first suggested by Judge (see 1991, Vivian 1990, for references) seems reasonable, we must now ponder the evolutionary implications of the Chaco phenomenon. If the Chaco rituality cannot be tidily encompassed in the available neo-evolutionary typology, is it a unique social evolutionary occurrence?

While such comparative research cannot be undertaken in this paper, Near Eastern archaeologists might consider the site of Çatal Hüyük a possible "rituality." This site (see Mellaart 1978, Roaf 1990; Todd 1976), which flourished from ca. 6500–5700 B.C., is known mainly for its precocious size and for the elaborate artistic representations reported to have been found there (compare Hodder 1990 with Hays 1993 on interpretations of these symbols). Whereas Jane Jacobs (1969) has proposed an ingenious economic scenario to explain the size, importance, and in her view the "success" of Çatal Hüyük, Kelley Hays (1993) regards the size of the site, unparalleled in its time, as creating social problems. One means of dealing with the organization of large numbers of people and possibly differing cultural orientations is to invest in ritual behavior, negotiating identity through ceremony, and providing a new, or at least improved, context for community integration.

Following the collapse of Çatal Hüyük there was a disaggregation from which new developments emerged in the mid to late fourth millennium (e.g., Frangipane and Palmieri 1988). In the late fourth millennium, the "Uruk expansion" from southern Mesopotamia (Algaze 1993, Stein 1994, Yoffee 1995b) influenced local Anatolian sites. A state in the region emerged only in the second millennium, itself a complicated response to new movements of Hurrians and Indo-Europeans, as well as interactions with Old Assyrian merchant colonies.

Finally, in returning to the SW, one concludes that the Classic period Hohokam platform mound sites were not like the Chacoan rituality in the important respect of residential stability. Most of these platform mound sites that were the centers of communities were relatively long-lived and the community itself was integrated through a fixity and loyalty to place that is uncharacteristic of its Anasazi contemporaries (or for that matter of many SE chiefdoms, see Scarry, Chapter 5). Indeed, in the prehistoric Pueblo world, the normal adaptive strategy was of residential mobility, and aggregation was the prelude to abandonment (even though the size of the largest aggregated settlements increased through time).

POSTHUMOUS PRINCES AND COMPETITIVE CHIEFS IN SE SOCIAL SYSTEMS

If the SE archaeologists at Dragoon were impressed by the size of Hohokam canals and the uniqueness of Chaco, SW archaeologists were correspondingly awed by the largest Mississippian sites, particularly Cahokia with its immense Monks Mound and the rich burial accompaniments, including many human sacrifices, in nearby Mound 72. Nothing remotely like these finds exists in the SW, so it was hard for SE archaeologists—to a man,

downsizers—to convince their colleagues that the society dominated by Cahokia was not fundamentally different than its Mississippian counterparts elsewhere, at least the largest ones like Moundville in western Alabama. Yet, despite big piles of earth and many fancy artifacts, no hard data support claims for a highly centralized and populous society with the means to direct trade among distant folk, to exploit them for resources required by Cahokia's teeming masses, and to ship vast quantities of goods regularly and safely over long distances (Milner 1986).

SW archaeologists were also envious of historic—typically called ethnohistoric—accounts of SE societies by the adventurers who took part in the sixteenth century Spanish expeditions of de Soto, Luna, and Pardo, as well as by later explorers of other nationalities. Whereas SE archaeologists are, or should be, skeptical of reports in which Frenchmen encountered the rough equivalents of sun kings and Englishmen parliamentary councils (see Muller, Chapter 11), confidence in some aspects of early historic accounts has been bolstered by a careful linkage of documentary evidence with archaeological data (Hally et al. 1990; Hudson et al. 1985, 1990). Muller (1994 and Chapter 11) argues that historic groups offer good analogues for prehistoric societies, at least in some characteristics such as settlement size. Knight (1990) also believes that certain fundamental integrative elements of these societies survived into historic times. Nevertheless, it is still true that descriptions of historic groups, particularly the great bulk of materials that date from the eighteenth century and later, do not adequately depict the societies of much earlier times. Most SW archaeologists likewise agree that historic SW societies were less politically centralized and economically specialized than at least some of their prehistoric forebears (see Levy 1994; Yoffee 1994).

If SE archaeologists might agree that Hohokam societies were not classic chiefdoms—and not tribes or states either—and would go along with the idea that Chaco was a "rituality," no one doubts that SE societies conformed to many (but not all) of the attributes commonly thought of as defining a chiefdom. SE chiefdoms consisted of multiple communities in reasonably well defined territories that were more-or-less under a chief's authority. These territories can often be detected archaeologically through the spatial distribution of sites and distinctive pottery varieties. Chief's domains (or simply, chiefdoms) are generally small—a few tens of kilometers long up to just over a hundred kilometers. Populations were correspondingly small, often numbering in the thousands, but no more than a few tens of thousands (that is, no bigger than the largest historic tribes).

These were kin-based societies with offices ranked through genealogical principles. An emphasis on identification with the illustrious ancestors of leading people is archaeologically evident in buildings, often called "temples," built on flat-topped mounds, and hence referred to as "temple mounds." These structures were, in fact, charnel houses where the remains of important people and their near relatives were kept: these are the "posthumous princes" of the Dragoon discussions. Located in prominent places, typically fronting plazas where community events took place, the bone houses legitimized the exalted social standing of leading figures and their lineages. The highly visible "temples" and the stories told about these ancients presumably formed the rationale for claims to the superordinate positions of the living.

Feasting and attendant ceremonies took place at these principal places, and these events required food and sumptuary items as donations. The line between voluntary and coerced gifts was undoubtedly fuzzy, since obligations among kinfolk blended into transactions among more distantly related and even unrelated people who were motivated by the possibility of currying favor with their social superiors and their fear of retribution for non-compliance. There is some evidence for the movement of highly valued and symbol-laden items down social hierarchies, but such distribution was undoubtedly undertaken more for political than economic purposes. A chief sought to perpetuate and expand support by establishing relations with important local leaders who, in turn, jealously guarded their own prerogatives and constituencies. The downward exchange of goods, therefore, was neither a wealth-leveling mechanism nor a means of providing goods for people's basic needs. It was, instead, a way to garner the support necessary to back positions obtained through adroit manipulation of potential supporters.

Large buildings in prominent locations near or on mounds at several major sites have been identified as council houses. In at least some places, local authority structures, vested in councils, were never marginalized by the rise of chiefs. These were places where leading figures congregated to make certain key decisions.

Judging from historic accounts—although doubtless also true of prehistoric times—the power of chiefs (while varying greatly) was limited, both in the range of permissible actions and in the means available for carrying them out. Even the most powerful chiefs had to be skillful manipulators of social situations, negotiating among established but always mutable customs, providing incentives for cooperation and compliance, and checking the power of both potential and real rivals who were backed by their own support groups.

Evidence for economic specialization is at best equivocal, although the subject is hotly debated. Of course, there have been numerous discoveries of fancy objects made by skilled hands, and many of those items were fashioned from highly valued non-local materials. Most of them come from features that were associated with high-ranking people. These artifacts, however, are greatly over-represented in our collective archaeological consciousness. They tend to occur in sites and contexts, especially mound centers and cemeteries, that have been the traditional targets of excavations. Aesthetically pleasing ornaments and the like are naturally exhibited in museums and illustrated in archaeological reports where they seem even more abundant than they were in the excavations themselves.

Labor was certainly mobilized by leading people for major projects undertaken for the common good, such as defensive enclosures, and for the benefit of the superordinate group, such as monumental architecture that included mounds. A common layout of principal places was shared by sites across a broad geographic area. The demarcation of space and placement of important architecture figuratively and literally reinforced the high standing of chiefs and their close kinfolk (see Holley, Chapter 2). Impressive architecture reminded the populace of the leader's ability to intercede with the supernatural world, provide protection from threatening enemies, and moderate relations among fractious social groups.

Settlements great and small were essentially self-sufficient in that their residents were able to support themselves with the necessities of life. Although to some variable extent the goals and whims of major chiefs affected the inhabitants of outlying communities, these people had a great deal of freedom in the conduct of their daily lives. In fact, the political and social linkages among settlements (or in complex chiefdoms, constellations of settlements) were weak enough that they formed cleavage planes along which these sociopolitical systems would fragment.

The territories of chiefdoms tended to be made up of concentrations of settlements, and these site clusters were surrounded by sparsely occupied areas used for hunting. Such rarely frequented areas doubled as no-man's lands between antagonistic groups. To be sure, such zones were often resource-poor uplands situated between resource-rich river valleys. However, even prime land along major rivers was not occupied at all times. The overall picture is one of a discontinuous population distribution with pockets of people mostly along the rivers that cut their way through the Eastern Woodlands.

SW archaeologists find it remarkable that both large and small Mississippian sites scattered across much of the southern Eastern Woodlands shared so many easily recognizable organizational features. There is no SW equivalent to such geographically widespread social commonality: it is the fact of geographic proximity that enfolds the Hohokam and Anasazi as "SW" societies.

The self-sufficiency and organizational similarities among Mississippian sites—from villages to mound centers—are naturally dramatically different from the spatial organization of the landscape in early states. The formation of city-states typically entailed a systematic reorganization of the countryside; indeed, one may say that the process of "ruralization" is the twin of "urbanization" (Yoffee 1995a,b, 1996). In states, therefore, villages and towns were not residuals of a pre-state countryside, left behind in the centripetal tendencies that resulted in cities. Rather, the countryside was created in the process of state formation, and villages and towns became special purpose settlements that were located in relation to urban central places. In the Mississippian world, where large-scale social systems were essentially bigger versions of smaller systems, it is not at all clear that there was a fundamental hierarchical restructuring of the landscape such as characterized the formation of early states.

Cycling in the SE

With recent improvements in chronological controls and better coverages of broad geographical areas, researchers have begun to recognize that sociopolitical and demographic landscapes changed considerably over the course of the Late Prehistoric period in the southern Eastern Woodlands. The term "cycling" is now often applied to such phenomena, following Anderson's (1996a) lengthy exposition of the term. This concept was earlier elaborated by Henry Wright (1971:381–382, 1984:42–43, re-printed with emendations in 1994) as part of his distinction between simple chiefdoms and complex chiefdoms. The former refers to chiefdoms with one level of administrative hierarchy above the local level whereas in the latter there are two such levels. By their very nature, complex chiefdoms are considered unstable and likely to fission or devolve into simple chiefdoms. A fundamentally different kind of sociopolitical system, the state, arose only when this "cycle" was interrupted by successful paramount chiefs who somehow surmounted the divisive and inconclusive conflicts among near equals and managed to transform the basic administrative apparatus of the chiefdom (see Yoffee 1993).

In brief, Anderson (1996a) sees cycling in the late prehistoric SE as fluctuations in administrative levels between simpler and more complex forms of chiefdom organization. Complex chiefdoms emerged against the backdrop of simple ones, expanded, and finally fragmented. Individual components then went their own way or aligned themselves elsewhere as local circumstances dictated. The volatile nature of sociopolitical relations was largely a function of the inherently unstable properties of chiefdoms, especially the kin-based nature of authority, in which potential rivals could and did struggle for positions of limited power. Despite the ideal of a fixed successional progression, successful chiefs needed to combine personal charisma, good judgment, wariness over potential rivals, clever handling of followers and enemies, willingness to act decisively at the right moment with whatever means were immediately available, and downright good luck. Individual chiefs began their passage to regional dominance by gaining competitive advantage over neighboring societies that were smaller, less centrally organized, or both. They spread by incorporating new groups largely through the fear inspired by their greater size and the chance that affiliation might offset threats from other expanding chiefdoms. We refrain from calling this process of incorporation one of conquest, because relations among the structurally similar components of complex chiefdoms resembled alliances (if unequal alliances) more than outright subjugation. Still, there was a cost associated with incorporating ever greater numbers of non-kin into geographically large chiefdoms. The simple addition of structurally similar social units, each self-sufficient and led by high-ranking leaders drawn from locally influential lineages, created problems for paramount chiefs. SE societies seem never to have resolved the fundamental contradiction that must have risen repeatedly: a chief's strength was built on successful territorial expansion and population incorporation, but that very success created the potential for serious rifts in the fabric of society, including ones severe enough to bring him or her down.

Dominant elite groups were those that could attract the most followers and hence mobilize the labor needed to procure resources that guaranteed their high standing. These material benefits, however, had the potential for turning kin-related groups into contentious factions and accentuating friction over succession to the highest ranks in these societies. Thus, as chiefdoms became more successful, the stress on basic structures of kinship and the authority of leaders mounted, threatening the long-term viability of large-scale social formations. In the SE, alternative avenues for the legitimate participation of those individuals and lineages competing for high status and power were quite limited, with the notable exception of a man's chance to achieve renown and influence through good judgment, prowess, and good luck in war.

Even in the most complex chiefdoms, support for the highest ranked people was always contestable because the constituent parts of the social system were fully capable of operating on their own, and local interests often ran counter to the goals of principal chiefs. Factionalism was such an important component of SE life that Anderson (1990:81) can claim that it is the "competition for prestige and power between rival elites . . . [that] initiates and drives the cycling process.. . ." Fundamentally different ways of organizing and administering these societies might have arisen given sufficient time, reliable systems of agricultural production, further increases in population, more intensive warfare, and new mechanisms for creating and sustaining economic and social dependencies. We shall never know. The arrival of Europeans starting in the sixteenth century cut short any such possibilities and opened an entirely unprecedented chapter in Native American ways of life.

Archaeological data on late prehistoric SE societies and European eyewitness accounts of their early historic period descendants support the cycling model. Complex chiefdoms formed and dissolved in different places because the defensive alliances and social relations that served as the glue holding them together were based on flexible kinship structures susceptible to reinterpretation as circumstances dictated. Household economies were little differentiated, political offices were neither specialized nor particularly diverse, and chiefly alliances between leaders of structurally similar groups were situationally expedient and typically short-lived. Mounds were built by community labor for the use of important people, and clues to administrative coercion are negligibly present. Centripetal forces, such as nucleation to meet defensive needs, were matched by equally strong centrifugal forces, including flight stemming from factional competition. Endemic regional competition leading to the ascendancy and eclipse of individual chiefdoms had a correspondingly great effect on the establishment and abandonment of Mississippian mound centers.

Conclusion

The implication of the argument that chiefdoms are inherently unstable and far likelier to "cycle" than to be transformed into states (or city-states, the dominant form of ancient states) is that the pathway to states does not lie inevitably through the chiefdoms that have been documented in recent (ethnographic) or more distant (archaeological) times. Pre-state societies cannot be modeled adequately by analogy with ethnographic cases that themselves were not, and might never have become, states. Archaeologically known chiefdoms, for the same reasons, cannot be simply assumed to have been much like the precursors of societies that did become states. SE sequences may lend credibility to this line of thinking, although their cycling was abruptly terminated about half a millennium after the rather sudden emergence of chiefdoms across a broad geographic area.

The SW sequences are similarly important because they highlight the difficulty in labeling every society a chiefdom just because it is neither tribe nor state. The dimensions of complexity in Hohokam "communities" and the Chaco "rituality" deserve study on their own terms. Similar kinds of social organizations and evolutionary trajectories might have occurred elsewhere, but they will only be identified if archaeologists shed the shackles of customary classifications and look more closely at the evidence at hand.

From an inspection of SW and SE data and the perspectives presented in this volume, it is asserted that the following similarities between the two regions are superficial (all were raised for discussion in Dragoon): late prehistoric societies and sites were larger than what had come before; they shaped what came afterwards; they were pretty close in time and perhaps had minor, indirect (but debatable) contact; high status burials were present, although the ones in the East are more numerous and more splendid than the ones in the West; and there were sites with populations that presumably surpassed a threshold of local decision-making capability, indicating the existence of organizations that exceeded local authority structures. There are also, of course, many more obvious differences between the two regions—in environmental settings, histories of development, contacts with Mesoamerica—but this is not the place to enumerate them all.

Last, it is astonishing how archaeological knowledge and social evolutionary theory have converged in the last few decades. Old rocks and pots are, by any measure, now making solid contributions to our understanding of social evolution. This development has taken place as researchers have moved away from societal archetypes and toward studies of the many dimensions of complexity in ancient societies that are identifiable and sometimes quantifiable in the archaeological record. While the comparative method has become increasingly a feature of archaeological research, these cross-cultural studies have tended less to homogenize examples than once was the case. Adhering to the honorable principles of "controlled comparison" (sensu Eggan), archaeologists are refusing to de-historicize cultures. This emphasis, however, should not be confused with the old direct historical approach in which prehistoric societies were viewed merely as earlier versions of their historic counterparts extending far back into the mists of time.

We hope that our criticism of certain comparative perspectives in this chapter does not mark us in the eyes of readers as particularists, for that would be missing the point. By expanding the purview of social evolutionary theory, but rejecting categories of comparison that are both too specific and restrictive, we have sought to devalue all notions of progress in social evolutionary thinking and so to understand "development" and "evolutionary trajectories" in new ways. If the prehistoric societies in the SW and SE and elsewhere can no longer be seen as stages in a great chain of becoming (read Western nation-states), then our reflections on the Dragoon proceedings may have captured the higher purposes for which the conference was organized.

ACKNOWLEDGMENTS

Suzanne Fish and Norman Yoffee thank the editors of the proceedings of the 1993 Chacmool conference, published as "Debating Complexity" (Meyer et al. 1996), for permission to excerpt parts of the first section of this paper from our essay in that volume. We all thank Steve Lekson for his critical reading of an early draft of this chapter.

Contributors

David G. Anderson, National Park Service, Atlanta, Florida

Charles R. Cobb, Department of Anthropology, State University of New York, Binghamton, New York

Linda S. Cordell, University Museum, University of Colorado, Boulder, Colorado

Robert D. Drennan, Department of Anthropology, University of Pittsburgh, Pittsburgh, Pennsylvania

Suzanne K. Fish, Arizona State Museum, University of Arizona, Tucson, Arizona

George R. Holley, Office of Contract Archaeology, Southern Illinois University, Edwardsville, Illinois

Stephen H. Lekson, University Museum, University of Colorado, Boulder, Colorado

Randall H. McGuire, Department of Anthropology, State University of New York, Binghamton, New York

Jeffrey H. Maymon, R. Christopher Goodwin & Associates, Frederick, Maryland.

George R Milner, Department of Anthropology, Pennsylvania State University, University Park, Pennsylvania

Jon Muller, Department of Anthropology, Southern Illinois University, Carbondale, Illinois

Jill E. Neitzel, Department of Anthropology, University of Delaware, Newark, Delaware

John F. Scarry, Department of Anthropology, University of North Carolina, Chapel Hill, North Carolina

Sissel Schroeder, Department of Anthropology, Pennsylvania State University, University Park, Pennsylvania

David R. Wilcox, Museum of Northern Arizona, Flagstaff, Arizona

Norman Yoffee, Museum of Anthropology, University of Michigan, Ann Arbor, Michigan

Anne I. Woosley, Amerind Foundation, Inc., Dragoon, Arizona

Bibliography

Abbott, David R.
1996   Ceramic Exchange and a Strategy for Reconstructing Organizational Developments Among the Hohokam. In Interpreting *Southwestern Diversity: Underlying Principles and Overarching Patterns*, edited by Paul R. Fish and J. Jefferson Reid, pp.147–158, Arizona State University, Anthropological Research Papers No. 48, Tempe.

Abbott, David R., Kim E. Beckwith, Patricia L. Crown, R. Thomas Euler, David Gregory, J. Ronald London, Marilyn B. Saul, Larry A. Schwalb, and Mary Bernard-Shaw
1988   *The 1982–1984 Excavations at Las Colinas, Volume 4, Material Culture*. Arizona State Museum Archaeological Series No. 162. University of Arizona, Tucson.

Ackerly, Neal W.
1988   False Causality in the Hohokam Collapse. *The Kiva* 53:305–319.

Adair, James
1775   *The History of the American Indians: Particularly Those Nations Adjoining the Mississippi, East and West Florida, Georgia, South and North Carolina, and Virginia*. Edward and Charles Dilly, London. Reprinted 1930 by the Society of Colonial Dames, facsimile edition by Promontory Press, New York.

Adams, E. Charles
1991   *The Origin and Development of the Pueblo Katsina Cult*. University of Arizona Press, Tucson.

Adams, E. Charles, and Kelley A. Hays (editors)
1991   *Homol'ovi II: Archaeology of an Ancestral Hopi Village*. Anthropological Papers of the University of Arizona No. 55. University of Arizona Press, Tucson.

Adams, Robert McC.
1977   World Picture, Anthropological Frame. *American Anthropologist* 79:265–279.

Adler, Michael A.
1990   *Communities of Soil and Stone: An Archaeological Investigation of Population Aggregation among the Mesa Verde Anasazi A.D. 900 to 1300*. Unpublished Ph.D. dissertation, Department of Anthropology, University of Michigan, Ann Arbor.

Adler, Michael A. (editor)
1996   *The Prehistoric Pueblo World, A.D. 1150–1350*. University of Arizona Press, Tucson.

Ahlstrom, Gosta W.
1993   *The History of Ancient Palestine*. Fortress Press, Minneapolis.

Ahlstrom, Richard Van Ness
1985   *The Interpretation of Archaeological Tree-Ring Dates*. Unpublished Ph.D. dissertation, Department of Anthropology, University of Arizona, Tucson.

Ahlstrom, Richard Van Ness, and Heidi Roberts
1994   *Prehistory of Perry Mesa: The Short-Lived Settlement of a Mesa-Canyon Complex in Central Arizona, ca. A.D. 1200–1400*. SWCA Archaeological Report No. 93–48, Tucson.

Akins, Nancy J.

1984   Temporal Variation in Faunal Assemblages from Chaco Canyon. *In Recent Research on Chaco Prehistory*, edited by W. James Judge and John D. Schelberg, pp. 225–240. Reports of the Chaco Center No. 8. Division of Cultural Research, National Park Service, Albuquerque.

1986   *A Biocultural Approach to Human Burials from Chaco Canyon, New Mexico.* Reports of the Chaco Center No. 9. Branch of Cultural Research, National Park Service, Santa Fe.

Algaze, Guillermo

1993   *The Uruk World System.* University of Chicago Press, Chicago.

Altschul, Jeffrey

1993   Review of *Chaco and Hohokam: Prehistoric Regional Systems in the American Southwest*, edited by Patricia L. Crown and W. James Judge. *Anthropos* 88:573–574.

Alvarez, Ana María

1985   Sociedades Agrícolas. In *Historia General de Sonora*, vol. 1, edited by J. C. Montané, pp. 225–262. Gobierno del Estado de Sonora, Hermosillo.

Ambler, J. Richard

1985   Northern Kayenta Ceramic Chronology. *In Archaeological Investigations near Rainbow City, Navajo Mountain, Utah*, edited by Phil Geib, J. Richard Ambler, and Martha M. Callahan, pp. 28–68. Northern Arizona Archaeological Research Report No. 576. Northern Arizona University Archaeology Laboratory, Flagstaff.

Ambler, J. Richard, and Mark Q. Sutton

1989   The Anasazi Abandonment of the San Juan Drainage and the Numic Expansion. *North American Archaeologist* 10(1):39–53.

Anderson, David G.

1990   Stability and Change in Chiefdom-Level Societies: An Examination of Mississippian Political Evolution on the South Atlantic Slope. In *Lamar Archaeology: Mississippian Chiefdoms in the Deep South*, edited by J. Mark Williams and Gary Shapiro, pp.187–213. The University of Alabama Press, Tuscaloosa.

1994   *The Savannah River Chiefdoms: Political Change in the Late Prehistoric Southeast.* University of Alabama Press, Tuscaloosa.

1996a   Chiefly Cycling Behavior and Large-Scale Abandonments as Viewed from the Savannah River Basin. In *Political Structure and Change in the Prehistoric Southeastern United States*, edited by John F. Scarry, pp. 150–191. University Presses of Florida, Gainesville.

1996b   Factional Competition and the Political Evolution of Mississippian Chiefdoms in the Southeastern United States. In *Factional Competition and Political Development in the New World*, edited by Elizabeth M. Brumfiel and John W. Fox, pp. 61–76. University of Cambridge Press, Cambridge.

1996c   Fluctuations Between Simple and Complex Chiefdoms: Cycling in the Late Prehistoric Southwest. In *Political Structure and Change in the Prehistoric Southeastern United States*, edited by John F. Scarry, pp. 231–252. University Press of Florida, Gainesville.

1997a   A National Commitment to Archaeology. In *Common Ground: Archaeology and Ethnography in the Public Interest 2(1).* National Park Service Archeology and Ethnology Program, Washington, D.C.

1997b   The Role of Cahokia in the Evolution of Southeastern Mississippian Society. In *Cahokia: Domination and Ideology in the Mississippian World*, edited by Timothy R. Pauketat and Thomas E. Emerson. University of Nebraska Press, Lincoln.

Anderson, David G., and Joseph Schuldenrein (editors)

1985   *Prehistoric Human Ecology Along the Upper Savannah River: Excavations at the Rucker's Bottom, Abbeville and Bullard Site Groups.* National Park Service, Interagency Archaeological Services. Atlanta, Georgia.

Anderson, David G., David J. Hally, and James L. Rudolph

1986   The Mississippian Occupation of the Savannah River Valley. *Southeastern Archaeology* 5:32–51.

Anderson, David G., David W. Stahle, and Malcolm R. Cleaveland

1995   Paleoclimate and the Potential Food Reserves of Mississippian Systems: A Case Study from the Savannah River Valley. *American Antiquity* 60:258–286.

Anderson, Keith M.

1980   *Highway Salvage on Arizona State Highway 98: Kayenta Anasazi Sites Between Kaibito and the Klethla Valley.* Arizona State Museum Archaeological Series No. 140. University of Arizona, Tucson.

Anscheutz, Kurt F.

1995   Saving a Rainy Day: The Integration of Diverse Agricultural Technologies to Harvest and Conserve Water in the Lower Río Chama Valley, New Mexico. In *Soil, Water, Biology, and Belief in Prehistoric and Traditional Southwestern Agriculture*, edited by H. Wolcott Toll, pp. 25–39. New Mexico Archaeological Council Special Publication No. 2, Albuquerque.

Antieau, John M.

1981   *The Palo Verde Archaeological Investigations, Arizona Nuclear Power Project: Hohokam Settlement at the Confluence: Excavations Along the Palo Verde Pipeline.* Museum of Northern Arizona Research Paper No. 20, Flagstaff.

Anyon, Roger, Patricia A. Gilman, and Steven A. LeBlanc
1981   A Reevaluation of the Mogollon-Mimbres Archaeological Sequence. *The Kiva* 46:209–226.

Anyon, Roger and Steven A. LeBlanc
1980   The Evolution of Mogollon-Mimbres Communal Structures. *The Kiva* 45:253–277.
1984   *The Galaz Ruin: A Prehistoric Mimbres Village in Southwestern New Mexico*. University of New Mexico Press, Albuquerque.

Arensberg, Conrad
1961   The Community as Object and Sample. *American Anthropologist* 63:241–264.

Asch, David B., and Nancy B. Asch
1985   Prehistoric Plant Cultivation in West-Central Illinois. In *Prehistoric Food Production in North America*, edited by Richard I. Ford, pp. 149–203. Museum of Anthropology Anthropological Papers No. 75. University of Michigan, Ann Arbor.

Bandelier, Adolph F. A.
1890   *Final Report of Investigations among the Indians of the Southwestern United States, Carried out Mainly in the Years from 1880 to 1885*. Papers of the Archaeological Institute of America, American Series III (pt. 1), Cambridge.
1892   *Final Report of Investigations among the Indians of the Southwestern United States, Carried out Mainly in the Years from 1880 to 1885*. Papers of the Archaeological Institute of America, American Series IV (pt. 2), Cambridge.

Bannister, Bryant, William J. Robinson, and Richard L. Warren
1970   *Tree-ring Dates from New Mexico A, G-H, Shiprock-Zuni-Mt. Taylor Area*. Laboratory of Tree-ring Research, University of Arizona, Tucson.

Barbour, Philip L. (editor)
1969   *The Jamestown Voyages Under the First Charter 1606–1609, Volume I*. Hakluyt Society Second Series No. 136. Cambridge University Press, Cambridge.

Barker, Alex W., and Timothy R. Pauketat (editors)
1992   *Lords of the Southeast: Social Inequality and the Native Elites of Southeastern North America*. Archaeological Papers of the American Anthropological Association No. 3, Washington, D.C.

Barnett, Franklin
1974   *Excavation of Main Pueblo at Fitzmaurice Ruin, Prescott Culture in Yavapai County, Arizona*. Museum of Northern Arizona Special Publication, Flagstaff.
1978   *Las Vegas Ranch Ruin-East and Las Vegas Ranch Ruin-West—Two Small Prehistoric Prescott Indian Culture Ruins in West Central Arizona*. Museum of Northern Arizona Bulletin No. 51, Flagstaff.

Baugh, Timothy G.
1986   Cultural History and Protohistoric Societies in the Southern Plains. *Memoir No. 21, Plains Anthropologist* 31: (114:Pt. 2).

Bayman, James M.
1992   The Circulation of Exotics in a Tucson Basin Platform Mound Community. In *Proceedings of the Second Salado Conference*, edited by Richard C. Lange and Stephen Germick, pp. 22–30. Occasional Paper of the Arizona Archaeological Society, Phoenix.
1993   The Circulation of Exotics in a Tucson Basin Platform Mound Community. In *Proceedings of the Second Salado Conference, Globe, Arizona*, edited by Richard C. Lange and Stephen Germick, pp. 31–37. Occaional Paper of the Arizona Archaeological Society, Phoenix.
1994   *Craft Production and Political Economy at the Marana Platform Mound Community*. Unpublished Ph.D. dissertation, Department of Anthropology, Arizona State University, Tempe.
1996   Reservoirs and Political Integration in the Hohokam Classic Period. In *Debating Complexity: Proceedings of the Twenty-sixth Annual Chacmool Conference*, edited by Daniel A. Meyer, Peter C. Dawson, and Donald T. Hanna, pp. 119–124. The Archaeological Association of the University of Calgary, Alberta.

Beal, John D.
1987   *Foundations of the Rio Grande Classic: The Lower Chama River A.D. 1300–1500*. Southwest Archaeological Consultants Research Series, Santa Fe.

Beals, Ralph L., George W. Brainerd, and Watson Smith
1945   *Archaeological Studies in Northeast Arizona; a Report on the Archaeological Work of the Rainbow Bridge-Monument Valley Expedition*. University of California Publications in American Archaeology and Ethnology 44(1), Berkeley.

Beckwith, Kim E.
1988   Intrusive Ceramic Wares and Types. In *The 1982–1984 Excavations at Las Colinas: Material Culture*, by David R. Abbott, Kim E. Beckwith, Patricia L. Crown, T. Robert Euler, David Gregory, J. Ronald London, Marilyn B. Saul, Larry A. Schwalb, Mary Bernard-Shaw, Christine R. Szuter, and Arthur Vokes, pp. 199–256. Arizona State Museum Archaeological Series No. 162(4). University of Arizona, Tucson.

Bennett, Charles E. (translator)
1975   *Three Voyages, Rene Laudonniere*. University Presses of Florida, Gainesville.

Bennett, John W.
1944   Middle American Influences on Cultures of the Southeastern United States. *Acta Americana* 2:25–50.

Bense, Judith A.
1994 *Archaeology of the Southeastern United States: Paleoindian to World War I*. Academic Press, San Diego.

Bentley, Mark T.
1987 Masked Anthropomorphic Representations and Mogollon Cultural Ceremonialism: A Possible Pacific Coastal Influence Through Exchange. *The Artifact* 25(4):61–120.

Berdan, Frances F.
1982 *The Aztecs of Central Mexico: An Imperial Society*. Holt, Rinehart, and Winston, New York.

Berry, Michael S.
1982 *Time, Space, and Transition in Anasazi Prehistory*. University of Utah Press, Salt Lake City.

Billideau, Jenny
1986 On the Trail of the Turquoise Toad. Ms. on file, Museum of Northern Arizona Library, Flagstaff.

Binford, Lewis R.
1983 *Working at Archaeology*. Studies in Archaeology, Academic Press, New York.

1989 *Debating Archaeology*. Studies in Archaeology, Academic Press, San Diego.

Black, G. A.
1967 *Angel Site: An Archaeological, Historical and Ethnological Study*. Indiana Historical Society, Indianapolis.

Black, Kevin D.
1991 Archaic Continuity in the Colorado Rockies: The Mountain Tradition. *Plains Anthropologist* 36(133):1–30.

Blake, Michael, Stephen A. LeBlanc, and Paul E. Minnis
1986 Changing Settlement and Population in the Mimbres Valley, Southwest New Mexico. *Journal of Field Archaeology* 13:439–464.

Blanton, Richard E.
1976 Anthropological Studies of Cities. *Annual Review of Anthropology* 5:249–264.

1983 The Founding of Monte Alban. In *The Cloud People: Divergent Evolution of the Zapotec and Mixtec Civilizations*, edited by Kent V. Flannery and Joyce Marcus, pp. 83–87; (see also editors' notes, pp. 79–83). Academic Press, New York.

Blanton, Richard E., Gary M. Feinman, Stephen A. Kowalewski, and Peter N. Peregrine
1996 Agency, Ideology, and Power in Archaeological Theory I: A Dual-Processual Theory for the Evolution of Mesoamerican Civilization. *Current Anthropology* 37(1):1–14.

Blinman, Eric
1989 Potluck or Protokiva: Ceramics and Ceremonialism in Pueblo I Villages. In *The Architecture of Social Integration in Prehistoric Pueblos*, edited by William D. Lipe and Michelle Hegmon, pp. 113–124. Occasional Papers, No. 1. Crow Canyon Archaeological Center, Cortez, Colorado.

Blinman, Eric, and C. Dean Wilson
1989 Mesa Verde Region Ceramic Types. Paper presented at the NMAC Ceramic Workshop, Red Rock State Park, Minnesota, 3 June 1989.

1993 Ceramic Perspectives on Northern Anasazi Exchange. In *The American Southwest and Mesoamerica: Systems of Prehistoric Exchange*, edited by Jonathon E. Ericson and Timothy G. Baugh, pp. 65–94. Plenum Press, New York.

Blitz, John H.
1993 *Ancient Chiefdoms of the Tombigbee*. University of Alabama Press, Tuscaloosa.

Bloch, Marc
1953 *The Historian's Craft*. Vintage Books, New York.

Bourne, Edward G. (translator)
1904 *Narratives of the Career of De Soto, Volume II*. A. S. Barnes, New York.

Bozeman, T. K.
1981 *Moundville Phase Communities in the Black Warrior River Valley, Alabama*. Ph.D. dissertation, University of California, Santa Barbara. University Microfilms, Ann Arbor.

Bradfield, Wesley
1931 *Cameron Creek Village: A Site in the Mimbres Area in Grant County, New Mexico*. Monographs of the School of American Research 1, Santa Fe.

Bradley, Bruce A.
1992 Excavations at Sand Canyon Pueblo. In *The Sand Canyon Archaeological Project: A Progress Report*, edited by William D. Lipe, pp. 79–97. Occasional Papers, No. 2. Crow Canyon Archaeological Center, Cortez, Colorado.

Brain, Jeffrey P.
1978 Late Prehistoric Settlement Patterning in the Yazoo Basin and Natchez Bluff Regions of the Lower Mississippi Valley. In *Mississippian Settlement Patterns*, edited by Bruce D. Smith, pp. 331–368. Academic Press, New York.

1988 *Tunica Archaeology*. Papers of the Peabody Museum of American Archaeology and Ethnology 78. Harvard University, Cambridge.

1989 *Winterville: Late Prehistoric Culture Contact in the Lower Mississippi Valley*. Archaeological Report No. 23. Mississippi Department of Archives and History, Jackson.

Brain, Jeffery P., and Phillip Phillips
1996 *Shell Gorgets: Styles of the Late Prehistoric and Protohistoric Southeast*. Peabody Museum Press, Cambridge.

Brand, Donald D.
1935 Prehistoric Trade in the Southwest. *New Mexico Business Review* 4(4):202–209.

1938 Aboriginal Trade Routes for Sea Shells in the Southwest. *Yearbook of the Association of Pacific Coast Geographers* 4:3–10.

Braniff, Beatriz

1974   Sequencias Arqueológicas en Guanajuato y la Cuenca de México: Intento de Correlacíon. In *Teotihuacan: XI Mesa Redonda*, pp. 273–323. Sociedad Mexicana de Antropología, Mexico City.

Braun, David P., and Stephen E. Plog

1982   Evolution of Tribal Social Networks: Theory and Prehistoric North American Evidence. *American Antiquity* 47:504–525.

Breternitz, Cory D.

1982   Introduction to the Bis sa' ani Community Sites. In *Bis sa'ani: A Late Bonito Phase Community on Escavada Wash, Northwest New Mexico*, edited by Cory D. Breternitz, David E. Doyel, and Michael P. Marshall, pp.453–458. Navajo Nation Papers in Anthropology 14. Navajo Nation Cultural Resource Program, Window Rock.

Breternitz, Cory D. (editor)

1991   *Prehistoric Irrigation in Arizona: 1988 Symposium*. Soil Systems Publications in Archaeology 17. Soil Systems, Phoenix.

Breternitz, Cory D., David E. Doyel, and Michael P. Marshall (editors)

1982   *Bis sa' ani: A Late Bonito Phase Community on Escavada Wash, Northwest New Mexico*. Navajo Nation Papers in Anthropology 14. Navajo Nation Cultural Resource Program, Window Rock.

Breternitz, David A., Arthur H. Rohn, Jr., and Elizabeth A. Morris (compilers)

1974   *Prehistoric Ceramics of the Mesa Verde Region*. Museum of Northern Arizona Ceramic Series No. 5, Flagstaff.

Brose, David S.

1989   From the Southeastern Ceremonial Complex to the Southern Cult: "You Can't Tell the Players without a Program." In *The Southeastern Ceremonial Complex: Artifacts and Analysis*, edited by Patricia Galloway, pp.27–37. University of Nebraska Press, Lincoln.

Brown, I. W.

1993   Bottle Creek Journal 1993: An Account of Archaeological Research Conducted by the Alabama Museum of Natural History in the Mobile-Tensaw Delta. Ms. on file, Alabama Museum of Natural History, Tuscaloosa.

Brown, James A.

1971   The Dimensions of Status in the Burials at Spiro. In *Approaches to the Social Dimensions of Mortuary Practices*, edited by James A. Brown, pp. 92–112. Memoir 25. Society for American Archaeology, Washington, D.C.

1975   Spiro Art and Its Mortuary Contexts. In *Death and the Afterlife in Pre-Columbian America*, edited by Elizabeth P. Benson, pp. 1–32. Dumbarton Oaks, Washington, D.C.

1976   The Southern Cult Reconsidered. *Midcontinental Journal of Archaeology* 1:115–135.

1978   Charnel Houses and Mortuary Crypts: Disposal of the Dead in the Middle Woodland Period. In *Hopewell Archaeology: the Chillicothe Conference*, edited by David S. Brose and N'omi Greber, pp. 211–219. Kent State University Press, Kent, Ohio.

1985   The Mississippian Period. In *Ancient Art of the American Woodland Indians*, pp. 93–145. Harry N. Abrams, New York.

1989   On Style Divisions of the Southeastern Ceremonial Complex: A Revisionist Perspective. In *The Southeastern Ceremonial Complex: Artifacts and Analysis*, edited by Patricia Galloway, pp. 183–204. University of Nebraska Press, Lincoln.

1991   Afterword. In *Stability, Transformation, and Variation: The Late Woodland Southeast*, edited by Michael S. Nassaney and Charles R. Cobb, pp. 323–327. Plenum Press, New York.

Brown, James A., Richard A. Kerber, and Howard D. Winters

1990   Trade and the Evolution of Exchange Relations at the Beginning of the Mississippian Period. In *The Mississippian Emergence*, edited by Bruce D. Smith, pp. 251–280. Smithsonian Press, Washington, D.C.

Brunson, Judy L.

1989   *The Social Organization of the Los Muertos Hohokam: A Reanalysis of Cushing's Hemenway Expedition Data*. Unpublished Ph.D. dissertation, Arizona State University, Tempe.

Bryan, Kirk

1954   *The Geology of Chaco Canyon, New Mexico, in Relation to the Life and Remains of the Prehistoric Peoples of Pueblo Bonito*. Smithsonian Miscellaneous Collections 122(7). Washington, D.C.

Bryson, Reid A.

1988   Civilization and Rapid Climate Change. *Environmental Conservation* 15:7–15.

Bryson, Reid A., and Thomas J. Murray

1977   *Climates of Hunger: Mankind and the World's Changing Weather*. The University of Wisconsin Press, Madison.

Bullen, Ripley P.

1966   Stelae at the Crystal River Site, Florida. *American Antiquity* 31:861–865.

Burchett, Tim W.

1990   *Household Organization at Wupatki Pueblo*. Unpublished Master's thesis, Department of Anthropology, Northern Arizona University, Flagstaff.

Butler, Brian M.

1977   *Mississippian Settlement in the Black Bottom, Pope and Massac Counties, Illinois*. Ph.D. dissertation, Department of Anthropology, Southern

Illinois University, Carbondale. University Microfilms, Ann Arbor.

Cable, John S., and David E. Doyel
1987   Pioneer Period Village Structure and Settlement Pattern in the Phoenix Basin. In *The Hohokam Village: Site Structure and Organization*, edited by David E. Doyel, pp. 21–70. Southwest and Rocky Mountain Division of the American Association for the Advancement of Science Monograph, Glenwood Springs, Colorado.

Cameron, Catherine M.
1984   A Regional View of Chipped Stone Raw Material Use in Chaco Canyon. In *Recent Research on Chaco Prehistory*, edited by W. James Judge and John D. Schelberg, pp. 137–152. Reports of the Chaco Center No. 8. Division of Cultural Research, National Park Service, Albuquerque.

Camilli, Eileen L.
1983   *Site Occupational History and Lithic Assemblage Structure: An Example from Southeastern Utah.* Unpublished Ph.D. dissertation, Department of Anthropology, University of New Mexico, Albuquerque.

Canouts, Veletta (assembler)
1975   *An Archaeological Survey of the Orme Reservoir.* Arizona State Museum Archaeological Series No. 92. University of Arizona, Tucson.

Carlson, Roy L.
1982   The Polychrome Complexes. In *Southwestern Ceramics: A Comparative Review*, edited by Albert H. Schroeder, pp. 201–234. The Arizona Archaeologist No. 15. Arizona Archaeological Society, Phoenix.

Carneiro, Robert L.
1970   A Theory of the Origin of the State. *Science* 169:733–738.
1981   The Chiefdom as Precursor of the State. In *The Transition to Statehood in the New World*, edited by Grant D. Jones and Robert R. Krautz, pp. 37–79. Cambridge University Press, Cambridge.

Carrasco, David
1982   *Quetzalcoatl and the Irony of Empire.* University of Chicago Press, Chicago.

Casagrande, Joseph B., Stephen I. Thompson, and Philip D. Young
1964   Colonization as a Research Frontier: The Ecuadorian Case. In *Process and Pattern in Culture: Essays in Honor of Julian H. Steward*, edited by Robert A. Manners, pp. 281–325. Aldine, Chicago.

Castetter, Edward F., and Willis H. Bell
1942   *Pima and Papago Indian Agriculture.* Interamericana Studies No. 1, University of New Mexico Press, Albuquerque.

Casti, John L.
1994   *The Cognitive Revolution?* Santa Fe Institute Paper No. 93–05–030. Santa Fe Institute, Santa Fe.

Caywood, Louis R., and Edward H. Spicer
1935   *Tuzigoot: The Excavation and Repair of a Ruin on the Verde River near Clarkdale, Arizona.* USDI, National Park Service, Berkeley.

Chang, K. C.
1961   *Rethinking Archaeology.* Yale University Press, New Haven.
1980   *Shang Civilization.* Yale University Press, New Haven.

Chapman, Carl H.
1980   *The Archaeology of Missouri, II.* University of Missouri Press, Columbia and London.

Chapman, Carl H., John W. Cottier, David Denman, David R. Evans, Dennis E. Harvey, Michael J. Reagan, Bradford L. Rope, Michael D. Southard, and Gregory A. Waselkov
1977   Investigation and Comparison of Two Fortified Mississippi Tradition Archaeological Sites in Southeastern Missouri: A Preliminary Compilation. *The Missouri Archaeologist* 38 (whole volume).

Chapman, Jefferson, and Gary D. Crites
1987   Evidence for Early Maize (*Zea mays*) from the Icehouse Bottom Site, Tennessee. *American Antiquity* 52:352–354.

Cherry, John F.
1978   Generalisation and the Archaeology of the State. In *Social Organisation and Settlement: Contributions from Anthropology, Archaeology and Geography*, edited by David R. Green, Colin Haselgrove, and Matthew Spriggs, pp. 411–437. BAR series 47. Oxford.

Chisolm, Michael
1979   *Rural Settlement and Land Use: An Essay on Location.* Hutchinson University Library, London.

Clark, Jeffery
1967   *A Preliminary Analysis of Burial Clusters at the Grasshopper Site, East-Central Arizona.* Unpublished Master's thesis, Department of Anthropology, University of Arizona, Tucson.
1995   The Role of Migration in Social Change. In *The Roosevelt Community Development Study: New Perspectives on Tonto Basin Prehistory*, edited by Mark D. Elson, Miriam T. Stark, and David A. Gregory, pp. 369–384. Center for Desert Archaeology Anthropological Papers No. 15. Center for Desert Archaeology, Tucson.

Clark, Wayne E., and Helen C. Rountree
1993   The Powhatans and the Maryland Mainland. In *Powhatan Foreign Relations: 1500–1722*, edited by Helen C. Rountree, pp. 112–135. University of Virginia Press, Charlottesville.

Cobb, Charles R.
1988   *Mill Creek Chert Biface Production: Mississippian Political Economy in Illinois.* Unpublished Ph.D. dissertation, Department of Anthropology, Southern Illinois University at Carbondale.

1989 An Appraisal of the Role of Mill Creek Chert Hoes in Mississippian Exchange Systems. *Southeastern Archaeology* 8:79–92.

1991 100 Years of Investigations on the Linn Site in Southern Illinois. *Illinois Archaeology* 3:56–76.

Coe, Joffre L.
1995 *Town Creek Indian Mound: A Native American Legacy*. University of North Carolina Press, Chapel Hill.

Cole, Fay-Cooper and others
1951 *Kincaid: A Prehistoric Illinois Metropolis*. The University of Chicago Press, Chicago.

Collins, J. M.
1990 *Cahokia Interpretive Center Tract—Location II Project Description and Feature Analysis*. Illinois Cultural Resources Study 10. Illinois Historic Preservation Agency, Springfield.

Colton, Harold S.
1918 Geography of Certain Ruins near the San Francisco Mountains, Arizona. *Bulletin of the Geographical Society of Philadelphia* 16(2):37–60.

1939 Prehistoric Culture Units and Their Relationships in Northern Arizona. *Museum of Northern Arizona Bulletin* No. 17, Flagstaff.

1941 Prehistoric Trade in the Southwest. *Scientific Monthly* 52:308–319.

1946 *The Sinagua: A Summary of the Archaeology of the Region of Flagstaff, Arizona*. Museum of Northern Arizona, Bulletin No. 22, Flagstaff.

1960 *Black Sand: Prehistory in Northern Arizona*. University of New Mexico Press, Albuquerque.

Conrad, Lawrence A.
1989 The Southeastern Ceremonial Complex in the Northern Middle Mississippian Frontier: Late Prehistoric Politico-Religious Systems in the Central Illinois River Valley. In *The Southeastern Ceremonial Complex: Artifacts and Analysis*, edited by Patricia Galloway, pp. 93–113. University of Nebraska Press, Lincoln.

Cooper, Laurel M.
1992 Space Syntax in Chaco Canyon, New Mexico. Poster presented at the Third Southwestern Symposium, University of Arizona, Tucson.

Cordell, Linda S.
1979 *Cultural Resources Overview of the Middle Rio Grande Valley, New Mexico*. USDA Forest Service, Albuquerue.

1981 The Wetherill Mesa Simulation: A Retrospective. In *Simulations in Archaeology*, edited by Jeremy A. Sabloff, pp. 119–141. University of New Mexico Press, Albuquerque.

1984 *Prehistory of the Southwest*. Academic Press, Orlando.

1989a History and Theory in Reconstructing Southwestern Sociopolitical Organization. In *The Sociopolitical Structure of Prehistoric Southwestern Societies*, edited by Steadman Upham, Kent G. Lightfoot, and Roberta A. Jewett, pp. 33–54. Westview Press, Boulder.

1989b Northern and Central Rio Grande. In *Dynamics of Southwest Prehistory*, edited by Linda S. Cordell and George J. Gumerman, pp. 293–336. Smithsonian Institution Press, Washington, D.C.

1991 Anna O. Shepard and Southwestern Archaeology: Ignoring a Cautious Heretic. In *The Ceramic Legacy of Anna O. Shepard*, edited by Ronald L. Bishop and Frederick W. Lange, pp. 132–153. University Press of Colorado, Niwot, Colorado.

1994a The Nature of Explanation in Archaeology: A Position Paper. In *Understanding Complexity in the Prehistoric Southwest*, Santa Fe Institute, Studies in the Sciences of Complexity, vol. XIV, edited by George J. Gummerman and Murray Gell-Mann, pp. 149–162. Addison-Wesley, Reading, Massachusetts.

1994b Tracing Migration Pathways from the Receiving End. Paper presented at the Third Southwest Symposium, Arizona State University, Tempe.

Cordell, Linda S., and George J. Gumerman
1989a Cultural Interaction in the Prehistoric Southwest. In *Dynamics of Southwest Prehistory*, edited by Linda S. Cordell and George J. Gumerman, pp. 1–18. Smithsonian Institution Press, Washington, D.C.

Cordell, Linda S., and Fred Plog
1979 Escaping the Confines of Normative Thought: A Reevaluation of Puebloan Prehistory. *American Antiquity* 44:405–429.

Cordell, Linda S., and Steadman Upham
1989 Culture and Cultural Behavior: One More Time, Please. *American Antiquity* 54:815–819.

Cordell, Linda S., and George J. Gumerman (editors)
1989b *Dynamics of Southwest Prehistory*. Smithsonian Institution Press, Washington, D.C.

Cordell, Linda S., David E. Doyel, and Keith W. Kintigh
1994a Processes of Aggregation in the Prehistoric Southwest. In *Themes in Southwest Prehistory*, edited by George J. Gumerman, pp. 109–134. School of American Research Press, Santa Fe.

Cordell, Linda S., Jane H. Kelley, Keith W. Kintigh, Stephen H. Lekson, and Rolf M. Sinclair
1994b Toward Increasing Our Knowledge of the Past: A Discussion. In *Understanding Complexity in the Prehistoric Southwest*, Santa Fe Institute, Studies in the Sciences of Complexity, vol. XIV, edited by George J. Gummerman and Murray Gell-Mann, pp. 163–192. Addison-Wesley, Reading, Massachusetts.

Cosgrove, Hattie S., and C. Burton Cosgrove
1932 *The Swarts Ruin: A Typical Mimbres Site in Southwestern New Mexico*. Papers of the Peabody Museum of American Archaeology and Ethnology 15(1). Harvard University, Cambridge.

Covarrubias, Miguel
1954   *The Eagle, the Jaguar, and the Serpent: Indian Art of the Americas.* Knopf, New York.

Craig, Douglas B., Mark D. Elson, and Scott Wood
1992   The Growth and Development of a Platform Mound Community in the Eastern Tonto Basin. In *Proceedings of the Second Salado Conference*, edited by Richard C. Lange and Stephen Germick, pp. 38–49. Occasional Paper of the Arizona Archaeological Society, Phoenix.

Creamer, Winifred
1990   The Study of Prehistoric Demography in the Northern Rio Grande Valley. Paper presented at the 59th Annual Meeting of the American Association of Physical Anthropologists, Miami.

1991   Demographic Implications of Changing Use of Space in Pueblo Settlements of Northern New Mexico during the Protohistoric, A.D. 1450–1680. Paper presented at the 56th Annual Meeting of the Society for American Archaeology, New Orleans.

1992a   Demography and the Proto-Historic Pueblos of the Northern Rio Grande: A.D. 1450–1680. In *Late Prehistoric and Early Historic New Mexico*, edited by B. Vierra. New Mexico Archaeological Council, Albuquerque.

1992b   The Transition to History in the Rio Grande: Recent Work at Pueblo Blanco, New Mexico. Paper presented at the 65th Annual Pecos Conference, Pecos, New Mexico.

1993a   A Tale of Two Villages: Protohistoric Demography at Pueblo Blanco (LA 40) and San Marcos Pueblo (LA 98). Paper presented at the 58th Annual Meeting of the Society for American Archaeology, St. Louis.

1993b   *The Architecture of Arroyo Hondo Pueblo, New Mexico.* School of American Research Press, Santa Fe.

1994   Re-examining the Black Legend: Recent Research on Contact Period Demography in the Rio Grande Valley of New Mexico. *New Mexico Historic Review*, July:263–278.

Creamer, Winifred, and Judith Habicht-Mauche
1989   Analysis of Room Use and Residence Units at Arroyo Hondo. Paper presented at the 54th Annual Meeting of the Society for American Archaeology, Atlanta.

Creamer, Winifred, and Lisa Renken
1994   Testing Conventional Wisdom: Prehistoric Ceramics and Chronology in the Northern Rio Grande. Paper presented at the 59th Annual Meeting of the Society for American Archaeology, Anaheim.

Creamer, Winifred, Janna Brown, Tom Durkin, and Michael Taylor
1992   *Interim Report on Salvage Excavations at Pueblo Blanco (LA 40).* Report submitted to the New Mexico State Land Office, Santa Fe.

Creel, Darrell G.
1993   *Status Report on Excavations at the Old Town Site (LA 1113), Luna County, New Mexico, Summer 1993.* Report submitted to the Bureau of Land Management, New Mexico State Office by The Texas Archaeological Research Laboratory, University of Texas, Austin.

1994   Interpreting the End of the Mimbres Classic. Paper presented at the Spring Meeting of the Arizona Archaeological Council, Tucson.

Creel, Darrell G., and Charmion McKusick R.
1994   Prehistoric Macaws and Parrots in the Mimbres Area, New Mexico. *American Antiquity* 59:510–524.

Crown, Patricia L.
1981   *Variability in Ceramic Manufacture at Chodistaas Site, East-Central Arizona.* Unpublished Ph.D. dissertation, Department of Anthropology, University of Arizona, Tucson.

1987   Classic Period Hohokam Settlement and Land Use in the Casa Grande Ruins Area, Arizona. *Journal of Field Archaeology* 14:147–162.

1989   The Role of Exchange and Interaction in Salt-Gila Basin Hohokam Prehistory. In *Exploring the Hohokam: Prehistoric Desert Peoples of the American Southwest*, edited by George J. Gumerman, pp. 383–415. University of New Mexico Press, Albuquerque.

1990a   The Hohokam of the American Southwest. *Journal of World Prehistory* 4:223–355.

1990b   The Chronology of the Taos Area Anasazi. In *Clues to the Past: Papers in Honor of William M. Sundt*, edited by Meliha S. Duran and David T. Kirkpatrick, pp. 63–74. Papers of the Archaeological Society of New Mexico No. 16, Albuquerque.

1991a   The Hohokam: Current Views of Prehistory and the Regional System. In *Chaco and Hohokam: Prehistoric Regional Systems in the American Southwest*, edited by Patricia L. Crown and W. James Judge, pp. 135–157. School of American Research Press, Santa Fe.

1991b   Evaluating the Construction Sequence and Population of Pot Creek Pueblo, Northern New Mexico. *American Antiquity* 56(2):291–314.

1994   *Ceramics and Ideology: Salado Polychrome Pottery.* University of New Mexico Press, Albuquerque.

Crown, Patricia L., and Timothy A. Kohler
1994   Community Dynamics, Site Structure, and Aggregation in the Northern Rio Grande. In *The Ancient Southwestern Community*, edited by Wirt H. Wills and Robert D. Leonard, pp. 103–117. University of New Mexico Press, Albuquerque.

Crown, Patricia L., and W. James Judge (editors)
1991   *Chaco and Hohokam: Prehistoric Regional Systems in the American Southwest.* School of American Research Press, Santa Fe.

Crumrine, N. Ross

1977   *The Mayo Indians of Sonora: A People Who Refuse to Die.* University of Arizona Press, Tucson

Cully, Anne C., Marcia L. Donaldson, Mollie S. Toll, and Klara B. Kelley

1982   Agriculture in the Bis sa' ani community. In *Bis sa' ani: A Late Bonito Phase Community on Escavada Wash, Northwest New Mexico*, edited by Cory D. Breternitz, David E. Doyel, and Michael P. Marshall, pp. 115–166. Navajo Nation Papers in Anthropology 14. Navajo Nation Cultural Resource Program, Window Rock.

Cushing, Frank H.

1888   Preliminary Notes on the Origin, Working Hypothesis and Primary Researches of the Hemenway Southwestern Archaeological Expedition. In *Proceedings: 7th Congres Internacional Des Americanistes*, pp. 151–194. Congres Internacional Des Americanistes, Berlin.

Dalan, Rinita A.

1993   *Landscape Modification at the Cahokia Mounds Site: Geophysical Evidence of Culture Change.* Unpublished Ph.D. dissertation, Department of Ancient Studies, University of Minnesota.

Dalan, Rinita A., H. W. Watters, Jr., George R. Holley, and William I. Woods

1994   *Sixth Annual Cahokia Mounds Field School: Understanding Mound Construction.* Unpublished report submitted to the Illinois Historic Preservation Agency, Springfield.

Danson, Edward B.

1957   *An Archaeological Survey of West Central New Mexico and East Central Arizona.* Papers of the Peabody Museum of American Archaeology and Ethnology 44(1). Harvard University, Cambridge.

Davis, Emma Lou

1965   Small Pressures and Cultural Drift as Explanation for Abandonment of the San Juan Area, New Mexico. *American Antiquity* 30:353–355.

Dean, Jeffrey S.

1969   Chronological Analysis of Tsegi Phase Sites in Northeastern Arizona. *Papers of the Laboratory of Tree-Ring Research* No. 3. University of Arizona, Tucson.

1978   Independent Dating in Archaeological Analysis. In *Advances in Archaeological Method and Theory 1*, edited by Michael B. Schiffer, pp. 223–255. Academic Press, New York.

1991   Thoughts on Hohokam Chronology. In *Exploring the Hohokam: Prehistoric Desert Peoples of the American Southwest*, edited by George J. Gumerman, pp. 61–149. Amerind Foundation New World Studies Series 1. Amerind Foundation, Dragoon, Arizona, and University of New Mexico Press.

1992   Environmental Factors in the Evolution of the Chacoan Sociopolitical System. In *Anasazi Regional Organization and the Chaco System*, edited by David E. Doyel, pp. 35–44. Maxwell Museum of Anthropology, Anthropological Papers No. 5, Albuquerque.

Dean, Jeffrey S., and John C. Ravesloot

1993   The Chronology of Cultural Interaction in the Gran Chichimeca. In *Culture and Contact: Charles Di Peso's Gran Chichimeca*, edited by Anne I. Woosley and John C. Ravesloot, pp. 83–103. Amerind Foundation New World Studies Series 2. Amerind Foundation, Dragoon, Arizona, and University of New Mexico Press, Albuquerque.

Dean, Jeffrey S., and Richard L. Warren

1983   Dendrochronology. In *The Architecture and Dendrochronology of Chetro Ketl*, edited by Stephen H. Lekson, pp. 105–240. Reports of the Chaco Center No. 6. Division of Cultural Research, National Park Service, Albuquerque.

Dean, Jeffery S., William H. Doelle, and Janet Orcutt

1996   Adaptive Stress: Environment and Demography. In *Themes in Southwestern Prehistory*, edited by George J. Gumerman, pp. 53–86. School of American Research Press, Santa Fe.

DeAtley, Suzanne P.

1980   *Regional Interaction of the Animas Phase Settlements on the Northern Casas Grandes Frontier.* Unpublished Ph.D. dissertation, Department of Anthropology, University of California, Los Angeles.

Debowski, Sharon S., Anique George, Richard Goddard, and Deborah Mullon

1976   *An Archaeological Survey of the Buttes Reservoir.* Arizona State Museum Archaeological Series No. 93. University of Arizona, Tucson.

DeJarnette, David L., and Steve B. Wimberly

1941   *The Bessemer Site: Excavation of Three Mounds and Surrounding Village Areas near Bessemer, Alabama.* Paper 17. Geological Survey of Alabama Museum, Tuscaloosa.

DePratter, Chester B.

1991   *Late Prehistoric and Early Historic Chiefdoms in the Southeastern United States.* Garland Press, New York.

Dice, Michael H.

1993   *A Disarticulated Human Bone Assemblage from Leroux Wash, Arizona.* Unpublished Master's thesis, Arizona State University, Tempe.

Dick, Herbert W.

1965   *Picuris Pueblo Excavations.* Clearinghouse for Federal, Scientific, and Technical Information, Document No. PB-177047. National Technical Information Service, Springfield, Virginia.

1980   Cohesive and Dispersive Configurations in Settlement Patterns of the Northern Anasazi: A Hypothesis. In *Collected Papers in Honor of Helen Blumenschein*, edited by Albert H. Schroeder, pp. 57–82. Papers of the Archaeological Society of New Mexico, No. 5, Albuquerque.

Dickens, Roy S., Jr.
1978   Mississippian Settlement Patterns in the Appalachian Summit Area: The Pisgah and Qualla Phases. In *Mississippian Settlement Patterns*, edited by Bruce D. Smith, pp. 115–140. Academic Press, New York.

Dickson, D. Bruce, Jr.
1980   *Prehistoric Pueblo Settlement Patterns: The Arroyo Hondo, New Mexico, Site Survey.* School of American Research Press, Santa Fe.

Dincauze, Dena F., and R. J. Hasenstab
1989   Explaining the Iroquois: Tribalization on a Prehistoric Periphery. In *Centre and Periphery: Comparative Studies in Archaeology*, edited by T. Champion, pp. 67–87. Unwin Hyman, London.

Di Peso, Charles C.
1956   *The Upper Pima of San Cayetano del Tumacacori: An Archaeological Reconstruction of the Ootam of Pimeria Alta.* Amerind Foundation Publication No. 7. Dragoon, Arizona.
1968   Casas Grandes: A Fallen Trading Center of the Gran Chichimeca. *Masterkey* 42(1):20–37.
1974   *Casas Grandes: A Fallen Trading Center of the Gran Chichimeca.* vol. 1–3, Amerind Foundation Publication No. 9, Amerind Foundation, Dragoon, Arizona, and Northland Press, Flagstaff.
1979   Prehistory: Southern Periphery. In *Southwest*, edited by Alfonso Ortiz, pp. 152–161, Handbook of North American Indians, vol. 9, William C. Sturtevant, general editor. Smithsonian Institution, Washington D.C.
1983   The Northern Sector of the Mesoamerican World System. In *Forgotten Places and Things: Archaeological Perspectives on American History*, edited by Albert E. Ward, pp. 11–21. Contributions to Anthropological Studies 3. Center for Anthropological Research, Albuquerque.

Di Peso, Charles C., John B. Rinaldo, and Gloria J. Fenner
1974   *Casas Grandes: A Fallen Trading Center of the Gran Chichimeca.* vol. 4–8. Amerind Foundation Publication No. 9, Amerind Foundation, Dragoon, Arizona, and Northland Press, Flagstaff.

Dittert, Alfred E., Jr.
1959   *Culture Change in the Cebolleta Mesa Region, Central Western New Mexico.* Unpublished Ph.D. dissertation, Department of Anthropology, University of Arizona, Tempe.

Dobyns, Henry F.
1983   *Their Number Become Thinned: Native American Population Dynamics in Eastern North America.* University of Tennessee Press, Knoxville.

Doelle, William H.
1988   Preclassic Community Patterns in the Tucson Basin. In *Recent Research on Tucson Basin Prehistory*, edited by William H. Doelle and Paul R. Fish, pp. 277–312. Anthropological Papers No. 10, Institute for American Research, Tucson.

Doelle, William H., and Henry D. Wallace
1991   The Changing Role of the Tucson Basin in the Hohokam Regional System. In *Exploring the Hohokam: Prehistoric Desert Peoples of the American Southwest*, edited by George J. Gumerman, pp. 279–345. Amerind Foundation New World Studies Series 1. Amerind Foundation, Dragoon, Arizona, and University of New Mexico Press, Albuquerque.

Doelle, William H., Douglas B. Craig, and Henry D. Wallace
1992   Measuring Prehistoric Demographic Trends. Paper presented at the 57th Annual Meeting of the Society for American Archaeology, Pittsburgh.

Doolittle, William E.
1988   *Pre-Hispanic Occupance in the Valley of Sonora, Mexico: Archaeological Confirmation of Early Spanish Reports.* Anthropological Papers of the University of Arizona No. 48. University of Arizona Press, Tucson.
1990   *Canal Irrigation in Prehistoric Mexico: The Sequence of Technological Change.* University of Texas Press, Austin.
1992   Agriculture in North America on the Eve of Contact: A Reassessment. *Annals of the Association of American Geographers* 82:386–401.

Douglas, John E.
1992   Distant Sources, Local Contexts: Interpreting Nonlocal Ceramics at Paquime (Casas Grandes), Chihuahua. *Journal of Anthropological Research* 48(1):1–24.

Douglass, Andrew E.
1929   The Secret of the Southwest Solved by Talkative Tree Rings. *National Geographic* 56(6):736–770.

Downum, Christian E.
1988   *"One Grand History": A Critical Review of Flagstaff Archaeology, 1851 to 1988.* Unpublished Ph.D. dissertation, Department of Anthropology, University of Arizona, Tucson.
1993   *Between Desert and River: Hohokam Settlement and Land Use in the Los Robles Community.* Anthropological Papers of the University of Arizona No. 57. University of Arizona Press, Tucson.
n.d.   *Archaeology of the Pueblo Grande Platform Mound and Surrounding Features, Volume 4: The Pueblo Grande Platform Mound Compound.* Pueblo Grande Museum Anthropological Papers No. 1. Pueblo Grande Museum, Phoenix, (in press).

Downum, Christian E., and John H. Madsen
1993   Classic Period Platform Mounds South of the Gila River. In *The Northern Tucson Basin Survey: Research Directions and Background Studies*, edited by John H. Madsen, Paul R. Fish and Suzanne K. Fish, pp. 125–142. Arizona State Museum Archaeological Series No. 182. University of Arizona, Tucson.

Downum, Christian E., and Todd W. Bostwick (editors)
1993   *Archaeology of the Pueblo Grande Platform Mound and Surrounding Features, Volume 1: Introduction to the Archival Project and History of Archaeological Research*. Pueblo Grande Museum Anthropological Papers No. 1, Phoenix.

Downum, Christian E., Paul R. Fish, and Suzanne K. Fish
1994   Refining the Role of Cerros de Trincheras in Southern Arizona. *Kiva* 59:271–296.

Doyel, David E.
1974   *Excavations in the Escalante Ruin Group, Southern Arizona*. Arizona State Museum Archaeological Series No. 37. University of Arizona, Tucson.

1979   The Prehistoric Hohokam of the Arizona Desert. *American Scientist* 67:544–554.

1980   Hohokam Social Organization and the Sedentary to Classic transition. In *Current Issues in Hohokam Prehistory: Proceedings of a Symposium,* edited by David E. Doyel and Fred Plog, pp. 23–40. Arizona State University, Anthropological Research Papers No. 23, Tempe.

1981   *Late Hohokam Prehistory in Southern Arizona*. Contributions to Archaeology 2. Gila Press, Scottsdale, Arizona.

1991   Hohokam Cultural Evolution in the Phoenix Basin. In *Exploring the Hohokam: Desert Peoples of the American Southwest*, edited by George J. Gumerman, pp. 231–278. Amerind Foundation New World Studies Series 1. Amerind Foundation, Dragoon, Arizona, and University of New Mexico Press, Albuquerque.

1992   Introduction. In *Anasazi Regional Organization and the Chaco System*, edited by David E. Doyel, pp. 3–14. Maxwell Museum of Anthropology, Anthropological Papers No. 5. University of New Mexico, Albuquerque.

Doyel, David E. (editor)
1987   *The Hohokam Village: Site Structure and Organization*. Southwest and Rocky Mountain Division of the American Association for the Advancement of Science Monograph, Glenwood Springs, Colorado.

1992   *Anasazi Regional Organization and the Chaco System*. Maxwell Museum of Anthropology, Anthropological Papers No. 5, University of New Mexico, Albuquerque.

Doyel, David E., and Stephen H. Lekson
1992   Regional Organization in the American Southwest. In *Anasazi Regional Organization and the Chaco System*, edited by David E. Doyel, pp. 15–22. Maxwell Museum of Anthropology, Anthropological Papers No. 5. University of New Mexico, Albuquerque.

Doyel, David E., and Fred Plog (editors)
1980   *Current Issues in Hohokam Prehistory: Proceedings of a Symposium*. Arizona State University, Anthropological Research Papers No. 23, Tempe.

Doyel, David E., Cory D. Breternitz, and Michael P. Marshall
1984   Chacoan Community Structure: Bis sa' ani Pueblo and the Chaco Halo. In *Recent Research on Chaco Prehistory*, edited by W. James Judge and John D. Schelberg, pp. 37–54. Reports of the Chaco Center No. 8. Division of Cultural Research, National Park Service, Albuquerque.

Drennan, Robert D.
1984   Long-Distance Transport Cost in Pre-Hispanic Mesoamerica. *American Anthropologist* 86(1):105–112.

1991   Pre-Hispanic Chiefdom Trajectories in Mesoamerica, Central America, and Northern South America. In *Chiefdoms: Power, Economy, and Ideology*, edited by Timothy K. Earle, pp. 263–287. Cambridge University Press, Cambridge.

Drennan, Robert D., and Carlos A. Uribe (editors)
1987   *Chiefdoms in the Americas*. University Press of America, Lanham, Maryland.

Dunnell, Robert C.
1990   The Role of the Southeast in American Archaeology. *Southeastern Archaeology* 9:11–22.

Dutton, Bertha P.
1963   *Sun Father's Way: The Kiva Murals of Kuaua, a Pueblo Ruin, Coronado State Monument, New Mexico*. University of New Mexico Press, Albuquerque, School of American Research, Santa Fe, and Museum of New Mexico Press, Santa Fe.

Dyson, Stephen L.
1989   The Role of Ideology and Institutions in Shaping Classical Archaeology in the Nineteenth and Twentieth Centuries. In *Tracing Archaeology's Past: the Historiography of Anthropology*, edited by Andrew L. Christenson, pp. 127–136. Southern Illinois University Press, Carbondale.

Earle, Timothy K.
1977   A Reappraisal of Redistribution: Complex Hawaiian Chiefdoms. In *Exchange Systems in Prehistory*, edited by Timothy K. Earle and Jonathon E. Ericson, pp. 213–229. Academic Press, New York.

1978   *Economic and Social Organization of a Complex Chiefdom: The Halalea District, Kaua'i, Hawaii*. Anthropological Papers, Museum of Anthropology, University of Michigan No. 63, Ann Arbor.

1987a   Chiefdoms in Archaeological and Ethnohistorical Perspective. *Annual Review of Anthropology* 16:279–308.

1987b   Specialization and the Production and Exchange of Wealth: Hawaiian Chiefdoms and the Inka Empire. In *Specialization, Exchange, and Complex Societies*, edited by Elizabeth M. Brumfiel and Timothy K. Earle, pp. 64–75. Cambridge University Press, Cambridge.

1991a   The Evolution of Chiefdoms. In *Chiefdoms: Power, Economy, and Ideology*, edited by Timothy K. Earle, pp. 1–15. Cambridge University Press, Cambridge.

Earle, Timothy K. (editor)

1991b   *Chiefdoms: Power, Economy, and Ideology*. Cambridge University Press, Cambridge.

Eddy, Frank W.

1966   *Prehistory in the Navajo Reservoir District in Northwestern New Mexico*. Museum of New Mexico Papers in Anthropology 4, Santa Fe.

1993   *Recent Research at Chimney Rock*. The Chimney Rock Archaeological Symposium, USDA Forest Service, Technical Report No. RM-227, Fort Collins, Colorado.

Effland, Richard W., Jr., A. Trinkle Jones, and Robert C. Euler

1982   *The Archaeology of Powell Plateau: Regional Interaction at Grand Canyon*. Grand Canyon Natural History Association Monograph No. 3, Prescott.

Eggan, Fred

1950   *Social Organization of the Western Pueblos*. University of Chicago Press, Chicago.

Eighmy, Jeffrey L., and Robert S. Sternberg (editors)

1990   *Archaeomagnetic Dating*. University of Arizona Press, Tucson.

Emerson, Thomas E.

1989   Water, Serpents, and the Underworld: An Exploration into Cahokian Symbolism. In *The Southeastern Ceremonial Complex: Artifacts and Analysis*, edited by Patricia Galloway, pp. 45–92. University of Nebraska Press, Lincoln.

1991   Some Perspectives on Cahokia and the Northern Mississippian Expansion. In *Cahokia and the Hinterlands: Middle Mississippian Cultures of the Midwest*, edited by Thomas E. Emerson and R. Barry Lewis, pp. 221–236. University of Illinois Press, Urbana.

1997   Mississippian Ideology. In *Cahokia: Domination and Ideology in the Mississippian World*, edited by Timothy R. Pauketat and Thomas E. Emerson. University of Nebraska Press, Lincoln.

Emerson, Thomas E., and R. Barry Lewis (editors)

1991   *Cahokia and the Hinterlands: Middle Mississippian Cultures of the Midwest*. University of Illinois Press, Urbana.

Esarey, Duane, and T. W. Good

1981   *Final Report on FAI-270 and Illinois Route 460 Related Excavations at the Lohmann Site, 11-S-49, St. Clair County, Illinois*. FAI-270 Archaeological Mitigation Project Report 39.

Department of Sociology and Anthropology, Western Illinois University.

Fagan, Brian

1994   A Case of Cannibalism. *Archaeology* 47(1):11–16.

Fairbanks, C.

1946   The Macon Earthlodge. *American Antiquity* 12:94–108.

1956   *Archaeology of the Funeral Mound, Ocmulgee*. Archaeological Research Series 3. National Park Service, United States Department of the Interior, Washington, D.C.

Fairley, Helen C., and Phil R. Geib

1989   Data Gaps and Research Issues in Arizona Strip Prehistory. In *Man, Models, and Management: An Overview of the Archaeology of the Arizona Strip and the Management of its Cultural Resources*, edited by Jeffrey H. Altschul and Helen C. Fairley, pp. 219–244. Statistical Research, Tucson.

Farmer, Malcolm F.

1935   The Mojave Trade Route. *The Masterkey* 9(5):155–157.

Feinman, Gary M.

1991   Hohokam Archaeology in the Eighties: An Outside View. In *Exploring the Hohokam: Prehistoric Desert Peoples in the American Southwest*, edited by George J. Gumerman, pp. 461–485. Amerind Foundation New World Stidies Series 1. Amerind Foundation New World Studies Series 1. Amerind Foundation, Dragoon, Arizona, and University of New Mexico Press, Albuquerque.

1995   The Emergence of Inequality: A Focus on Strategies and Processes. In *Foundations of Social Inequality*, edited by T. Douglas Price and Gary M. Feinman, pp. 255–279. Plenum Press, New York.

Feinman, Gary M., and Jill E. Neitzel

1984   Too Many Types: An Overview of Sedentary Prestate Societies in the Americas. In *Advances in Archaeological Method and Theory 7*, edited by Michael B. Schiffer, pp. 39–102. Academic Press, New York.

Ferdon, Edwin N., Jr.

1955   *A Trial Survey of Mexican-Southwestern Architectural Parallels*. Monographs of the School of American Research No. 21. Santa Fe.

Ferguson, William M., and Arthur H. Rohn

1987   *Anasazi Ruins of the Southwest in Color*. University of New Mexico Press, Albuquerque.

Fewkes, Jesse W.

1912a   *Antiquities of the Upper Verde River and Walnut Creek Valleys, Arizona*. Twenty-eighth Annual Report of the Bureau of American Ethnology for the Years 1906–1907, pp. 181–220. Smithsonian Institution, Washington, D.C.

1912b   *Casa Grande, Arizona*. Twenty-eighth Annual Report of the Bureau of American Ethnology for the Years 1906–1907, pp. 25–180. Smithsonian Institution, Washington, D.C.

Findlow, Frank, and Suzanne P. DeAtley
1978　An Ecological Analysis of Animas Phase Assemblages in Southwestern New Mexico. *Journal of New World Archaeology* 2(5):6–18.

Fischer, Fred W.
1972　Recent Archaeological Investigations on the Fourth Elevation of Monk's Mound, Madison County, Illinois. Ms. on file, Department of Anthropology, Washington University, St. Louis.

Fish, Paul R.
1989　The Hohokam: 1000 Years of Prehistory in the Sonoran Desert. In *Dynamics of Southwest Prehistory*, edited by Linda S. Cordell and George J. Gumerman, pp. 19–63. Smithsonian Institution Press, Washington, D.C.

Fish, Paul R., and Suzanne K. Fish
1989　Hohokam Warfare from a Regional Perspective. In *Cultures in Conflict: Current Archaeological Perspectives, Proceedings of the Twentieth Annual Chacmool Conference*, edited by Diana C. Tkaczuk and Brian C. Vivian, pp. 112–129. The Archaeological Association of the University of Calgary, Alberta.
1991　Hohokam Political and Social Organization. In *Exploring the Hohokam: Prehistoric Desert Peoples of the American Southwest*, edited by George J. Gumerman, pp. 151–175. Amerind Foundation New World Studies Series 1. Amerind Foundation, Dragoon, Arizona, and University of New Mexico Press, Albuquerque.
1994　Southwest and Northwest: Recent Research at the Juncture of the United States and Mexico. *Journal of Archaeological Research* 2:3–44.

Fish, Paul R., Suzanne K. Fish, Curtiss Brennan, Douglas Gann, and James M. Baymen
1992a　Marana: Configuration of an Early Classic Period Hohokam Platform Mound Site. In *Proceedings of the Second Salado Conference*, edited by Richard C. Lange and Stephen Germick, pp. 62–68. Occasional Paper of the Arizona Archaeological Society, Phoenix.

Fish, Paul R., Suzanne K. Fish, Stephanie Whittlesey, Hector Neff, Michael D. Glasscock, and J. Michael Elam
1992b　An Evaluation of the Production and Exchange of Tanque Verde Red-on-Brown Ceramics in Southern Arizona. In *Chemical Characterization of Ceramic Pastes in Archaeology*, edited by Hector Neff. Monographs in World Archaeology 7:233–254. Prehistory Press, Madison.

Fish, Suzanne K.
1996　Dynamics of Scale in the Southern Deserts. In *Interpreting Southwestern Diversity: Underlying Principles and Overarching Patterns*, edited by Paul R. Fish and J. Jefferson Reid, pp. 107–114.

Arizona State University, Anthropological Research Papers No. 48, Tempe.

Fish, Suzanne K., and Marcia Donaldson
1991　Production and Consumption in the Archaeological Record: A Hohokam Example. *Kiva* 56:255–275.

Fish, Suzanne K., and Paul R. Fish
1990　An Archaeological Assessment of Ecosystems in the Tucson Basin of Southern Arizona. In *The Ecosystem Concept in Anthropology*, edited by Emilio F. Moran, pp. 159–190. University of Michigan Press, Ann Arbor.
1993　An Assessment of Classic Period Hohokam Abandonment in the Tucson Basin. In *The Abandonment of Settlements and Regions*, edited by Catherine M. Cameron and Steve A. Tomka, pp. 99–109. Cambridge University Press, Cambridge.
1994　Multisite Communities as Measures of Hohokam Aggregation. In *The Ancient Southwestern Community*, edited by Wirt H. Wills and Robert D. Leonard, pp. 119–130. University of New Mexico Press, Albuquerque.

Fish, Suzanne K., and Gary P. Nabhan
1991　Desert as Context: the Hohokam Environment. In *Exploring the Hohokam: Prehistoric Desert Peoples of the Southwest*, edited by George J. Gumerman, pp. 29–60. Amerind Foundation New World Studies Series 1. Amerind Foundation, Dragoon, Arizona, and University of New Mexico Press, Albuquerque.

Fish, Suzanne K., and Norman Yoffee
1995　The Hohokam "State." In *Debating Complexity: Proceedings of the Twenty-sixth Annual Chacmool Conference*, edited by Daniel A. Meyer, Peter C. Dawson, and Donald T. Hanna. The Archaeological Association of the University of Calgary, Alberta.

Fish, Suzanne K., and Paul R. Fish (editors)
1984　*Prehistoric Agricultural Strategies in the Southwest*. Arizona State University, Anthropological Research Papers No. 33, Tempe.

Fish, Suzanne K., Paul R. Fish, and Christian E. Downum
1984　Hohokam Terraces and Agricultural Production in the Tucson Basin. In *Prehistoric Agricultural Strategies in the Southwest*, edited by Suzanne K. Fish and Paul R. Fish, pp. 55–72. Arizona State University, Anthropological Research Papers No. 33, Tempe.

Fish, Suzanne K., Paul R. Fish, and John H. Madsen
1989　Classic Period Hohokam Community Integration in the Tucson Basin. In *the Sociopolitical Structure of Prehistoric Southwestern Societies*, edited by Steadman Upham, Kent G. Lightfoot, and Roberta A. Jewett, pp. 237–267. Westview Press, Boulder.
1990　Analyzing Regional Agriculture: A Hohokam Example. In *The Archaeology of Regions: The*

Case for Full Coverage Survey, edited by Suzanne K. Fish and Stephen A. Kowalewski, pp. 189–218. Smithsonian Institution Press, Washington, D.C.

Fish, Suzanne K., Paul R. Fish, and John H. Madsen (editors)

1992   *The Marana Community in the Hohokam World.* Anthropological Papers of the University of Arizona No. 56. University of Arizona Press, Tucson.

Fish, Suzanne K., Paul R. Fish, Charles H. Miksicek, and John H. Madsen

1985   Prehistoric Agave Cultivation in Southern Arizona. *Desert Plants* 7(2):100,107–112.

Flannery, Kent V.

1968   Archaeological Systems Theory and Early Mesoamerica. In *Anthropological Archaeology in the Americas*, edited by Betty J. Meggers, pp. 67–87. Anthropological Society of Washington, Washington, D.C.

1972a   The Cultural Evolution of Civilizations. *Annual Review of Ecology and Systematics* 3:399–426.

1972b   The Origins of the Village as a Settlement Type in Mesoamerica and the Near East: A Comparative Approach. In *Man, Settlement, and Urbanism: Proceedings of a Meeting of the Research Seminar in Archaeology and Related Subjects held at Institute of Archaeology, London University*, edited by Peter J. Ucko, Ruth Tringham, and George W. Dimbleby, pp. 23–53. Duckworth, Cambridge.

Flannery, Kent V. (editor)

1976   *The Early Mesoamerican Village.* Academic Press, New York.

Ford, Richard I.

1985   Patterns of Prehistoric Food Production in North America. In *Prehistoric Food Production in North America*, edited by Richard I. Ford, pp. 341–364. Museum of Anthropology Anthropological Papers No. 75. University of Michigan, Ann Arbor.

Ford, Richard I., Albert H. Schroeder, and Stewart L. Peckham

1972   Three Perspectives on Puebloan Prehistory. In *New Perspectives on the Pueblos*, edited by Alfonso Ortiz, pp. 19–39. University of New Mexico Press, Albuquerque.

Fowler, Andrew P., and John R. Stein

1992   The Anasazi Great House in Space, Time, and Paradigm. In *Anasazi Regional Organization and the Chaco System*, edited by David E. Doyel, pp. 101–122. Maxwell Museum of Anthropology, Anthropological Papers No. 5. University of New Mexico, Albuquerque.

Fowler, Andrew P., John R. Stein, and Roger Anyon

1987   An Archaeological Reconnaissance of West-Central New Mexico: the Anasazi Monuments Project. Ms. on file, Zuni Archaeological Program, Zuni, New Mexico.

Fowler, Melvin L.

1974   *Cahokia: Ancient Capital of the Midwest.* Addison-Wesley Module in Anthropology 48. Cummings Publishers, Menlo Park, California.

1975a   Footnote to "A Population Estimate for Cahokia," by M. L. Gregg. In *Perspectives in Cahokia Archaeology*, edited by James A. Brown, pp. 126–136. Illinois Archaeological Survey Bulletin No. 10, Urbana.

1975b   A Pre-Columbian Urban Center on the Mississippi. *Scientific American* 233(2):92–101.

1978   Cahokia and the American Bottom: Settlement Archeology. In *Mississippian Settlement Patterns*, edited by Bruce D. Smith, pp. 455–478. Academic Press, New York.

1989   *The Cahokia Atlas: A Historical Atlas of Cahokia Archaeology.* Studies in Illinois Archaeology No. 6. Illinois Historic Preservation Agency, Springfield.

1991   Mound 72 and Early Mississippian at Cahokia. In *New Perspectives on Cakokia: Views from the Periphery*, edited by James B. Stoltman, pp. 1–28. Prehistory Press, Madison, Wisconsin.

Frangipane, M., and A. Palmieri

1988   Aspects of Centralization in the Lake Uruk Period in Mesopotamian Periphery. *Origini* 14:539–560.

Fried, Morton H.

1967   *The Evolution of Political Society.* Random House, New York.

1975   *The Notion of Tribe.* Cummings Publishing Company, Menlo Park, California.

Frisbie, Theodore

1978   High Status Burials in the Greater Southwest: An Interpretive Synthesis. In *Across the Chichimec Sea: Papers in Honor of J. Charles Kelley*, edited by Carroll L. Riley and Basil C. Hedrick, pp. 202–232. Southern Illinois University Press, Carbondale.

Fritz, Gayle J.

1990   Multiple Pathways to Farming in Precontact Eastern North America. *Journal of World Prehistory* 4:387–435.

Fritz, John M.

1978   Paleopsychology Today: Ideational Systems and Human Adaptation in Prehistory. In *Social Archaeology: Beyond Subsistence and Dating*, edited by Charles L. Redman, Mary Jane Berman, Edward V. Curtin, William T. Langhorne, Jr., Nina M. Versaggi, and Jeffery C. Wanser, pp. 37–60. Academic Press, New York.

Fuller, R. S., and I. W. Brown

1992   Recent Research at the Bottle Creek Mounds, SW Alabama. *LAMAR Briefs* 19:5–6.

Galloway, Patricia (editor)

1989   *The Southeastern Ceremonial Complex: Artifacts and Analysis.* University of Nebraska Press, Lincoln.

Garland, E. B.
1992   *The Obion Site: An Early Mississippian Center in Western Tennessee*. Report of Investigations 7. Cobb Institute of Archaeology, Mississippi State University.

Gasser, Robert E., and Scott M. Kwiatkowski
1991   Food for Thought: Recognizing Patterns in Hohokam Subsistence. In *Exploring the Hohokam: Prehistoric Desert Peoples of the American Southwest*, edited by George J. Gumerman, pp. 417–459. Amerind Foundation New World Studies Series 1. Amerind Foundation, Dragoon, Arizona, and University of New Mexico Press, Albuquerque.

Gearing, Fred
1962   Priests and Warriors: Social Structures for Cherokee Politics in the 18th Century. *American Anthropological Association, Memoir 93*, Menasha, Wisconsin.

Geib, Phil R.
1993   New Evidence for the Antiquity of Fremont Occupation in Glen Canyon, South-central Utah. In *Proceedings of the First Biennial Conference on Research in Colorado Plateau National Parks*, edited by Peter G. Rowlands, Charles van Riper III, and Mark K. Sogge, pp. 154–165. Northern Arizona University, Flagstaff.

Gell-Mann, Murray
1990   Santa Fe Institute lecture, January 9, 1990, Santa Fe, New Mexico.

Gibbon, Guy E.
1974   A Model of Mississippian Development and Its Implications for the Red Wing Area. In *Aspects of Upper Great Lakes Anthropology*, edited by Elden Johnson, pp. 129–137. Minneapolis Historical Society, St. Paul.

Gilman, Patricia A.
1991   Changing Land Use and Pit Structure Seasonalitiy Along the San Simon Drainage in Southeastern Arizona. In *Mogollon V*, edited by Patrick H. Beckett, pp. 11–27. COAS Publishing and Research, Las Cruces.

Gilpin, Dennis
1989   Great Houses and Pueblos in Northeastern Arizona. Paper presented at the 1989 Pecos Conference, Bandelier National Monument, August 17–20, 1989. Ms. on file, Museum of Northern Arizona Library, Flagstaff.

Gladwin, Harold S., Emil W. Haury, Edwin B. Sayles, and Nora Gladwin
1937   *Excavations at Snaketown: Material Culture*. Medallion Papers No. 25. Gila Pueblo, Globe, Arizona.

Goldman, Irving
1970   *Ancient Polynesian Society*. The University of Chicago Press, Chicago.

Goldstein, Lynne G.
1980   *Mississippian Mortuary Practices: A Case Study of Two Cemeteries in the Lower Illinois Valley*. Scientific Papers 4. Northwestern University Archaeological Program, Evanston.

Goodman, A. H., and George J. Armelagos
1985   Disease and Death at Dr. Dickson's Mounds. *Natural History* 94:12–18.

Goodman, A. H., J. Lallo, George J. Armelagos, and J. C. Rose
1984   Health Changes at Dickson Mounds, Illinois (A.D. 950–1300). In *Paleopathology at the Origins of Agriculture*, edited by Mark N. Cohen and George J. Armelagos, pp. 271–305. Academic Press, Orlando.

Goodwin, Grenville
1942   *The Social Organization of the Western Apache*. University of Chicago Press, Chicago.

Goodyear, Albert C.
1975   *Hecla II and III: An Interpretive Study of Archaeological Remains from the Lakeshore Project, Papago Indian Reservation, South-Central, Arizona*. Arizona State University, Anthropological Research Papers No. 9, Tempe.

Graves, Michael W.
1987   Rending Reality in Archaeological Analyses: A Reply to Upham and Plog. *Journal of Field Archaeology* 14:243–249.
1994   Community Boundaries in Late Prehistoric Puebloan Society: Kalinga Ethnoarchaeology as a Model for the Southwestern Production and Exchange of Pottery. In *The Ancient Southwestern Community: Models and Methods for the Study of Prehistoric Social Organization*, edited by Wirt H. Wills and Robert D. Leonard, pp. 149–170. The University of New Mexico Press, Albuquerque.

Graves, Michael W., William A. Longacre, and Sally J. Holbrook
1982   Aggregation and Abandonment at Grasshopper Pueblo, Arizona. *Journal of Field Archaeology* 9:193–206.

Graybill, Donald A.
1975   *Mimbres-Mogollon Adaptations in the Gila National Forest, Mimbres District, New Mexico*. Archaeological Report No. 9. U.S. Forest Service, Southwest Region, Albuquerque.

Graybill, Donald A., and Fred L. Nials
1989   Aspects of Climate, Streamflows, and Geomorphology Affecting Irrigation Patterns in the Salt River Valley. In *The 1982–1984 Excavations at Las Colinas: Environment and Subsistence*, by Donald A. Graybill, David A. Gregory, Fred L. Nials, Suzanne K. Fish, Robert E. Gasser, Charles H. Miksicek. Arizona State Museum Archaeological Series No. 162(5). University of Arizona, Tucson.

Green, Ernestene L.
1976   *Valdez Phase Occupation near Taos, New Mexico*. Fort Burgwin Research Center, Publication No. 10, Southern Methodist University, Dallas.

Green, T. J., and C. Munson
1978   Mississippian Settlement Patterns in Southwestern Indiana. In *Mississippian Settlement Patterns*, edited by Bruce D. Smith, pp. 293–330. Academic Press, New York.

Gregg, Michael L.
1975   A Population Estimate for Cahokia. In *Perspectives in Cahokia Archaeology*, edited by James A. Brown, pp. 126–136. Illinois Archaeological Survey Bulletin No. 10, Urbana.

Gregory, David A.
1987   The Morphology of Platform Mounds and the Structure of Classic Period Hohokam Sites. In *The Hohokam Village: Site Structure and Organization*, edited by David E. Doyel, pp. 183–210. Southwest and Rocky Mountain Division of the American Association for the Advancement of Science Monograph, Glenwood Springs, Colorado.
1991   Form and Variation in Hohokam Settlement Patterns. In *Chaco & Hohokam: Prehistoric Regional Systems in the American Southwest*, edited by Patricia L. Crown and W. James Judge, pp. 159–194. School of American Research Press, Santa Fe.

Gregory, David A., and Gary Huckleberry
1994   *An Archaeological Survey of the Blackwater Area, Volume 1: The History of Human Settlement in the Blackwater Area*. Archaeological Consulting Services Cultural Resources Report No. 86, Tempe.

Gregory, David A., and Fred L. Nials
1985   Observations Concerning the Distribution of Classic Period Platform Mounds. In *Proceedings of the 1983 Hohokam Symposium, Part 1*, edited by Alfred E. Dittert, Jr., and Donald E. Dove, pp. 373–388. Occasional Paper of the Arizona Archaeological Society, Phoenix.

Gregory, David A., David R. Abbott, Deni J. Seymour, and Nancy M. Bannister
1988   *The 1982–1984 Excavations at Las Colinas: The Mound 8 Precinct*. Arizona State Museum Archaeological Series No. 162(3). University of Arizona, Tucson.

Griffin, James B.
1966   Mesoamerica and the Eastern United States in Prehistoric Times. In *Archaeological Frontiers and External Connections*, edited by Gordon F. Ekholm and Gordon R. Willey, pp. 111–131. Handbook of Middle American Indians, Robert Wauchope, general editor. University of Texas Press, Austin.
1967   Eastern North American Archaeology: A Summary. *Science* 156:175–191.
1980   The Mesoamerican-Southeastern U.S. Connection. *Early Man* 2(3):12–18.
1993   Cahokia Interaction with Contemporary Southeastern and Eastern Societies. *Midcontinental Journal of Archaeology* 18:3–17.

Griffin, James B., and Volney H. Jones
1977   The University of Michigan Excavations at the Pulcher Site in 1970 (*sic*). *American Antiquity* 42:462–490.

Griffin, John W.
1950   Test Excavations at the Lake Jackson Site. *American Antiquity* 16:99–112.

Gross, G. Timothy
1990   Mollusks Recovered at La Lomita. In *The La Lomita Excavations: 10th Century Hohokam Occupation in South-Central Arizona*, edited by Douglas R. Mitchell, pp. 127–144. Soil Systems Publications in Archaeology No. 15, Phoenix.

Gumerman, George J.
1991   Understanding the Hohokam. In *Exploring the Hohokam: Prehistoric Desert Peoples of the American Southwest*, edited by George J. Gumerman, pp. 1–27. Amerind Foundation New World Studies Series 1. Amerind Foundation, Dragoon, Arizona, and University of New Mexico Press, Albuquerque.

Gumerman, George J. (editor)
1988   *The Anasazi in a Changing Environment*. Cambridge University Press, Cambridge.
1991   *Exploring the Hohokam: Prehistoric Desert Peoples of the American Southwest*. Amerind Foundation New World Studies Series 1. Amerind Foundation, Dragoon, Arizona, and University of New Mexico Press, Albuquerque.
1994   *Themes in Southwest Prehistory*. School of American Research Press, Santa Fe.

Gumerman, George J., and Jeffrey S. Dean
1989   Prehistoric Cooperation and Competition in the Western Anasazi Area. In *Dynamics of Southwest Prehistory*, edited by Linda S. Cordell and George J. Gumerman, pp. 99–148. Smithsonian Institution Press, Washington, D.C.

Gumerman, George J., and Murray Gell-Mann
1993   Cultural Evolution in the Prehistoric Southwest. In *Themes in Southwest Prehistory*, edited by George J. Gumerman, pp.11–32. School of American Research Press, Santa Fe.

Gums, Bonnie L.
1993   Groundstone Tools, Modified Rock, and Exotic Materials. In *The Archaeology of the Cahokia Mounds ICT-II: Testing and Lithics*. Illinois Cultural Resources Study No. 9. Illinois Historic Preservation Agency, Springfield.

Gunnerson, Dolores A.
1956   The Southern Athabascans: Their Arrival in the Southwest. *El Palacio* 63:346–365.

Habicht-Mauche, Judith

1993 *The Pottery from Arroyo Hondo Pueblo, New Mexico, Tribalization and Trade in the Northern Rio Grande.* School of American Research Press, Santa Fe.

n.d. Town and Province: Sociopolitical Change among the Northern Rio Grande Pueblos. Ms. on file, Department of Anthropology, University of California, Santa Cruz.

Hafen, LeRoy R., and Ann W. Hafen

1954 *Old Spanish Trail.* Arthur H. Clark, Glendale, California.

Hall, Robert L.

1980 A Demographic Interpretation of the Two-climax Model of Illinois Prehistory. In *Early Native Americans,* edited by David L. Borowman pp. 401–162. Mouton, The Hague.

1989 The Cultural Background of Mississippian Symbolism. In *The Southeastern Ceremonial Complex: Artifacts and Analysis,* edited by Patricia Galloway, pp. 239–278. University of Nebraska Press, Lincoln

Hally, David J.

1988 Archaeology and Settlement Plan of the King Site. In *The King Site: Continuity and Contact in Sixteenth-Century Georgia,* edited by Robert L. Blakely, pp. 3–16. University of Georgia Press, Athens.

1993 The Territorial Size of Mississippian Chiefdoms. In *Archaeology of Eastern North America: Papers in Honor of Stephen Williams,* edited by James B. Stoltman, pp. 143–168. Mississippi Department of Archives and History, Jackson, Mississippi.

1996a Abandoned Centers and Change in Mississippian Societies. In *Political Structure and Change in the Prehistoric Southeastern United States,* edited by John F. Scarry. University Presses of Florida, Gainesville.

1996b Platform Mound Construction and the Instability of Mississippian Chiefdoms. In *Political Structure and Change in the Prehistoric Southeastern United States,* edited by John F. Scarry, pp. 92–127. University Presses of Florida, Gainesville.

Hally, David J., and James L. Rudolph

1986 *Mississippi Period Archaeology of the Georgia Piedmont.* Laboratory of Archaeology Report No. 24. University of Georgia, Athens.

Hally, David J., Marvin T. Smith, and James B. Langford, Jr.

1990 The Archaeological Reality of de Soto's Coosa. In *Columbian Consequences, Volume 2: Archaeolgical and Historical Perspectives on the Spanish Borderlands East,* edited by David Hurst Thomas, pp. 121–138. Smithsonian Institution Press, Washington, D.C.

Hally, David J., B. H. Connor, G. Funkhouser, J. A. Roth, and Marvin T. Smith

1980 *Archaeological Investigation of the Little Egypt site (9 Mu 102) Murry County, Georgia 1970–72 Seasons.* Report submitted to the Heritage Conservation and Recreation Service, United States Department of the Interior.

Hamlen, Patricia L.

1993 *Patterns of Life at Pueblo Blanco, New Mexico: Determining Occupation and Abandonment Through the Use of Ceramic Surface Collection Analysis.* Unpublished Master's thesis, Department of Anthropology, Northern Illinois University.

Hammack, Laurens C., and Nancy S. Hammack

1981 Architecture. In *The 1968 Excavations at Mound 8, Las Colinas Ruins Group, Phoenix, Arizona,* edited and assembled by Laurens C. Hammack and Alan P. Sullivan, pp. 15–86. Arizona State Museum Archaeological Series No. 154. University of Arizona, Tucson.

Hann, J. H.

1988 *Apalachee: The Land Between the Rivers.* Ripley P. Bullen Monographs in Anthropology and History 7. University Presses of Florida, Gainesville.

Hardin, M. A.

1981 The Identification of Individual Style on Moundville Engraved Vessels: A Preliminary Note. *Southeastern Archaeological Conference Bulletin* 24:108–110.

Hargrave, Lyndon L.

1970 *Mexican Macaws: Comparative Osteology and Survey of Remains from the Southwest.* Anthropological Papers of the University of Arizona No. 20. University of Arizona Press, Tucson.

Harn, Alan D.

1971 An Archaeological Survey of the American Bottoms in Madison and St. Clair Counties, Illinois. In *An Archaeological Survey of the American Bottoms and Wood River Terrace,* by Patrick J. Munson and Alan D. Harn, pp. 19–39. Illinois State Museum, Reports of Investigations No. 21(2).

Harner, Michael J.

1958 *Lowland Patayan Phases in the Lower Colorado River Region.* University of California Archaeological Survey Reports 42:93–99. Berkeley.

Harvey, David

1973 Urbanism and the City—An Interpretative Essay. In *Social Justice and the City,* edited by David Harvey, pp. 195–284. Johns Hopkins University Press, Baltimore.

Hatch, James W.

1987 Mortuary Indicators of Organizational Variability Among Late Prehistoric Chiefdoms in the Southeastern U.S. Interior. In *Chiefdoms in the Americas*, edited by Robert D. Drennan and Carlos A. Uribe, pp. 9–18. University Press of America, Lanham, Maryland.

1936   *The Mogollon Culture of Southwestern New Mexico.* Medallion Papers 20. Gila Pueblo, Globe.

1937   Shell. In *Excavations at Snaketown 1: Material Culture*, by Harold S. Gladwin, Emil W. Haury, Edwin B. Sayles, and Nora Gladwin, pp. 135–153. Medallion Papers 25. Gila Pueblo, Globe.

1945a   *The Excavation of Los Muertos and Neighboring Ruins in the Salt River Valley, Southern Arizona.* Papers of the American Archaeology and Ethonology 25(1). Harvard University, Cambridge.

1945b   The Problem of Contacts Between the Southwestern United States and Mexico. *Southwestern Journal of Anthropology* 1:55–74.

1950   *The Stratigraphy and Archaeology of Ventana Cave, Arizona.* University of Arizona Press, Tucson.

1958   Evidence at Point of Pines for a Prehistoric Migration From Northern Arizona. In *Migrations in New World Culture History*, edited by Raymond H. Thompson, pp. 1–8. University of Arizona Bulletin 29(2), Tucson.

1976   *The Hohokam: Desert Farmers and Craftsmen: Excavations at Snaketown, 1964–1965.* University of Arizona Press, Tucson.

1985   *Mogollon Culture in the Forestdale Valley, East-Central Arizona.* University of Arizona Press, Tucson.

1987   Comments on Symposium Papers. In *The Hohokam Village: Site Structure and Organization*, edited by David E. Doyel, pp. 249–252. Southwest and Rocky Mountain Division of the American Association for the Advancement of Science Monograph, Glenwood Springs, Colorado.

Hawkins, Benjamin

1848   *The Creek Country Collections of the Georgia Historical Society. Vol. III, Part I.* Reprinted 1971, Kraus Reprint Company, New York.

Hawley, Florence M.

1936   *Manual of Prehistoric Pottery Types.* University of New Mexico Bulletin, Anthropological Series 1(4).

Hayes, Alden C.

1981   A Survey of Chaco Canyon Archaeology. In *Archaeological Surveys of Chaco Canyon, New Mexico*, edited by Alden C. Hayes, David M. Brugge, and W. James Judge, pp. 1–68. Publications in Archaeology 18-A, Chaco Canyon Studies. National Park Service, Washington, D.C.

Hayes, Alden C., Jon N. Young, and A. Helene Warren

1981a   *Excavations in Mound 7, Gran Quivira National Monument, New Mexico.* Publications in Archaeology 16. National Park Service, Washington, D.C.

Hayes, Alden C., David M. Brugge, and W. James Judge (editors)

1981b   *Archaeological Surveys of Chaco Canyon, New Mexico.* Publications in Archaeology 18A, Chaco Canyon Studies. National Park Service, Washington, D.C.

Hays, Kelley A.

1993   When is a Symbol Archaeologically Meaningful? In *Archaeological Theory: Who Sets the Agenda?*, edited by Norman Yoffee and Andrew Sherratt, pp. 81–92. Cambridge University Press, Cambridge.

Henderson, T. Kathleen

1986   *Site Structure and Development at La Ciudad: A Study of Community Organization.* Unpublished Ph.D. dissertation, Department of Anthropology, Arizona State University, Tempe.

Herold, Laurance C.

1965   *Trincheras and Physical Environment along the Rio Gavilan, Chihuahua, Mexico.* University of Denver Publications in Geography Technical Paper 65–1, Denver.

Herrington, Selma LaVerne

1982   Water Control Systems of the Mimbres Classic Phase. In *Mogollon Archaeology: Proceedings of the 1980 Mogollon Conference*, edited by Patrick H. Beckett, pp. 75–90. Acoma Books, Ramona, California.

Hill, James N.

1970a   Prehistoric Social Organization in the American Southwest, Method and Theory. In *Reconstructing Prehistoric Pueblo Societies*, edited by William A. Longacre, pp. 11–58. University of New Mexico Press, Albuquerque.

1970b   *Broken K Pueblo: Prehistoric Social Organization in the American Southwest.* Anthropological Papers of the University of Arizona No. 18. University of Arizona Press, Tucson.

Hill, James N., and Joel Gunn

1977   *The Individual in Prehistory: Studies in Variability in Style in Prehistoric Technology.* Academic Press, New York.

Hinsley, Curtis M., Jr.

1981   *Savages and Scientists: The Smithsonian Institution and the Development of American Anthropology 1846–1910.* Smithsonian Institution Press, Washington, D.C.

1983   Ethnographic Charisma and Scientific Routine: Cushing and Fewkes in the American Southwest, 1879–1893. *In Observers Observed: Essays on Ethnographic Fieldwork.* edited by George W. Stocking, Jr., pp. 53–60. The University of Wisconsin Press, Madison.

1989   Revising and Revisioning the History of Archaeology: Reflections on Region and Context. In *Tracing Archaeology's Past: the Historiography* of Archaeology, edited by Andrew L. Christenson, pp. 79–96. Southern Illinois University Press, Carbondale.

Hirth, Kenneth
1978   Interregional Trade and the Formation of Prehistoric Gateway Communities. *American Antiquity* 43:35–45.

Hobsbawm, Eric
1983   Introduction: Inventing Traditions. In *The Invention of Tradition*, edited by Eric Hobsbawm and Terence Ranger, pp. 1–14. Cambridge University Press, Cambridge.

Hodder, Ian
1990   *The Domestication of Europe*. Blackwells, Oxford.

Hodder, Ian, and Clive Orton
1976   *Spatial Analysis in Archaeology*. University of Cambridge Press, Cambridge.

Holley, George R.
1978   *Mississippian Agriculture at Kincaid: An Economic Approach*. Unpublished Master's thesis, Department of Anthropology, Southern Illinois University, Carbondale.
1991   Cahokia as a State? Paper presented at the 56th Annual Meeting of the Society for American Archaeology, New Orleans.
1993   Observations Regarding Sedentism in Central Silver Creek and the Enduring Significance of the FAI-64 Archaeological Mitigation Program. In *Highways of the Past: Essays in Honor of Charles J. Bareis*, edited by T. E. Emerson, A. C. Fortier, and D. L. McElrath. *Illinois Archaeology* 5(1–2):276–284.

Holley, George R., Rinita A. Dalan, and Phillip A. Smith
1993   Investigations in the Cahokia Site Grand Plaza. *American Antiquity* 58:306–319.

Holley, George R., Rinita A. Dalan, and H. W. Watters, Jr.
1992   Archaeological Investigations at the Rouch Mound Group, Cahokia Mounds State Historic Site. Unpublished report submitted to the Illinois Historic Preservation Agency, Springfield.

Holley, George R., N. H. Lopinot, William I. Woods, and J. E. Kelly
1989   Dynamics of Community Organization at Prehistoric Cahokia. In *Households and Communities: Proceedings of the Twenty-first Annual Chacmool Conference*, edited by Scott MacEachern, David J. W. Archer, and Richard D. Garvin, pp. 339–349. The Archaeological Association of the University of Calgary, Alberta.

Holmes, William H.
1903   *Aboriginal Pottery of Eastern United States*. Twentieth Annual Report of the Bureau of American Ethnology, pp. 1–201. Smithsonian Institution, Washington, D.C.

Hough, Walter
1903   *Archaeological Field Work in Northeastern Arizona: The Museum-Gates Expedition of 1901*. Report of the United States National Museum for 1901, pp. 279–358. Washington, D.C.

Howard, James H.
1968   *The Southern Ceremonial Complex and Its Interpretation*. Memoir 6. Missouri Archaeological Society, Columbia.

Howard, Jerry B.
1987   The Lehi Canal System Organization of a Classic Period Irrigation Community. In *The Hohokam Village: Site Structure and Organization*, edited by David E. Doyel, pp. 211–221. Southwest and Rocky Mountain Division of the American Association for the Advancement of Science Monograph. Glenwood Springs, Colorado.
1992   Architecture and Ideology: An Approach to the Functional Analysis of Platform Mounds. In *Proceedings of the Second Salado Conference*, edited by Richard C. Lange and Stephen Germick, pp. 69–77. Occasional Paper of the Arizona Archaeological Society, Phoenix.
1993   A Paleohydraulic Approach to Examining Agricultural Intensification in Hohokam Irrigation Systems. In *Economic Aspects of Water Management in the Prehispanic New World*, edited by Vernon L. Scarborough and Barry L. Isaac, pp. 263–324. Research in Economic Anthropology, Supplement No. 7. JAI Press, Greenwich, Connecticut.

Hudson, Charles M.
1976   *The Southeastern Indians*. University of Tennessee Press, Knoxville.
1990   *The Juan Pardo Expeditions: Exploration of the Carolinas and Tennessee, 1566–1568*. Smithsonian Institution Press, Washington, D.C.

Hudson, Charles M., Marvin T. Smith, and Chester B. DePratter
1990a   The Hernando de Soto Expedition: From Mabila to the Mississippi River. In *Towns and Temples along the Mississippi*, edited by David H. Dye and Cheryl A. Cox, pp. 181–207. University of Alabama Press, Tuscaloosa.

Hudson, Charles M., John E. Worth, and Chester B. DePratter
1990b   Refinements in Hernando de Soto's Route Through Georgia and South Carolina. In *Columbian Consequences, Volume 2: Archaeological and Historical Perspectives on the Spanish Borderlands East*, edited by David Hurst Thomas, pp. 107–119. Smithsonian Institution Press, Washington, D.C.

Hudson, Charles M., Marvin T. Smith, David J. Hally, Richard R. Polhemus, and Chester B. DePratter
1985   Coosa: A Chiefdom in the Sixteenth-Century

Southeastern United States. *American Antiquity* 50:723–737.

1987 In Search of Coosa: Reply to Schroedl and Boyd. *American Antiquity* 52:840–857.

Irwin-Williams, Cynthia

1983 Socio-Economic Order and Authority Structure in the Chacoan Community at Salmon Ruin. Paper presented at the 1983 Anasazi Symposium, Salmon Ruins, Farmington, New Mexico.

Irwin-Williams, Cynthia and Phillip H. Shelley (editors)

1980 *Investigations at the Salmon Site: The Structure of Chacoan Society in the Northern Southwest.* Eastern New Mexico University Printing Services, Portales.

Iseminger, W. R., Timothy R. Pauketat, B. Koldehoff, L. Kelly, and L. Blake

1990 East Palisade Excavations. In *The Archaeology of the Cahokia Palisade.* Illinois Cultural Resource Study 14. Illinois Historic Preservation Agency, Springfield.

Jacobs, David

1994 *Archaeology of the Salado in the Livingston Area of Tonto Basin.* Arizona State University, Anthropological Field Studies No. 32, Tempe.

n.d. *A Salado Platform Mound on Tonto Creek: A Report on Cline Terrace Mound.* Arizona State University, Anthropological Field Studies, Tempe (in press).

Jacobs, Jane

1969 *The Economy of Cities.* Jonathan Cape, London.

Jackson, H. Edwin, and Susan L. Scott

1995 The Faunal Record of the Southeastern Elite: The Implications of Economy, Social Relations, and Ideology. *Southeastern Archaeology* 14:103–119.

Jeançon, Jean A.

1929 Archaeological Investigations in the Taos Valley, New Mexico, during 1920. Smithsonian Miscellaneous Collections 81(12):1–21. Washington, D.C.

Jefferies, Richard W., and Brian M. Butler (editors)

1982 *The Carrier Mills Archaeological Project.* Center for Archaeological Investigations Research Paper 33. Southern Illinois University, Carbondale.

Jennings, Frances

1975 *The Invasion of America: Indians, Colonialism, and the Cant of Conquest.* University of North Carolina, Chapel Hill.

Jennings, Jesse D.

1978 *Prehistory of Utah and the Eastern Great Basin.* University of Utah Anthropological Papers No. 98, Salt Lake City.

Jett, Stephen C., and Peter B. Moyle

1986 The Exotic Origins of Fishes Depicted on Prehistoric Mimbres Pottery from New Mexico. *American Antiquity* 51:688–720.

Jewett, Roberta A.

1989 Distance, Integration, and Complexity: The Spatial Organization of Pan-Regional Settlement Clusters in the American Southwest. In *The Sociopolitical Structure of Prehistoric Southwestern Societies,* edited by Steadman Upham, Kent G. Lightfoot, and Roberta A. Jewett, pp. 363–388. Westview Press, Boulder.

Johannessen, Sissel

1984 Paleoethnobotany. In *American Bottom Archaeology,* edited by Charles J. Bareis and James W. Porter, pp. 197–214. University of Illinois Press, Urbana.

Johnson, Alfred E.

1961 A Ball Court at Point of Pines, Arizona. *American Antiquity* 26:563–567.

Johnson, Allen W., and Timothy K. Earle

1987 *The Evolution of Human Societies.* Stanford University Press, Palo Alto.

Johnson, Gregory A.

1977 Aspects of Regional Analysis in Archaeology. *Annual Review of Anthropology* 6:479–508.

1980 Rank-Size Convexity and System Integration: A View from Archaeology. *Economic Geography* 56(3):234–247.

1982 Organizational Structure and Scalar Stress. In *Theory and Explanation in Archaeology: The Southampton Conference,* edited by Colin Renfrew, Michael J. Rowland, and Barbara A. Segraves, pp. 389–421. Academic Press, New York.

1987 The Changing Organization of Uruk Administration on the Susiana Plain. In *The Archaeology of Western Iran: Settlement and Society from Prehistory to the Islamic Conquest,* edited by Frank Hole, pp. 107–140. Smithsonian Institution Press, Washington, D.C.

1989 Far Outside—Looking In. In *Dynamics of Southwest Prehistory,* edited by Linda S. Cordell and George J. Gumerman, pp. 371–389. Smithsonian Institution Press, Washington, D.C.

Jones, B. C.

1982 Southern Cult Manifestations at the Lake Jackson Site, Leon County, Florida: Salvage Excavation of Mound 3. *Midcontinental Journal of Archaeology* 7:3–44.

1990 A Late Mississippian Collector. *Soto States Anthropologist* 90(2):83–86.

Jorde, L. B.

1977 Precipitation Cycles and Cultural Buffering in the Prehistoric Southwest. In *For Theory Building in Archaeology: Essays on Faunal Remains, Aquatic Resources, Spatial Analysis, and Systemic Modeling,* edited by Lewis R. Binford, pp. 385–396. Academic Press, New York.

Judd, Neil M.

1954 *The Material Culture of Pueblo Bonito.* Smithsonian Miscellaneous Collections 124. Washington, D.C.

1959 *Pueblo del Arroyo, Chaco Canyon, New Mexico.*

Smithsonian Miscellaneous Collections 138(1), Washington, D.C.

1964 *The Architecture of Pueblo Bonito*. Smithsonian Miscellaneous Collections 147(1), Washington, D.C.

Judge, Christopher

1991 Some Preliminary Thoughts on Barbacoas and the Importance of Food and Tribute Storage in Late Mississippian Times. *South Carolina Antiquities* 23:19–29.

Judge, W. James

1979 The Development of a Complex Cultural Ecosystem in the Chaco Basin, New Mexico. In *Proceedings of the First Conference on Scientific Research in National Parks, Volume II*, edited by Robert M. Linn, pp. 901–906. National Park Service Transactions and Proceedings Series 5, Washington, D.C.

1984 New Light on Chaco Canyon. In *New Light on Chaco Canyon*, edited by David G. Noble, pp. 1–12. School of American Research Press, Santa Fe.

1989 Chaco Canyon-San Juan Basin. In *Dynamics of Southwest Prehistory*, edited by Linda S. Cordell and George J. Gumerman, pp. 209–261. Smithsonian Institution Press, Washington, D.C.

1991 Chaco: Current Views of Prehistory and the Regional System. In *Chaco and Hohokam: Prehistoric Regional Systems in the American Southwest*, edited by Patricia L. Crown and W. James Judge, pp. 11–30. School of American Research Press, Santa Fe.

Judge, W. James, William B. Gillespie, Stephen H. Lekson, and H. Wolcott Toll

1981 Tenth Century Developments in Chaco Canyon. In *Collected Papers in Honor of Eric Kellerman Reed*, edited by Albert H. Schroeder, pp. 65–98. Papers of the Archaeological Society of New Mexico No. 6, Albuquerque.

Judge, W. James, and John D. Schelberg (editors)

1984 *Recent Research on Chaco Prehistory*. Reports of the Chaco Center No. 8. Division of Cultural Research, National Park Service, Albuquerque.

Kane, Allen E.

1988 McPhee Community Cluster Introduction. In *Dolores Archaeological Program: Anasazi Communities at Dolores, McPhee Village*, edited by Allen E. Kane and C. K. Robinson, pp. 3–62. U.S. Department of the Interior, Bureau of Reclamation, Denver.

1989 Did the Sheep Look Up? Sociopolitical Complexity in Ninth Century Dolores Society. In *The Sociopolitical Structure of Prehistoric Southwestern Societies*, edited by Steadman Upham, Kent G. Lightfoot, and Roberta A. Jewett, pp. 307–362. Westview Press, Boulder.

1993 Settlement Analogues for Chimney Rock: Models of 11th and 12th Century Northern Anasazi

Society. In *The Chimney Rock Archaeological Symposium*, edited by J. McKim Malville and Gary Matlock, pp. 43–60. General Technical Report RM-227, USDA Forest Service Rocky Mountain Forest and Range Experiment Station, Fort Collins.

Kanter, John

n.d. Political Competition among the Chaco Anasazi of the American Southwest. *Journal of Anthropological Archaeology* (in press).

Kelley, J. Charles

1952a Factors Involved in the Abandonment of Certain Peripheral Southwestern Settlements. *American Anthropologist* 54:356–387.

1952b Some Geographic and Cultural Factors Involved in Mexican-Southeastern Contacts. In *Indian Tribes of Aboriginal America*, edited by Sol Tax, pp. 139–144. Selected Papers of the Twenty-ninth International Congress of Americanists 3. University of Chicago Press, Chicago.

1966 Mesoamerica and the Southwestern United States. In *Archaeological Frontiers and External Connections*, edited by Gordon F. Ekholm and Gordon R. Willey, pp. 95–110. Handbook of Middle American Indians, Vol. 4, Robert Wauchope, general editor. University of Texas Press, Austin.

1986a The Mobile Merchants of Molino. In *Ripples in the Chichimec Sea: New Considerations of Southwestern-Mesoamerican Interactions*, edited by Francis J. Mathien and Randall H. McGuire, pp. 81–104. Southern Illinois University Press, Carbondale.

1986b *Jumano and Patarabueye: Relations at La Junta de Los Rios*. Anthropological Papers No. 77, Museum of Anthropology, University of Michigan, Ann Arbor.

Kelley, J. Charles, and Ellen A. Kelley

1975 An Alternative Hypothesis for the Explanation of Anasazi Culture History. In *Collected Papers in Honor of Florence Hawley Ellis*, edited by Theodore R. Frisbie, pp. 178–223. Papers of the Archaeological Society of New Mexico 2, Santa Fe.

Kelley, John E.

1990a The Emergence of Mississippian Culture in the American Bottom Region. In *The Mississippian Emergence*, edited by Bruce D. Smith, pp. 113–152. Smithsonian Institution Press, Washington, D.C.

1990b Range Site Community Patterns and the Mississippian Emergence. In *The Mississippian Emergence*, edited by Bruce D. Smith, pp. 67–112. Smithsonian Institution Press, Washington, D.C.

1991 Cahokia and Its Role as a Gateway Center in Interregional Exchange. In *Cahokia and the Hinterlands: Middle Mississippian Cultures of the Midwest*, edited by Thomas E. Emerson and

R. Barry Lewis, pp. 61–80. University of Illinois Press, Urbana.

Kelley, N. Edmund
1979   *The Contemporary Ecology of Arroyo Hondo, New Mexico*. School of American Research Press, Santa Fe.

Kelly, Klara B.
1976   Dendritic Central-Place Systems and the Regional Organization of Navajo Trading Posts. In *Regional Analysis, Volume 1, Economic Systems*, edited by Carol A. Smith, pp. 219–254. Academic Press, New York.

Kent, Kate Peck
1957   *The Cultivation and Weaving of Cotton in the Prehistoric Southwestern United States*. Transactions of the American Philosophical Society 47(3). Washington, D.C.

Kidder, Alfred V.
1924   *An Introduction to the Study of Southwestern Archaeology with a Preliminary Account of the Excavations at Pecos*. Papers of the Southwestern Expedition No. 1. Department of Archaeology, Phillips Academy, Yale University Press, New Haven.
1927   Southwestern Archaeological Conference. *Science* 66(1716):489–491.
1936   The Archaeology of Peripheral Regions. *Southwestern Lore* 2(3):46–48.

Kincaid, Chris (editor)
1983   *Chaco Roads Project Phase I: A Reappraisal of Prehistoric Roads in the San Juan Basin, 1983*. Bureau of Land Management, Albuquerque.

King, Adam
1991   *Excavations at Mound B, Etowah: 1954–1958*. Unpublished Master's thesis, Department of Anthropology, University of Georgia, Athens.

King, Chester D.
1983   Beads and Selected Ornaments. In *Archaeological Studies at Oro Grande, Mohave Desert, California*, edited by Carol H. Rector, James D. Swenson, and Philip J. Wilke, pp. 68–87. San Bernardino County Museum Association, Redlands.

King, David
1949   *Nlakihu: Excavations at a Pueblo III Site on Wupatki National Monument, Arizona*. Museum of Northern Arizona, Bulletin No. 23, Flagstaff.

King, Mary E. and Joan S. Gardner
1981   The Analysis of Textiles from Spiro Mound, Oklahoma. In *The Research Potential of Anthropological Museum Collections*, edited by Anna-Marie E. Cantwell, James B. Griffin, and Nan A. Rothschild. *Annals of the New York Academy of Science* 376:123–139.

Kintigh, Keith W.
1985   *Settlement, Subsistence, and Society in Late Zuni Prehistory*. Anthropological Papers of the University of Arizona No. 44. University of Arizona Press, Tucson.
1994   Chaco, Communal Architecture, and Cibolan Aggregation. In *The Ancient Southwestern Community, Models and Methods for the Study of Prehistoric Social Organization*, edited by Wirt H. Wills and Robert D. Leonard, pp. 131–140. University of New Mexico Press, Albuquerque.

Kirch, Patrick V.
1984   *The Evolution of Polynesian Chiefdoms*. Cambridge University Press, Cambridge.
1991   Prehistoric Exchange in Western Melanesia. *Annual Review of Anthropology* 20:141–166.

Kirchhoff, Paul
1943   Mesoamerica: Sus Limites Geographicas, Composition Ethnica y Caracteres Culturales. *Acta Americana* 1:92–107.

Knight, Vernon James, Jr.
1981   *Mississippian Ritual*. Ph.D. dissertation, Department of Anthropology, University of Florida. University Microfilms, Ann Arbor.
1986   The Institutional Organization of Mississippian Religion. *American Antiquity* 51:675–687.
1989   Certain Aboriginal Mounds at Moundville: 1937 Excavations in Mounds H, I, J, K, and L. Paper presented at the 46th Annual Southeastern Archaeological Conference, Tampa.
1990   Social Organization and the Evolution of Hierarchy in Southeastern Chiefdoms. *Journal of Anthropological Research* 46:1–23.
1992   Preliminary Report on Excavations at Mound Q, Moundville. Paper presented at the 49th Annual Southeastern Archaeological Conference, Little Rock.
1993   Moundville as a Diagrammatic Ceremonial Center. Paper presented at the 58th Annual Meeting of the Society for American Archaeology, St. Louis.

Kohler, Timothy A.
1993   News from the Northern American Southwest: Prehistory on the edge of Chaos. *Journal of Archaeological Research* 1(4):267–321.

Kosse, Krisztina
1990   Group Size and Societal Complexity: Thresholds in the Long-term Memory. *Journal of Anthropological Archaeology* 9:275–303.
1992   Middle Range Societies from a Scalar Perspective. Paper presented at the Third Southwest Symposium, Tucson.

Kowalewski, Stephen A.
1990   The Evolution of Complexity in the Valley of Oaxaca. *Annual Review of Anthropology* 19:39–58.

Krieger, Alex D.
1945   An Inquiry Into Supposed Mexican Influence on a Prehistoric "Cult" in the Southern United States. *American Anthropologist* 47:483–515.

1947a   *Culture Complexes and Chronology in Northern Texas.* University of Texas Publication No. 4640, Austin.

1947b   The Eastward Extension of Puebloan Datings toward Cultures of the Mississippi Valley. *American Antiquity* 12:141–148.

Kroeber, Alfred L.

1928   Native Culture of the Southwest. *University of California Publications in American Archaeology and Ethnology* 33:375–398, Berkeley.

1939   Cultural and Natural Areas of Native North America. *University of California Publications in American Archaeology and Ethnology* 38:1–242, Berkeley.

Lafferty, Robert H, III.

1994   Prehistoric Exchange in the Lower Mississippi Valley. In *Prehistoric Exchange Systems in North America*, edited by Timothy G. Baugh and Jonathon E. Ericson, pp. 177–213. Plenum Press, New York.

Lang, Richard W.

1988   Ceramics from the North Reservoir of Pueblo Blanco. In *Reflections on Southwestern Culture History in Honor of Charles H. Lange*, edited by Anne van Arsdell Poore, pp. 184–192. Papers of the Archaeological Society of New Mexico No. 14, Albuquerque.

Lange, Frederick, Nancy Mahaney, Joe Ben Wheat, and Mark L. Chenault

1986   *Yellow Jacket: A Four Corners Anasazi Ceremonial Center.* Johnson Books, Boulder.

Lange, Richard C., and Stephen Germick (editors)

1992   *Proceedings of the Second Salado Conference.* Occasional Paper of the Arizona Archaeological Society, Phoenix.

Larsen, Clark S., Margaret J. Schoeninger, Nikolaas J. van der Merwe, Katherine M. Moore, and Julia A. Lee-Thorp

1992   Carbon and Nitrogen Stable Isotope Signatures of Human Dietary Change in the Georgia Bight. *American Journal of Physical Anthropology* 89:197–214.

Larson, Lewis H., Jr.

1971a   Archaeological Implications of Social Stratification at the Etowah Site, Georgia. In *Approaches to the Social Dimensions of Mortuary Practices*, edited by James A. Brown, pp. 58–67. Memoir 25. Society for American Archaeology, Washington, D.C.

1971b   Settlement Distribution during the Mississippi Period. *Southeastern Archaeological Conference Bulletin* 13:19–25.

1972   Functional Considerations of Warfare in the Southeast During the Mississippian Period. *American Antiquity* 37:383–392.

1989   The Etowah Site. In *The Southeastern Ceremonial Complex: Artifacts and Analysis*, edited by Patricia Galloway, pp. 133–141. University of Nebraska Press, Lincoln.

Lathrap, Donald W.

1987   The Introduction of Maize in Prehistoric Eastern North America: The View from Amazonia and the Santa Elena Peninsula. In *Emergent Horticultural Economies of the Eastern Woodlands*, edited by William F. Keegan, pp. 345–371. Center for Archaeological Investigations Occasional Paper 7. Southern Illinois University, Carbondale.

Lawson, John

1709   *A New Voyage to Carolina.* Reprint edition, 1967. Editing, introduction, and notes by Hugh T. Lefler. University of North Carolina Press, Chapel Hill.

Leader, J. M.

1988   *Technological Continuities and Specialization in Prehistoric Metalwork in the Eastern United States.* Ph.D. dissertation, University of Florida. University Microfilms, Ann Arbor.

LeBlanc, Stephen A.

1980   The Dating of Casas Grandes. *American Antiquity* 45:799–806.

1982   Temporal Change in Mogollon Ceramics. In *Southwestern Ceramics: A Comparative View*, edited by Albert H. Schroeder, *The Arizona Archaeologist* 15:107–128, Arizona Archaeological Society, Phoenix.

1983   *The Mimbres People.* Thames and Hudson, London.

1986   Development of Archaeological Thought on the Mimbres Mogollon. In *Emil W. Haury's Prehistory of the American Southwest*, edited by J. Jefferson Reid and David E. Doyel, pp. 297–304. University of Arizona Press, Tucson.

1989   Cultural Dynamics in the Southern Mogollon Area. In *Dynamics of Southwest Prehistory*, edited by Linda S. Cordell and George J. Gumerman, pp. 279–208. Smithsonian Institution Press, Washington, D.C.

LeBlanc, Steven A., and Ben A. Nelson

1976   The Salado in Southwestern New Mexico. *The Kiva* 42:71–80.

LeBlanc, Stephen A., and Michael E. Whalen

1980   *An Archeological Synthesis of South-Central and Southwestern New Mexico.* Office of Contract Archeology, University of New Mexico, Albuquerque.

Lee, Richard B.

1992   Art, Science, or Politics? The Crisis in Hunter-Gatherer Studies. *American Anthropologist* 94(1):31–54.

Lekson, Stephen H.

1982   Architecture and Settlement Plan in the Redrock Valley of the Gila River, Southwestern

New Mexico. In Mogollon Archaeology, edited by Patrick H. Beckett, pp. 61–73. Acoma Books, Ramona, California.

1984a   Great Pueblo Architecture of Chaco Canyon, New Mexico. Publications in Archaeology 18B, Chaco Canyon Studies. National Park Service, and University of New Mexico Press, Albuquerque.

1984b   Standing Architecture at Chaco Canyon and the Interpretation of Local and Regional Organization. In Recent Research on Chaco Prehistory, edited by W. James Judge and John D. Schelberg, pp. 55–74. Reports of the Chaco Center No. 8. Division of Cultural Research, National Park Service, Albuquerque.

1984c   Mimbres Settlement Size in Southwestern New Mexico. In Recent Research in Mogollon Archaeology, edited by Steadman Upham, Fred Plog, David G. Batcho, and Barbara E. Kauffman, pp. 68–74. The University Museum, New Mexico State University, Occasional Papers No. 10, Las Cruces.

1986a   Mimbres Riverine Adaptations. In Mogollon Variability, edited by Charlotte Benson and Steadman Upham, pp. 181–190. The University Museum, New Mexico State University, Occasional Papers No. 15, Las Cruces.

1986b   The Mimbres Region. In Mogollon Variability, edited by Charlotte Benson and Steadman Upham, pp. 145–155. The University Museum, New Mexico State University, Occasional Papers No. 15, Las Cruces.

1986c   Great Pueblo Architecture of Chaco Canyon. University of New Mexico Press, Albuquerque.

1988a   The Idea of the Kiva in Anasazi Archaeology. The Kiva 53:213–234.

1988b   The Mangas Phase in Mimbres Archaeology. The Kiva 53:129–145.

1989   The Community in Anasazi Archaeology. In Households and Communities: Proceedings of the Twenty-first Annual Chacmool Conference, edited by Scott MacEachern, David J. W. Archer, and Richard D. Garvin, pp. 181–185. The Archaeological Association of the University of Calgary, Alberta.

1990a   Cross-Cultural Perspectives on the Community. In Vernacular Architecture: Paradigms of Environmental Response, edited by Mete Turan, pp.122–145. Avebury, Aldershot.

1990b   The Great Pueblo Period in Southwestern Archaeology. In Pueblo Style and Regional Architecture, edited by Nicholas C. Markovich, Wolfgang F. E. Preiser, and Fred G. Sturm, pp. 64–77. Van Nostrand Reinhold, New York.

1990c   Mimbres Archaeology of the Upper Gila, New Mexico. Anthropological Papers of the University of Arizona No. 53. University of Arizona Press, Tucson.

1990d   Sedentism and Aggregation in Anasazi Archaeology. In Perspectives on Southwestern Prehistory, edited by Paul E. Minnis and Charles L. Redman, pp. 333–340. Westview Press, Boulder.

1991   Settlement Patterns and the Chaco Region. In Chaco and Hohokam: Prehistoric Regional Systems in the American Southwest, edited by Patricia L. Crown and W. James Judge, pp. 31–55. School of American Research Press, Santa Fe.

1992a   Archaeological Overview of Southwestern New Mexico. New Mexico Historic Preservation Division, Santa Fe.

1992b   Mimbres Art and Archaeology. In Archaeology, Art, and Anthropology: Papers in Honor of J. J. Brody, edited by Meliha S. Duran and David T. Kirkpatrick, pp. 111–122. The Archaeological Society of New Mexico No.18, Albuquerque.

1992c   Salado of the East. In Proceedings of the Second Salado Conference, edited by Richard C. Lange and Stephen Germick, pp. 17–21. Occasional Paper of the Arizona Archaeological Society, Phoenix.

1992d   The Surface Archaeology of Southwestern New Mexico. The Artifact 30(3):1–36.

1993   Chaco, Hohokam and Mimbres: The Southwest in the 11th and 12th Centuries. Expedition 35(1):44–52.

1994   Thinking about Chaco. In Chaco Canyon: A Center and its World, pp. 11–42. Photographs by Mary Peck, with essays by Stephen H. Lekson, John R. Stein, and Simon J. Ortiz. Museum of New Mexico Press, Santa Fe.

Lekson, Stephen H., and Catherine M. Cameron

1993   The Abandonment of Chaco Canyon and the Reorganization of the Anasazi World. Paper presented at the American Anthropological Association Annual Meeting, Washington, D.C.

Lekson, Stephen H., and Alan Rorex

1987   Archaeological Survey of the Cottonwood Spring and Indian Tank Sites, Dona Ana County, New Mexico. Human Systems Research, Tularosa.

1994   Ethnographic Analogs: Strategies for Reconstructing Archaeological Cultures. In Understanding Complexity in the Prehistoric Southwest, edited by George J. Gumerman and Murray Gell-Mann, pp. 233–244. Addison-Wesley, Reading, Massachusetts.

Lewis, R. Barry

1990   The Late Prehistory of the Ohio-Mississippi Rivers Confluence Region, Kentucky and Missouri. In Towns and Temples along the Mississippi, edited by David H. Dye and Cheryl A. Cox, pp. 38–58. University of Alabama Press, Tuscaloosa.

Lewis, R. Barry (editor)

1986   Mississippian Towns of the Western Kentucky Border: The Adams, Wickliffe, and Sassafras

Ridge Sites. Kentucky Heritage Council, Frankfort.

Lewis, Thomas M. N., and Madeline K. Kneberg
1946　*Hiwassee Island: An Archaeological Account of Four Tennessee Indian Peoples*. University of Tennessee Press, Knoxville.

Lewis, Thomas M. N., and Madeline Kneberg Lewis
1961　*Eva: An Archaic Site*. The University of Tennessee Press, Knoxville.

Lightfoot, Kent G.
1984　*Prehistoric Political Dynamics: A Case Study from the American Southwest*. Northern Illinois University Press, De Kalb.

1987　A Consideration of Complex Prehistoric Societies in the U.S. Southwest. In *Chiefdoms in the Americas*, edited by Robert D. Drennan and Carlos A. Uribe, pp. 43–57. University Press of America, Lanham, Maryland.

Lightfoot, Kent G., and Gary M. Feinman
1982　Social Differentiation and Leadership Development in Early Pithouse Villages in the Mogollon Region of the American Southwest. *American Antiquity* 47:64–86.

Lightfoot, Kent G., and Rachel Most
1989　Interpreting Settlement Hierarchies: A Reassessment of Pinedale and Snowflake Settlement Patterns. In *The Sociopolitical Structure of Prehistoric Southwestern Societies*, edited by Steadman Upham, Kent G. Lightfoot, and Roberta A. Jewett, pp. 389–418. Westview Press, Boulder.

Lightfoot, Ricky R., and Mary C. Etzkorn (editors)
1993　*The Duckfoot Site, Volume 1, Descriptive Archaeology*. Occasional Papers, No. 3. Crow Canyon Archaeological Center, Cortez, Colorado.

Lindauer, Owen
1992　Architectural Engineering and Variation Among Salado Platform Mounds. In *Proceedings of the Second Salado Conference*, edited by Richard C. Lange and Stephen Germick, pp. 50–56. Occasional Paper of the Arizona Archaeological Society, Phoenix.

1995　*Where the Rivers Converge: A Report on the Bass Point Mound*. Arizona State University, Anthropological Field Studies No. 33, Tempe.

n.d.a　*The Place of the Storehouses: A Report on the Schoolhouse Point Mound*. Arizona State University, Anthropological Field Studies, Tempe (in press).

n.d.b　*The Archaeology of Schoolhouse Mesa*. Arizona State University, Anthropological Field Studies, Tempe (in press).

Lipe, William D.
1970　Anasazi Communities in the Red Rock Plateau, Southeastern Utah. In *Reconstructing Prehistoric Pueblo Societies*, edited by William A. Longacre, pp. 84–139. School of American Research, Santa Fe, and University of New Mexico Press, Albuquerque.

1989　Social Scale of Mesa Verde Anasazi Kivas. In *The Architecture of Social Integration in Prehistoric Pueblos*, edited by William D. Lipe and Michelle Hegmon, pp. 53–71. Occasional Papers No 1. Crow Canyon Archaeological Center, Cortez, Colorado.

Lipe, William D., and Michelle Hegmon (editors)
1989　*The Architecture of Social Integration in Prehistoric Pueblos*. Occasional Papers No. 1. Crow Canyon Archaeological Center, Cortez, Colorado.

Lister, Florence C.
1964　*Kaiparowits Plateau and Glen Canyon Prehistory: An Interpretation Based on Ceramics*. University of Utah Anthropological Paper No. 71, Salt Lake City.

Lister, Robert H.
1978　Mesoamerican Influences at Chaco Canyon, New Mexico. In *Across the Chichimec Sea: Papers in Honor of J. Charles Kelley*, edited by Carroll L. Riley and Basil C. Hedrick, pp. 233–241. Southern Illinois University Press, Carbondale.

Little, Elizabeth A.
1987　Inland Waterways in the Northeast. *Midcontinental Journal of Archaeology* 12:55–76.

Liverani, M. (editor)
1993　*Akkad: The First World Empire*. Sargon, Padova.

Longacre, William A.
1970a　*Archaeology as Anthropology: A Case Study*. Anthropological Papers of the University of Arizona No. 17. University of Arizona Press, Tucson.

Longacre, William A. (editor)
1970b　*Reconstructing Prehistoric Pueblo Societies*. School of American Research and University of New Mexico Press, Santa Fe.

Longacre, William A., and J. Jefferson Reid
1974　The University of Arizona Field School at Grasshopper. *The Kiva* 40(1–2):3–38.

Longacre, William A., Sally J. Holbrook, and Michael W. Graves (editors)
1982　*Multidisciplinary Research at Grasshopper Pueblo, Arizona*. Anthropological Papers of the University of Arizona No. 40. University of Arizona Press, Tucson.

Loose, Anne A.
1974　*Archaeological Excavations Near Arroyo Hondo, Carson National Forest, New Mexico*. Archaeological Report No. 4, U.S.D.A. Forest Service, Southwestern Region.

Lopinot, N. H.
1991　Archaeobotanical Remains. In *The Archaeology of Cahokia Mounds ICT-II: Biological Remains*. Illinois Cultural Resources Study 13. Illinois Historic Preservation Agency, Springfield.

Lopinot, N. H., and William I. Woods
1993   Wood Overexploitation and the Collapse of
        Cahokia. In *Foraging and Farming in the East-
        ern Woodlands*, edited by C. Margaret Scarry,
        pp. 206–231. University of Florida Press,
        Gainesville.

Lyneis, Margaret M.
1984   The Western Anasazi Frontier: Cultural Pro-
        cesses Along a Prehistoric Boundary. In *Explor-
        ing the Limits: Frontiers and Boundaries in
        Prehistory*, edited by Suzanne P. DeAtley and
        Frank J. Findlow, No. 92. BAR International
        Series 223, London.

Lyneis, Margaret M., Mary K. Rusco, and Keith Myhrer
1989   *Investigations at Adam 2 (26Ck2059): A Mesa
        House Phase Site in the Moapa Valley, Nevada.*
        Nevada State Museum Anthropological Papers
        No. 22, Carson City.

Lynott, Mark J., Thomas W. Boutton, James E. Price, and
Dwight E. Nelson
1986   Stable Carbon Isotopic Evidence for Maize
        Agriculture in Southeast Missouri and North-
        east Arkansas. *American Antiquity* 51:51–65.

McGregor, John C.
1943   Burial of an Early American Magician. *Proceed-
        ings of the American Philosophical Society*
        86(2):270–298.

McGuire, Randall H.
1980   The Mesoamerican Connection in the South-
        west. *The Kiva* 46:3–38.
1983   Breaking Down Cultural Complexity: Inequal-
        ity and Heterogeneity. *Advances in Archaeologi-
        cal Method and Theory 6*, edited by Michael B.
        Schiffer, pp. 91–142. Academic Press, New York.
1987   A Gila Butte Ballcourt at La Ciudad. In *The
        Hohokam Community of La Ciudad*, edited by
        Glen E. Rice, pp. 69–110. OCRM Report No. 69,
        Arizona State University, Tempe.
1989   The Greater Southwest as a Periphery of
        Mesoamerica. In *Centre and Periphery: Com-
        parative Studies in Archaeology*, edited by T. C.
        Champion, pp. 40–66. Unwin Hyman, London.
1991   On the Outside Looking In: The Concept of
        Periphery in Hohokam Archaeology. In *Explor-
        ing the Hohokam: Prehistoric Desert Peoples of
        the American Southwest*, edited by George J.
        Gumerman, pp. 347–382. Amerind Foundation
        New World Studies Series 1. Amerind Founda-
        tion, Dragoon, Arizona, and University of New
        Mexico Press, Albuquerque.
1992a   *Death, Society, and Ideology in a Hohokam
        Community.* Westview Press, Boulder.
1992b   *A Marxist Archaeology.* Academic Press, Orlando.

McGuire, Randall H., and Anne V. Howard
1987   The Structure and Organization of Hohokam
        Shell Exchange. *The Kiva* 52:113–146.

McGuire, Randall H., and Dean J. Saitta
1996   Although They Have Petty Captains, They
        Obey Them Badly: The Dialectics of Pre-
        hispanic Western Pueblo Social Organization.
        American Antiquity 61:197–216.

McGuire, Randall H., and Michael B. Schiffer
1983   A Theory of Architectural Design. *Journal of
        Anthropological Archaeology* 2:277–303.

McGuire, Randall H., E. Charles Adams, Ben A. Nelson,
and Katherine A. Spielmann
1994   Drawing the Southwest to Scale: Perspectives
        on Macroregional Relations. In *Themes in
        Southwest Prehistory*, edited by George J.
        Gumerman, pp. 267–324. School of American
        Research Press, Santa Fe.

McKenna, Peter J., and H. Wolcott Toll
1992   Regional Patterns of Great House Development
        among the Totah Anasazi, New Mexico. In
        *Anasazi Regional Organization and the Chaco
        System*, edited by David E. Doyel, pp. 133–146.
        Maxwell Museum of Anthropology, Anthropo-
        logical Papers No. 5, Albuquerque.

McKenzie, D. H.
1966   A Summary of the Moundville Phase. *Journal of
        Alabama Archaeology* 12:1–58.

McKusick, Charmion R.
1992   Evidences of Hereditary High Status at Gila
        Pueblo. In *Proceedings of the Second Salado
        Conference*, edited by Richard C. Lange and
        Stephen Germick, pp. 86–91. Occasional Paper
        of the Arizona Archaeological Society, Phoenix.

McMichael, Edward V.
1964   Veracruz, the Crystal River Complex, and the
        Hopewellian Climax. In *Hopewellian Studies*,
        edited by Joseph R. Caldwell and Robert L.
        Hall, pp. 123–132. Scientific Papers No. 12. Illi-
        nois State Museum, Springfield.

Mainfort, Robert C., Jr.
1986   *Pinson Mounds: A Middle Woodland Ceremonial
        Center.* Division of Archaeology Research Series
        No. 7. Tennessee Department of Conservation,
        Nashville.

Malinowski, Bronislaw
1932   *Argonauts of the Western Pacific.* Routledge,
        London.

Malouf, Carling
1940   Prehistoric Exchange in the Northern Periphery
        of the Southwest. *American Antiquity* 6:115–122.

Mann, Michael
1986   *The Sources of Social Power.* Cambridge Univer-
        sity Press, Cambridge.

Marcus, Joyce, Kent V. Flannery, and Ronald Spores
1983   The Cultural Legacy of the Oaxacan Pre-
        ceramic. In *The Cloud People*, edited by Kent V.
        Flannery and Joyce Marcus, pp. 36–39. Aca-
        demic Press, New York.

Marshall, Michael P.
1973   The Jornada Culture Area. In *1973 Survey of the Tularosa Basin*, pp. 49–120. Human Systems Research, Albuquerque.

Marshall, Michael P., and Henry J. Walt
1984   *Rio Abajo: Prehistory and History of a Rio Grande Province*. New Mexico Historic Preservation Division, Santa Fe.

Marshall, Michael P., David E. Doyel, and Cory D. Breternitz
1982   A Regional Perspective on the Late Bonito Phase. In *Bis sa' ani: A Late Bonito Phase Community on Escavada Wash, Northwest New Mexico*, edited by Cory D. Breternitz, David E. Doyel, and Michael P. Marshall, pp. 1227–1240. Navajo Nation Papers in Anthropology 14. Navajo Nation Cultural Resource Program, Window Rock.

Marshall, Michael P., John R. Stein, Richard W. Loose, and Judith E. Novotny
1979   *Anasazi Communities of the San Juan Basin*. Public Service Company of New Mexico and New Mexico Historic Preservation Division, Albuquerque and Santa Fe.

Martin, Paul S., and Fred Plog
1973   *The Archaeology of Arizona: A Study of the Southwest Region*. The American Museum of Natural History, Doubleday-Natural History Press, Garden City, New York.

Mason, Ronald J., and Gregory Perino
1961   Microblades at Cahokia, Illinois. *American Antiquity* 26:553–557.

Masse, W. Bruce
1981   Prehistoric Irrigation Systems in the Salt River Valley, Arizona. *Science* 214:408–415
1991   The Quest for Subsistence Sufficiency and Civilization in the Sonoran Desert. In *Chaco & Hohokam: Prehistoric Regional Systems in the American Southwest*, edited by Patricia L. Crown and W. James Judge, pp. 195–223. The School of American Research Press, Santa Fe.

Mathien, Frances J.
1984   Social and Economic Implications of Jewelry Items of the Chaco Anasazi. In *Recent Research on Chaco Prehistory*, edited by W. James Judge and John D. Schelberg, pp. 173–186. Reports of the Chaco Center No. 8. Division of Cultural Research, National Park Service, Albuquerque, New Mexico.
1993   Exchange Systems and Social Stratification among the Chaco Anasazi. In *The American Southwest and Mesoamerica: Systems of Prehistoric Exchange*, edited by Jonathan E. Ericson and Timothy G. Baugh, pp. 27–63. Plenum Press, New York.

Mathien, Frances J., and Randall H. McGuire (editors)
1986   *Ripples in the Chichimec Sea: New Consider-*ations of Southwestern-Mesoamerican Interactions. Southern Illinois University Press, Carbondale.

Matson, Richard G., William D. Lipe, and William R. Haase, IV
1988   Adaptational Continuities and Occupational Discontinuities: The Anasazi on Cedar Mesa. *Journal of Field Archaeology* 15:245–264.

Meillassoux, Claude
1981   *Maidens, Meal, and Money: Capitalism and the Domestic Economy*. [translation: 1977; *Femmes, Grenier, et Capitaux*. Maspero, Paris]. Cambridge University Press, Cambridge.

Mellaart, James
1978   *Çatal Hüyük: A Neolithic Town in Anatolia*. Thames and Hudson, London.

Meyer, Daniel A., Peter C. Dawson, and Donald T. Hanna (editors)
1996   Debating Complexity: Proceedings of the Twenty-sixth Annual Chacmool Conference. The Archaeological Association of the University of Calgary, Alberta.

Milfort, General (Louis LeClerc de)
1802   *Mémoire ou Coup-d'oeil Rapide Sur Mes Différens Voyages et Mon Séjour dans la Nation Crëck*. Giguet et Michaud, Paris. [translation: 1956; *Memoir: or A Cursory Glance at My Different Travels & My Sojourn in the Creek Nation*, translated by G. de Courcey]. The Lakeside Press, Chicago.

Milner, George R.
1984   Social and Temporal Implications of Variation among American Bottom Mississippian Cemeteries. *American Antiquity* 49:468–488.
1986   Mississippian Period Population Density in a Segment of the Central Mississippi River Valley. *American Antiquity* 51:227–238.
1991a   American Bottom Mississippian Cultures: Internal Developments and External Relationships. In *New Perspectives on Cakokia: Views from the Periphery*, edited by James B. Stoltman, pp. 29–47. Prehistory Press, Madison, Wisconsin.
1991b   Health and Cultural Change in the Late Prehistoric American Bottom, Illinois. In *What Mean These Bones? Studies in Southeastern Bioarchaeology*, edited by Mary L. Powell, Patricia S. Bridges, and Ann M. Mires, pp. 52–69. University of Alabama Press, Tuscaloosa.
1993   Settlements Amidst Swamps. *Illinois Archaeology* 5:374–380.
1996   Development and Dissolution of a Mississippian Society in the American Bottom, Illinois. In *Political Structure and Change in the Prehistoric Southeastern United States*, edited by John F. Scarry. University Presses of Florida, Gainesville.

Milner, George R., Eve Anderson, and Virginia G. Smith
1991   Warfare in Late Prehistoric West-Central Illinois. *American Antiquity* 56:581–603.

Mindeleff, Victor
1891   *A Study of Pueblo Architecture: Tusayan and Cibola.* Eighth Annual Report of the Bureau of American Ethnology for the Years 1886–1887, pp. 3–228. Smithsonian Institution Press, Washington, D.C.

Minnis, Paul E.
1984   Peeking Under the Tortilla Curtain: Regional Interaction and Integration on the Northeastern Periphery of Casas Grandes. *American Archaeology* 4(3):181–193.

1985   *Social Adaptation to Food Stress: A Prehistoric Southwestern Example.* University of Chicago Press, Chicago.

1988   Four Examples of Specialized Production at Casas Grandes, Northwestern Chihuahua. *The Kiva* 53:181–194.

1989   The Casas Grandes Polity in the International Four Corners. In *The Sociopolitical Structure of Prehistoric Southwestern Societies,* edited by Steadman Upham, Kent G. Lightfoot, and Roberta A. Jewett, pp. 269–305, Westview Press, Boulder.

Minnis, Paul E., and Michael E. Whalen
1992   *El Sistema Regional de Casas Grandes, Chihuahua: Informe Presentado al Instituto Nacional de Antropologia e Historia.* Department of Anthropology, University of Oklahoma and Department of Anthropology, University of Tulsa.

Moore, Clarence B.
1905   Aboriginal Remains of the Black Warrior River, Lower Tombigbee River, Mobile Bay and Mississippi Sound, and Miscellaneous Investigations in Florida. *Journal of the Academy of Natural Sciences of Philadelphia* 13:125–244.

1907   Moundville Revisited. *Journal of the Academy of Natural Sciences of Philadelphia* 13:337–405.

Moorehead, Warren K.
1928   *The Cahokia Mounds.* Bulletin of the University of Illinois No. 26(4).

Moratto, Michael J.
1984   *California Archaeology.* Academic Press, Orlando.

Morgan, William N.
1980   *Prehistoric Architecture in the Eastern United States.* MIT Press, Cambridge.

Morley, Slvanius G., and George W. Brainerd
(revised by Robert J. Sharer)
1983   *The Ancient Maya.* Stanford University Press, Palo Alto.

Morris, Earl H.
1939   Archaeological Studies in the La Plata District: Southwestern Colorado and Northwestern New Mexico. *Carnegie Institution of Washington Publication* 519, Washington, D.C.

Morrow, Carol A., and Mary McCorvie
1983   Layers of Trail Systems in the Midwestern U.S.: Archaeological, Historical, and Modern Environment. Paper presented at 58th Annual Meeting of the Society for American Archaeology, St. Louis.

Morse, Dan F.
1990   The Nodena Phase. In *Towns and Temples Along the Mississippi,* edited by David H. Dye and Cheryl A. Cox, pp. 69–97. University of Alabama Press, Tuscaloosa.

Morse, Dan F., and Phyllis A. Morse
1983   *Archaeology of the Central Mississippi Valley.* Academic Press, New York.

Morse, Phyllis A.
1990   The Parkin Site and the Parkin Phase. In *Towns and Temples Along the Mississippi,* edited by David H. Dye and Cheryl A. Cox, pp. 118–134. University of Alabama Press, Tuscaloosa.

Morss, Noel
1931   *The Ancient Culture of the Fremont River in Utah: Report on the Explorations Under the Claflen-Emerson Fund, 1928–29.* Papers of the Peabody Museum of American Archaeology and Ethnology 12(3). Harvard University, Cambridge.

Muller, Jon
1966a   Archaeological Analysis of Art Styles. *Tennessee Archaeologist* 22(1):25–39.

1966b   *An Experimental Theory of Stylistic Analysis.* Unpublished Ph.D. dissertation, Department of Anthropology, Harvard University, Cambridge.

1978   The Kincaid System: Mississippian Settlement in the Environs of a Large Site. In *Mississippian Settlement Patterns,* edited by Bruce D. Smith, pp. 269–292. Academic Press, New York.

1979   Structural Studies of Art Styles. In *The Visual Arts: Plastic and Graphic,* edited by Justine Cordwell, pp. 139–211. Mouton Publishers, New York.

1984   Mississippian Specialization and Salt. *American Antiquity* 49:489–507.

1986a   *Archaeology of the Lower Ohio River Valley.* Academic Press, Orlando, Florida.

1986b   Pans and a Grain of Salt: Mississippian Specialization Revisited. *American Antiquity* 51:405–408.

1986c   Serpents and Dancers: Art of the Mud Glyph Cave. In *The Prehistoric Native American Art of Mud Glyph Cave,* edited by Charles H. Faulkner, pp. 36–80, University of Tennessee Press, Knoxville.

1987   Salt, Chert, and Shell: Mississippian Exchange and Economy. In *Specialization, Exchange, and Complex Societies,* edited by Elizabeth M. Brumfiel and Timothy K. Earle, pp. 10–21. Cambridge University Press, Cambridge.

1989   The Southern Cult. In *The Southeastern Ceremonial Complex: Artifacts and Analysis,* edited by Patricia Galloway, pp. 11–26. University of Nebraska Press, Lincoln.

1993a Eastern North American Population Dynamics. *Illinois Archaeology* 5:84–99.

1993b Towns along the Lower Ohio. Paper presented at the 58th Annual Meeting of the Society for American Archaeology, St. Louis.

1994 Native Eastern American Population Stability. Paper presented Visiting Scholar Conference, Center for Archaeological Investigations, Southern Illinois University, Carbondale.

1995 Regional Interaction in the Southeast. In *Native American Interactions: Multiscalar Analyses and Interpretations in the Eastern Woodlands*, edited by Michael S. Nassaney and Kenneth E. Sassaman, pp. 317–340. University of Nebraska Press, Lincoln.

1997 *Mississippian Political Economy*. Plenum Press, New York.

Muller, Jon (editor)

1992 The Great Salt Spring: Mississippian Production and Specialization. Draft Report of March, 1992. Ms. on file, Shawnee National Forest, U.S. Forest Service, Harrisburg, Illinois.

Muller, Jon, and Jeanette E. Stephens

1991 Mississippian Sociocultural Adaptation. In *Cahokia and the Hinterlands: Middle Mississippian Cultures of the Midwest*, edited by Thomas E. Emerson and R. Barry Lewis, pp. 297–310. University of Illinois Press, Urbana.

Myer, William E.

1928 *Indian Trails of the Southeast*. Forty-second Annual Report of the Bureau of American Ethnology, pp. 727–857. Smithsonian Institution, Washington, D.C.

Naroll, Robert

1962 Floor Area and Settlement Population. *American Antiquity* 27:587–589.

Nassaney, Michael S.

1991 Spatio-Temporal Dimensions of Social Integration During the Coles Creek Period in Central Arkansas. In *Stability, Transformation, and Variation: The Late Woodland Southeast*, edited by Michael S. Nassaney and Charles R. Cobb, pp. 177–220. Plenum Press, New York.

Nassaney, Michael S., and Charles R. Cobb (editors)

1991 *Stability, Transformation, and Variation: The Late Woodland Southeast*. Plenum Press, New York.

Neely, James A.

1974 *The Prehistoric Lunt and Stove Canyon Sites, Point of Pines, Arizona*. Unpublished Ph.D. dissertation, Department of Anthropology, University of Arizona, Tucson.

Neitzel, Jill E.

1989a The Chacoan Regional System: Interpreting the Evidence for Sociopolitical Complexity. In *The Sociopolitical Structure of Prehistoric Southwestern Societies*, edited by Steadman Upham, Kent G. Lightfoot, and Roberta A. Jewett, pp. 509–556. Westview Press, Boulder.

1989b Regional Exchange Networks in the American Southwest: A Comparative Analysis of Long Distance Trade. In *The Sociopolitical Structure of Prehistoric Southwestern Societies*, edited by Steadman Upham, Kent G. Lightfoot, and Roberta A. Jewett, pp. 149–195. Westview Press, Boulder.

1991 Hohokam Material Culture and Behavior: The Dimensions of Organizational Change. In *Exploring the Hohokam: Prehistoric Desert Peoples of the American Southwest*, edited by George J. Gumerman, pp. 177–230. Amerind Foundation New World Studies Series 1. Amerind Foundation, Dragoon, Arizona, and University of New Mexico Press, Albuquerque.

1994 Boundary Dynamics in the Chacoan Regional System. In *The Ancient Southwestern Community: Models and Methods for the Study of Prehistoric Social Organization*, edited by Wirt H. Wills and Robert D. Leonard, pp. 209–240. University of New Mexico Press, Albuquerque.

Neitzel, Jill E., and Ronald L. Bishop

1990 Neutron Activation of Dogoszhi Style Ceramics: Production and Exchange in the Chacoan Regional System. *Kiva* 56:67–85.

Neitzel, Robert S.

1965 *Archaeology of the Fatherland Site: The Grand Village of the Natchez*. Anthropological Papers No. 51, pt. 1. The American Museum of Natural History, New York.

1983 *The Grand Village of the Natchez Revisited: Excavations at the Fatherland Site, Adams County, Mississippi, 1972*. Archaeological Report No. 12. Mississippi Department of Archives and History, Jackson.

Nelson, Ben A.

1990 Observaciones Acerca de la Presencia Tolteca en La Quemada, Zacatecas. In *Mesoamérica y Norte de México, Siglo IX-XII, Volume 2*, edited by F. Sodi Miranda, pp. 521–540. Instituto Nacional de Antropología e Historia, México City.

1994 Complexity, Hierarchy, and Scale: A Controlled Comparison Between Chaco Canyon, New Mexico, and La Quemada, Zacatecas. *American Antiquity* 60:597–618.

Nelson, Ben A., and Stephen A. LeBlanc

1986 *Short-Term Sedentism in the American Southwest; The Mimbres Valley Salado*. Maxwell Museum of Anthropology and University of New Mexico Press, Albuquerque.

Nelson, Ben A., Debra Martin, Alan Swedlund, Paul R. Fish, and George Armelegos

1994 Studies in Disruption: Demography and Health in the Prehistoric Southwest. In *Understanding*

Complexity in the Prehistoric Southwest, edited
by George J. Gumerman and Murrey Gell-man,
pp. 39–58. Santa Fe Institute Studies in Sciences
of Complexity Proceedings, vol. 24. Addison-
Wesley, Reading, Massachusetts.

Nelson, Bonnie K.
1977   *A Spatial Analysis of the Classic Mimbres Sites
        along the Rio Mimbres of Southwestern New
        Mexico.* Unpublished Master's thesis, Depart-
        ment of Geography, Florida State University,
        Tallahassee.

Nelson, Margaret C.
1993   Changing Occupational Pattern among Prehis-
        toric Horticulturalists in SW New Mexico.
        Journal of Field Archaeology 20:43–57.

Nelson, Nels
1914   *Pueblo Ruins of the Galisteo Basin, New Mexico.*
        Anthropological Papers of the American Mu-
        seum of Natural History No. 15 (pt. 1).

Nelson, Richard S.
1981   *The Role of a Puchteca System in Hohokam
        Exchange.* Unpublished Ph.D. dissertation,
        Department of Anthropology, New York Uni-
        versity, New York.

Netting, R. McC.
1993   *Smallholders, Householders: Farm Families and
        the Ecology of Intensive, Sustainable Agriculture.*
        Stanford University Press, Palo Alto.

Nials, Fred L., John R. Stein, and John Roney
1987   *Chacoan Roads in the Southern Periphery: Re-
        sults of Phase II of the BLM Chaco Roads Project.*
        Cultural Resources Series No. 1. Bureau of Land
        Management, Albuquerque.

Nicholas, Linda M., and Gary M. Feinman
1989   A Regional Perspective on Hohokam Irrigation
        in the Lower Salt River Valley. In *The
        Sociopolitical Structure of Prehistoric Southwest-
        ern Societies*, edited by Steadman Upham, Kent
        G. Lightfoot, and Roberta A. Jewett, pp. 199–
        236. Westview Press, Boulder.

Nicholas, Linda M., and Jill E. Neitzel
1984   Canal Irrigation and Sociopolitical Organiza-
        tion in the Lower Salt River Valley: A Dia-
        chronic Analysis. In *Prehistoric Agricultural
        Strategies of the Southwest*, edited by Suzanne K.
        Fish and Paul R. Fish, pp. 161–178. Arizona State
        University, Anthropological Research Papers
        No. 32, Tempe.

Nuñez Cabeza de Vaca, Alvar
1542   *La Relacion que Dio Alvar Nuñez Cabeza de
        Vaca de lo Acaescido en las Indias en la Armada.*
        Translated by Buckingham Smith 1871, Relation
        of Alvar Nuñez Cabeza de Vaca, New York

O'Brien, Patricia J.
1972a   *A Formal Analysis of Cahokia Ceramics from the
        Powell Tract.* Illinois Archaeological Survey
        Monograph No. 3, Urbana.

1972b   Urbanism, Cahokia and Middle Mississippian.
        Archaeology 25:189–197.

1989   Cahokia: The Political Capital of the "Ramey"
        State? *North American Archaeologist* 10:275–292.

1991   Early State Economics: Cahokia, Capital of the
        Ramey State. In *Early State Economics*, edited by
        Henri J. M. Claessen and Pieter van de Velde,
        pp. 143–175. Political and Legal Anthropology 8.
        Transaction Publishers, New Brunswick.

Oliver, Theodore J.
n.d.   *Classic Period Settlement in the Uplands of Tonto
        Basin.* Arizona State University, Anthropologi-
        cal Field Studies, Tempe (in press).

Oliver, Theodore J., and David Jacobs
n.d.   *Salado Residential Settlements on Tonto Creek.*
        Arizona State University Anthropological Field
        Studies, Tempe (in press).

Orcutt, Jan D., Eric Blinman, and Timothy A. Kohler
1990   Explanations of Population Aggregation in the
        Mesa Verde Region Prior to A.D. 900. In *Perspec-
        tives on Southwestern Prehistory*, edited by Paul
        E. Minnis and Charles L. Redman, pp. 76–91.
        Westview Press, Boulder.

Ottoway, Lucretia V.
1975   Some Architectural Features Characteristic of
        the Taos, New Mexico Area: Early Manifesta-
        tions at TA-26. In *Collected Papers in Honor of
        Florence Hawley Ellis*, edited by Theodore R.
        Frisbie, pp. 407–436. Papers of the Archaeologi-
        cal Society of New Mexico No. 2. Hooper Pub-
        lishing, Norman.

Palkowvich, Ann M.
1980   *Pueblo Population and Society: The Arroyo
        Hondo Skeletal and Mortuary Remains.* School
        of American Research Press, Santa Fe.

Parsons, Elsie C.
1923   *Laguna Genealogies.* Anthropological Papers of
        the American Museum of Natural History,
        19(5):133–292. New York.

Pauketat, Timothy R.
1987   Mississippian Domestic Economy and Forma-
        tion Processes: A Response to Prentice. *Mid-
        continental Journal of Archaeology* 12:77–88.

1989   Monitoring Mississippian Homestead Occupa-
        tion Span and Economy Using Ceramic Refuse.
        American Antiquity 54:288–310.

1991   *The Dynamics of Pre-State Political Centraliza-
        tion in the North American Midcontinent.* Un-
        published Ph.D. dissertation, Department of
        Anthropology, University of Michigan, Ann
        Arbor.

1992   The Reign and Ruin of the Lords of Cahokia: A
        Dialectic of Dominance. In *Lords of the South-
        east: Social Inequality and the Native Elites of
        Southeastern North America*, edited by Alex W.
        Barker and Timothy R. Pauketat, pp. 31–51.

Archaeological Papers of the American Anthropological Association No. 3, Washington, D.C.

1994　*The Ascent of Chiefs: Cahokia and Mississippian Polities in Native North America*. The University of Alabama Press, Tuscaloosa.

1997　Mississippian Political Economy. In *Cahokia: Domination and Ideology in the Mississippian World*, edited by Timothy R. Pauketat and Thomas E. Emerson. University of Nebraska Press, Lincoln.

Pauketat, Timothy R., and Thomas E. Emerson (editors)

1997　*Cahokia: Domination and Ideology in the Mississippian World*. University of Nebraska Press, Lincoln.

Payne, Claudine

1994a　Fifty Years of Archaeological Research at the Lake Jackson Site. *The Florida Anthropologist* 47:107–119.

1994b　*Mississippian Capitals: An Archaeological Investigation of Precolumbian Political Structure*. Unpublished Ph.D. dissertation, Department of Anthropology, University of Florida.

Payne, Claudine, and John F. Scarry

1994　Town Structure at the Edge of the Mississippian World. In *Mississippian Towns and Central Places*, edited by R. Barry Lewis and C. B. Stout. Ms. submitted to the University of Alabama Press, Tuscaloosa.

Paynter, Robert

1982　*Models of Spatial Inequality: Settlement Patterns in Historical Archeology*. Academic Press, New York.

1989　The Archaeology of Equality and Inequality. *Annual Review of Anthropology* 18:369–399.

Peckham, Stewart

1969　An Archaeological Site Inventory of New Mexico, Part 1.

Ms. on file, Laboratory of Anthropology, Santa Fe.

1981　The Palisade Ruin (LA 3505): A Coalition Period Pueblo Near Abiquiu Dam, New Mexico. In *Collected Papers in Honor of Erik Kellerman Reed*, edited by Albert H. Schroeder, pp. 113–147. Papers of the Archaeological Society of New Mexico No. 6, Albuquerque.

Peebles, Christopher S.

1971　Moundville and Surrounding Sites: Some Structural Considerations of Mortuary Practices II. In *Approaches to the Social Dimensions of Mortuary Practices*, edited by James A. Brown, pp. 68–91. Memoir 25. Society for American Archaeology, Washington, D.C.

1978　Determinants of Settlement Size and Location in the Moundville Phase. In *Mississippian Settlement Patterns*, edited by Bruce D. Smith, pp. 369–416. Academic Press, New York.

1983　Moundville: Late Prehistoric Sociopolitical Organization in the Southeastern United States. In *The Development of Political Organization in Native North America*, edited by Elisabeth Tooker, pp. 183–198. American Ethnological Society.

1986　Paradise Lost, Strayed, and Stolen: Prehistoric Social Devolution in the Southeast. In *The Burden of Being Civilized: an Anthropological Perspective on the Discontents of Civilization*, edited by Miles Richardson and Malcolm Webb, pp. 24–40. Southern Anthropological Society Proceedings 18. University of Georgia Press, Athens.

1987a　Moundville from 1000 to 1500 A.D. as seen from 1840 to 1985 A.D. In *Chiefdoms in the Americas*, edited by Robert D. Drennan and Carlos A. Uribe, pp. 21–42. University Press of America, Lanham, Maryland.

1987b　The Rise and Fall of the Mississippian in Western Alabama: The Moundville and Summerville Phases, A.D. 1000 to 1600. *Mississippi Archaeology* 22:1–31.

1990　From History to Hermeneutics: The Place of Theory in the Later Prehistory of the Southeast. *Southeastern Archaeology* 9:23–34.

Peebles, Christopher S., and Susan M. Kus

1977　Some Archaeological Correlates of Ranked Societies. *American Antiquity* 42:421–448.

Pendergast, David M.

1960　*The Distribution of Metal Artifacts in Pre-Hispanic Mesoamerica*. Unpublished Ph.D. dissertation, Department of Anthropology, University of California, Los Angeles.

Pepper, George H.

1909　The Exploration of a Burial-Room in Pueblo Bonito, New Mexico. In *Putnum Anniversary Volume: Anthropological Essays Presented to Frederic Ward Putnam*, edited by Franz Boas, pp. 196–252. Cedar Rapids, Iowa.

1920　*Pueblo Bonito*. Anthropological Papers of the American Museum of Natural History 27, New York.

Peregrine, Peter N.

1991　Prehistoric Chiefdoms on the American Midcontinent: A World System Based on Prestige Goods. In *Core/Periphery Relations in Precapitalist Worlds*, edited by Christopher Chase-Dunn and Thomas D. Hall, pp. 193–211. Westview Press, Boulder.

1992　*Mississippian Evolution: A World-System Perspective*. Prehistory Press, Madison, Wisconsin.

Phillips, Philip

1940　Middle American Influences on the Archaeology of the Southeastern United States. In *The Maya and Their Neighbors*, edited by Clarence L. Hay, Ralph L. Linton, Samuel K. Lothrop, Harry L. Shapiro, and George C. Vaillant, pp. 349–367. Appleton-Century, New York.

Phillips, Philip, and James A. Brown

1975 –   *Pre-Columbian Shell Engravings from the*
1984   *Craig Mound at 1982 Spiro, Oklahoma* (volumes
        1–6). Peabody Museum Press, Cambridge.

1984   *Pre-Columbian Shell Engravings from the Craig
        Mound at Spiro, Oklahoma.* (2-volume edition)
        Peabody Museum Press, Cambridge.

Phillips, Philip., James A. Ford, and James B. Griffin

1951   *Archaeological Survey in the Lower Mississippi
        Alluvial Valley, 1940–1947.* Papers of the Pea-
        body Museum of American Archaeology and
        Ethnology 25. Harvard University, Cambridge.

Plog, Fred

1974   *The Study of Prehistoric Change.* Academic
        Press, New York.

1979   Alternative Models of Prehistoric Change. In
        *Transformations: Mathematical Approaches to
        Culture Change,* edited by Colin Renfrew and
        Kenneth L. Cooke, pp. 221–236. Academic Press,
        New York.

1983   Political and Economic Alliances on the Colo-
        rado Plateaus, A.D. 400–1450. *Advances in World
        Archaeology* 2:289–330.

1985   Status and Death at Grasshopper: The Homog-
        enization of Reality. In *Status, Structure, and
        Stratification: Current Archaeological Recon-
        structions: Proceedings of the Sixteenth Annual
        Chacmool Conference,* edited by Marc Thomp-
        son, Maria T. Garcia, and Francois J. Kense, pp.
        161–167. The Archaeological Association of the
        University of Calgary, Alberta.

1989   Studying Complexity. In *The Sociopolitical
        Structure of Prehistoric Southwestern Societies,*
        edited by Steadman Upham, Kent G. Lightfoot,
        and Roberta A. Jewett, pp. 103–128. Westview
        Press, Boulder.

Plog, Fred, and Cheryl Garrett

1972   Explaining Variability in Prehistoric Southwest-
        ern Water Systems. In *Contemporary Archaeol-
        ogy: A Guide to Theory and Contributions,*
        edited by Mark P. Leone, pp. 280–288. Southern
        Illinois University Press, Carbondale.

Plog, Fred, Steadman Upham, and Phillip C. Weigand

1982   A Perspective on Mogollon-Mesoamerican
        Interaction. In *Mogollon Archaeology: Proceed-
        ings of the 1980 Conference,* edited by Patrick H.
        Beckett, pp. 227–238. Acoma Books, Ramona.

Plog, Stephen E.

1980   *Stylistic Variation in Prehistoric Ceramics: De-
        sign Analysis in the American Southwest.* Cam-
        bridge University Press, New York.

Plog, Stephen E., and Julie Solomento

1995   Alternative Pathways in the Evolution of West-
        ern Pueblo Ritual. In *Debating Complexity:
        Proceedings of the Twenty-sixth Annual
        Chacmool Conference,* edited by Daniel A.

Meyer, Peter C. Dawson, and Donald T. Hanna.
        The Archaeological Association of the Univer-
        sity Calgary, Alberta.

Polhemus, Richard R.

1990   Dallas Phase Architecture and Sociopolitical
        Structure. In *Lamar Archaeology: Mississippian
        Chiefdoms in the Deep South,* edited by J. Mark
        Williams and Gary Shapiro, pp. 125–138. The
        University of Alabama Press, Tuscaloosa.

Polhemus, Richard R., Arthur E. Bogan, Jefferson Chapman,
Kenneth R. Parham, A. Reed, Wayne D. Roberts,
Gary T. Scott, and Andrea B. Shea

1987   *The Toqua Site: 40MR6: A Late Mississippian,
        Dallas Phase Town.* Report of Investigations No.
        41. Department of Anthropology, University of
        Tennessee, Knoxville.

Porter, James W.

1969   The Mitchell Site and Prehistoric Exchange
        Systems at Cahokia: A.D. 1000"300. In *Explora-
        tions into Cahokia Archaeology,* edited by
        Melvin L. Fowler, pp. 137–164. Illinois Archaeo-
        logical Survey Bulletin No. 7,Urbana.

1974   *Cahokia Archaeology as Viewed from the
        Mitchell Site: A Satellite Community at A.D. 1150–
        1200.* Ph.D. dissertation. Department of An-
        thropology, University of Wisconsin, Madison.
        University Microfilms, Ann Arbor.

1984   Thin Section Analysis of Ceramics. In *The
        Robinson's Lake Site (11-Ms–582),* by George R.
        Milner, pp. 133–170. American Bottom Archae-
        ology FAI-270 Site Report No. 7. University of
        Illinois Press, Urbana.

Postgate, J. N.

1992   *Early Mesopotamia: Society and Economy at the
        Dawn of History.* Routledge, London.

Potter, Stephen R.

1993   *Commoners, Tribute, and Chiefs: The Development
        of Algonquian Culture in the Potomac Valley.* Uni-
        versity of Virginia Press, Charlottesville.

Powell, Mary L.

1988   *Status and Health in Prehistory: A Case Study of
        the Moundville Chiefdom.* Smithsonian Series in
        Archaeological Inquiry. Smithsonian Institu-
        tion Press, Washington, D.C.

Powers, Robert P., William B. Gillespie, and
Stephen H. Lekson

1983   *The Outlier Survey: a Regional View of Settle-
        ment in the San Juan Basin.* Reports of the
        Chaco Center No. 3. Division of Cultural Re-
        search, National Park Service, Albuquerque.

Prentice, Guy

1983   Cottage Industries: Concepts and Implications.
        Midcontinental Journal of Archaeology 8:17–48.

1985   Economic Differentiation among Mississippian
        Farmsteads. *Midcontinental Journal of Archaeol-
        ogy* 10:77–122.

1986   An Analysis of the Symbolism Expressed by the Birger Figurine. *American Antiquity* 51:239–266.

1987   Marine Shells as Wealth Items in Mississippian Societies. *Midcontinental Journal of Archaeology* 12:193–223.

Price, James E.

1978   The Settlement Pattern of the Powers Phase. In *Mississippian Settlement Patterns*, edited by Bruce D. Smith, pp. 201–231. Academic Press, New York.

Price, James E., and James B. Griffin

1979   *The Snodgrass Site of the Powers Phase of Southeast Missouri.* Anthropological Papers No. 66. University of Michigan Museum of Anthropology, Ann Arbor.

Quinn, David B. (editor)

1955   *The Roanoke Voyages 1584–1590, Volume I.* Hakluyt Society Second Series No. 104. Cambridge University Press, Cambridge.

Rands, Robert L.

1957   Comparative Notes on the Hand-Eye and Related Motifs. *American Antiquity* 22:247–257.

Ravesloot, John C.

1988   *Mortuary Practices and Social Differentiation at Casas Grandes, Chihuahua, Mexico.* Anthropological Papers of the University of Arizona No. 49. University of Arizona Press, Tucson.

Reed, Erik K.

1948   *Fractional Burials, Trophy Skulls, and Cannibalism.* National Park Service, Region 3, Anthropological Notes No. 79, Santa Fe.

1953   Appendix III: Human Skeletal Remains from Te'ewi. In *Salvage Archaeology in the Chama Valley, New Mexico*, by Fred Wendorf, pp. 104–118. Monographs of the School of American Research No. 17, Santa Fe.

Reed, Lori

1990   X-Ray Diffraction Analysis of Glaze Painted Ceramics from the Northern Rio Grande Region, New Mexico: Implications of Glazeware Production and Exchange. In *Economy and Polity in Late Rio Grande Prehistory*, edited by Steadman Upham and Barbara D. Staley, pp. 90–149. The University Museum, New Mexico State University, Occasional Papers No. 16, Las Cruces.

Reed, Nelson A., John W. Bennett, and James W. Porter

1968   Solid Core Drilling of Monks Mound: Technique and Findings. *American Antiquity* 33:137–148.

Reed, Paul F.

1990   A Spatial Analysis of the Northern Rio Grande Region, New Mexico: Implications for Sociopolitical and Economic Development. In *Economy and Polity in Late Rio Grande Prehistory*, edited by Steadman Upham and Barbara D. Staley, pp. 1–89. The University Museum, New Mexico State University, Occasional Papers No. 16, Las Cruces.

Reid, J. Jefferson

1973   *Growth and Response to Stress at Grasshopper Pueblo, Arizona.* Unpublished Ph.D. dissertation, Department of Anthropology, University of Arizona, Tucson.

1978   Response to Stress at Grasshopper Pueblo, Arizona. In *Discovering Past Behavior: Experiments in the Archaeology of the American Southwest*, edited by Paul F. Grebinger, pp. 195–213. Gordon and Breach, London.

1984   Implications of Mogollon Settlement Variability in Grasshopper and Adjacent Regions. In *Recent Research in Mogollon Archaeology*, edited by Steadman Upham, Fred Plog, David G. Batcho, and Barbara E. Kauffman, pp. 59–67. The University Museum, New Mexico State University, Occasional Papers No. 10, Las Cruces.

1985   Measuring Social Complexity in the American Southwest. In *Status, Structure, and Stratification: Current Archaeological Reconstructions, Proceedings of the Sixteenth Annual Chacmool Conference*, edited by Marc Thompson, Marcia T. Garcia, and Francois J. Kense, pp. 167–174. The Archaeological Association of the University of Calgary, Alberta.

1989   A Grasshopper Perspective on the Mogollon of the Arizona Mountains. In *Dynamics of Southwest Prehistory*, edited by Linda S. Cordell and George J. Gumerman, pp. 65–98. Smithsonian Institution Press, Washington, D.C.

Reid, J. Jefferson, and Stephanie M. Whittlesey

1982   Households at Grasshopper Pueblo. *American Behavioral Scientist* 25(6):687–703.

1990   The Complicated and the Complex: Observations on the Archaeological Record of Large Pueblos. In *Perspectives on Southwestern Prehistory*, edited by Paul E. Minnis and Charles L. Redman, pp. 184–195. Westview Press, Boulder.

Reid, J. Jefferson, Michael B. Schiffer, Stephanie M. Whittlesey, Madeleine J. M. Hinkes, Alan P. Sullivan, and Christian E. Downum

1989   Perception and Interpretation in Contemporary Southwestern Archaeology: Comments on Cordell, Upham, and Brock. *American Antiquity* 54:802–814.

Renfrew, Colin

1969   Trade and Cultural Process in European Prehistory. *Current Anthropology* 10:151–69.

1974   Beyond a Subsistence Economy, the Evolution of Social Organization in Prehistoric Europe. In *Reconstructing Complex Societies: An Archaeological Colloquium*, edited by Charlotte B. Moore, pp. 69–95. Bulletin of the American School of Oriental Research No. 20, Chicago

1977   Alternative Models for Exchange and Spatial Distributions. In *Exchange Systems in Prehistory*, edited by Timothy K. Earle and Jonathon E. Ericson, pp. 78–89. Academic Press, New York.

Renfrew, Colin, and John F. Cherry (editors)

1986   *Peer Polity Interaction and Socio-Political Change.* Cambridge University Press, Cambridge.

Renfrew, Colin, and E. V. Level

1979   Exploring Dominance: Predicting Polities from Centers. In *Transformations: Mathematical Approaches to Culture Change*, edited by Colin Renfrew and Kenneth L. Cooke, pp. 145–167. Academic Press, New York.

Reyman, Jonathan E.

1976   Astronomy, Architecture, and Adaptation at Pueblo Bonito. *Science* 193(4257):957–962.

1978   Pochteca Burials at Anasazi Sites? In *Across the Chichimec Sea: Papers in Honor of J. Charles Kelley*, edited by Carroll L. Riley and Basil C. Hedrick, pp. 242–262. Southern Illinois University Press, Carbondale.

1985   A Re-evaluation of Bi-wall and Tri-wall Structures in the Anasazi Area. In *Contributions to the Archaeology and Ethnohistory of Greater Mesoamerica*, edited by William J. Folan, pp. 293–334. Southern Illinois Press, Carbondale.

Reyman, Jonathan E. (editor)

1995   *The Gran Chichimeca: Essays on the Archaeology and History of Northern Mexico.* Ashgate Press, Brookfield, Vermont.

Reyna, Stephen P.

1994   A Mode of Domination Approach to Organized Violence. In *Studying War: Anthropological Perspectives*, edited by Stephen P. Reyna and R. E. Downs, pp. 29–65. Gordon and Breach, Langhorne, Pennsylvania.

Rice, Glen E., and Charles L. Redman

1993   Platform Mounds of the Arizona Desert. *Expedition* 35(1):53–63.

Riley, Carroll L.

1987   *The Frontier People: the Greater Southwest in the Protohistoric Period.* University of New Mexico Press, Albuquerque.

Roaf, Michael

1990   *A Cultural Atlas of Mesopotamia and the Ancient Near East.* Facts on File, New York.

Roberts, Frank H. H., Jr.

1935   A Survey of Southwestern Archaeology. *American Anthropologist* 37(1):1–33.

1937   Archaeology in the Southwest. *American Antiquity* 3:3–33.

Rogers, Malcolm J.

1941   Aboriginal Cultural Relations Between Southern California and the Southwest. *San Diego Museum Bulletin No. 5*(3):1–6.

Rohn, Arthur H.

1977   *Cultural Change and Continuity on Chapin Mesa.* The Regents Press of Kansas, Lawrence.

1983   Budding Urban Settlements in the Northern San Juan. In *Proceedings of the Anasazi Symposium*, edited by Jack E. Smith, pp. 175–180. Mesa Verde Museum Association, Mesa Verde National Park, Colorado.

1989   Northern San Juan Prehistory. In *Dynamics of Southwest Prehistory*, edited by Linda S. Cordell and George J. Gumerman, pp. 149–178. Smithsonian Institution Press, Washington, D.C.

Rolingson, Martha A.

1990a   Excavations of Mound S at the Toltec Mounds Site: Preliminary Report. *The Arkansas Archeologist* 31:1–27.

1990b   The Toltec Mounds Site: A Ceremonial Center in the Arkansas River Lowland. In *The Mississippian Emergence*, edited by Bruce D. Smith, pp. 27–49. Smithsonian Institution Press, Washington, D.C.

Romans, Bernard

1775   *A Concise Natural History of East and West Florida.* New York.

Roney, John R.

1992   Prehistoric Roads and Regional Integration in the Chacoan System. In *Anasazi Regional Organization and the Chaco System*, edited by David E. Doyel, pp. 123–132. Maxwell Museum of Anthropology, Anthropological Papers No. 5, Albuquerque.

Roosevelt, Anna C.

1991   *Moundbuilders of the Amazon: Geophysical Archaeology on Marajoara Island, Brazil.* Academic Press, San Diego.

Rose, J. C., M. K. Marks, and L. L. Tieszen

1991   Bioarchaeology and Subsistence in the Central and Lower Portions of the Mississippi Valley. In *What Mean These Bones? Studies in Southeastern Bioarchaeology*, edited by Mary L. Powell, Patricia S. Bridges, and Ann M. Mires, pp. 7–21. University of Alabama Press, Tuscaloosa.

Rose, Martin R., Jeffery S. Dean, and William J. Robinson

1981   *The Past Climate of Arroyo Hondo, New Mexico, Reconstructed from Tree Rings.* School of American Research Press, Santa Fe.

Rountree, Helen C.

1989   *The Powhatan Indians of Virginia.* University of Oklahoma Press, Norman.

Rudy, Jack R.

1953   *Archeological Survey of Western Utah.* University of Utah Anthropological Papers No. 12, Salt Lake City.

Runciman, Walter G.

1982   Origins of States: The Case of Archaic Greece. *Comparative Studies in Society and History* 24:351–377.

1989   *A Treatise on Social Theory.* Cambridge University Press, Cambridge.

Russell, Frank
1975   *The Pima Indians*. University of Arizona Press, Tucson.

Saggs, H. W. F.
1984   *The Might That Was Assyria*. Sidgwick and Jackson, London.

Sahlins, Marshall D.
1958   *Social Stratification in Polynesia*. American Ethnological Society Monograph 29. University of Washington Press, Seattle.

1963   Poor Man, Rich Man, Big Man, Chief: Political Types in Melanesia and Polynesia. *Comparative Studies in Society and History* 5:285–303.

1972   *Stone-Age Economics*. Chicago, Aldine.

1976   *Culture and Practical Reason*. University of Chicago Press, Chicago.

1985   *Islands of History*. University of Chicago Press, Chicago.

Sanders, William T.
1972   Population, Agricultural History, and Societal Evolution in Mesoamerica. In *Population Growth: Anthropological Implications*, edited by Brian Spooner. MIT Press, Cambridge, Massachusetts.

1984   Pre-Industrial Demography and Social Evolution. In *On the Evolution of Complex Societies: Essays in Honor of Harry Hoijer, 1982*, edited by Timothy K. Earle, pp. 7–40. Undena Publications, Malibu, California.

Sanders, William T., and Barbara Price
1968   *Mesoamerica: The Evolution of a Civilization*. Random House, New York.

Sando, Joe S.
1992   *Pueblo Nations: Eight Centuries of Pueblo Indian History*. Clear Light Publishers, Santa Fe.

Santure, Sharron K.
1981   The Changing Community Plan of Settlement C. In *The Orendorf Site: Preliminary Working Papers*, edited by Duane Esarey and Lawrence A. Conrad, pp. 5–80. Archaeological Research Laboratory, Western Illinois University, Macomb.

Santure, Sharron K., Alan D. Horn, and Duane Esarey (editors)
1990   Archaeological Investigations at the Morton Village and Norris Farms 36 Cemetery. Reports of Investigations No. 45, Illinois State Museum, Springfield.

Sauer, Carl O., and Donald R. Brand
1931   *Prehistoric Settlement of Sonora with Special Reference to Cerros de Trincheras*. University of California Publications in Geography 5:67–148.

Scarry, C. Margaret
1986   *Change in Plant Procurement and Production during the Emergence of the Moundville Chiefdom*. Ph.D. dissertation, University of Michigan. University Microfilms, Ann Arbor.

1993a   Agricultural Risk and the Development of Mississippian Chiefdoms: Prehistoric Moundville a Case Study. In *Foraging and Farming in the Eastern Woodlands*, edited by C. Margaret Scarry, pp. 157–181. University Presses of Florida, Gainesville.

1993b   Variability in Mississippian Crop Production Strategies. In *Foraging and Farmers in the Eastern Woodlands*, edited by C. Margaret Scarry, pp. 78–90. University Presses of Florida, Gainesville.

1994   Variability in Late Prehistoric Corn from the Lower Southeast. In *Corn and Culture in the Prehistoric New World*, edited by Sissel Johannessen and Christine A. Hastorf, pp. 347–367. Westview Press, Boulder.

1995   *Excavations on the Northwest Riverbank at Moundville: Investigations of a Moundville I Residential Area*. Report of Investigations No. 72. University of Alabama Museums Office of Archaeological Services, Tuscaloosa.

Scarry, John F.
1985   A Proposed Revision of the Fort Walton Ceramic Typology: A Type-variety System. *The Florida Anthropologist* 38:199–233.

1990a   Mississippian Emergence in the Fort Walton Area: The Evolution of the Cayson and Lake Jackson Phases. In *The Mississippian Emergence*, edited by Bruce D. Smith, pp. 227–250. Smithsonian Institution Press, Washington, D.C.

1990b   The Rise, Transformation, and Fall of Apalachee: A Case Study of Political Change in a Chiefly Society. In *Lamar Archaeology: Mississippian Cheifdoms in the Deep South*, edited by J. Mark Williams and Gary Shapiro, pp. 175–186. University of Alabama Press, Tuscaloosa.

1991   Mound 3 and the Political Structure of the Lake Jackson Chiefdom. Paper presented at the 48th Annual Southeastern Archaeological Conference, Jackson, Mississippi.

1992   Political Offices and Political Structure: Ethnohistoric and Archaeological Perspectives on the Native Lords of Apalachee. In *Lords of the Southeast: Social Inequality and the Native Elites of Southeastern North America*, edited by Alex W. Barker and Timothy R. Pauketat, pp. 163–183. Archeological Papers of the American Anthropological Association No. 3, Washington, D.C.

1996   Stability and Change in the Apalachee Chiefdom: Centralization, Decentralization, and Social Reproduction. In *Political Structure and Change in the Prehistoric Southeastern United States*, edited by John F. Scarry, pp. 192–227. University Presses of Florida, Gainesville.

Scarry, John F., and Claudine Payne
1986   Mississippian Polities in the Fort Walton Area: A Model Generated from the Renfrew-Level

XTENT Algorithm. *Southeastern Archaeology* 5:79–90.

Schaafsma, Polly

1980   *Indian Rock Art of the Southwest*. University of New Mexico Press, Albuquerque.

1992   *Rock Art of New Mexico*. Museum of New Mexico Press, Santa Fe.

1994   The Prehistoric Kachina Cult and Its Origins as Suggested by Southwestern Rock Art. In *Kachinas in the Pueblo World*, edited by Polly Shaafsma, pp. 63–79. Museum of New Mexico Press, Santa Fe.

Schelberg, John D.

1984   Analogy, Complexity, and Regionally-Based Perspectives. In *Recent Research on Chaco Prehistory*, edited by W. James Judge and John D. Schelberg, pp. 5–22. Reports of the Chaco Center No. 8. Division of Cultural Research, National Park Service, Albuquerque.

Schiffer, Michael B.

1976   *Behavioral Archaeology*. Studies in Archaeology, Academic Press, New York.

1982   Hohokam Chronology: An Essay on History and Method. In *Hohokam and Patayan: Prehistory of Southwestern Arizona*, edited by Randall H. McGuire and Michael B. Schiffer, pp. 299–344. Academic Press, New York.

Schnell, Frank T., Vernon J. Knight, Jr., and Gail S. Schnell

1981   *Cemochechobee: Archaeology of a Mississippian Ceremonial Center on the Chattahoochee River*. Ripley P. Bullen Monographs in Anthropology and History No. 3. University Presses of Florida, Gainesville.

Schroeder, Albert H.

1940   *A Stratigraphic Survey of Pre-Spanish Trash Mounds of the Salt River Valley, Arizona*. Unpublished Master's thesis, Department of Anthropology, University of Arizona, Tucson.

1965   Unregulated Diffusion from Mexico into the Southwest Prior to A.D. 700. *American Antiquity* 30:297–309.

1966   Pattern Diffusion from Mexico into the Southwest after A.D. 600. *American Antiquity* 31:683–704.

1979   Pueblos Abandoned in Historic Times. In *Southwest*, edited by Alfonso Ortiz, pp. 236–254. Handbook of North American Indians, vol. 9, William C. Sturtevant, general editor. Smithsonian Institution Press, Washington D.C.

1981   How Far Can a Pochteca Leap Without Leaving Foot Prints? In *Collected Papers in Honor of Erik Kellerman Reed*, edited by Albert H. Schroeder, pp. 43–64. Papers of the Archaeological Society of New Mexico No. 6, Albuquerque.

Scott, Stuart D.

1966   *Dendrochronology in Mexico*. Papers of the Laboratory of Tree-ring Research No. 2. University of Arizona, Tucson.

Sears, William H.

1955   Creek and Cherokee Culture in the Eighteenth Century. *American Antiquity* 21:143–149.

1961   The Study of Social and Religious Systems in North American Archaeology. *Current Anthropology* 12:223–246.

1968   The State and Settlement Patterns in the New World. In *Settlement Archaeology*, edited by K. C. Chang, pp. 134–153. National Press, Palo Alto.

1973   The Sacred and the Secular in Prehistoric Ceramics. In *Variation in Anthropology: Essays in Honor of John C. McGregor*, edited by Donald W. Lathrap and Jody Douglas, pp. 31–42. Illinois Archaeological Survey Publications, Urbana.

1977   Seaborne Contacts Between Early Cultures in Lower Southeastern United States and Middle Through South America. In *The Sea in the Pre-Columbian World: A Conference at Dumbarton Oaks, October 26th and 27th, 1974*, edited by Elizabeth P. Benson, pp. 1–13. Dumbarton Oaks, Washington, D.C.

Sebastian, Lynne

1991   Sociopolitical Complexity and the Chaco System. In *Chaco & Hohokam: Prehistoric Regional Systems in the American Southwest*, edited by Patricia L. Crown and W. James Judge, pp. 109–134. School of American Research Press, Santa Fe.

1992   *The Chaco Anasazi: Sociopolitical Evolution in the Prehistoric Southwest*. Cambridge University Press, Cambridge.

Service, Elman R.

1962   *Primitive Social Organization: An Evolutionary Perspective*. New York, Random House.

1971   *Primitive Social Organization: An Evolutionary Perspective*, 2nd edition. Random House, New York.

1975   *Origins of the State and Civilization*. W. W. Norton, New York.

Shafer, Harry J., and Anna J. Taylor

1986   Mimbres Mogollon Pueblo Dynamics and Ceramic Style Change. *Journal of Field Archaeology* 13:43–68.

Shepard, Anna O.

1942   *Rio Grande Glaze Paint Ware: A Study Illustrating the Place of Ceramic Technological Analysis in Archaeological Research*. Contributions to American Anthropology and History, No. 39, Publication 528. Carnegie Institution of Washington, Washington, D.C.

Sires, Earl W., Jr.

1987   Hohokam Architectural Variability and Site Structure During the Sedentary-Classic Transition. In *The Hohokam Village: Site Structure and Organization*, edited by David E. Doyel, pp. 171–

182. Southwest and Rocky Mountain Division of the American Association for the Advancement of Science Monograph, Glenwood Springs, Colorado.

Slatter, Edwin D.
1979   *Drought and Demographic Change in the Prehistoric Southwest United States: A Preliminary Quantitative Assessment.* Unpublished Ph.D. dissertation, University of California, Los Angeles.

Smiley, Francis E., IV
1985   *The Chronometrics of Early Agricultural Sites in Northeastern Arizona: Approaches to the Interpretation of Radiocarbon Dates.* Unpublished Ph.D. dissertation, Department of Anthropology, University of Michigan, Ann Arbor.

Smith, Bruce D.
1978a   Variation in Mississippian Settlement Patterns. In *Mississippian Settlement Patterns*, edited by Bruce D. Smith, pp. 479–503. Academic Press, New York.

1984   Mississippian Expansion: Tracing the Historical Development of an Explanatory Model. *Southeastern Archaeology* 3:13–32.

1985a   The Archaeology of the Southeastern United States: From Dalton to De Soto, 10,500–500 B.P. *Advances in World Archaeology* 5:1–88.

1985b   Mississippian Patterns of Subsistence and Settlement. In *Alabama and the Borderlands: From Prehistory to Statehood*, edited by R. Reid Badger and Lawrence A. Clayton, pp. 64–79. University of Alabama Press, Tuscaloosa.

1992   Mississippian Elites and Solar Alignments—A Reflection of Managerial Necessity, or Levers of Social Inequality? In *Lords of the Southeast: Social Inequality and the Native Elites of Southeastern North America*, edited by Alex W. Barker and Timothy R. Pauketat, pp. 11–30. Archaeological Papers of the American Anthropological Association No. 3, Washington, D.C.

Smith, Bruce D. (editor)
1978b   *Mississippian Settlement Patterns.* Academic Press, New York.

1990   *Mississippian Emergence.* Smithsonian Institution Press, Washington, D.C.

Smith, Buckingham (translator)
1968   *Narratives of De Soto in the Conquest of Florida.* Palmetto Books, Gainesville.

Smith, Harriet M.
1973   The Murdock Mound: Cahokia Site. In *Explorations into Cahokia Archaeology*, edited by Melvin L. Fowler, pp. 49–88. Illinois Archaeological Survey Bulletin No. 7, Urbana.

Smith, Marvin T.
1987   *Archaeology of Aboriginal Culture Change in the Interior Southeast.* University Presses of Florida, Gainesville.

1989   Indian Responses to European Contact: The Coosa Example. In *First Encounters: Spanish Explorations in the Caribbean and the United States, 1492–1570*, edited by Jerald T. Milanich and Susan Milbrath, pp. 135–149. Ripley P. Bullen Monographs in Anthropology and History No. 9. Florida Museum of Natural History, Gainesville.

Smith, Marvin T., and Stephen A. Kowalewski
1981   Tentative Identification of a Prehistoric 'Province' in Piedmont Georgia. *Early Georgia* 8:1–13.

Smith, Watson
1952   *Excavations in Big Hawk Valley: Wupatki National Monument, Arizona.* Museum of Northern Arizona Bulletin No. 24, Flagstaff.

Southall, Aidan
1956   *Alur Society: A Study in Processes and Types of Domination.* Heffer, Cambridge.

1988a   On Mode of Production Theory: The Foraging Mode of Production and the Kinship Mode of Production. *Dialectical Anthropology* 12:165–192.

1988b   The Segmentary State in Africa and Asia. *Comparative Studies in Society and History* 30(1):52–82.

1991   The Segmentary State: From the Imaginary to the Material Means of Production. In *Political and Legal Anthropology, Volume 8: Early State Economics*, edited by Henri J. M. Claessen and Pieter van de Velde, pp. 75–95. Transactions Publishers, New Brunswick.

Speck, Frank G.
1907   Notes on Chickasaw Ethnology and Folk-lore. *Journal of American Folk-Lore* 20:50–58.

Spencer, Charles S.
1987   Rethinking the Chiefdom. In *Chiefdoms in the Americas*, edited by Robert D. Drennan and Carlos A. Uribe, pp. 369–389. University Press of America, Lanham, Maryland.

1990   On the Tempo and Mode of State Formation: Neoevolutionism Reconsidered. *Journal of Anthropological Archaeology* 9:1–30.

Speth, John D.
1988   Do We Need Concepts Like "Mogollon," "Anasazi," and "Hohokam" Today? A Cultural Anthropological Perspective. *The Kiva* 53:201–204.

Speth, John D., and Susan L. Scott
1985   The Role of Large Mammals in Late Prehistoric Horticultural Adaptations: The View from Southeastern New Mexico. *Archaeological Survey of Alberta Occasional Paper* 26:233–266.

Spicer, Edward H., and Louis P. Caywood
1936   *Two Pueblo Ruins in West Central Arizona.* University of Arizona Bulletin 7(1); Social Science Bulletin No. 10, Tucson.

Spielmann, Katherine A.
1982   *Inter-Societal Food Acquisition Among Egalitarian Societies: An Ecological Study of Plains/*

Pueblo Interaction in the American Southwest. Unpublished Ph.D. dissertation, Department of Anthropology, University of Michigan, Ann Arbor.

1994 Clustered Confederacies: Sociopolitical Organization in the Prehistoric Rio Grande. In *The Ancient Southwestern Community: Models and Methods for the Study of Prehistoric Social Organization*, edited by Wirt H. Wills and Robert D. Leonard, pp. 45–54. The University of New Mexico Press, Albuquerque.

Spielmann, Katherine A. (editor)
1991 *Farmers, Hunters and Colonists: Interaction between the Southwest and the Southern Plains.* University of Arizona Press, Tucson.

Spoerl, Patricia M.
1984 Prehistoric Fortifications in Central Arizona. In *Prehistoric Cultural Development in Central Arizona: Archaeology of the Upper New River Region*, edited by Patricia M. Spoerl and George J. Gumerman, pp. 261–278. Southern Illinois University at Carbondale Center for Archaeological Investigations Occasional Paper No. 5, Carbondale.

Spores, Ronald
1967 *The Mixtec Kings and Their People.* University of Oklahoma Press, Norman.

Sprague, Roderick, and Aldo Signori
1963 Inventory of Prehistoric Southwestern Copper Bells. *The Kiva* 28(4):1–20.

Stanislawski, Michael B.
1963 *Wupatki Pueblo: A Study in Cultural Fusion and Change in Sinagua and Hopi Prehistory.* Unpublished Ph.D. dissertation, Department of Anthropology, University of Arizona, Tucson.

Stein, G.
1994 Ethnicity, Exchange, and Emulation: Mesopotamian-Anatolian Interaction at Hacinebi, Turkey. Ms. in possession of the author.

Stein, John R.
1989 The Chaco Roads—Clues to an Ancient Riddle? *El Palacio* 94(3):4–17.

Stein, John R., and Stephen H. Lekson
1992 Anasazi Ritual Landscapes. In *Anasazi Regional Organization and the Chaco System*, edited by David E. Doyel, pp. 101–122. Maxwell Museum of Anthropology, Anthropological Papers No. 5, Albuquerque.

1994 Anasazi Ritual Landscape. In *Chaco Canyon: A Center and its Landscape*. Photographs by Mary Peck, with essays by Stephen H. Lekson, John R. Stein, and Simon J. Ortiz, pp. 45–58. Museum of New Mexico Press, Santa Fe.

Stein, John R., and Peter J. McKenna
1988 *An Archaeological Reconnaissance of a Late Bonito Phase Occupation Near Aztec Ruins*

National Monument, New Mexico. National Park Service, Southwest Cultural Resources Center, Division of Anthropology, Santa Fe.

Steponaitis, Vincas P.
1978 Location Theory and Complex Chiefdoms: A Mississippian Example. In *Mississippian Settlement Patterns*, edited by Bruce D. Smith, pp. 417–453. Academic Press, New York.

1983 *Ceramics, Chronology, and Community Patterns: An Archaeological Study at Moundville.* Academic Press, New York.

1986 Prehistoric Archaeology in the Southeastern United States, 1970–1985. *Annual Review of Anthropology* 15:363–404.

1991 Contrasting Patterns of Mississippian Development. In *Chiefdoms: Power, Economy, and Ideology*, edited by Timothy K. Earle, pp. 193–228. Cambridge University Press, Cambridge.

1992 Excavations at 1Tu50, An Early Mississippian Center Near Moundville. *Southeastern Archaeology* 11:1–13.

1993 Population Trends at Moundville. Paper presented at the 58th Annual Meeting of the Society for American Archaeology, St. Louis.

Stevenson, Matilda C.
1904 *The Zuni Indians: Their Mythology, Esoteric Fraternities, and Ceremonies.* Twenty-third Annual Report of the Bureau of American Ethnology for the Years 1908–1909, pp. 31–102. Smithsonian Institution, Washington D.C.

Steward, Julian D.
1933 *Archaeological Problems of the Northern Periphery.* Museum of Northern Arizona Bulletin No. 5, Flagstaff.

Stewart, Omar C.
1966 Ute Indians: Before and After White Contact. *Utah Historical Quarterly* 34(1):38–61.

Stoltman, James B. (editor)
1991 *New Perspectives on Cahokia: Views from the Periphery.* Prehistory Press, Madison, Wisconsin.

Strong, John A.
1989 The Mississippian Bird-Man Theme in Cross-Cultural Perspective. In *The Southeastern Ceremonial Complex: Artifacts and Analysis*, edited by Patricia Galloway, pp. 211–238. University of Nebraska Press, Lincoln.

Stubbs, Stanley A.
1950 *Bird's Eye View of the Pueblos.* University of Oklahoma Press, Norman.

Sullivan, Alan P.
1980 *Prehistoric Settlement Variability in the Grasshopper Area, East-Central Arizona.* Unpublished Ph.D. dissertation, Department of Anthropology, University of Arizona, Tucson.

Sullivan, Lynne P.
1987 The Mouse Creek Phase Household. *Southeastern Archaeology* 6:16–29.

Sussenbach, T.
1993   *Agricultural Intensification and Mississippian Developments in the Confluence Region of the Mississippi River Valley*. Ph.D. dissertation, University of Illinois. University Microfilms, Ann Arbor.

Sussenbach, T., and R. Barry Lewis
1987   *Archaeological Investigations in Carlisle, Hickman, and Fulton Counties, Kentucky*. Western Kentucky Project Report No. 4, University of Illinois Department of Anthropology, Urbana.

Swanton, John R.
1911   *Indian Tribes of the Lower Mississippi Valley and Adjacent Coast of the Gulf of Mexico*. Bureau of American Ethnology Bulletin No. 43. Smithsonian Intitution, Washington, D.C.
1922   *Early History of the Creek Indians and Their Neighbors*. Bureau of American Ethnology Bulletin No. 73. Smithsonian Institution, Washington, D.C.
1946   *The Indians of the Southeastern United States*. Bureau of American Ethnology Bulletin No. 137. Smithsonian Institution, Washington, D.C.

Tainter, Joseph A.
1978   Mortuary Practices and the Study of Prehistoric Social Systems. In *Advances in Archaeological Method and Theory 1*, edited by Michael B. Schiffer, pp. 106–141. Academic Press, Orlando.
1988   *The Collapse of Complex Societies*. Cambridge University Press, Cambridge.

Tainter, Joseph A., and Fred Plog
1994   Structure and Patterning: The Formation of Puebloan Archaeology. In *Themes in Southwest Prehistory*, edited by George J. Gumerman, pp. 163–182. School of American Research Press, Santa Fe.

Taylor, Donna
1974   *Some Locational Aspects of Middle-Range Hierarchical Societies*. Ph.D. dissertation, Department of Anthropology, City University of New York. University Microfilms, Ann Arbor.

Teague, Lynn S.
1984   Role and Ritual in Hohokam Society. In *Hohokam Archaeology along the Salt Gila Aqueduct Central Arizona Project Volume IX: Synthesis and Conclusions*, edited by Lynn S. Teague and Patricia L. Crown, pp. 155–185. Arizona State Museum Archaeological Series No. 150. University of Arizona, Tucson.

Tedlock, Dennis
1979   Zuni Religion and World View. In *Southwest*, edited by Alfonso Ortiz, pp. 499–508. Handbook of North American Indians, vol. 9, William C. Sturtevant, general editor. Smithsonian Institution Press, Washington D.C.

Thorne, Tanis C.
1993   Black Bird, "King of the Mahars": Autocrat, Big Man, Chief. *Ethnohistory* 40:410–437.

Tiffany, Joseph A.
1991   Modeling Mill Creek-Mississippian Interaction. In *New Perspectives on Cahokia: Views from the Periphery*, edited by James B. Stoltman, pp. 319–347. Prehistory Press, Madison, Wisconsin.

Todd, Ian A.
1976   *Çatal Hüyük In Perspective*. Cummings Publishing Co., Menlo Park.

Toll, H. Wolcott
1985   *Pottery, Production, Public Architecture, and the Chaco Anasazi System*. Unpublished Ph.D. dissertation, Department of Anthropology, University of Colorado, Boulder.
1991   Material Distributions and Exchange in the Chaco System. In *Chaco & Hohokam: Prehistoric Regional Systems in the American Southwest*, edited by Patricia L. Crown and W. James Judge, pp. 77–107. School of American Research Press, Santa Fe.

Toll, H. Wolcott, Thomas C. Windes, and Peter J. McKenna
1980   Late Ceramic Patterns in Chaco Canyon: The Pragmatics of Modeling Ceramic Exchange. In *Models and Methods in Regional Exchange*, edited by Robert E. Fry, pp. 95–118. Society of American Archaeology Papers No. 1, Washington, D.C.

Toll, Mollie S.
1984   Taxonomic Diversity in Flotation and Macrobotanical Assemblages from Chaco Canyon. In *Recent Research on Chaco Prehistory*, edited by W. James Judge and John D. Schelberg, pp. 241–250. Reports of the Chaco Center No. 8. National Park Service, Albuquerque.

Toth, Alan
1975   *Archaeology and Ceramics at the Marksville Site*. Museum of Anthropology Anthropological Papers No. 56. University of Michigan, Ann Arbor.

Tower, Donald B.
1945   The Use of Marine Mollusca and Their Value in Reconstructing Prehistoric Trade Routes in the American Southwest. *Papers of the Excavators Club* 2(3), Cambridge.

Tregle, Joseph G. (editor)
1975   *The History of Louisiana*. Louisiana State University Press, Baton Rouge.

Triadan, Daniela
1994   *White Mountain Redware: Exotic Trade Pots or Local Commodity*? Unpublished Ph.D. dissertation. Freie Universitat, Berlin, Germany.

Trigger, Bruce G.
1985   Marxism in Archaeology: Real or Spurious? *Reviews in Anthropology* 12:114–123.

Truell, Marcia L.
1986   A Summary of Small Site Architecture in Chaco Canyon, New Mexico. In *Small Site Architecture of Chaco Canyon, New Mexico*, edited by Peter McKenna and Marcia Truell, pp. 115–508. Publi-

cations in Anthropology 18-D, Chaco Canyon Studies. National Park Service, Santa Fe.

Tuggle, H. David
1970 *Prehistoric Community Relationships in East-Central Arizona*. Unpublished Ph.D. dissertation, Department of Anthropology, University of Arizona, Tucson.

Tuggle, H. David, J. Jefferson Reid, and Robert C. Cole, Jr.
1984 Fourteenth Century Mogollon Agriculture in the Grasshopper Region of Arizona. In *Prehistoric Agricultural Strategies in the Southwest*, edited by Suzanne F. Fish and Paul R. Fish, pp. 101–110. Arizona State University, Anthropological Research Papers No. 33, Tempe.

Turner, Christy G., II
1993 Cannibalism in Chaco Canyon: The Charnel Pit Excavated in 1926 at Small House Ruin by Frank H. H. Roberts, Jr. *American Journal of Physical Anthropology* 91:421–439.

Turner, Christy G., II, and Jacqueline A. Turner
1990 Perimortem Damage to Human Skeletal Remains from Wupatki National Monument. *Kiva* 55:187–212.

Turney, Omar A.
1929 *Prehistoric Irrigation in Arizona*. Office of Arizona State Historian, Phoenix.

Underhill, Ruth M.
1939 *Social Organization of the Papago Indians*. Columbia University Contributions to Anthropology 30, New York.

Upham, Steadman
1982 *Polities and Power: An Economic and Political History of the Western Pueblo*. Academic Press, New York.
1983 Intensification and Exchange: An Evolutionary Model of Non-Egalitarian Sociopolitical Organization for the Prehistoric Plateau Southwest. In *Ecological Models in Economic Prehistory*, edited by Gordon Bronitsky, pp. 219–245. Arizona State University, Anthropological Research Papers No. 29, Tempe.
1984 Adaptive Diversity and Southwestern Abandonment. *Journal of Anthropological Research*, 40:235–256.
1986 Imperialists, Isolationists, World Systems and Political Realities: Perspectives on Mesoamerican-Southwestern Interactions. In *Ripples in the Chichimec Sea: New Considerations of Southwestern-Mesoamerican Interactions*, edited by Frances J. Mathien and Randall H. McGuire, pp. 205–219. Southern Illinois University Press, Carbondale.
1990a Analog or Digital? Toward a Generic Framework for Explaining the Development of Emergent Political Systems. In *The Evolution of Political Systems: Sociopolitics in Small Scale Societies*, edited by Steadman Upham, pp. 87–115. Cambridge University Press, Cambridge.

Upham, Steadman (editor)
1990b *The Evolution of Political Systems: Sociopolitics in Small-Scale Sedentary Societies*. Cambridge University Press, Cambridge.

Upham, Steadman, and Gail M. Bockley
1989 The Chronologies of Nuvakwewtaqa: Implications for Social Processes. In *The Sociopolitical Structure of Prehistoric Southwestern Societies*, edited by Steadman Upham, Kent G. Lightfoot, and Roberta A. Jewett, pp. 447–490. Westview Press, Boulder.

Upham, Steadman, and Fred Plog
1986 The Interpretation of Prehistoric Political Complexity in the Central and Northern Southwest: Toward a Mending of the Models. *Journal of Field Archaeology* 13(2):223–238.

Upham, Steadman, and Lori Stephens Reed
1989 Regional Systems in the Central and Northern Southwest: Demography, Economy, and Sociopolitics Preceding Contact. In *Columbian Consequences, Volume 1: Archaeological and Historical Perspectives on the Spanish Borderlands*, edited by David Hurst Thomas, pp. 57–76. Smithsonian Institution Press, Washington, D.C.

Upham, Steadman, and Glen E. Rice
1980 Up the Canal without a Pattern: Modeling Hohokam Interaction and Exchange. In *Current Issues in Hohokam Prehistory: Proceedings of a Symposium*, edited by David E. Doyel and Fred Plog, pp. 78–105. Arizona State University, Anthropological Research Papers No. 23, Tempe.

Upham, Steadman, Patricia L. Crown, and Stephen E. Plog
1994 Alliance Formation and Cultural Identity in the American Southwest. In *Themes in Southwest Prehistory*, edited by George J. Gumerman, pp. 183–210. School of American Research Press, Santa Fe.

Upham, Steadman, Kent G. Lightfoot, and Roberta A. Jewett (editors)
1989 *The Sociopolitical Structure of Prehistoric Southwestern Societies*. Westview Press, Boulder, Colorado.

van der Leeuw, Sander E.
1981 Preliminary Report on the Analysis of Moundville Phase Ceramic Technology. *Southeastern Archaeological Conference Bulletin* 24:105–108.

van Warden, Nora
1984 *Hilltop Sites in Central Arizona: An Analysis of Their Functional Relationships*. Unpublished Master's thesis, Arizona State University, Tempe.

Varner, John T., and Jeannette J. Varner (translators)
1951 *The Florida of the Inca*. University of Texas Press, Austin.

Vivian, Gordon R.
1959   The Hubbard Site and Other Tri-wall Struc-
        tures in New Mexico and Colorado. *Archeologi-
        cal Research Series No. 5*. National Park Service,
        Washington, D.C.

Vivian, Gordon R., and Tom W. Matthews
1964   Kin Kletso: A Pueblo III Community in Chaco
        Canyon, New Mexico. *Southwestern Monuments
        Association Technical Series* 6(1), Globe, Arizona.

Vivian, Gordon R., and Paul Reiter
1960   *The Great Kivas of Chaco Canyon and Their
        Relationships*, School of American Research
        Monograph, No. 22, Santa Fe.

Vivian, R. Gwinn
1974   Conservation and Diversion: Water-control
        Systems in the Anasazi Southwest. In *Irrigation's
        Impact on Society*, edited by Theodore E. Down-
        ing and McGuire Gibson, pp. 95–112. Anthropo-
        logical Papers of the University of Arizona No.
        25. University of Arizona Press, Tucson.

1990   *The Chacoan Prehistory of the San Juan Basin*.
        Academic Press, New York.

1991   Chacoan Subsistence. In *Chaco & Hohokam:
        Prehistoric Regional Systems in the American
        Southwest*, edited by Patricia L. Crown and W.
        James Judge, pp. 57–75. School of American
        Research Press, Santa Fe.

Vokes, Arthur
1984   The Shell Assemblages of the Salt-Gila Aque-
        duct Sites. In *Hohokam Archaeology Along the
        Salt-Gila Aqueduct, Central Arizona Project:
        Material Culture*, edited by Lynn S. Teague and
        Patricia L. Crown, pp. 463–574. Arizona State
        Museum Archaeological Series, No. 150(8).
        University of Arizona, Tucson.

Walker, Winslow M., and Robert Mc. Adams
1946   *Excavations in the Matthews Site, New Madrid
        County, Missouri*. Transactions of the Academy
        of Science of St. Louis, 31(4), St. Louis.

Wallace, Henry D.
1994   An Iconographic Perspective on the Sequence
        of Culture Change in Central and Southern
        Arizona. Paper presented at the Fourth South-
        west Symposium, Tempe.

1986   *Petroglyphs of the Picacho Mountains, South
        Central Arizona*. Institute for American Re-
        search Anthropological Papers No. 6, Tucson.

Walthall, John A.
1980   *Prehistoric Indians of the Southeast: Archaeology
        of Alabama and the Middle South*. University of
        Alabama Press, Tuscaloosa.

Waring, Antonio J.
1968   *The Waring Papers: The Collected Works of Antonio
        J. Waring*, edited by Stephen Williams. Papers of
        the Peabody Museum of Archaeology and Ethnol-
        ogy 58. Harvard University, Cambridge.

Waring, Antonio J., and Preston Holder
1945   A Prehistoric Ceremonial Complex in the
        Southeastern United States. *American Anthro-
        pologist* 47:1–34.

Warren, Claude N.
1984   The Desert Region. In *California Archaeology*, by
        Michael J. Moratto, pp. 339–430. New World
        Archaeological Record, Academic Press, New York.

Warren, A. Helene
1979   The Glaze Paint Wares of the Upper Middle Rio
        Grande. In *Archaeological Investigations in
        Cochiti Reservoir, New Mexico, Volume 4: Adap-
        tive Change in the Northern Rio Grande Valley*,
        edited by Jan V. Biella and Richard C. Chap-
        man, pp. 187–216. Office of Contract Archeol-
        ogy, University of New Mexico, Albuquerque.

Waselkov, Gregory A.
1989   Indian Maps of the Colonial Southeast. In
        *Powhatan's Mantle: Indians in the Colonial
        Southeast*, edited by Peter H. Wood, Gregory A.
        Waselkov, and M. Thomas Hatley, pp. 292–343.
        University of Nebraska Press, Lincoln.

Wasley, William W., and Alfred Johnson
1965   *Salvage Archaeology in Painted Rocks Reservoir,
        Western Arizona*. Anthropological Papers of the
        University of Arizona No. 9. University of
        Arizona Press, Tucson.

Watson, Patty Jo
1990   Trend and Tradition in Southeastern Archaeol-
        ogy. *Southeastern Archaeology* 9:43–55.

Webb, Clarence H.
1968   The Extent and Content of Poverty Point Cul-
        ture. *American Antiquity* 33:297–321.

Webb, Malcolm C.
1989   Functional and Historical Parallelisms Between
        Mesoamerican and Mississippian Cultures. In
        *The Southeastern Ceremonial Complex: Artifacts
        and Analysis*, edited by Patricia Galloway, pp.
        279–293. University of Nebraska Press, Lincoln.

Webb, William S., and David J. DeJarnette
1942   *An Archeological Survey of Pickwick Basin and
        the Adjacent Portions of the States of Alabama,
        Mississippi, and Tennessee*. Bureau of American
        Ethnology Bulletin No. 129. Smithsonian Insti-
        tution, Washington, D.C.

Webb, William S., and Charles E. Snow
1945   *The Adena People*. Reports in Anthropology and
        Archaeology, Vol. 6. University of Kentucky,
        Lexington.

Weigand, Phillip C., and Garman Harbottle
1993   The Role of Turquoises in the Ancient Meso-
        american Trade Structure. In *The American
        Southwest and Mesoamerica: Systems of Prehis-
        toric Exchange*, edited by Jonathon E. Ericson
        and Timothy G. Baugh, pp. 159–177. Plenum
        Press, New York.

Weigand, Phil C., Garman Harbottle, and Edward V. Sayre
1977   Turquoise Sources and Source Analysis: Meso-america and the Southwestern U.S.A. In *Exchange Systems in Prehistory*, edited by Timothy K. Earle and Jonathon E. Ericson, pp. 15–34. Academic Press, New York.

Weiner, Annette
1976   *Women of Value, Men of Renown.* University of Texas Press, Austin.

Welch, Paul D.
1990a   Mississippian Emergence in West Central Alabama. In *The Mississippian Emergence*, edited by Bruce D. Smith, pp. 197–225. Smithsonian Institution Press, Washington, D.C.
1990b   The Vacant Quarter and Other Events in the Lower Valley. In *Towns and Temples along the Mississippi*, edited by David H. Dye and Cheryl A. Cox, pp. 170–180. University of Alabama Press, Tuscaloosa.
1991   *Moundville's Economy.* University of Alabama Press, Tuscaloosa.
1994   The Occupational History of the Bessemer Site. *Southeastern Archaeology* 13:1–26.
1996   Control over Goods and the Political Stability of the Moundville Chiefdom. In *Political Structure and Change in the Prehistoric Southeastern United States*, edited by John F. Scarry, pp. 69–91. University Presses of Florida, Gainesville.

Welch, Paul D., and C. Margaret Scarry
1994   Status-related Variation in Foodways in the Moundville Chiefdom. *American Antiquity* 60:397–419.

Wendorf, Fred
1953   Excavations at Te'ewi. In *Salvage Archaeology in the Chama Valley, New Mexico*, edited by Fred Wendorf, pp. 34–93. Monographs of the School of American Research No. 17, Santa Fe.

Wendorf, Fred, and Erik K. Reed
1955   An Alternative Reconstruction of Northern Rio Grande Prehistory. *El Palacio* 62(2):131–173.

Wetherington, Ronald K.
1968   *Excavations at Pot Creek Pueblo.* Fort Burgwin Research Center, Publication No. 6, Southern Methodist University, Dallas.

Wesler, K. W.
1991   Aspects of Settlement Patterning at Wickliffe (15BA4). In *The Human Landscape in Kentucky's Past: Site Structure and Settlement Patterns*, edited by C. Stout and C. K. Hensley, pp. 106–127. Kentucky Heritage Council, Frankfort.

Wetterstrom, Wilma
1986   *Food, Diet, and Population at Prehistoric Arroyo Hondo Pueblo, New Mexico.* School of American Research Press, Santa Fe.

Whalen, Michael E., and Paul E. Minnis
1996a   Studying Complexity in Northern Mexico: The Paquime Regional System. In *Debating Complexity: Proceedings of the Twenty-sixth Annual Chacmool Conference*, edited by Daniel A. Meyer, Peter C. Dawson, and Donald T. Hanna, pp. 173–184. The Archaeological Association of the University of Calgary, Alberta.
1996b   Ball Courts and Political Centralization in the Casas Grandes Region. *American Antiquity* 61(4):732–746.
1996   The Context of Production in and Around Paquime, Chihuahua, Mexico. In *Interpreting Southwestern Diversity: Underlying Principles and Overarching Patterns*, edited by Paul R. Fish and J. Jefferson Reid, pp. 173–182, Arizona State University, Anthropological Research Papers No. 48, Tempe.

Wheat, Joe Ben
1955   Mogollon Culture Prior to A.D. 1000. Memoirs of the Society for American Archaeology No. 10; Memoirs of the American Anthropological Association 82. *American Antiquity* 20(4)pt. 2.
1983   Anasazi Who? In *Proceedings of the Anasazi Symposium, 1981*, edited by Jack E. Smith. Mesa Verde Museum, Mesa Verde, Colorado.

White, Leslie A.
1942   Lewis Henry Morgan's Journal of a Trip to Southwestern Colorado and New Mexico, June 21 to August 7, 1878. *American Antiquity* 8:1–26.

White, T. D.
1992   *Prehistoric Cannibalism at Mancos 5MTUMR-2346.* Princeton University Press, Princeton.

Whitecotton, Joseph W.
1977   *The Zapotecs: Princes, Priests, and Peasants.* University of Oklahoma Press, Norman.

Whittlesey, Stephanie M.
1978   *Status and Death at Grasshopper Pueblo: Experiments Towards and Archaeological Theory of Correlates.* Unpublished Ph.D. dissertation, Department of Anthropology, University of Arizona, Tucson.
1984   Uses and Abuses of Mogollon Mortuary Data. In *Recent Research in Mogollon Archaeology*, edited by Steadman Upham, Fred Plog, David G. Batcho, and Barbara E. Kauffman, pp. 276–284. The University Museum, New Mexico State University, Occasional Papers No. 10, Las Cruces.
1993   Chihuahuan Threads Among the Bowls: Stylistic Discontinuities in Roosevelt Redware. Paper presented at the Arizona Archaeological Council Meetings, Flagstaff.

Whittlesey, Stephanie M., and Richard Ciolek-Torrello
1992   A Revolt Against Rampant Elites: Toward an Alternative Paradigm. In *Proceedings of the Second Salado Conference*, edited by Richard C. Lange and Stephen Germick, pp. 312–324. Occa-

sional Paper of the Arizona Archaeological
Society, Phoenix.

Wicke, Charles R.

1965   Pyramids and Temple Mounds: Mesoamerican
Ceremonial Architecture in Eastern North
America. *American Antiquity* 30:409–420.

Wicklein, John

1994   Spirit Paths of the Anasazi. *Archaeology*
47(1):36–41.

Widmer, Randolph J.

1988   *The Evolution of the Calusa.* University of Alabama Press, Tuscaloosa.

Wilcox, David R.

1975   A Strategy for Perceiving Social Groups in Puebloan Sites. *Fieldiana: Anthropology* 65:120–159.

1979a   The Hohokam Regional System. In *An Archaeological Test of Sites in the Gila Butte-Santan
Region, South-central Arizona*, edited by Glen E.
Rice, pp. 77–116. Arizona State University, Anthropological Field Studies No. 19, Tempe.

1979b   The Warfare Implications of Dry-laid Masonry
Walls on Tumamoc Hill. *The Kiva* 45:15–38.

1980   The Current Status of the Hohokam Concept.
In *Current Issues in Hohokam Prehistory: Pro-
ceedings of a Conference*, edited by David E.
Doyel and Fred Plog, pp. 236–242. Arizona State
University, Anthropological Research Papers
No. 23, Tempe.

1981a   Changing Perspectives on the Protohistoric
Pueblos, A.D. 1450–1700. In *The Protohistoric
Period in the North American Southwest, A.D.
1450–1700*, edited by David R. Wilcox and W.
Bruce Masse, pp. 378–409. Arizona State University, Anthropological Research Papers No.
24, Tempe.

1981b   The Entry of Athapaskan Speakers into the
American Southwest: The Problem Today. In
*The Protohistoric Period in the North American
Southwest, A.D. 1450–1700*, edited by David R.
Wilcox and W. Bruce Masse, pp. 213–256. Ari-
zona State University, Anthropological Research
Papers No. 24, Tempe.

1984   Multi-Ethnic Division of Labor in the Protohistoric Southwest. In *Collected Papers in Honor
of Harry L. Hadlock*, edited by Nancy L. Fox, pp.
141–156. Papers of the New Mexico Archaeological Society No. 9, Albuquerque.

1986a   Excavations on Three Sites on Bottomless Pits
Mesa, Flagstaff, Arizona. Ms. on file, Coconino
National Forest, Flagstaff.

1986b   A Historical Analysis of the Problem of Southwestern-Mesoamerican Connections. In *Ripples
in the Chichimec Sea: New Considerations of
Southwestern-Mesoamerican Interactions*, edited
by Frances J. Mathian and Randall H. McGuire,
pp. 9–44. Southern Illinois University Press,
Carbondale.

1987a   The Evolution of Hohokam Ceremonial Sys-
tems. In *Astronomy and Ceremony in the Prehis-
toric Southwest*, edited by John Carlson and W.
James Judge, pp. 149–168. Maxwell Museum of
Anthropology, Anthropological Papers No. 2,
Albuquerque.

1987b   *Frank Midvale's Investigation of the Site of La
Ciudad.* Arizona State University, Anthropological Field Studies No. l9, Tempe.

1988a   The Regional Context of the Brady Wash and
Picacho Area Sites. In *Hohokam Settlement
Along the Slopes of the Picacho Mountains:
Synthesis and Conclusions, Tucson Aqueduct
Project*, edited by Richard Ciolek-Torrello and
David R. Wilcox, pp. 244–267. Museum of
Northern Arizona Research Paper No. 35(6),
Flagstaff.

1988b   Rethinking the Mogollon Concept. *The Kiva*
53:205–209.

1989   Hohokam Warfare. In *Cultures in Conflict:
Current Archaeological Perspectives, Proceedings
of the Twentieth Annual Chacmool Conference*,
edited by Diana C. Tkaczuk and Brian C.
Vivian, pp. 163–172. The Archaeological Association of the University of Calgary, Alberta.

1991a   Changing Context of Pueblo Adaptations, A.D.
1250–1600. In *Farmers, Hunters and Colonists:
Interaction Between the Southwest and the
Southern Plains*, edited by Katherine A.
Spielmann, pp. 128–154. University of Arizona
Press, Tucson.

1991b   The Changing Structure of Macroregional
Organization. In *The North American Southwest: A New World Perspective.* Ms. in possession of author.

1991c   Hohokam Religion: An Archaeologist's Perspec-
tive. In *The Hohokam: Ancient People of the
Desert*, edited by David G. Noble, pp. 47–61.
School of American Research Press, Santa Fe.

1991d   Hohokam Social Complexity. In *Chaco &
Hohokam: Prehistoric Regional Systems in the
American Southwest*, edited by Patricia L.
Crown and W. James Judge, pp. 253–275. School
of American Research Press, Santa Fe.

1991e   The Mesoamerican Ballgame in the American
Southwest. In *The Mesoamerican Ballgame*,
edited by Vernon L. Scarborough and David R.
Wilcox, pp. 101–125. University of Arizona Press,
Tucson.

1993   The Evolution of the Chacoan Polity. In *The
Chimney Rock Symposium*, edited by J. McKim
Malville and Gary Matlock. Rocky Mountain
Forest and Range Experiment Station, U.S.D.A.
Forest Service, Ft. Collins, Colorado.

1995   A Processual Model of Charles C. Di Peso's
Babocomari Site and Related Systems. In *The

Gran Chichimeca: Essays on the Archaeology and Ethnohistory of Northern Mesoamerica, edited by Jonathan E. Reyman, pp. 281–319. Avebury, London.

1996a   The Diversity of Regional and Macroregional Systems in the American Southwest. In *Debating Complexity: Proceedings of the Twenty-sixth Annual Chacmool Conference*, edited by Daniel A. Meyer, Peter C. Dawson, and Donald T. Hanna. The Archaeological Association of the University of Calgary, Alberta.

1996b   Pueblo III People and Polity in Relational Context. In *The Prehistoric Pueblo World, A.D. 1150–1350*, edited by Michael A. Adler, pp. 241–254. University of Arizona Press, Tucson.

1996c   The Wupatki Nexus: Chaco-Hohokam-Chumash Connectivity, A.D. 1150–1225. In *Proceedings of the Twenty-fifth Chacmool Meetings*. The Archaeological Association of the University of Calgary, Alberta.

Wilcox, David R., and Jonathan Haas

1994a   The Reality of Competition and Conflict in the Prehistoric Southwest. In *Themes in Southwestern Prehistory*, edited by George J. Gumerman. School of American Research Press, Santa Fe.

1994b   The Scream of the Butterfly: Competition and Conflict in the Prehistoric Southwest. In *Themes in Southwest Prehistory*, edited by George J. Gumerman, pp. 211–238. School of American Research Press, Santa Fe.

Wilcox, David R., and Lynette O. Shenk

1977   *The Architecture of the Casa Grande and Its Interpretation*. Arizona State Museum Archaeological Series No. 146. University of Arizona, Tucson.

Wilcox, David R., and Robert Sternberg

1983   *Hohokam Ballcourts and Their Interpretation*. Arizona State Museum Archaeological Series No. 160. University of Arizona, Tucson.

Wilcox, David R., and Phil C. Weigand

1993   Chacoan Capitals: Centers of Competing Polities. Paper presented at 58th Annual Meeting of the Society for American Archaeology, St. Louis.

Wilcox, David R., Jerry B. Howard, and Rueben H. Nelson

1990   *One Hundred Years of Archaeology at La Ciudad de los Hornos*. Soil Systems Publications in Archaeology No. 16, Phoenix.

Wilcox, David R., Donald Keller, and David Ortiz

n.d.   Walnut Creek, the Indian Peak Ruin and Long Distance Exchange in the Greater Southwest. Ms. in possession of the author.

Wilcox, David R., Thomas R. McGuire, and Charles Sternberg

1981   *Snaketown Revisited*. Arizona State Museum Archaeological Series No. 155. University of Arizona, Tucson.

Wilcox, David R., Terry Samples, Donald Keller, and Maria Laughner

1996   The Wagner Hill Ballcourt Community and Other Cohonina Sites. *Kiva* 61:433–455.

Willey, Gordon R., and Phillip Phillips

1958   *Method and Theory in American Archaeology*. University of Chicago Press, Chicago.

Willey, Gordon R., and Jeremy A. Sabloff

1980   *A History of American Archaeology*. W. H. Freeman and Company, San Francisco.

Williams, J. Mark, and Gary Shapiro

1990   Paired Towns. In *Lamar Archaeology: Mississippian Chiefdoms in the Deep South*, edited by J. Mark Williams and Gary Shapiro, pp. 163–174. University of Alabama Press, Tuscaloosa.

1996   Mississippian Political Dynamics in the Oconee Valley, Georgia. In *Political Structure and Change in the Prehistoric Southeastern United States*, edited by John F. Scarry, pp. 128–149. University Presses of Florida, Gainesville.

Williams, Stephen

1990   The Vacant Quarter and Other Late Events in the Lower Valley. In *Towns and Temples along the Mississippi*, edited by David H. Dye and Cheryl A. Cox, pp. 170–180. University of Alabama Press, Tuscaloosa.

Williams, Stephen, and Jeffery P. Brain

1983   *Excavations at the Lake George Site, Yazoo County, Mississippi, 1958–1960*. Papers of the Peabody Museum of American Archaeology and Ethnology 74. Harvard University, Cambridge.

Williams, Stephen, and John M. Goggin

1956   The Long Nosed God Mask in Eastern United States. *Missouri Archaeologist* 18:4–72.

Williamson, Ray A.

1984   *Living the Sky: The Cosmos of the American Indian*. University of Oklahoma Press, Norman.

Wills, Wirt H.

1988a   Early Agriculture and Sedentism in the American Southwest, Evidence and Interpretations. *Journal of World Prehistory* 2:445–489.

1988b   *Early Prehistoric Agriculture in the American Southwest*. School of American Research Press, Santa Fe.

1994   Evolutionary and Ecological Modeling in Southwestern Archaeology. In *Understanding Complexity in the Prehistoric Southwest*, edited by George J. Gumerman and Murray Gell-Mann, pp. 287–296. Addison-Wesley, Reading, Massachusetts.

Wills, Wirt H., and Thomas C. Windes

1989   Evidence for Population Aggregation and Dispersal During the Basketmaker III Period in Chaco Canyon, New Mexico. *American Antiquity* 54:347–369.

Wilshusen, Richard H.

1989   Unstuffing the Estufa: Ritual Floor Features in Anasazi Pit Structures and Pueblo Kivas. In *The Architecture of Social Integration in Prehistoric Pueblos*, edited by William D. Lipe and Michelle Hegmon, pp. 89–111. Occasional Paper No. 1, Crow Canyon Archaeological Center, Cortez, Colorado.

1990   *Early Villages in the American Southwest: Cross-Cultural and Archaeological Perspectives*. Unpublished Ph.D. dissertation, Department of Anthropology, University of Colorado, Boulder.

Wilshusen, Richard H., and Eric Blinman

1992   Pueblo I Village Formation: A Reevaluation of Sites Recorded by Earl Morris on the Ute Mountain Tribal Lands. *Kiva* 57:251–269.

Windes, Thomas C.

1977   Typology and Technology of Anasazi Ceramics. In *Settlement and Subsistence along the Lower Chaco River: The CGP Survey*, edited by Charles A. Reher, pp. 279–370. University of New Mexico Press, Albuquerque.

1984a   A New Look at Population in Chaco Canyon. In *Recent Research in Chaco Prehistory*, edited by W. James Judge and John D. Schelburg, pp. 75–88. Reports of the Chaco Center No. 5. Division of Cultural Research, National Park Service, Albuquerque.

1984b   A View of the Cibola Whiteware from Chaco Canyon. In *Regional Analysis of Prehistoric Ceramic Variation: Contemporary Studies of the Cibola Whitewares*, edited by Alan P. Sullivan and Jeffrey L. Hantman, pp. 94–119. Arizona State University, Anthropological Research Papers No. 31, Tempe.

1985   Chaco-McElmo Black-on-white from Chaco Canyon with an Emphasis on the Pueblo del Arroyo Collection. In *Prehistory and History in the Southwest: Collected Papers in Honor of Alden C. Hayes*, edited by Nancy L. Fox, pp. 19–42. Papers of the Archaeological Society of New Mexico No. 11, Albuquerque.

1993   *The Spadefoot Toad Site: Investigations at 29SJ629 in Marcia's Rincon and Fajada Gap Pueblo II Community, Chaco Canyon, New Mexico*, Reports of the Chaco Center No. 12, Santa Fe.

Windes, Thomas C., and Dabney Ford

1992   The Nature of the Early Bonito Phase. In *Anasazi Regional Organization and the Chaco System*, edited by David E. Doyel, pp. 75–85. Maxwell Museum of Anthropology, Anthropological Papers No. 5, Albuquerque.

Windes, Thomas C., and Peter J. McKenna

1989   Cibola Whiteware and Cibola Grayware. Paper presented at the NMAC Ceramics Workshop, Red Rock State Park, New Mexico.

Wissler, Clark

1914   Material Cultures of the North American Indian. *American Anthropologist* 16(3):447–505.

Witthoft, John

1949   *Green Corn Ceremonialism in the Eastern Woodlands*. Museum of Anthropology Occasional Contributions No. 13. University of Michigan, Ann Arbor.

Wolf, Eric R.

1966   *Peasants*. Prentice-Hall, Englewood Cliffs, New Jersey.

1982   *Europe and the People Without History*. University of California Press, Berkeley.

1990   Distinguished Lecture: Facing Power—Old Insights, New Questions. *American Anthropologist* 92:586–596.

Wood, Jon S.

1985   The Northeastern Periphery. In *Proceedings of the 1983 Hohokam Symposium, Part 1*, edited by Alfred E. Dittert, Jr., and Donald E. Dove, pp. 239–262. Occasional Paper of the Arizona Archaeological Society, Phoenix.

Woodbury, Richard B.

1961   A Reappraisal of Hohokam Irrigation. *American Anthropologist* 63:550–560.

1991   A Brief History of Hohokam Archaeology. In *The Hohokam: Ancient People of the Desert*, edited by David G. Noble, pp. 27–38. School of American Research Press, Santa Fe.

Woods, William I., and George R. Holley

1989   Current Research at the Cahokia Site (1984–1989). In *The Cahokia Atlas: A Historical Atlas of Cahokia Archaeology*, by Melvin L. Fowler, pp. 227–232. Studies in Illinois Archaeology No. 6. Illinois Historic Preservation Agency, Springfield.

1991   Upland Mississippian Settlement in the American Bottom Region. In *Cahokia and the Hinterlands: Middle Mississippian Cultures of the Midwest*, edited by Thomas E. Emerson and R. Barry Lewis, pp. 46–60. University of Illinois Press, Urbana.

Woosley, Anne I.

1980   Agricultural Diversity in the Prehistoric Southwest. *The Kiva* 45:317–335.

1986   Puebloan Prehistory of the Northern Rio Grande: Settlement, Population, Subsistence. *The Kiva* 51:143–164.

Woosley, Anne I., and Allan J. McIntyre

1996   *Mimbres Mogollon Archaeology: Charles C. Di Peso's Excavations at Wind Mountain*. Amerind Foundation Archaeology Series No. 10. Amerind Foundation, Dragoon, Arizona, and University of New Mexico Press, Albuquerque.

Woosley, Anne I., and Bart Olinger

1993   The Casas Grandes Ceramic Tradition: Production and Interregional Exchange of Ramos Polychrome. In *Culture and Contact: Charles C. Di Peso's Gran Chichimeca*, edited by Anne I. Woosley and John C. Ravesloot, pp. 105–131. Amerind Foundation New World Studies Series 2. Amerind Foundation, Dragoon, Arizona, and University of New Mexico Press, Albuquerque.

Woosley, Anne I., and John C. Ravesloot (editors)

1993   *Culture and Contact: Charles C. Di Peso's Gran Chichimeca*. Amerind Foundation New World Studies Series 2. Amerind Foundation, Dragoon, Arizona, and University of New Mexico Press, Albuquerque.

Wormington, H. M.

1947   *Prehistoric Indians of the Southwest*. Colorado Museum of Natural History, Popular Series No.7, Denver.

Wright, Henry T.

1971   Recent Research on the Origin of the State. *Annual Review of Anthropology* 6:379–397.

1984   Prestate Political Formations. In *On the Evolution of Complex Societies: Essays in Honor of Harry Hoijer*, by William Sanders, Henry Wright, and Robert McC. Adams, edited by Timothy K. Earle, pp. 43–77 (reprinted 1994 in *Chiefdoms and Early States in the Near East: The Organizational Dynamics of Complexity*, edited by Gil Stein and Mitchell S. Rothman, pp. 67–84. Prehistory Press, Madison.

1986   The Evolution of Civilizations. In *American Archaeology Past and Future: A Celebration of the Society for American Archaeology, 1935–1985*, edited by David J. Meltzer, Don D. Fowler, and Jeremy A. Sabloff, pp. 323–365. Smithsonian Institution Press, Washington, D.C.

Yerkes, Richard W.

1983   Microwear, Microdrills, and Mississippian Craft Specialization. *American Antiquity* 48:499–518.

1986   Licks, Pans, and Chiefs: A Comment on Mississippian Specialization and Salt. *American Antiquity* 51:402–404.

1989   Mississippian Craft Specialization on the American Bottom. *Southeastern Archaeology* 8:93–106.

1991   Specialization in Shell Artifact Production at Cahokia. In *New Perspectives on Cakokia: Views from the Periphery*, edited by James B. Stoltman, pp. 49–64. Prehistory Press, Madison, Wisconsin.

Yoffee, Norman

1985   Perspectives on 'Trends Towards Social Complexity in Prehistoric Australia and Papua, New Guinea.' *Archaeology in Oceania* 20:41–49.

1993   Too Many Chiefs? (Or, Safe Texts for the '90s). In *Archaeological Theory: Who Sets the Agenda?*, edited by Norman Yoffee and Andrew Sherratt, pp. 60–78. Cambridge University Press, Cambridge.

1994   *Memorandum to Murray Gell-Mann Concerning: the Complications of Complexity in the Prehistoric Southwest*, edited by George J. Gumerman and Murray Gell-Mann, pp. 341–358. Addison-Wesley, Reading, Massachusetts.

1995a   A Mass in Celebration of the Conference. In *The Archaeology of Society in the Holy Land*, edited by Thomas E. Levy, pp. 242–248. Leicester University Press, London.

1995b   Political Economy in Early Mesopotamian States. *Annual Review of Anthropology* 24:281–311.

1996   Codifying the Obvious. In *The Archaeology of City-States: Cross-Cultural Approaches*, edited by D. Nichols and T. Charlton, Smithsonian Institution Press, Washington, D.C.

Yoffee, Norman, and George L. Cowgill (editors)

1988   *The Collapse of Ancient States and Civilizations*. University of Arizona Press, Tucson.

Yoffee, Norman, and Andrew Sherratt

1993   Introduction: the Sources of Archaeological Theory. In *Archaeological Theory: Who Sets the Agenda?*, edited by Norman Yoffee and Andrew Sherratt, pp.1–11. Cambridge University Press, Cambridge.

Zantwijk, Rudolph van

1985   *The Aztec Arrangement: The Social History of Pre-Spanish Mexico*. University of Oklahoma Press, Norman.

Zedeno, Maria N.

1991   *Refining Inferences of Ceramic Circulation: A Stylistic, Technological, and Compositional Analysis of Whole Vessels from Chodistaas, Arizona*. Unpublished Ph.D. dissertation, Department of Anthropology, Southern Methodist University, Dallas.

Index

Abandonment: in Southeast, 219; in Southwest, 20, 89, 204, 247
Adams site, Kentucky, 24
Adena, 172
Alkali Ridge, Utah, 14
Allentown site, Arizona, 133, 135
American Bottom. *See* Cahokia site/region, Illinois
Anasazi: abandonment and aggregation by, 17–18, 89; "balkanization" of, 19–20; public buildings and facilities, 6–7; residential structures, 3–4; shell trade to, 117; site permanence, 17–18; site layouts, 9, 13, 14; site size, 15–16. *See also* Chaco Canyon, New Mexico; Mesa Verde, Colorado; *under specific site names*
Angel site/region, Indiana, 24, 31, 230, 232, 239, 241
Apalachee, 64–65, 68, 71, 74. *See also* Lake Jackson phase
Archeotekopa II site, New Mexico, 16
Arroyo Hondo site, New Mexico: agricultural intensification at, 210; craft specialization at, 211; layout of, 11, 14; organizational change at, 207; population change at, 208; prestige goods exchange at, 212; warfare at, 213
Aztec, 171, 178
Aztec Ruins, New Mexico, 12, 50, 133, 135, 136

Bass Point site, Arizona, 8
BBB Motor site, Illinois, 177
Beckwith's Fort, Missouri, 24, 34
Betatakin site, Arizona, 140
Big Bend area, Florida. *See* Apalachee; Lake Jackson phase
Bis sa'ani site, New Mexico, 52, 136
Borrow Pit site, Florida, 73
Box S site, New Mexico, 11

Caddo, 154
Cahokia site/region, Illinois: agricultural intensification in, 234; appearance and collapse of chiefdoms in, 34, 35, 36, 106, 241; chief's mound at, 28; circular buildings at, 30; commerce regulation lacking in, 100–101, 152; compared with Chaco Canyon, 40–42, 251; as complex chiefdom, 150; craft specialization in, 69–70, 238; economic interdependence in, 100; elites at, 33, 77, 102, 157; extent of power of, 149; farmsteads around, 105; longevity and stability of, 66, 67; as Mega-center, 23–24; mortuary patterns at, 73, 102; organizational change in, 230; polity size of, 60–61, 78, 162; population of, 32, 33, 64, 79, 232; prestige goods exchange in, 101, 154, 155, 236; settlement hierarchy in, 71; site complexity of, 71, 76; site layout, 26, 32, 41; storage facilities at, 33; warfare in, 239
Canals: Hohokam, 8, 9, 51, 85–86, 87, 189, 191, 192, 193; Mimbres, 8, 17
Carrier Mills site, Illinois, 172
Carter Ranch Pueblo, Arizona, 137
Casa Grande site, Arizona, 8, 14, 51, 52, 56, 79
Çatal Hüyük, Turkey, 266–67
Chaco Canyon, New Mexico: agricultural intensification in, 196–97; chronology of, 120–21; class system in, 127; compared with Cahokia, 40–42, 251; compared with Hohokam, 198–99; craft specialization in, 211; decline of, 12; great houses in, 4, 49, 128, 132, 133–36; macroregional system of, 123–24; map of, 40; Mesoamerican contacts of, 136, 170; mounds in, 76; organization of, 86–87, 194, 206; population of, 15, 51, 194–96, 197, 208; prestige goods exchange in, 212; as "proto-urban," 21, 39, 130; public buildings and facilities in, 7, 8; as "rituality," 265–66;